GERMAN SECRET
FLIGHT TEST CENTRES
to 1945

Johannisthal, Lipetsk, Rechlin, Travemünde, Tarnewitz, Peenemünde-West

German Secret Flight Test Centres to 1945
© Bernard & Graefe Verlag 1998, 2002

ISBN 1 85780 127 X

First published 1998 in Germany by
Bernard & Graefe Verlag, Bonn

Translation from original German text
by Ted Oliver

English language edition published 2002 by
Midland Publishing
4 Watling Drive, Hinckley, LE10 3EY, England.
Tel: 01455 254 490 Fax: 01455 254 495

Midland Publishing is an imprint of
Ian Allan Publishing Ltd.

Worldwide distribution (except North America):
Midland Counties Publications
4 Watling Drive, Hinckley, LE10 3EY, England
Tel: 01455 233 747   Fax: 01455 233 737
E-mail: midlandbooks@compuserve.com

North America trade distribution:
Specialty Press Publishers & Wholesalers Inc.
39966 Grand Avenue
North Branch, MN 55056, USA
Tel: 651 277 1400   Fax: 651 277 1203
Toll free telephone: 800 895 4585
www.specialtypress.com

Design concept and editorial layout
© Midland Publishing and
Stephen Thompson Associates.

Printed by Ian Allan Printing Ltd
Riverdene Business Park, Molesey Road
Hersham, Surrey, KT12 4RG, England.

Jacket illustration:
*This specially commissioned painting from
Keith Woodcock GAvA portrays an imagined
scene at Rechlin during 1944.*

Half-title page illustration:
*The Ha 140V-1D-AUTO, Werk-Nr.281 takes off
from the water on 7th February 1938 piloted by
Flugbaumeister Gerhard Geike.*

Title page illustration:
An ejection seat firing from a Heinkel 219.

GERMAN SECRET FLIGHT TEST CENTRES
to 1945

Johannisthal, Lipetsk, Rechlin, Travemünde, Tarnewitz, Peenemünde-West

Heinrich Beauvais, Karl Kössler, Max Mayer, Christoph Regel

In co-operation with Heinz Borsdorff,
Mathias Jens, Dr Volker Koos, Hanfried Schliephake

Midland Publishing

Contents

Photo Credits

Air Force Historical Research Agency	1
Bundesarchiv/Militärarchiv Freiburg	2
Blumberg/Kössler collection	57
H Borsdorff collection	1
P Cohausz collection	2
E Creek collection	2
B Dirschauer collection	4
M Griehl collection	6
G Hentschel collection	4
H Heyligenstädt collection	1
M Jens collection	1
K Koessler collection	6
V Koos collection	26
M Mayer collection	54
G Ott collection	3
P Petrick collection	6
H Rebelski collection	1
C Regel collection	61
H Schaefer collection	15
H Schliephake collection	7
B Stüwe collection	4
C Trampert collection	1
Deutsches Museum	38
Dornier Archives	4
Förderverein Luftfahrttechn. Museum Rechlin	2
Förderverein Peenemünde	1
Foto Adrion	2
Gemeindeverwaltung Peenemünde	1
Kreisarchiv Neustrelitz	1
Landesvermessungamt Mecklenburg-Vorpommern	1
National Archives Washington	1
Schmetz	1
Schöning-Verlag	1

About the Authors

Dipl.-Ing. Heinrich Beauvais

Born in Mainz on 25th May 1908. Upon completion of his matriculation in 1927, he commenced his Mechanical Engineering studies at the TH München, obtaining his Diploma of Engineering (Dipl.-Ing.) degree in 1932. He then spent 3 years as a designer with the firm of MAN (Maschinen Augsburg-Nürnberg) in Mainz-Gustavsburg, during which time he trained as a pilot at his own expense, obtaining his A2 license in 1934.

From 1935 he was engaged at the E-Stelle Rechlin, initially as a specialist, then as Group Leader for Fighters and Heavy Fighters, responsible especially for flight measurements and judgement of the performance of such types. From 1945 to 1949 he was engaged in a rural occupation, interrupted by his involvement on the 'German Aviation Medicine World War Two' Report in the US Aero Medical Center in Heidelberg. From 1949 to 1953 he again worked as a designer at MAN in Mainz. From 1953 to 1958 he was engaged as a Scientific Contributor in the 'Preliminary Federal Centre for Aircraft and Air Accident Investigation' in Bonn and in the DFS München-Riem, during which period as an Assessor, he provided technical appraisals for the first training aircraft to be selected for the Bundeswehr and the Federal Aviation Office (LBA) aircraft flight certification and evaluation requirements, also providing his assessment on the flying qualities of the HA 200 for Professor Messerschmitt in Spain.

From 1958 he worked at the 'E-Stelle for Aircraft' in Oberpfaffenhofen and later at Manching (currently the WTD 61) on establishment of the 'Aircraft Group', becoming their first pilot and instructor, as well as being involved in helicopter selection for the Bundeswehr.

In 1967 he became Administrative Chief of the Interpretation of Aircraft Accidents and Malfunctions at the Bundeswehr Aircraft Type-Test Centre (MBL), and from 1968, Scientific Advisor to the Commander and Administration Chief

of Operations Research and Flight Mechanics in the Luftwaffe Specialist College in Neubiberg. From 1956 to 1973 he lectured at the TU München on the subject of 'Piloting', thereafter going into retirement.

Dipl.-Ing. Max Mayer

Born on 30th June 1913 in Regensburg, he studied Mechanical Engineering in the TH München from 1932 to 1936, when he obtained his Dipl.-Ing. degree. He was thereafter engaged in the DVL Berlin-Adlershof as a 'Flugbauführer' during which period he qualified as an Engineer-Pilot, obtaining his 'Land C' pilot licence. His next involvement was on the Focke-Wulf wind-tunnel in Bremen, in the Junkers 'Ju 88' design office at Dessau and at the Luftwaffe Versuchsstelle Peenemünde-West, absolving his second State Examination as 'Flugbaumeister' (Master of Aircraft Engineering) in Autumn 1939.

During the period 1938 to 1945 at the Versuchsstelle, he functioned initially as Test Pilot and Specialist for unmanned missiles and later as Head of the Department E2 concerned with 'automatically or remotely-guided missiles and rocket-propelled aircraft', including the testing of 'carrier-aircraft for missile systems'. On 1st June 1943 he obtained his Blind-flying Licence Class II, and in 1944, his higher-graded Luftwaffe pilot licence for land-based aircraft, accomplishing some 3,500 flights and 2,500 flying hours. The most important aircraft types he flew included the Ar 68, Ar 96, Ar 234: Do 17, Do 17Z, Do 217E, K and M; Fw 44, Fw 58, Fw 190, Fw 200; He 51, He 70, He 111B, H and Z, He 177A-1 and A-3; Ju F13, A48, W33, W34, Ju 52, Ju 88, Ju 90, Ju 188 and Ju 290; Messerschmitt Bf 108, Bf 109, Bf 110 and Si 204.

He spent time in an internment camp in England from July 1945 to February 1946, following which he

became an independent engineer for mechanical drain cleaning of drainage systems near coastal regions, and in 1948-49, had an Engineering Office for the statics of high-rise buildings.

From 1949, on the Reconstruction Staff of the German Patent Office, he undertook legal training in the field of Patent Rights, becoming a civil servant 'Member of the German Patent Office' in 1954.

Between 1957 and 1962 he was at the Federal German Defence Ministry in Bonn. In the 'Department for Military Technology' he headed the 'Army, Navy and Air Force Missiles Systems' Advisory Board. From 1962-1971, at the Federal German Ministry for Science and Further Education, he established the new 'Space Research and Space Flight Technology' group to an active, capable and internationally-respected Ministerial Department and promoted the formation and expansion of a national, competent organisation possessing research and industrial capacity as the basis for international cooperation as well as several space research projects.

From 1957-1971 he served as a delegate on several official panels, and during the period 1972-1976 was the Aviation and Space Advisor of the Board of Directors of the Dresdner Bank, Frankfurt am Main, among others for the Airbus Development proposal.

From 1974-1980, he was responsible for the formation and leadership of the German Representation of a large US electronics company. The author is an Honorary Member of the Senate of the DGLR – Lilienthal-Oberth Society, and since 1959, member and long-serving Vice President – and from 1994, President of the 'German Aero-Club' and is also a Member of the 'Air and Space' Specialist Committee of the Deutsches Museum since 1973.

From 1978-1993, he was Chairman of the Board of Trustees of the Lilienthal Foundation and since 1981, member of the 'Alte Adler' (Old Eagles) Traditional Society, and since 1995, Member of the Board of the DLR Society of Friends and the Lilienthal Foundation.

Dipl.-Ing. Karl Kössler

Born in 1924, he studied Mechanical Engineering at the TH München, obtaining his Dipl.-Ing. degree in 1950. After two years as a designer at BMW, he was engaged as a Test Engineer with the Auto-Union in Ingolstadt until 1956, after which he went to Dornier in

Friedrichshafen and Oberpfaffenhofen as a Flight Test Engineer. Following his motorized flight instruction as a Test Pilot, he undertook flight tests with the Do 27, Do 28A and B, Do 29 and the Do 32 small helicopter. A crowning achievement was his maiden flight and testing of the German 'Flying Bedstead' equivalent for the Do 31 vertical take-off transport aircraft.

In 1969 he entered the Federal German Aviation Office (LBA) as Head of the 'Certification of Aircraft and Helicopters' Advisory Board. In 1970 he was a Section Head in the 'Technology' department and from 1971 until his retirement at the end of 1987 functioned as its Office Chief.

He was a founder-member and currently Honorary Member of the 'U52 Interessengemeinschaft' (Community of Interests) in Wunstorf and is active on the Board of the Aviation Luftfahrt-Museum in Laatzen. His long period of involvement with German aviation history has led to his authorship of numerous articles in magazines and two books.

Christoph Regel

Born in Aschaffenburg in 1959, he matriculated in 1979 in the Kronberg-Gymnasium of Humanistics, Aschaffenburg and from 1980-1985, he studied at the Fachhochschule für Technik in Esslingen, specializing in Propulsion Technology. Simultaneously, he began his freelance journalistic career for various newspapers. At the conclusion of his studies, he joined the Süddeutsche Kühlerfabrik Julius Behr GmbH & Co in Stuttgart as a Development Engineer in the Aviation Department, becoming in 1993 Head of this specialist field responsible for Design, Development and Product Support for heat-exchangers for aeronautical applications.

Through his father, who from 1935-1945 had been engaged as a Test Engineer for Engine Installations at the E-Stelle Rechlin, his interest in aviation history was awakened at an early age, leading to contact with many 'old Rechliners', and to building-up extensive archives on the history of the E-Stelle Rechlin. He is an active Member of the Board of the Förderverein Luftfahrttechnisches Museum e.V. in Rechlin. (Aerotechnical Promotional Association Museum).

Dipl.-Ing. Heinz Borsdorff

Born in Bad Warmbrunn, Silesia, on 30th August 1909, following matriculation he absolved various courses of practical work before studying general Mechanical Engineering at the TH Breslau (now in Poland). Interrupted by a two-year voluntary term of military service, he finally obtained his Dipl.-Ing. engineering degree. Whilst engaged at the Argus Motorenwerke in Berlin-Reinickendorf from March 1936 onwards he undertook pilot-training, obtaining his C-licence which enabled him to undertake flight testing work in the Argus Flight Test Department.

Following call-up for World War Two military service, he became a flying instructor and took part in the Norwegian Campaign with KGr z.b.V.101, thereafter qualifying as a blind-flying instructor. In August 1941 he was transferred to the Luftwaffe E-Stelle Rechlin Engine Test Department where he was involved as a specialist and Test Pilot. From December 1941 to February 1942 he saw active service with the KGr z.b.V. 800 on the Russian front.

From January 1944 he undertook jet-engine testing in Rechlin-Roggentin, this activity being transferred to Lechfeld in February 1945. His last flights were with the He 162 until 22nd April 1944 and was engaged also in ground operations in support of JG 7. Taken prisoner by the US Army on 5th May 1945, he was held in captivity and subsequently interrogated in the USA.

Following his release in July 1946, he joined the 'Gruppe O' (led by former Dr.-Ing. Hermann Oestrich of BMW) in France, where he remained for the next 5 years. In 1950 he was granted a normal work contract with SNECMA in Paris as Head of the ATAR Turbojet Flight Test Department, where he remained until August 1948 before he returned to Germany, entering the Bundeswehr as an Oberstleutnant.

During his service, he occupied various posts in the Führungsstab, the Luftwaffenamt and the Bundesamt für Wehrtechnik und Beschaffung (Federal Office for Military Technology and Procurement).

Following his departure from the Military with the rank of Oberst in July 1969 he became the Lärmschutz-Beauftragter (Noise Protection Commissioner) for Stuttgart Airport until 1973.

Mathias Jens

The youngest of the contributing authors, he was born in 1977 in Wismar. Following completion of his schooling in his home town, he served his customary 10 months of military service in the Bundeswehr. During the preparation of this book he was a student in the specialist field of Measurement Technology at the FH Hamburg. Encouraged and supported by his family, at an early age he developed an enthusiasm for aviation and its

history. Following the unification of East and West Germany, he at first devoted himself out of curiosity to the Research Project Tarnewitz, which resulted in detailed research on this subject. His aim is to accumulate a comprehensive chronicle of activities of the Tarnewitz semi-peninsula from the very beginning up to the present, his contribution here representing a first step in this undertaking.

Dr. Volker Koos

Born in 1947 in Göhren/Rügen, he obtained his Doctor of Physics degree at the University of Rostock in 1975, being engaged thereafter until 1992 as Scientific Assistant and Head of the Lecturing Group at the Pädagogische Hochschule in Güstrow and in the specialist sphere of Physics at the University of Rostock.

Already as a scholar during his school years, he started to build up an extensive archive on German aviation history, especially for the Northern Germany sector. The result of this past-time activity has been a series of lectures, books and magazine articles.

Johann-Friedrich Schliephake

Born in 1922, upon completion of his schooling he entered service with the Luftwaffe where he was trained as a W/T operator, becoming an instructor on the subject at the LNS Halle/Saale. During World War Two, he was engaged in frontline operations as a W/T operator with the 1st Mine Detection Squadron (Minensuchstaffel 1, Sondergruppe 'Mausi').

Following a period of captivity after the surrender, he became a Customs Inspector until 1956, when he joined the Bundeswehr Luftwaffe as an Air Navigation and Communications Officer, serving on operations with Lufttransportgeschwader 61 and later, with the Flugvermessungsstaffel until his retirement.

From his early youth he became interested in the history of aviation, and has been the author, co-author, translator and partaker on foreign aviation publications, his speciality being the subject of aircraft armament. He is also active as a free-lance aviation journalist. Since 1970 he is a member of the Aviation Press-Club, and member of the Gesellschaft zur Bewahrung von Stätten Deutscher Luftfahrtgeschichte (Society for the Preservation of Repositories of German Aviation History).

The author has contributed to other volumes in the Bernhard & Gräfe 'Die Deutsche Luftfahrt' series, in particular to Volume 9 'Typenhandbuch der Deutschen Luftfahrt-Technik' (Compendium of German Aviation Technology) and Volume 10 'Flugkörper und Lenkraketen' (Missiles and Guided Rockets).

Preface and Acknowledgements

In the first half of the Twentieth Century, testing new aircraft took on an even greater importance with the rapid development of aviation. As with other technical devices, testing aircraft and missiles is unavoidable, for even with highly advanced technology and a wealth of experience, not all deficiencies which can appear during use can be predicted during the design phase. Fundamentally, testing was undertaken by the manufacturer, but the purchaser and later user – primarily the government – displayed an interest in verifying the suitability of the item concerned for its intended purpose and where necessary, putting forward suggestions for alterations, thus exerting an influence in its development.

With this goal in mind, state-owned Experimental and Test Establishments were created in Germany, encompassing an increasingly specialized sphere of tasks. Moreover, the state supervised the inception process of the aeronautical item with the assistance of both the Prüfstelle für Luftfahrzeuge (Aircraft Evaluation Centre) which examined the bases for certification principally from the flight-safety aspect, and the RLM Bauaufsicht für Luftfahrtgerät (Aircraft Construction Authority) which supervised the requirement that the article to be delivered was in conformity with that which had been certificated.

These centres worked closely together with each other as well with the eventual user, ie, the Luftwaffe units. At the end of World War Two, all of these centres had to terminate their activities.

Although the Erprobungsstellen (Test Centres) played an important role in the development of each new aircraft, a thorough and comprehensive portrayal of their activities has up to now been missing. This book is intended to close that gap in historical accounts of German aviation up to 1945.

In view of the extensive destruction of documents at the end of World War Two and in particular, those referring to the aviation sphere, the desire to describe the erection, the activities and the tasks of these Test Centres more than 50 years later, appeared at first to be almost impossible. In spite of this, the authors took up the chal-

lenge. Their accounts are based partially upon their own experiences as former members of a Test Centre and partially drawing upon years of research and the intensive study of archival and source material as well as several conversations with contemporaries. That several questions nevertheless remain unanswered was unavoidable, and results from the loss of irretrievable documents.

An important principle for the authors was to base their evidence almost exclusively upon the use of primary sources. The actual events which describe the realities of the time, was of particular concern to the authors of this publication.

The authors express their thanks to the support received from several contemporaries and their families as well as from experienced aviation historians which enabled an almost complete summary of the activities of German Test Establishments up to 1945.

Especial thanks are expressed to the following: Heinrich Ahrens, Walter Ballerstedt (†), Dr.-Ing. Walter Baist, Hans Beitel (†), Horst Beythien (†), Hans Blumberg, Heinrich Böbs, Friedrich Böhle, Harry Böttcher (†), Hans Boye (†), Rudolf Brée, Dr. Fritz v. Burger-Scheidlin, Leo Conrad (†), Otto Cuno (†), Helmut Czolbe (†), Erich Damrau, Dr.-Ing. Josef Dantscher (†), Prof. Wilhelm Dettmering, Prof. Karl Doetsch, Otto Dumke, Joachim Eisermann (†), Hermann Gatzemeier (†), Gerhard Geike (†), Rudolf von Gordon (†), Horst Hädrich (†), Dr.-Ing. Georg Hentschel, Helmut Heyligenstädt, Röttger Hilleke, Karl-Friedrich Königs, Walter Kröger (†), Alfred Kuhn, Ewald Kursch, Rita Mayer-Schoen, Fritz Mittelstädt, Adolf Mlodoch, Hugo Parlow, Uvo Pauls (†), Uwe Petersen (†), Heinrich Reck (†), Walter Reibisch (†), Felix Ries, Martin Ruck (†), Heinz Schaefer (†), Heinrich Schiemann, Otto Schneider, Hans Schröder (†), Bernhard Schultze, Helmuth Schuster (†), Heinz Simon, Günter Sinram (†), Heinrich Stawinoga, Walter Strobl, Botho Stüwe, Fritz Taucher (†), Heinz Westphal and Erich Wilts.

Significant contributions were also received by the authors from: Peter Achs, Ulf Balke, Heinz Birkholz, Helmut Bukowski,

Steve Coates, Peter W Cohausz, Bodo R Dirschauer (†), Ralf Elbelt, Anne Firk, Günter Frost, Edith Gatzemeier, Peter M Grosz, Horst Günter, Jan Horn, Dieter Heinskill, L Hiller, Gerhard Kaschuba, Winfried Kirschke, Rolf Mehner, Frederic Müller-Romminger, Ursula Marie Mossner-Lechner, Günter Ott, Peter Petrick, Reinhard Petry, Hans-Günter Ploes, Hans Rebeski, Herta Reccius, Heinz Riediger, Irene Rodig, Berta Schabert, Thorsten Schaefer, Paul Schenck, Rolf Schippers, Dr. Günter Schmitt, Franz Selinger, Ursula Spies, Heidewig Sternberg-Damasko, Christian Stopsack, Marton Szigeti, Oliver Thiele, Dr. Jürgen Thoenes, Axel Urbanke and Jürgen Zapf.

Thanks are also expressed to the numerous Archives which consistently aided the authors' researches and in particular the: Air Force Historical Research Agency, Maxwell AFB, Alabama; the Bundesarchiv/ Militärarchiv Freiburg; the Deutsche Dienststelle Berlin (formerly the Wehrmacht Information Centre); the DGLR-Lilienthal-Oberth, Bonn; Deutsches Museum, Munich; Kreisarchiv Neustrelitz; Mecklenburgisches Landeshauptarchiv, Schwerin; National Archives and Records Administration, Washington, and the Gesellschaft zur Bewahrung von Stätten Deutscher Luftfahrtgeschichte (Society for the Preservation of Places of German Aeronautical History), Berlin.

In particular, the authors thank their wives and families who showed considerable understanding and patience for the time-consuming activities of their spouses.

Our appreciation is also expressed to the Bernard & Gräfe Verlag for including this work in 'Die Deutsche Luftfahrt' series of volumes and for their generous contents support. The deceased initiator and editor of this series, Dr. Theodor Benecke, is also remembered here for encouraging the realization of this volume.

Heinrich Beauvais, Munich
Karl Kössler, Cremlingen
Max Mayer, Bonn
Christoph Regel, Stuttgart

Spring 1998

Abbreviations

Additionally, quick reference abbreviations appear at the beginning of most chapters

Aircraft Equipment

			Example
BK	Bordkanone	*Airborne cannon*	BK 3.7, BK 7.5
BZA	Bombenzielaggregat	*Bomb-aiming apparatus*	BZA 1, BZA 20
EZ	Einheitszielvorrichtung	*Unified bomb-aiming apparatus*	EZ 42 gunsight
FA	Fernantrieb	*Remote drive motor*	FA 15
FDL	Ferngelenkte Drehringlafette	*Remote-controlled rotatable turret*	FDL 131Z
FDL-B../2	Ferngelenkte Drehringlafette für B-Stand/2	*Remote-controlled rotatable turret for B-position with 2 guns*	FDL-B 131/2
FDSL-B 131	Ferngelenkte Doppelseiten-lafette für MG 131	*Remote-controlled twin-turrets for MG 131*	FDSL-B 131
FHL	Ferngelenkte Hecklafette	*Remote-controlled tail turret*	FHL 131Z
FuG	Funkgerät	*W/T Equipment*	FuG 203, 230
FuMG	Funkmessgerät	*Radar set*	FuMG 65, 404
FZG	Flakzielgerät	*Anti-aircraft target device*	FZG 76 (V-1)
GM	so called: 'Göring-Mischung'	*Engine performance enhancement system GM-1*	
HD	Hydraulische Drehringlafette	*Hydraulically-operated rotatable turret*	HD 151
HL	Hecklafette	*Tail turret*	HL 131
HL..V	Hecklafette für Vierling	*Tail turret for quadruple gun-mount*	HL 131V
HL..Z	Hecklafette für Zwilling	*Tail turret for twin gun mount*	HL 151Z
KWK	Kampfwagenkanone	*Combat vehicle (Tank) cannon*	KWK 39
Lotfe	Lotfernrohr (Bombenvisier)	*Telescopic bombsight*	Lotfe 7D
MG	Maschinengewehr	*Machine gun*	MG 131, MG 151
MK	Maschinenkanone	*Machine cannon*	MK 103, MK 108
MW	Methanol-Wasser	*Engine performance enhancement*	MW 50
PDS	Patin-Dreiachsen-Steuerung	*Patin three-axis steering*	
PVE	Periskopvisier-Einrichtung	*Periscope sighting device (gunsight)*	
Revi	Reflexvisier	*Reflector (mirror) sight*	
RZ	Rauchzylinder (Bordrakete)	*Smoke cylinder (airborne rocket)*	RZ 65, RZ 73
SG	Sondergerät	*Special device (multi-barreled gun)*	SG 113, 500
Stuvi	Sturzkampfvisier	*Dive bombing gunsight*	
TL	Turbinen-Luftstrahl	*Turbojet*	TL 003, TL 004
VE	Visier, eigengeschwindigkeits-gesteuert	*Gunsight, airspeed-controlled*	
VSE	Visierstand, elektrisch	*Electrical gunsight stand*	
WB	Waffenbehälter	*Weapons container*	WB 81A, WB 151
WGr	Werfergranate	*Mortar grenade (Rocket projectile)*	WGr. 21
ZFR	Zielfernrohr	*Target telescope*	

Firms and Organisations

AEG	Allgemeine Elektrizitäts-Gesellschaft	*General Electric Company*
APK	Artillerie Prüfungskommission	*Artillery Evaluation Commission*
BAL	Bauaufsicht des RLM	*German Air Ministry Construction Inspectorate*
BFW	Bayerische Flugzeug-Werke	*Bavarian Aircraft Works*
BMW	Bayerische Motorenwerke	*Bavarian Motor Works*
DFS	Deutsches Forschungsinstitut für Segelflug	*German Research Institute for Sailplane Flight*
DLH	Deutsche Lufthansa	*German Airlines*
DVL	Deutsche Versuchsanstalt für Luftfahrt	*German Experimental Institute for Aeronautics*
DVS	Deutsche Verkehrsflieger Schule	*German Transport Pilots School*
EHF	Ernst Heinkel Flugzeugwerke	*Ernst Heinkel Aircraft Company*
FLZ	Flugzeugmeisterei	*Aircraft Engineering Centre*
GWF	Gothaer Waggonfabrik	*Gotha Waggon Factory*
HAP	Heeresanstalt Peenemünde (Heimat Artillerie-Park 11)	*Army Institute Peenemünde (Homeland Artillery Park 11)*

HWA	Heereswaffenamt (HWaA)	*Army Ordnance Office*
HWK	Hellmuth Walter-Werke KG	*Hellmuth Walter-Works, Kiel*
LFG	Luft-Fahrzeug-Gesellschaft	*Aviation Vehicles Company*
LGL	Lilienthal Gesellschaft für Luftfahrt	*Lilienthal Society for Aeronautics*
LVG	Luftverkehrsgesellschaft	*Air Transport Company*
OKH	Oberkommando des Heeres	*Supreme Command of the Army*
OKL	Oberkommando der Luftwaffe	*Supreme Command of the Air Force*
OKM	Oberkommando der Marine	*Supreme Command of the Navy*
OKW	Oberkommando der Wehrmacht	*Supreme Command of the Armed Forces*
PuW	Prüfanstalt & Werft der Fliegertruppe	*Evaluation Institute & Flying Corps Facility*
RDL	Reichsverband der Deutschen Luftfahrt-Industrie	*Reich Association of German Aviation Industry*
RLM	Reichsluftfahrtministerium	*German Air Ministry*
RMA	Reichsmarineamt	*Reich Navy Office*
RMF	Reichministerium der Finanzen	*Reich Finance Ministry (Treasury Office)*
RPF	Reichspost-Forschungsanstalt	*Reich Post Office Research Institute*
RVM	Reichsverkehrsministerium	*Reich Transport Ministry*
RWM	Reichswehrministerium	*Reich Army & Navy Ministry*
SAK	Seeflugzeug-Abnahmekommission	*Seaplane Acceptance Commission*
SES	Seeflugzeug-Erprobungsstelle	*Seaplane Test Centre*
SSW	Siemens-Schuckert-Werke	*Siemens-Schuckert-Works*
SVK	Seeflugzeug-Versuchskommando	*Seaplane Test Detachment*
TLR	Technische Luftrüstung (RLM-TLR)	*Technical Air Armament Office*
TVA	Torpedo Versuchsanstalt, Eckernförde	*Torpedo Test Institute*
TVK	Technisches Versuchskommando	*Technical Test Detachment*
VPK	Verkehrstechnische Prüfungskommission	*Technical Transport Evaluation Commission*
DGLR	Deutsche Gesellschaft für Luft-u. Raumfahrt	*German Aviation & Space Society*
NSDAP	National Sozialistische Deutsche Arbeiter Partei	*National Socialist German Workers Party*

Luftwaffe Units

EK	Erprobungskommando	*Test Detachment*
EKL	Erprobungskommando Lärz	*Test Detachment Lärz*
FAGr	Fernaufklärungsgruppe	*Long-range Reconnaissance Wing*
FdF	Fliegerstaffel des Führers	*The Führer's Air Squadron*
FKG	Fernkampfgeschwader	*Long-rage Bomber Wing*
JG	Jagdgeschwader	*Fighter Wing*
JV	Jagdverband	*Fighter Formation*
KdE	Kommandeur der Erprobungsstelle	*Test Centre Commander*
Kdo.d.E	Kommando der Erprobungsstelle	*Test Centre Detachment*
KG	Kampfgeschwader	*Bomber Wing*
LG	Lehrgeschwader	*Test & Training Unit*
NJG	Nachtjagdgeschwader	*Night Fighter Wing*
SG	Schlachtgeschwader	*Ground-attack Wing*
TG	Transportgeschwader	*Transport Wing*
ZG	Zerstörergeschwader	*Heavy Fighter Wing*

Notes

Manufacturers

The Reichsluftfahrtministerium (RLM) adopted a series of (mostly) two-letter prefixes to act as design or manufacturer codes for aircraft. These mostly consisted of one upper and one lower case letter (eg Fw) but there were a handful of exceptions which used all capitals (eg BV):

Al	Albatros
Ao	AGO-Flugzeugwerke
Ar	Arado
Ba	Bachem
Bf	Bayerische Flugzeugwerke
Bü	Bücker
BV	Blohm und Voss
DFS	Deutsche Forschungsanstalt für Segelflug
Do	Dornier
FA	Focke-Achgelis
Fh	Flugzeugbau Halle
Fi	Fieseler
FK	Flugzeugbau Kiel
Fl	Flettner
Fw	Focke-Wulf
Go	Gothaer Waggonfabrik
Ha	Hamburger Flugzeugbau
He	Heinkel
Ho	Horten
Hs	Henschel
Hü	Hütter
Ju	Junkers
Ka	Kalkert
Kl	Klemm
Me	Messerschmitt
NR	Nagler-Rolz
Si	Siebel
Sk	Skoda-Kauba
Ta	Tank
WNF	Wiener-Neustädter-Flugzeugbau *
ZMe	Zeppelin/Messerschmitt
ZSO	Zeppelin/SNCASO

The RLM adopted a similar series of abbreviations for the design and/or manufacturers of engines:

As	Argus
BMW	Bayerische Motorenwerke
Bramo	Brandenburgische Motorenwerke
DB	Daimler-Benz
DZ	Deutz
HM	Heinkel/Hirth
Jumo	Junkers
Sh	Siemens
Z	Zündapp

Messerschmitt Aircraft Designations

This brings us to the inevitable 'chestnut' of 'Bf' or 'Me' for Messerschmitt's earlier designs. This work is very much a study of official documentation and RLM nomenclature has been adhered to.

For the RLM the transition from 'Bf' to 'Me' occurs between the unsuccessful Bf 162 Jaguar (whose number was subsequently allocated to the He 162 Volksjäger) and the Me 163 Komet. The 'Me'155 avoids the issue by having been transferred at a very early stage to Blohm und Voss.

Then there is the 'grey area' of projected developments of 'Bf' types (eg the Bf 109G) initiated after the change to 'Me'. This is tempting (eg Me 109H) but since later operational variants of the '109 retained the 'Bf' prefix (Bf 109K circa 1944-45) this work has standardised on all Messerschmitt types below the RLM number 162 being prefixed 'Bf' and all those from 163 and upwards being prefixed 'Me'.

Publisher's and Translator's Note

In preparing this English edition and translation from the German original some changes, hopefully beneficial to the reader, have been made.

In particular some of the material contained in the appendices to the German book have been moved so that they accompany the relevant chapters in this version. Additionally, at the beginning of each chapter a short list of standard German abbreviations (with English equivalents) which occur frequently in the original text has been provided, as these pertain to the relevant narrative that follows.

As much of the original text was written by elderly authors who in many instances participated in the events described, their sometimes abrupt or conversely lengthy sentences have been restructured to provide a more flowing narrative in the translation. Although some portions may still appear to be less than easy reading, this results from adhering as closely as possible to the original content in order to preserve the style of the individual authors.

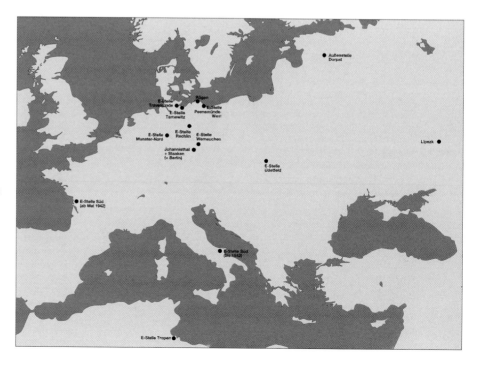

Chapter One
by Heinrich Beauvais

Aircraft Flight Testing at an Erprobungsstelle (Test Centre)

The flight testing spectrum related here has been drawn from original experiences during the period 1935 to 1945 at the Luftwaffe E-Stellen (Test Centres) in Rechlin, Travemünde, and elsewhere. Even today, all aircraft undergo testing in a similar manner, but needless to say, installations and procedures, including organisational, have been further developed.

Quick-Reference Abbreviations

DVL   Deutsche Versuchsanstalt für Luftfahrt
          German Experimental Institute for Aviation

GL/C   Generalluftzeugmeister C-Amt
          Chief of Procurement & Supply, RLM C-Office

INA   Internationale Norm-Atmosphäre
          International Standard Atmosphere (ISA)

KBA   Kurzbetriebsanleitungen
          Brief Operating Instructions

KdE   Kommandeur der Erprobungsstelle
          Test Centre Commander

LGL   Lilienthal-Gesellschaft für Luftfahrt
          Lilienthal Society for Aviation

PfL   Prüfstelle für Luftfahrzeuge
          Evaluation Centre for Aircraft

RLM   Reichsluftfahrtministerium
          German Air Ministry

TAGL   Technische Anweisung des GL
          Technical Instructions of the GL

TATT   Technische Anweisungen des Generals der
          Truppentechnik – *Technical Instructions of the*
          General for Military Technology

Characterizing briefly the tasks of an E-Stelle is frequently related to the phrase 'proof of technical usefulness' as opposed to 'military usefulness'. It is convenient to imagine, however, that there is only one all-embracing indivisible usefulness. Over and above technical requirements, the E-Stelle was certainly expected to concern itself with military aspects, but which for various reasons, was not well entertained.

Testing has to involve, in particular, examining the usefulness of a specific type of aircraft, systems, or article of equipment within the shortest period of time, thus serving as one of the bases for the decision-making authorities. Test results basically encompass the cooperative efforts within the Test Centre and provides its consolidated opinion – not that of an individual employee. Exactness and considered judge-

ment within the specified limits are therefore of importance for test-work.

Using the same bases of the evolution of an aircraft for the evolution process of a particular item of equipment[1] as a standard, the testing phase thus portrays a part of its development. The E-Stellen accordingly, were placed under the aegis of the RLM Development Department, and although they possessed no powers of authorization during the course of development, were nevertheless closely connected with the evolution of every 'Gerät' (aircraft, contrivance, or item of equipment). For example, for evaluation of the article to be tested, newly-defined requirements were important. The article thus developed should not be contrary to existing experience and standards, so that it appeared advisable to involve the E-Stelle with its development at an early date.

During World War Two, testing was accelerated through the provision of more than three 'Versuchsmuster' (prototypes) or of a '0-Serie' (pre-production series). However, the long-valid principle of involving three or more competing firms in the contest to provide a new aircraft was no longer consistently followed, or alternatively, was reverted back to the drawing-board. The E-Stelle thus lost the possibility of comparison between the various project submissions and consequently exercised a much smaller influence upon development.

The bases for testing were the Work Orders. These were assigned by superior specialist departments in the RLM Technisches Amt (Technical Office) and were often prepared with the collaboration of the E-Stelle. During the war, it was often only in the form of a telegram in which individual testing, often bearing the highest priority, was required. Procurement of the necessary material, such as having suitable aircraft made available by the RLM, seldom caused difficulties. Rather, it became a question of the ever-growing limitations in the testing capacity of the E-Stelle. At irregular intervals, the RLM Technical Office issued survey lists containing those tests that were to be cancelled, thus providing the E-Stelle with a little more breathing-space.

As a rule, the preliminary stage in the manufacture of 'Versuchsmuster' (prototypes) of a new aircraft was the construction of a mock-up, whose inspection was the actual beginning of E-Stelle involvement with a new aircraft, and which had already been preceded by its participation during the reading of the 'Baubeschreibung' (Construction Description)[2] of the aircraft concerned, together with the RLM Technisches Amt specialist department. The E-Stelle was also involved at an early date in the project and development conferences.

From mock-up inspection onwards, responsibility for aircraft type-testing lay in the hands of Section E2.[3] In the 1920s, subsequent inspections of the bare prototype airframe still took place during the early prototype construction stage, but not any more during my years of service in Rechlin.

The most significant event that followed was inspection of the completed first prototype at the manufacturer's premises. This proceeded in a similar manner to the mock-up inspection whereby, at the concluding meeting the same principles applied. In addition, the following points had to be heeded: (a) the completed mock-up served as the basis for the prototype completion inspection, (b) in many instances the first prototype might not be identical in all respects to the mock-up, and (c) a distinction had to be made between individual components and prototype deficiencies.

The results of meetings, mock-up and finished-product inspections, flight testing and so on, were recorded in Minutes which were compiled and signed-off by representatives of the RLM, the E-Stelle, and the manufacturers. The E-Stelle itself was only allowed to express its opinion to the manufacturers in the form of an 'Aktenvermerk' (File Remark) since the purchaser of course, was the RLM. We were only able to lend emphasis to our demands or suggestions upon the manufacturer by appealing to his insight, but perhaps also in the form of threats by citing 'Big Brother', ie, the RLM.

First and subsequent test flights were generally accomplished by the manufacturer's own Works pilots. In later years especially, this initial phase was soon followed by pilots from the E-Stelle, the RLM, and also partly by combat pilots in order to obtain first impressions.

After a particular period of Works testing – mostly lasting a few months, the first V-models arrived at the E-Stelle, ferried over as a rule by the manufacturer. When new aircraft types arrived at an E-Stelle, test flights were usually carried out, mainly to determine its characteristics in spins and dives (pull-out, controllability, flutter) and even involving tracking by cinetheodolite.

Each aircraft taken over by the E-Stelle was subjected to an 'Eingangskontrolle' (reception check). With prototypes, it was particularly thorough in the sense of an 'item' check and involved the participation of specialist groups. The final acceptance meeting took place together with the manufacturer.

During the period of relatively peaceful development, namely, before World War Two, endeavours were made to bring together the prototypes of the competing firms so as to conduct direct comparisons between them. Comparative flying was really mainly of significance with fighter aircraft. During testing, which was expected to reveal important arguments for or against a decision regarding procurement and series production, the prototypes were evaluated by various departments. Test programmes, roughly in the form of a completed review upon the expiration of testing of a particular aircraft, were not usual. The duration depended largely upon whether only one or two prototypes had been made available which were successively passed to the specialist sections, or whether a large number of aircraft could be evaluated in parallel. The process, nevertheless, took place in a regulated manner. Exactly how the individual steps followed in succession, were contained in the so-called 'Travemünder-Ringbuch' (loose-leaf or ring-book)[4] prepared by Dipl.-Ing. Carl Francke. Successive steps to be undertaken during testing often resulted from preceding ones, so that it was appropriate to apply flexibility when considering intermediate results achieved to date, particularly regarding urgent questions, eg, from the military aspect, and available capacity of the specialist groups. On the other hand, depending on circumstances, it became necessary to evaluate measurements as soon as possible. Naturally, problems of co-operation or intervention by external official departments also occurred.

For the purpose of carrying out individual tasks, the possibility was presented of drawing-up largely comprehensive checklists. This was the case for example, for determining flight characteristics of performance noted on a card-index. Over and above the standardized questionnaire, the test specialist had to be wary enough to be able to recognize new dangers or situations at the earliest possible moment.

In the course of its activities, the E-Stelle also accomplished a portion of prototype acceptance testing, such as determination of flight performance and characteristics as a 'sub-contractor' to the DVL's PfL (Evaluation Center for Aircraft), where examiners at the latter presented appropriate prototype check-programmes to the E-Stelle and received the results.

Testing and prototype acceptance represented an important part of official controls in the development of a new aircraft. 'Musterprüfung' (type-testing) with safety as the main aim, as well as 'Erprobung' (testing) of which, above all, usefulness was the criteria, was based on optimization.

For various as well as historical reasons, the 'Musterprüfung' and not the 'Erprobung' serves as the basis in Germany for the 'Zulassung' (certification) of an aircraft. Proof in terms of flight safety, reliability and efficiency – including all component parts of the aircraft, has to be provided. The main tasks of a 'Musterprüfstelle' (type-test and certification center) are: (a) establishment and further development of relevant regulations, (b) examination and checking of documents (calculations, construction details, handbooks) as well as laboratory and flight test results, and (c) taking experiences into consideration (flying activity, breakdowns and accidents).

The 'Musterprüfer' (type-test examiner) does not therefore 'actively' participate as in the case of those involved in flight testing. But this by no means constitutes a downgrading, as a high degree of judgement is required of the examiner who must not systematically apply regulations which are often contradictory, but must secure a balance.

The 'Musterprüfstelle' (type-test centre), in the course of its duties, examined the documentation and laboratory investigations provided by the manufacturers. Some examiners also tended to take into account flight test results, since these were also available 'in-house' in the firms' records. Basically, however, flight test results ascertained by the E-Stelle were authoritative.

Flight Testing in General
An E-Stelle is not a combat airfield, and accordingly, the method of testing does not follow a set pattern and is so to speak 'indirect'. The aircraft types are not compared directly, but by means of measurements calculated using normal conditions or limiting values. The measurements methods are specific for a particular sphere of tasks of the various departments. Tests are often conducted under conditions which exceed the otherwise permissible standard, eg, in endurance tests or flight characteristics with extended centre of gravity and flight parameters with increased load factors. It must also be frequently checked whether certain data or limits have been observed, eg, through cg checks, or the fine-tuning of flight regulators or weapons.

Since testing, as already mentioned, can hardly follow a set pattern, problems always arise which have to be subject to operational testing. But even the involvement of an 'Erprobungskommando' (Test Detachment) within the sphere of activity of an E-Stelle, is almost impossible for the former to carry out testing as is possible by an E-Stelle, as certain facilities such as a repair workshop have to be resorted to time and again.

As far we were able to observe, a large proportion of the efforts of such a Test Detachment concentrated on getting used to a new aircraft type and mastering it, instead of testing it from a feeling of superiority. Even after the conclusion of military follow-on testing by the E-Stelle with the aircraft type concerned, the work was not as a rule finished. Examples of aircraft which entered large-scale production such as the Bf 109 and the Ju 88, were constantly developed into newer series models with standard equipment sets and thus required further testing.

The individual steps applied at that time for type-testing an aircraft are described below.

Mock-up Inspection
Mock-up evaluation was based on the tactical-technical guidelines issued by the Luftwaffe leadership or alternatively, the 'Baubeschreibung' (construction description), KBA (works resumé) as well as the equipment and component lists (AG-Liste) issued by the manufacturer. Generally known compulsory instructions or 'checklists' for the evaluation of an aircraft did not exist. Many facets were, however, standardized, such as the arrangement of the most important instrument dials, levers and various external connections. Standards also existed for specific installations such as for cockpit instrument panels and oxygen equipment, but not all systems had by far been included. Documentation of this nature were mostly known completely only by the specialists, but only partially known to the controlling aircraft type-specialists. It would have been necessary for the latter to acquire full knowledge of all instructional guidelines, thus making the specialist redundant as the latter sometimes feared.

The most important part of the mock-up was the crew compartment. Principally, but at the very least, the engine installation

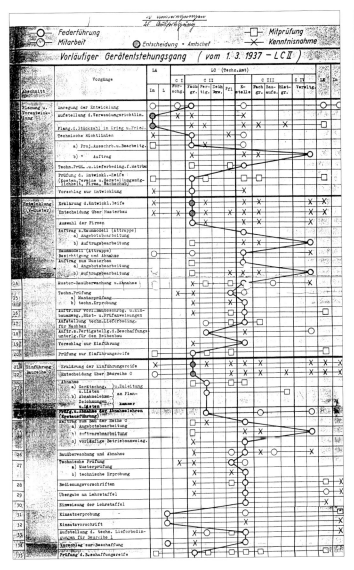

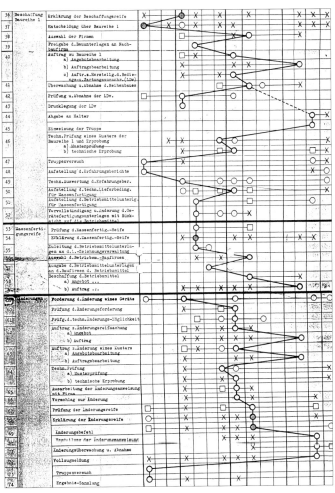

The RLM LC II 'Preliminary Equipment Generation Process' of 1st March 1937, which appeared 9 months after the assumption of Ernst Udet as 'Chef des Technischen Amtes' (Chief of the RLM Technical Office), shows the multitudinous tasks and responsibilities performed by the Erprobungsstellen (Test Centres) concerned with the development of a new item of equipment.

An important partial aspect of mock-up inspection was the clear and systematic arrangement of all instrumentation. The growing number of aircraft systems and equipment sets required the installation of auxiliary instrument panels and consoles in order to provide space for the numerous instruments and operating controls.

and significant parts of other equipment such as the wireless/telegraphy (W/T) equipment and remote-controlled weapons bays were displayed and reviewed. The mock-up was generally built of wood, whereas the installations consisted of actual hardware.

As an 'operating centre', the pilot's seat featured prominently, especially its suitability for various human statures and differing personal equipment, the positioning of instruments and levers, as well as internal and external visibility. At that time – as would be termed today – 'ergonomic' standards also applied.

During mock-up inspection, both tall and short individuals fitted with personal equipment and parachute, evaluated the seat. A seat adjustable in flight was not a general requirement but had to be adjustable in height on the ground. Instead of an adjustment in seat length, rudder pedal adjustment was deemed sufficient.

One of the main criteria, especially involving the pilot's seat, was his external and internal visibility in which the dividing line is always a compromise. For this, there was no objective or generally-valid optimum but was influenced by various parameters, among them personal experience, in-flight tasks and the interpretation of priorities. The question of visibility involved two concepts – that of the full-view fuselage nose and raised dorsal cockpit – the former being independent as to whether the aircraft has a high- or a low-positioned wing, whereas a cabin set on top of a high wing such as in the Ar 198 had an extremely unorganic effect. The 'full-view cockpit' arose from the need to release bombs during various flight attitudes as well as the endeavour to house the crew as close as possible together, but had the disadvantage of difficult protection under enemy fire from ahead and from being blinded by searchlights, added to the fact that the pilot had a very poor overall view of the aircraft – especially wings and engines.

The dorsal cockpit provided the pilot with a good view, especially over the upper portion of the aircraft. During flight in a bank, the wing allowed vision at a downward angle, whereas with a normal high wing, the field of vision was obstructed. The nose-mounted engine offered protection against frontal attack, enhanced through the provision of an armour-proof front windscreen. In a fighter, it was still acceptable when the engine disturbed the view during taxying on the runway or when firing the guns in flight, but made aiming for dropping bombs in horizontal flight hardly possible. The ventral window in the Ju 87 was of little help and was often covered with oil.

The field of vision was captured with the so-called 'field of vision camera' – a Leica equipped with a special objective. Windscreen heating was provided by warm air, but also by electrical means. Windscreen wiping was by means of an alcohol-water mixture, and on fighters, with petrol – to wash away oil splashes from the enemy aircraft.

Internal view is closely connected with external view, hence the question: where to place the instrument panel in the full-view canopy of a bomber or helicopter?

The next point of interest with mock-up inspection was the arrangement of the indicator instruments and operating controls. As a rule, one hand – mainly the right one – held the control stick or steering wheel, and the other hand the engine throttle. From this point on, all the other controls ought to lie within reach and without being easily mistaken. Since the instrument panel was hardly able to contain the whole host of necessary instruments, it was therefore avoided to include operating controls on it, even though it appeared to be advantageous to group related indicator dials and control instruments together. In general, 'clock-face' dials were required for the indicators; oblong strip screens and numeric indicators were only permitted exceptionally. In order to relieve the instrument panel, a portion of the engine indicators were relocated for a trial period to the engine nacelle itself, but this led to illumination problems and made overall awareness more difficult, so that the idea was soon abandoned. As opposed to the basic separation of indicators from operating controls, the various switchboxes for armament and bombs contained both.

As adopted for small aircraft from the very beginning, rudder and elevator controls were incorporated on the control stick with standardized handgrips, and on larger aircraft, on the control pedestal's handwheel. Rudder control was performed using standardized foot pedals equipped with toe-cap brakes. The radio communication button was placed forward and directly below the control stick handgrip. If the aircraft happened to be fitted with variable-pitch propellers, these were operated by thumb switches on the engine throttle – if not set in the 'automatic' mode. As a rule, ignition switches and fuel-cocks were located at front left, and fuel injection-pumps behind the throttle.

Whereas up to about 1940, the cockpit exterior extended to the fuselage skin, cockpits were thereafter fitted with an additional inner skinning onto which lateral banks of controls were attached as a continuation of the instrument panels. In aircraft with several crew members, each workplace had to be reviewed separately, whereby the same criteria applied as related above.

Important aspects in the layout and arrangement of the instruments and control levers were their conspicuousness and unmistakability which in part contradicted the desire for increased standardization.

After about 1935, although no longer developed, aircraft with open cockpits were still flown, such as the Hs 123 employed on operations in Russia until 1942.

In aircraft having enclosed cockpits in particular, air-conditioning and illumination became of importance. Oxygen equipment was necessary in the cockpit and was further developed, whilst problematical protective clothing – too hot or too cold – was dispensed with.

The next stage of development was a pressure cabin. Its introduction into series production was delayed as the cabin could not be held sufficiently air-tight and the air in it was less comfortable.

Dependent on cabin internal pressure and for emergencies, oxygen supply had to be maintained. One further aspect, which could not always be definitely evaluated during mock-up inspection, was the question of illumination. Maintaining safety through comprehensive adjustability and the provision of self-illuminating instruments and various types of emergency lighting (white, red, and ultra-violet light), had to be weighed against each other and co-ordinated.

Review of the Complete Mock-up

The question of making provision for emergencies is very complex and far exceeds that of mock-up inspection, and for the E-Stelle, a new aircraft type provided the first opportunity to exercise and introduce the experience gained to date. Problems of jettisoning the cockpit hood then surfaced. On the Fw 190 for instance, the cockpit hood could scarcely be opened by hand at 250km/h (155mph), so that an explosive release mechanism had to be developed. Questions also involved emergency undercarriage extension, ejection seats, and explosive release of the tail surfaces or parts thereof.

With regard to the overall layout of the new aircraft, the general arrangement of wings, tail surfaces, undercarriage and powerplant as also numerous individual aspects had to be evaluated. Related to these were the design of entry/exit hatches, suspension mechanisms for internal and external loads, the arrangement of cameras, ammunition installations, the type of aerodynamic or weight balance, trimming possibilities, landing flaps, and leading edge slats – to mention only a few.

The specialists from Section E3[5] concerned themselves especially with the engine mock-up, which included partial installations such as engine components

An example of a Test and Development Order to the E-Stelle Rechlin.

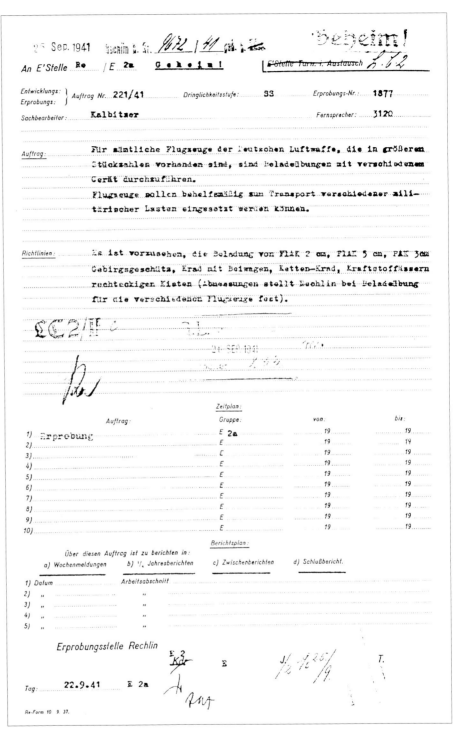

and storage, ignition, air aspiration, exhaust, cooling and oil systems, and not least, the propellers as the focal point of interest. Criteria included protection against overload through heat or pressure, eg, bypass oil, loss of cooling (evaporation only – no fluid ejection), dirt (filters), power peaks (flexible positioning) and serviceability.

In co-ordinated agreement with other specialist departments, questions were clarified relating to aerodynamics, cg positions, motor ignition and interference elimination, power supply via generators, and so on. Finally, the aspects involving wireless, radio direction-finding, navigation equipment installation and interference elimination, and the entire electrical or hydraulic installations as well as the armament and bomb-release systems, had to be evaluated by the specialist groups.

During the mock-up inspection closing meeting, all participants were able to speak. In deciding upon measures to be taken, consideration was given to importance (re usefulness, safety, standardization) as well as to feasibility (re costs, time involved, material and manufacturing capability).

This was followed-up by laying down a time schedule. It had to be determined which alterations, eg, for safety considerations, had to be definitely carried out in the prototypes and which alterations could be progressively introduced, and in particular circumstances, in connection with ongoing developments. On occasions when extensive alterations had been decided, a renewed mock-up inspection took place, but with fewer participants.

Flight Testing Commencement by the E-Stelle

As already mentioned, during the course of Works testing (by the manufacturer) pilots from the E-Stelle, the RLM, and the armed forces became involved. The RLM pilots were mostly former colleagues, such as Flugbaumeister, so that differences in their evaluations were not greater than those made by E-Stelle pilots. Participation of combat pilots on the other hand was not unproblematic, since they were mostly not able to distinguish sufficiently the positive as well as negative deviations between a prototype compared to a later series production aircraft. Thus, for example, Werner Mölders was disappointed with the Fw 190 when he later got to fly it in its series version equipped with weapons, armour-plating, and large auxiliary fuel tanks, etc.

On what basis the timing was selected for handing over to the E-Stelle, was not known to us. Both manufacturer and the RLM had to display an interest in making a speedy decision for the early commencement of testing by the E-Stelle. When, however, an aircraft type like the first Ju 86 passed to Rechlin possessed such bad stalling characteristics, it was probably due more to lack of suspicion or pressure of time than to a feeling of ill-will.

The prototypes, or those machines intended for testing by the E-Stelle, were mostly ferried over by the manufacturer. During the war, these were also collected by crews from the E-Stelle or the 'Erprobungskommandos' (Test Detachments).

Fundamentally, every aircraft that came to Rechlin was subjected to the 'entry control' which included balance and loading plan control. The loading plans were needed for general flying operations and were mandatory to be able to establish flying weights and flight conditions such as flight performance measurements or undercarriage tests, or to establish extreme

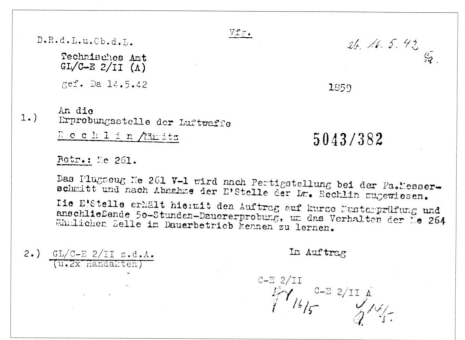

```
D.R.d.L.u.Ob.d.L.                    Vfg.
     Technisches Amt                              26. 16. 5. 42
     GL/C-E 2/II (A)                                       G2.
     gef. Da 14.5.42                       1359

1.)  An die
     Erprobungsstelle der Luftwaffe
     R e c h l i n /Müritz              5043/382

     Betr.: Me 261.

     Das Flugzeug Me 261 V-1 wird nach Fertigstellung bei der Fa.Messer-
     schmitt und nach Abnahme der E'Stelle der Lw. Rechlin zugewiesen.
     Die E'Stelle erhält hiermit den Auftrag auf kurze Musterprüfung und
     anschließende 50-Stunden-Dauererprobung, um das Verhalten der Me 264
     ähnlicher Zelle im Dauerbetrieb kennen zu lernen.

2.)  GL/C-E 2/II z.d.A.                  In Auftrag
     (u.2x Handakten)
                                         C-E 2/II
                                              C-E 2/II A
```

As the war progressed, Development Orders were often issued in the form of a short letter or telegram.

cg positions for checking flight characteristics. With a new aircraft type, entry control was particularly important, since it played a part as one aspect in the overall evaluation. When all hatches and covers were laid open, the specialist groups were then invited to continue.

The same principles applied at the concluding meeting as at the complete mock-up inspection, when experience gathered in the meantime on detailed points had to be taken into account. In the beginning – in other words, around 1935/36 – the manufacturers frequently made the equipment contractors responsible for deficiencies. The RLM, however, soon put a stop to that. In general, only a portion of the deficiencies could be eliminated immediately on prototypes, in the sense of component deficiencies which affected flight safety.

Following completion of the entry controls or after completion of immediate alterations deemed necessary, the aircraft were handed over to the specialist units and flight testing could commence.

Flight Performance
One of the most important duties of the E-Stelle was measuring flight performance. The latter is understood to mean the 'movement of a point mass', ie, the movement of the aircraft's centre of gravity.

With flight performance measurement, there were two characteristic tendencies, namely, the least amount of expense on auxiliary instrumentation and the detailed, comprehensive and uninterrupted recording involved. The former required specially-trained pilots and in the evaluation, considerations of control and estimation of deviations from everyday conditions.[6]

Recording began with the traditional barograph which became used in the end more for control than for evaluation purposes. The Askania 4-track recorder, as far as I can remember, was scarcely used for this purpose. From around 1937/38, we photographed the instrument panel – referred to occasionally as the 'automatic observer', using a Leica or Robot camera activated by the pilot, but which experienced illumination problems. As far as I am aware, 'Schaltuhr' (time-switches) were not used. The next step, to employ instrument panels with artificial illumination, was seldom used at that time. Take-off and landing measurements were continually registered with the Zeiss-Startmess camera.

One of the basic prerequisites for speed measurements was calibration of the speedometer on the so-called 'measurement tracks'. In Rechlin, these consisted of two stretches each of 8km (5 miles) and 6.5km (4 miles) in length, lying almost rectangular to one another along the line of the railway track emanating from Mirow. These were overflown successively to-and-fro at constant speed, the time taken recorded by stop-watch. On an evaluation sheet, upon which the respective direction of the measurement stretches were given, the speeds thus recorded could be entered and the central point of the circle determined via the four 'measurement points', which enabled determination of the actual aircraft speed and mean wind speed. Even simple mean-speed values obtained from flight in each direction back and forth, proved mostly adequate. This held good for speeds up to 600km/h (373mph) or so, but with the Me 262, it proved necessary

to install approach-markers along the stretch. Using the so-called 'Tower Method' the error caused by measurement of the static pressure could be determined.[7] In rare instances, measurements using cine-theodolites were also made, whereas radar measurements were only considered but not used at that time.

Flight speeds near the ground were obtained by speedometer calibration described above. The speed indications at various altitudes were mostly calculated without reference to the Mach number. Atmospheric compressibility was only given consideration with high diving speeds. We seldom used the Junkers Air-log.[8] Use of the tracking station was mostly confined to important proving flights, since the cost of measurement and evaluation as well as the difficulty of determining wind direction was a deterrent.

Conducting repeated flights over the measurement stretch for horizontal speed measurements was always very time-consuming, if one did not know this fairly precisely beforehand. This validity held independently of whether it was approached from 'above' or 'below', above all, in single-engine flight, since in such cases the optimum value of bank or side-slip had to be taken into consideration, and because the effect of 'snaking' caused by following variometer displacements had to be definitely avoided. If the value was known, it was simplest to set it up from 'above' and to check whether everything agreed.

The next most important aspect in determining flight performance was rate-of-climb measurement. The best climb was understood to be attainment of the highest altitude. The highest gain in energy was not particularly taken notice of, and is surely only relevant with jet aircraft. During the early period of flight, the so-called 'Gasuhr' (gas-clock) was used for altitude measurement, consisting of a scaled drum-barometer of roughly 20cm (8in) diameter, calibrated in millimetres of mercury (Torr) and connected to the static pressure. Thus exact values as with the barograph were obtainable. For temperature measurements, the so-called 'Stiel' (strut) thermometer was used with biplanes. With monoplanes, temperature determination became a problem since heating-up caused by the engine or its exhaust had to be avoided and furthermore, it was not known which portion of the energy transformation caused by ram-pressure or friction needed to be taken into consideration for the increase in temperature. Later on, the Colsmann altimeter was employed, otherwise series-produced devices were deemed sufficient. We then allowed ourselves to be advised of temperatures by the weather forecasters.

The indicator for 'best climb rate', for example with the Ar 68, was made initially with the so-called 'saw-tooth' barograph. An altitude step of perhaps 300m (984ft) was flown out at various, but each time constant altimeter indications. The speed-curves thus showed a maximum for each altitude step flown.

With the Bf 109, this turned out to be very time-consuming since for a constant climbing speed, a long approach run was necessary. We later determined the desired climbing speed under the following considerations:

The optimum climbing speed (w) as a function of the altitude (h) from experience is almost a straight line. The indicated air-speed (v) varies and in general, decreases with altitude. If one climbs with constant speed (v), w.h then becomes a rising convex curve or hump whose tangent is the above-mentioned straight line. By an apt choice of two constant airspeed indicators, it was possible in two climbs to determine the optimum straight line, the result being confirmed in a third climbing flight. Absolutely decisive for this was an exact and disturbance-free flight. The required flightpath speed had to be held with the smallest possible control movements so that only a few points recorded were sufficient. We mainly noted the times from 1,000m (3,280ft) to the next thousand. We even attempted to convey our readings by wireless, but the unavoidable return queries were so disturbing that this method proved unsuccessful.

The w.h curve (tangent) showed flying errors very sensitively. From the barograph curve of climbing time, it cannot be seen where the error lies and the exact determination of climbing speed up to full-pressure altitude which is dependent upon engine performance, is very time-consuming. We therefore satisfied ourselves mostly with determination of the mean climbing speed in this respect. In the early days after 1935, for climbing-flight evaluation, pre-printed tables from the 'Travemünder-Ringbuch' were used.

An important aid was the atmospheric diagram having co-ordinates b (air pressure) and t (temperature) plus the line p

(air density) being a constant, as also the INA (international standard atmosphere) curve which we entered in. The INA y-altitude was the basis altitude initially used. Later, a change-over to 'air pressure altitude' was made and calculated simply with indicated altitude differences. Based on the daily temperatures entered by ourselves in the atmospheric diagram we estimated the adjusting corrections to be made.

For take-off and landing measurements, the Zeiss camera was used exclusively, set up in the vertical plane of the flightpath using the wingspan as the basic element of size. Transverse axis systems such as developed by Dornier and Messerschmitt, were not employed in Rechlin. Aircraft-

installed systems were not known to me at that time. Measurements of take-off run length with variable take-off weights at various temperature and air-pressure conditions were determined by the ground-run tables contained in the aircraft type-sheet. Take-off measurements required the steepest – but not the best – climb values. Undercarriage measurements were to denote the highest permissible sink speeds which were not to be exceeded. Performance in turning flight was not viewed at that time as a constituent of performance measurement.

As far as I recall, performance in single-engined flight, ie, multi-engined aircraft suffering engine failure – was not systemat-

This type of 'Operation Chart' represented one of a number of results of measurement flights obtained by the E-Stelle Rechlin for each new aircraft type entering operational service.

ically investigated. It was deemed sufficient to determine whether or how climbing or horizontal flight was still possible at particular weight conditions.

Take-off power was still only measured in the early years after 1935, since 'constant-speed' propellers indicated inferior values in particular circumstances. Later, when variable-pitch propellers had been introduced, there was no longer a need to carry out such measurements.

Measurements of flying range were carried out by Section E3. The aircraft type compilers in Section E2, besides flight distance and duration under constant flight conditions, were interested in data obtained under various types of operating or loading conditions. We took pains to develop a suitable presentation. New was the fact that a jet aircraft at 10,000m (32,800ft) altitude covered twice as great a distance than near the ground, and compared with propeller-driven aircraft, throttling had little influence on the range.

It appeared tempting to us to measure flight polars, eg, as the basis for performance calculations for range measurement control, for estimating the emergency landing possibilities caused by engine failure and so on. However, we faced definition difficulties (influence of the engine) and the measurement and particular dangers (such as through windmilling propellers) which constantly hindered these being carried out. These measurements and the development of suitable methodology was certainly one of the tasks of research.

Flight performance judgement was obtained by comparison of the requirements contained in the tactical-technical guidelines and with corresponding indigenous and foreign aircraft. By balancing the diverse components of flight performance of an aircraft type, it appeared that speed was unconsciously given a certain priority, despite certain disadvantages such as the longer turn-around time of our fighters compared with the Spitfire. It thus appeared very difficult to undertake even the slightest step which would sacrifice speed, and was one reason why we did not get away from the He 177's coupled engines. The introduction of the Fw 190 with its 18.3m² (197ft²) wing area appeared improbable and the altered wingtips of the Bf 109F which improved its stalling characteristics, were pushed through only with difficulty. As a whole, it appeared that concepts had been unwillingly altered, which then raised the question: were they really so good? Did manufacturing aspects provide the impetus (alterations which disturbed smooth production) or were there too few important reasons for an alternative compromise?

Comparative Flight Trials

Comparative flights were of direct significance only for judging fighter aircraft. One could well hold such tests with aircraft designed for other purposes such as flying in parallel in climbing or horizontal flight and gaining impressions of differences in performance, but it was not extremely important for evaluation. In conducting comparative flights with fighters, two procedures could in principle be adopted. The one could be termed 'analytical' and would follow the British example described by Alfred Price in his book 'Air Combat'. These included climbing, horizontal flight, acceleration and dives, turning radius and rate of roll – especially by breaking-off combat by rolling in the opposite direction, and could be conducted partly under the same initial conditions or partly with an initially more favourable condition to one of the participants.

With the other, one particular situation was allowed to develop out of another, similar to how it happens during air combat. This procedure was less apparent but was felt to be much nearer to reality. Compared to an air combat situation, this type of comparison dispensed with a one-sided superiority stemming from the initial situation such as an attack from above or out of the sun, and thus giving one of the pilots a significant advantage. It therefore became customary with us to meet at a pre-arranged spot at a pre-determined altitude and geographical location, approach each other in opposite directions in level flight and attempt to out-turn one's opponent. This served as the main criteria for the possibilities offered in combat turns, perhaps not strictly correct – although 'dogfighting' even today is not yet obsolescent, but well in the sense of flying tradition. As to exactly how an advantage was to be achieved, there were two differing points of view. One could be construed as being 'energy conscious' and the other as 'trick-oriented'. It appeared clear to us that in turning flight, the highest possible 'angular gain' was dependent upon the energy transformed producing the highest efficiency, so that all superfluous manoeuvres only led to a loss in speed. One could thus achieve the best and smallest turning radius at constant speed, and if this did not lead to success, it meant that this aircraft type was inferior to its opponent in turning dogfights. Despite this energy exercise, we many times observed – without asking ourselves or others – that the rate of turn formed a component of the aircraft's manoeuvrability as one of its flight characteristics. The momentary optimum appeared to us to be more or less one of flying feeling. It was also suggested whether or in which instances it would be useful to extend the landing flaps,

but this question produced no clear answer. In his 'Travemünder-Ringbuch', Carl Francke treated the measurement of the 'tightest circles'. With the aid of performance equations, Dr. Jodlbauer calculated better curvature times for the He 51 and Ar 68 biplanes than for the newer Bf 109 and He 112 monoplanes. But all this was 'secret' and was currently insufficient to enable us to conduct systematic measurements to obtain optimum times for curvature. I well remember having recorded the time to fly a full circle in a Bf 109, but of what use was an isolated figure without anything to compare it with?

The 'trick-oriented' variant is well-covered by Carl Francke's remark: 'The roll is the fastest turn'. This determination is doubtlessly correct when one aircraft makes a level turn and the other rolls vertically around its axis. With the Bf 109 for example, the rate of roll was about five seconds for 360°, whereas a full-circle turn required about 12 seconds. It never became clear to me, however, what length of time was needed for the 'rolling aircraft' to transition from and to level flight from the initial altitude. I unfortunately let the opportunity slip by for Francke to show this to me. Whoever broke-off a turning dogfight, appeared to be at a hopeless disadvantage. I have no recollection of systematic tests conducted to change that. The higher rate of roll of the Fw 190 against that of the Bf 109 appeared to us to offer only a small advantage.

It is of course important to know the turning behaviour of one's own aircraft as well as the opponent's, but it appeared to be of greater importance to recognize and to take advantage of the short time available for opening fire. This was valid in turning dogfights with tricks, in curving in and out of formations, but also when making attacks with an excess of speed such as in a dive. Recording such situations as well as the effectiveness of defensive manoeuvres such as through rapid rudder movements was not possible for us due to the lack of a suitable gun-camera. The ESK 2000 was much too clumsy!

We regretted at that time that we had no 'Theory of Air Combat' available in the sense of 'operational research'. It was a question as to whether one existed at all which went beyond a few sentences of experience. Perhaps it should have been a task for the RLM to seek out suitable individuals to work on this problem. We aircraft type-testers were well aware of the questions, but had neither the time nor the theoretical expertise to work on it.

There were certainly starting points as shown by the above-mentioned work of Flugbaumeister Dr. Jodlbauer who concerned himself with the question as to which effective conclusions were to be drawn from the inferior turns albeit higher speeds of the newer aircraft. This work, however, never appeared to have found the attention it deserved. It was certainly classified secret, and this hindered its dissemination.

Comparative flights with combat pilots resulted in a welcome mutual acquaintanceship, but factually brought nothing new, as instanced by the comparative flights of the Bf109 and Fw190 in 1941. Even there, the 'test of ability' was carried out through an exchange of pilots, but we were not able at that time to ascertain much comprehension for a 'Theory of Air Combat'.

Flight Characteristics

The second most important task in flight testing is the measurement and judgement of flight characteristics. They involve a whole series of specialist areas and alternating relationships such that they can be perceived under various viewpoints, and only a few basic aspects will be touched upon here.

Flight characteristics and the purpose of use of the aircraft have two types of relationships. The first requires – for both civil and military aircraft – particular qualities for the type of operational use envisaged, whilst the second requires flight characteristics together with other criteria which are partly enhancing and partly contradictory.

Specific military requirements such as high manoeuvrability were, and still are, the characteristic goals with fighters and bombers and take into account: an unequivocal neutral point, method of lateral movement, frequency, damping, and control surface effectiveness. Flight characteristics have to be seen in connection with flight performance. Concerning manoeuvrability, for instance, the rate of roll, turning radius, level speed and rate of climb, are all of significance. Even structural strength has to be considered, with single-engine flight based equally upon flight characteristics and performance. For all-weather flight, the equipment installed besides the flight characteristics, are decisive factors. For use as a weapons carrier, the appropriate targeting devices also come into consideration. In particular types of employment, special slow-flying characteristics were of value.

Stalling tests ought to indicate, among other things, how altitude losses which are incurred can be kept within limits and possible methods of recovery taken. In these type of tests, it is important to achieve a lateral stall and then try out effective measures – as a rule – the 'hard vertical rudder' displacement. Limiting the elevator effectiveness alone offers no safety, as the acci-

dent with Heinz Bär in the Zaunkönig (wren) in 1957 showed.[9] Each aircraft to be certificated had to be controllable with 'aileron alone' or with 'rudder alone'. If this requirement had been met with the He 70, the accident involving Generalleutnant Walter Wever (take-off crash with fixed ailerons) would in all probability not have happened. These are all experiences gained from our experimental activities, some 60 years old, but apparently still not so well known today as they should be. Particular blind-flying characteristics were not a requirement at that time, and the term 'blind-flying capability' far exceeds the domain of flight characteristics. Here, the equipment is much more decisive as well as the division of tasks by the aircrew. Equally important are the ground services. In earlier years, multi-engined aircraft were used – with a few exceptions such as the JuW34. Later, blind-flying was also required of single-seaters (fighters), fitted with the appropriate equipment.

The flight mechanics of flying characteristics were worked upon by numerous authors and each filled an imposing volume. But that is not the subject of discussion here. Rather, a mere definition from the flight-mechanical standpoint ought to be introduced. The term 'flight characteristic' is valid for everything which causes the aircraft as a fixed body to move; in other words, its movement and momentum around the cg, where the control surface and turning impetus is taken into consideration. A short look into history will suffice:

With all manned aircraft one can speak – using the terminology of today – of a 'man-machine-system'. To the objectively available characteristics of the aircraft there appears in opposition, the capabilities of the more or less subjective judgement of the pilot. The history of objective comprehension and that of expression of opinion is as old and lasting as the history of aviation itself, even when many pilots happily mix this all up together.

When the aircraft became an object serving a purpose, requirements were placed on its use. To cite but one example: In the first fighter comparison made in January 1918 in Adlershof, Manfred von Richthofen judged the flying characteristics of the Fokker V11 as being unsatisfactory. 'The aircraft has to be outwitted; it is directionally unstable and difficult to hold straight in a dive. That is not acceptable in a fighter. Its stalling characteristics are unfavourable

and accident-prone'. In strict secrecy, Fokker lengthened the fuselage by 40cm (15¾in), moved the upper wing rearward and made modifications to the control surfaces, and thus created the precursor of the famous Fokker DVII. This shows that Fokker had an understanding of flight characteristics and knew how one could influence them. Terms like stability, controllability and stalling behaviour were certainly known, even when far from being tackled systematically.

During the period 1927-1933, Dipl.-Ing. Walter Hübner published several reports on the subject of flight characteristics. He took into detailed account the topics of balance, stability with fixed and moving control surfaces, load alterations caused through throttling, controllability and manoeuvrability (influencing performance), and various types of spin dependent upon configuration features and development of checking methods as well as pertinent guidelines and directives. An overview of the 'Development Direction of Flight Characteristics' was given by Joachim von Koeppen in the 1933 DVL-Jahrbuch (Annual). Unfortunately, it did not feature a 'Literature Index', and therefore gave no indication of the article by Walter Hübner. Nevertheless, von Koeppen mentioned Hübner as his collaborator and stated in his Introduction that the development of flight characteristics, ie, the controllability and stability, despite the possibility of measuring some of its distinctive values, can only be immediately established by the pilot.

On the subject of longitudinal stability and control, he mentioned that development tended towards longer fuselages and larger tail surface aspect ratios; of improved aerodynamic control surface balances; of influences on the aircraft cg and the elevators; on behaviour of the aircraft with fixed and movable controls, as well as differences in idling- and maximum-power

Engineers at the E-Stelle Rechlin still appeared in civilian clothes at the end of the 1930s. Talking shop prior to the next flight (from left to right) are Bäumler, Wittmann, Weigand, Ullrich and Arlt.

flight. He discussed the subject of the desired degree of longitudinal stability and damping. With reference to lateral movement, the achieved reduction in aileron forces through improved effectiveness and the increased directional stability (mainly through longer fuselages and larger vertical tail surfaces) were emphasized. Harmonizing of control forces and control surface effectiveness were regarded as important. The dependence of lateral movement on the angle of attack and on the propeller slipstream was equally alluded to, as also to longitudinal moments. The author established in conclusion that 'laterally-stable aircraft are characterized by enhanced dihedral or wing sweep and through large damping, but possess moderate stability around the vertical (yaw) axis'. Finally, the 'Behaviour at Large Angles of Attack' and 'Landing Characteristics' were also dealt with.

Whether I was aware at that time of von Koeppen's statements, I am not able to recall, but am of the opinion that they were certainly of interest with regard to the status of general knowledge, but were of limited use in practise.

One fundamental contribution to the development of flight characteristics evaluation was the study by Dr. A Kuppers entitled 'Measures for The Assessment of Flight Characteristics'. Although this treatise was based on quantitative determinations, ie, measurements, it provided an excellent starting point for what were in practice still mainly qualitative methods used for a systematic examination.

In the early days (1935/36), a report on spinning also existed which, as far as I can remember, was a compilation of experiences from chiefly foreign sources. Significance was attached to the importance of the cg position and above all, the decisive rudder effectiveness at the point of recovery. Up to the present, I know of no experience to the contrary, although by retaining rudder deflection for too long during the recovery process, the danger exists of a change in the direction of rotation.

When Carl Francke came to Rechlin from the E-Stelle Travemünde, he brought his 1937 'Ring Book' with him. We were only interested at that time in the evaluation of flight characteristics, so that I only mainly recall this portion of it.

On 15th February 1938, our Rechlin colleague Dipl.-Ing. Alexander Thoenes completed a contribution to the 'Technical Aeronautics Ring-Book' entitled 'The Essence and Significance of Flight Characteristics and their Examination'. The summary portrayed very well the status at that time. Like several others, however, Thoenes envisaged future solution of the problem as being rather too simple. With the establish-

ment of numerical values via measurements, only one aspect of the questions raised is answered. The other aspect – that of determination, is not answered as one would imagine in establishing only a few figures independent of each other. This was shown quite clearly during a conference lasting several days in Marienehe on the subject of a '100-tonne Aircraft'. Unfortunately, I have not been able to discover any report about it, even by the LGL which normally covered such matters. As far as I remember, the lecture notes did not stem from Heinkel but from Berlin, and appeared to contain incorrect information, but we did not know whether this was due to the author's failing or was deliberate. In any case, what came to hand at that time, served as an example of how unreliable 'documents' could be. Although all records are missing, I shall attempt to list a few recollections.

The numerous visitors came from official departments, from research and industry, and a diversity of problems were discussed. The majority of participants were of the unanimous view that most of the questions raised could only be answered through trial-and-error solutions and experience. The categorical statement of one of those present to the effect that 'the pilots must also provide clear numerical details, according to which we then design' appeared reasonable as a wish but was unrealistic at that time. Only a few measurement values could be made available and exorbitant requirements were either unrealizable or could only be considered with undue effort.

The discussion was very lively and comprehensive, obviously, since we were aware how dependent the solution of special problems was with those that were generally valid. The example was given of a Dornier transport aircraft with fully-balanced controls, with the conclusion that it was certainly flyable but highly unpleasant. This 'power-free' steering was deemed an advantageous method by a large number of participants as a 'relief' if only the effectiveness depended continually on the force involved. We were also convinced that for normal flight, particularly with very large aircraft, that the aerodynamic balance or aerodynamic power increase in the manner of Heinkel or Blohm & Voss could be operated up to their limits. There existed doubts concerning extreme cases such as with turbulent airflow, ground tailwinds, icing conditions as also elastic deformation of the control surfaces. Questions of loading changes through variation of the flight attitude such as through load release in rotatable turrets, were also raised. For such cases, emergency control possibilities were considered, for example, by altering

the gear-ratio in the flying controls through distribution of loads over other crew members, and by braking. On the question of servo-controls, it concerned performance, angular speeds, reliability, multi-systems (how and which part of the installation), tied up with the question of switch-on and switch-off capability. In order to avoid surprises, an attempt was made to consider all possible flight conditions and configurations.

A further conference on the topic of flight characteristics was held on 8th and 9th April 1943 in Berlin (LGL Report 163). In his introduction, Flugbaumeister Walter Friebel of GL/C-E2 spoke briefly over the RLM's concerns and desires on the subject of flight characteristics in the following categories: General military significance of flight characteristics, (2) ground-looping (or swinging) on take-off, (3) slow flight, (4) dead-stick landing, ie, due to engine-failure, (5) directional qualities in the neutral position, (6) stability, (7) the impact of deformations, (8) correct sychronization of flight characteristics, (9) withdrawal of the dive-bombing requirement, and (10) retention of the flight characteristics of series-built aircraft, the ease of exchangeability of control surfaces, etc.

The expositions of Prof. K H Doetsch and his collaborators (Friedrichs, Lugner and Höhler) concerning the new establishment of flight characteristic standards found the widest interest. Most noteworthy by the above were the separation between basic characteristics checks and measurement checks. These standards had hardly any influence in practise in Rechlin, but gave good cause for reflection.

On the topic of flight characteristics measurements, Flugbaumeister Lorenz Schmid from the E-Stelle Rechlin reported in particular on the lateral movement of the Do 217. In these tests, three angular speeds and three control surface positions were mechanically recorded, whereas speed, altitude, temperature, manifold pressure and rpm had to be noted manually.

Other reports delivered during the conference were by Flugbaumeister Paul Bader of Rechlin on 'Flight Characteristics of Captured Enemy Aircraft', W Liebe of Prague on 'Sideslip Measurements in Flight', P Höhler of Adlershof on 'On Conducting Spin Tests', H Schorn of Brunswick on 'Formula-related Connections between Airframe Size and Lateral Stability Requirements', and Flugbaumeister G Full of Travemünde on 'Characteristics of Seaplanes on Water'. From the discussions which followed each dissertation, it appeared noteworthy that whereas the 'Prüfstelle' (Examination Centre) tended towards 'Vorschrift' (Regulation), the E-Stelle wanted 'Richtlinien' (Guiding Principles) in order not to hinder development. The viewpoints of the remaining participants also differed.

It was generally established that the new guiding principles were 'Acceptance Test' aligned, whilst the tasks of industry and research could in individual cases stipulate other procedures.

Vigorously discussed was also the question of control effectiveness limitation as a safety factor and the levelling-out with aileron operation, especially with fighter aircraft having a safety factor of 7.0, and roll duration of 3-4 seconds. Further questions were directed at the requirements for tailless aircraft and large transport aircraft, and whether flight performance or characteristics in single-engine flight or landing were a decisive factor. From various participants a unification of measuring devices and methods were suggested, which ought to be worked upon by a central establishment.

Measurement checks were initially still problematic so that practical application of the new guidelines were rather limited. The perceptions of various pilots were generally in close agreement. Where differences of opinion occasionally surfaced, clarification was hindered more by self-consciousness or departmental egoisms than by factual arguments.

Advances in aircraft development hardly influenced the determination of flight characteristics, but made a large number of individual verifications necessary, so that the testing programme constantly broadened. One only has to bear in mind 'inventions' such as retractable undercarriages, landing flaps, wing leading-edge slats, reverse-thrust propellers, brake-parachutes, particular air-tow methods, helicopters, jet propulsion, and so on; furthermore, the influence of higher wing-loadings, higher speeds and increasing aircraft dimensions.

A particular role played in the 'man-machine-system' is the flight control technique. Initially, it seemed to relieve the pilot in the form of course-control and three-axis autopilot control. With its assistance, thought was also given to improving pure flying behaviour, as had been offered by Siemens to Messerschmitt for the Me 210, and by expanding its effectiveness to avoid critical flight situations from developing.

The subject of pilot training also belongs to these considerations. As we would term it today, it was and still is a 'man-machine-problem', where man places demands on the machine and vice-versa. The incidents of 'accident-prone' aircraft has continually been spoken of. Such frequent occurrences could have been avoided not so much from lengthy practice time (flying hours, take-offs and landings) as from useful instruction.

With adequate space available, auxiliary measuring instruments could be assembled together on a simple wooden panel which enabled rapid mounting, dismantling and usage possible in various types of aircraft.

Borderline cases are also problematic and can only be very basically touched upon here by citing a few examples. There was the case of the Me 210 which 'unintentionally' went into a flat spin but which also had other faults which led to its rejection. Accidents have been described as a result of peculiar characteristics, one of which I myself witnessed. In my experience, these occurrences were 'unnecessary' and could have been avoided with appropriate instruction. The in-flight behaviour of the Fw 190 on take-off when fitted with bombs was the reason why I was called to go to Russia. I was able to demonstrate better take-offs, but the combat pilots took no notice.

Another problem in this connection was and is the mastering of trimming of powerful single-seat aircraft at take-off. Adequate control surface effectiveness is not sufficient; it has to be used sensibly.

If the question is now raised, what has all that got to do with flight characteristics, the answer can only be 'very much, for the momentary handling required of an aircraft is a direct result of its flight characteristics'.

The E-Stelle had as good as no influence on the training of flight crews. The examples illustrated, however, that a need certainly existed in this respect. We had talked about this difficulty in Rechlin, but had neither the time nor the authorization to do anything about it. To this set of questions belongs also Carl Francke's intention to connect a 'fast-flight school' to the E-Stelle. At this point, a remark of a general nature to the theory is necessary:

What we were missing was an expansion of the usual theoretical methods of presentation with graphic illustrations. I shall try somewhat to explain the problem by taking a simple example, namely, the considerations on the longitudinal moments.

The books available at that time appear not to have contained sufficient information, otherwise what would have been the need at the end of the 1930s for the dissertations from Doetsch, Doetsch-Lange and Bock on the subject of longitudinal stability? But even these accounts provide no clearly visible model. When some 20 years later Just in Germany and Elkin in Canada in pages-long calculations finally determined that 'the distance between the cg and the neutral point is a measure of stationary longitudinal stability', but for such a simple fact no equally simple model can be

provided, then in the 'physical' sense something is not quite right – as correct as the calculations may well be. There thus exists a gap here. The theoretician is too good to provide a vivid representation or, he is afraid in front of colleagues who may accuse him of triviality. On the other hand, the practician does not have the time to obtain the necessary overall picture. He is happy when he can follow the presentation step by step. With complicated problems, the theoretician's help by providing transparent presentations is even more important!

The aim in Rechlin was to bridge gaps with the aid of research. In Dr. Kuppers' time – as long as the DVL outstation Rechlin existed under his leadership, that was still possible to some extent. The military basic training of Rechlin engineers was at a later stage apparently more important than a closer contact with the DVL.

At that time, we had neither flight simulators for the development phase nor for training purposes. The intention to create something of this nature was obvious, as we had been required to provide numerical values of flight characteristics. But that was not always possible, hence, for the evaluation of an aircraft, the only course remaining was flight testing.

Testing Flying Qualities in Practice

The sequence of tests to be carried out during a flight is determined from the state of the aircraft, eg, load distribution and cg position, and on the natural discharge of the flight. The pilot takes along with him the appropriate programme of tests to be conducted.

Flight characteristics are determined in a series of single tasks and as a rule run basically as follows:

An initial commencement status is first established (speed, engine-power, trim,

Rechlin E 7b₅	Mustererprobung	Schlußbericht
Erpr.Nr. 1334	Fi 156	LC II 1 Nr. 153/36 Blatt 2

Zusammenfassende Beurteilung.

Die Harmlosigkeit der Flugeigenschaften ist unübertroffen. Vervollkommnung der Eigenschaften um Längsachse wird für spätere Serie vorbereitet.

Die Start- und Landemöglichkeiten lassen Benutzung fast jeder offenen Geländeform und auch mittlerer Waldwiesen zu. Das Einsinken der Laufräder in stark aufgeweichten Ackerboden läßt sich zwar ohne unerträgliches Mehrgewicht nicht herabsetzen. Um das Einsinken und Hängenbleiben des Sporns zu verringern, erhält die Serie ab 50.Maschine eine geänderte Spornausführung.

Die Sicht genügt in beiden Hauptsitzen den hier besonders hohen Anforderungen.

Wünschenswert wäre noch eine Verbesserung der Reise- bzw. Höchstgeschwindigkeit.

Das als FT-Ausrüstung zuerst vorgesehene FuG XXIII (Telefunken Spez. 901 II) erwies sich in endgültiger Ausführung als unbrauchbar. Es wurde daher die Ausrüstung mit FuG XVII (UKW) vorgesehen. Bis zur Serienlieferung dieses Gerätes wurde die provisorische Verwendung des FuG VII ermöglicht.

Verzeichnis der Berichte.

Datum	Bericht	Nr.	Inhalt	D-Nr.	W.Nr.	Muster
17.8.36	-	-	Nachfliegen der V 1	IBXY	601	V 1
15.10.36	Akt.Verm.	-	Untersuchung des FT-Einbaus	IGII	602	V 2
16.10.36	Z-Bericht	1	Kontrollbeanstandungen	IGII	602	V 2
24.11.36	Akt.Verm.	-	Kurzerprobung des Langwellensprechgerätes	IGII	602	V 2
17.12.36	Z-Bericht	2	Bisheriges Erprobungsergebnis bei Einsatz als Verbindungsflugzeug	IBXY	601	V 1
20.1.37	Niederschr.	-	Besprechung der Fi 156 O-Serie	-	-	-

Rechlin E 7b₅	Mustererprobung	Schlußbericht
Erpr.Nr. 1334	Fi 156	LC II 1 Nr. 153/36 Blatt 3

Datum	Bericht	Nr.	Inhalt	D-Nr.	W.Nr.	Muster
24.2.37	Akt.Verm.	1037	Funktionserprobung der Kompasse	IGLI	602	V 2
2.3.37	"	1021	Transportfähigkeit der Fi 156	-	-	-
27.2.37	"	1012	Nachfliegen der Fi 156 V 2 in Kassel	IGLI	602	V 2
12.3.37	Niederschr.	-	Besprechung der Fi 156 O-Serie	-	-	-
15.3.37	Akt.Verm.	1035	Nachfliegen der V 2 in Kassel	IGLI	602	V 2
12.4.37	"	1068	CO-Messungen	IBXY	601	V 1
24.4.37	"		"	IGQE	603	V 3
24.4.37	"	4	Nachfliegen (O-Serie) in Kassel		605	O-Serie
24.5.37	"	2049	Langwellentelefoniegerät Spez 901	IGQE	603	V 3
2.6.37	"	5	Fahrwerkserprobung	IGLI	602	V 2
4.6.37	"	2082	Staurohr-Einbauort	IBXY	601	V 1
25.6.37	"	6	Reichweitenbestimmung	IBXY	601	V 1
11.8.37	"	7	FT-Erprobung FuG XXII	IGQE	603	V 3
5.8.37	Niederschr.	-	Besprechung am 5.8.37 in Rechlin	-	-	-
6.8.37	Akt.Verm.	8	Flugleistungen	IGQE	603	V 3
13.8.37	Bericht	-	Konstruktionsbeanstandungen			
7.9.37	Teilbericht	9	Elektr. Bordnetz	IHKT	607	O-Serie
3.9.37	"	10	Nachtflugbeurteilung	IHKT	607	O-Serie
3.9.37	Niederschr.	-	Besprechung am 3.9.37 in Kassel	-	-	-
12.9.37	"	-	Einbaubesichtigung FuG XXII	IIFN	612	O-Serie
20.9.37	Teilbericht	11	Serien-Besprechung am 20.9.37 in Re			
11.12.37	"	12	Mustereinbau des Abgassammlers	IIFN	612	O-Serie
21.1.38	"	13	Besprechungsniederschrift			

Rechlin E 7b₅	Mustererprobung	Schlußbericht
Erpr.Nr. 1334	Fi 156	LC II 1 Nr. 153/36 Blatt 4

Datum	Bericht	Nr.	Inhalt	D-Nr.	W.Nr.	Muster
18.1.38	Teilbericht	14	Kohlenoxydmessungen	IIFN	612	O-Serie
8.2.38	"	15	Rotierende Klarsichtscheibe	IGQE	603	V 3
17.2.38	"		Erprobung des massefreien FuG XXII	IIFN	612	O-Serie
5.3.38	"	16	Einbaubesprechung FuG VII	IGQE	603	V 3
23.3.38	"	17	Fi 156 Weiterentwicklung (Flugeigenschaften)	IBXY	601	V 1
5.4.38	Niederschr.		Niederschrift über Einbaubesprechung FuG VII	IIFN	612	O-Serie
2.6.38	"		Niederschrift über Nachfliegen der Serie C-1 und Besprechung kleiner Änderungspunkte. Schlußbericht.		629	C-1

Weiterentwicklung.

Zunächst läuft die Fi 156 in bisheriger Ausführung als C-1-Serie. Nach Beendigung der Vorversuche an W.Nr. 601 werden die vorgesehenen aerodynamischen Verbesserungen zusammen mit anderen kleinen Änderungen frühestens ab 250. Maschine durchgeführt.

One of the rare instances in which a listing of all partial reports, file remarks and minutes of conferences have been annotated on the Rechlin Concluding Report on type-testing conducted with the Fieseler Fi 156.

rpm, aircraft attitude, etc) leading to the intended change in the aircraft's attitude or state, and observing the accompanying change in motion, the required control movements or effort required, and making the desired notations according to what the recording instruments are able or not able to capture. A strong distinction must be made between observance and judgement. When recording instruments are not available, the pilot must always keep this in mind. With recording instruments, one can improve on substitute observance of developments. With manned aircraft, the pilot's judgement is never superfluous. The evaluation of flight characteristics is an important part of the test flight, and resulting recommendations such as changes to the aircraft are then the concern of the aircraft's development. Similar basic principles hold true in these instances as with those described in the final acceptance conferences.

Although the topic of 'aeroelasticity'[10] is an important part of flight mechanics and its forms of appearance such as flutter and control effectiveness reversal are significant risk factors, it was only dealt with in

Rechlin when this was unavoidable in certain instances. To these observations regarding flight characteristics belongs the change-over to series production, ie, acceptance flight tests. As a rule, the flight characteristics of series-built aircraft should be the same as the prototypes, but an official procedure to ensure this did not exist. Hence, the pilots conducting acceptance flights were not regularly summoned to Rechlin and reliance was placed upon the manufacturer.

Difficulties which surfaced, as for instance with the Messerschmitt wing leading-edge slats or the Fw 190 aileron setting adjustments, were rectified on a case-by-case basis.

In other respects, the functions of all subsystems were checked in the course of acceptance tests and check-flights. This was especially the case for the powerplant and all 'automatics' involving the propellers, the gearing, governor and its manual override.

Endurance Testing
The meanwhile well-known definition that 'reliability is the ability of a unit to withstand the requirement it is called upon to fulfil for a definite length of time' was not known in those words at that time, but certainly its content. Endurance testing, such as the 100-hour engine flight test, were carried out. Endurance tests with other new components such as undercarriages and tyres, subject to a particular load factor, were also conducted. In order to shorten or to make it more safe, endurance tests were often conducted under more controlled conditions.

Work at the E-Stelle
In conclusion, I shall attempt to describe the activities of the individual Sections of an E-Stelle such as Rechlin, admittedly with the serious limitation that I can only do this from an aircraft type-tester's point of view.

In retrospect, it is appropriate to consider the testing work conducted on a typical day by an individual, such as in Section E2. But there was no such type of day, since the tasks were many and varied. How the day ran, was determined by the main task to be performed. The equally-inherited 'small stuff' was mostly that which of necessity remained unattended or just by chance (mail, telephone) happened to come by and was often regarded as a nuisance or interruption. At best, the main activities should be considered in view of the two most important workplaces – the aircraft and the writing-desk.

One of the main tasks at Section E2 was the method of carrying out aircraft type-tests. I obviously did not limit this to the office, but it all started from the writing-desk. By and large, conducting an aircraft type-test in this way worked out very well. However, there were exceptions whose reasons could be easily recognized. 'Project Management' – even in a small way as at the E-Stelle, is certainly a necessity for a complex system such as an aircraft, but individualists in the specialist sections had little sense of co-operation with one another and the chief 'director' as a rule only served incompletely the ideal of a 'Project Manager'. Added to this, the E-Stelle specialist departments were occasionally allocated tasks which had a bearing on aircraft type-testing, direct from 'their' department in the RLM and hence circumventing GL/C-E2 alias Section E2. Even there, one did not always stick to the rules! The friendly, unbureaucratic method of working in Rechlin undoubtedly contributed to the fact that 'evasive' possibilities existed. This was all eventually superimposed and disrupted by the direct intervention of the KdE or of the 'Kommandos der Erprobungsstellen' (Test Centre Detachments). For example, all mock-up inspections were to be led by the 'Delegate for Mock-up and Installation Matters'. The 'Sonderbeauftragte' (Special Delegate) who would act as his support, was to be selected from the ranks of the E-Stelle concerned or from a frontline Detachment so that although Section E2 was not fundamentally excluded, it suffered much intrusion upon its sphere of activity. The GL/C Order No 75 of autumn 1942 was probably responsible for creating the KdE instead of lending support to the entrusted organisation. A further step was the introduction of the 'Typenbegleiter' (Type Escort) who reported directly to the KdE. These belonged partly to the 'Stab' (HQ staff) of the KdE such as Major Otto Behrens for the Me 262, or partly to the E-Stelle such as Leutnant Kurt Zechner for the Ar 234. Organisationally, it was all rather confusing, without definite demarcations vis-à-vis the E-Stelle or the RLM Development Departments. Thus Behrens wrote in a Report on the Me 262: 'Through the provisional appointment of Oberst Petersen as 'Gruppenleiter des Sachgebietes Jäger' (Group Leader on the special field of Fighters), he was afforded the necessity to concern himself in detail with the state of activity of this aircraft. But since the duties went far beyond the general framework of the E-Stelle, this activity resulted in the creation of the 'Typenbegleiter'.

Our attention is thus drawn to the title 'Gruppenleiter des Sachgebietes Jäger', which must be expanded to read 'bei KdE' (in the KdE), since there still existed simultaneously in Rechlin the position of 'Gruppenleiter Jäger' (Group Leader for Fighters), namely H Beauvais at the E-Stelle. Furthermore, since the tasks exceeded the general framework of the E-Stelle, they could also affect other E-Stellen such as Tarnewitz. That was nothing new, as E2 had worked together with Tarnewitz from the earliest days. But it could also have effects on RLM authorizations to industry, research and the armed forces. How the RLM, to be precise, the GL/C-E, came to terms with such 'Commissar Orders' was not known to us. In any case, disregarding this organisation held hidden dangers, and was probably the cause of a serious crash during a weapons release test in March 1945 in Rechlin due to a 'provisional commissarial intervention order' which had insufficient knowledge of the actual situation. So much said for the change in 'direction' concerning aircraft type-testing.

Nevertheless, detail work performed by the E-Stelle's separate sections continued as before, even when under less favourable conditions. A further and singularly professional chief task of E2's teams working on aircraft, was the test work undertaken on aircraft performance and characteristics. Besides the flying, that naturally required a lot of paperwork for preparations and evaluations.

In a similar manner ran the activities of E2's specialist groups concerned with undercarriages, aircraft protection and systems, as also all other E-Stelle specialist groups and departments, even if pursued without a central direction of effort. Extremely important and unavoidable in addition was the much higher percentage of involvement in laboratory and test-bed checks conducted by other E-Stellen units on engines and related ancilliaries, on equipment, electrics, controls, wireless and target-finding installations.

The second 'work-station' at E2 was the aircraft itself. Flight testing encompassed the entire spectrum of airframe, engine and equipment, and showed how multifarious the tasks during flight could be. There were nevertheless a series of tasks which had to be performed together with the pilot, as each test flight had to be minutely prepared, especially when one flew alone. Among these were:
- Preparation of the aircraft and its clearance for flight.
- Regular preparation by the pilot, such as obtaining weather forecast information, carrying personal equipment including knee-pad, pencil and necessary recording sheets.
- Special preparations, such as reaching agreement with remaining aircrew and personnel from the ground station, firing- and dropping-ranges and accompanying aircraft.
- Orientation concerning operation of the measuring instruments.
- Knowledge of the tasks involving maintaining or re-establishing the status quo for testing and safety.

In carrying out the test flight, the navigational and other routine components of pilot activity should not endanger the test flying priorities. Much more decisive is the maintenance of specific 'static' values such as the heading, altitude, flight-path, angle of inclination and sinking speed during the flight. For dynamical considerations, finite control measures of a particular value in a definite series of actions, dependent upon observation of the existing flight condition or instrument readings have to be immediately and exactly carried out. This is all not only necessary during a test flight, but also for equipment testing.

Certainly, test flights were often carried out in good visibility under normal flying conditions, but there were also many instances were severe conditions were imposed, such as overload, cg positions outside the normal range, new types of installations, take-off and landing aids, and unusual flight conditions such as spins, high loadings, induced vibrations, short take-offs and landings, unusual environmental conditions such as lack of vision outside the cockpit or icing conditions. Attention was particularly required when flying captured enemy aircraft which, although series-produced models, had to be flown without any instructions or manuals.

The test pilot had to master all of this. With unexpected occurrences, he had to make decisions promising successful corrective measures and act accordingly. Post-flight action by the pilot included reporting on deficiencies or disturbances, instrument readings and evaluation notes and where needed, expand upon these. If he undertook the evaluation duty himself, this again was a writing-desk activity which would eventually lead to an interim or closing report.

The above portrayal does not pretend to be complete, but provides an impression of everything connected with a test flight. These tasks are of course – besides the pure flying aspect – also valid for the accompanying measurement engineers, and with limitations for the checkers, mechanics and aircrew operators.

Shooting-practice on moving target surfaces required a certain amount of training on estimating the distance. Releasing bombs in level flight using the Lotfe[11] or alternatively, the X-or Y-system[12] was strictly the domain of the specialist. Aircraft range determination flights were more a matter of careful preparation than flying aptitude, and cross-country flights in a single-engine fighter under the most economical cruise conditions, eg, at 280km/h (174mph), was more a test of patience than ability. Deck-landing trials in Travemünde were more absorbing than difficult. Catapult take-offs using a so-called 'land aircraft catapult' with overloaded aircraft were only carried out by a few pilots in Rechlin.

In sea emergency-rescue trials using the Fi 156, Fw 58 and Ju 52, it was necessary to bring the marker-buoy into position flying the tightest full-power wind-compensated turns using the throttle or altitude change – where observation showed that many pilots found this extremely uncomfortable. It should be mentioned that diving flights were also performed until the destruction of wooden auxiliary containers occurred, billowing of the vertical rudder, testing Mach effect on longitudinal trim, demonstrating the flutter safety of control surfaces and auxiliary control tabs, checking on their stiffness, wing torsion and overloading, and not least, pull-out and roll movements for checking aileron forces. Steep and even vertical dives in the Mach 0.8 region and over were only exceptionally undertaken in Rechlin. Lessons had been learned from such related dangers and notice was taken of maximum allowable speed data, although that was not to be regarded as a solution to the problem.

Following conclusion or the result of the tests – or an incremental part of it – there followed the preparation of Interim and Final Reports, Aircraft Type-Sheet Range Tables or Cold-Start Instructions. They represented the outgoing documentation on the expiration of testing and were used partly by the services and partly to serve as the basis for alteration of operating instructions and regulations. A few remarks are necessary here on the printed notifications, since there existed the same problems as the above-mentioned 'theory' term.

The most important of the printed notifications were in the KBA (Short Operating Instructions), together with their control lists, but which were nowhere given the worthy attention they deserved. In other respects, the printed notifications – construction manuals, handbooks, servicing and repair manuals, substitute parts lists, etc – were extremely voluminous items. In order to retain the value of these items and make effective use of them, as well as establishing their necessary understanding through training courses requiring the least possible expenditure of time and material, a fundamental optimization of these notifications would have been a useful task to undertake. Endeavours to this end on my part were commented upon by Carl Francke with the words: 'No-one will thank you for occupying yourself with such things!' Hence, application for such educational deliberations was very low, and the habit of moving in set tracks was preferred. A discussion with Graf Baudissin, the so-called 'Regulations Pope' confirmed this. We also had the task of conducting examinations, but this was limited in practice to technical details. My critique was aimed at the arrangement of the printed matter which was haphazardly composed without regard to placing related parts in a consistent sequence. The weapons directives appeared to be a typical case in point. As far as I remember, there was, for example a chapter on 'Firing Procedures'. Item by item was described of everything that could happen, instead of providing an explanation of the functions of components such as arming/disarming, ammunition loading/unloading, firing-mechanism function, and so on. If I am not mistaken, it was a similar situation with presentation of the other directives, where the putting together, handling, maintenance and checking of the equipment items was not listed in a sensible functional arrangement.

The Siebel Fh 104 (GM+AG) of the E-Stelle Rechlin was not only used as a communications aircraft, but was also employed on test flights. The place, date, and purpose of the test in this photograph are unfortunately not known, but conceivably depicts preliminary trials of a towed fuel tank.

Safety measures on the bomb-release ranges of the E-Stelle required exacting preparation of the daily jettison programme.

```
                    Programm für den 2. Sept. 1941
                    -.-.-.-.-.-.-.-.-.-.-.-.-.-.-.-

 52 554             Flugzeug: Do 217 NFUW
 Messbasis!         Flugzeugführer: Wiegand
 FT-Abriss!         Beobachter:     Kaule/Riebold/Feldw. Müller
 Erdvermessung!        1. Start: auf Abruf. 2.-4.Start: anschl.
                    Höhe: 1000 - 4000 m/Ziel: Mitte /Anfl. 6
                    Bomben: 6 SC 50, Zdr. 15 o.V.
                    -------------------------
                    Flugzeug: Ju 88 BJNP und Do 17 BGNT und Do 17 GMAE
                    Flugzeugführer: Darré/Rank
                    Beobachter:     Claassen/Lenz/Heinrichs
                       1. Start: auf Abruf, weitere Starts anschl.
                    Abwurf auf Ost und West/ Beladung nach besonderer Angabe
                    -------------------------
                    Flugzeug: Ju 88 NDEE
                    Flugzeugführer: Voigt
                    Beobachter:     Heinemann/Noch
                    H'Beobachter:   Gefr. Ulbricht
                       1. Start: auf Abruf
                    Höhe: 80 m/Ziel: B-Platte / Anfl: 2
                    Bomben: 4 SC 250 Üb, Zdr. Ex
 52264                 2. Start: anschl. wie oben, jedoch
                    Bomben: 4 SD 250 Üb.
 52432 52542           3. Start: anschl. wie oben, jedoch
                    Bomben: 6 SC 50 Üb, + 1 SD 250 Üb + 1 SC 250 Üb.
                    -------------------------
                    Flugzeug: He 111 GPAY
                    Flugzeugführer: Voigt
                    Beobachter:     Gluska
                       1. Start: auf Abruf
                    Höhe:80/200/3500m/Ziel: Ost/B-Platte/Müritz/Anfl: 8
                    Bomben: 3 BSK B 2 El + 2 SC 50 Üb verst. Zdr. + 20 SC 50 Üb +
                            2 ZC 50 mit Farbrauch, Zdr. 63, 17A, 79
                       2. Start: anschl.
 52462             Höhe: 1000 m / Ziel: Mitte / Anfl: 2
                    Bomben: 8 Flam C 250, Zdr. 26 o.V.
                    -------------------------
                    Flugzeug: He 111 TUAP
                    Flugzeugführer: Wiegand/Kaule (Beobachter)
                       1. Start: auf Abruf
                    Höhe: 2000 m/ Ziel: Mitte /  Anfl: 1
                    Bomben: 1 BM 1000, Zdr. ?? o.V.
                       2. Start: anschl.   wie 1. Start
                    Höhe: 4000 m / Ziel: Mitte / Anfl. 1
                       3. Start: anschl.  wie 1. Start: jedoch
                    Höhe: 1000 m / Ziel: Mitte
                    -------------------------
                    Flugzeug: Me 210 PEPB
                    Flugzeugführer: Ballerstedt/Beobachter:    Schulz
 1669                  1. Start: auf Abruf, 2. Start: anschl.
 Messbasis!         Höhe: 4000 auf 1000 m/ Ziel: Mitte /  Anfl: je 2
 FT-Abriss!         Bomben: je 2 SC 250 Üb verst. Zdr. 15 o.V.
   Erdvermessg.!    -------------------------
                    Flugzeug: Do 17 GMAE
                    Flugzeugführer: Voigt / Beobachter: Gluska
 52510                 1. Start: auf Abruf, 2.-4. Start: anschl.
                    Höhe: 50/ 5m/Ziel: West /Anfl: je 5
                    Bomben: je 40 SD 2Üb, Zdr. 41 AZ
                    -------------------------

                                            Flugkapitän
```

Relations with Other Centres

By reason of its organisational and time-connected involvement in the course of development, the E-Stellen were in constant contact with departments of the RLM, industrial firms, and not least the Services. All of these differing relationships are briefly summarized below.

Testing and Development

Certainly the most intensive contact took place with the RLM Development Departments as immediate superior, and already during the early phase of development. Based on the E-Stelle's experiences, this appeared to be sensible and ensured a certain degree of influence, at least insofar as new developments and competitive requirements were concerned and a decision between various proposals or designs had to be taken. Diversion from this principle limited the E-Stelle's possibility of exerting influence. Systematic thinking – which was certainly known but not mentioned – contradicted the tendency of the manufacturers (supported partially by certain RLM individuals and by way of pressing demands from military sources) to conduct early first flights. The aircraft were smooth and light and therefore displayed a good flying performance – but then came the disappointment! Warnings in this regard by the E-Stelle were disregarded. The longer the war lasted, arguments became effective to an even lesser extent against the driving force of the troops or party higher-ups. To cite an example of this:

The E-Stelle pointed out that additional weights, such as the armour-plating on the Me 210 would not only negatively influence its speed and rate of climb but also its manoeuvrability, failed to hinder the greatest of efforts expended in their installation – and on the battlefield, they were again removed! Expressions such as 'standardization' possessing advantages for the manufacture, supply, handling or 'simplification', appeared enormously sensible. But its realization pre-supposed the foreseeable answer to a number of questions as to whether the correct compromise between quality and quantity was discernible. It was thus not possible to say which was the 'best fighter'. Neither the E-Stelle nor Gordon Gollob with his crews by comparing the Fw 190 with the Bf 109 in 1941 could do this. The evaluation depended upon too many parameters and the then extant priorities such as performance, characteristics, armament, and the enemy and his oppor-

tunities. Attempts had also been made to balance all of this by means of awarding points such as suggested by Woldemar Voigt of Messerschmitt.

The understanding to 'develop to a conclusion', initially unburdened by a series production, was too little. Series manufacture continued apace without sufficient development and testing – the He 177 and Me 210 are examples where unpleasant setbacks resulted. On the other hand, developments took place which, without pressure, would not have led to series production, eg, the Me 262.

Testing and Industry

It goes without saying that relationships between the manufacturers and the E-Stelle were very lively, as there existed a series of common interests in the sense of an optimum product, except that there was not always agreement over the standards. Messerschmitt's main aim for example was speed, to which everything else gave way. The ordering authority and with it, the

E-Stelle, did not completely share this viewpoint. Despite a high rating for speed, other aspects such as flight characteristics, strength, maintenance, reliability, etc should not be neglected. Not every report of deficiency by the E-Stelle was accepted by the firm concerned. There were, however, E-Stelle personnel on whose judgements the firm placed due recognition. It was easier to reach an agreement with the engineers concerned with prototype flight test evaluation, the project- and design offices, than with those concerned with series manufacture since changes obviously resulted in more problems, even when these were explicitly demanded from an official source. Even so, the firms tended to exercise their influence upon the introduction and time schedule for the changes required. In addition to this, there was a rapid succession of series models which, during the war, led to a short average 'life' of a particular aircraft, so that it often happened that the importance of specific changes in an often very short space of time were discarded and thus difficult to ascertain. The firms, of course, took advantage of this in several instances.

On the question of the correct set of development steps for series production at that time, I based my thoughts on the Bf 109 and the later Ta 152. Based on similar considerations and experiences as on the official side 'Firmen Typenbegleiter' (Works Type Escorts) were also introduced, who actually became the point of contact for the E-Stelle. Besides this, the RLM appointed to the firms as their 'out-station' representatives the 'Bauaufsichten' (Construction Supervisors) or 'Entwicklungs-Bauaufsichten' (Development/Construction Supervisors) alias BAL or EBAL. E-Stellen personnel who wished to visit the manufacturers were obliged to first meet with these representatives.

Testing and the Services

Attached to prototype testing for various aircraft types were the so-called 'Erprobungskommandos' (Test Detachments) established in Rechlin. These formed the foundation stone for the first operational units to be equipped with a new aircraft type, and after a while, were transferred complete to the frontline. In addition to that, service pilots participated in familiarization or comparative flights with German as well as captured enemy aircraft, eg, Werner Mölders with the Fw 190 and later, Otto Behrens with the Ta 154. Concerning difficulties with flight characteristics which were mostly traceable to insufficiently-tested aircraft (resulting from control surface alterations and so forth), several visits were made to operational units such as in France or Russia. One operation of a particular type involved demonstration flights with a captured Boeing B-17 (Otto Behrens

with Heinrich Beauvais as pilot) on a series of airfields ranging from Husum right up to Poix in France. Extensive trips were also made by E3 personnel for training frontline formations in the use of the 'cold-start' procedure, but also in Rechlin, a series of 'cold-start' courses were held for technical officers and foremen belonging to frontline units. The introduction of performance-boosting using GM-1[13] also required extensive assistance. Co-operation was very close between Department F and service units when the order was given to find, erect, and put into operation emplacements for the X- and Y-beam transmitters.

In a broad sense, the examinations of faults and accidents occurring in operations also formed part of the relationships with field units, although these were not a part of the E-Stelle's tasks, neither were the related methods to be applied. The E-Stelle, however, was on the distribution list on reports of faults and accidents and was also made aware of objections and complaints, not confined to accidents and crashes which occurred during flight test operations. The result was that the E-Stelle became continually involved, including the creation of 'Alterations Directives' set out in the 'Technical Instructions of the Inspector General' (TAGL) and in the 'Technical Instructions of the General for Military Technology' (TATT). Alteration directives resulted partly from complaints and partly in the train of development. In several cases, it was the task of the E-Stelle to undertake functional efficiency checks prior to series production. Finally, the aircraft operated by an E-Stelle also had to be treated in accordance with these directives.

Footnotes

1 Schematic description of the development, testing and manufacturing phases of a new aircraft (equipment item or device) listing all centres involved in responsibility, participation or information.

2 Comprehensive document in which the manufacturing firm provides for the potential purchaser all details concerning design and construction, including drawings or illustrations or mock-up photographs.

3 Designation valid from 1939 denoting the E-Stelle Rechlin Section responsible for airframe testing as well as exercising leadership of aircraft prototype testing.

4 A flight test manual, compiled and issued by Dipl.-Ing. Carl Francke at the E-Stelle Travemünde.

5 Designation valid from 1939 denoting the E-Stelle Rechlin Section responsible for the testing of powerplants and their accessories.

6 Standard conditions for day temperature and air pressure, alias ISA or INA (International Standard/Normal Atmosphere).

7 Method whereby an aircraft flies at the same height past a building (tower) equipped with recording instruments which register the measurement values within the aircraft. A comparison of the measurements enables calculations to be made of the actual airspeed.

8 Instrument which simultaneously measured the true airspeed and the wing angles of incidence and sideslip. To obtain correct measurement in the undisturbed airstream ahead of the aircraft, it had to be mounted at the extremity of a long probe.

9 Oberstleutnant a.D. (retired) Heinz Bär, World War Two fighter ace with 220 victories, crashed and was killed on 28th April 1957 in Brunswick in a test flight with the Zaunkönig (wren) light aircraft.

10 Observation of elastic deformations on an aircraft due to aerodynamic forces acting on the aircraft in flight.

11 Abbreviation for 'Lotfernrohr' (telescopic bombsight), an optical target-sighting instrument used for bomb-release in horizontal flight.

12 X- and Y-systems: guiding-beam system to enable an aimed blind bomb-release to be effected, developed by the E-Stelle Rechlin Section F.

13 System for increasing the performance of reciprocating engines at high altitudes through the injection of an oxygen-carrying agent in the engine air scoop.

Filming from an accompanying aircraft was frequently necessary during flight tests. The work of the cameraman was not easy standing in a modified open MG-position and secured only by a waist-harness, he had to operate the camera mounted on the rotatable gun-mount whilst subjected to the slipstream.

Chapter Two
by Volker Koos

Flight Testing to the End
of World War One

Quick-Reference Abbreviations

AKO   Allerhöchste Kabinetts-Ordre
Supreme Cabinet Order

APK   Artillerie-Prüfungs-Kommission
Artillery Evaluation Commission

BdL   Befehlshaber der Marine-Luftfahrt-Abteilungen
Supreme Commander, Navy Aviation Department

BLV   Bau- und Lieferungsvorschriften
Construction & Delivery Regulations

BMW   Bayerische Motoren-Werke
Bavarian Motor Works

DFW   Deutsche Flugzeugwerft
German Aircraft Dockyard

DVL   Deutsche Versuchsanstalt für Luftfahrt
German Experimental Institute for Aviation

FLZ   Flugzeugmeisterei
Aircraft Engineering Centre

Goe   Goebel Motoren Werke
Goebel Motor Works

LFG   Luft-Fahrzeug-Gesellschaft
Aeronautical Vehicles Company

LVM   Lehr- und Versuchsanstalt für Militärflugwesen
Military Training & Test Institute

LVG   Luft-Verkehrs-Gesellschaft
Air Traffic Company

LVL   Lehr- und Versuchsabteilung für Luftbildwesen
Air Photography Instruction & Test Department

MFA   Marinefliegerabteilung
Navy Aviation Department

PuW   Prüfanstalt und Werft der Fliegertruppe
Flying Corps Evaluation Institute & Workshops

RMA   Reichsmarineamt
Reich Navy Office

SAK   Seeflugzeug-Abnahmekommission
Seaplane Acceptance Commission

SSW   Siemens-Schuckert Werke
Siemens-Schuckert Works

SVK   Seeflugzeug-Versuchskommando
Seaplane Test Detachment

VMK   Versuchsabteilung des Militär-Verkehrswesens
Military Traffic Services Test Department

VPK   Versuchstechnische Prüfungs-Kommission
Vehicle Technical Evaluation Commission

Efka   Fernlenk-u.Kreiselversuchsabteilung
Remote Guidance & Gyroscopic Test Department

Idflieg   Inspektion der Fliegertruppe
Flying Corps Inspectorate

Idlicht   Inspektion des Lichtbildwesens
Inspectorate of Photography

Idverk   Inspektion der Verkehrstruppen
Inspectorate of the Motorized Troops

Iluk   Inspektion des Militär-Luft-und Kraftfahrwesens
Inspectorate of Military Air & Road Vehicles

Lubia   Lichtbildabteilung
Air Photography Department

Lubiko   Luftbildkommando
Air Photography Detachment

KoGenLuft   Kommandierender General der Luftstreitkräfte
Commanding General of the Air Forces

Early Flight Testing by the Army and Navy

The earliest aircraft were products of empirical development, and spectacular accidents caused pressing demands for the urgent introduction of methods which would replace ignorance with increased knowledge, spontaneity with methodology, and indiscipline with binding regulations. This demanded the establishment, alongside the growing number of aircraft manufacturing centres, of an independent or even superior organisation which, as a result of its increasing specialist competence, would be in a position to set standards for manufacturing and application techniques and undertake aircraft certification checks. The breakthrough first occurred when the military administrative bodies began to occupy themselves with the military usage of such vehicles, which prior to purchase and service operation, had been subjected to suitability tests by testing establishments independent from the manufacturers. Thus, from the very beginning, the basic principle was adopted of applying private inventor and manufacturer's initiatives for the solution of design and technological problems to examine the results obtained from military testing and to place contracts for construction and delivery of the most suitable aircraft. This advance, resulted in at least three important facts: Firstly, the close interweaving of interests between private manufacturers and military users; secondly, the establishment of the first aeronautical Army and Navy testing and evaluation establishments, and thirdly, the increasing influence of military requirements exerted on the quality and performance capability of the aircraft.

Army Flight Test Centres

The very first military test centre was established after the foundation of the Airship Department of the Prussian Army on 9th May 1884 on the Tegel firing-range near Berlin. This later became the Airship Battalion, joined by a 100-man Test Company on 1st April 1907. At the Tegel base the Army developed, built and tested semi-rigid military airships of its own design based on the Gross-Bassenach system.

At this time, when airships were still used exclusively by the Prussian Army, the preliminary history of military aircraft testing began in Döberitz.

On 14th April 1906, when the Prussian War Ministry received a letter from Orville and Wilbur Wright from the USA offering to sell them aircraft; in keeping with their responsibility, the offer was passed to the Test Department of the Idverk (Inspectorate of the Motorized Troops) which recommended rejection of the Wright offer.

In May 1907, Hauptmann Wolfram de le Roi, who had served in the Tegel Test Centre and who had obtained his Free-Balloon Pilot's Licence there in March 1899, commenced his duties as Referent (Specialist Advisor) in the Idverk Experimental Department.

In the summer of 1907, the Wright Brothers again offered their aircraft which still possessed the best performance worldwide. Following discussions with Wilbur Wright, the military administration again decided upon rejection as the price demanded appeared to be too exorbitant. On the strength of this, de le Roi in August 1908 presented a study in which he alluded to progress made in other countries on powered flight and recommended that the previously-adopted waiting tactic be altered and suggested that the military administration themselves tackle the advancement of flying problems.

A beginning was made, however, with a hopeless attempt. The Stuttgart Government Construction Engineer W Siegfried Hoffmann had submitted a triplane proposal. On 18th February 1909, the Kaiser, accompanied by his War Minister, was informed by the Chief of Idverk, Alfred von Lyncker and Hauptmann de le Roi of the projected goal and method of construction of the Hoffmann aircraft, and agreed to financing it. It was expected that this aircraft would exceed the Wright's perfor-

Besides the older spherical-shaped APK-bombs at right, three of the various Carbonit-bombs introduced even before World War One can be seen here.

The Albatros C II with pusher propeller did not enter series production. This photo of the C 27/15, taken in Adlershof, displays the PuW Flying Corps inscription on the forward fuselage.

as well as trials with aerial photography and bomb release. The examination and testing spectrum was thus extensive.[2]

When aircraft took part for the very first time in the autumn manoeuvres in 1911 and showed their value for aerial reconnaissance, voices became louder demanding the establishment of a central 'Versuchsanstalt für Luftfahrt' (Aviation Experimental Institute), under authoritative state influence. On 20th April 1912, at the Reich Ministry of the Interior, the DVL was established, whose provisional President, Oberst Hugo Schmiedecke was the Chief of Staff of the Inspectorate-General of Military Vehicle Transport. The next day, Prinz Heinrich von Preussen called for a 'National Aviation Donation' out of which over 500,000 Marks flowed into the DVL. The first notable task of the DVL was the evaluation of aero-engines which had been submitted in the competition for the 'Kaiser's Prize for the best German aero-engine'. This evaluation, published on 27th January 1912, lasted a whole year. Besides the Aero-engine Department, the DVL had an Aircraft and a Physics Department. From 1913, breaking-load tests on aircraft were conducted at the DVL, which erected its installations on the Adlershof side of the Berlin-Johannisthal airfield.

Organised as a 'registered Association', to which as foundation members besides Reich Offices and industrial firms the War Ministry and the Navy Department also belonged, the DVL became the centre for the clarification of scientific problems met in aeronautical engineering development.

On 1st October 1912, the Flying Corps made their debut as a part of the Guards Corps. One year later, as a Flying Corps they became an independent unit known as the Flying Corps Inspectorate (Idflieg). At the end of 1913, out of the 'Test Department of the Motorized Troops' was formed the above-mentioned VPK, which supervised the entire technical development and testing of military aircraft. The VPK for example, formulated for the first time, construction and safety regulations for the aircraft industry; conducted the first W/T (wireless/telegraphy) tests in 1913 with Army aircraft in Döberitz and checked their equipment with air-drop weapons.

mance, which at that time had flown for almost three hours and a distance of 124.7km (77.5 miles).

On 18th March 1910, the Army test aircraft, with de le Roi at the controls was demonstrated before a 'high-ranking military commission'. After take-off, the machine, now completed as a biplane, climbed to a height of 3.5m (11½ft), winged-over on its side, crashed and disintegrated. The very first military aircraft to be built and tested in Germany had cost 50,000 Marks and was a write-off.

The military administration, still without a far-reaching concept, now appeared to wake up. The Army-owned grounds beside Döberitz village near Berlin, used as a troop training ground by the Spandau Garrison, received a few aircraft tents for its northwest corner. In that same year, the first of five aircraft sheds appeared there. On 1st April 1910, the 'Fliegerkommando' (Flying Detachment) Döberitz as a structural element of the 'Versuchsabteilung der Verkehrstruppen' (Test Department of the Motorized Troops) was founded and placed under the direct charge of de le Roi.[1]

In July 1910, training of military pilots began in the Provisional Flying School with a Farman biplane, presented as a gift by Dr. Walter Huth, founder of the 'Albatros-Flugzeugwerke' (Aircraft Factory), and on 15th July 1910, became the first military aircraft in the service of the Prussian Army.

On 1st April 1911, the Idverk, hitherto responsible for aviation matters, now became the 'General Inspectorate of the Motorized Troops' to which the Iluk (Inspectorate of Military Air & Road Vehicles) belonged. At the same time, the 'Fliegerkommando' (Flight Detachment) Döberitz was given the title of LVM (Military Training & Test Institute). They were subordinated to the initially-entitled 'Test Department of the Traffic Corps' which in 1911 became the VMK (Military Traffic Services Test Department), made finally subordinate to the VPK (Vehicle Technical Evaluation Commission).

In accordance with the duties allocated to it, the training of a growing number of suitable officers as pilots and observers took place in Döberitz. Training rules were improved, hangar personnel underwent instruction for checking and acceptance tests for aircraft, acceptance conditions for military aircraft being instituted, and aircraft breaking-load tests were carried out

In addition to that, beginning in 1912, release trials were conducted with spherical bombs of 5kg (11lb) and 10kg (22lb) which had been developed by the 'Artillerie-Prüfungs-Kommission' (Artillery Evaluation Commission) – the so-called APK-bombs, prior to the introduction of 'Carbonit' bombs at the beginning of 1914. These consisted of teardrop-shaped bombs fitted with an annular ring at the tail-end and containing 4.5kg (9.9lb), 10kg (22lb), 20kg (44lb), and 50kg (110lb) of explosives made by the firm of Sprengstoff AG 'Carbonit' Schlebusch.

On 14th April 1914, it was agreed between the VPK and the DVL that the latter would assume the scientific testing and certification work for the Flying Corps, and on the grounds of the DVL in Adlershof, the first barracks for a 'Versuchskompanie' (Test Company) was erected.

Based on the experiences of the DVL, the Idflieg issued for the first time the 'Load Acceptances for Military Aircraft'. Load factors, as a multiple of the aircraft's weight, were determined by loading the wings with sandbags until they eventually collapsed. At the beginning of 1916 the Construction and Delivery Regulations for Military Aircraft (BLV) followed, revised in 1916 and 1918, taking into account the latest research results and requiring for the first time proof of fatigue-strength calculations. Each new aircraft type and initial version built under licence and versions with design changes had to undergo a type-test performed by the Idflieg. This consisted of a static strength test, a flight test, and a general engineering technical examination. The type-test, whose results were recorded in a 'Baubeschreibung' (Construction Description) report, together with the most important technical and design details, was the prerequisite for the operational acceptance of the aircraft.

The multiplicity of flight tests is apparent from the various categories of aircraft which appeared in the course of World War One, based on military needs and their further development. In designations, the Army and Navy adopted different systems.

Army Aircraft Categories

A   unarmed two-seat monoplane
E   single-seat monoplane fighter with MG
B   unarmed two-seat biplane
F   originally-used category for Dr-types
C   two-seat biplane with MG
G   twin-engine large aircraft
CL lightened C-aircraft
GL lightened G-aircraft
D   single-seat fighter with fixed MG
N   two-seat night bomber (biplane or triplane)
Dr single-seat triplane fighter with MG
R   giant aircraft with two and more engines
(Navy Aircraft Categories are listed on page 34)

Since at the beginning of the war, only unarmed monoplanes and biplanes for reconnaissance and training purposes were available, further variants following in rapid succession which, after undergoing thorough technical, flying, and equipment-related trials (the so-called type-tests) were introduced at the frontline.

Upon the outbreak of war in 1914 the VPK took over the DVL's buildings and installations and its members were called up for military service. At Adlershof, there initially appeared a flying school, a spare-parts depot, and a repair and disassembly shed. On the DVL premises was the PuW, established in 1915 under Major Felix Wagenführ, who had a number of the DVL's leading individuals and other engineers and scientists recalled from the front for service in his establishment. Whilst the DVL originally measured 34,000m^2 (365,960ft^2) in area, the military expanded it to around 77,000m^2 (828,800ft^2).

The evermore apparent necessity during the war for a uniformly-led independent air force and the related restructuring it required, had effects on technical demands and on flight testing. On 11th March 1915, the Office of the 'Chef des Feldflugwesens' (Chief of Combat Aviation) was established under Oberst von der Lieth-Thomsen, and intensive endeavours were made to introduce machine-guns into air force use, where in the years prior to the war, relatively little had been done to put existing patents into practical use.

On the 19th and 20th May 1915, however, the VPK in Döberitz demonstrated to military and industry representatives the MG-control system developed by the Fokker

Test pilot Ernst Wendler standing in front of a new Fokker D II in Adlershof, behind which are the Aircraft Works and Transport Park vehicles.

Aircraft Company which, based upon knowledge of the French deflection system, was developed as a result of the emergency landing of the pilot Roland Garros.

Besides the Johannisthal airfield, which became largely overloaded due to the aircraft companies stationed there, the PuW and later the FLZ also used the Döberitz airfield for flight testing, and from the end of 1916, laid plans for the erection of a test centre on the Müritzsee.

Due to the loss of the majority of relevant documents, the administration and command-related structure of the test centre's equipment and organisation which worked within the scope of the Idflieg, are still not fully clear, even today. A subordinate structure existed, set out according to duties such as for wireless technology and weapons test and development, whereby the different categories of machine-guns, bombs, etc were worked upon separately. Even here, it had taken until 1916/17 before special aircraft armament developed by the Army weapons advisors made use of the Idflieg's installations.

On 1st January 1917, the FLZ was created through amalgamation by the Idflieg of previously existing aircraft workshops and the Testing Institute and Workshops into one unit, which consisted of four Departments: A for Aircraft, B for Aero-engines and Propellers, C for Technical Equipment, and D for the Physics Department as well as an Adlershof garrison headquarters. The FLZ was directly subordinate to the Idflieg, which was also the case with the following Detachments, each of which had an Instruction and Test Department:

a) Aircraft-Armaments-Departments.
b) Aircraft-Wireless-Departments.
c) Aircraft-Bombs-Departments.
d) Aerial Photography Departments.

To investigate the flow pattern, this LFG Roland D III has long streamers attached to the wings and interplane bracing. Visible in the background is an LFG hangar.

Flow-pattern investigations were likewise undertaken in Adlershof with this Albatros B II on which small streamers attached to vertical strands have been laid out on a segment between the biplane wings. The results were also registered photographically, as seen by the recording camera mounting at the side of the pilot's cockpit.

In a number of areas, the dividing line between the military Idflieg activities and the civilian DVL cannot now be clearly established. Whereas the pre- and post-war DVL members, Dr.-Ing. Wilhelm Hoff and Georg Madelung worked out the construction and delivery directives within the scope of work conducted by the PuW and the FLZ and issued the 'Flugzeugmeisterei' Technical Reports, Dr.-Ing. Friedrich Bendemann, who had been the DVL Director since 21st June 1912, following his release from military service at the end of 1915, again took on its leadership and without any influence exercised by the PuW's work, was able to put a small part of its original installations back into operation. The DVL also performed sub-contracts and services for the Idflieg and industrial firms.

An interesting project was the construction of rail-track towing-tests for complete aircraft and full-scale parts which had already been taken up in 1914. On a suitable stretch of the military track between Zossen and Jüterborg, it was planned to undertake measurements from a specially-designed fast carriage equipped with a measurement tower, and in Dümde near Schönefeld a Test Hangar was erected for the 'Test Track' Department. From the end of 1916, however, since work on completion of the stretch for high speeds had to be broken off due to lack of military priority, speeds only up to twice that of normal fast trains could be reached, which was insufficient for testing purposes.

As a result of a military directive, the DVL was authorized from October 1916 to undertake checking and testing of propellers for the Army's military aircraft. Through the establishment of a service unit of the Kogenluft under Generalleutnant Ernst von Hoeppner on 8th October 1916, the Flying Corps became an independent activity within the Army. From the end of 1916, Idflieg construction inspectorates at aircraft and equipment manufacturing centres were established.

Due to the enemy's ever-increasing numerical superiority, aircraft technical development took on greater importance, since only a technical superiority promised a status of equality. This meant undertaking wide-ranging development and testing, and in the spheres of wireless-telegraphy and photography, a leap ahead of the enemy was successfully achieved and upheld during the entire war. Following initial trials with radio equipment in September and October 1914, these became operational on the Western Front in December 1914, and in June 1915, the first exchange of radio traffic took place between an aircraft and a ground station. The airborne transmitters and receiving station were introduced from November 1915 as 'Type D'. In August 1917, the W/T Test Department concluded its tests with W/T equipment for single-seat fighters after 204 test flights had taken place in Döberitz, which included a three-part 'umbrella antenna' mounted on a 1.40m (4½ft) high mast on the Halberstadt D V 401/16 that had been found suitable after successful flight tests. For tests conducted in frontline operations, the W/T Test Department formed a special single-seat combat aircraft squadron under Leutnant Gericke, and in September 1918 an ancillary device for wireless picture transmission which had taken two years to develop by the W/T Test Department, was successfully demonstrated in Döberitz. By this means, map contours and shaded outlines could be transmitted, but did not come into operational use.

The Remote-control and Gyro Test Department (Efka) in August 1917 tested from the Anschütz firm a new Turn- and Position Indicator which displayed its suitability for all types of aircraft. In the Efka laboratories stood a working model of a gyroscopic steering device for manned aircraft. Trials with remote-control installations bearing the code name 'Fledermaus Apparate' (Bat contrivance) developed by Wirt & Röver for installation in remote-controlled aircraft and missiles, were produced up to the end of the war by the Mannesmann-Mulag-Werke and by Siemens.

A direction-finding (D/F) receiver, the so-called 'Airship and Aircraft Position Finder' was operationally capable at the end of the war.

On the subject of aerial photography technique, particularly noteworthy was the development by Oberleutnant Oskar Messter of an automatic aerial camera which underwent trials in November 1916 in the Training and Test Department for Aerial Photography (LVM). From this unit was formed, at the end of the year, the Idflieg 'Air Photography Detachment' (Lubiko) as a central supply, training, test and development centre, out of which was later developed the 'Air Photography Inspectorate' (Idlicht) to which a Photographic Centre was subordinated. In May 1917, the Air Photography Department (Lubia) of the Idflieg Aircraft Detachment I, reported the conclusion of trials for a particular camera installation in single-seat combat aircraft, so that operational trials could be undertaken.

In 1915, the Bomb Test Department had developed a new type of bomb, which in collaboration with the Goerz firm of Friedenau, was completed at the end of the year. Known as the PuW-bomb, it became operational from mid 1916 onwards and replaced the Carbonit-bomb. Introduced for the first time for operational use with the PuW bombs were target telescopes and sights, and bomb-dropping mechanisms developed by the Goerz firm. Bomb weights rose to 1,000kg (2,205 lb) and bomb-release trials with these devices began in December 1917.

Following ongoing series manufacture in 1916 of the Paulus rescue parachute for use by balloon observers, Otto Heinicke attached to the 'Flugmeisterei's' Department A6 in Adlershof undertook on 1st May 1917 the first jump-test of a parachute he had developed for aircraft use. Further demonstration jumps from various altitudes and speeds followed on 5th May 1917 and 21st February 1918, and after concluding trials at the FLZ, the firm of Schröder & Co in Berlin began series production of the Heinicke parachute for the military administration.

After the machine-gun (MG) had been introduced as aircraft armament in 1915, firearms development was concentrated on improving weapons steering mechanisms, turret mounting and raising the calibres, in the course of which a whole series of special turret installations underwent trials. Besides ground-based tests, air firing-trials were always necessary. A few examples below served to indicate the various types of tests undertaken.

In May 1917, a machine-gun coupled with an aero-engine (Kändler System) was installed in an Albatros D-fighter and test-fired statically with good results. At the same time, a twin-barrelled MG (Gast System) was undergoing trials. Electrical MG steering mechanisms from Voigt & Haeffner and Siemens were under test. The first-named firm worked on a mechanism which would interrupt the firing of the mov-

able MGs in 'Riesenflugzeugen' (giant aircraft) when parts of the aircraft traversed the line of fire. The electrical MG steering mechanism was demonstrated in September 1917 at the Aviatik Werke in Leipzig, where 50 examples were installed for operational trials in the DFW licence-built Aviatik C V reconnaissance biplane. On 15th October 1917 a static firing test of a Siemens motor-MG took place in Döberitz in the presence of Manfred von Richthofen, and installations in the Albatros D III and D V were tested in the air. In November 1917, in-flight firing trials against ground targets with a 20mm Becker MG, mounted to fire downwards at a fixed angle in an Albatros C V, were successfully concluded by Leutnant Umlauf.

In the following month, the first air-firing trials took place with the 20mm Becker MG Type II and the GG (Geschütz-Giesserei)

Preparations being made for the test release of a Heinicke parachute in Adlershof in the presence of Rittmeister (Captain) Manfred von Richthofen and his brother Lothar.

In the early armed observation aircraft, the observer was situated ahead of the pilot. Only 12 examples were ordered of the Albatros C IV C.850/15 seen here with pilot Ernst Wendler in front of the Adlershof hangars during flight testing.

The Nieuport N.16 (serial No 959), forced to land in 1916, had launching rails for incendiary rockets on the interplane bracing. It was repaired and flight tested in Adlershof.

After flight testing was completed, the method of construction was studied. The fabric skinning was first removed, followed later by loading and breaking-load tests.

Type III on the Albatros J I 710/17. The movable installation of a 20mm MG was also tested. Examples of flight trials with 'special' armament were:
- Testing a Halberstadt D II in summer 1916 in Döberitz with rockets mounted on guide rails on the wing struts for attacks against balloons. Frontline trials undertaken in October 1916 were unsuccessful because of unsolved problems with the rockets.
- Flight trials with a flame-thrower for operations against ground targets were conducted on an 'infantry' aircraft. The flame-thrower was ordered in November 1917 and initial flights using non-flammable oil to determine the behaviour of the jet, took place the following month. In the Idflieg monthly report of December it mentioned that the first combustion tests were scheduled for the second week of January 1918.

Likewise, at the turn of the year 1917/18, tests were carried out with vertically-mounted MGs fixed to fire downwards at a 45° angle for attacking ground targets. This arrangement was installed in the Junkers J I 816/17 ground-attack aircraft.

For further increasing the performance from industry, the Idflieg strengthened its endeavours at 'normalizing' aircraft from summer 1916. For this purpose, the DVL erected a 'standards' station, and organised a conduit-switch contest for fuel-cocks. A further comparison intended to cover aircraft fabrics did not get that far.

From 13th March to 18th May 1918, a series of C-aircraft underwent comparative trials in Adlershof. The best-known, however, were the so-called D-aircraft contests in Adlershof, intended to enable selection of the most suitable fighters, where compara-

tive flights were carried out by manufacturer's pilots, those from the 'Flugmeisterei' military workshops as well as experienced combat pilots, with the most successful type recommended for production. In all, three such contests were held, at which evaluation conferences partially formed a part.

In the first D-aircraft comparison flights undertaken from 20th January to 12th February 1918, 21 experimental machines from eight companies took part. The winner was the Fokker D VII prototype. In the second contest from 27th May to 21st June 1918, in which 38 aircraft took part, the winner was the Fokker V 28, the prototype of the E V (later D VIII). In July, the machines were test flown by combat pilots and the results evaluated on 6th and 14th July 1918. For the third elimination contest from 10th October to 18th November 1918, only aircraft powered by the BMW IIIa engine were permitted to participate. This contest, in which service pilots took part, was terminated earlier than planned because of the approaching national revolution.

A substantial part of flight testing had to do with engine testing, where the lack of certain raw materials caused problems. Turbo-compressor testing, intended to raise engine performance, was concluded by the Idflieg in September 1918 and an order for 20 of these exhaust-gas superchargers was placed for testing under combat conditions, but was too late for operational use. On 29th August 1918, the 'Pilot- Test- and Training Institute' (FVL) on the Müritzsee – consisting of an 'Aircraft Department Rechlin', an 'Engine Department Roggentin', and the 'Pilot- W/T Operator Test Department Lärz' – was inaugurated by the Grand Duke of Mecklenburg in the presence of the Flying Corps Inspector Oberleutnant Wilhelm Siegert and the Flugzeugmeisterei Commander Major Wagenführ, and formed the basis of the later reactivated E-Stelle Rechlin. In October 1918, comparative test flights took place in Rechlin with the Fokker D VII prototype V11 both with and without N-struts on the wings.

On 16th January 1919, the office of the Commanding General of the Air Forces (Kogenluft) was disbanded, and in the summer, the DVL received back all the installations used by the FLZ, together with a few new buildings, the latter as compensation for military usage during World War One.

List of Participants – 1st D-Aircraft Contest,
Adlershof: 20th Jan to 12th Feb 1918

Builder	Type	Motor	Series (Werk) No
Albatros	DVa	BMW IIIa	7117/17
Albatros	DVa	DIIIaü	(4563)
Albatros	DVa	DIII	7089/17
Albatros	DVa	DIII	7090/17
Aviatik	DIII	Bz IIIb	
Fokker	V9	Ur II	(1831)
Fokker	V11	DIII	(1883)
Fokker	V13	Ur III	(1983)
Fokker	V13	Sh III	(2054)
Fokker	V17	Ur II	
Fokker	V18	DIII	(2116)
Fokker	DrI	Goe III	201/17 (1920)
Fokker	DrI	Ur III	469/17 (2095)
Junkers	J7	DIII	
LFG	DVIa	DIII	
LFG	DVIb	Bz IIIa	
LFG	DVII	Bz IIIb	
LFG	DIX	Sh III	
Pfalz	DIIIa	DIII	5935/17
Pfalz	DIIIa	DIII	6033/17
Pfalz	DVI	Ur II	
Pfalz	DVII	Sh III	
Pfalz	DVIII	Sh III	
Pfalz	DrI		
Rumpler	DI	DIII	
Rumpler	D	DIII	
Schütte-Lanz	DIII	DIII	
SSW	DIIe	Sh III	7553/17
SSW	DIII	Sh III	7551/17
SSW	DIII	Sh III	7552/17
SSW	DIII	Sh III	8340/17
Pfalz	DXII	BMW IIIa	1387/18
Pfalz	DXIIa	Bz III boü	
Pfalz	DXIV	Bz IVa	2800/18
Rumpler	DI	DIII	1552/18
Rumpler	DI	DIIIü	1553/18 (4402)
Schütte-Lanz	DVII	DIIIaü	
SSW	DIII	Sh III	1626/18
SSW	DIII	Sh III	1627/18
SSW	DIII	Sh III	3008/18
SSW	DIII	Sh III	1629/18
SSW	DIIIa	Sh III	1622/18
SSW	DIV	Sh III	7555/17
SSW	DIVa	Sh III	7554/17
SSW	DV	Sh III	557/17

Note: The Fokker V28 was flown with different engines.

List of Participants – 3rd D-Aircraft Contest,
Adlershof: 10th Oct to 2nd Nov 1918.

Builder	Type	Motor	Series (Werk) No
Albatros	DXI	Sh III	2208/18
Albatros	DXII	BMW IIIa	2210/18
Fokker	V28	Sh III	
Fokker	V29	BMW IIIa	
Fokker	V36	BMW IIIa	
Fokker	DVIII	Ur III	
Junkers	DI	BMW IIIa	
LFG	DXVI	Sh III	
LFG	DXVII	BMW IIIa	
Kondor	EIII	Ur III	
Kondor	EIIIa	Goe III	
Pfalz	DIIIa	DIII	
Pfalz	DXVI	BMW IIIa	8364/17
Pfalz	DXV	BMW IIIa	
Rumpler	DI	BMW IIIa	
Zeppelin	DI	BMW IIIa	

List of Participants – 2nd D-Aircraft Contest,
Adlershof: 27th May to 21st June 1918.

Builder	Type	Motor	Series (Werk) No
Albatros	DX	Bz IIIbm	2206/18 (4914)
Albatros	DXI	Sh III	2209/18 (5045)
Aviatik	DIII	Bz III bo	3550/18 (10012)
Aviatik	DIII	Bz III bo	(10005)
Aviatik	DIV	Bz IIIbv	(10008)
Daimler	DI	DIII bv	(60)
Fokker	V21	DIIIü	(2310)
Fokker	V23	DIII	(2443)
Fokker	V24	Bz IVü	(2612)
Fokker	V25	Ur II	(2732)
Fokker	V27	Bz IIIboü	(2734)
Fokker	DVII	DIII	(2268)
			wooden fuselage
Fokker	DVII Alb.	DIII	527/18 (5148)
Fokker	V28	Ur II	(2735)
Fokker	V28	Ur III	(2735)
Fokker	V28	Goe III	(2735)
Junkers	J7	DIIIa	
Junkers	J9/I	DIIIaü	
Kondor	DI	Ur II	(200)
Kondor	DII	Ur II	(201)
LFG	DVIb	Bz IIIaü	
LFG	DVII	Bz IIIbo	224/18 (3780)
LFG	DIX	Sh III	3001/18 (3900)
LVG	DIV	Bz IIIbo	
Pfalz	DVIII	Sh III(RH)	150/18
Pfalz	DVIII	Ur III	158/18
Pfalz	DXII	DIIIa	1371/17
Pfalz	DXII	DIIIaü	1375/18

Navy Flight Test Centres

Whilst those in responsible positions in the Army and Navy hierarchy at the turn of the century preferred to use the rigid airships built by Graf Zeppelin for military purposes, the Navy authorities were less interested in the large and relatively limited manoeuvrability of the Zeppelins and attentively followed aircraft developments.

At the end of 1910, Alfred von Tirpitz, the State Secretary of the Reich Navy Office (RMA) agreed to preliminary tests leading to the design of an aircraft suitable for use by the Navy. Development was to take place at the Kaiserlichen Werft (Imperial Shipyard), Danzig. In the RMA Shipyard Department, Fregattenkapitän Lübbert was the Dezernent (Administrative Department Head) having responsibility for aeronautical equipment matters.

In 1911, an aircraft test centre was erected at the KW Danzig, under the leadership of Kapitänleutnant Max Hering,

Test pilot Ernst Wendler standing by a British Sopwith bomber forced to land in October 1916. The Adlershof field fire-brigade was located in the centre building in the background.

A valuable capture was examined in Adlershof, consisting of the third prototype Handley Page 0/100 which appeared on the Western Front and soon afterwards fell undamaged into German hands.

succeeded from June 1912 by Korvetten-kapitän Gygas. Responsible for matters relating to design was Marinebaumeister Wilhelm Coulmann, supported by Marine-Obering. Carl Loew as aeronautical adviser with Oberleutnant zur See Walter von Langfeld as pilot. In September 1911, the Navy received its first aircraft as a gift from Otto Fritzsche, and was set on floats, which after conversion by the Rumpler firm, resembled the well-known Taube (dove) of the period. Loew carried out land-based take-offs and landings with it and demonstrated its floatation capabilities. In winter 1911, a flight test station was brought into operation in Putzig near Danzig.

In summer 1912, trials took place there with the first Albatros-Farman biplanes to be set on floats. On 3rd May 1912, Walter von Langfeld carried out the first landing on water with the Albatros D2 biplane equipped with a Coulmann central float and landing-gear, and on 5th June 1912, he successfully made the first take-off from water without the landing-gear with the D3.

The Navy chose to number its aircraft with navy numbers which were consecutively allocated. A distinction was initially made between Eindecker (monoplanes) and Doppeldecker (biplanes), but this was later discarded. In accordance with this system, the Fritzsche-Rumpler monoplane carried the Marinenummer E1, followed by the Albatros-Farman biplanes with D2 and D3. Navy land-based aircraft had a separate numbering system prefixed with the letters LF to distinguish them.

During the period 29th August to 5th September 1912, the first German water-based aircraft contest was held in Heiligendamm near Doberan on the Baltic coast, where the competition and performance requirements were laid down by the Navy which had also put up the prize money.

Navy Aircraft Categories

B	two-seat bomber
BFT	B-aircraft with transmitter
HFT	aircraft with transmitter & receiver
C	two-seat aircraft with movable MG
C2MG	C-aircraft with 1 fixed and 1 movable MG
C3MG	C-aircraft with 2 fixed and 1 movable MG
CHFT	armed HFT aircraft
S	Schulflugzeug (basic trainer)
U	Übungsflugzeug (practice aircraft)
V	Versuchsflugzeug (test aircraft)
FL	guidance aircraft for wire-guided explosive boats
Bu	U-boat (submarine-based) aircraft
E	single-seat flying boat with 1-2 fixed MGs
ED	single-seat twin-float aircraft with 1-2 fixed MGs
T	torpedo aircraft, also usable as bomber and minelayer
G	twin-engined Grossflugzeug (large aircraft)
R	Riesenflugzeug (giant aircraft) with three and more engines

The presence of the Iron Cross and the stencilled name Emil on the rear fuselage indicates that this Sopwith Baby, number 8153, fell into German hands. It is seen here during tests undertaken by the SVK in Warnemünde.

A view in a north-westerly direction above the hangars of the Seaplane Test Detachment in Warnemünde. The large Hangar VI (front), Hangar V (rear right) and Hangar IV (rear centre) were first erected during the war and only the small Hangar III (partly hidden at top left) was already completed in Summer 1914.

The first provisional trials of torpedo-carrying aircraft for operational use were carried out with this LVG D IV Zig. test aircraft flown by Flugmeister Herz in June 1915.

List of Participants – 1st German Water-based Aircraft Contest,
Heiligendamm: 29th August to 5th September 1912

Builder	Type	Engine	Pilot
Ago	Biplane	100hp (74kW) Argus	Ellery von Gorrissen
Albatros	Biplane	100hp (74kW) Argus	Robert Thelen
Alk	Monoplane	100hp (74kW) Argus	Ellie Dunetz
Aviatik	Biplane	100hp (74kW) Argus	Bruno Büchner
Goedecker	Flying-boat	70hp (52kW) Daimler	Bernard de Waal
Dr. Hübner	Monoplane	100hp (74kW) Argus	Paul Senge

On 12th October 1912, the RMA established its Shipyard Department, a new 'Dezernat für Luftschiff- und Fliegerwesen' (Administrative Department for Airships and Aircraft) alias B X, headed by Kapitän zur See Lübbert. At the end of 1912, comparison and evaluation flights took place in Putzig with the Ago, Albatros and Aviatik aircraft that had previously been flown in Heiligendamm and resulted in the Navy giving up its existing requirement that its aircraft should be capable of landing on both land and water.

In order to compare foreign designs with German types in the years up to 1919, the Navy purchased individual examples of Curtiss, Sopwith, AV Roe and Lohner aircraft and tested them in Putzig, Kiel, and Wismar. The main problem in naval aircraft development, besides the design of suitable floats, was increasing engine performance and load-carrying capacity. The decision as to which aircraft type was the best of all possibilities – flying-boat, single- or twin-float seaplanes – also required numerous test flights, and eventually led to the adoption of mainly twin-float aircraft without an additional tail-float.

At the beginning of 1913, the Navy installed W/T equipment of the Signal Company, Kiel, on the Albatros WMZ biplane (Navy code D 5) and tested it in Kiel, the aircraft having a long bamboo antenna mast 6.5m (21¼ft) long. During the 'Kieler Flugwoche' (Kiel Flying Week) in July 1913, the first bomb-dropping tests on the target ship 'Bayern' also took place.

Following the formation on 1st April 1913 of the 'Aviation Section' in the Shipyard Department of the RMA (B X), divided into Administrative Departments B Xa for military and B Xb for technical matters, a Supreme Cabinet Decree (AKO) resulted, between 3rd May 1913 and 1st June 1913, in the establishment – besides a Navy Airship Department – of a new Navy Flying Department (MFA) under Korvettenkapitän Gygas

in Putzig, which reported in all test and technical matters directly to the RMA State Secretary. In 1914, the Section received the status of a Department (B X) in the RMA. Following a waterborne aircraft contest which had taken place on Lake Constance in 1913, the second German seaplane contest called the 'Ostseeflug' (Baltic Sea Flight) was scheduled to be held in Warnemünde in 1914. At the latter location from 1913, a combined sea- and land airfield facility between the Baltic and the Breitling – an extension of the Warnow lagoon – had been erected, catering for Navy needs.[3]

An examination of the preliminary performance test requirements for the 'Ostseeflug' reveals the technical status of waterborne aircraft at that time. Besides take-off on water with zero windspeed followed by a straight-line flight course, the aircraft was to attain an altitude of 500m (1,640ft) in a maximum of 15 mins with a maximum speed of 80km/h (50mph), be able to manoeuvre and anchor at a windspeed of at least 4m/sec (9mph) and demonstrate ability to stay afloat for 24 hours.

When the order for general mobilization was received on the evening of 1st August 1914 – the first day of the contest – the 'Ostseeflug' was cancelled and the Navy took possession of the 21 aircraft available as well as the airfield. From its initial provisional beginnings, the Navy Aircraft Test

Centre eventually developed at the airfield. A 'Seaplane Acceptance Commission (SAK) was set up by Kapitänleutnant (retd) Walter Hormel. On 22nd September 1915, the Navy officially took over the Warnemünde airfield, and Korvettenkapitän Max Hering become Kommandant of what was still known as the 'Navy Flight and Test Station' which soon became renamed the Seaplane Test Detachment (SVK). Hectic construction activity began, where, besides barrack blocks, officers' quarters and workshops, a series of large aircraft hangars and 14 engine test-beds were erected. Particularly noteworthy were the two large so-called harbour hangars which stood on pylons in the water on the banks of the Breitling. Erected in 1918, they were suitable for housing the multi-engined G- and R-aircraft.

An experimental hangar was also built in 1918 with an 8 x 10m (26¼ x 32⅔ft) water tank for testing aircraft floats, in addition to which were laboratories and other experimental rooms in the building that was to house a wind-tunnel, but the latter had not been completed up to the end of the war. Equally incomplete internally was the Giant Aircraft Hangar VII which, with a length of 140m (459ft), width 66m (216½ft) and height 18m (59ft), was the largest building of all.

After 1914, when initial attempts to produce a torpedo-carrying aircraft using the LVG D IV Zig. and Albatros B I Torp. landplanes had to be discontinued because of inadequate performance, the performance requirements for future torpedo aircraft were laid out. The abbreviations Zig and Torp stood for 'cigar-shaped' and 'torpedo-shaped' appearance of the experimental torpedo mock-ups flown. When World War One began, the command structure was again revised where at first, the B X Department was separated from the main Ship-

The first prototype Sablatnig SF 2 (Navy number 580) was completely destroyed during testing in Warnemünde and is seen here in front of the SVK Hangars I and II.

yard Department and became the autonomous 'Abteilung für Luftfahrtwesen' (Department for Aviation) reporting to the State Secretary. In the military service echelons, the Navy Aircraft and Airship Departments of the newly-established office was subordinated to the Supreme Commander of the Navy Aviation Departments (BdL).

At the SVK in Warnemünde, all naval aircraft underwent sea testing, ie, taking-off and landing three times at Force 4. One after another, various types of aircraft were promoted and developed. Initially, reconnaissance aircraft with high-seas capability, led to the development of more powerful engines as well as air-dropped weapons and W/T equipment, followed by single-seat naval combat aircraft with fixed offensive armament. In the next category, Grossflugzeuge (large aircraft) were developed which later served as bombers, minelayers, and long-range reconnaissance aircraft. The Riesenflugzeuge (giant aircraft) whose development then followed, served in these roles also. Technical examination and testing of water-based aircraft produced by the industrial firms were also tested by the SVK on water and in the air. Simultaneously, the entire range of equipment – armament, bombs, W/T, cameras, navigational and signals aids as well as crew equipment were tested on the ground, and after installation in the aircraft, were tested in flight.

These checks resulted in special tests and Navy-instituted developments particularly with regard to equipment. As an example, in 1915, at the Torpedo Special Detachment in Warnemünde, the first instrument test flights with Anschütz gyrohorizons were carried out. Aerial photography had made such advances by the end of

the war that with the use of various filters and sensitive photo plates, even minefields and submarines at small underwater depths could be recognized.

From May to September 1917, flight trials were conducted with a DWM 37mm cannon on the twin-engined Gotha WD 7 (Navy number 676). The 20mm Becker MG and the electrically-operated MG-steering previously mentioned in the Army Aircraft section above, were also tested by the SVK for the Navy, and in June 1918, testing was concluded on a Navy-developed multiple-bomb-release mechanism for 12 x 50kg (110 lb) bombs for torpedo aircraft.

From 1916, the manufacture and test of an aircraft catapult driven by compressed air took place not in Warnemünde but in the KW Danzig, designed and produced by Dr. Stein, the Technical Officer of the Zeebrugge Naval Air Station. The first catapult take-offs were carried out by Leutnant zur See von Reppert in 1918 with a Rumpler naval single-seat fighter and a Hansa-Brandenburg monoplane.

When the office of the 'Navy Flight Chief' established on 30th July 1917 was abolished on 12th February 1919, all naval flying activities were terminated upon instructions from the Victorious Powers. A government commission which inspected the SVK installations in Warnemünde at the end of May 1919, decided that 'these were to be transferred on 1st October 1919 to the DVL in one form or another, so as to retain the testing installations for the German nation!' However, when airfield administration was transferred on 1st October 1919 from the Navy to the Reich Ministry of the Treasury, plans for take over by the DVL were shattered due to the high rental/lease demands.

Footnotes

1   Up to this point, the presentation is that of the unpublished manuscript entitled 'Erprobungsstellen für Luftfahrtzeuge – die Anfänge' (Aircraft Test Centres – the Beginning) by Dr. Günter Schmitt from which extracts are cited verbatim. The text, originally prepared for inclusion in this book, was placed at the author's disposal.
2   Taken from the abovementioned document.
3   Preliminary history and development of Warnemünde airfield including Navy activities and the aircraft companies operating there were extensively described by the author in the book 'Luftfahrt zwischen Ostsee und Breitling' (Aviation between the Baltic and Breitling), Transpress Verlag, Berlin, 1990, and by the Nara-Verlag, Allershausen.

Literature List

Buchholtz: Die Geburt und erste Kindheit der preussischen Militär-Luftschiffer-Abteilung (The birth and initial childhood of the Prussian Military Airship Department), in Illustrierte Aeronautische Mittheilungen, Nr.4/1900.

Braunbeck, G: Braunbecks Sport-Lexikon 1911/1912 issue, Berlin, 1911.

Carganico: History of the first German military airfield – (Döberitz until March 1912) and the first out-station on the Western border (Metz from 10th April 1912). Recollections of a Lieutenant in the Flying Corps. Manuscript dated 1st December 1912. Stiasny-Archiv, Deutsches Technikmuseum, Berlin.

Koos V: 'Luftfahrt zwischen Ostsee und Breitling', Transpress Verlag, Berlin, 1990.

Kroschel, G/Stützer, H: 'Die deutschen Militärflugzeuge 1910-1918', Wilhelmshaven, 1977.

Schmitt, G: Berlin-Johannisthal 1912: 'Die Gründung der Deutsche Versuchsanstalt für Luftfahrt' (The Founding of the DVL), in Flieger-Review, Nr.7/1994.

Developed by Hansa-Brandenburg for use as a submarine-based aircraft seen here is the second W 20 (Navy number 1552) during its trials at the SVK in Warnemünde.

Chapter Three
by Christoph Regel

Organisation and Responsibility for Development & Testing 1920-1945

Under the restrictions imposed by the Treaty of Versailles after the end of World War One, development and manufacture of aircraft was forbidden in Germany. Despite this, the RWM had as early as 1920 set up disguised Referate (Advisory Boards) responsible for undertaking preparations for the establishment of a 'Fliegertruppe' (Flying Corps) and for the creation of related development and testing centres. The following account provides an overall picture of the origin and organisational changes of these civilian and military centres up to 1945.

Quick-Reference Abbreviations

Heer *Army;* Luftwaffe *Air Force;* Marine *Navy;*
Referat *Advisory Board;* Wehrmacht *Armed Forces*

BA/MA   Bundesarchiv/Militärarchiv
        (Federal/Military Archives), Freiburg

DLV   Deutscher Luftsport Verband
        German Airsports Association

DVL   Deutsche Versuchsanstalt für Luftfahrt
        German Experimental Institute for Aviation

DVS   Deutsche Verkehrsflieger-Schule
        German Commercial Pilots School

E-Stelle Erprobungsstelle
        Experimental/Test Establishment/Centre

EdL   Erprobungsstelle der Luftwaffe
        Luftwaffe E-Stelle

EKL   Erprobungskommando Lärz
        Test Detachment Lärz

HWA (HwaA) Heereswaffenamt
        Army Ordnance Office, successor to the RWM

HWA Wa.A Waffenamt
        Ordnance Office

HWA Wa.B.6 Waffenamt Beschaffung, Referat 6
        Wa. Procurement, Advisory Board 6

HWA Wa.L Waffenamt-Organisation, Prüfwesen und
        Beschaffung – *Organisation, Evaluation,
        Procurement, Sub-Sections Wa.L.1/L.II/L.III*

HWA Wa.Prw. Waffenamt Prüfwesen
        *Checking/Testing/Certification Office Sub-Sections
        Wa.Prw.6F, 8*

IWG (InWG) Inspektion für Waffen und Gerät
        Armament & Equipment Inspectorate Sub-Section 6F

KdE   Kommandeur der Erprobungsstellen
        E-Stellen Commander

Kdo.d.E. Kommando der Erprobungsstellen
        E-Stellen Detachments

RDL (RDLI) Reichsverband der Deutschen Luftfahrt-Industrie
        Reich Association of German Aviation Industry

RLM   Reichsluftfahrtministerium
        German Air Ministry

RLM GL Generalluftzeugmeister
        Chief of Procurement & Supply

RLM LA Luftschutzamt, later Luftkommandoamt
        Air Defence Office, later Air Detachment Office

RLM LB Allgemeines Amt
        General Office, Sub-Section LBII

RLM LC Technisches Amt
        Technical Office, Sub-Sections LCI/LCII/LCIII

RVM   Reichsverkehrsministerium
        Reich Ministry of Transport

RWM   Reichswehrministerium
        Imperial Army & Navy Ministry, later the HWA

RWM TA Truppenamt
        Armed Forces Office

RWM TA(L) Truppenamt Luftschutz-Referat (early)
        Air Defence Advisory Board

RWM TA(L) Truppenamt Luftfahrt-Referat (later)
        Aeronautical Advisory Board

TLR   Technische Luftrüstung
        Technical Air Armament, usually: Chef TLR

As mentioned also in Chapter 4, the RWM Truppenamt on 1st March 1920 had established a so-called TA(L) Luftschutz-Referat headed by Hauptmann Hellmuth Wilberg and simultaneously within the IWG organisation, a Referat 'Flugtechnik' (Aviation) headed by Hauptmann Kurt Student. Because of the existing bans and limitations, the early activities of these new bodies were of a purely theoretical nature. Nevertheless, basic principles were able to be established which defined the equipment needs of a future Flying Corps and which led from 1923 onwards to the first development orders for new aircraft and aero-engines.

Around the beginning of 1927, the IWG was combined with the RWM Wa.A, and the Aviation Referat – probably previously designated as IWG 6F – received the title Wa.Prw.6F, still headed by Hauptmann Kurt Student. The Development Advisory Boards which formed a part of it, for external appearances, were camouflaged as independent civilian firms. The 'Flugzeugreferat' (Aircraft Advisory Board) for example, was called the 'Ingenieurbüro Nicolaus' but was subordinate to the Wa.Prw.6F as were the Erprobungsgruppen (Testing Units) in Johannisthal, Staaken and Rechlin. Testing thus became a part of Development and Control in the

HWA. The Procurement Office on the other hand, was an independent branch. This twin-track organisation thus existed in accordance with the classical structure of the Ordnance Office, but with the build-up of aviation interests, suffered from deficiencies caused by rivalry and performance delays which in the long term were unacceptable and soon led to the idea of creating a single responsible body to take care of Development and Procurement. That there were obviously attempts made along these lines to subordinate the Wa.Prw.6F and the DVL to the RVM is indicated in an undated document[1] in which a contrary attitude was expressed. In this, the unknown author feared that military needs would no longer receive sufficient consideration, and that a 'Centre for Air Power together with Evaluation, Procurement, and Industrial Armament' could well arise.

Such endeavours were certainly not misguided since the RVM, whose Aviation Department headed by its foresighted Director Ministerialdirigent Ernst Brandenburg, provided the main source of funds for Development in the aviation sector, and in any case, development was pursued in the DVL as 'Department M'. In the event, the military was able to have its way so that the technical aviation portion of the HWA was retained, except that in accordance with the decree of 29th November 1928, the Organisational, Evaluation and Procurement Departments were amalgamated under a new 'roof' called the Wa.L[2] headed by Hauptmann Hellmuth Volkmann – the former Chef Wa.B.6. The 'Prüfwesen' section retained its former composition, but instead of Hauptmann Kurt Student, was now headed by Hauptmann Dr. Paul Jeschonnek.

The 'Entwicklungsreferate' (Development Advisory Boards), formerly disguised as civilian 'Ingenieurbüros' (engineering offices), had already been apparently dissolved during the summer of 1928 and were incorporated organisationally into the Wa.Prw.6F, as can be discerned from a letter dated 2nd August 1928, written by the Ingenieurbüro Nicolaus and addressed to the Rohrbach firm.[3] Hence, the Wa.L Prüfwesen office at the end of 1928, besides having Staff HQ Advisory Boards for organisational, technical and budgeting matters, had five 'Entwicklungsreferate', whilst on an equal organisational level, handled two 'Erprobungsgruppen' as out-stations and formed the Referate VI and VII. Soon afterwards, the Wa.L.Prw organisation was concentrated into only 4 Development Test Advisory Boards as well as Air Squadrons known as the 'Flieger-Staffel Berlin', headed by Ing. Hans Leutert and the 'Fliegerstaffel' Rechlin, headed by Oberleutnant (retd) Eberhard Mohnicke.

In the summer of 1929, the entire HWA was restructured, which also affected the technical aviation section. In accordance with growing demands on development and testing during the period of secret 'Fliegerrüstung' (air armament), the 'Prüfwesen' section was divided (by the decree of 30th July 1929) into 3 equi-authorized sections: the Wa.L.I (Aircraft Development), Wa.L.II (Weapons, Photographic and W/T-Development) and Wa.L.III (Testing).[4] Other Wa.L. sections remained as before, but with new designations. The 'Erprobungsgruppe' (Testing Unit) was now headed by Dipl.-Ing. Dietrich Freiherr von Massenbach, who is said to have played a significant role in the erection and expansion of the E-Stelle Rechlin.

As successor to Hauptmann Volkmann, after summer 1929, Major Wilhelm Wimmer took over the aviation section. At the same time, and certainly before summer 1931, the Wa.L. was again re-designated as the Wa.Prw.8 but without any organisational changes.[5] This separation of development, test, armament and procurement offices for the future Flying Corps remained largely unaltered until the establishment of the RLM (German Air Ministry) in 1933. Already prior to the take over by the NSDAP (Nazi Party) on 30th January 1933, officers concerned with secret air armament were able to convince the RWM leadership that it was absolutely mandatory at the highest level, to establish a central organisation which would be concerned with all matters dealing with military aviation.

On 8th February 1933, the Reichswehrminister Generaloberst Werner von Blomberg issued the decree setting-up and reporting directly to himself, the 'Luftschutzamt' (Air Defence Office), created out of the 'Aviation & Air Defence' section of the Heer (Army) and Marine (Navy)[6] whose formation was to be carried out by 1st April 1933. The tasks of this new organisation included the 'development, testing and procurement of aircraft, aero-engines and special flying equipment'.

In accordance with this edict, the Wa.Prw.8 Department previously responsible for such matters, was extracted and incorporated as Department L2 'Technik' in the 'Luftschutzamt'. As the detailed Establishment Order of 21st March 1933 confirmed,[7] out-stations of the departments taken over were assimilated into the new organisation. Specifically mentioned were the E-Stellen Staaken and Rechlin, the Naval Aircraft E-Stelle Travemünde and the Fertigung GmbH (Manufacturing Co Ltd). Thus, although for the very first time, a central directorate for military aviation was established in Germany, it still lay within the organisational confines of the RWM and hence within the sphere of influence by the Army and Navy leadership. A step towards its independence as a separate Ministry – driven energetically by the new Reichskommissar für Luftfahrt (Reich Commissioner for Aviation) Hermann Göring – did not have to wait long, and took place with the Reichspräsident edict of 27th April 1933, which brought the RLM into being.[8] Shortly thereafter, effective 15th May 1933, Generaloberst von Blomberg gave the order for the Luftschutzamt to be transferred in its entirety from the RWM into the new RLM. This is generally regarded as the date of origin of the new, even if still disguised Luftwaffe (Air Force).

When this step had taken place, the majority of the Technical Flying Department left the Luftschutzamt and was subordinated to the RLM's LB (General Office) as the LB II (Technical Department). The sphere of development for the aviation sector henceforth outwardly belonged to a civilian Ministry, whilst at the same time, testing was carried out under the equally disguised cover of the civilian RDL E-Stelle. Spearheading the new and enlarged Department as hitherto was Major Wimmer, whilst besides the inspectorates Prüfwesen (Pr), with its combined responsibility and equality of authorization for development, testing and manufacture, headed by Korvettenkapitän Hans Siburg, there existed the subordinate munitions department Rüstung (R), and the newly-formed research department Forschung (F).[9]

An important upgrading of Technical Flying activity took place in the course of another RLM restructuring on 1st October 1933, when it was raised to the status of a Technical Department known as the LC Technisches Amt (Technical Office). It stood on the same organisational level as that of the Luftkommandoamt (LA) and the Allgemeine Amt (LB), reporting directly to the Staatssekretär für Luftfahrt (State Secretary for Aviation) Erhard Milch. Under this constellation, the Technisches Amt retained its position even after the announcement of the existence of the Luftwaffe.

The LC Department was likewise subdivided into the Research Department LC I (Forschung), Inspectorate LC II (Prüfwesen) and Procurement LC III (Beschaffung), as well as the organisation of the Prüfwesen itself. Oberst Wilhelm Wimmer retained his current responsibility for Technical Flying, whilst from June 1934, Dr.-Ing. Wolfram Freiherr von Richthofen headed the Department LC II and in reality thus became head of the development centres and the E-Stellen.

The last existing camouflage, termed the 'RDL E-Stelle' became superfluous with the declaration of military power and establishment of the Luftwaffe as the third arm of the Armed Forces in March 1935. During the course of that year, Rechlin and Travemünde were also officially designated as Luftwaffe E-Stellen. During this period, erection of installations at the weapons proving grounds began in Tarnewitz, initially operated as an out-station of Travemünde, but soon afterwards receiving the status of an independent E-Stelle.

To improve control and harmonization of the tasks of an E-Stelle, a 'Kommando der Fliegererprobungsstelle' (Flight Test Centre Detachment) based in Rechlin had also been established in summer 1934.[10] At its head was the KdE Commander whose function was also that of Head of the E-Stelle Rechlin and who simultaneously became the superior of the Head of the E-Stelle Travemünde. The KdE itself was subordinate to the RLM LC II Department Head. The first holder of this position was Walter Stahr – formerly Chief of the Fliegerschule Stahr in Lipetsk and now holding the rank of 'Flight Commodore' in the DLV – who was appointed officially on 1st July 1934, after taking over such duties as early as February 1934.[11]

The creation of this central E-Stelle Detachment was obviously aimed at being able to improve co-ordination of the growing range of tasks that were performed by existing and anticipated new E-Stellen which would have a common point of contact with superiors of the RLM Technisches Amt Development Departments as well as the responsible regional Luftwaffe command authorities.

In June 1936, embracing the leadership of the RLM Technisches Amt was an individual who was to greatly influence the further development of aeronautical technology and the entire spectrum of German aviation armaments, namely, Oberst Ernst Udet. As the most successful surviving World War One fighter pilot, daring stunt-flyer, film-idol and 'bonvivant' he enjoyed enormous popularity in Germany as well as having several contacts and friendships abroad. For Göring, it was therefore not least, ultimately a question of prestige to induce Udet to join the Luftwaffe and to entrust him with leadership of one of the most important posts in the RLM. On the other hand, Udet disliked desk-work and administrative duties, and from his training and preferences, was neither technician nor organiser – something he himself often stressed. Nevertheless, as successor to Oberst Wimmer, he was responsible for development, testing and procurement of aviation equipment, and as such, was the highest professional superior of all the Luftwaffe E-Stellen.

A substantial upgrading in the sphere of testing took place through the 'Re-organisation of Development'[12] which Udet had produced and ordered to be carried out in December 1936, according to which:
'The E-Stellen Rechlin, Travemünde and Tarnewitz are immediately subordinate to the Chief of the Technical Office and are entrusted with conducting the development and technical testing of Luftwaffe equipment'.

From the definitions contained therein, it was now the task of the E-Stellen 'on the basis of development proposals, working in collaboration with appropriate branches of industry, to carry out the development tasks assigned to them and their technical testing'. Based on this, the LC II was to dedicate itself increasingly to foreseeable development planning. This re-organisation clearly carries Udet's signature in which testing took on a significant responsibility in a rather flat hierarchy under his direct control. Related to this were numerous transfers of personnel from LC II to the E-Stellen.

However, it only lasted just over one year until the next organisational change. The starting point was a new structuring of the entire RLM in the course of which the Technisches Amt was placed directly under Hermann Göring, and no longer under the Staatssekretär für Luftfahrt Erhard Milch.

Udet himself as 'Amtschef' (Organisation Chief) abolished the existing organisations in May 1938 and placed under his control no less than 13 independent Departments, among them 7 different Development Departments – a seemingly very problematic step in view of the necessary leadership and overview needed in this sphere of importance. This action also dissolved the position of E-Stellen Commander (KdE) which, after being held by Major Stahr had meanwhile been filled by Oberstleutnant Kurt Student and finally, Major Carl-August von Schönebeck. The E-Stellen each now had an independent commandant's office reporting to the Chef LC, besides which there existed an Erprobungsleitung (Testing Directorate) and a Militärische Prüfung (Military Evaluation Centre) with an identical reporting structure.[13] As if this accumulation of direct reporting lines to the Amtschef (Udet) was not already confusing enough, it was even more exacerbated by the fact that the Head of the Test Detach-

ments within the E-Stellen, effective immediately, was made directly responsible for technical matters to the Head of the Specialist Groups in the Technisches Amt. Whilst this certainly allowed work to proceed rapidly and unbureaucratically, a tightly-controlled and foreseeable plan of research, development and testing, was increasingly impaired.

Yet again, one year later in spring 1939, noticeable changes took place in the Luftwaffe leadership structure. Of special significance for aeronautical technology was creation of the position of Generalluftzeugmeister or GL, which embraced the Technisches Amt (Technical Office), the Nachschubamt (Supply Office) and the Amtsgruppe Industrie und Wirtschaft (Office of Industry and Economy). Generalleutnant Udet became the first GL combined with the office of Chief of the Technisches Amt, but had to again be contented to remain subordinate to Generaloberst Milch, the State Secretary for Aviation.

In the spring of 1939, no changes were made to the position of the E-Stellen which merely underwent some renaming internally in conformity with new designations of RLM Development Departments. This situation remained largely unaltered right up until 1944.

In autumn 1941, there were noticeable effects in the Testing sphere with the establishment of a Kdo.d.E (E-Stellen Detachment) led by a KdE (E-Stellen Commander), which technically and operationally had the task of controlling a total of 9 Test- and Experimental Centres. The KdE himself reported to the Chief of the Technical Office. Noteworthy is that this position was assigned to Major Edgar Petersen, who as KG 40 Commodore and pilot possessed pertinent combat experience, but no previous knowledge. In the leadership of the Luftwaffe, Göring and Milch believed, in view of the evermore apparent problems being faced with Luftwaffe armament and battlefield setbacks, that with a tightened military organisation and command structure, they would be able to make sudden changes of worth. Following Udet's suicide, Göring strived to establish a military Court of Enquiry which would uncover mistakes and failures of the responsible engineers in the Technisches Amt. The result, however, was that the faults were found to lie primarily in the uppermost echelons of leadership, less in the Development Departments, and none at all in the E-Stellen which had also been subject to scrutiny. Nevertheless, the E-Stellen Commander posts were soon afterwards filled with officers having combat experience, whilst the positions of Heads of Testing were no longer filled.

During this time also, the so-called Erprobungskommandos (Test Detachments) or Erprobungsstaffeln (Test Squadrons) were introduced and which could be regarded as successors of the former 'Abteilung M' and 'Militärische Prüfung' that already existed in 1937/38 in the E-Stellen Rechlin and Travemünde respectively. They were intended to guarantee rapid testing under realistic conditions of particular new types of aircraft involving airmen and Luftwaffe units and thus lay the foundations for the first operational squadrons equipped with the aircraft concerned. These Detachments were mostly formed in Lärz, near Rechlin, where the EKL (Test Detachment Lärz), stationed there since its formation in 1942, held a somewhat special status. It took care of the new Detachments, and in addition, assumed the increasing flight test and transportation duties for the E-Stelle Rechlin and Kdo.d.E.

The last decisive changes in the armament sphere of the Luftwaffe occurred at the end of July 1944 with the establishment of an organisation known as the 'Chef der Technischen Luftrüstung' (Head of Technical Air Armament)[14] or Chef TLR. The catastrophic situation in all the theatres of war, the non-appearance of new types of aircraft and equipment, the inroads made upon production caused by the effect of Allied bombing raids, appeared to leave no other alternative than the creation of a central TLR office in a much-too-late attempt to counter the enemy's quantitative superiority with improved quality of armament and equipment on the home front. When it was finally recognized that technology could not be 'governed' using the principle of 'Order and Obey' it was now expected that the 'engineers would come to the rescue'. An all-encompassing organisation was now created, responsible for research, development, testing, procurement, production and acceptance of Luftwaffe equipment items, inclusive now of anti-aircraft weapon and fuels. The position of GL was absorbed by the Chef TLR who reported to the Luftwaffe General Staff, which in turn was subordinate to the OKL or Oberkommando der Luftwaffe (Supreme Command of the Air Force). From this time onwards, the KdE reported directly to the Chef TLR.

Testing activity, however, was made more difficult through the parallel existence of various Sonderbeauftragten (Special Commissioners) and Generalbevollmächtigten (General Plenipotentiaries) of Reichsmarschall Hermann Göring or of the Führer Adolf Hitler, as well as by the Jägerstab (Fighter HQ) and individual Waffengeneräle (Armaments Generals) who were partly authorized directly to issue development orders or requirements to the E-Stellen and thus further added to the already prevailing chaos caused by enemy action.

A final re-organisation occurred only a few weeks before the end of the war by subordinating the Kdo.d.E. to the Befehlshaber der Ersatz-Luftwaffe (Commander of the Replacement Air Force)[15] at a time when the majority of E-Stellen Detachments had already been dissolved. For what reasons these organisational changes were made and whether they had an effect on testing work, cannot be established from available documentation relating to that period.

A review of chronological events shows how often and multifarious were the consecutive changes in the sphere of Luftwaffe Development and Testing which took place in the space of rather more than 20 years. It shows clearly that pursuance of clear technical goals and appropriate planning was missing in the Luftwaffe leadership, and equally so, that the significance of technology and its inherent laws were not comprehended by those in positions of responsibility. Soon after the outbreak of World War Two, the first signs of failures began to appear which could no longer be recovered, especially since the opposing countries more and more gained the upper hand and the German aviation and armaments industry – in an increasingly limited capacity – were compelled to react. Nevertheless, under these conditions, astonishing achievements in the field of technical development and testing were realized to which the enemy also paid tribute, and whose effects are still recognizable in aeronautical technology even decades after the end of the war.

Footnotes

1 BA/MA Freiburg, File RH8v/3601.

2 BA/MA Freiburg, File RH8v/3599: HWaA, WaB6 Nr.2840/28 gKdos'z' of 29.11.1928.

3 BA/MA Freiburg, File RH8v/3678: Letter Ingenieurbüro Nicolaus of 02.08.1928 to Firma Rohrbach, Berlin.

4 BA/MA Freiburg, File RH8v/3599: Gruppenbefehl (Group Order) Wa.L. Nr.452/29.A gKdos'z' of 30.07.1929.

5 BA/MA Freiburg, File RH8v/3599. Arbeitsplan (Work-plan) Wa.Prw8 of 29.05.1931 with description and occupation of work-positions.

6 Der Reichswehrminister T.A. Nr.109/33 gKdos T 2 III B/In(L) of 08.02.1933 re Establishment of an Air Defence Office (Luftschutzamt), reproduced by Karl-Heinz Völker: Die Entwicklung der Militärischen Luftfahrt in Deutschland 1920-1933, Stuttgart, 1962.

7 Der Reichswehrminister, Nr.401/33 gKdos In 1(L)V of 21.03.1933 re Formation of an Air Defence Office (Luftschutzamt), reproduced by Karl-Heinz Völker: Die Entwicklung der Militärischen Luftfahrt in Deutschland 1920-1933, Stuttgart, 1962.

8 Cited by Karl-Heinz Völker: Die Entwicklung der Militärischen Luftfahrt in Deutschland 1920-1933, Stuttgart, 1962, p204.

9 BA/MA Freiburg, File RL 3/2220. Organigramme of the RLM Technisches Amt (B.II) as of 15.06.1933.

10 BA/MA Freiburg, File RL 3/2234.

11 BA/MA Freiburg, File Pers 6/1928: Personnel Record of Walter Stahr.

12 BA/MA Freiburg, File RL 3/1246: LC/LA Nr.4140/36 gKdos. L.A. II 1 of 14.12.1936 re Reorganisation of Sphere of Development in Department LC.

13 BA/MA Freiburg, File RL 3/2323: Technisches Amt LC Adj. Nr.2250/38 geheim (secret) of 28.05.1938 (Transcript): re New Organisational Structure of the Technisches Amt.

14 Attachment II to OKL Gen.Qu.Nr.19327/44 geheim (secret) (2.Abt.[I]) of 27.04.1944 (Transcript): Preliminary Office Instructions for the Chef der Technischen Luftrüstung.

15 Horst Boog: Die Deutsche Luftwaffenführung 1935-45, Stuttgart, 1982, p334 and p586.

Chapter Four
by Hanfried Schliephake

Secret Flight Testing in Lipetsk, Russia

With the signing of the Treaty of Versailles, the German Reich was forbidden to possess aircraft, tanks, and submarines. The 100,000-man Army was only allowed to carry out manoeuvres with appropriate dummies and provisional artifacts, without being able to ascertain the actual operational value of these weapons. As a result of a secret Treaty between the Reich government and the Soviet Union, four E-Stellen of the Reichswehr were brought into being in the mid 1920s on Soviet territory, which introduced a close co-operation between the Reichswehr and the Red Army. One of these Test Centres was Lipetsk. In the period that followed and remote from the Allied Control Commissions, the military and their equipment and aircraft, developed in the strictest of secrecy by German aviation firms under contracts placed by the Reichswehr, could be tested there for their combat capabilities. Lipetsk also served as the training centre for German fighter pilots and observers. It was only in 1933 that activities in Lipetsk were terminated, and the testing teams together with their whole inventory were relocated to Rechlin.

Quick-Reference Abbreviations

BFW   Bayerische Flugzeugwerke
       Bavarian Aircraft Works

BMW   Bayerische Motoren-Werke
       Bavarian Motor Works

DVS   Deutsche Verkehrs-Flieger Schule
       German Commercial Pilots School

HDV   Heeresdienstvorschrift
       Army Service Regulation

HwaA(HWA) Heereswaffenamt
       Army Ordnance Office

ILÜK   Interallierten-Luftfahrt-Überwachungs-Kommission
       Inter-Allied Aviation Supervisory Commission

IMKK   Interalliierte Militär-Kontroll-Kommission
       Inter-Allied Military Control Commission

IWG(InWG) Inspektion für Waffen und Gerät
       Inspectorate for Ordnance & Equipment

KoGenLuft Kommandierender General der Luftstreitkräfte
       General-in-Command of the Air Forces

LGK   Luftfahrt-Garantie-Kommittee
       Aviation Security Committee

Luftriko Luftfahrtfriedenskommission
       Aviation Peace Commission

RWM   Reichswehrministerium
       Imperial Army & Navy Ministry

TA(L) Truppenamt (Luftfahrtreferat)
       Armed Forces Office (Aviation Advisory Board)

Wivupal Wissenschaftliche Versuchs- und
       Prüfanstalt für Luftfahrzeuge
       Aircraft Scientific Test & Evaluation Institute

Early History

With the signing of the Treaty of Versailles on 28th June 1919, the German Reich was forbidden to have aviation contingents of the Army and Navy. Even the manufacture and import of aircraft and related individual components were forbidden for an initial period of six months following the coming into force of the Treaty. This length of time was later extended to 15th May 1922. Furthermore, Article 202 stipulated that the handover and destruction of the entire stock of military aircraft materials had to take place within three months from the effective date of the Treaty. Control of all designated measures was assigned to the IMKK, the aviation sector being controlled by the ILÜK. Both control organs were placed under the 'Permanent Legation Conference'. On the German side, the Luftriko was formed and attached to the Truppenamt (Armed Forces Office) which was incorporated into the RWM newly-established on 1st October 1919. A delay in the disarmament process resulted in presentation of a 'Disarmament Note' on 29th January 1921, and the London Ultimatum Reminder of 5th May 1921 which referred once more to the precise instructions on immediate action demanded in the Disarmament Note.

After almost one year, on 9th February 1922, the Reich government was informed that from 5th May 1922 onwards, aircraft for purely civilian purposes may again be built in Germany. This consent, however, prior to official permission being granted, was limited by the Begriffsbestimmungen (Definitions of Understanding) contained in a Note from the 'Permanent Legation Conference' of 14th April 1921. It limited the performance of new aircraft to 170km/h (106mph) speed, 300km (186 miles) range, 2.5 hours flight duration, 600kg (1,323lb) useful load, and 4,000m (13,120ft) ceiling. In addition, the aircraft were to be neither armed nor carry armour-plating. Control

responsibility for the observance of these and other restrictions following the dissolution of the ILÜK on 5th May 1922 passed to the newly-established LGK (Aviation Guarantee Committee). A few German aircraft firms by-passed all of these measures by establishing branch offices in neighbouring countries.[1]

German military power was undoubtedly the hardest hit by the Treaty of Versailles. Customary military service was abolished and the Army limited to 100,000 men. Generalmajor Hans von Seeckt was appointed Chef des Truppenamtes (Head of the Armed Forces Office) in the RWM, and against all bans that had been imposed, on 1st March 1920 he had already established a TA(L) Luftfahrtreferat (Aviation Advisory Board) which would be concerned with all matters in connection with military aviation. Head of the Advisory Board was Hauptmann Helmuth Wilberg and for technical military aviation matters, the InWG Referat 'Flugtechnik' under Hauptmann Kurt Student was established. In addition to that, there was the Advisory Board for 'Domestic Air Armament' led by Hauptmann Leopold Vogt and the Advisory Board for 'Foreign Aviation Matters'. The Navy also created a camouflaged Fliegerreferat (Aviation Advisory Board) headed by Kapitänleutnant Walther Faber.

One of the first activities of these secret Advisory Boards was formulating the HDV (Army Service Regulations) entitled 'Leadership and Combat Engagement of Allied Ordnance Weapons (F and G)' which contained the unmistakable outline of an operative air-warfare leadership having close Army support. It was approved by General von Seeckt on 1st September 1921. These HDV contained for the first time particulars of the aircraft to be selected for such purposes – single- and two-seat combat aircraft, heavy- and light ground-attack aircraft, day- and night bombers, long- and close-range reconnaissance aircraft and finally, armoured infantry aircraft. These ideas may have seemed fully utopian at that time; however, von Seeckt had already in March 1920 given consideration to a close co-operation between the Reichswehr and the Red Army in which he saw the only chance, undisturbed by Allied controls, in distant Russia to realize his measures for the re-establishment of an efficient 100,000-man Army. Based on these ideas, the Sondergruppe R (Special Group R for Russia) was created in December 1920, entrusted with responsibility for all future contacts with Moscow.[2]

On 8th December 1920, von Seeckt headed initial negotiations with Soviet intermediaries[3] concerning expansion of the Russian armaments industry with German assistance. Following the conclusion of the Treaty of Rapallo on 16th April 1922, these negotiations were continued and allowed the Reichswehr the possibility of obtaining military practice and test facilities on Russian soil. In exchange, German knowledge and experience, in particular in the field of aircraft construction, would be made available to the Red Armed Forces. With this undertaking, there thus began one of the best-kept secrets of the Weimar Republic, namely the co-operation between the Reichswehr and the Red Army.

On 1st January 1923, Germany was given back sovereignty over its airspace. The RWM viewed this as an opportunity to partake in the visibly-rising trend of aviation development to provide financial support to still-extant German aircraft firms to encourage them to develop military aircraft. Under the utmost secrecy, Hauptmann Kurt Student held the first contacts with the aircraft industry and gave the first development orders to Heinkel, Albatros and Arado.[4] One year later, BMW received an order for development of an aero-engine similar to the British 12-cylinder Napier Lion. As a direct result of the Ruhr crisis,[5] Student, with the agreement of the Reich Chancellor Wilhelm Cuno, placed an order with the Fokker firm for the delivery of 100 fighter aircraft, intended for use in the event of complications arising. At the same time, through the offices of the disguised Referat A II 1 – the later Gruppe BsX of the Navy Command, an order was placed with Heinkel for 10 HE 1/S 1 marine combat aircraft whose assembly and storage, for reasons of secrecy, took place in Sweden.

Beginning of Co-operation between the Reichswehr and the Red Army in Russia

On 17th February 1923, a six-man RWM delegation travelled to Moscow to negotiate with Red Army representatives on the subject of armament and economic co-operation. Main priority was given to the allocation of specific locations for the training of special Reichswehr personnel and for testing weapons that were forbidden in Germany. The Soviets initially offered the Reichswehr the aircraft land- and sea-base Odessa on the Black Sea, but since the Navy had already conducted negotiations

with Sweden, it was finally decided upon the airfield of Lipetsk[6] situated 400km (242 miles) south of Moscow.

As a result of these negotiations, a German liaison office called the 'Moscow Centre' was established, which worked together with Russian officialdom and the military directly and independently of the German Embassy. Its first head, code-named 'von der Lieth' was Oberst (retd) Hermann Thomsen,[7] the former Chief of the General Staff of KoGenLuft in World War One. The Moscow Centre was subordinated to the Department Fremde Heere (Foreign Armies) T3.

In 1924, work began with the erection of the Lipetsk flight centre.[8] A deserted factory building was the central point of the installations that were in an altogether derelict state. At the beginning of March 1925, Major (retd) Walter Stahr, the head of the future Reichswehr Flying School, travelled to Lipetsk together with Heinz von Beaulieu in order to reach agreement on the take over conditions. Finally, on 15th April 1924, the foundation contract for the School was signed. In addition to the available installations, a number of new buildings had to be erected. The flight centre was camouflaged as the 4th Eskadrille (Squadron) of a Red Air Fleet unit. The base itself received the cover designation 'Wivupal' (Scientific Test and Experimental Institute for Aircraft).

All expenditures incurred in Russia by the Reichswehr were financed from the so-called 'blue budget' which by-passed the Reich parliamentary controls, and for the Lipetsk centre, an annual sum of RM 2 million was set aside.

Since the Reich government had given up the notion of organising active resistance in the Ruhr, a number of Fokker fighters that had been ordered could thus be used for aircrew training purposes. Hence, at the suggestion of Major Stahr, the RWM decided to transfer 50 Fokker D XIII fighters[9] to Lipetsk.

The 'Stahr' Flying School

In mid June 1925, Walter Stahr and Flying Instructor Werner Junck travelled together with four other pilots to Lipetsk. They were followed by Carl-August von Schönebeck, Hans Leutert, Egloff Freiherr von Freyberg, Hermann Frommherz and Ernst Bormann. After arming the Fokker fighters which had been packed in crates, flight testing commenced immediately, whereupon serious instances of damage came to light. Eliminating them took up so much time that it was only in spring 1926 that fighter-pilot training could be started. Test flying and establishing the performance envelope of the new Fokker fighters before being able to release them for fighter-pilot training was in fact the beginning of flight testing.

The range of duties of the Lipetsk flight centre were:
- Training of flying personnel to become fighter pilots and instructors.
- Training of technical flight personnel.
- Conducting courses for fighter pilots.
- Conducting courses for aircrew observers.
- Conducting tactical and technical combat testing of military aircraft.
- Accumulating experience of a tactical, technical and organisational nature in all regimes.

Training of technical ground crews of the Red Air Fleet was also conducted. In 1930, Major Stahr relinquished his position as head of the School, being succeeded by Major (retd) Max Mohr until the beginning of 1932 and subsequently, by Hauptmann Gottlob Müller, who headed the School until its dissolution in 1933.

Initial Relaxations despite further Official Controls

In a Note issued by the Permanent Legation Conference on 24th June 1925, the demand was made to firmly establish the number of aircraft, aero-engines, pilots and trainees by the ILÜK (Inter-Allied Control Commission). Simultaneously, the 'Regulations' were relaxed, raising the permitted maximum speed to 180km/h (112mph) and payload to 900kg (1,984lb). The 4000m (13,120ft) ceiling remained unchanged. When the Paris Aviation Agreement was signed on 21st May 1926, these 'Regulations' were eliminated. The German aircraft industry was now even allowed once more to manufacture aircraft which possessed the characteristics of fighters. However, the ban on military aircraft development still remained in force. The Paris Agreement ended the activities of the ILÜK, but despite these positive prospects, a strained political atmosphere still prevailed between Germany and the former enemy countries such that the Reich government decided to institute immediate measures in the event of a self-defence contingency arising. Measures included the procurement of combat aircraft for whose specifications the RWM brought into being a Prüfstelle (Evaluation Centre) under the cover-name of 'Fertigungs-GmbH' (Manufacturing Co Ltd) on whose staff was Hauptmann Kurt Student, the head of Wa Prüf 6F (Aeronautical Technical Development Advisory Board) in the HWA. It was here that the Technical Requirements were drawn up for aircraft to be developed and tenders placed with the aircraft industry. The orders concerned the development of fighters, reconnaissance aircraft and medium bombers, on which construction work was begun by Arado, Albatros, BFW, Heinkel and Dornier.

A partial view of the Reichswehr Lipetsk Flight Test Centre showing aircraft hangars and repair workshops, and (at right) the firing-range for testing aircraft armament following optical centring. Some of the Fokker D XIII fighters of the Fighter Squadron can be discerned in front of the hangar buildings.

Organisation of the Lipetsk Test Unit

The pure flight testing of military aircraft newly developed by the industrial firms could be performed in Germany but without their military equipment. For reasons of secrecy, all tests and experiments of a military nature, as well as the German obligation to the Allied Powers not to conduct any weapons testing on German soil, were transferred to Lipetsk where the aircraft, fitted with appropriate military equipment, were put through their paces. In a concluding 'Combat Test' under the harshest conditions, they were evaluated for their combat usefulness and fitness for series production.

A Versuchsgruppe (Test Unit) was earmarked for this purpose in the Flieger-schule Stahr whose personnel strength was matched to the pertaining needs. From the commencement of testing in 1928, this unit was divided into:

- Testing of bombs and bomb-release mechanisms, under Dipl.-Ing. Ernst A Marquard (HWaA).
- Testing of aircraft armament and installations, under Oberleutnant (retd) Emil Thuy (HWaA).
- Aircraft testing, under Leutnant (retd) Carl-August von Schönebeck.

In the first three years, the personnel strength of this Test Unit lay between 50 and 100 men when testing took place during the summer months. They were supported with varying degrees of strength by qualified Russian specialists, some of whom were highly-qualified officers of the Red Air Fleet and who almost all possessed a good knowledge of the German language but gave no indication of this.

Transport and Ferry Flights

Transportation of personnel and materials between Germany and Russia was selectively undertaken by land, sea, and air, whereby Poland, graded politically as being hostile, had to be avoided. Personnel travel was accomplished in small unobtrusive groups by rail from Berlin over the Königsberg, Kovno, Dunaburg, Smolensk and Moscow route to Lipetsk. The air route approximated that of the land route. Air-

craft scheduled for testing were flown over at high altitude, wherever possible without intermediate landings, to Lipetsk. Those aircraft having shorter ranges were crated and transported by sea.

The personnel groups, whether airmen or firms' representatives, travelled with genuine passports and transit visas, except that names and professional occupations were occasionally altered. For the duration of their stay in Russia, military personnel were excluded from the Active Service Lists, whilst the civilian workers were deleted from their firms' personnel lists. Correspondence was also handled via disguised addresses, mail between Lipetsk and Berlin being transported solely by a courier aircraft.

The Beginning of Frontline Testing in Summer 1928

The first flight trials under frontline conditions commenced in Lipetsk in summer 1928. For this purpose, a 16-man-strong Test Unit journeyed to the Lipetsk Flight Test Centre in July 1928, headed by Ernst Marquard and Emil Thuy – the specialist advisors on bombs and armament. It was their task to establish whether the Lufthansa-operated Rohrbach Roland and Junkers G 24 civilian aircraft, foreseen as

The Rohrbach Ro VIII Roland which had been selected for use as an Auxiliary Bomber under the Emergency Armament Programme. Following rapid modification, this civil aircraft was able to carry three 300kg (661 lb) PuW bombs beneath the fuselage.

A frontal view of the bomb suspension-gear beneath the fuselage of the Roland Auxiliary Bomber.

The fully-equipped Roland Auxiliary Bomber in flight. Clearly visible are the two MG cupola positions at the rear of the engine nacelles and the fuselage-mounted bombs.

possible Auxiliary Bombers as part of an emergency air equipment programme in the event of hostilities could, after a very short period of conversion, be operated as night bombers.

For the bomb-release trials, a large 2 x 2km (1.2 x 1.2 miles) square bombing range equipped with observation towers and simulated targets as well as a 50 x 50m (165 x 165ft) square and 50cm (20in) thick concrete slab were available to assess bomb penetration capabilities.

Due to pressure of time, recourse had to be made for the 'emergency conversions' to the PuW-designed high-explosive bombs of World War One vintage, even though it was known that these types of bombs disintegrated in the air when dropped from altitudes above 3,000m (9,840ft). The new cylindrical C-bombs designed by Ernst Marquard in collaboration with Wa.Prw.8, were still in the early development stage at this time. It was a similar story with aircraft machine-guns. Although more modern developments had been proposed, the tried-and-tested 1. MG 08/15 of World War One was utilized.

After all the military equipment for the two transport aircraft had undergone functional testing, it was removed, packed in crates, and sent on the 3-week journey to Lipetsk. The equipment arrived in Lipetsk at about the same time as the aircraft which had been flown over. The Junkers G 24[10] and the Rohrbach Roland[11] arrived in Lipetsk in the last week of June, supplemented by a Junkers A 35.[12]

The two Auxiliary Bombers each flew 10 sorties into the month of September, in which 40 releases of practice-bombs as well as 8 releases with live PuW bombs were made. The Junkers A 35 made 8 sorties and dropped 100 practice-bombs. Evaluation of this series of releases showed that the PuW bombs could only be dropped from altitudes below 3,000m (9,840ft), since at higher altitudes they broke into pieces. The results of tests with both transport aircraft as Auxiliary Bombers showed

Above: *The Junkers G 24 ge (D 878) Auxiliary Bomber with its Lipetsk ID No 78. To maintain undercover flight test operations in Lipetsk, the national letter D and one or two of the following digits were painted over.*

Far right: *A view of the starboard MG-Stand in the engine nacelle cupola of the Roland with its MG 08/15 mounted on the Vickers-Scharff D 29 turntable, the 100-cartridge ammunition box and gunsight installation with its circular bead sight and wind-vane.*

Bottom: *Out of six examples of the Albatros L 78 'Erkudista' reconnaissance aircraft sent to Lipetsk to supplement the six L 76s undergoing combat testing there, at least four were written-off in crashes.*

Above: *Another view of the Junkers G 24 ge. The combined observer and bomb-aimer is seen here opening the Goerz mechanical bombsight.*

that for a final judgement, further testing during the following summer was necessary in Lipetsk. Both aircraft were thereupon returned to Germany.

For the reconnaissance role, Heinkel harboured some expectations that a variant of his 'Zeitungsbomber' (newspaper-bomber), the HD 40/II,[13] would prove suitable. On its transfer flight to Lipetsk, however, the biplane was severely damaged in a crash and required considerable time for repairs. An Albatros prototype, the L 76 Aeolus[14] as well as the experimental L 74 Adlershof,[15] the latter with negative success, rounded off the 1928 flight test programme.

Frontline Testing 1929 to 1933
The Auxiliary Bomber testing programme was resumed in the summer of 1929. On 14th June 1929, the Junkers G 24 took off from Berlin on its way to Lipetsk, the Rohrbach Roland following one day later. During the previous winter, the necessary structural modifications to both aircraft had been carried out. The undercarriage struts of the Roland for example, had been lengthened by 50cm (19¾in) so that with its increased ground-clearance, three of the 2.75m (10½ft) long, 300kg (661 lb)-weight PuW bombs could now be carried beneath the fuselage.

This page:

A flight test of a message-capture apparatus fitted beneath the Heinkel HD 17 'III' in summer 1930 in Lipetsk.

Group photograph of the entire German contingent in the Lipetsk airfield officers mess during the 1931 training and testing period.

Opposite page, left column, top to bottom:

Abundant use was made of the Heinkel HD 38 twin-float single-seat naval fighter seen here with fixed undercarriage during operational dogfight trials in Lipetsk. Its opponents were the Lipetsk-based Fokker fighters which were still a good match against modern fighters.

The Heinkel HD 45 (D-2064) 'Erkunigros' reconnaissance aircraft with Lipetsk ID No 64, equipped with a 50kg (110 lb) SC 50 bomb during combat flight testing in Lipetsk. At this time it still featured a four-bladed propeller, collective exhaust tubes and an undercarriage which were all altered in the course of later mass-production.

Front view of the Heinkel HD 45 (D-2064) showing the SC 50 bomb beneath the fuselage.

A view of the Heinkel HD 45 (D-2064) upon a visit to the DVS Schleißheim after its return to Germany. It had meanwhile been fitted with new individual exhaust outlets and a two-bladed propeller to enable forward firing of an MG through the propeller disc, which with a three- or four-bladed propeller was technically not possible.

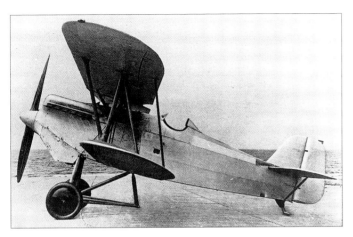

Photographs above, top to bottom:

The Dornier Do P four-engined aircraft intended as a 'Gronabo' large close-combat bomber seen prior to leaving for operational testing in Lipetsk in 1932.

In response to the specification for a 'Minabo' bomber, the twin-engined Dornier F (alias Do 11) was sent for combat testing to Lipetsk in 1932. It was the first bomber to be equipped from the outset to carry the new cylindrical C-bombs.

The Heinkel He 59 (D-2215) water-based multi-purpose aircraft, bearing its Lipetsk ID No 22 and fitted with a fixed trousered undercarriage for its operational trials in Lipetsk. For the long overland ferry flight from Warnemünde to Lipetsk, the streamlined undercarriage housings contained auxiliary fuel tanks. Frontline testing served for the transport and release of a heavy anti-shipping bomb.

The Test Unit had a strength of 20 men, and the equipment and armament which had been brought by sea, had increased considerably in amount compared to the year before. In the months of July and August alone, over 1,200 practice-bombs were dropped by the two Auxiliary Bombers. In addition, tests were carried out with the modified bomb-release mechanisms, the bomb detonators, new bombsights, and several other items of equipment. In the final report, both aircraft were declared 'in the corresponding circumstances' to be suitable, but only the Junkers G 24 really fitted the role of Auxiliary Bomber. Their conversion occupied only a little time as it consisted merely of installing a steel-tube grate to support the bombs in factory-mounted metal fittings beneath the fuselage and beneath the MG positions. The Albatros firm sent a number of L 76/L 77[16] and L 78[17] aircraft to Lipetsk which came through the tests with mixed success and with only partially usable results.

The first German fighters to commence frontline testing in the summer of 1930 were the Arado SD III and SSD I (Land),[18] but both aircraft failed to fulfil the requirements laid down. In contrast, the three Ju K 47 (A 48)[19] aircraft were liked by the pilots. Heinkel made an appearance in Lipetsk with his HD 40/II[20] multi-purpose aircraft that had suffered damage two years before, together with an HD 41a[21] Army reconnaissance aircraft.

A notable occurrence was testing the cylindrical C-bombs, for which purpose the two Junkers W 34[22] aircraft, specially equipped for bomb and armament tests, had been sent to Lipetsk.

This summer in Lipetsk was overshadowed by the tragic accident experienced by Oberleutnant (retd) Emil Thuy, the head of the Advisory Group for Air Armament and holder of the Pour le Mérite, and his accompanying aircraft mechanic Hundorf. They crashed due to engine failure in an Albatros L 76[23] on 11th June at Jarzewo near Smolensk on the flight to Lipetsk. The observer, Rittmeister (Cavalry Captain) Amlinger was also killed on 30th August in a practice air combat.

Flight testing during that summer ended with demonstration of new aircraft types, airborne bombs and their release mechanisms, bombsights, and photometric records of bomb releases and airborne armament. The Russians for their part, reciprocated with presentations of their own developments.

In 1931, the first of the military aircraft types developed by German industry commenced testing in Lipetsk, during the period of air armament between 1929 and 1933. The Testing Unit, compared to previous year, had risen to almost 200 men. On top of that, the Russians supplemented the strength of the unit with over 50 engineer-officers and flight technicians and provided over 200,000 litres of aviation fuel without charge.

Aircraft which arrived in Lipetsk were the Arado Ar 64 single-seat fighters,[24] the Heinkel HD 38 land- and seaborne fighter,[25] an Albatros L 84 two-seat fighter,[26] the Heinkel HD 45 long-range reconnaissance aircraft[27] and an Albatros L 77v[28] which was to serve the Armament Unit as a test-carrier for a 20mm Oerlikon machine-gun. Release tests with the cylindrical C-bombs which had began the previous year, were continued with two Junkers W 34s. In July and August, there followed comprehensive test- and comparative flights as well as air combat practice flights between the Ar 64, the HD 38 and the Fokker D XIII. Test-pilots were: Blumensaat, Bollmann, von Cramon, Dick, Hoppe, Knäser, von Massenbach, von Schönebeck, Schwencke, Simon, Spies and Wiborg.

Good results had been obtained for the first time this year in accordance with the HDV F. and G. in fighter-bomber operational trials with the Fokker D XIII and the Junkers K 47 two-seat fighters which laid the foundations for dive-bombing techniques. Due to supposedly excessive procurement costs, the K 47 was eliminated from the armament programme, the Ar 64 being judged as partially suitable for frontline use, doubtless in view of the improved Ar 65.

At the beginning of September 1931, another two-day exhibition and flying demonstration of all test aircraft took place in front of Russian aviation experts as a concluding event to summer flight testing. Experimental test pilots of the Red Air Fleet were able to use the opportunity to fly the aircraft.

Although German-Russian co-operation continually improved, the RWM decided to reduce training and operational trials in Lipetsk in gradual stages. The first effects of this became visible at the end of the year when the entire observer training curriculum was relocated back to Brunswick, and became even more apparent in the flight test summer of 1932.

At that time, aircraft which had arrived in Lipetsk were the four-engined Dornier Do P,[29] the twin-engined Do F = Do 11,[30] and the seaborne multi-purpose He 59[31] intended specially for flight testing bombs developed for attacking ship targets. Instead of floats, this large biplane had been fitted with an undercarriage for the trials. Close-reconnaissance aircraft were represented by the He 46,[32] the Focke-Wulf W 7 and the unusual-looking Albatros L 81 'Electra'[33] with its one-and-a-half biplane wings. The latter two aircraft types, however, were clearly inferior to the He 46. The robustly-designed W 7[34] biplane had made such a good impression on the Russians during operational flight trials that they acquired it.

The Dornier Do P was already practically outmoded in 1932 since it was only equipped to carry PuW bombs, and with this aircraft, only a few firing trials with the new MG 15, mounted in nose and tail positions, were carried out. In its place, the Do F (alias Do 11) medium bomber had already undergone thorough technical and operational trials in Rechlin. From the outset, it was capable of being equipped with the new C-bombs. What appeared to be new and unusual was that the 50kg (110 lb) and 250kg (551 lb) bombs were loaded nose-up into vertical magazines, whilst the 500kg (1102 lb) bombs were suspended in individual frames beneath the fuselage, the bombs being released electrically. Defensive armament consisted of three MG 15 machine-guns. Tests with the He 59 extended principally to the new electrically-operated jettison equipment[35] and their automatic release. Comparative tests were also conducted with the Zeiss-Lotfernrohr (Lotfe) and the fully-automatic Goerz-Boykow bombsights.

At the end of August 1932, the customary two-day demonstration of all test aircraft, armament and equipment was again held, at which the Russian observers were full of praise for the exhibits displayed.

Although the political situation had completely changed in Germany in 1933, military co-operation between the Reichswehr and the Red Army remained still relatively unaffected. Operational trials continued in Lipetsk with the He 45[36] and the He 46 reconnaissance aircraft, the Do 11 bomber and the Ar 65[37] fighter. The large Do P bomber was still there, but was handed over to the Russians as a gift. Precedence was being given to the final selection of military equipment earmarked for aircraft types which had reached combat maturity and intended for mass-production. In terms of fixed aircraft armament, the 1 MG 08/15, with improvements, was to be used. The Ar 65 fighter was accordingly equipped with two of these machine-guns as well as a reflex sight, and a vertical magazine in the fuselage able to accommodate six C 10 10kg (22 lb) bombs. The Heinkel reconnaissance aircraft were each equipped with one fixed 1 MG 08/15 and a movable MG 15 in a Drehkranz 30 rotatable turret. The He 46 could also carry twelve C 10 bombs.

Dissolution of the Lipetsk Flight Test Centre

After the situation in Lipetsk in mid-summer 1933 had become visibly critical, Hauptmann Wilhelm Speidel was ordered by the RWM to travel to Russia to close down the Lipetsk centre. Thus, following completion of the last fighter-pilot training course and the last operational trials, flying activities were terminated on 14th August 1933. Following difficult negotiations, all movable German-owned property, including all the test aircraft, were able to be transported back to Germany, whilst all fixed items such as the entire airfield installations remained behind with the Russians, including the still usable but meanwhile outmoded 30 Fokker fighters.

The German Flight Centre at Lipetsk had therefore ceased to exist. For the build-up of the new Luftwaffe the aircraft, together with their equipment which had been operationally tested in Lipetsk, now served as standard types and formed the basis, prepared down to the smallest details, for mass-production by the German aircraft industry. Without Lipetsk and without the Kampfwagenschule (Tank and Combat Vehicle School) in Kazan, neither the Luftwaffe formations nor the first Army Panzer-divisions could have been brought into being.[38]

Footnotes

1 Dornier in Pisa (Italy), Altenrhein (Switzerland), Kobe (Japan), Madrid and Cadiz (Spain) and Papendrecht (Holland); Junkers in Limhamn (Sweden) and Fili (Russia); Rohrbach in Copenhagen (Denmark).

2 Epstein: 'The Seekt Plan' in Manfred Zeitler's 'The Reichswehr und Rote Armee, 1920-33'.

3 In the presence of Karl B Radek, expert on Germany and associate of V I Lenin.

4 Heinkel developed the HD 32 and HD 35 basic trainers and the HD 17 close-reconnaissance aircraft; Albatros the L 65 I 'Memel' (AFG-1) scout, Arado a fighter, and BMW the BMW VI aero-engine.

5 On 11.01.1923 French and Belgian troops occupied the Ruhr region in order to exert force on their reparations demands.

6 The Tank troops were allocated to Kazan in the central Volga region and for anti-gas combat training to a location with the cover-name Tomka near Zaratov.

7 From 1924 to 1928 'von der Lieth'; 1928 to autumn 1931, Major (retd) Oskar Ritter von Niedermayer and 1932 to 1933 Oberleutnant (retd) Lothar Schüttel.

8 A well-known health and bathing resort in the Tsarist period.

9 The Fokker D XIII, first flown on 23.09.1923, was considered to be the best fighter aircraft available at that time.

10 Ju G 24ge (D-878, Werk-Nr.844) coded 78.

11 Ro VIII Mb (D-991, Werk-Nr.18) coded 91.

12 Ju A 35 (D-987, Werk-Nr.1059) coded 9.

13 HD 40/II alias HD 40/-02 (D-1180, Werk-Nr.274).

14 L 76 (D-1127, Werk-Nr.10.101).

15 L 74 (D-1100, Werk-Nr.10.095).

16 L 76/77 (Werk-Nr.10.102, 10.103, 10.122 to 125), coded 1 to 6.

17 L 78 (Werk-Nr.10.151 to 10.156; D-1524, Werk-Nr.10.121, coded 15; D-1791, Werk-Nr.10.157, coded 17).

18 Ar SSD I (D-1905, Werk-Nr.53); Ar SD III (D-1973, Werk-Nr.54).

19 Ju K 47 (Werk-Nr.3361 to 3363) alphabet-coded eg, J.

20 The HD 40/II, following combat testing in Lipetsk, was used as a poison-gas test-bed aircraft in the Tomka research centre.

21 HD 41a (D-1694, Werk-Nr.321).

22 Ju W 34 (D-1844, Werk-Nr.2589) with Jupiter radials (D-1845, Werk-Nr.2590) with Hornet radials. Both aircraft were flown by Leutert, von Rochow, Mohnike, Hoppe and von Boltenstern. Observers were Marquard, Peter, Pflugbeil, Holm and Koch.

23 L 76 (D-1127, Werk-Nr.10.101).

24 Ar 64 (D-2470, Werk-Nr.65) coded 103; (D-2338, Werk-Nr.66) coded 104. Their four-bladed propellers rendered armament improbable and only a small series were manufactured.

25 HD 38 (D-2272, Werk-Nr.369).

26 L 84 (D-1899, Werk-Nr.10.187) coded 18.

27 HD 45 (D-2064, Werk-Nr.364) coded 64.

28 L 77v built by Heinkel and fitted with MG rotatable turret fittings.

29 Do P 'Harry Piel' (D-1982, Werk-Nr.180).

30 Do 11 (D-2270, Werk-Nr.230).

31 He 59 (D-2215, Werk-Nr.379) coded 22. Crew were: Heinz Simon, pilot; Waschko, flight mechanic; Rudolf Gessner, escort.

32 He 46 (D-1702, Werk-Nr.376) and (D-1028, Werk-Nr.377).

33 L 81 (D-2198, Werk-Nr.10.164).

34 Fw W 7 (D-2216, Werk-Nr.112).

35 Because of possible icing-up of the under-fuselage release mechanism in seaborne operations, release was electrically activated via an electrically-ignited powder cartridge (PVC device). The cartridge blew away all types of icing.

36 He 45 (D-2238, Werk-Nr.391).

37 Ar 65 (D-2218, Werk-Nr.71?).

38 W Speidel / M Zeidler (see Literature below).

Literature List

Epstein, Julius: The Seekt Plan. From unpublished documents in: Der Monat (1948) 2.

E-Stelle See: Die Geschichte der Erprobungsstellen (History of the Flight Test Centres) Travemünde and Tarnewitz, Vols 1-3, Luftfahrt-Verlag Walter Zuerl, Steinbach/Wörthsee.

Fischer, Ruth: Stalin und der deutsche Kommunismus. Der Übergang zur Konterrevolution (Stalin and German communism. The transition to counter-revolution), Frankfurt/Main, 1950.

Koos, Dr. V: Luftfahrt zwischen Ostsee und Breitling (Aviation between the Baltic and Breitling), Nara Verlag, Allershausen, 1990.

Kosin, Rudiger: Die Entwicklung der deutschen Jagdflugzeuge (German Fighter Aircraft Development), Bernard & Gräfe Verlag, Koblenz, 1983.

Lange, Bruno: Typenbuch der deutschen Luftfahrttechnik (German Aircraft & Aero-engines), Bernard & Gräfe Verlag, Koblenz, 1986.

Meier, Hans-Justus: Rohrbach Ro VIII Mb, alias 'Militär-Roland', in Luftfahrt International, 4/1974.

Rechliner Briefe, Series 1-5. Published by Franz Kirch & Heinrich Beauvais, 1976-1984.

Ries, Karl: Recherchen zur deutschen Luftfahrtzeugrolle (Researches on the Role of German Aircraft), Verlag Dieter Hoffmann, Mainz, 1977.

Roeder, Jean: Bombenflugzeuge und Aufklärer (Bombers & Reconnaissance Aircraft), Bernard & Graefe Verlag, Koblenz, 1990.

Schliephake, Hanfried: The Birth of the Luftwaffe, London, 1971 and Chicago,1972.

Schliephake, Hanfried: Wie die Luftwaffe wirklich Entstand. Der Aufbau zwischen den beiden Weltkriegen (How the Luftwaffe arose. Its build-up between the two World Wars), Motorbuch Verlag, Stuttgart, 1972.

Schliephake, Hanfried: Flugzeugbewaffnung (Aircraft Armament), Motorbuch Verlag, Stuttgart, 1977.

Speidel, Wilhelm: Reichswehr und Roter Armee (The Reichswehr and the Red Army), in: Vierteljahreshefte für Zeitgeschichte, 1/1953, pp9-45.

Völker, Karl-Heinz: Die Entwicklung der militärischen Luftfahrt in Deutschland 1920-1933. Planung und Massnahmen zur Schaffung einer Fliegertruppe in der Reichswehr The development of military aviation in Germany, 1920-1933. Planning and measures for the establishment of a Flying Corps in the Reichswehr), in: Beiträge zur Militär-geschichte, Vol 3, Stuttgart, 1962.

Völker, Karl-Heinz: Die geheime Rüstung der Reichswehr und ihre Auswirkung auf den Flugzeugbestand der Luftwaffe bis zum Beginn des Zweiten Weltkrieges (Secret Air Armament of the Reichswehr and its effect on the quantity of Luftwaffe aircraft up to the beginning of World War Two) in: Wehrwissenschaftliche Rundschau, 9/1962, pp540-549.

Völker, Karl-Heinz: Dokumente und Dokumentarfotos zur Geschichte der deutschen Luftwaffe. Aus den Geheimakten der Reichswehrministeriums 1919-1933 und des Reichluftfahrtministeriums 1933-39 (Documents and photographs on the history of the Luftwaffe. From the secret archives of the RWM 1919-1933 and the RLM 1933-1939) in: Beiträge zur Militärgeschichte, Vol 9, Stuttgart, 1968.

Zeidler, Manfred: Reichswehr und Roter Armee 1920-33. Wege und Stationen einer ungewöhnlichen Zusammenarbeit (The Reichswehr and the Red Army. Paths and Stations of an unusual Co-operation) in: Beiträge zur Militärgeschichte, Vol 26, 2nd Ed, Oldenbourg Verlag, Munich, 1994.

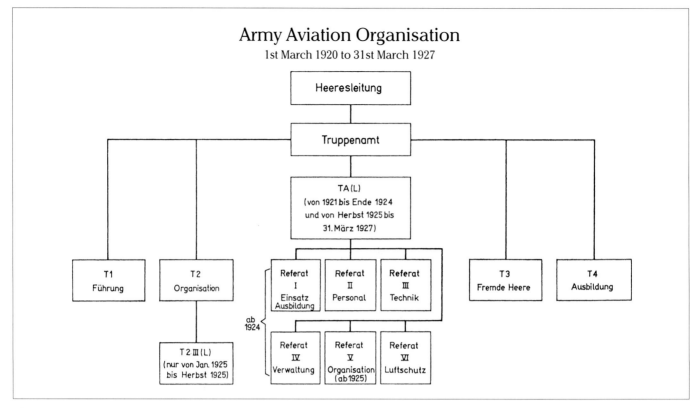

Army Aviation Organisation
1st March 1920 to 31st March 1927

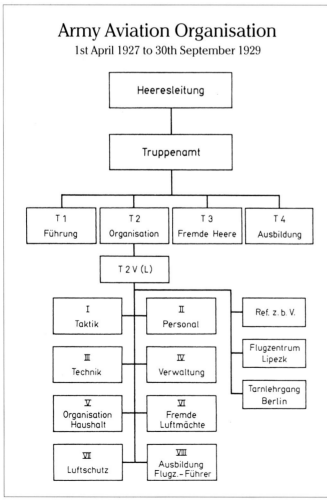

Army Aviation Organisation
1st April 1927 to 30th September 1929

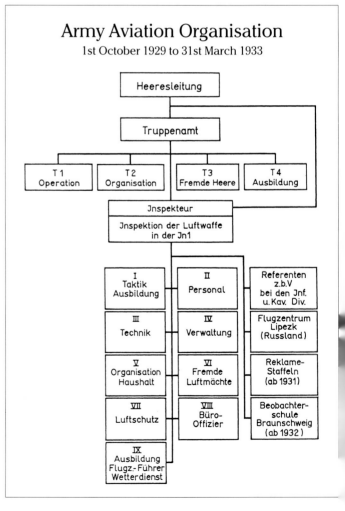

Army Aviation Organisation
1st October 1929 to 31st March 1933

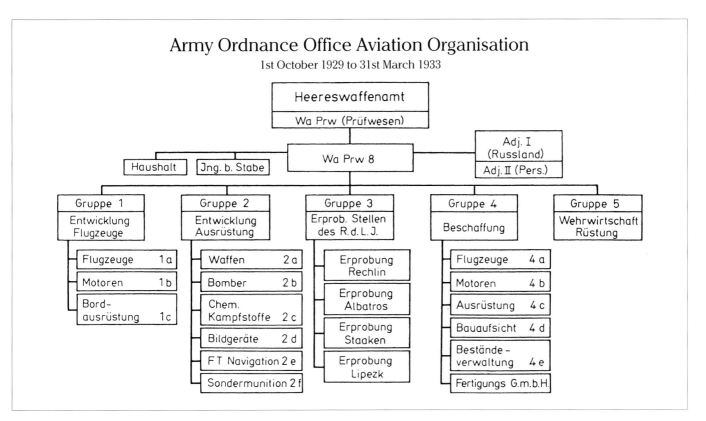

Army Ordnance Office Aviation Organisation
1st October 1929 to 31st March 1933

Taken from Karl-Heinz Völker:

Die Entwicklung der militärischen Luftfahrt in Deutschland 1920-1933

(Planning & Measures for the Creation of a Flying Corps in the Reichswehr)

Cited in: Beiträge zur Militär- und Kriegsgeschichte, Volume 3, Deutsche Verlags-Anstalt GmbH,

Chapter Five
by Christoph Regel

The Erprobungsstelle Rechlin

After the necessity had already been recognized during World War One to establish a central Test Centre for the aircraft and equipment of the Flying Corps, construction of such an establishment was begun in Rechlin on the shore of Lake Müritz. Following the forced interruption of work on it in 1918, a new start was made in the mid 1920s to testing activities under strict secrecy. In just a little over 10 years, Rechlin rose and expanded to become the largest German aeronautical Erprobungsstelle (Test Centre), whose work met a sudden and final end at the close of World War Two in 1945.

Quick-Reference Abbreviations

BA/MA   Bundesarchiv/Militärarchiv
        (Federal/Military Archives), Freiburg
BFW   Bayerische Flugzeug-Werke
        Bavarian Aircraft Works
BMW   Bayerische Motoren-Werke
        Bavarian Motor Works
DDR   Deutsche Demokratische Republik
        German Democratic Republic
DFS   Deutsche Forschungsanstalt für Segelflug
        German Research Institute for Gliding Flight
DLH   Deutsche Lufthansa
        German Airlines
DVL   Deutsche Versuchanstalt für Luftfahrt
        German Aviation Research Institute
DVS   Deutsche Verkehrsflieger-Schule
        German Commercial Pilots School
EKL   Erprobungskommando Lärz
        Test Detachment Lärz
FDJ   Freie Deutsche Jugend
        Free German Youth (DDR)
FVL   Flieger-Versuchs- und Lehranstalt
        Aviator Test & Training Institute
GST   Gesellschaft für Sport und Technik
        Society for Sports & Technics (DDR)
GWF   Gothaer Waggonfabrik
        Gotha Wagon Works
HWA   Heereswaffenamt
        Army Ordnance Office
KdE   Kommandeur der Erprobungsstelle
        E-Stelle Commander
LGW   Luftfahrtgerätewerk
        Aviation Equipment Works
OKL   Oberkommando der Luftwaffe
        Supreme Command of the Air Force
OKW   Oberkommando der Wehrmacht
        Supreme Command of the Armed Forces

PfL   Prüfstelle für Luftfahrzeuge
        Aircraft Evaluation Centre
RDL   Reichsverband d. Deutschen Luftfahrtindustrie
        Association of German Aircraft Industry
RLM   Reichsluftfahrtministerium
        German Air Ministry
RWM   Reichswehrministerium
        The Imperial Army and Navy Ministry
VEB   Volkseigene Betriebe
        People-owned Enterprises (DDR)

The Müritzsee Aviation Test- and Training Institute

The growing number of aircraft types and the rapid development of aeronautical technology, clearly indicated to those responsible in the Aviation Department of the Prussian War Ministry as early as 1916 that the existing Army Flugzeugmeisterei (Aircraft Engineering Centre) in Berlin-Johannisthal and the DVL in Berlin-Adlershof, would be insufficient to conduct thorough testing of all the new aircraft making their appearance.

A search was therefore made and found, for a suitable location not too far from Berlin, and at the same time, completely isolated in a thinly-populated area owned by Freiherr von Hammerstein in Retzow.

In the oldest document discovered so far, in a War Ministry letter from Berlin dated 29th November 1916 addressed to the Grand Duchy's Ministry of the Interior in Schwerin, planning was described[1] in more detail:

'The Army Administration proposes to erect comprehensive aeronautical installations on the south shore of the Müritzsee … Hauptmann Joly from the Flying Corps Inspectorate has been authorized to clarify preliminary questions regarding the acquisition of property there'.

For this 'acquisition', the War Ministry cited a law from the year 1845 (!) allowing them to expropriate the property they needed. From the record of the dispossession discussions which took place on 25th June 1917 in Mirow, it concerned portions of property from the 'boundaries of the village of Lärz and the large hereditary estates of: Retzow and adjoining property in Rechlin; Klopzow and adjoining property of Bolter Mühle, Leppin with adjoining property in Roggentin, respectively the Knightly

estate Ludorf … having a total land area of some 1,377 Hectares 18.5 Ares (5.32mls[2])'.

Because of the war situation, a whole year went by before Hauptmann August Joly, meanwhile appointed as 'Müritzsee Airfield Commander' was in the position to state in a letter dated 25th July 1918:[2]

'His Royal Highness (ie, The Grand Duke Friedrich-Franz von Mecklenburg-Schwerin) is most humbly requested to give the signal for airfield operations to commence, and as Sovereign, to travel on the new stretch of railway and to confer on the Flying Corps the right of abode on the grounds of the airfields … '.

In the words of Hauptmann Joly, the installations would represent 'the future central point of all German military flying activity'. The properties belonging to it meanwhile encompassed three airfields in Mirow, Lärz and Müritz, of 7,000 Morgen (6.9mls[2]) in extent. Construction of buildings and preliminary installations had by this time commenced and important tests already undertaken.

Inspection and inauguration by the Grand Duke, suggested in the above-mentioned letter, took place on 29th August 1918 in the presence of Flying Corps Inspector Oberstleutnant Wilhelm Siegert and the Flugmeisterei Commander Major Felix Wagenführ, so that this date may be regarded as the 'official' establishment of the FVL (Aviation Test & Training Institute) on the Müritzsee. At this point, the FVL consisted of an Aviation Department Rechlin (Leutnant Heidelberg), an Engine Department Roggentin (Leutnant Hoffmann) and an Aviation W/T Test Department Lärz (Oberleutnant Baldus). Commander of the Airfields was Hauptmann Joly who, prior to erection of the Müritzsee installations, was Commander of Döberitz airfield, with Oberstleutnant Bauer acting as his adjutant. The inauguration ceremony obviously provided the impetus for expanding the installations, for already in September 1918, plans had been drawn up for the erection and extension of new steel-and-concrete aircraft hangars in Müritz. These, however, came to nothing since the signing of the Armistice in Compiègne on 11th November 1918 put a sudden end to all these proposals.

The oldest-known pictorial record of Rechlin dating from 1st July 1917, showing the Vorkommando (Preliminary Detachment) of the 'Flieger-Versuchs- und Lehranstalt' at the Müritzsee.

At the inauguration ceremony of the above-mentioned Aviator Test- and Training Institute on 29th August 1918, a vantage platform was erected on the Sprottsche Berg which, at an elevation of 106m (348ft) above sea-level was the highest point in the surroundings of Rechlin, the occasion being used to provide a commentary to the local dignitaries about all three airfields belonging to the unit.

The Treaty of Versailles, which had forbidden flying activities of any kind in Germany, meant that there was no possible future for an Aviation Test and Training Institute, and the installations – including the new stretch of railway – were dismantled. A rural quiet subsequently returned to Müritz.

Disguised New Beginning

At about the same time that contacts had commenced since 1923 with Russia for the establishment of a Training and Test Centre under the camouflage name of 'Flying School Stahr' in Lipetsk, at the initiative of Hauptmann Student, the DVL in Berlin-Adlershof had in late autumn 1925 set up the new 'Department M'[3]. Its first four members – Dipl.-Ing. Wilhelm Degen, Dr. Karl Genthe, Ing. Bruno Gollhammer and Dipl.-Ing. Schaper – worked out the concept for the future spheres of activity and erection of a Flight Test Centre in Rechlin. The 'Luftfahrtverein Waren e.V.' (Aviation Association) had already been established there in 1925. Commissioned by the Reich government, it now negotiated purchase of the necessary property in Müritz and took over operation of the newly-opened airfield,[4] which consisted of the same extent of property used in 1918 by the FVL in Müritz. Since nothing of the former installations still existed, the first action taken by the DVL was to erect next to the Rechlin stables a 42 x 21m (138 x 69ft) aircraft hangar featuring a workshop and living quarters annex at its rear – the so-called 'Swiss House'. At the end of May 1926, the first usability acceptance of this new building took place, so that the workshops and flying activities could commence in Rechlin in summer 1926.

At the turn of the year 1927/28,[5] the Albatros Flugzeugwerke GmbH of Berlin-Johannisthal rented the airfield and undertook – at a moderate pace at first – further expansion of the installations. In 1929, a second aircraft hangar featuring the Junkers ribbed

sheet-metal type of construction was erected, with a third and larger hangar begun at the beginning of 1933.

Since it had been learned from experience that aero-engines to be developed required not only testing in aircraft but also extensively on static test-stands, project work commenced in autumn 1930 on a large engine test-stand in Rechlin, the plans being submitted to the responsible Police Construction Authorities in December that year. Its intended site was the south-east

corner of the airfield, far from all existing installations. Construction work, however, proceeded at a slow pace, for in autumn 1931, work was still being done on the machinery foundations, and in spring 1933, parts of the internal installations were still not available. Nevertheless, the foundations for the later Luftwaffe E-Stelle (Test Centre) were thus laid on Rechlin airfield.

It was only at the end of 1928, nine months after the appearance of the Albatros Werke as lessee, that the official affiliation to the

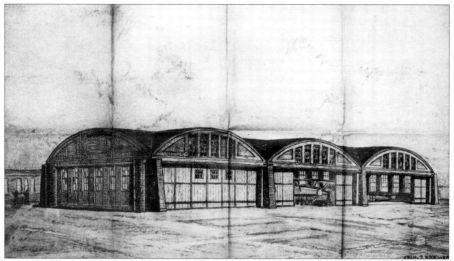

According to the plans of the Government- and Building Counsellor Friedrichs, head of the Administrative Department 'Müritzsee' of the Air Arm Superintendent's Office in Berlin, several of these steel-and-concrete aircraft hangars were to have been erected at the Müritzsee Airfield, but were not realized due to the end of World War One.

There was almost no indication at the end of 1926 that flight testing was being secretly conducted immediately on the banks of the Müritzsee. The Rechlin scene was still dominated by the church, alongside which were the building of the Rechlin estate, blacksmith, farm workers' housing quarters, and two larger farm buildings. The very first aircraft hangar with its rear annex appeared almost unpretentious between the stables and a small shed.

DVL in the shape of 'Department M' was dropped and replaced with the new title of 'Test Department of the Albatros Aircraft Company, Johannisthal'. For the members of the Testing team, this change had no effect on either housing or work.

The purely superficial affinity to the Albatros firm did not last long, for as early as autumn 1929, the Reichswehr Truppenamt approached the RDL with the request that the RDL should use its name as of 1st October 1929 as a cover to camouflage the Test Centres at Staaken and Müritz, as had been the case with the E-Stelle Travemünde since the beginning of the year.[6] After initial

hesitation by the RDL, this step had not been taken by the planned date, but must have occurred very shortly afterwards, since from December 1929, the 'RDL E-Stelle Staaken' appeared as the owner of new test aircraft, whilst negotiations under the 'Test Department of the Albatros Aircraft Company' can only be traced until autumn 1928. (A summary of aircraft operated by the DVL, Albatros, and the RDL E-Stelle, is listed at the end of this chapter, from page 113.)

As recalled by some Rechlin 'oldtimers', the RWM military aviation activities had already been concentrated in a 'stronghold' at the Berlin-Staaken airfield some years

before. Whether it had consisted of an independent installation or had perhaps been a resident Flying School or Training Station can no longer be established. When the DVS moved from Staaken to Brunswick in October 1929, the Test Unit's offices that had been located in Adlershof were definitely moved to Staaken where more space was available for further expansion. In accordance with this, testing was now conducted under the voluminous title of 'RDL-Gruppe Flugzeugbau – Berlin Erprobungsstelle – Berlin-Staaken' (Reich Association of German Industries – Aircraft Manufacturing Group – Test Station Berlin –

Berlin-Staaken). For a short intermediate period – at least theoretically – it seems that a sub-division into 'Erprobung Albatros' and 'Erprobung Staaken' existed in parallel,[7] but the name Albatros thereafter disappeared entirely. During this period, purely aeronautical testing activity was transferred more and more to Rechlin, whilst armament and bomb-testing took place in Lipetsk exclusively.

Testing Activity in the 1920s

In the initial expansion phase of Rechlin airfield, the infrastructure was conceivably poor, not only because of lack of financing. There were no houses or apartments, personnel accommodation consisted only of the 'Swiss House' and a ground-floor barracks, to which was later added the 'Café Achteck', each equipped with furniture. There were also no streets and footpaths, and no firm parking areas in front of the aircraft hangars. The few buildings had been built with only the minimum of fittings, when considering heating for instance, so that under these conditions, testing on an all-year-round basis was not possible.

These disadvantages, however, were not so critical, since in the Adlershof/Johannisthal and Staaken airfield locations, all the necessary installations were available, added to the fact that they were not far away from the HWA centres of activity. A large proportion of testing tasks still had to be taken care of by HWA specialists, so that the proximity of office space at Staaken was a great advantage.

An impression of testing tasks undertaken at that time is given in a surviving proposal recorded in the 'Test Programme 1.2.25 – 30.6.25' Bb.Nr.25/2.25 F,[8] which lists the following:
- J28.
- L70.
- Large aircraft.
- Observer cabin development in fast aircraft.
- Tests with fire-proof fuel-tanks.
- Tests with variable-pitch propellers.
- Dinos-motor.
- WGL-motor.
- Grübler-motor.
- Exhaust-gas turbine.
- BMW IV air-test.
- BMW VI endurance test.
- Gast verification firing.
- Siemens air-test.
- Lübbe.
- Training Deutscher Rundflug.

The J28 consisted of a 'military aircraft and two-seat fighter powered by the BMW VI', whose design was begun by Junkers in March 1925 but was then discontinued. The Albatros L70, serving the same purpose and powered by the same engine, was to have been ready for flight testing in Sep-

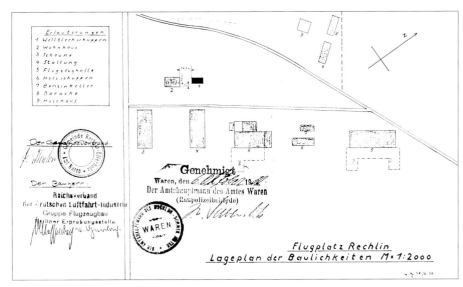

The oldest-known site-plan of Rechlin airfield is contained in the Construction Application tendered by the RDLI for the erection of the small (Number 1) corrugated metal shed, approved on 6th October 1930 by the Amtshauptmann (Department Chief) in Waren – the town responsible for the region at that time. The earliest of the site-plan buildings numbered 2 to 6 are visible nearest the right-hand edge of the lake in the preceding photograph.

In the rear annex of the first Rechlin aircraft hangar, the workshops were on the ground floor, with the living quarters housing the mechanics and members of the Testing Unit coming to Rechlin situated on the floor above. Because of its structural appearance, the building was usually referred to as the 'Swiss House'.

Equally known to all 'Rechliners' in 1930 was the completed 'Café Achteck' (eight-sided café) which featured accommodation rooms and a community centre. In order to house the growing number of Test personnel, however, it became necessary to erect an additional housing barracks and a canteen beside it.

Left: From at least May 1927 onwards, the 1926-built Dornier Do B-Bal (Werk-Nr.96, D-970) received its DVL certification. The aircraft was used for flight testing by the DVL 'Abteilung M' as well as in Lipetsk from 1929 to 1932. Upon its return, it was assigned to the RDL.

Above: Early diving tests with an Albatros L 76 in 1927. To determine the angle of inclination, a mirror with a graduated scale was installed ahead of the pilot, and diving angles of over 60° were flown.

Left: The second structural expansion undertaken in Rechlin in 1929 was the erection of a larger aircraft hangar built according to the Junkers segment system, and was ready for use the following year.

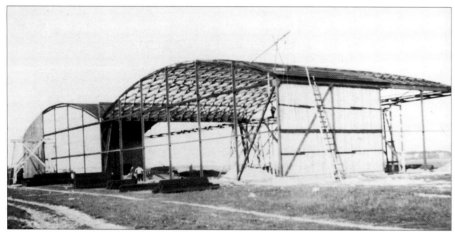

tember 1925. Evidently inspired by the revolutionary war theses of the Italian Giulio Douhet in 1921, of interest in this test programme is that besides the contract placed in the meantime by the Navy with Dornier for a large flying-boat – the later Do X, with the same aim in mind the Army began negotiations with Rohrbach, which obviously led to the design of the four-engined Ro XII Roska large bomber.

In 1925, a good deal of interest was aroused in responsible circles by further aircraft developments such as the Dornier Do C, Do N, and the Falke (falcon or hawk), and the Albatros L 65 I and L 65 II. As series of tests took place in August 1925 with the Do C and the Falke in Dübendorf; flights with the Do Komet (comet) in Staaken, and with the L 65 in Memel. For the L 65 I, the range of tasks included: checking its flight characteristics, maximum speed, landing speed, climbing speed, ceiling, take-off and landing-run length, and demonstration flights (figure-flying).

Personnel came mostly from the DVL and from their 'Department M'. In the following year, the nucleus of tasks was altered – clearly established in the 1925/26 Test Programme which defined that emphasis be placed upon engine develop-

ment.[9] This involved in particular the BMW VI, the development of an 800-1200hp engine as an interim stage towards one of 1500hp, the development of a Schweröl (Diesel-type) engine as well as fundamental improvements to the basic layout of engines and fuels. In the aircraft field, only those tests should be carried out which were necessary to serve as preliminary stages for future development. The aim at that time was to create four basic types of aircraft, namely:
- Long-range reconnaissance aircraft, and simultaneously day-bombers.
- Two-seat fighters – with limited suitability for reconnaissance.
- Night-reconnaissance and night-fighters, together with artillery aircraft.
- Medium-range night-bombers.

In this programme, emphasis was also laid on the necessity to establish a 'numerically large entity for independent air warfare' whereby it was recognized that to achieve this goal, development of interim types was essential. Where before the majority of tests had up until then been conducted at the aircraft factories, in the years that followed, these were transferred more and more to Adlershof. The oldest surviving Test

Reports from spring 1927, show that speed measurement flights had been conducted on two measurement stretches between Adlershof and Marienfelde as well as Waltersdorf.

The HWA had meanwhile put into practice the Truppenamt's desire for the four basic types of aircraft outlined, in evaluating the proposals received from the various aircraft firms and placing contracts accordingly. The Reichswehr thus wanted to gain knowledge of the aircraft industry's manufacturing and performance capabilities. At the same time, the aircraft firms were to be provided with the basis for military aircraft design and establish future tactical and technical needs. In contrast to the 1925 plans, it is noticeable that the demands for a day-bomber and a night-bomber were discarded, and that the following types of aircraft were now to be developed:[10]
- A homeland day-fighter (Heitag), the Arado SD I.
- A reconnaissance aircraft (Erkudista) for the Divisionsstaffel, the Albatros L 76 or L 77.
- A night-fighter and reconnaissance aircraft (Najaku) the BFW M 22.
- A reconnaissance aircraft for medium altitude and long ranges, the Heinkel HD 41.

Except for the BFW M 22, all the others mentioned arrived for testing in Rechlin. The Arado SD I, of which only the first prototype (Werk-Nr.31) was completed in summer 1927, crashed after 20 flights on 11th October 1927 in the middle of Rechlin airfield killing the pilot – an official DVL Department Head – Dr.-Ing. Theodor Bienen. In the sphere of development and testing then being built up, this represented not only a serious loss but is also the first recorded aircraft crash in Rechlin. There had, however, been two previous fatalities during flight testing elsewhere. The first occurred on 19th October 1926, when Dipl.-Ing. Max Seefeld of the DVL 'Department M' was unable to leave his spinning Albatros L 47b (D-586) and was killed upon impact in Adlershof. A similar incident occurred on the afternoon of 27th July 1927 to the crew of the Albatros L 76a (RR-32, Werk-Nr.10.106). In this instance, upon completion of a W/T test flight, the aircraft entered a spin from which the pilot, only able to recover just above the ground, had clipped several trees so that the aircraft crashed near Rudow, resulting in the deaths of both the pilot Fritz Mühlhan (who probably belonged to the DVL Department M) and his accompanying Telefunken technician Erich Wedekind.

But to return now to the aircraft of the Notrüstungsperiode (emergency equipment period). The crashes of the Arado SD I and the Albatros L 76a in 1927 showed that these were both the first to be completed and undergo testing. The Heinkel HD 41a (Werk-Nr.321) on the other hand, received its D-1694 certification only in July 1929 whilst the BFW M 22 accomplished its

maiden flight as late as April 1930. Similar to the 'Heitag' prototype, the latter also had a short life, for on 14th October 1930, it crashed near Augsburg on an acceptance flight after a propeller blade had broken off, killing its pilot Eberhard Mohnicke, who had been a fighter pilot in World War One in the Jagdgeschwader Richthofen, and as a test pilot for several years thereafter in Rechlin, Adlershof and Staaken, had already become an 'old Rechliner'.

Of the four types of development aircraft mentioned, besides the Albatros L 76 – the sole type to be produced in quantity, there remained only the Heinkel HD 41 (alternatively HD 45) of which only three further examples were delivered in 1930. The HD 41c (Werk-Nr.363) registered later as the HD 45 (D-1011), went to the RDL E-Stelle in Staaken, the HD 41 (Werk-Nr.364) being used in Lipetsk for bomb-release tests before being registered in May 1931 as the HD 45a (D-2064) at the DVL in Adlershof.

The longest-recorded aircraft is the second prototype, built as the HD 41b (D-1795, Werk-Nr.342) which was still in Rechlin in June 1936 (as D-IXAZ) and following the installation of another engine, the Sh 20, was subjected to additional prototype certification trials.[11]

Nevertheless, the Truppenamt, building upon the test results of these aircraft, was able to lay down precise guidelines for the intended first-generation aircraft to form its main flying equipment, which had led the partaking firms to develop the Arado Ar 64, the Heinkel HD 45 and HD 46, the Albatros L 76 and L 77, and the Dornier Do 11. In keeping with their notions on operational use by the Flying Corps, all of these designs were intended to provide direct support for the Army units, where, instead of a night-fighter or night reconnaissance aircraft, a new medium bomber was to be used. On the whole, it appears noteworthy that the majority of aircraft types promoted, had no strategically offensive role to fulfil. Testing of these aircraft was of particular impor-

tance during the build-up of the Flying-Corps. It was only after the ban had been lifted on the aircraft 'Definition of Understanding' in May 1926 and the dissolution of the IMKK (Inter-Allied Military Control Commission) at the end of January 1927 that aircraft manufacture had a foreseeable future, although under the Treaty of Versailles military aircraft were still forbidden. The capacity of the aircraft firms, however, was only sufficient for manufacturing anything from single prototypes to a limited series. Predetermined standards for the manufacture of aircraft, aero-engines and equipment did not exist at all. Accordingly, aircraft flight testing was still in its infancy, and even here there were no guidelines. As recalled by former Rechliners, in the early days the head of testing drew up the testing programme and carried out the majority of flight testing himself. Foremost at this period and without any tactical and technical demands, was test flying the aircraft and engines delivered by the manufacturers in order to accumulate knowledge of the technical status of the fledgling German aircraft industry. It was necessary above all, to ascertain maximum speed, rate of climb, ceiling, length of the take-off and landing runs, each time with various loadings, engine performance and propellers, partially even with different powerplants. All in all, the primary aim lay on examining the flying qualities which had been limited for several years by the so-called aircraft 'Definition of Understanding' restrictions. Testing flight characteristics took on a wider spectrum later, after preliminary work on the subject had been done by the DVL. This was made all the more difficult since aircraft instruments, flying clothing, safety and rescue equipment and not least, measurement techniques, were still all of the standards reached after the end of World War One and had to be painstakingly developed anew. Hence, the conditions under which flight testing was undertaken from the mid 1920s, were anything but safe or comfortable.

A Caspar C 30 biplane at the end of the 1920s being prepared for a flight in Rechlin. In the background is the first aircraft hangar at whose rear was located the 'Swiss House' not visible from this position.

The Albatros L 78 was exhaustively tested in Rechlin in 1928. It was the first aircraft type to be built based on the criteria supplied by the 'Fertigung GmbH', a cover-name for the HWA Department Wa. Prw. 8, which drew up regulations for construction particulars and arrangements to ease licence manufacture and exchangeability of equivalent construction items.

At Rechlin in 1929, performing as an engine flying test-bed, the Heinkel HD 41 was nothing other than the predecessor of the He 45 reconnaissance aircraft. The photograph presumably depicts the first HD 41 a (Werk-Nr.321, D-1694) completed in July 1929.

time and have only one yearning – to ascend as fast as possible after take-off to a bearable external temperature. Until the engine has been started and warmed up, the sun is beating down on us. Finally, we are ready and roll to the take-off point. Our actual work begins right after lift-off. For safety reasons we note continually the time with several stop-watches, register the ambient temperatures from a thermometer on the wing strut, note the airscrew rpm and other measurement values. Joyfully I read off the sinking outside temperature. The dewpoint is just exactly what one needs now! But the 'bird' has to ascend higher, into even colder regions. The increasing cold incessantly penetrates through leather and fur, and the sweat-drenched underwear. We begin to shiver miserably. Time seems to stretch endlessly, with retarding climbing speed the ceiling still has to be reached first. Nothing helps other than patiently holding on, all the time continually making recordings. At about 7,000m (23,000ft) we don't appear to be climbing any further, so that we break-off at this point. With idling engine we again descend earthwards in large spirals. When we finally touch-down, the sticky hot summer air again envelops us. We taxi right up to the hangar, shut the engine down and rip off the head gear and leather mask from our faces, fling off the gloves and loosen the parachute straps. Stiff and clumsy, we raise ourselves out of the seats, let the mechanics help us out of our boots and flying combinations and then have only one thing in mind: move as fast as possible to the bathing room and get under the shower!'

Dipl.-Ing. Georg Wollé, working in Rechlin since summer 1926, describes in a picturesque way, the course of a typical flight test at that time:[12]

'A hot, summer day! The air over the airfield is shimmering! A climb to ceiling altitude has been ordered and we know what that means for us – a long flight in the icy cold in an open cockpit. Ignoring the prevailing heat, we have already donned warm underwear and to protect the kidneys, have wrapped around a warm truss as well. On top of that, normal clothing. In the shadow of the hangar and with the help of our mechanics, we slip into the fur-lined leather combinations. Our legs disappear into high, fur-lined boots which we have stuffed with old newspaper for additional warmth. The head will be protected by a

woollen hood, the face being covered by a leather mask with inner lining, with apertures for the eyes and mouth. Over the head, we put on the usual fur-lined flying helmet and flying goggles. At the very least, we cover our hands with thin silk gloves and fur-lined leather gloves with high armshields. We are then finished with our clothing 'magic' and stand there like prehistoric monsters.

In front of the hangar, our excellent mechanics have checked out the 'bird' and made it flight-ready whilst we slip on our parachutes and knee-pads on which we have to note measurement results during the flight. Since we are hardly able to move with all this gear on, strong-armed mechanics push and lift us up the fuselage into our seats. We are bathed in sweat in the mean-

In ways similar to these, the aircraft delivered by the manufacturers were tested one after another in Staaken and Rechlin, among them prototypes of the Albatros L 59, L 76, L 76a, L 77, L 78, L 79, L 80, L 81, L 82 and L 84, and the Heinkel HD 20, HD 21, HD 22, HD 40, HD 41 and HD 45, the two firms providing numerically the largest number of aircraft.

Exactly when flight testing recommenced in Rechlin in the 1920s cannot be determined from surviving documents. The later Generalingenieur der Luftwaffe Heinz Marquard, reported that he made the first landing in Rechlin 'in autumn 1925'[13] and Georg Wollé recalls that immediately after his arrival in Rechlin in July 1926, he had to make stop-watch flight-time recordings of an Albatros prototype flown by Hauptmann Student himself, not to mention the previously-cited crash of the Arado SD I on 11th October 1927. Despite the lack of documentation and flight log-book entries for the period, it can be assumed that from 1928, flight test operations increased dramatically. In the aircraft parks in Staaken and Rechlin at that time, Georg Wollé and Walter Hertel recall that among others, there were the Albatros L 65, L 68, L 76, L 78, Heinkel HD 20, HD 21, Udet U 12a, Junkers F 13, A 35, K 47, G 24 and Dornier Merkur (Mercury). Besides these, there were those prototypes that had been subjected to flight testing which formed the first part of the 'chief equipment period'[14] begun in 1929, ie, the He 46 for close-reconnaissance, HD 45 for long-range reconnaissance, Ar 64 and Ar 65 as single-seat fighters and the Do 11 (later the Do 13 and Do 23) as night-bombers.

The increase in development activity in the course of secret aerial armament with its resulting increase in test flying, made the latter and the especial need for disguise in the nation's capital city more difficult so that flight testing at the beginning of the 1930s had to be transferred more and more to Rechlin.

Ever since the timorous beginning in 1926, Erprobungsgruppe personnel had been continuously increased. Its core at that time included Dipl.-Ing. Bruno Gollhammer, Ing. Karl Haubold, Dipl.-Ing. Walter Hertel, Ing. Fritz Klemm, Dipl.-Ing. Theo Schröder and Dipl.-Ing. Georg Wollé. Head of the Gruppe

The earliest known 'official' demonstration flights for the HWA took place in Rechlin on 23rd/24th August 1928. During the hours of darkness, take-offs and landings using various optical aids, reconnaissance, and bomb-releases with the aid of illuminated bombs were conducted. In the course of these, the pilot, Ing. Hans Leutert, crashed at 0100hrs in the HD 22 (Werk-Nr.293, D-1147) which suffered 100% damage. He himself remained uninjured.

Organisation Chart of Gruppe III, Wa. Prw.8, on 1st June 1931. In the Overall Summary, it was termed a 'disguised Section'. The sub-division of the Test Section into 5 Referate corresponds almost exactly to the later initial organisation of the E-Stelle Rechlin (T1 to T5).

Gruppe III

(Erprobungsstelle des Reichsverbandes der Deutschen Luftfahrtindustrie Staaken - Rechlin).

Geschäftsführer:

Dipl.Ing.Frhr.v.Massenbach,
Flz.Flu.

Verwaltungsreferat:

Brandt,	Referent
Müller,Fr.,	Kassenführer
Goerth,	Einkäufer
Hackbusch,Lohnbuchhalter	
Grosse)	
Ising) Sekretärin-	
Segeletz) nen	

Erprobungsgruppe:

a) Ref.Flugzeuge:
Hoppe,Ref.,Flz.Fhr.
Schröder,Dipl.Ing.Vers.Beob.
Gollhammer) Ingenieure
Klemm)
b) Ref.Motoren:+)
............,Referent
............,Ingenieur
c) Ref.Ausrüstung:
Schwencke,Dipl.Ing.,Ref.
Schade,) Ingenieure
Haubold)
d) Ref.F.T.:
v.Seelen,Dr.phil.,Ref.
Müller,A., Ingenieur
e) Ref.L.B.:
Poetsch,Referent
Riebold, Ingenieur
Schmidt, Techniker
Feige)
Mayer)
Otterbein)Fotografen
Braungard)

Betriebsgruppe:

Leitung: Dipl.Ing.v.Gerlach
Flz.Fhr.

Betrieb Staaken	Betrieb Rechlin
Leiter: Ing.Leutert Flz.Fhr. Drewsky, Flz.Fhr. v.Bornstedt,Flz.Fhr.	Leiter: Dipl.Ing. Bader, Flz.Fhr.

Lager	Werft	Flugbetr.	
Verwalter Heppner	Meister Bengsch	Meister Redding	Meister Schubert

47 Arbeiter
(durchschnittlich)

Wa Prw 8 (Zentrale) zugeteilt und
dort aufgeführt:
Ing.Sachse
Dr.Genthe
Briefbuchfhr.Hermann
Stenotypistin Georges.

+) Beide Stellen im Referat Motoren sind z.Zt.
unbesetzt.Wiederbesetzung demnächst.

and hence the first head of testing since World War One was Ing. Stephan von Prondzynski, a retired Kapitänleutnant and Navy flyer, who after the war spent many years at Junkers.

Highly regarded by his team members as a colleague, pilot and engineer, and referred to by the nickname of 'Professeur' he guided the skills of the Gruppe until his move to the Heinkel firm in May 1928 where shortly afterwards, he met with a fatal accident with the HE 8 on 27th September 1928 in Warnemünde.[15] His successor was Dipl.-Ing. Freiherr von Massenbach, who as 'managing director' of the RDL E-Stelle Staaken and Rechlin, and later as Technical Head in Rechlin, authoritatively accompanied the build-up of the E-Stelle there. In summer 1931, the Erprobungsgruppe had grown to a strength of 80 in Staaken and Rechlin.

Testing in the majority of cases took the form of individual items to be verified on the various prototype aircraft, the results being compared with each other for a final evaluation. It seems that November 1928 was the first occasion after the end of World War One when direct comparison flights were carried out. As recorded in the flight log-book of pilot Heinz Simon, participating aircraft from the E-Stelle Travemünde were the Ar 64 (D-2355), Ar 65A (D-2218), Ar 65B (D-1898), HD 38 (D-2346), HD 38c (D-2340) and the He 49a (D-2363). After a few test flights in these aircraft and with a Fokker D XIII on 7th and 8th November 1932, comparative 'air battles' with each other took place on all the types

Maintenance work at the beginning of the 1930s had to be performed mainly without special tools. Here, an Sh VI 'Jupiter' engine of the Do 11A (Werk-Nr.230, D-2270) is being exchanged, the photo taken in the old maintenance hangar in Rechlin-North.

named on the 9th, 10th, and 12th November 1932. In the days that followed, formation- and low-level flights and a further simulated air battle were conducted. It is unfortunately not known whether the He 49 and the HD 38 were equipped with floats or wheels on these flights, since these were exchangeable on both aircraft. Certainly as a result of these comparisons, the Ar 65B fighter was selected as the aircraft to equip the intended fighter formations – camouflaged as 'publicity squadrons' – but which were soon replaced by the He 51 and latterly, by the improved Ar 68.

Besides testing the various aircraft types, equipment items were also thoroughly examined for use by the crews of the almost exclusively open-cockpits, including not only flying clothing but also rescue equipment, since the aircraft flew ever faster and were able to attain higher ceiling altitudes.

The subject of intensive and sometimes dangerous testing, were all types of manual and automatic crew parachutes, on which Dipl.-Ing. Georg Wollé again comments:

'One day, a special parachute release-test was to be carried out, whose result would show whether an exit could be made by parachute from the Albatros L 76 when it got into a spin. For this test, I had my customary seat in the rear crew-compartment behind the pilot removed and replaced with a broad harness serving as a makeshift seat. I now sat in reverse, facing the tailplane. A 75 kg (165 lb)-weight dummy, complete with full flying clothing, boots and gloves, and equipped with an automatically-opening parachute, served as the 'test person', that had to be positioned on my lap until the moment of release. Considerably tense, I took off with Hoppe on this test flight on 11th May 1929. At a higher altitude than usual, the pilot gave me the signal over Rechlin airfield that he would now enter a steep spin. What a different feeling it is to a 'normal' spin, to be watching the tail surfaces rotating at seemingly enormous speed! I lie with my back to the wall separating me from the pilot and am pressed hard against the cockpit side wall due to the acceleration forces. The same forces now pressed the dummy which is still in my lap even further, its weight appearing to have multiplied several times. But the dummy has to go, regardless of what it takes! I was only able with the greatest exertion, to raise it to the

top of the fuselage. Taking a last deep breath – the tension has now reached its highest peak – one last push with both hands, and hurray! With an elegant turn, the dummy falls just clear of the outermost edge of the lower wing and is soon swaying beneath the billowing parachute!'

These tests did not always take place so easily, as evidenced by the fatal crash of Walter Kneeser and Ing. Karl Haubold on 15th December 1933 in Rechlin when releasing a parachute-equipped dummy. At this time, however, the scope of conditions for aircraft construction and also for aircraft testing had already undergone substantial changes in Germany.

The Construction of Rechlin from 1933

After 30th January 1933, the new rulers of the Reich uninterruptedly pursued a policy of establishing a Luftwaffe and its corresponding aircraft industry. The newly-appointed Reichskommissar für Luftfahrt (Commissioner for Aviation), Hermann Göring, paid a visit at the end of March 1933 to the RDL E-Stelle Rechlin,[16] accompanied by the Reich Defence Minister Generaloberst Werner von Blomberg, Admiral Erich Raeder, and the Army and Navy Department Chiefs. As recollected by Oberst Helmuth Felmy who was present, Göring appeared most surprised at the status of work and commented on what he had seen with the words: 'I had no idea that you are so far advanced...'.

Whether it was due to this positive impression which had its effect on Rechlin's further expansion is a matter of conjecture. In any event, money poured in from 1933 onwards to an extent unimaginable until then, and enabled the installations surrounding the airfield to be rapidly expanded. Four closed groups of buildings could soon be recognized which, situated at 90° to each other, spattered around the almost circular airstrip, this grouping dominating the picture of the E-Stelle Rechlin until the end of World War Two. Planning work for its expansion was carried out by Rechlin's Luftwaffe Construction Department, headed by Regierungsbaurat Kamecke, whose department already occupied its own building completed before 1935 at the southern tip of the Claas-See.

Construction work was begun in this later-designated 'Gruppe Nord' on what was until then the largest hangar building (Halle 105) adjoining the existing Junkers hangar. In the course of time, with the ever increasing number of test aircraft, hangar space proved insufficient, so that the Junkers hangar was dismantled and rebuilt on the western periphery of the Roggentin airfield. In its old position, the new Halle 105 hangar was erected connected to an office

wing which housed the meteorological and air traffic control personnel. The oldest southern-situated hangar with its attached 'Swiss House', both of which no longer sufficed to fulfil needs, had to make way. In their place, a second repair hangar was erected and like the one built in 1933, was connected to adjoining office premises which housed the head of the Management Department. Behind these hangars, office buildings and workshops were built, as well as the main guard-house, the Base Command HQ building, the automobile park, the central heating works, a large hangar, and last but not least, the emergency power station. Thus, up to 1936, a wide-ranging and nevertheless enclosed installation had been erected, which initially housed almost all of the test and administration departments of the E-Stelle.

Parallel with the expansion of Gruppe Nord, the so-called 'Halle Ost' (East Hangar) took shape a few hundred metres eastward, intended to accommodate the Testing Departments for air-launched weapons and aircraft ammunition. For security reasons, it was obviously separated from the other buildings on the northern edge of the airfield. Still further eastward and beyond the ring road, a 'Muna' or bunkered ammunition institute was erected. Between this and the Halle Ost was the bomb-loading area. The hangar was so configured as to be economically 'self-sufficient' but nevertheless, on its left side had available a 2-storey office wing, with a built-in air traffic control; on its right side, several garages for the fire brigade and miscellaneous vehicles, and at its rear face the ground-level workshop rooms. Except for a few items of interior

Brisk constructional activity at Rechlin airfield around 1933/34. Another aircraft hangar between the Junkers hangar (far right) and the old aircraft workshops was almost completed. Behind the hangars, the foundations were laid for the first maintenance buildings and garrison headquarters. The foundations for the so-called 'Meistersiedlung' (specialists' colony) housing area between the Class-See and Müritz was also laid (far left).

The first engine Prüfstand (Test Stand) completed in Rechlin about 1933, was the so-called 'Engine Measurement Stand I'. Energy for the installation was supplied by a Diesel engine, generator, cooling towers and a spring-water installation. Engines up to 1200hp (880kW) could be tested. Later, Test Stands for engines up to 4000hp (2950kW) were added.

work remaining to be done, the Halle Ost became available for testing functions from summer 1934. Around 1936, two single-storey office and workshop buildings were erected behind this hangar in which the armament and bomb-centres were housed, and still further eastward, two parallel firing-ranges were erected in which fixed aircraft armament could be centred and firing trials conducted.

Because of the separation of activities into a 'technical' E-Stelle and an Airbase (described elsewhere) responsible for installations and ground location functions, erection of accommodation for military personnel was given an equally high priority as the Gruppe Nord. For this purpose, barrack blocks were to be built, receiving its name from the Ellerholz grounds lying alongside, which together with an additional large aircraft hangar, became known as the Gruppe West. Upon conclusion of related planning, the so-called Fliegerge-bäude (flight personnel building) was the first to be completed – a large single-storey building which later contained the air intelligence unit and officers quarters. In late spring 1934 construction work began on the first barrack block, a mess building, a medical centre, several dwelling houses, garages and a guard-house. In summer 1934, foundation work was started on the second barrack block and on the Halle West hangar situated directly beside the airstrip, the installations becoming ready for use by spring 1935. In the barrack block area, a large mess hall and canteen, a sports centre and sports field as well as more dwellings were later built. Beside the Halle West was a garage complex which housed the vehicles of the fire-fighting and rescue, salvage and recovery teams. One of the single-storey buildings housed the E-Stelle training workshops having the most modern equipment and fittings, in which from 1937, experienced shop-floor instructors and specialists led by Flieger- (later Ober-) stabsing. Friedrich Jahn, trained between 20 and 30 trainees annually to become proficient as electro-mechanics, precision mechanics, metal aircraft builders and technical illustrators, who by reason of their high standard of knowledge displayed in national and district contests, had attained excellent placings. The training workshops were re-located to Mirow in 1944. Because of the critical war situation, the last batch of trainees were not able to complete their training course and were called-up for frontline service.

The expansion of Gruppe Süd was likewise begun in 1934 and at the end of the year, next to the sole existing engine test-stand, a whole row of construction excavations and foundations were to be seen. Out of all this arose the northern aircraft hangar ready for use in 1935, behind which were

the two long, flat engine workshop buildings and the fuel laboratory, completed to the building skeleton state by the end of the year. Behind the laboratory, the first of four twin-motor test-stands shot up, and further away from the airfield, a further engine test-stand. Heating for this group of buildings was provided from a central heating installation which was put into operation. The first expansion stage, completed around the beginning of 1936, preceded construction of the administration building and the second large hangar, whilst on the oldest engine test-stand, work began to convert it into an altitude test-stand. Alongside, work was begun on further test-stands for air- and liquid-cooled engines as well as propellers and engine accessories. The erection of several workshops, mainly completed the picture of this group of buildings by the end of 1938.

In the meantime, a further building complex arose between the Gruppe Nord and the Müritzsee, whose location and the two large hangars – one large hangar with convex roofing and one of rectangular shape, led to it being called the 'seaplane hangar group'. Beside these hangars was a launch and slipway. In fact, water-based aircraft were never tested in Rechlin and the presence of such aircraft was confined to occasional visits from Travemünde. Consequently, the hangar in close proximity to the Müritz shoreline, originally called the 'water hangar' was converted into a 'control' hangar in 1936 and later turned over to the ground installations section for their use. Besides these large buildings, a number of office buildings were erected and on the shore of the Claas-See, accommodation and moorings for the E-Stelle's boat group was provided.

To connect the four building complexes on Rechlin airfield, a ring road and a parallel normal-track railway were built which, emanating from the terminus in Mirow, connected Lärz, Ellerholz and Rechlin together – the same stretch that had earlier been built in 1918. Directly in front of the Main Watch at the entrance to Gruppe Nord was the E-Stelle Rechlin railway station with two platforms and a large canteen. There were also auxiliary narrow-gauge rail connections to the C-Platz, into the 'Muna' as well as to an explosives quarry lying east of the Gruppe Süd complex. Airfield installations were made complete through the emplacement of two compensating compass-bases near the Gruppe Nord and from subterranean fuel mixing chambers near to the four groups of buildings that beside the Gruppe Süd alone, had a capacity of over 150,000 litres (33,000 Imperial gallons) connected to each other by a ring-shaped conduit as well as with Roggentin and Lärz. In 1943, the capacity of the normal tank installations was 800,000 litres (176,000 Imperial

gallons) as well as a further 1.3 million litres (286,000 Imperial gallons) in remotely-located tanks.

It was not only the region in the direct neighbourhood of Rechlin airfield which suffered alterations due to construction work, as considerable inroads into outlying areas had been made as well. The most unobtrusive of these was expansion of the extensive property covered only by low-lying shrubbery between the Gruppe Nord and Ost, the roadway to Bock, the Bolter canal and the Müritz shore on which the so-called C-Platz had been laid out. It was used by the ammunition testing section, which from 1936 onwards, built office and storage rooms there, the latter partly in bunkers, as well as armament and ammunition workshops, laboratories and shooting ranges. A speciality here was a walled acceleration test-stand and a rail-mounted centrifuge of some 15m (49ft) external diameter, an extinguishing chamber to burn-off or extinguish punctured fuel tanks as well as a velocity tower.

Villages make way for Bombing Ranges
Expansion of the E-Stelle to include bombing ranges resulted in serious consequences for existing villages and estates north and east of the airfield. This region, interspersed with woodlands and lakes, was only sparsely populated and hence ideal for this purpose. It must be borne in mind that the Luftwaffe build-up had still to be conducted in secrecy, since the Treaty of Versailles forbidding the establishment of air power in Germany was officially still in force. However, since the possibility of conducting bombing trials in Lipetsk had disappeared since the summer of 1933, a new range had to be sought within Germany. The Reichswehr artillery shooting-range in Jüterborg was used on a shared basis at first, but was too small and not capable of extension. It was therefore advantageous to have such facilities near to the new E-Stelle for land-based aircraft.

The first to give way to the expansion plans was Rechlin village with its estate-workers dwellings for the erection of the large Halle 105 hangar of Gruppe Nord. After the occupants had been suitably relocated, the houses were destroyed on 15th April 1934 in a series of bomb-release tests and subsequently demolished. The same fate was later met by the village of Leppin. The evacuated buildings were suitably prepared by the responsible RLM Department in order to test the effectiveness of safety measures against various types of incendiary bombs in a large-scale test. This took place on 5th and 6th December 1934 and sealed the fate of the settlement. The Roggentin estate seems to have been eradicated in the same manner shortly after-

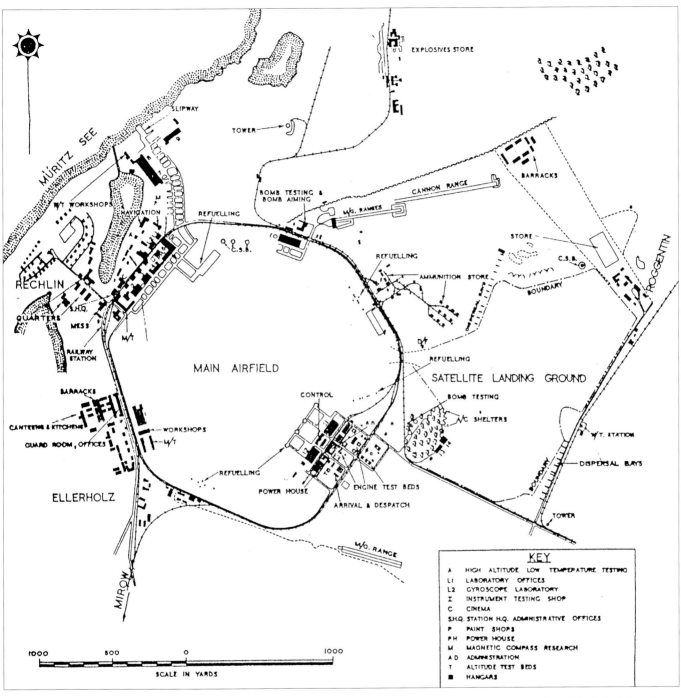

KEY

A	HIGH ALTITUDE LOW TEMPERATURE TESTING
L1	LABORATORY OFFICES
L2	GYROSCOPE LABORATORY
I	INSTRUMENT TESTING SHOP
C	CINEMA
S.H.Q.	STATION H.Q. ADMINISTRATIVE OFFICES
P	PAINT SHOPS
PH	POWER HOUSE
M	MAGNETIC COMPASS RESEARCH
A D	ADMINISTRATION
T	ALTITUDE TEST BEDS
■	HANGARS

wards. All these villages lay west of the Leppin lake on the grounds of the first E-Stelle bombing range, designated as 'B-Platz West'. It soon became evident that this did not suffice, so that further expansion east of the Leppin-See commenced on what later became known as 'B-Platz Mitte' and 'B-Platz Ost'. The B-Platte concrete slab, roughly the size of a football field and over 2m (6½ft) thick, built for testing bomb fuses and bomb casings, was laid out in 1934. As a further consequence, the occupants of Schillersdorf, Qualzow and Zartwitz hamlets had to vacate their homes and relocate as far as Neustrelitz up to the end of 1935.

The Air Defence Department began immediately to setup special target- and observation emplacements near Schillersdorf and laid out the village to cater for extensive incendiary bomb tests which took place at the end of October 1936. By the end of the year, expansion of the B-Plätze were largely completed and included the erection of a so-called 'Sprenggarten' (blast garden) near Qualzow in which not only duds were exploded but also other tests could be undertaken. In addition, several tower-like cinetheodolite measuring stations to track the flightpaths of descending bombs were also erected.

An overall view of the E-Stelle Rechlin as it existed in 1944 is shown on this target-chart prepared by the 8th USAAF. Based on reconnaissance photographs and probably assisted via espionage, the Allies had an exact picture of the tasks of individual departments as well as the purpose served by the various groups of buildings.

The 'Rechlin Colony' between the Class-See and Müritz in its final stage of expansion as seen in this aerial photograph taken around 1942.

Rapid expansion of the E-Stelle caused a sizeable requirement for housing quarters. The large number of building-site labourers at the beginning were housed in barracks directly next to the sites, but as work progressed, the need arose for an ever-increasing number of permanent houses and apartments. Up until 1933, the few accommodation possibilities available were the 'Swiss House', the 'Café Achteck' and the nearby barrack blocks, so that probably as early as 1933, construction work had started on the Rechlin-Nord settlement area with single- and two-family houses, situated on both sides of the 1832-vintage church. In 1935 and 1936, two accommodation buildings for singles – colloquially called 'bull-cloisters', with some 40 single rooms, were erected on the southern edge of the Claas-See. A third building of similar type was later added, but was by no means adequate, so that a large number of employees had to be housed in private

dwellings in Röbel, Mirow, Wesenberg and even in Neustrelitz. From there, they were able to commute to their workplaces by a special railway train service which had been introduced since at least spring 1934.

From an early date, plans had already been made for the erection of a generous housing settlement area between the southern edge of Rechlin airfield and Vietzen village, which lent its name to the new settlement. The first 34 single- and two-family houses were ready for occupation during 1935, the next building phase up to spring 1937 adding a further 60 apartments. Simultaneously, for the E-Stellen workers, a settlement consisting of large blocks shot up on the eastern edge of Mirow which brought about a further improvement to the housing situation. The final stage of expansion in 1938 doubled the amount of houses in Vietzen as well as in the Rechlin-Nord community. Although more space was available, the housing areas were not further enlarged, which meant that until the end of the war, a sizeable proportion of E-Stelle personnel had to commute daily between a distant dwelling and their workplaces.

Lärz Airfield and E-Hafen Roggentin

Although Lärz airfield already had a Test Department stationed there as part of the FVL on the Müritzsee in 1918, the dismantling requirements of the Allied Powers left nothing other than a few foundations of the former installations visible. The 1918 dispossessions had apparently been subsequently nullified, as in the mid 1930s, new negotiations became necessary for the purchase of land to enable construction work on the airfield to begin. This work was largely completed in 1935 after the 'Lärzer canal' – a part of the Müritz-Havel waterway had been completed. It was originally only intended to have a grass surface but with provision for drainage. Construction of the east-west concrete runway, according to eye-witnesses, first took place in 1939, that of the north-west south-east runway following later.[17] The needs of continually increasing take-off weights and speeds were thus catered for which a grass field was no longer adequate. The primarily-used east-west runway became a permanent 'building-site' until the end of the war due to continual length increases, especially when jet aircraft appeared from summer 1944. In its early years of operation, in contrast to Rechlin, the location did not have to make allowances for Test Departments offices and workshops, so that the number of buildings remained low. Two aircraft hangars of different sizes were erected at 90° to each other on the southern edge, plus a solidly-built air traffic control building and a row of barrack blocks. During World War Two, anti-shrapnel protective boxes were built there, especially at the eastern edge of the woodlands, where construction of a massive concrete bunker was started in 1944. The bunker itself was completed but the entrance gates, according to contemporaries, were never delivered. The bunker was nevertheless intensively used for maintenance and modification work on jet aircraft. At the south-western edge of the field, a series of single-family houses were built, occupied chiefly by personnel from the E-Stelle Rechlin.

From about 1942, the Erprobungskommando Lärz, belonging to the E-Stelle Rechlin, was stationed in Lärz. Its members were at first housed in a barracks complex in the nearby village of Retzow, but were later moved to barracks in Lärz itself, where other units of long- and short-term duration stationed in Lärz were also housed. The inclusion of Lärz in the 'Reichsverteidigung' (homeland defence) and the often-present combat units necessitated dispersal of part of the Technical and Workshops Company from Rechlin to Lärz from mid 1944, the contingents moving into newly-erected barracks in the woods on the eastern edge of the airfield. This location remained largely in the memory of those housed there for the simple reason that in order to maintain natural camouflage, the barracks were built around the trees which were not felled, so that the main tree trunks sometimes protruded from the midst of some of the buildings.

Since the buildings and hangars survived both American air raids almost entirely intact, it must be assumed that at the end of the war the hangars had been blown up or subsequently demolished. The air traffic control building remained untouched and was in continual use by Russian Air Force units until their withdrawal. After several unsuccessful attempts, the concrete bunker on the eastern edge of the airfield was blown up towards the end of 1945, using several warheads from Mistel combinations which survived the war in Rechlin and Lärz, but which were only able to bring about the collapse of the roofing. In this state, the bunker still survives to this day.

The Roggentin airfield was not intended to be regarded as an independent entity even though it was designated in Luftwaffe erection plans in the 1930s as an 'Einsatz-Hafen' (Operational Field) or auxiliary field in the event of general mobilization and

was used during that period as a transfer exercise by Luftwaffe units.[18] The territory lay directly next to the north-eastern edge of Rechlin and was separated from the latter only by the circular road and railway. For the E-Stelle, this represented a fortuitous extension of the principally-used east-west runway in the direction of the Müritzsee, the Roggentin airfield deriving its name from the estate that formerly existed on its north-eastern perimeter. Although there were no airfield-type installations at the beginning, an underground fuel depot was, however, built and connected to the overall Rechlin and Lärz supply system. The erection of a new aircraft hangar in the Gruppe Nord, bestowed upon Roggentin the 'gift' of its own building, erected on the site of the old 1929 Junkers hangar, to which was later added a large tent for housing aircraft. Since these hangars stood immediately behind the rear of the Gruppe Süd complex, separated from it only by the so-called 'Krähenwäldchen' (crows mini-woodland) the location proved eminently suitable from 1943 onwards for testing the new reaction or TL-Triebwerke (turbojet) engines. Physical separation from the normal testing environment of Section E3 ensured the necessary degree of secrecy, at the same time affording unhindered access to Rechlin airfield. Roggentin also proved useful after the first heavy bombing raids on the E-Stelle, when Rechlin airfield became unusable for a while, and flying operations were then able to be organised from Roggentin.

At some intermediate point of time, Rechlin also received its own rotatable compass-base whose remains are still visible; otherwise, nothing more is left to indicate the former use of the location.

Flight Testing in Rechlin from 1933

From the end of the 1920s, the scope of flight testing activity in Rechlin increased steadily. In 1932, the requirements for the second main armament phase had been firmly laid down. The aircraft consisted of a medium bomber and long-range reconnaissance aircraft, a single-seat fighter, a light dive-bomber, a close-reconnaissance aircraft, new trainer aircraft and a heavy long-range bomber. Development of these types begun by the aircraft firms, did not reach the testing stage before 1934/35. Thus in 1933, the principal types available were the already-mentioned Albatros L 76 and L 78, Ar 65, He 45, He 46 and Do 11, partly with new standard equipment sets or with improved engines. In addition to these, attempts were made to convert available civil aircraft such as the Dornier Merkur, Junkers G 24 and Ju 52 and Rohrbach Ro VIII into auxiliary bombers. Unfortunately, with few exceptions, no documents

of the 1933/34 period exist which permit further details to be cited.

One of these exceptions is the Monthly Report from 26th July to 25th August 1934 of Department M[19] that was responsible for military testing in Rechlin and which states:

'In the reporting month from 26th July to 25th August 1934, Department M participated in the following tests:
- Static firing-tests with the F 13 (D-2063) and He 63 (D-2329).
- Testing the special equipment of the Ju 52 (D-2640).
- 100-hour test of the He 51 (D-2726).
- 100-hour test of the Ar 65 (D-2858) variable-pitch propellers.
- Testing the Askania automatic-control device and determining its suitability as a target-approach device with the Do 11 (D-2230 and D 3025).
- Testing the T5B in Jüterborg from 1st August to 11th August 1934 with an He 70 (D-UBEQ) and a Ju W 33 (D-OKEH).
- Department M also carried out comparison tests with the Fw 56 (D-ISOT, D-ILAR and D-IGIR) and Ar 76 (D-IBET) single-seat trainer aircraft ...'

On 9th November 1934, a demonstration took place at the E-Stelle with the He 45, He 46, He 70, Ju W 34 and Do 11, each with full equipment which were to serve as initial aircraft types for the first flying units of the Luftwaffe. Whilst participants in this demonstration are unknown, it is known that at the end of 1934, DLH carried out performance measurements with the Ju 52 in Rechlin.[20]

In 1935, new aircraft arrived in large numbers in Rechlin, as well as older models such as the Do 17, Ju 86 and He 111 whose development dated back to the 1932 tactical requirements for a medium bomber. The time pressure under which development and testing were conducted at that time, can be seen from the following example:

After the first flight on 23rd November 1934 of the Do 17 V1 (D-AJUN, Werk-Nr.256) which subsequently had to be repaired following two undercarriage mishaps during company testing, both this and the second prototype were test flown less than six months later at the end of June 1935 by E-Stelle pilots Dipl.-Ing. Erich Fleischhauer and Dipl.-Ing. Alexander Thoenes at the Dornier works. At the end of August 1935, the Do 17 V1 landed for the first time in Rechlin[21] for a further series of flight trials before being handed over to the E-Stelle on 30th October 1935. The Ju 86 V1 (D-AHEH, Werk-Nr.4910) progressed even more rapidly, having made its first flight on 4th November 1934 and tested in Rechlin since the beginning of June 1935.[22] The speediness record, however, was held by the He 111 V1 (D-ADAP, Werk-Nr.713) whose first flight had taken place on 24th February 1935 and only two

A further contest for whose outcome trials in Rechlin were a decisive factor, concerned the new twin-engined trainer aircraft required for B2, W/T-operator, and air-gunnery training. The Fw 58 competed in this case with the Ar 77, prototypes of both aircraft arriving in Rechlin in 1935. Incidentally, contrary to information related in published literature, two prototypes of the Ar 77 were built – the V1 (D-ABIM, Werk-Nr.845) and the V2 (D-AJAZ, Werk-Nr.846). After the decision had fallen in favour of the Fw 58, they remained in Rechlin until at least summer 1937, being used as test-beds for W/T equipment. The Fw 58 on the other hand, was built in large numbers for use by Luftwaffe training schools. In the last year of World War Two, a few much-liked Fw 58s belonging to the E-Stelle, were employed on communications duties and as test-beds for flight instruments.

The Hs 122 close-reconnaissance aircraft, designed as a successor to the He 46, also arrived for testing in 1935. Following comprehensive trials in Rechlin, the RLM decided against this aircraft since its further development, the Hs 126, promised to have better performance.

For the Luftwaffe E-Stelle Rechlin the year 1935 was an extremely busy period, which faced difficulties not only from uncompleted installations but also from a dearth of qualified personnel. Despite this, remarkably enough, there was only one fatal accident in the course of testing, when the Kl 35 V1 (D-EHXE, Werk-Nr.959) crashed on the airfield as a result of wing failure on 18th July 1935, killing its two-man crew Helmuth König and Gefreiter Alfred Lipke.

weeks later, had been flown from Rechlin on 9th March 1935[23] before remaining at the E-Stelle for a long period from July onwards.

These details constitute but a sample of the fast pace of prototype testing at that time, which subsequently lasted for several months or even years. Besides these known medium bomber designs built in large numbers and in further-developed versions used operationally by the Luftwaffe almost to the end of World War Two, there came in 1935 yet another world-renowned aircraft for testing at the E-Stelle on the Müritz – the Bf 109! After its first flight on 28th May 1935, it was demonstrated in Rechlin in October. Its further development and direct comparison flights with its rival, the He 112 (described later in this book) took place largely in Travemünde. It was only after the final decision had been made

in favour of the Bf 109 that Rechlin, as the responsible centre for land-based aircraft, took over further work on it.

In 1935, testing was also begun in Rechlin of aircraft that had been developed to the competition for a light dive-bomber. In the course of the year, the first prototypes of the Ha 137 and the Hs 123 arrived. Comparative trials lasted until the end of 1936, the winning Henschel prototype staying on until 1938. Whether the third aircraft in this competition, the Fi 98, ever arrived for trials in Rechlin is questionable, as it has not so far been established from documents. The fact is, the Fi 98 V1 flew in summer 1935 and that the V2 prototype crashed on 23rd April 1936 in Kassel killing the pilot Theo Schröder – a real 'old Rechliner' from the earliest days who had meanwhile switched to the Fieseler firm.

In 1935, the first prototype of the new 'pursuit fighter' the Bf 109 V1 (Werk-Nr.758, D-IABI), arrived at the E-Stelle Rechlin. Its first landing resulted in a nose-over but without substantial damage, and had little effect on the later history of this aircraft.

The Ha 137 V3 (Werk-Nr.109, D-IZIQ), powered by a Rolls-Royce Kestrel engine, and seen here at take-off in Rechlin, was unsuccessful in the competition for a light dive-bomber.

One of the first mechanically-operated retractable main undercarriages of its period was that on the Do 11. This close-up view was taken during maintenance work on the first prototype, the Do 11A (Werk-Nr.230, D-2270) during tests at Rechlin. Functional problems led to follow-on types such as the Do 13 and Do 23 reverting to fixed undercarriages.

Below left and right: In the 1930s, the E-Stelle Rechlin undertook flight testing commissioned by the PfL (Aircraft Evaluation Centre) including prototype testing of new aircraft. The tasks listed above depict the Fw 187 V2 Prototype Test Report 1402 of 16.8.1937.

Among the leadership, a change took place in the E-Stelle Rechlin that year, when its first KdE and Airbase Commander Oberst Stahr was transferred to the RLM as of 1st August 1935. His place was assumed by none other than the then HWA head of the Technical Aviation Referat, Oberst Kurt Student. Its technical head since the beginning of the year was Dipl.-Ing. Gottfried Reidenbach, who had previously served in Lipetsk as a pilot under Oberst Stahr. Worthy of mention for 1935, is that at the end of the year, a DVL liaison office was opened in Rechlin, whereby a mutual exchange of information and accumulation of suggestions resulting from testing would find useful application in future research and was probably at the initiative of Oberst Stahr. Since 1st April 1933, the latter had been Geschäftsführer (Business Manager) at the DVL Adlershof when he assumed the post of KdE Detachment Head in Rechlin in 1934. Whatever the reason may be, the DVL out-station had its office between Halle 105 and the Junkers hangar in Rechlin-Nord,

directly next to the PfL liaison office. The presence of the PfL in Rechlin was obviously due to the fact that in those years, the E-Stelle conducted a portion of evaluating new prototype aircraft as a 'sub-contractor' to the PfL. Exactly how long the PfL office functioned in Rechlin is not known, save that a concluding Evaluation Report on the Fw 187 V2 was submitted by the E-Stelle to the PfL in June 1938.[24] The DVL out-station still existed in 1938 even after its first head Dr. August Kupper, was killed on 12th June 1937 when he crashed in a glider of his own design, the out-station being led thereafter by Dipl.-Ing. Julius Henrici who had come from Junkers in 1936 to the DVL Rechlin as the responsible specialist on aero-engines. Shortly after his departure to industry at the beginning of 1939, however, the out-station was closed.[25]

Returning to the year 1936, it is apparent that the workload for the E-Stelle increased noticeably, illustrated in the list overleaf of aircraft on hand for November 1935 and June 1936 that had been evaluated:

Rechlin E 7c_p Erpr.Nr. 1402 Teilbericht 10	Flugzeug Fw 187 V 2 Musterprüfung und Flugleistungen.	Musterprüfbericht 152 f. PfL-Auftr. v. 16.8.37 Blatt 1

Ka/Vr.

Zusammenfassung.

Die Abflugleistung entspricht den PfL-Prüfbedingungen. Bei der Landung wird die vorgeschriebene 600 m-Grenze stark überschritten (726 m von 20 m Höhe bis Stillstand).

Die CO-Messungen ergaben Werte, die in den zulässigen Grenzen liegen.

Die E'Stelle hat gegen eine Zulassung der Fw 187 V 2 keine Bedenken.

Bearbeiter: ....   Gesehen: ....

Dienststelle: Mitarbeiter.   Abt. E 7.

Verteiler:
2 x LC 7 (1 x LC 7 Aussenstelle)
4 x LC 4 (1 x Abnahme)
1 x Fachgruppe (E 7b_3)
1 x Firma über BAL
1 x Greifswald
1 x Travemünde z. Austausch
3 x E 7 (1 x Reserve)

Rechlin, den 24.6.38

Bearbeitet:	Geprüft:	Geprüft:	Gelesen:
			J:

Kalbitzer

Gruppe	Bearbeiter	Tag		

Rechlin E 7c_p Erpr.Nr. 1402 Teilbericht 10	Flugzeug Fw 187 V 2 Musterprüfung und Flugleistungen.	Musterprüfbericht 152 f. PfL-Auftr. vom 16.8.37 Blatt 2

Inhalt!

1.) Allgemeines
2.) Abflugleistung
3.) Landeleistung
4.) Steigleistung
5.) Geschwindigkeitsleistung
6.) Einmotorenleistung
7.) CO-Messung
8.) Flugeigenschaftprüfung
9.) Kunstflugprüfung.

1.) Allgemeines:

Flugzeug: Fw 187 V 2
       Werk-Nr. 950

Motoren: 2 x Jumo 210 D
       Werk-Nr. 40155
       Werk-Nr. 40610

Luftschrauben: 2 x HKW Verstellschraube 3 flg.
       Werk-Nr. 17310
       Werk-Nr. 17311   D = 3000 mm
       12^{00} Uhr = 25^0 Blattwinkel

Fluggewicht: G = 3850 kg

2.) Abflugleistung:

Start Nr.	Anlauf m sec	Von Stand bis 20 m Höhe m sec	Abhebegeschw. km/h	Luftschrauben- stellung
1	163 10,50	421 17,70	117	12.00
2	142 9,7	386 16,80	103	12.00
3	153 10,2	402 17,20	111	12.00

	Bearbeiter	Tag		

Department	Flights (Nov 1935)	in% (Nov 1935)	Flying hrs (Nov 1935)	in% (Nov 1935)	Flights (Jun 1936)	in% (Jun 1936)	Flying hrs (Jun 1936)	in% (Jun 1936)
T1 (later E1)	1230	49.7	223	27.9	810	23.1	344	20.8
T2 (later E2)	382	15.4	262	2.8	659	18.9	536	32.4
T3 (later E3)	269	10.9	175	1.9	950	27.2	494	29.8
T5 (later E5)	211	8.5	51	6.4	346	9.9	112	6.8
B (Betrieb)	363	14.7	76	9.5	560	16.0	70	4.3
M (mil.test)	21	0.8	12	1.5	170	4.9	98	5.9
Total	**2476**	**100**	**802**	**100**	**3495**	**100**	**1655**	**100**

In November 1935, the E-Stelle had a total of 182 aircraft available for test purposes. Of these, 142 were in active use, the remainder either undergoing conversion, repairs, etc at the manufacturers, at operational units, or were not airworthy. In June 1936 the number had risen to 211 – a plus of 16% of which 104 were not in active use. Total take-offs had risen by 41%.[26]

From this, it can be seen that there was not only a general increase in testing activity, but also that the number of take-offs for airframe test purposes, although proportionally the greatest, was lower than the average duration of flying hours. In comparison, engine testing took up 32% of the total flying hours. Also noteworthy is the sharp increase in flights devoted to equipment testing (by T3/E3) and the large number of flights of the Department B, responsible for verification, certification and transport flights, and enables conclusions to be drawn as to where activity was focused at that time.

Unfortunately, this type of information is not available for subsequent years.

In 1936, principal aircraft undergoing further testing consisted of those types already in active military service, namely, the He 45, He 46, He 70, Do 13 and Do 23, and the He 51 and Ar 68, the latter two already having accomplished trials with fixed, obliquely-firing armament[27] later utilized during World War Two on night-fighters, this type of armament becoming generally known as 'Schräge Musik' (Jazz music). In addition, there were numerous experimental and pre-production variants of the new Bf 109, Do 17, He 111, Hs 123 and Ju 86. But there also appeared a whole new set of aircraft at the E-Stelle.

In response to the requirement for a heavy dive-bomber, the Arado, Heinkel and Junkers firms sent their Ar 81, He 118 and Ju 87. During the course of 1936, prototypes of almost all of these aircraft arrived in Rechlin – first the Ju 87 V2 (D-UHUH, Werk-Nr.4922) in March, then the He 118 V2 at the beginning of July. Exactly when the first Ar 81 was flown at the E-Stelle is not known at this juncture. In any case, the Ar 81 V3 (D-UDEX) was still in Department T1/E1 in October 1936. At this point, however, after comparative flights had been made in Rechlin at the beginning of July,[28] the contest had been decided in favour of the Ju 87. Ernst Udet had already flown the Ju 87 on 19th March 1936 in Rechlin, but on 27th July in Rostock, had to make a parachute exit from the He 118 V1 when the propeller

flew off during a dive. The Ar 81, as the sole bi-plane and despite certain technical advances, hardly stood a chance.

Rechlin was the showplace in summer that year for several large exhibitions. On 22nd May 1936, the Reichsminister der Luftfahrt and Oberbefehlshaber der Luftwaffe, Hermann Göring, inspected the newest aircraft on the ground and saw them demonstrated in flight – the Ju 86 with BMW 132 and Jumo 205 engines; the He 111 and Do 17 with BMW VI engines; the Fw 58, He 70, Hs 123, Ha 137, Ju 87, Ar 68, Bf 109, He 112 and the Fw 159. A short time later, on 6th July 1936, the Reichskriegsminister Generalfeldmarschall Werner von Blomberg and the Staatssekretär für Luftfahrt Erhard Milch together with various high officers and officials were guests at the Müritz. They saw the same aircraft as well as the Ar 81 and the He 118. At the end of the intrinsic demonstration, comparative flights between the Ar 68, Fw 159 and Bf 109 had been planned. Whether this actually took place is not certain. Equally unrecorded is whether the same programme, scheduled on 10th July 1936 for Adolf Hitler, and on 15th July 1936 for the three Wehrmacht Commanders-in-Chief and the Commanding Generals, in fact took place. Planning for these events was only completed and distributed less than a fortnight before the scheduled events. Nevertheless, it is clear that in these circumstances and in follow-on visits and demonstrations that year, the E-Stelle Rechlin had become the 'sign-board' of the Luftwaffe and the RLM. On the other hand, it had to contend with problems of maintaining the necessary secrecy which these visits caused, plus the frequent delays to ongoing testing which was inevitably under time pressure.

Besides all this, the year in retrospect also experienced changes in the E-Stelle leadership. The Commander, Oberst Student, departed from Rechlin to take over command of the Fliegerwaffenschulen (Aircraft Armament Schools) with effect from 1st October 1936. He was succeeded by Major Werner Junck who only exercised this office for one month before handing it over to Major Carl-August von Schönebeck. There was continuity at least in the E-Stelle technical leadership under Fliegerober-stabsing. Gottfried Reidenbach. But even in the uppermost levels of aviation technology there was a significant change, when

Seen here from an unusual perspective is the He 111 V3 (Werk-Nr.715, D-ALES), which arrived for testing in Rechlin in 1936 together with the Do 17 and Ju 86. A lowered nose profile and DB 600 engines were characteristics of early He 111 variants.

Oberst Ernst Udet took over the leadership of the RLM Technisches Amt from Oberst Wimmer in June 1936.

Towards the end of 1936, testing of a new aircraft began in Rechlin – the world-renowned and well-liked Fieseler Fi 156 Storch (stork). For the sake of completeness, it should be mentioned that the rival Si 201 from the Flugzeugbau Halle and the Messerschmitt Bf 163 both lost out. Their prototypes were first flown by E-Stelle pilots as late as spring 1938 (!) and most probably never arrived in Rechlin.

Finally, 1936 also experienced the first flights of other newer aircraft which were later used in large numbers by the Luft-waffe and which from 1937 were part of the daily scene in Rechlin – the Ju 88 and the Bf 110. The latter emanated from the General Staff requirement for a land-based high-altitude medium-range reconnaissance aircraft cum Flugzeugzerstörer, ie, a twin-engined aircraft designed to pursue and destroy enemy aircraft. Following a conference between the Luftkommandoamt (Air Command Office) and the RLM Technisches Amt on 11th May 1934, besides the large bomber, a heavy dive-bomber, and a medium bomber (all three land-based) this new hybrid was also placed on the top-priority Class I – above that of the single-seat pursuit fighter.[29] In the meantime, the emphasis had obviously again shifted, as the aircraft already under test serve to indicate.

In the contest for a Flugzeugzerstörer, the Fw 57, Hs 124 and Bf 110 were submitted. Messerschmitt was the only one who had so designed his new aircraft that with only minor alterations, a high-altitude medium-range reconnaissance aircraft and fast bomber could be rapidly developed. Three examples of the Bf 110 had already flown in 1936 so that testing was able to commence in Rechlin the following year. It can be assumed, even though until now not verifiable from documents, that the competitive aircraft came at the same time to the E-Stelle. The Bf 110, however, was able to win the race for itself. In contrast, the Bf 162, which had been derived from the Bf 110 in the contest for a future fast bomber, proved inferior to the Ju 88, and with the third competitor the Hs 127, the story was no different. Apparently Heinkel had also tendered a design in this contest – the unconventional He 119, but this aircraft and the Hs 127, described as a 'SV-Flugzeuge' in the Aircraft Development Programme of 1st April 1937, were not planned to be purchased nor built in a 0-series. In accordance with conference notes made by the Development Department LC II on 16th December 1937[30] the SV-aircraft were 'for the present not be handed over to Rechlin', probably to limit work overload at the E-

Only two photographs of the Ar 81 V1 (D-UJOX) exist of it in Rechlin, probably taken during the summer of 1936. In the competition for a heavy dive-bomber, it was unsuccessful against the Ju 87.

On 26th February 1936, Dipl.-Ing. Walter Baist was to have carried out an engine test flight with one of the first Jumo 210s installed in the He 45 (D-IHIT, Werk-Nr.300). Following engine failure on take-off, the pilot was just able to circle the airfield and land again before the

aircraft crashed – its 4-letter registration proving eminently appropriate on this occasion! Both crew members escaped with some broken limbs.

In aircraft with open cockpits, the engine exhaust gases had to be safely diverted past the crew compartments. For this purpose, extensive measurements were carried out by the E-Stelle Rechlin in 1936 with a smoke-generator and various chemicals on the He 46D (D-IQAV, Werk-Nr.843).

Stelle. Thus left the Bf 162 and the Ju 88, whose prototype appeared in Rechlin in 1937. Karl-Heinz Völker has stated[31] that the Ju 88 emerged as the victor in comparison flights of both aircraft in August 1937. Whether such trials were in fact undertaken is questionable, but the fact remains that the Ju 88 was selected and that this aircraft, also used until the end of World War Two, was continuously in Rechlin for testing its numerous variants.

Known to a lesser extent was the Hs 126, derived from the Hs 122 close-reconnaissance aircraft which was to have replaced the He 46 in frontline service. Its trials also began in 1937 and were completed without major difficulties. Finally, the Ar 96 prototypes which arrived in Rechlin in 1937 should not go unmentioned; with these the manufacturer from Brandenburg succeeded in creating yet another excellent

trainer as successor to the Ar 66. At least since the summer of that year, the Ar 96 V1 had undergone exhaustive testing in Rechlin, as a result of which several modifications were made and with further prototypes, was intensively tested further during the following year.

The continually-growing development and testing activities at all the Luftwaffe E-Stellen and in the Technisches Amt in Berlin led to an ever-increasing number of conferences, meetings, and official trips by members of the various departments involved. In order to accelerate progress and not always call upon the services of testing establishments – who were then unable to carry-out their own obligations – the DLH in spring 1937 at the RLM's request, organised a special to-and-fro flight service between Berlin, Rechlin and Travemünde. Principally catered for were members of

the RLM, the E-Stellen and aviation industry representatives, but also included Luftwaffe servicemen and those going on leave. For this flight service, the RLM provided DLH with the government-owned Ju 52/3m (D-AQAU, Werk-Nr.5650). In spring 1938, this aircraft was replaced by the Ju 52/3m (D-AIMA, Werk-Nr.5848) belonging to the Kdo.d.E. Following the outbreak of World War Two, the Ju 52/3mge (D-AHAL, Werk-Nr.5034) christened 'Otto Bernert' finally operated this special DLH service route until it was cancelled in May 1942.[32]

But to return now to the year 1937. Besides the increasingly multifarious testing duties, there were some aviation highlights to be recorded for members of the E-Stelle in a quite different field of activity. In the International Flying Meeting which was held from 23rd July to 1st August 1937 in Dübendorf, Switzerland, a number of Rechliners formed a part of the German team. These brought over with them the Do 17 M V1, a few Bf 108s and Bf 109s, an He 112, an Hs 123 and the Fi 156A-0. The Storch had been fetched from Kassel on 23rd July by Dipl.-Ing. Otto Cuno, head of the Powerplant Department and flown to Zürich, where he also demonstrated it in flight. Even more attention was achieved by the head of Department E1, Dipl.-Ing. Carl Francke, who with a Bf 109, won the speed, climb, and diving contests, with Dipl.-Ing. Otmar Schürfeld of Department E5, taking second place to the last-named contender with the Hs 123. Major Seidemann won the 'Alpenrundflug' – the closed-circuit flight for single-seat military aircraft in a Bf 109, and the Polte/Milch team in the Do 17 won the contest for multi-seat aircraft, thus rounding off a great success for the German participants at this Flying Meeting.

Besides these aviation highlights, 1937 also brought severe losses during flight testing. In six crashes, a total of 18 E-Stellen members were killed, testifying to the more hazardous situations encountered in flight testing.

The year 1938 brought a new round of changes in the top echelons of the Luftwaffe. The most direct effects felt by the E-Stellen was the abolishment of the post of KdE (E-Stellen Commander). With its dissolution, the acting KdE, Major von Schönebeck, was transferred to the post of Military Attaché in Belgrade.

```
Generalluftzeugmeister                 Berlin, den 12. Mai 1939
    G L / Adj. 2
Nr.: 2041/39 Adj.2


                         F l u g p l a n

       für den Sonderflugdienst Berlin - Rechlin - Travemünde,
                       Gültig ab 15. Mai 1939.


                            M o n t a g

ab Bln.-Tempelhof   7 00 )Bedarfslandung  ab Bln.-Tempelhof  15 20
an Rechlin          7 40 )in Tarnewitz    an Rechlin         15 00
ab Rechlin          7 50 )auf d. Strecke  ab Rechlin         16 10
an Travemünde       8 40 )Rechlin-Tra-    an Bln.-Tempelhof  16 50
ab Travemünde       8 50 )vemünde bzw.
an Rechlin          9 40 )auf dem Rück-
ab Rechlin          9 50 )flug.
an Bln.-Tempelhof  10 30 )


                     Dienstag und Freitag

ab Bln.-Tempelhof   8 00 )Bedarfslandung  ab Travemünde      15 10
an Rechlin          8 40 )in Tarnewitz    an Rechlin         16 00
ab Rechlin          8 50 )auf d. Strecke  ab Rechlin         16 10
an Tarnewitz        9 35 )Rechlin-Tra-    an Bln.-Tempelhof  16 50
                         )vemünde bzw.
ab Tarnewitz        9 45 )auf d.Rückflug.
an Travemünde       9 50 )


                   Mittwoch und Donnerstag

ab Bln.-Tempelhof   8 00      ab Bln.-Tempelhof  15 20
an Rechlin          8 40      an Rechlin         16 00
ab Rechlin         12 00      ab Rechlin         16 10
an Bln.-Tempelhof  12 40      an Bln.-Tempelhof  16 50


                                    Im Auftrag


Verteiler:
GL/Chef des Stabes   LC 1    P.f.L.           E.St.Peenemünde
GL/Chef-Ing          LC 2    L E              DLH (Flugleitung)
GL/Adj.2             LC 3    ZA (Kurierstelle) DLH (Vertragsverw.)
GL/B.f.S.            LC 4    ZA (Reisebüro)   DLH (Buchungsst.)
GL/B.f.S.(A)         LC 5    F.V.Z.           DLH (Bezirksltg Mitte)
GL 1                 LC 6    L In 5           R.D.L.I.
GL 2                 LC 7    E.St.Rechlin
GL 3                 LC 8    E.St.Tarnewitz
GL 4  1 u. 2         B.f.L.  E.St.Travemünde
```

A Flight-Plan Timetable, valid from 15th May 1939, of the Deutsche Lufthansa Special Service operated between Berlin and the various E-Stellen, which had been instituted by DLH in January 1937 at RLM request. Notice that the E-Stelle Peenemünde is on the distribution list.

The E-Stelle Rechlin's Airbase Commander was now Major (E) Rudolf Haagen, formerly at the E-Stelle Travemünde. As activity head of the E-Stelle, the RLM LC initially appointed the long-standing Technical Chief Flieger-Hauptstabsing. Gottfried Reidenbach who, however, in mid 1938, switched to the Development Department of the RLM Technisches Amt. He was succeeded by Dipl.-Ing. Karl Fritsche, who like Haagen, came from Travemünde. Leadership of 'Military Testing' in Rechlin was assumed by Hauptmann Werner Restemeyer.

At this time, E-Stelle personnel strength consisted of 754 officers and men in uniform and 2,559 officials and employees in civilian sectors, or altogether 3,113 individuals.[33] Reorganisation of the RLM in 1938 resulted in designation changes and a stronger upgrading of Test Departments and formed the basic final structure of the organisation.

In addition to essential testing activities, the year introduced a number of special flying experiences for some E-Stelle Rechlin aircrew members where W Altrogge, C Dietrich, E Kettler, Uske and Waschischek

took first place in the 3rd Italian Rundflug with the Fh 104 (D-IQPG). Rechlin itself became the showplace for film scenes in the Luftwaffe cine-film 'Pour le Mérite', and it is possible that scenes in the film 'D III 88' were also taken in the E-Stelle. Unfortunately, a serious accident occurred during filming, when Dipl.-Ing. Ernst Holtermann of Department E7 and Unteroffizier Horst Selter of the Technische Kompanie – certainly due to being blinded by the sun – collided over the airfield and crashed with fatal results.

Quite a different type of activity was undertaken simultaneously by an E-Stellen team made up of Alexander Thoenes, Otto Spengler, Heinz Schwendler, Alfred Ebermann and Rudolf Mense. A German mountain-climbing team again attempted to reach the peak of the 8,162m (26,660ft) high Nanga Parbat in the Himalayan chain. Ernst Udet, himself an enthusiastic mountaineering fan, had promised Luftwaffe support and placed an aircraft from Rechlin at its disposal. The Ju 52 (D-ABWR) with BMW 132c high-altitude engines and three-bladed propellers, was furnished for this special operation with auxiliary oxygen

This photograph of the E-Stelle Rechlin's Technische Kompanie (with more than 180 men visible), was taken around 1936 with an early Ju 86 prototype in front of the West Hangar. The semi-circular building projection housed the Testing Unit and Air Traffic Control personnel. The building wing (at right) housed the Training Workshops on the ground floor and the Sailplane Workshops on the upper floor.

equipment and low-temperature insulation inside the fuselage. It was stationed from May 1938 in Srinagar in Kashmir from where supply flights were undertaken for the climbers making their way to the peak. The Rechlin crew carried out this support task very successfully and in addition to accumulating experience in high-altitude flights, brought back a quantity of ancillary experiences with regard to navigation, oxygen equipment, and dropping loads by parachute. Even though the peak could not be reached because of prevailing weather conditions, their enterprise received a great deal of respect and recognition. All the participants returned in good spirits to Ger-

The unusual face of the Ju 52/3m (D-AWBR) with which a Rechlin crew assisted the German Himalaya Expedition in its attempt to climb Nanga Parbat with supplies in summer 1938. The photograph was taken on the airfield at Lahore.

drawn up requirements for a successor capable of also being used in the low-level strike role. Whilst Arado and Focke-Wulf offered their submissions in response, the Hamburger Flugzeugbau entered the contest on their own initiative, resulting in the Ha 141 (later BV 141), the Ar 198 and the Fw 189, whose first prototypes all arrived in Rechlin in 1938. A particularly noticeable design was that of the asymmetrical Ha 141, which after its initial proving flights, indicated that difficulties which could be expected from this type of construction, were not experienced.[34] In October, the RLM Development Department requested that a direct comparison of all three designs be made with the participation of Lufwaffe Instruction Units in Rechlin. Whereas the Ar 198 lost out, despite a basically good showing, the Ha 141 in the end was not accepted. This left the Fw 189 whose programme of trials was completed.

This last year of peace, filled with rises and falls for the E-Stelle Rechlin, alongside successes, was fraught with new, painful losses due to accidents and crashes.

Another round of reorganisations in the development sphere took place in January 1939 with the creation of the office of 'Generalluftzeugmeister' (Chief of Procurement and Supply) to which the RLM Technisches Amt reported. As a consequence, the individual Test Departments in all E-Stellen were renamed. In Rechlin, the previously-known departments E7 to E13 were now replaced by the designations E2 to E8 and remained as such until the end of World War Two.

Testing work continued to run at a fast pace; above all, the Ju 88 had to be made operationally mature as soon as possible, for which reason the 0-series aircraft on hand were incorporated into a Test Detachment Ju 88 under Hauptmann Pohle stationed in Rechlin.[35]

A further new aircraft, the Do 217, began to make its appearance in increasing numbers. Only a few days after its first flight, the first prototype had crashed in October 1938,

many at the beginning of September via Rhodes and Rome. There was no depreciation in testing activity, even though fundamentally little new found its way to Rechlin. The year was marked principally in evaluating newer series production models of the Do 17, Bf 109 and He 111. Testing work made good progress after the arrival of the Ju 88 V2 (D-ASAZ, Werk-Nr.4942), Ju 88 V4 (D-ASYI, Werk-Nr.4944), Ju 88 V5 (D-ATYU, Werk-Nr.4945) and the Ju 88 V7 (D-ARNC,

Werk-Nr.4947). Test work was also vigorously pursued with the Ar 96 V1 (D-IRUU, Werk-Nr.2067), Ar 96 V3 (D-IGME, Werk-Nr.2069) and the Ar 96 V4 (D-IZIE, Werk-Nr.2070), whilst another Arado aircraft, the Ar 79, found its way to Rechlin. It was criticized because of its narrow cabin, but was nevertheless later used alongside the Bü 181 for communications duties.

To replace the Hs 126 close-reconnaissance aircraft in service use, the RLM had

but succeeding machines, nevertheless, soon arrived at the E-Stelle. It was essentially a further development of the meanwhile obsolete Do 17, but bore only a faint resemblance to its forbear. As well as the He 111 and Ju 88, the Do 217 was now the third twin-engined bomber undergoing trials prior to entering Luftwaffe service and thus absorbing precious testing capacity. Alongside of these, there were no important newcomers in the skies over Rechlin, except perhaps for the He 100 and various types of Czech aircraft which, following the establishment of the Protectorate of Bohemia and Moravia in March, were examined more closely. This work was thereafter transferred in 1940 to the E-Stelle Travemünde.

A particular well-known event which took place, caused the E-Stelle Rechlin to draw headline attention in the news media, namely, the much-cited 'Führer Visit' of 3rd July 1939. It concerned an extensive demonstration of Luftwaffe aircraft and equipment at which, besides Hitler, Göring, Milch, Udet, Keitel and their entourages, various Luftwaffe generals and department heads from the Technisches Amt were present. Practically everything that was undergoing trials at that time was displayed, accompanied by brief enunciations from the responsible department heads or from Udet himself. Unfortunately, a complete record of the programme is no longer available, and even the 15-minute documentary film entitled 'The Führer in Berlin' which

A 'rare bird' that was flown for a long time in Rechlin, was one of the two Boeing 247 aircraft purchased by DLH in the USA in 1934. The D-AKIN, Werk-Nr.1944, was in Rechlin since at least as early as August 1934, where, following detailed flight testing, it was used as a flying test-bed for automatic course-control tests. During this series of tests, it crashed on 13th August 1937 during take-off at Hannover-Vahrenwald on the return flight to Rechlin. Of the eight crew members, only one man, seriously injured, survived.

On 7th April 1937, an unknown pilot set down the prototype Bf 109 V11 (D-IIBA, Werk-Nr.808) in the middle of Rechlin's runway. The telephone inscription 'Fernruf Mirow 230' on the rudder confirms that this aircraft had been assigned to the E-Stelle Rechlin. In the background is the West Hangar, the control tower and building wing shown earlier and behind it the Technical Company's barracks.

Spring 1938: Upon the departure of the until then acting E-Stellen Commander Major von Schönebeck, the Technical Company Music Corps and Troopers lined up in the courtyard of the Ellerholz-Kaserne. In the background is the rear edifice of the West Hangar.

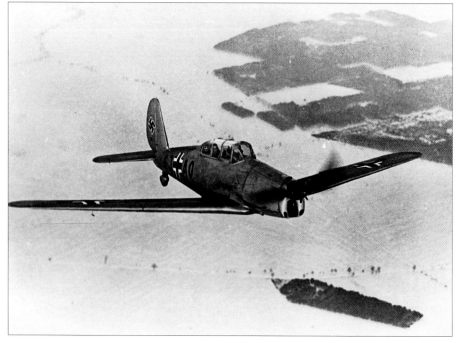

Belly-landing of the Fw 189 V1 (D-OPVN, Werk-Nr.1997) in Rechlin, probably on 8th November 1939 following rupture of the elevator through oscillation. The ground-attack variant of this design with its armoured cockpit was unsuccessful against the Hs 129.

The Ar 96 (GJ+AO) during a test flight. The E-Stelle Rechlin call-sign letters G+A indicates that this aircraft was already undergoing testing in November 1939.

nected with the fact that hardly nine weeks after that 3rd of July 1939, the Second World War broke out.

In Rechlin, work proceeded as usual despite the necessary restrictions imposed by wartime conditions. Before the year was through, however, there were three new aircraft designs flown in trials or on proving flights by E-Stelle pilots. On 12th October 1939, Dipl.-Ing. Karl-Gustav Neidhardt of Department E2 had the opportunity in Augsburg to test fly the Me 210 V1, whilst on 31st October 1939, Dipl.-Ing. Heinrich Beauvais, also from Department E2, flew the Fw 190 V1 for the first time in Bremen, followed on 20th November[37] – according to other sources on the 19th – by Dipl.-Ing. Carl Francke, head of Department E2, who accomplished the maiden flight of the He 177 V1 in Rostock-Marienehe. All three prototypes came to Rechlin in 1940, but suffered from a number of teething troubles which required extensive testing and modifications and kept the E-Stelle occupied for several years thereafter.

Prior to that, in late summer 1939, a new system of identification for military aircraft was introduced in Germany. Instead of that previously used, consisting of the country letter D- followed by 4 alphabet letters, there now appeared the so-called SKZ or 'Stammkennzeichen' – a core or root designator together with the 'Balkenkreuz' Luftwaffe emblem. It differed from civilian aircraft designations in that the first letter of an SKZ was always a consonant. Since the SKZ was allocated from a central office in the various E-Stellen, Flying Schools and so on, to use on their aircraft as well as to the aircraft manufacturers for their newest products, it is possible to derive a picture of the quantity of aircraft on hand in Rechlin during the period in question. According to this, there were at least 260 (!) test aircraft in use by the E-Stelle departments. A listing of the known SKZs is provided in the tables on pages 116-119.

At the beginning of 1940, test flying activity almost came to a standstill. The reason for this was the winter weather conditions which had often lasted into March and led to closure of the airfield. Since the Müritz

had been made at Udet's request by the E-Stelle Photographic Department that same evening and had certainly existed in several copies, has since disappeared.[36] It is therefore only possible from various descriptions and flight log-book entries, to attempt a partial reconstruction of what was shown. It included among others, the Rechlin engine 'Kaltstartverfahren' (cold start-up system), an engine quick-change procedure, RATO assisted take-off of heavily-loaded aircraft, firing tests with the 30-mm MK 101 cannon, bullet-proof fuel tanks, the effects of various types of bombs against armoured targets, the first radar sets, and the X-beam system. As far as is known, aircraft displayed were the BV 141 V1, the Fl 265 helicopter, the Fw 190 V1, the Hs 128 V1, a dive-bombing attack by three Ju 88s flying in wedge formation, rocket-powered bombs jettisoned in level flight from a Ju 88, as well as the rocket-powered He 176 which had accomplished its first flight a short time earlier, and the jet-propelled He 178. The programme, run through in rapid succession

within the four hours between arrival and departure of the guests, had been through a practice-run two days previous to the visit. The demonstration quite obviously impressed everyone involved, but did not lead to the desired aim, namely, the establishment of higher priorities and raw material distribution for arming the Luftwaffe. The reasons for this would require detailed observations which exceed the scope of this book. In this respect, it will merely be noted that the lack of consequences drawn at the highest leadership level from the demonstration cannot be traced back to any 'blame' on the part of the E-Stelle and their staffs since the latter had merely showed the status and the successes of their testing activity. Years later, the rebuke advanced by Göring – certainly to defend himself – that he was 'deceived' at this demonstration, was in no way justified.

Interestingly enough, after this event and until May 1942 no further official exhibitions of large extent are known to have taken place in Rechlin. This may also be con-

was also frozen over, it was possible in limited measure to conduct ice-landing tests with various aircraft and continue trials with snow-skids.

Aircraft which were tested included the Bücker Bü 181, a two-seat trainer with side-by-side seats. It had been first flown in 1939 and in the autumn of that year, the Bü 181 (D-ERBV) had undergone brief flight testing in Rechlin. Further prototypes were now available and after snow conditions permitted flying to resume, trials at the E-Stelle were continued. The flight log-book, still available, of Ing. Helmuth Kirschke, the responsible prototype specialist at E2, details the progress of such testing very well and is reproduced below.

The aircraft listed, as well as subsequent prototypes, were subsequently employed by Department E3 primarily on engine tests.

In the first quarter of 1940, the E-Stelle had also begun He 177 testing with the first four prototypes, but which suffered significant delays and numerous difficulties, among them: problems of vibration, undercarriage, powerplant and aircraft stability, and the loss of two prototypes in crashes. Nevertheless, discussions with firms concerning licence-manufacture had already taken place and in the E2 Weekly Report of 4th April 1940,[38] it can be seen that the 'series can be released for production, with certain reservations on construction parts on which alterations are to be expected in

the course of testing'. It can be thus clearly seen here, under what pressures the development and testing of new aircraft were being experienced following a period of years where only improvements to existing types had been undertaken.

Initial operational experiences in World War Two on both the British and the German side, soon led to according higher priority to further testing tasks over and above those that were already in progress. One in particular, was the necessity to improve the defensive capabilities of the Do 17, Ju 88 and He 111 bombers against enemy fire. In order to break through barrage-balloon defences, the introduction of balloon repellents was demanded. At the end of Febru-

Aircraft	Code	Date	From	To	Crew	Task	Remarks
Bü 181 V3	CO+DI	26.03.40	Rechlin	Rechlin	Kirschke	Workshop test flight	-
Bü 181 V3	CO+DI	29.03.40	Rechlin	Rechlin	Kirschke	Workshop test flight (2nd)	-
Bü 181 V3	CO+DI	30.03.40	Rechlin	Rechlin	Kirschke	Test flight max. rear cg	-
Bü 181 V3	CO+DI	01.04.40	Rechlin	Rechlin	Kuhn	Test flight	-
Bü 181 V4	CO+DH	25.04.40	Rechlin	Rechlin	Altrogge	Test flight	-
Bü 181 V4	CO+DH	08.05.40	Rechlin	Rechlin	Kirschke	T.o. landing characteristics for instruction purposes	-
Bü 181 V4	CO+DH	09.05.40	Rechlin	Rechlin	Kirschke	Test flight, min. rear cg	-
Bü 181 V4	CO+DH	10.05.40	Rechlin	Rechlin	Kirschke, Heller	Sortie & cross-country.	Meeting: V4 deficiencies/mock-up Hs 125
Bü 181 V3	CO+DI	15.05.40	Rechlin	Rechlin	Kirschke	Wing l.e. slats	-
Bü 181 V3	CO+DI	20.05.40	Rechlin	Rechlin	Kirschke, Görges	Climbing test.	Broken off due to leaky fuel-injection pipe.
Bü 181 V3	CO+DI	22.05.40	Rechlin	Rechlin	Schneider	Test flight	-
Bü 181 V3	CO+DI	25.05.40	Rechlin	Rechlin	Kirschke, Görges	Climbing test.	-
Bü 181 V3	CO+DI	27.05.40	Rechlin	Braunschw / Völkenrode	Kirschke	Sortie & cross-country	Parachute test M14 in LFA
Bü 181 V3	CO+DI	29.05.40	Braunschw / Völkenrode	Rechlin	Kirschke	Cross-country flight	-
Bü 181 V4	CO+DH	30.05.40	Rechlin	Prag	Kirschke	Cross-country flight	Discussion Zlin 14 prototype test
Bü 181 V3	CO+DI	30.05.40	Rechlin	Rechlin	Kuhn	Cross-country flight	-
Bü 181 V4	CO+DH	01.06.40	Prag/Gbell	Olmütz	Kirschke, Regel	Cross-country flight	Discussion Zlin 14 prototype test
Bü 181 V4	CO+DH	02.06.40	Olmütz	Rechlin	Kirschke, Regel	Cross-country flight	Discussion Zlin 14 prototype test
Bü 181 V4	CO+DH	08.06.40	Rechlin	Rechlin	Kirschke, Reinsch	Measurement stretch	-
Bü 181 V4	CO+DH	25.06.40	Rechlin	Rechlin	Kirschke	Workshop test flight	-
Bü 181 V3	CO+DI	27.06.40	Rechlin	Rechlin	Kirschke	Cross-country flight	Air bombardment DFS 229
Bü 181 V3	CO+DI	18.07.40	Rechlin	Gotha	Kirschke, Werner	Endurance test	Mock-up inspection Go 240
Bü 181 V4	CO+DH	01.08.40	Rechlin	Rechlin	Schneider	Workshop test flight	-
Bü 181 V4	CO+DH	03.08.40	Rechlin	Rechlin	Schneider	Towed flight	-
Bü 181 V4	CO+DH	09.09.40	Rechlin	Rechlin	Kirschke, Heller	T.o. & landing in rain	-
Bü 181 V4	CO+DH	10.09.40	Rechlin	Bremen	Kirschke	Duration flight	Inspection DFS 329 mock-up
Bü 181 V4	CO+DH	11.09.40	Bremen	Rechlin	Kirschke, Heller	Duration flight	Inspection Fw 191 mock-up
Bü 181 V4	CO+DH	14.09.40	Rechlin	Rechlin	Schneider	Test flight	-
Bü 181 V5	KK+MU	28.09.40	Rechlin	Schönefeld	Kirschke	Duration flight	Inspection Go 242 mock-up
Bü 181 V5	KK+MU	29.09.40	Schönefeld	Schönefeld	Kirschke, Stein	Duration flight	Flight test M09C
Bü 181 V5	KK+MU	30.09.40	Schönefeld	Rechlin	Kirschke	Duration flight	-
Bü 181 V4	CO+DH	01.10.40	Rechlin	Prag	Beauvais	Duration flight	-
Bü 181 V5	KK+MU	01.10.40	Rechlin	Prag	Kirschke, Heller	Duration flight	Zlin 15 prototype test
Bü 181 V4	CO+DH	02.10.40	Augsburg	Regensburg	Beauvais	Cross-country flight	-
Bü 181 V5	KK+MU	03.10.40	Prag	Zlin	Kirschke	Duration flight	Mock-up inspection
Bü 181 V5	KK+MU	04.10.40	Zlin	Zlin	Kirschke	Duration flight	-
Bü 181 V5	KK+MU	05.10.40	Zlin	Rangsdorf	Kirschke, Heller	Duration flight	-
Bü 181 V5	KK+MU	18.10.40	Rechlin	Gotha	Kirschke	Duration flight	Go 242 mock-up inspection
Bü 181 V5	KK+MU	11.11.40	Rechlin	Nürnberg	Kirschke	Duration flight	Go 242 V1 inspection
Bü 181 V5	KK+MU	13.11.40	Nürnberg	Böblingen	Kirschke	Duration flight	Test flight Kl 105
Bü 181 V5	KK+MU	15.11.40	Böblingen	Rechlin	Kirschke	Duration flight	-
Bü 181 V5	KK+MU	16.11.40	Rechlin	Rechlin	Kirschke, Behrmann	Test flight max. rear cg	-
Bü 181 V5	KK+MU	19.11.40	Rechlin	Rechlin	Kirschke, Behrmann	Test flight without cabin	-
Bü 181	KK+MV	12.03.41	Rechlin	Rechlin	Bergmann	Engine test	-
Bü 181	GL+AF	27.03.41	Rechlin	Rechlin	Bode	Duration flight	-
Bü 181	KK+MV	27.03.41	Rechlin	Rechlin	Reck, Bode	Range-measurement flight	-

After the beginning of World War Two various camouflage measures were tried out and evaluated by the E-Stelle Rechlin's Department E8 (Ground Equipment). Camouflaging the hangars of the Gruppe Nord as a 'housing colony' was discarded as it proved ineffective when the hangar doors were open. Despite this, the paint scheme remained unchanged throughout the war years.

ary 1940, the first such aircraft, the He 111R[39] together with a barrage-balloon arrived in Rechlin, followed three weeks later by a Do 17 and the Ju 88 V8 shortly afterwards. An initial approach flight at 260km/h (162mph) towards the balloon cable with the He 111R took place on 17th March 1940 where 'no influence on the aircraft and its flight path' could be determined. Further tests with strengthened balloon cables followed where in the April 1940 tests, the cable was cut through and the balloon continuously drifted away. It was simultaneously established that the wire cable-repellent previously employed on the aircraft was insufficient at higher speeds, so that a change had to be made to fixed steel-tube profiles with which the balloon was not only repelled but which cut the cable as well. This installation, however, not only led to a noticeable loss in aircraft speed, but significantly influenced its flight characteristics as well. Finally, it became possible to integrate the balloon repulsor in the form of

a 'Kuto-Nase' (balloon cable-cutter) on the fuselage and wing leading-edges. Hanna Reitsch is also reported to have undertaken some of the flight tests involving these balloon cable-cutters.

For defence against enemy aircraft attacking from the rear, the installation of rearward-directed flame-throwers were examined, but because of lack of capacity for the modifications in the Rechlin workshops was delayed until at least mid 1940, and in the end was not used operationally. So-called 'Störkörper' (interference bodies) were also developed, consisting of small explosive charges ejected from two barrels in the tail of the aircraft and suspended on parachutes, were to have been detonated with the aid of time fuses in front of the pursuing fighter. Flight testing this installation was also necessary, but the devices were rejected from an operational standpoint as being inadequate, being replaced by two rearward-firing machine-guns instead. This type of rearward armament is rather well documented through photographs and written reports, whereas the defensive method now related remains still widely unknown.

In summer 1940, the E-Stelle Rechlin tested a device known as the 'Ente' (duck) which supposedly is traceable to an idea from Ernst Udet. It apparently consisted of a rotating body suspended on the end of a rope or cable trailed behind the aircraft, that would damage or at least be a hindrance to an attacking aircraft. The first

release-test with the 'Ente' in cast-iron form, took place on 7th June 1940 with the Do 17P (DK+DN) which suffered severe damage to its rudders and elevators. Further release-tests with a pre-production 0-series followed until August 1940. Both the E-Stelle and the Heinkel firm developed 'Ente' designs in parallel but the minutes of a conference on 9th August 1940 recorded that, following a demonstration in Rechlin, the 'Rechlin variant' should be produced. In spite of this, the first and second prototype 'Heinkel-Ente' were air-dropped on 30th and 31st August 1940. At the end of September, Heinkel received a preliminary ruling on the 'Manufacture of the design and works drawings of the Rechlin-Ente, including installation drawings for the He 111, completion of prototypes in the He 111, and the manufacture of 100 Enten.'

Release-tests with the 'Ente' were continued in Rechlin from 6th November 1940, this time with the BV 141 (GL+AH). Testing stretched into April 1941 but thereafter suffered a long interruption, due no doubt to the fatal crash of the specialist pilot Ing. Helmuth Kuschke in a Go 242. Together with Dipl.-Ing. Werner Altrogge, he had been chiefly conducting the 'Ente' flight tests. At the beginning of 1942, the subject was again snatched up by order of the KdE, as the summary report of 15th March 1942 and Altrogge's related flight log-book entries contain: 'Ente comparison with the He 111' and 'Ente testing with the Do 217'. Nothing further is heard of the project thereafter, so it remains provisionally unknown, what the 'Rechlin-Ente' looked like and whether it achieved operational status. It may, however, serve as a further example of how the E-Stelle Rechlin continually conceived developments on its own initiative in all spheres of testing, such as the 'Rechlin-Emil' unified three-axis steering control, the 'System Rechlin' special slide-rule for evaluating flight performance, the Rechlin 'Kaltstartverfahren' engine cold-starting procedure, the HM 51 high-altitude breathing-mask and the 'Rechlin Ignition-sequence' for the Jumo 213 engine without whose introduction this powerplant would not have entered operational use.

Experience gained in initial wartime missions led to a further new task for the E-Stelle. It was soon manifest that the available medium bombers possessed too low a range or bomb-carrying capacity. The aircraft were often overloaded, leading to an increased risk at take-off and in flight, a deficiency for which various aids were sought to compensate. One of these was the use of jettisonable RATO units that had been tested at the Luftwaffe Test Establishment Peenemünde-West, and which was in fact adopted. Another method was the use of catapults for land-based aircraft which had been tested in Rechlin. This consisted of a jettisonable cable which was wound around a profiled cable-drum serving as a source of energy, capable of enabling an aircraft to become airborne in a very short distance. At the end of March 1940 various types of catapults, the KL 12/3, KL 12/4 and KL 12/5 were purchased through Department E8 and prepared for take-off trials and for crew training. It can be assumed that, as mentioned in the E2 Weekly Report of 25th April 1940, that the first catapult test with the Ju 88 V18 referred to these catapults. The August 1940 Terminal Report 'catapult take-off with the KL 12/6 from the catapult pit' shows that testing had been concluded, operational use having begun from January 1941. The order for testing a larger catapult – the Heinkel K 18 for aircraft up to 18 tonnes (39,680 lb)

weight proceeded apace only slowly, and in 1943, was included in the list of work to be cancelled. In summer 1943 a similar-working principle was tested in Rechlin, known as the 'Vorspann-Starthilfe' ATO system. It appears that a rolling tow-craft transferred its dynamic energy over a multiple-wound cable to an aircraft preparing to take off, before the aircraft itself loosened the cable and rolled out. In co-operation with the FGZ (Graf Zeppelin Research Institute) in Ruit near Stuttgart, initial trials were continued by the E-Stelle Lärz, which had also been closely involved in the development of catapults for land-based aircraft. Initial trials were conducted by the E-Stelle in Lärz, where an aircraft weighing 9 tonnes (19,840 lb) was accelerated to a take-off speed of 220km/h (137mph) in a take-off distance of 350m (1,148ft). Trials were scheduled to be continued, but as mentioned earlier, the RATO system was adopted because of its simplicity and flexibility.

Returning once more to the year 1940, when trials at Rechlin with the Me 210 V3, V5 and V8 prototypes were ongoing, a number of faults were encountered (oscillations, flight characteristics, undercarriage)

so that this design became a problem case. Particularly explosive during the testing phase was that at an early stage of the trials, the jigs and tools for series production had already been ordered far into the year 1941, but testing, accompanied by many failures and crashes required so many modifications and led to such serious delays that manufacture was finally terminated. It was a serious blow for the Messerschmitt firm and for the Luftwaffe, which had accorded this aircraft the highest 'Sonderstufe' (special status) priority in its 1939/40 procurement programme.[40]

Equally great difficulties were faced in the initial development phase of another new aircraft – the Fw 190. At the beginning of 1940, the first two prototypes developed engine cooling problems. Following replacement of the BMW 139 by the BMW 801 and redesign of the propeller boss, the Fw 190 V1 (RM+CA, Werk-Nr.0001) again arrived in summer 1940[41] in Rechlin for flight testing. The Fw 190 V2 (RM+CB), appeared in autumn at the E-Stelle Tarnewitz. The next prototype to be flight tested, the Fw 190 V5, came in the summer and then not to Rechlin, so that testing on a wider scale could not be accomplished.

Signs of lively activity in front of the East Hangar, with a Do 17, Ju 87, Hs 126 and various communications aircraft parked around. A different type of camouflage was tried out for this hangar, intended to be more in harmony with the surroundings. The strict geometrical form of the building, however, hindered its effectiveness.

The hydraulics of the BV 141 caused considerable problems. During the landing run, the starboard mainwheel unexpectedly retracted as seen here in the middle of the runway.

This is all the more astounding, since in the 1939/40 Procurement Programme, like the Me 210, the Fw 190 had also been accorded the highest 'Sonderstufe' priority.

The really new aircraft were therefore far from being thoroughly tested in 1940, E-Stelle activity being concentrated on the Ju 88, the Bf 109F-series, the new Bf 110 variants, and on the various Do 217 proto-types and 0-series aircraft. As an interim solution to the He 177 long-range bomber and reconnaissance aircraft which was not yet available, accelerated testing was undertaken of a military version of the Fw 200 civilian transport, known as the 'Kurier' (courier). Flight- and acceptance-tests with the new variant were conducted in a relatively short time in the first half of the year, partly through the presence of E-Stelle staff at the manufacturing centre. Nevertheless, because of the new demand placed on it, continual modifications were necessary – new engines, auxiliary fuel tanks due to the installation of weapon bays, fire-fighting and W/T equipment, all caused weight increases requiring strengthening of the airframe and under-carriage. Despite this, the necessary mea-surement flights were concluded by April 1940.

In retrospect, the year 1940 should not be forgotten with respect to a quite different type of aircraft which had undergone thor-ough testing since the beginning of the year – the Hs 129 ground-attack aircraft. Initial difficulties with its W/T, weapons installa-tions and electrical equipment had all been rapidly overcome. Not so, however, the mediocre performance in flight resulting from the weak powerplants and poor view for the pilot. Even so, the aircraft proved more successful than the competitive ground-attack version of the Fw 189, and following the installation of French Gnôme & Rhône radials and revised crew cabin, became a suitable ground-attack aircraft which, in its later B and C versions, contin-ually equipped with stronger armament and in operational use right up to and including 1945, was always present at the E-Stelle.

For the Rechliners, a year of consider-able activity came to an end in the course of which almost 30 members of the E-Stelle lost their lives in 1940. From the military aspect, the victories in Denmark, Norway, Belgium, Holland and France were fol-lowed by severe setbacks in the air war against the British Isles. Omissions in previ-ous rearmament planning now became highly apparent and indicated the urgent need for new types of aircraft, and were to lead to a further increase in testing activity in 1941.

Testing work, currently with the He 177 V4 to V8 prototypes inclusive, was substan-tially intensified. Alongside it, trials were to be continued with the Fw 190, Do 217 and the Me 210, as also with the D-version of the long-obsolete Ju 87. Although no serious deficiencies were encountered, the lack of a suitable ground-attack aircraft was clearly shown, since the Hs 129 and the Fw 190 in their ground-attack roles were still far from being combat-ready. The theatres of war had meanwhile fanned out and reached the Balkans, the Mediterranean and North Africa, and in June 1941, the USSR to the East. The E-Stelle thus received an increased number of foreign aircraft which it had to examine. As a result of a GL-Order issued in 1940,[42] every captured enemy air-craft, whether it was intended to be granted flight certification in Germany and whether used for training purposes or otherwise, had to undergo a brief evaluation in Rech-lin. It therefore created new and exacting tasks for the E-Stelle pilots!

In the 'Rechlin Letters', Flieger-Oberstab-sing. Harry Böttcher, the former head of Department E2, described the flight trials with a captured British Vickers Wellington bomber and gives an impression of the carelessness exercised in flight by a certain Ernst Udet who at that time was the Reich's Generalluftzeugmeister.

'... the workshops had made the night-bomber ready for flight. The initial aim was to become familiar with the aircraft and to gain a first impression of its flying qualities. After a few take-offs and landings, I then made somewhat longer flights between heights of 500m (1,640ft) and 1,000m (3,280ft) in order to determine whether its behaviour in straight flight, in turns or by disturbances, agreed with our expecta-tions. The first take-offs already indicated that the honeycomb type of construction lent the wings and even greater flexibility than we had been accustomed to with the Ju 52. On the ground, the wingtips hung really low, whilst in flight, they bend upwards and become noticeably warped. The lateral rolling moments were of course positive, but not particularly remarkable, so that the aircraft was not very responsive in turns and required some degree of effort. But perhaps I had not yet got everything out of the aircraft in these early flights.

I was on the point of taking off on an extended test flight when a Fieseler Storch landed right next to the starting flag, Udet stepping out hurriedly and indicating by signs that the take-off should be inter-rupted. A little later, he sat in the cockpit and let himself be familiarized by me with the handling procedures. I had known Udet for his stunt-flying ever since I was a student and was therefore prepared for all sorts of flying surprises. We had hardly taken off and had just begun to pick up speed when I saw that we were surrounded by cloud. I felt a little reassured that my seat still felt comfortable and that we had no untoward flight attitude. I was then pressed down enormously into the seat when we entered into a sharp turn and then came out of the clouds. Hardly had we left the clouds below us, when Udet with a sharp turn to the right and with raised tail surfaces descended into the clouds again. Because of the clouds, I could not see the wingtips and therefore could not know what deflexions were taking place. However, the opportu-nity to make such observations soon presented itself, for in the next move, Udet depressed the nose into a long straight flight in order to raise it again at a higher speed. Since he pulled up above the clouds, I was able to clearly see the folds and the 'Wellen' (waves, ripples, or undulations) on the upper surface of the wings and made Udet aware of this. When he saw the effects on the skinning of the upper wing surface, he adjusted the steering wheel very unobtrusively and then said laconically 'now I know why it is called the Wellington'. I don't know whether the sight of the rippled wing upper surface or whether the satisfaction of his curiosity was the cause for terminating the flight, but anyhow, we now descended calmly towards the landing-cross on the airfield. When the landing attitude as well as the altitude and speed threatened to get out of hand, I wanted to increase power by pushing the throttles forward, but Udet called out 'I am doing the flying'. We then heard a terrible bump, the machine groaned in all its joints and came momentarily to a standstill. Udet again calmly remarked ' It was indeed too high'. After a few taxying tests, we took off once more to make a circuit of the airfield. The eventual landing then proved that Udet had now got to know the Wellington.'

For captured enemy aircraft that arrived in Rechlin, there was also a specific identification code system in use from 1940. Evidently, such aircraft became successively numbered whereby the second digit was separated from the first by the 'Balkenkreuz' – the Luftwaffe cross insignia. The lowest known aircraft identifier of this type is 0+9 for a Dutch Fokker G Ia, the highest being 8+7 for a North American Mustang captured in France. This does not necessarily mean that only some 90 captured aircraft or so were flown at the E-Stelle, since a large number of foreign types, above all Czech, French and Italian, already bore specific markings when they arrived in Rechlin. In several flight log-book entries, no markings at all are indicated – at the most a Balkenkreuz – so that it is still not clear under what criteria and when, if at all,

special identification codes were allocated to captured aircraft. A list of known identification codes assigned to captured aircraft is given on page 118.

The ever-widening Luftwaffe operational theatres led increasingly to supply problems for the ground troops who often made very rapid advances in the field, but still the Luftwaffe had to make do with the reliable but yet aged and slow Ju 52. Load-carrying gliders like the DFS 230 originally conceived for setting down airborne troops at pinpoint locations, had to be called upon more and more to fulfil supply tasks. Already during the 1940 Western Campaign, the Ju 52 squadrons and especially during the occupation of Crete in May 1941, suffered enormous losses. A successor was not in sight. At first, development of larger load-carrying gliders were taken up. The Gotha aircraft company designed the Go 242, whose mock-up inspection took place on 18th July and 18th October 1940, the V1 prototype being inspected on 11th November 1940.

The V2 prototype had already been flown in January 1941 at the manufacturer's by E-Stelle personnel, and shortly afterwards, the first test aircraft arrived at the E-Stelle. Testing showed that it was necessary to strengthen the airframe, and Fliegerstabsing. Helmut Czolbe, whose sphere of activity included transport-glider testing, made a report about a crucial incident:

'One day, towed by an He 111, the Go 242 was to undertake a measurement flight at its fully-loaded weight. I went out to the airfield to witness the take-off. The tow-pair were positioned at the south-eastern corner in order to have a sufficient ground run. The surface there, however, was not quite even, and a disadvantage. The unloaded He 111 lifted off, whilst the fully-loaded Go 242 continued to bounce over the uneven surface. It was already a hazardous situation, but the Go 242 eventually rose from the ground. At the approximate landing time of the Go 242, I again made my way to the airfield. I saw Udet who occasionally

An Hs 129B (possibly DQ+ZO) on Rechlin airfield covered in deep snow in winter 1942. The B-series, equipped with French Gnôme & Rhône engines arrived for testing from 1941 onwards, fitted with various Rüstsätze (standard equipment sets), in this case with a ventral fuselage MK 103 cannon.

One of the earliest captured American aircraft in Rechlin was the Curtiss H 75 A, at least five of which came to the E-Stelle. Following exhaustive tests and use in propaganda film scenarios, the aircraft were handed over to fighter training schools.

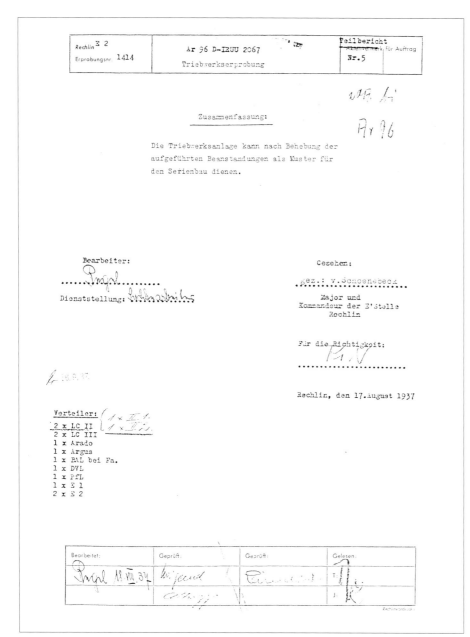

An example of an E-Stelle Rechlin Partial Report of 17th August 1937, in this case for the Ar 96 (D-IRUU, Werk-Nr.2067).

weeks later at the hands of the E-Stelle pilots B Flinsch, C Francke and H Reitsch. Even these tests suffered accidents, when Feldwebel Bernhard Flinsch of E2 was killed when he crashed in an Me 321 on 28th May 1941 on a landing approach to Obertraubling. Although the Me 321 came to the E-Stelle during 1941, the considerable preparations required for take-off, coupled with the inflexibility of this giant glider following a landing, resulted in interest soon shifting in favour of a motorized version, the Me 323. Even though the Me 323, equipped with four as well as six engines had also flown in 1941, flight trials only commenced in Rechlin the following year.

The deficit in transport space was expected to be overcome by means other than through load-carrying gliders. In September 1941, the E-Stelle Rechlin received the commission 'on all Luftwaffe aircraft which are available in large numbers, to carry out loading trials with various items'. That this could only serve as a temporary solution was clear from the further text contained in the order. Within a short time, the E-Stelle thereupon developed a transport container which became known as the 'Dobbas'. Dipl.-Ing. Ernst Hirschberg from the Advisory Group Referat E2f (Undercarriage Testing), who had been closely connected with Dobbas trials, recalls that:

'The maximum payload for each aircraft type had to be tested in flight, and was found to be 2 tonnes (4,409 lb) for the He 111 and Ju 88, 1 tonne (2,205 lb) for the Bf 110 and 600 kg (1,323 lb) for the Ju 87. Due to high air drag, there was a speed loss of 50 to 70 km/h (31 to 43 mph) depending on the type of aircraft, together with a considerable increase in the take-off run. Added to this were often unpleasant deteriorations to the flying characteristics. Series production was to have been undertaken by a small firm near Königgrätz in whose neighbourhood there was no airfield, so with special approval to fetch the 'Dobbas' containers, I landed and took off from a forest clearing of about 1 km (3,280 ft) in length and 200 m (650 ft) in width with the Ju 88, Bf 110 and Ju 87, also in winter snow conditions. Testing stretched out over almost the whole of 1942 and when it was finally completed, operational use of it became uninteresting because of the changed war situation.'

Among aircraft employed on 'Dobbas' testing were the Bf 110D (CG+OV), Bf 110F (TM+OS), He 111H-6 (RD+ZQ), Ju 87D

enthusiastically watched our flying operations, standing at one corner of a hangar and beside him, the head of our department. I placed myself in such a position that I could observe the expected landing stretch without hindrance. When the Go 242 touched the ground upon a flawless landing, both tail-booms broke off simultaneously immediately aft of the wings. The tailless fuselage continued to roll until it came to a halt in a cloud of dust. Udet angrily ordered the pilot to report to him. It was only after the pilot had no choice but to listen to a stormy reprimand about his miserable landing with its consequential damage, that I was able to explain to Udet the facts about the take-off and the unimpeachable landing – events that he was not able to observe from his vantage point. The investigation undertaken immediately,

revealed that the sturdily-built twin-booms, at the point where they overlapped with the continuation of the wing, and weakened by two holes which had been bored for the connecting bolts transmitting the forces, had broken-off at exactly this point – in other words, a design error!'

Unfortunately, within a very short time during trials with this aircraft, there were two fatal accidents in which the two Rechlin experts for load-carrying gliders, Ing. Helmut Kirschke and Ing. Rolf Quitter, were killed.

Dimensionally much larger than the Go 242 was a further project, to which the Messerschmitt and Junkers firms submitted proposals. In the end, only the Me 321, the largest glider aircraft in the world, which had accomplished its maiden flight in February 1941, was test flown a mere two

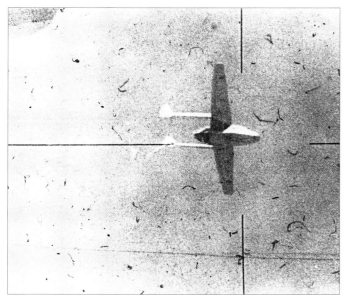

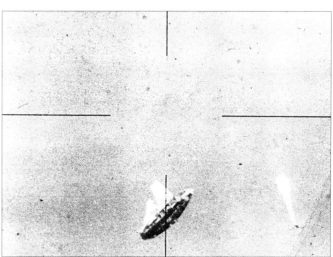

A spectacular film sequence taken by cinetheodolite at the Lärz Tracking Station on 18th March 1941. In a maximum-speed test flight with an early Go 242 prototype, the tailplane disintegrated, followed by the twin-booms and the starboard wing. The GWF company pilot Harmens was able to escape with his parachute, but flight mechanic Thomas was not able to leave the tumbling aircraft.

An He 177A (possibly VE+UN, Werk-Nr.15214), in summer 1942 on the Gruppe Nord compass-base. Behind it are the East Hangar and far beyond, the armoury.

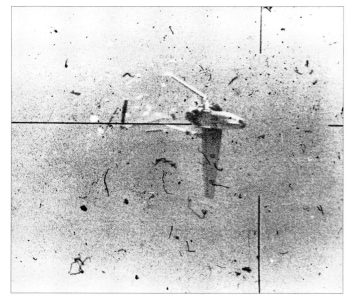

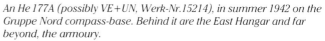

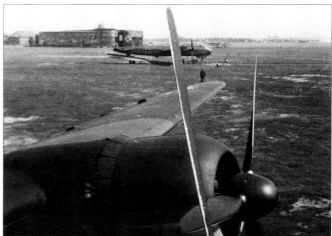

(CE+EN and DN+ZT) and the Ju 88A-4 (KA+ET) and Ju 88A-5 (VB+XH).

A reconstruction relating to the leadership of the E-Stelle Rechlin in 1941 presents some difficulty since official documents on the subject are missing. Definitely known is that on a flight on 31st August 1941 from Derna to Athens over the Mediterranean with an He 111, Fliegerstabsing. Kurt Fritsche and its entire crew from Rechlin were reported as missing. Fritsche's death meant a particularly heavy loss for the E-Stelle since, based on secondary information, from the end of 1939/beginning of 1940, he had been not only the head of testing, but the head of the E-Stelle as well. It is possible that at that time, both positions had been merged into one. However, beginning from June 1941, Fliegeroberstabsing. Francke – formerly head of Department E2, had already signed documents as head of the E-Stelle Rechlin, and it must be assumed that Fritsche at this time had already taken over a new task – possibly the erection of the E-Stelle Tropen (Tropics). Francke remained until at least the beginning of 1942 as head of the E-Stelle Rechlin (switching thereafter to the Heinkel firm) whilst from autumn 1941, the post of 'Kommando der E-Stellen der Luftwaffe' was resurrected and responsibilities handed over to Major Edgar Petersen, the former Kom-

modore of KG 40. This change, which brought about a considerably stronger military influence upon the course of development and testing, was certainly connected with the suicide of Generaloberst Udet on 17th November 1941.

The year 1941 finally came to an end with further drum-beating which did not augur well for the future: the German advance in Russia was halted short of Moscow in the icy winter, and the German Reich had declared war on the USA (on 11th December 1941).

In Rechlin, testing operations forged ahead at a rapid pace in 1942. Pre-eminently, there were the new series-models and variants of earlier types undergoing testing, among them the Bf 109G, Bf 110F and G, Do 217K, M and N, Fw 190, He 111H, He 177 and Ju 88A, B and C. The first prototypes of an improved aircraft, the Ju 188, arrived at the E-Stelle during the year, alongside a few new types which, despite good evaluation results, were eventually not produced in large numbers. Here was already a sign of lack of capacity in the German aircraft industry which was hardly able to replace training and frontline losses, not to mention large-scale production of newer designs. Added to this, there existed an increasing chaos in planning, whereby newer types, cancelled from the procure-

ment programme today, were re-instated the next day with the highest priority status. This was the case with the Ar 232, Ar 240, Fi 256, Go 244, Ju 252 and eventually the He 219, whose first examples arrived at the Müritz in 1942 but of which only a few prototypes or at best a small series were produced. Additionally, there was the Si 204D version with which the Luftwaffe finally obtained a suitable training aircraft for W/T operators and blind-flying training. An exotic type appearing in Rechlin during the same period was the He 111Z, conceived as a towing-craft for the Me 321 large transport glider. Relevant flight testing was carried out in Rechlin, as well as with two Go 242 gliders towed simultaneously. For jet-propelled aircraft undergoing development, the year 1942 finally resulted in progress. The Me 262 was able to accomplish its first pure jet flight in July 1942, after its rival the He 280 with Heinkel turbojets had already achieved this on 30th March 1941. From the very outset, the E-Stelle was closely connected with flight testing, and its pilots soon had the opportunity to test fly the new prototypes. Whilst one of the earliest jet-propelled He 280 prototypes was able to be test flown in Rechlin in 1942, this first became possible with the Me 262 in 1943.

Typical Flight Testing Sequence with the Go 244

The deficit in towing-craft already mentioned, the inflexibility of gliders after landing and the lack of a successor to the aged Ju 52/3m, led to consideration in 1941 to motorize the Go 242 by use of the large quantities Gnôme & Rhône 14M captured engines available from France. This led to the twin-engined Go 244 whose development has been extremely sparsely covered in literature. On hand from existing documentation[43] covering reports on flight tests conducted in Rechlin, the course of testing can be extensively followed. Although it is not known with certainty how many test reports were compiled altogether, out of the first 19 reports 15 still exist, a fortunate situation that is not to be found for any other aircraft tested in Rechlin. This therefore enables an almost complete history of testing to be reconstructed, so that the Go 244 serves as an example for the innumerable other prototype tests conducted by the E-Stelle.

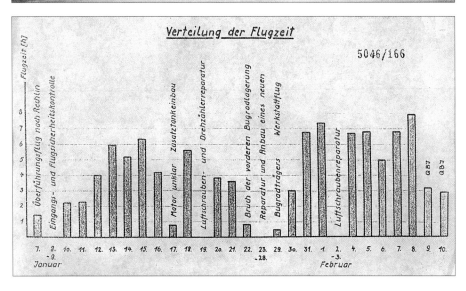

The last documented Go 244 at the E-Stelle Rechlin was RJ+II, used until April 1944 for transportation flights.

When a new prototype arrived at the E-Stelle, flight testing was conducted with it every day of the week, interrupted only by repairs or bad weather. The chart represents the 100-hour test sequence of the Go 244 V2.

On 7th January 1942, the Go 244 V2 (Werk-Nr.00019) was ferried over from Gotha to Rechlin, and was evidently the first prototype of this design that came to the E-Stelle. The entry-control procedure commenced immediately. Flight testing began from 10th January and already on 17th January, Partial Report No 2 on Test Number 1884 (Go 244 Development and Test) had been prepared. It commented upon some deficiencies but is unfortunately not available, neither is Partial Report No 1. The third Report (Go 244 Flight tests in Rechlin) contained an initial collective judgement in which the type was described as 'an aircraft easy to handle both on the ground and in the air'. Take-off and landing were conceivably simple and the flying qualities good, ignoring minor deficiencies. The aircraft was more pleasant to fly than the Ju 52, but its performance and flying characteristics in single-engine flight with a 1.2 tonne (2,646 lb) payload was found to be just possible for even skilled pilots. The maximum payload, however, was supposed to be 2.5 tonnes (5,512 lb)! Here, a problem had already been discovered, which was one of the reasons why the design did not enjoy success at a later date, ie, weak engine power and little payload. Besides these points, other minor deficiencies were listed which were able to be corrected with a minimum of effort.

As early as 10th February 1942, the first 100-hour duration testing was able to be completed without any significant airframe or engine problems, as confirmed in Partial Report No 4. The focal point of E-Stelle criticism centred on the poor undercarriage ground-roll characteristics. A weak point on the nosewheel support had already been criticized by the E-Stelle and modified by the manufacturer for series production machines. The other points criticized had also been taken up and rectified by the Gothaer Waggonfabrik (GWF) and incorporated in series production documentation, as shown in a communication of 31st January 1942. In Partial Report No 6 of 24th February, however, ten new deficiencies were listed after 140 hours of testing, of which three were to be rectified immediately – strengthening the rear fuselage locking mechanisms, redesign of the mass-balance support on the Flettner elevator servo-tab, and remodelling of specific shaped fittings for the fuselage coverings. For the remaining deficiencies, modification proposals were required to be presented by the GWF within one week. These included for example, rectifying the danger of injury due to the absence of a head cushion on a cross-brace, unacceptable draught from the door seal, and a fuel tank support which lay so low that the normal pipe-fitting could not be screwed onto it.

The next Test Report of 15th April 1942 stated that prototype evaluation, except for the W/T installation had been completed and that testing was 80% concluded. Take-off and range measurements as well as descents had been determined in which the values provided by the GWF had been confirmed. Still to be corrected were minor airframe deficiencies besides the single-engine flying characteristics, the fuel tank switching, and above all, the undercarriage which had been passed by the E-Stelle up to a maximum flying weight of 6.8 tonnes (14,992 lb), whereas another 1 tonne (2,205 lb) payload that was supposed to be carried, had not been catered for! Up to the end of April, Partial Report No 8 stated that flights to determine the cg regime had been carried out with various loadings. The poor flying qualities in single-engine flight continued to occupy the E-Stelle, so much so that in Partial Report No 10 of 15th May, demands for urgent improvements were again reiterated. The rectifications experimentally introduced by GWF to relieve spring loads on the elevator was shown to have been completely insufficient. Since the variable-pitch Gnôme & Rhône propellers employed up until then were all apparently required for the Hs 129, fixed-pitch wooden propellers of 2.7m (8¾ft) and 2.8m (9¼ft) diameter had been developed which were now to be tested on the Go 244 (VC+OJ, Werk-Nr.00010). Simultaneously, an improved undercarriage was also to be tested. Both together, however, reduced the cruising speed near the ground to only 170km/h (106mph), and hence to the level of the recommended climbing speed! Even at 1,000m (3,280ft) altitude, flying speed at maximum permissible continuous power at full load was no higher than 205km/h (127mph). Added to that, the noise discomfort caused by the fixed-pitch propellers had reached the limit of tolerability, according to Partial Report No 12 of 11th August 1942. Engine testing, which had in the meantime also begun with the Go 244 (VC+OJ) as well as the Go 244 (TE+UK, Werk-Nr.00047), indicated the necessity to reduce cylinder temperature by altering the mixture regulation, installing larger lubricating oil-coolers and greatly enlarging the lubricant tanks so that the cold-start-system requirements could be met. Also, inclusion of an engine starter injection system was necessary. The undercarriage, nevertheless, still remained the greatest problem with the Go 244. From testing results obtained in the meantime, the nosewheel undercarriage had been strengthened and the main undercarriage – formerly a fixed-axis arrangement, was replaced with an outrigger type, as noted in Partial Report No 17 of 17th August 1942. Larger wheels were also experimentally tried. Exhaustive

ground runs and landing-shock measurements had shown namely, that the undercarriage had been too weakly designed to cater for ground runs. The above measures taken greatly improved its roll and strength (stability) characteristics, but resulted in a weight increase of 140kg (309 lb) and a speed loss of up to 23km/h (14mph). The corresponding reduction experienced in climbing speed in loaded condition from 2.3m/sec (453ft/min) to a mere 1.25m/sec (246ft/min) was regarded as no longer acceptable, to which came a noticeable deterioration in the flight characteristics around the vertical and lateral axes. As the Partial Report No 19 of 20th September had established, re-equipping the Go 244 with Gnôme & Rhône engines and v-p propellers onto the 'improved' undercarriage was workwise not possible, and even less thinkable with the use of the unfavourable fixed-pitch propellers. Hence the lower loaded weight limit of 6.8 tonnes (14,992 lb) established by the E-Stelle had to remain in force. In order to turn the aircraft into a 'useful auxiliary transporter', it was necessary as the sole possibility imaginable, to equip it with the BMW 132L or M each having 170hp more than the current powerplants. But probably because of lack of availability of the BMW 132 for this purpose, this was never achieved. Hence, of the few hundred Go 244 examples built and according to the Modification Plan 223/1 of 1st December 1943, 324 aircraft were to be reconverted as Go 242 gliders. Altogether, 13 various Go 244s can be confirmed as having been at the E-Stelle Rechlin until May 1943 including one example until April 1944 that had been engaged in testing and transportation duties, and partially even been used in operational trials on the Eastern Front. No documents, however, are available concerning experiences gathered in the latter category.

Multiple Testing Tasks for the E-Stelle

On looking back on the activities of the E-Stelle, it should not be forgotten that besides the inherent need for flight testing new aircraft, a large measure of the daily tasks involved the examination of propulsion units, parts of systems and individual equipment. It was not without a purpose that besides the Department responsible for overall planning and type-testing, the sphere of tasks was initially divided among three subordinate sections, and with a further distribution of tasks, as many as eight specialist sections. For the E-Stelle Rechlin, a detailed list of these supporting groups is provided on pages 127-129.

Of particular significance, in view of the number of its Referate (specialist advisory groups) and personnel strength, was the Powerplant Department E3. Its obligations

concerned the testing not only of new engines, but also complete installations and systems, individual separate components, and airscrews as well as fuels and lubricants. Testing was conducted not only in numerous special static engine test-beds, but also in flight.

As already mentioned elsewhere, following its defeat at the end of World War One, there was an especial need felt in Germany for recovery and development in the aero-engine sector, caused particularly by the harsh limitations imposed by the Treaty of Versailles. The few German engines available in the 1920s that had been manufactured by BMW, Daimler, Junkers, and Siemens & Halske, were hardly advanced in their status of development beyond that of 1918.[44] With the manufacture and the licence of foreign engines such as the Gnôme Jupiter and the Pratt & Whitney Hornet, an attempt was made to once more attain the technical state achieved abroad. In the mid 1930s, however, it still proved necessary for the first prototypes of newer aircraft – the Ar 80, Bf 109, He 112, Ju 87, Hs 122 and so on – to be powered by the Rolls-Royce Kestrel engine in order to achieve a reasonably acceptable flying per-

formance. Examples of this engine had been previously evaluated at the E-Stelle Rechlin on the very first engine test-bed to be put into operation since 1933. A large number of German aircraft prototypes at this time had still been fitted with the BMW VI of 690 to 750hp (508 to 552kW) before, in gradual stages, the first DB 600 and Jumo 210 carburettor-engines became available. In mid 1936, these three engines were still the principal types undergoing testing, joined by the first examples of engines from Hirth (HM 4, HM 6, HM 60) and Argus (As 10) and the BMW 132. This meant conducting 100 hour and 200 hour duration tests to determine the operating safety and reliability of specific components parts or materials. For the new engines and powerplant installations, a large number of auxiliary equipment items, under development by the contracting companies, also had to be thoroughly tested. An extensive field of activity developed from the rapidly-growing demand for high-performance fuels and lubricants. The E-Stelle was also engaged at this time on a system which enabled engines to be cold-started at very low ambient temperatures. Becoming widely-known later as the KSV or 'Rechlin Kaltstartverfahren'[45]

Measurement engineers at work in a Ju 52 fuselage in Rechlin. Instead of the centrally-mounted BMW 132 in some aircraft, an engine due to undergo testing, eg, the DB 603, DB 605 or Jumo 213, was installed. The principal service of these flying test-beds was to measure performance and fuel consumption as well as to conduct endurance tests.

On the fully-rotatable Test Stand, propeller engines could be tested in various operating conditions.

it still took some time to be accepted by frontline service units. The basic aim of this method was thinning the lubricant with petrol (gasoline) which prevents the lubricating oil from becoming sluggish on the cold engine and causing the lubricating fluid to rupture upon starting. In an extensive series of tests, the staff of the Rechlin specialist department were able to prove that the system, in contrast to widely-held fears, was not dangerous and above all was effective. The 'Engine Starting in Winter' was finally published in the form of a Luftwaffe Regulation and its application made compulsory. All aircraft were hence forth equipped with 'cold-start' equipment, the E-Stelle Rechlin compiling a mixture table for each aircraft or engine, for which a large number of flight tests were necessary.

Whilst work on the KSV was proceeding, the first aero-engines with petrol-injection appeared in development, on whose testing the E-Stelle concentrated more and more from 1936/37. The 1,000hp (735kW) DB 601 and 730hp (535kW) Jumo 210 served as basic designs for the much-modified and higher-performance DB 603, DB 605, Jumo 211 and Jumo 213 which were built in large numbers. Until the end of World War Two, these were to have served as standard equipment in German aircraft and in their numerous variants, were correspondingly continually undergoing testing in Rechlin. Furthermore, from the As 10, Argus had developed the As 410 and As 411 in the 600hp (445kW) class, and at the end of the 1930s, there appeared the first German twin-row radial, the BMW 801, initially of 1,600hp (1,175kW), but which only matured sufficiently for series production in 1941/42. Alongside these were the BMW 132 and Bramo 323 radials, initially laid out as carburettor types but later as fuel-injector types which remained in operational use for many years and therefore also subject to testing in Rechlin.

With new engines or series production models, the test sequence was as follows: the 'bare' engines were initially subjected to measurement and duration runs on the static engine test-beds, and then installed as the central motor in the Ju 52 flying test-bed. At the E-Stelle Rechlin, among known Ju 52 flying engine test-beds were the D-AHOR (DB 600), DM+DX (DB 605), DT+GA (Jumo 222), GS+AP (Jumo 208), GS+AQ (DB 603), GS+AR (DB 601 and DB 605), GS+AU (Jumo 213), GS+AV (Jumo 222) and PB+UA (DB 603 and Jumo 213). As a final step, the engine, complete with all ancillary equipment needed for its operation and in flight (exhaust, ignition, lubrication, and cooling systems) were tested on the engine measurement test-stand followed by flight trials in aircraft intended to receive it.

In the course of flight trials in new aircraft, problems often came to light which could not have been anticipated on the test-stand, the reason for this lying in the various installation layouts. Well-known are the initial susceptibilities of the DB 606 (comprised of two coupled DB 601s) and the DB 610 (two coupled DB 605s) in the He 177. The E-Stelle Rechlin had already ascertained at an early date and pointed out the weak points of the engine installation and had put forward modification proposals (altering the position of the engines, the fire-proof bulkhead, the oil pipes to prevent foaming, the propeller-gearing oil tanks and the coverings of the inner exhaust stacks). Even so, it still took years until all these modifications were introduced and the aircraft relieved of its engine problems.[46]

A general problem at that time existed in the cooling system and the cooler for the lubricant or for the oil, whose effectiveness was strongly dependent upon the layout of the conduits, and as related above, were dependent upon the quantity of cooling air.

Comprehensive vibration tests conducted in Rechlin by members of Measurement Section E3e led by Dipl.-Ing. G Hentschel enabled design faults with the DB 603 and Jumo 213 to be discovered, corrected by means of a new ignition sequence.

Added to this were material and manufacturing problems from the licence-firms, which constantly caused delays and setbacks to testing schedules.

The continual increase in engine performance and power caused equal increases in material problems such as the configuration of crankshaft bearings and their lubrication, not to mention vibration problems encountered. During engine tests in Rechlin with the Jumo 213 for example, it was established that because the ignition sequence selected by the manufacturer resulted in strong vibrations, the engine was unsuitable for operational use. The Engine Department's Measuring Group had established that this was caused (for installation reasons) by a subsequently-introduced propeller-shaft extension which led to oscillation in the major rotational speed range of the engine and to overcome the problem, had put forward an altered ignition sequence which had been effectively tried out in Rechlin.[47] On the strength of this,

the Junkers firm was compelled to alter the design and recall the engines already delivered for retroactive modification. Similar problems with the DB 603 were also able to be eliminated as a consequence of testing results obtained by Rechlin's test engineers.

The E3 Measurement Unit also handled numerous other special tasks, including measuring engine torque, fuel-flow rates and fuel consumption, oil-scum measurements in the lubricating circuits, sound radiations from engines and exhausts, examinations on vibration occurrences during weapons-firing tests, airscrew vibration stresses, and fundamental questions relating to a possibly vibration-free engine installation in the airframe of the aircraft. In the course of this work conducted by Rechlin engineers and technicians – partly independently and partly in co-operation with industry, a series of measuring instruments were developed, such as the 'automatic observer' in 1944 – a recording camera

which registered the readings of a total of 13 important measuring instruments installed in a single instrument panel and provided with reflection-free lighting. Another was the 'Felgner-Dehnungsmesser' for measuring elongations/expansions.[48]

New tasks were added with the development of TL-Triebwerke (turbojet engines), the BMW 003 and Jumo 004. Within the Engine Department, the new Referat E3a5 was created, led by Fliegerstabsing. Johann Ruther, concerned exclusively with jet propulsion units. One of the few Rechlin engineers still alive who had taken an important part in this advance into the jet age was Dipl.-Ing. Heinz Borsdorff, who as pilot and expert, was transferred to the E-Stelle Department E3 in June 1941. As a former employee concerned with engine development at Argus and subsequently, a blind-flying instructor in the Luftwaffe, he possessed ideal qualifications for this task. Fifty years later, Heinz Borsdorff recalled the following:

'TL-engine testing began in Rechlin at the beginning of 1943. According to the Test Reports in front of me, the first measurements of the Jumo 004A V11 unit per Partial Report No 1, were concluded on 18th February 1943. The values supplied by the manufacturer were checked out and found to be in order.

TL-unit flight testing took place using several Ju 88s. The turbojets, each fitted with an intake cowling but otherwise left uncovered, hung on a special suspension beneath the port wing. Operating and measuring installations were located inside the crew compartment in the hands of the Test Engineer.

Partial Report No 2 of 4th June 1943 deals with further testing of the Jumo 004A V11. Until this date 14.5 hours of testing had taken place on static test-stands at Junkers and in Rechlin, 7.5 hours of static runs in the flying test-bed aircraft and 14 hours in flight tests, the flights also serving to calibrate the measuring instruments. On one flight at 8,300m (18,300ft) the compressor was found to function faultlessly at 8,450rpm in full-load operation, and no damage worth mentioning surfaced. After this, the V11 unit was exchanged for another one representing the latest state of development.

The first prototypes of the new TL-Triebwerke (turbojets) arrived in Rechlin in spring 1943 for testing, for which purpose a special Test Stand was built. The Jumo 004A V11 prototype engine is seen here undergoing testing in February 1943.

Test Stand runs were followed by flight testing where, as in this case, a Jumo 004A is seen suspended beneath the Ju 88A-5 (GF+HQ).

Stabsing. Borsdorff had luck despite misfortune when after a test flight on 8th October 1943 in the Bf 109G-6 (TR+GT) with a dead engine, it landed short of the runway in a soft field and overturned, the pilot escaping uninjured.

Following tests with other units, Partial Report No 4 of 27th August 1943 mentions the conclusion of the first 100 hour duration test with the Jumo 004A, Werk-Nr.A 015) in which the turbine wheel, due to blade cracks, had to be exchanged after 68 hours. Subsequent to dismantling, a number of defects were found which appeared to be capable of rectification.

Partial Report No 11 of 19th July 1944 describes Jumo 004 testing under icing conditions. There were no particular objections to be raised; the build-up of ice on the intake cowling and on the intake profiles broke away due to the airflow and were swallowed by the turbojet without untoward effects.

Testing of the BMW 003 first began a few months after the Jumo 004. Static test-bed measurements and initial test flights with the BMW 003A, Werk-Nr.012, were described in Partial Report No 1 of 27th October 1943. Starting behaviour on the ground as well as in flight was generally bad, and ignition above 3,000m (9,840ft) was not possible at all.

In the Report dated 29th June 1944, its poor starting behaviour, vibration and humming encountered when increasing the revolutions was again referred to. The intensity of the vibrations varied in the fuel-injection pump, governor, and engine systems. Testing was conducted with the BMW 003A Werk-Nr.035 and 040.

Partial Report No 6 of 30th September 1944 established that:
- Ignition was successful in tests up to 4,000m (13,120ft) altitude with the starting fuel.
- The engine governor did not function reliably. With the BMW 003A, Werk-Nr.061, there were rpm undulations at 7,000m (22,960ft). In climbing flight up to 6,000m (19,685ft) and 8,000m (26,250ft), the turbine-exhaust temperature control T5 remained constant with engine Nr.061 whereas with engine Nr.074 it increased above 6,000m (19,685ft).
- Testing with J2 fuel. With TL-unit Nr.061, the turbine wheel failed after 18 hours of operation, the compressor of TL-unit Nr.074 failing due to foreign object ingestion.

Partial Report No 11 of 22nd December 1944 established that the starting characteristics were dependent upon the fuel injection nozzles and injection pumps. With a nozzle diameter of 0.6mm (0.02in) and the Bar-

mag pump, results were tolerable. The idling behaviour was also improved with these nozzles.

Partial Report No 15 of 6th February 1945 contained a summary of tests over the previous 4 months. Damages encountered on a total of 28 engines were divided into: compressor 17%, turbine 19%, gearing failures 13%, thrust nozzle 13%, bullet nozzle mechanism 0%, oil consumption 12%, Riedel starter 11%, and labyrinth-feed 8%.

At the end of January 1944 I was transferred to Roggentin where Jumo 004 and BMW 003 flight testing had been conducted since mid 1943. I commenced my activities in this sphere with my flight number 3192 on 27th January 1944 in the Ju 88A-4 (DH+JX). In all, I undertook 13 flights with this aircraft until 3rd March 1944, including cross-country flights to Dessau for meetings with Junkers engineers.

In between, flights were very often carried out for the E3 Motoren-Referate. On 31st May 1944, my conversion-training took place in Lechfeld on the Me 262A (VI+AH) whose undercarriage was not retractable. In the meantime, our Department had received an Si 204D (BP+FK) powered by Argus As 411 engines for duration testing, and with this aircraft I flew to several conferences.

My first flight with the Me 262A (E3+01) in Lärz, followed on 19th June 1944. On 1st July 1944, I took off in the Ju 88 V41 (DE+EK) on a measurement flight to 8,000m (26,250ft) with the suspended Jumo 004. After that, the aircraft was utilized in the course of duration testing to fetch W/T equipment for the Me 262, for which purpose we flew to Grossenhain in Sachsen. Upon landing in Rechlin, the starboard undercarriage leg buckled.

Thanks to the BMW 801 engine, I was able to take off again successfully. After

examining the in-flight behaviour and checking instrument indicators, I made a renewed landing approach. Again the starboard undercarriage leg buckled, but did not fully close properly this time, remaining semi-suspended beneath the closed undercarriage doors. Hectic discussion followed, whereupon the W/T equipment in the underfuselage pannier was relocated to between the crew seats. The suspended Jumo 004 was the first to be equipped with double fuel-injection jets in the combustion chamber to prevent the flame being suddenly extinguished with too-rapid throttle movement and to improve the idling behaviour at altitude. We decided to jettison the turbojet near the bank of the Müritz so as to minimize damage to it upon impact. On the other hand, the turbojet suspended beneath the port wing and the semi-extended starboard undercarriage, gave us to some extent the possibility of making a horizontal landing. After jettisoning the cockpit canopy, I prepared for the landing which fortunately turned out well for us, except that the engine and aircraft were badly damaged. On 13th July 1944, I ferried over a Ju 388 from Rechlin via Dessau to Lechfeld. It was my first-ever flight in a pressure-cabin at 9,000m (29,530ft) altitude without an oxygen mask.

In flight number 3417 on 19th August 1944, I attained an altitude of 10,000m (32,800ft) in the Me 262A (E3+02). This flight was again in connection with the dual problem of flame-extinction caused by too-rapid movement of the fuel lever and the engine's idling behaviour. Further flights followed with this aircraft on 16th and 21st September, and on 2nd and 3rd October 1944 at altitudes between 10,000m (32,800ft) and 11,500m (37,730ft).

On 12th September 1944 I took off on a measurement flight in the Ju 88A-4 (VL+ZF).

Upon deciding to land after a trouble-free 13-minutes flight and upon extending the landing flaps, my control lever shifted to port and remained blocked there. Since upon extending the landing flaps the ailerons also became deflected, I immediately thought of the aileron blocking mechanism which the flight mechanic had probably forgotten. As I had developed the habit of bringing the Ju 88 in to land in a rather steep approach, I still had time to retract the landing flaps, circuit the airfield, and land in Lärz without the use of flaps. The aileron lock was indeed in place, but had exercised so much freedom that I had not noticed anything in flight. We removed it, the mechanic was given an orderly reprimand, and seven minutes later we took off in the direction of Roggentin where we landed without any problems.

In a flight with the Me 262A (E3+02) on 13th October 1944, I noticed a gentle vibration in one of the turbojets at 10,000m (32,800ft). However, I was not able to tell from reading the instruments, which engine it was. I shut down the starboard TL-unit, but the vibration still remained, so I had therefore shut the wrong one. As I had already carried out several start-up tests in test-bed aircraft as well as with the Me 262, I glided slowly down to 2,500m (8,200ft) altitude, where I first attempted an engine light-up, but without success. I repeated the same at 2,000m (6,560ft) and again at 1,500m (4,920ft), still without success. I consequently decided to make a power-off landing. The emergency compressed-air undercarriage extension worked, but I was still too high to reach the runway aligned at 340° and too low for the 260° runway. I decided upon a grass-landing in a roughly 300° heading. Upon nearing the ground, I noticed that the main landing strip was occupied. It so happened that work was at that time in progress to alter the take-off area, so that workshop trucks, wireless trucks, and a few Me 262s being towed by NSU tracked-vehicles were all on the way from the western end of the runway to the eastern. I had the greatest of good luck to

pass through a gap in this convoy. I was, of course, heavily berated for my landing, but I was happy to have made it unscathed. The loss of a turbine blade was later found to be the cause of the vibration.

In the meantime, we had also received a two-seater Me 262B (E3+04) on which I conducted instruction flights for several colleagues on the 18th and 23rd December 1944. On 28th December 1944, I was again up in the Me 262 (E3+01) on a test flight up to 11,000m (36,100ft) altitude.

In the final weeks, a few Me 262s were being re-equipped in the workshops in Lärz with BMW 003 turbojets. On three of these aircraft, I carried out the first 'works' flights, such as that on 20th January 1945 with the Me 262 (E3+32). The starboard engine failed, but the single-engine landing was without mishap. Since I had meanwhile had experience of single-engine landings with the Jumo 004-powered Me 262, I therefore knew that with extended landing flaps and undercarriage, ie, at low speeds of some 200km/h (124mph), applying full throttle when too short of the runway meant that the rudder was too small to hold the aircraft on course. I still remember this landing very well. I was too short and had to apply full power. In order not to turn to the right, I banked the aircraft to the left and accelerated the left turbojet. The ground crew visualized a crash and scattered in all directions. I returned the aircraft to the horizontal again and made a problem-free landing.

On 2nd February 1945 a fatal accident occurred with a BMW 003-powered machine. A Captain, delegated to Lärz for conversion training on the Me 262, was later to have been occupied with flight testing at BMW. The two-seater was not available and I had to continually console the Captain since there was no Jumo 004-powered Me 262 available either. Finally, I relented and had the BMW 003-powered Me 262 (E3+32) made ready for him.

Following detailed instruction and pointing out in particular to be very cautious with the throttle levers, he took off without any

problems. After a while, however, he reported that both engines had flamed out. I gave him the instruction to make a belly-landing on grass with the aircraft. Despite this, he attempted a normal landing approach and crashed with fatal results about 1km (0.62 miles) short of the airfield because flying speed was too low.

On 18th February 1945 I made the first 'works' flight with the BMW 003-powered Me 262 (E3+36). It was a very short flight – only about seven minutes. The aircraft lifted off very rapidly, and I had my hands full to slow down the climb by pushing the control stick to its maximum forward position. By reducing power I was able to make a furtive circuit of the airfield and land again. In the workshops, the weapons had been removed from the forward fuselage bay, but they had forgotten to replace them with the appropriate ballast so as to bring the aircraft cg back to the correct position. On the next flight on the afternoon of 19th February, the desired result was achieved.

With the Ju 88 (VL+ZF), I ferried over a Jumo 004 to Munich-Oberwiesenfeld on 1st March 1945 for examination. The BMW Works there had a high-altitude test-chamber where the following flight conditions with a running engine could be set: Air mass-flow 20kg/sec (44 lb/sec) at sea-level; altitudes 0 to 16km (52,500ft); speed 0 to 900km/h (559mph) and an air temperature of –60°C to +60°C. Measurements were carried out on the turbojet there, but could only be accomplished at night since the compressor, suction-pumps and so on, were electrically driven and we required the entire power supply for the town of Munich. On 6th March 1945, I flew the turbojet back to Lärz.

On the last flight with the Me 262 (E3+36), I flew the aircraft over from Lärz to Burg near Magdeburg, where shortly afterwards the first meeting took place concerning the relocation of Department E3 to southern Germany, as flight testing activity at Rechlin was approaching its end...'

Reciprocating engine development and testing had reached its peak in spring 1945. In Rechlin, the 2000hp (1470kW) DB 605 and the 2200hp (1620kW) BMW 801 engines had been test flown in the flying test-bed. These increases in performance were only possible by raising the rpm, the

A large number of tail brake-chute landing tests took place in Rechlin in summer 1942. In these, a Ju 52 (here the NI+NT) was to break through enemy defences as soon as possible in a steep dive with folded tail-chute, and immediately before contact with the runway, open the parachute and thus reduce the landing run.

Final preparations being made prior to the next test flight in an He 177. Measurement and control instruments were installed on an auxiliary panel ahead of the flight mechanic's position.

boost-pressures up to 2 atm, and by use of GM-1 (nitrous oxide) and MW-50 (water-methanol) injection. Documentary evidence of engine test flights which took place in the final month, included flights with the 2250hp (1655kW) DB 603EB units in the Ju 88 (SL+QW), the 2050hp (1500kW) Jumo 213 in the Ju 188 (DN+HF), and the 2000hp (1470kW) DB 605C in the Bf 109K-4 (VN+GV) and the Ju 52 (GS+AR).[49] Even when these tests had furnished positive results, they were no longer able to significantly alter the course of the war since they consisted mostly of special variants of engines available in only very small numbers.

The Department E5, responsible for testing aircraft equipment, had approximately the same personnel strength as the Power-plant Department E3. The multiplicity of their tasks were probably the greatest, and encompassed the spheres of: aircraft instruments; cameras, films and ancillaries; rescue- and safety-devices; electrical aircraft systems; autopilots and hydraulic installations. Hence, items to be tested ranged from the simple key switch or lever right up to complete automatic flight controls and gyro platforms. Its sub-division of activity spheres had mostly existed since the mid 1930s, except that the group dealing with hydraulic installations was formed later. Because of the vast spectrum of tasks which it had to handle, it is impossible to provide even a near all-round approximation of Department E5's activities. Participation by the E-Stelle Rechlin in the testing of rescue- and safety-devices, airborne equipment as well as automatic course controls, has been described in other volumes of 'Die Deutsche Luftfahrt' series already published.[50]

Attention will therefore be drawn here only to that portion of Rechlin involvement on the development of flight regulators conducted in the 1930s by the group led by Dr.-Ing. Waldemar Möller,[51] development of items for oxygen systems, as well as the testing of rescue- and load-carrying para-chutes and ejection seats.

In addition to a large number of the Department's own laboratories and work-shops, the E5 also had some test aircraft that had been set aside for its use. For the large number of parachute release tests, specially-equipped test aircraft were necessary. Likewise, new instruments, components for the hydraulic or electrical systems

and cameras could be installed in these aircraft as needed. Accordingly, E5 possessed far into the war years, aircraft such as the Do 17, Fw 58, He 111 or Ju 87, filled-out time and again with new items of equipment and which accomplished their daily flight tests. In addition, it was self-understood that the unit took part in the development and testing of the latest aircraft and their systems (on-board circuits, hydraulic, oxygen or anti-icing systems, pressure-cabins, etc) and exercising their judgements.

Department E4 operated in a similar manner, their activities encompassing navigation and communications systems. In these fields in particular, further technical development followed with considerable rapidity. The continually increasing flying altitudes and speeds of the newest aircraft placed even higher demands on industry. At the beginning of the 1930s, several aircraft were still not equipped with W/T equipment. Later, air-to-air and air-to-ground communication with press-keys were evolved, before voice communication methods eventually came into active use.

In navigational matters, ie, the approach to particular targets and the return flight to particular geographic points or to the original airfield in conditions of bad weather and poor visibility, required concentrated development and testing efforts.

Equipment items and antennae had to be kept small and light and generate little air resistance, at the same time possessing high performance and low susceptibility to disturbances. These requirements and the continual race with developments by the enemy led to an increasing number of laboratory and flight testing tasks to be conducted until the closing months of the war.

Of particular interest is the fact that as early as May 1942, Department E4 had already conducted tests whereby dipoles, ie, strips of aluminium sheet 8mm (0.315in) in width, 0.3mm (0.012in) in thickness and varying lengths had been ejected from a Fieseler Storch over the Müritz.[52] Tracking of these ejections had shown that with the 'Würzburg' radar installations, measurements of distance and bearing could be rendered impossible. Known as 'Düppel' (window or chaff), it was not put into operational use in order to preserve secrecy. On the Allied side, however, an equally effective system had been developed which was employed in large measure by the RAF in their air-raid attacks on Hamburg for the first time in July 1943, completely 'blacking-out' the German radar.

Over and above its own testing activities in Rechlin, department E4 also worked closely with the local airbase aerial navigation unit, with Department F (high-frequency research and guide-beam systems), and with the E-Stelle Werneuchen, taking over the Referat 'Funkstörtechnik' (radio-frequency disturbance engineering) from them in autumn 1944. In parallel, E4 staff members were often engaged in setting-up and putting into operation new radio and direction-finding installations all over Germany and Europe, especially as the continuing duration of the war resulted in the testing of newer prototypes which eventually came into operational service.

A 'special existence' was led by Department E6. Following erection of the E-Stelle Tarnewitz and relocation there of the weapons installation group formerly in Rechlin, they became a 'remnant'. Its members did not carry out any flight testing, and from the space point of view, were separated from the other centres and were quartered on the so-called C-Platz, a sparsely-built flat countryside area north of the Gruppe Nord. This department concerned itself exclusively with testing ammunition for aircraft weapons, smoke- and signal devices, explosives, self-destroying compositions, and – together with the expert Referat at E2 – matters dealing with aircraft (armour) protection. Towards the end of the war, testing was undertaken of air-to-air rocket projectiles, eg, the R4M and air-launched missiles as well as special weapons equipped with automatic projectile release such as the 'Panzerfaust', 'Panzerblitz', 'Panzerschreck' and 'Jägerfaust' which were all armour-penetration weapons. For carrying out such trials on the C-Platz, besides laboratories and workshops, there were a series of underground and surface firing ranges. A large number of the captured enemy aircraft available in Rechlin, upon completion of flight testing, were used as targets and destroyed in firing trials to determine the effectiveness of various types of ammunition.

Department E7 on the other hand, was responsible for testing air-launched weapons and ancillary devices. Its members were housed in the Halle Ost (east hangar) and in the buildings behind it. This Department had to carry out a considerable amount of flight testing and possessed its own test aircraft. Besides the essential testing of air-launched weapons as well as all types of bombs, multi-bomb containers, jettisonable tanks and fuses, it had to test their suspension on and in the various types of aircraft, as also target-sighting mechanisms and operating procedures.

On grounds of secrecy, tests such as these were conducted up until 1933 in Lipetsk, and it is not surprising that a large

number of its members who had formerly been engaged there, were now to be found in the appropriate specialist Department in Rechlin. Included in the course of testing were the proper functioning of detonators, bullet-proof safety of bombs, correct and problem-free bomb separation from aircraft in various flying attitudes (such as in dives), safe descent of the bomb bodies (no component separations), ground loading and unloading possibilities, effectiveness of the target-sighting installations, functional capabilities of the electrical circuitry and operating instruments related to the method of release (single- or multiple-bomb releases) and arming of the bombs. During the course of the war, bomb-release trials in connection with three-axis autopilots and with computer-supported partially automated weapon release installations such as the BZA and TSA were added. Trials were also latterly conducted involving methods whereby bombs or jettisonable containers for defence against enemy bomber formations were dropped on the latter and were made to explode with the aid of acoustic or barometric detonators. Actual use of such schemes did not take place since the development of guided and unguided air-to-air rockets had meanwhile progressed to the stage where these could have been used operationally.

Department E8 again, was another activity which was only indirectly connected with flight testing. Its range of tasks involved the examination and testing of all aeronautical ground equipment. This type of testing was partially conducted at first in the Powerplant Department and partly in the Operations Department. The expanding range of tasks as early as 1937 necessitated the establishment of a district organisational unit to handle 'airfield equipment', and

even here, the range of tasks was extraordinarily vast. Aside from fixed airfield ground installations such as power supply, runway lighting and fuel depots and an equal measure of mobile equipment, there was a growing quantity of special vehicles such as fuel tankers, transport and salvage vehicles, special trailers, cranes, mobile land catapults, mobile workshop and fire-brigade vehicles, and last but not least, a variety of miscellaneous items such as hand pumps, ladders, maintenance platforms, wheel chocks, camouflaging, protective and conservation materials for parked aircraft. With its extensive aircraft parks and three airfields, the E-Stelle Rechlin offered ideal pre-conditions for direct and efficient testing in daily flying operations.

In mid 1943, the new Department E10 responsible for 'Materials and Fuels' was formed out of the various expert Referate from other Departments. It consolidated foremostly, the former E3 Fuels Group with its own laboratory and test-stand together with some members of the Referate 'De-icing and Materials' from Department E2.

Because of the growing number of special materials (fuels, lubricants, hydraulic and de-icing fluids, axle-greases, and special propulsion fuels for rocket motors) and their declining availability and quality which necessitated development and testing of substitute materials, there were numerous testing tasks to be performed by the staff of E10 as the war progressed. Thus, in the last months of the war, aviation petrol of merely 58 to 60 Octane was tested, to which lead tetraethyl and aniline had to be added.[53] With this mixture, the Junkers and Daimler-Benz reciprocating engines certainly functioned, but had to have their manifold pressures reduced and thus suffer performance reductions. Even for the already low quality J2 fuel used in the Jumo 004 and BMW 003 turbojets, substitute fuels were to have been tested. In this instance, tests were undertaken in E10 with bituminous coal-tar oil, marine heating-oil and shale oils, but which could only be used as auxiliary mixing ingredients.

The aggressive nature of rocket motor propellants especially, called for the development of new materials for fuel conduits and seals which had to undergo a thorough series of tests. From the autumn of 1944, the activities of E10 were noticeably impaired, for after the bombing raid of 25th August

An Me 410A with open nose bomb-doors prior to its next flight in Lärz. Flight testing with the Me 410 began in March 1943 in Rechlin, and after overcoming problems with the engine lubricating and cooling system, extended into the summer of 1944.

A sample from the multifarious facets of air and ground testing undertaken by Section E5 at the E-Stelle Rechlin.

E'Stelle Rechlin
E 5

Rechlin, den 9.1o.1943

Über Kdr. an KdE.

Schwerpunkts – Erprobungsbericht.

Messtrupp:
Zügige Arbeit, keine Rückstände.

Druckanzug:
Vermessung der Druckluftanlage in He 111 durch-geführt. Die Regulierung der Temp. ist auch bei tiefsten Aussentemperaturen möglich, sodass mit mindestens + 2o°C im Druckanzug zu rechnen ist. Für die notwendige Kühlung in Bodennähe reicht der Wärmeaustauscher ebenfalls aus. Höhenflug mit angelegtem Druckanzug steht noch aus.

Höhenabsprung-gerät HAS 16:
Sicherstellung der Rohrflaschenfertigung bei VDM. Nullserie für HAS 16 wird noch in unge-schütztem Stahl ausgeliefert.

Lastenfallschirme:
Hochabwurf mit Misch-lastabwurfbehälter 1ooo:
Acht Abwürfe aus 3ooom Höhe bei 350 km/h mit KTh-Vermessung durchgeführt (Gesamt-gewicht 1ooo – 5oo kg). Funktion von 6 Abwürfen einwandfrei. 2, Abwürfe fielen aus, da Abwurfhöhe wegen zunehmender Be-wölkung nicht eingehalten werden konnte.

Schaltgeräte der Firma Hirth:
Erprobung der Schaltgetriebe der Fa. Hirth wurde nach flugklarwerden des Flugzeuges Ju 88 FL+SK bisher erfolgreich durchgeführt,

3 kW-Regler der Firma LGW:
Erprobung des 3 kW-Reglers der Fa. LGW im unab-geschirmten Bordnetz der Do 217 M bezüglich Ent-störung ergab, dass die Regler auch für einen Einsatz unter diesen Bedingungen genügend entstört sind. In Einzelfällen wird bei Bedarf ein zusätz-licher Entstörer vorgesehen.

FKZ 16:
In der Besprechung vom 6.1o.43 wurde von der Be-schaffungsabteilung zugesagt, dass der Serienan-schluss an die 15o Nullseriengeräte der Kurszen-trale FKZ 16 sichergestellt wird.

Schleudersitz-versuche He 219 V 6:
Sitzschleudern aus dem am Boden abgestellten Flugzeug mit Puppen und mittels Luftdrücken von 5o-12o atü verliefen positiv, d.h. die Abschüsse bestätigten die errechneten Werte der Wurfhöhe und Wurfweite. Schleuderversuche von Puppen aus dem fliegenden Flugzeug folgen kommende Woche.

Fl-Oberstabsing. und Abteilungsleiter E 5

1944, they had to be relocated as a whole to Neustrelitz and remained there until shortly before the end of the war.

Finally, there still remain two Depart-ments needing to be mentioned which also occupied a special status within the E-Stelle since they consisted chiefly of Research and Development Departments with ancil-lary flight testing functions. These were the Departments E Med and F.

The former had already been established in March 1934[54] and for a long time, reported directly to the E-Stelle or to the RLM Technisches Amt respectively. It was only in 1944 that it reported to the Luftwaffe Chef des Sanitätswesens (Medical Service Chief). Stimulated by the Department Head, relocation of the unit began at the end of the year to south-west Germany with the aim of strengthening closer co-opera-tion with the resident research institutes there, but because of the war situation, could not be effected. During its existence, the E Med was for a time affiliated to the Equipment Department E3 and worked together with the 'Rescue and Safety Equipment' group. Its tasks resulted from general developments in aviation. The attainment of ever higher altitudes required the application of special measures against low temperatures, and the incorporation of oxygen equipment and pressure-cabins. Psychological effects on aircrews had to be examined, as also the effects and protec-tive measures resulting from damage or loss of these safety installations. High flying speeds and the introduction of ejection seats led to high acceleration forces on human beings, and here too, it became necessary to develop and test out protec-tive measures. The carbon-monoxide (CO) content of air within the crew compart-ment, particularly in single-engined aircraft stationed for flight testing in Rechlin, were thoroughly investigated by the E Med in all aircraft types. Even so, problems were still encountered until the very end of the war, and resulted in related objections with the Ar 396 and Skoda-Kauba Sk V4 as also to crashes caused by CO-poisoning suffered by the pilot. Systematic treatment of ergonomical aspects, in other words, the layout and accessibility of operating con-trols in the crew compartments, only com-menced at a very late date and could not be intensively pursued even after E Med had evolved initial proposals and had passed these on to industry. The work of the Department, which included a large num-ber of flight trials and tests in its own labo-ratories, was summarized in a series of basic publications such as: 'Protection of Human Beings Against Conflagration Heat', 'High-Altitude Rescue Dive', 'Low Temper-atures in Aircraft', 'Apparel in Stratospheric Aircraft', 'Oxygen Supply During Parachute Descent', and 'Psychological Values for the Construction of Closed High-Altitude Chambers.'

The second and last of the above organi-sational units needing to be mentioned here is Department F. It originated from the Department RL of the Rechlin DVL out-sta-tion.[55] Its establishment was chiefly due to the initiative of Dr. Hans Plendl, who had been a member of the DVL since the 1920s, and from that period onwards, had occu-pied himself intensively on the subject of the expansion of ultra-short wavelengths in the atmosphere and the application of such wavelengths for radio navigation. Out of this, there emerged the main spheres of activity of the DVL Department RL, which as Department F, was taken over by the E-Stelle Rechlin in 1936, and comprised:

Development and Testing of localizing beam systems – the so-called X- and Y- Ver-fahren (X- and Y-beam systems) for the aiming and automatic release of bombs and the Y-Jägerleitverfahren (fighter con-trol system) for day- and night-fighters.

Study and exploration of atmospheric layers regarding their influence on the expansion of radio waves of various wave-lengths and erection of a radio advisory ser-vice for field crews.

Development of a system for indigenous homing with the aid of two rotating radio beacons – the 'Rechliner Drehbakenver-fahren, System Plendl' – as well as other special tasks in the sphere of aircraft identification and altitude measurement.

To accomplish these tasks, Department F, whose personnel was constantly being enlarged, had a number of its own flight test aircraft and laboratories. In addition to the work of development, its members were continually travelling for the purpose of erecting new radio-beam experimental stations and also accompanied the installation and operations performed at several X- and Y-stations throughout the whole of Europe.

The planned early dissolution of Department F – originally intended to take place upon conclusion of development of the X-Verfahren, finally followed in stages up to 1943. The radio advisory centre was relocated from Rechlin to Bad Vöslau, south of Vienna, in 1942. Remaining Department F personnel were distributed during the course of 1942 to institutes of the 'Reichsstelle für Hochfrequenzforschung' (Reich Centre for High-Frequency Research) established by Dr. Plendl who had meanwhile been appointed as the 'Bevollmächtigter für Hochfrequenzforschung' (Plenipotentiary for High-Frequency Research), thus bringing the activities of Department F in Rechlin to an end.

To return now to flight testing in Rechlin in 1942. In the spring of that year, the war reached the E-Stelle for the first time directly when a British night-bomber, apparently in an emergency, released its bombload, but fortunately caused only minor damage to buildings. This event may have been the impulse for the erection of a dummy airfield near Boek, a few kilometres north-east of Rechlin. A few mock-up hangars of wood and canvas were erected there, accompanied by a row of dummy aircraft. When air-raid sirens sounded, men

of the Technical Company had to drive around in vehicles on which green and red position lights were attached. The camouflage was obviously insufficient as the Allies became aware of this from their reconnaissance photographs as early as April 1942 and designated the area as a 'Dummy Aerodrome near Boek'.[56]

There were other ways by which Rechliners came more and more in direct contact with wartime events. The precarious situation on all fronts called for the greatest efforts from Transport Squadrons to provide frontline troops with the most urgent supplies. In this way, it often happened that flight test aircraft from the E-Stelle together with their crews were temporarily transferred to frontline duties. Mostly it involved Ju 52s, but Do 217s have also been confirmed. It was hardly to be expected otherwise that both personnel and aircraft suffered losses, so that this type of commitment was curtailed from summer 1943. It nevertheless happened that the E-Stelle crews were called upon at short notice to fly to operational theatres either to instruct servicemen, to transport new equipment requiring to be tested, or to return with reports of experience gained. On top of that, there were individual engineers who for various reasons reported for frontline service, and even here, losses were unfortunately suffered.

In September 1942, the E-Stelle received a new Commander. It was again a field officer, Major Edmund Daser, formerly Gruppenkommandeur of I./KG 40. This appointment can presumably be traced to the initiative of his former Kommodore Oberstleutnant Petersen, the current KdE, all the more so since, together with another officer from KG 40, Hauptmann Rudolf Mons, had since February 1942 left it to enter the KdE area of command – the former Staffelkapitän in KG 40 taking over the

leadership of the He 177 Test Squadron in Lärz. Despite a broadening of the basis for flight testing of the He 177 through this appointment, the fundamental oscillation problems with this aircraft still persisted, as illustrated in the recollection of the E-Stelle type specialist Dipl.-Ing. Friedrich Utech,[57] commenting upon a test flight at that time:

'Having arrived at Heinkel's, the Flight-test Unit confirmed that everything is now in order to a speed of 500km/h (310mph). Other than the flight mechanic, the aircraft carried fuel sufficient for a few hours, but no further payload. It was also not fitted with dive-brakes. We climbed slowly up to about 4,000m (13,120ft), trimmed out to cruising condition, and with engines running entered a shallow dive of some 15°. Everything functioned normally until we hit 500km/h (310mph), where upon the flight mechanic suddenly pulled back the throttles without being asked. Before I could even ask him to provide me with an explanation, I noticed that the aircraft had begun to exercise a slight undulating movement around the lateral axis, not dissimilar to a stability oscillation when the control column is let go. The only thing was, I was holding the control column very firmly! With every oscillation, the amplitude increased, and the aircraft rose and dipped rhythmically. Out of sheer habit, I at first attempted to suppress the oscillations by counter-movements with the elevator, but to my surprise, it seemed to have no effect. Since I had no success with my attempts at suppression, I decided it would be better to hold on firmly to the control column and by pulling-up very cautiously, reduce the speed. The amplitudes, however, continued to rise with ever-increasing frequency despite the reduction in speed – the throttle being at idling revs and with gradual pull-up. A complete oscillation cycle took some three seconds; acceleration remained below 5g, and vision disturbances did not occur. During the oscillations, the control column remained firm and no shaking or untoward movements with the elevator was felt. Ailerons and rudder were equally calm. Would the oscillations increase until something gave way, or not? Fortunately, they reached a maximum value and then began to subside. This, however, lasted much longer than the see-saw movement and only ended below 400km/h (250mph). We had got away with it! The cause of the oscillating behaviour was never discovered and the He 177 retained its upper speed limit.'

Mainwheel change on a Ju 188E, probably GB+CM, Werk-Nr.10009, in April 1944 in Rechlin. The aircraft was operated by Section E5 for testing the unified hydraulic system.

The year ended with gloomy prospects. The Afrikakorps was in retreat in North Africa, and in the East, a catastrophe was looming in Stalingrad. During flight testing, over 50 members of the E-Stelle and seconded servicemen were killed. Although revolutionary jet- and rocket-propelled aircraft such as the Ar 234, He 280, Me 163, Me 262, and Me 328 had all been accorded the highest priority, all of these aircraft were still far from reaching development – and still less, operational maturity.

Rechlin Focussed in the Allied Bombsights

At this point in the chronology, a retrospective glance at the stance of the former enemy towards the E-Stelle Rechlin is in order. When contemplating the events of World War Two, it becomes noticeable that although the E-Stelle Rechlin represented the largest and focal Test Centre for land-based aircraft and aviation equipment in Germany, it was only at a relatively late date that it became of interest to Allied reconnaissance and still later, the target for bombing raids. The location of Rechlin, nevertheless, must have been known to the Allies ever since the end of World War One, as a consequence of the enforced demolition of all aeronautical test and training institute installations imposed by the Treaty of Versailles. Efforts had therefore been made with increased intensity since 1926, to maintain strict secrecy concerning the emergence of forbidden flight testing activity.

On 27th June 1927, when a two-seater British sports aircraft crewed by officers landed supposedly 'off-course' completely by surprise on the Rechlin airstrip just at the time when the Arado SD I single-seat fighter was airborne on a test flight, it understandably caused great consternation to those in positions of responsibility![58] It has not been ascertained up to the present, whether it was really a coincidence or a disguised reconnaissance. Whatever the case, the event did not raise diplomatic consequences, and even in Allied target documents in 1944, it was merely appended that 'Rechlin existed since at least 1930'.[59]

Had the Victorious Powers taken a closer look at German aviation activities at the latest from 1929 onwards, they would have been able to establish that flying activities had been resumed in Rechlin. German daily newspapers had even freely published articles reporting on the crash on 6th March 1929 of the Arens/Düring crew on the 'Ellerholz Airfield' in Mecklenburg, as well as the fatal accident of Hauptmann Dr. Paul Jeschonnek at 'Rechlin Airfield' on 13th June 1929.

On the German side, efforts were naturally exerted to disguise the fact that the increase in flight testing activity was serving any military purpose. This underwent a fundamental change following revelation of the Luftwaffe's existence in March 1935. The E-Stelle Rechlin thereafter became a prestige showpiece, certainly with the ulterior motive of presenting foreign visitors with a deliberately 'intimidating' impression of the rapid technical progress made in the resurrection of the Luftwaffe. Thus, in spring 1936, when in short succession, the American Military Attaché and the British Air Attaché were invited guests in Rechlin, they became visibly impressed with what they had seen. In October 1938, none other than Captain Charles Lindbergh was accorded the opportunity to test fly a Bf 109 in Rechlin, and as already mentioned, the comprehensive exhibition that was held in Rechlin on 3rd July 1939, was widely publicized in the daily newspapers.

During the early years of World War Two, the RLM Technisches Amt still published the obituaries for deaths incurred in crashes by members of the E-Stelle, together with their full military grades. Understandably, no technical details or other reports concerning the E-Stelle's activities or any flying demonstrations were announced.

The Allies certainly displayed a great interest in Rechlin, but up until 1942, highest priority was given by RAF Bomber Command to German cities, as it was to U-Boat bases at the climax of the 'Battle of the Atlantic'. At that time, independent American air forces were not yet in action in Europe.

It was almost more through pure chance than intent that development work by German aircraft manufacturers and flight testing activities by the E-Stellen became more sharply focussed in the sights of British reconnaissance, when an aerial photograph of the Heinkel-Werke taken after the raid on Rostock at the end of April 1942 revealed for the first time, a new type of propellerless aircraft – the He 280.[60]

This led to the sober realization that up until then, no systematic reconnaissance of the aircraft industry had been carried out, and that not a single photograph was to hand for example, of the Junkers-Werke in Dessau, nor the Henschel- or Arado-Flugzeugwerke. Even from Rechlin, it was for the first time on 17th April 1942 that British reconnaissance aircraft had brought back useful photographs which the photo interpreters at RAF Medmenham began to study closely. From these, they were able to discover 114 different aircraft, almost half of which could be clearly identified.[61]

The next batch of informative reconnaissance photos only became available one year later, and this time 136 aircraft, among them several related types, could be identified. In the matching 'Interpretation Report', it was remarked especially, that no apparent efforts had been made to apply camouflage or protective measures to parked aircraft. Shortly after that, the Allied photo interpreters introduced a new system whereby the name 'Rechlin' thereafter featured more often in evaluation reports. As a consequence, from June 1943 onwards, all new and unknown aircraft types were provisionally designated by their place of discovery, followed by the approximate wingspan in feet.[62]

The first aircraft known to be designated under this system was the 'Rechlin 104' of which two examples were discovered in Rechlin on the Reconnaissance Sortie N/870 of 28th June 1943. In this case, it was none other than the Ar 232A, whose initial pre-production prototypes had been undergoing flight testing at the E-Stelle since autumn 1942. The sortie on 28th June 1943 was exceedingly successful, as it brought the Allies the first detailed knowledge of the Ju 252 as well as an often-seen aircraft, now designated 'Rechlin 33', and another known as 'Rechlin 60' similar to the Me 110 in appearance, plus a further 'newcomer' ie, the 'Rechlin 72' which in all probability was the Ju 188.

From further reconnaissance flights made on 4th October 1943 and 19th April 1944, such good photographs were brought back from Rechlin and Lärz that the Allies were able to prepare exact target information with overhead views and descriptions of airfield installations. Nevertheless, a considerable time was to elapse before the first air-raid took place.

Right at the beginning of the year, on 13th January 1943, the very first 'mission-related' use of an ejection seat in the history of aviation took place in Rechlin from an He 280, which saved the life of the pilot Schenk. Despite this, flight testing of this and other priority jet aircraft types progressed at a slow pace. In contrast, the same basic aircraft types as in the previous year governed the skies over Rechlin, night-fighter variants of the Bf 110, Do 217 and Ju 88 among others, appearing for flight testing. Components of new systems like pressure-cabins or ever more voluminous hydraulic systems expanded the range of tasks. Continually increasing flying ceilings required new heating as well as de-icing systems. Not only that, much effort was expended to gain every possible increase in speed, such as by installing coverings on the undercarriage bays.

At the same time, increased savings in materials and expenditure became necessary, so that the use of substitute materials and standardization of aircraft equipment and system brought further testing tasks. A new aircraft type in the shape of the He 219

Top left: *Secretly photographed from a Ju 188 in Rechlin were the Fw 190A-5 (GT+IH, Werk-Nr.41027) and the Si 204 V4 (KM+GB), which were used by Section E3 in 1943/44 for engine testing of the BMW 801D-2 and As 411 respectively. In the background is the northern-most twin Test Stand of Gruppe Süd (south).*

Left: *External auxiliary air intakes such as those seen on the port engine nacelle of this Ju 188 were experimentally tested during BMW 801 trials but were not adopted for production.*

Below left: *The E-Stelle Rechlin undertook a large part of ejection-seat testing. Evaluation of individual firings from He 219 flying test-beds were based on film sequences taken from an accompanying aircraft.*

Top right: *Unteroffizier Walter Würgler of the EKL (Lärz) seen climbing into the He 219 V6 (DH+PV, Werk-Nr.190006). This prototype was used for ejection-seat testing from 1943, joined later by the He 219 (DV+DI) pictured on the title page.*

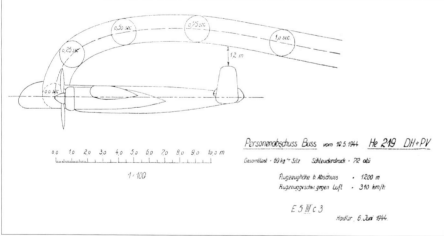

appeared – the first pure night-fighter development with which extensive ejection seat tests were carried out.

Since the transport aircraft problem had still not been solved, ie, a successor to the Ju 52, further tests were undertaken with the Ar 232, Go 244 and Ju 252. The same difficulty led to intensified tests with load-carrying gliders. In Rechlin, successful rigid-tow combinations were conducted with the DFS 230 towed by the Boeing B-17 and He 111, and the Go 242 towed by the

Ar 232. In towing tests behind the Ju 88A, the results were so bad that this combination was not further pursued. The Messerschmitt firm had meanwhile developed the Me 410, which resulted from suggestions for improvements emanating from flight testing of the unsuccessful Me 210, and delivered it to the E-Stelle for testing.

The Rechlin engineers were also able to examine a series of interesting captured enemy aircraft in 1943, such as the Bell P-39 Airacobra, two Boeing B-17s, a Convair

B-24 Liberator, a Martin B-26 Marauder, a Yakovlev Yak-7, a Lavochkin LaGG 3, a de Havilland Mosquito and a Republic P-47 Thunderbolt. Together with the newest German types developed, these were displayed on the occasion of an 'Armaments Conference' held from 3rd to 5th September 1943, to Reichsminister Albert Speer and leading personalities from the Luftwaffe and industry. Prior to that, on 24th July 1943, another extensive demonstration had already taken place in the presence of

Hermann Göring and high Luftwaffe officers, where an Me 163 and Me 262 were to be seen for the first time in the skies above Rechlin.

At the end of 1943, E-Stelle personnel totalled 4,078, made up of 1,831 officers, NCOs and men, 2,131 officials, employees, members of the Engineer Corps and wage-earners, and 116 trainees. The total land area of the E-Stelle was spread over not less than 151km² (58.3mls²) of which around 1.3% or 1.9 million m² (20.45 million ft²) were built-up areas.[63]

1944 – The War Reaches the E-Stelle
Intensification of the air war against Germany as well as the growing presence and strength of the 8th USAAF on the British Isles enabled the possibility of an American daylight attack to become ever greater as the war prolonged. Ever since the 'Big Week' in February 1944, it had become clear what danger this fighting force represented.[64]

Recognizing this danger, the E-Stellen Commands began to prepare dispersal measures in spring 1944. Where initially, special emphasis was laid on relaxed, and as far as possible, protected enclosures for the valuable test aircraft as well as dispersal of barracks away from the closely-knit complexes of the airfield, it was soon decided to disperse complete workshops, storage areas and offices into surrounding areas, and included training schools, factory buildings, restaurants and pubs, and even forestry houses and prison cells in a circle up to 40km (24 miles) distant. Through these measures, up until 1st May

1944, Rechlin was able to disperse about 50% of all machine-tools, 70% of all storage materials and 25% of technical equipment out of the immediate neighbourhood of the E-Stelle. For 700 members of the E-Stelle, this meant inconvenient travel to their workplaces and difficult working conditions, but were relatively safe from bombing attacks. At first, Rechlin remained spared from being attacked directly, but with the increasing daily bomber formations, above all, on their way to Berlin, the Rechliners were enveloped in the whirlpool of events. One of the first missions against approaching bomber formations has been documented for the 24th February 1944. In the battle against enemy air superiority, Leutnant Rudolf Pohl of the EKL in Lärz in his Bf 109G-6 had no chance. He fell in battle over the Plauer See. Soon afterwards, aircraft again took off from Lärz to fend off the large American air raid on the Reich capital on 6th March 1944. On this occasion there were also losses. Unteroffiziere Ernst Wachter and Lindenbaum in their Bf 109G-2 attacked the four-engined bombers. Northeast of Perleberg, Wachter was hit by enemy defensive fire and his radioman was wounded. In the same mission, Feldwebels Kamp and Fleige from the EKL shot down a B-17 from a formation of 20 bombers and damaged another, whilst Feldwebel Fischer managed to down one. For this action, he was promoted to Oberfeldwebel, but on his next defensive mission on 13th March 1944 died in the air battle.

In the face of Allied air superiority, these losses had apparently indicated to those

responsible, how ridiculous such missions with testing crews were, since further EKL operational sorties are not known. On the other hand, attempts were made to try and recognize an air attack on the E-Stelle at the earliest possible moment whereby individual machines functioning as 'early-warning aircraft' and 'probes' held contact with the bomber formations, as exemplified by Feldwebel Kamp in the Ju 88 V18 (BH + DA) on 22nd March 1944. The only possible countermeasure upon the approach of enemy aircraft was to leave the vicinity at the start of an alarm and disperse as many aircraft as possible to nearby airfields, an action accomplished on several occasions.

In low-level attacks, however, it was in any case too late for such measures, so that from spring 1944, strengthened local anti-aircraft defences – a detachment of light flak with 12 x 20mm guns and a total of 100 machine-guns of 7.5mm and 7.9mm calibre went into action when American long-range Lightning fighters of the 364th Fighter Group made a surprise attack on Lärz at midday on 21st May 1944. Several flight test aircraft on the ground were set on fire, but apparently there were no casualties of airfield personnel. The attackers lost a P-38J, Serial-No: 43-28272 which was hit by flak and had to make a belly-landing in the middle of Lärz airfield. The pilot, 2nd Lieutenant Lemar J Miller was wounded and taken into captivity.[65]

If these attacks were to be regarded almost as a warning, it was only a few days later that Rechlin received a taste of the effects of a deliberately-aimed large air attack on 24th May 1944, when 13 four-

A total of five of these enormous twin Engine Test Stands formed the most significant imprint of the Gruppe Süd installations in Rechlin.

Inside view of one of the Test Stands with final preparations being made for a Jumo 213 engine test run.

engined aircraft of the 388th Bombardment Group which had diverted away from a large formation attacking Berlin shortly before midday, dropped 31 tonnes of high-explosive bombs over Lärz airfield, which because of the weather, fell mostly on the airfield and surrounding fields but did not hit the buildings.[66] Only one workshop was destroyed, and this time too, there did not appear to be any casualties. Flying operations were hardly affected by this raid.

One week later, on 31st May 1944, the first mission of the US 7th Photo Group – previously only British reconnaissance aircraft appeared in the sky above Rechlin – brought to the Allies the first information about a completely new and unusual aircraft, initially designated as the 'Rechlin 66':

The accompanying evaluation report[67] stated 'The characteristics of this aircraft deviating completely from the normal are the sharply forward-swept wings and the very long and fat fuselage nose. There are no signs of engine nacelles attached, which leads to the assumption that this aircraft is either turbojet-powered, or is a glider'

It was believed that this aircraft had already been sighted somewhere else in Rechlin on 19th April 1944, but at that time was so hidden by tenting and strips of material that the Allied interpreter was not certain whether the 'object' was in fact an aircraft at all. The 31st May 1944 photographs now provided the confirmation. The subject of discovery was none other than the 4-jet Junkers Ju 287. This nevertheless points to an unsolved question, since according to Junkers documents, the Ju 287 V1 prototype was only completed in the second half of May 1944 and the first flight, as stated in the Department E2 Weekly Report of the E-Stelle Rechlin, first

took place on 8th August 1944. How it could therefore come about that a Ju 287 could have been sighted as early as April or end of May 1944 in Rechlin, or whether it consisted of a mock-up or the first prototype without engines remains still a mystery. Behind the next discovery which the Allies made during the course of their almost monthly rhythm in keeping a watch over Rechlin there remain no questions unanswered, for on 6th August 1944, a British reconnaissance aircraft brought back from the flight the first photograph of an Ar 234 which was parked beside two Me 262s in front of the large hangar in Lärz. Evidently the Allies had no previous knowledge of this aircraft whose first flight had already taken place on 30th July 1943 from the Arado Flugzeugwerke airfield in Brandenburg, so that it was provisionally designated 'Rechlin 46'. Because of the excellent quality of the photographs, they were soon able to determine its dimensions and overall appearance very accurately.

The reconnaissance results just mentioned show that the Allies were now in the position to be able to identify and to describe with great accuracy the new aircraft types that were arriving in Rechlin. The Ar 234 and the Me 262 for example, were to be found in the E-Stelle starting from June 1944 onwards. As early as spring 1944 delivery of several pre-production aircraft and prototypes of the Ju 388 as successor to the Ju 88 and Ju 188 had begun, planned to fulfil several roles – as bomber, reconnaissance, and night-fighter. Alongside these, there were also new series variants of the Ju 88 to be tested, particularly the G, S, and T-series. There were also new variants of the Bf 109 – the K-series, and the Fw 190 D-series. A completely new aircraft was the

The measurement observer's position in a Ju 88 engine flying test-bed, where every available space has been filled with engine measurement and control instruments.

Photographs of jet aircraft undergoing testing in Rechlin are extremely rare. Seen here is an Me 262A (probably E2+02, Werk-Nr.130170), being towed by a tractor from its protected revetment at the edge of the forest in Lärz to its take-off point.

Ta 154 of which the first, the V6 (TE+FJ, Werk-Nr.100006) and the Ta 154A-0 (TQ+XD, Werk-Nr.120004) have been confirmed at the E-Stelle in June 1944.[68] Equally as new was the Do 335, a design envisaged by Dornier as a reconnaissance, heavy-fighter, fast bomber and night-fighter. Initial tests with the type in Rechlin evidently began with the Do 335 V9 (CP+UI, Werk-Nr.230009) and was in Rechlin since at least 3rd August 1944.[69] Both of the latter types had already been test flown some time before at the manufacturers by pilots from Rechlin.

Besides all these during the course of the year, there were the Ju 352 V1, V2, V3, V7, V8, V9 and V13 prototypes, each employed over a long period on flight testing or transport duties at the E-Stelle. At the end of the year, the Ar 396 V4 (SO+DD) was able to commence its flight trials in Rechlin, followed shortly after by pre-production machines.

Of particular significance, however, was the commencement of flight trials in summer 1944 with the new Ar 234 and Me 262 jet aircraft. The first documented Messerschmitt machines were the Me 262 (VI+AR, Werk-Nr.130018) on 19th June, and the

SQ+XA, Werk-Nr.130188 on 28th June. With the Arado aircraft, it was the Ar 234B-0 (GM+BA, Werk-Nr.140101), and the first machine confirmed as having been in Rechlin per flight log-book entry under the date of 24th June. This was followed by GM+BB, Werk-Nr.140102, on 22nd July 1944. Until August some ten further examples of the new jet bomber appeared in quick succession. Immediately after the arrival of the first jet aircraft, comparison flights were made in Rechlin between the two designs. Interestingly enough, it was the Ar 234 in both its bomber and reconnaissance roles which was judged to be the better aircraft, above all, by virtue of its noticeably smaller turning radius, its higher rate of roll, and its lower aileron and elevator forces. The Me 262 was criticized due to unsatisfactory manufacturing methods – poor compatibility of external skin panels, plus Flettner servo-tabs not balanced, but its 80km/h (50mph) higher speed was in its favour. The Messerschmitt firm had in mind to eliminate the deficiencies by introducing immediate remedial measures.[70]

At the beginning of their flight trials, the new aircraft still had to contend with numerous problems. For one thing, there were the far from reliable novel jet engines which had to be inspected after only 12.5 hours of operation. Many failed even earlier due to damage suffered by the turbine stator or rotor blades. Added to that, there were continual problems with the Riedel starters, and on the engine components themselves, maintenance personnel had to contend with earthing connections,

Time Period	Remarks
29.07.-04.08.44	Acceptance checks, alterations to undercarriage spring suspension.
06.08.-12.08.44	PDS (Patin three-axis steering) trials by Department E5.
12.08.-19.08.44	In Rechlin since 12.08.44 for installations (2 flights) PDS modification. Due to high manufacturing inaccuracies inherent in the aircraft, it is not possible to work with the PDS in its present form. Ferry flight Rechlin to Lärz.
20.08.-26.08.44	Earthing connection check in the course control; installation by E5; engine change, Werk-Nr.254 installed, right turbine adjusted.
27.08.-01.09.44	Left engine Werk-Nr.254 removed, replaced by Werk-Nr.512. Both turbojets adjusted. Oil motor exchanged, new version of rpm indicator installed, larger brake footpumps installed (1 flight).
02.08.-08.09.44	Earthing connection check. Brake problems. Measuring instruments installed by E3 (7 flights).
09.09.-15.09.44	Installation of gyro course control. Change-over switch exchanged. Earthing connection checks (6 flights). Installation of 'Lotzentrale 7E'. Tests with new flying control gearing and new steering motor. Test gave improved steering behaviour.
23.09.-30.09.44	First flights with 'Lotzentrale 7E' and statoscope gave good results. In all aircraft, the missing spar rivets were replaced by bolts.
07.10.-13.10.44	Wing strengthening (6 flights).
21.10.-27.10.44	Two fuel tank pumps exchanged. Self-operating switch failed (1 flight)
28.10.-03.11.44	Check flights of course control. Left aileron exchanged (2 flights).
05.11.-12.11.44	Further flights conducted, hampered by bad weather.
11.11.-18.11.44	Elimination of undercarriage difficulties. (Brake shield, loose steering).
18.11.-25.11.44	One flight. Series-examination on statoscope for PDS.
26.11.-02.12.44	Flights with series-type statoscope switching.
08.12.-15.12.44	One flight to test simplified statoscope switching (PDS).
17.12.-23.12.44	Earthing connection checks. One flight with simplified statoscope switching.

Even though of poor quality, this is the only known photograph of an He 177 parked in front of the Gruppe Süd hangars at the E-Stelle Rechlin. The He 177 A-3 (DR+IS, Werk-Nr.2011) was used at least from 9th September 1942 to 24th June 1944 as an engine flying test-bed.

hydraulics system problems, manufacturing inaccuracies and bemoan the tact that most of the engines to hand were not in accordance with the latest alterations, and as a result, had to be suitably modified. An impression of these problems is furnished in the following extract[71] from the testing sequence of the Ar 234B-0 (GM+BF, Werk-Nr.140106) in the table above:

Exclusively for the jet-propelled aircraft, the E-Stelle Rechlin introduced its own aircraft code system. Numerals ahead of the 'Balkenkreuz' signified the Department to which the aircraft had been assigned, whilst behind it the numerals were consecutively applied in order of receipt of the aircraft. For the Me 262, the latter series commenced with 01, 02, 03 etc, and for the Ar 234, the series was 10, 20, 30, etc. Thus, at the time, Me 262s flew with the codes E2+01, E2+02, E3+01, E3+02 or E7+01

and the Ar 234s with E2+10, E2+20, E3+20 etc at the E-Stelle. It should be noted that these did not constitute the 'Stammkennzeichen' or parent company identification codes as these were already allocated at the manufacturing firm and remained unchanged. A list of all known Rechlin codes conforming to this scheme is provided in the table on page 119.

At about the same time that flight testing began with jet-propelled aircraft in Rechlin, another extensive exhibition took place in the presence of Generalfeldmarschall Milch, Reichsminister Speer, the Jägerstab, and other high Luftwaffe officers.

On the 12th and 13th June 1944, all Luftwaffe E-Stellen displayed the newest aircraft being worked upon. In-flight demonstrations were held with the He 177B-5, Ju 88S-3, Ta 154, He 219, Fw 190, Ar 232B, Do 335, Ar 234, Me 262 and Me 163. Besides

these, the latest captured enemy aircraft were to be seen – Fortress, Liberator, Lightning, Mustang, Mosquito, Spitfire, and Typhoon.

Participants at the inspection noticed immediately the difference between the superb and matching construction components of the American aircraft in comparison to the very imperfect manufacture of the German aircraft, as noted in a report compiled by Flugbaumeister Kröger of the Arado firm.

Scarcely half a month later, a portion of the aircraft types displayed were cancelled from the Procurement Programme, whilst for other designs which were partly still not yet even in the flight test stage, utopian production quantities had been laid down.

This to-and-fro between the most varied new Programme studies with continual changes in priorities can be traced back even further. In the coming months of 1944 until the end of the war in 1945, it was even further emphasized and flight testing continually impaired. But before that, an event happened that had far-reaching detrimental effects on the working capabilities of the E-Stelle Rechlin.

The First Large Air Raid

It has not so far been possible to establish exactly when planning for a large air attack on the E-Stelle Rechlin had begun, but measures to be put into action were certainly accelerated with growing testing activities with the new jet aircraft.

The date was the 25th August 1944. Already in the early morning hours, large formations of the 8th USAAF were beginning to take off from their bases in southeast England. More than 1,100 four-engined bombers of the 1st, 2nd and 3rd Bombardment Division (BD), protected by over 800 single- and twin-engined long-range escort fighters took off from 0730 hours to attack aircraft plants, airfields and a refinery in northern Germany.

For 179 aircraft of the 3rd BD flying B-17 Flying Fortresses on Mission AF 570, the target was 'Rechlin – German Air Force Experimental Station'. Aircraft of the 487th and 486th Bombardment Group (BG) as well as the Flying Fortresses of the 94th, 390th, 385th and 447th BG were in the air. After

more than a 3-hour flight, most of the aircraft had reached their designated altitude of 21,000ft (6,400 m). North of Husum, the bombers met up with the first of their escort fighters from the 339th and 357th Fighter Group (FG) equipped with P-51 Mustangs. One group with P-47 Thunderbolt fighters was to provide cover to the bombers on their return.

Shortly after midday the sirens sounded in Rechlin whilst the bombers turned on to a south-easterly course over Stettin at 1230 hours before turning on a north-westerly course some 20 minutes later on their approach course to Rechlin. At 1250 hours, the first bombs fell from the bomb-bays of the 487th and 486th BG in the region of the Gruppe Nord and the seaplane hangar. Bombs then followed in quick succession on emplacements of the Gruppe Ost, Gruppe West, and Gruppe Süd. Some 20 minutes later, it was all over.

Dipl.-Ing. Kurt Pflügel, at that time Works Engineer in Department B-Süd, recalls in the 'Rechliner Briefe' (Rechlin Letters):

'...the humming of engines faded. We now came out of our fox-holes. I had to get to my workplace. I pushed my bicycle over the partly patched-up ring road. Soon, there loomed ahead of me the tall shape of the Low-Temperature Chamber from whose roof smoke was belching. Since the installation was driven by ammonia, it could explode at any time and without oxygen masks it was impossible to enter. The heating supply station beside it to the left had also been hit by incendiary bombs. Penetration holes gaped from the roof out of which tongues of flame were visible. I ran in there and found two stokers. There was no water in the water pipes, but there was still water in containers. I climbed on the roof and had water in a bucket hauled up to me. The three of us were able to check the fire and finally, to douse it completely.

From my high position I now had the opportunity to survey the picture of destruction. The forefront of both hangars were destroyed, the Gruppe Süd administration building had collapsed, its concrete roof lying askew on the ruins. Beside me, the dining hall and canteen were burning in bright flames. Right behind it, nothing was left of our barracks office. It did not take long before the low-temperature chamber's large ammonia vaporizer on the upper floor burst, and thick black clouds of smoke whirled and swelled upwards. The pipe conduits, compressor and installations exploded, the cork insulation caught fire and even days later were still aglow and giving off smoke – a further visible sign of the destruction.'

Based on knowledge gathered at the time, some 20 had died, but the majority of personnel were able to be evacuated in

good time to the nearby surroundings. The flak positions stationed in Rechlin had apparently downed only one bomber of the formations – the B-17G, code R5, serial 43-37980, from the 487th BG. A part of the crew were able to jump out with their parachutes and were taken into captivity.[72] A large number of the bombers were damaged by the flak defences, which were described in the operational reports as 'weak, but relatively accurate'.

The massive inferiority of the Reich defences also revealed that the formation which had been ordered to Rechlin had met no fighter opposition whatsoever!

E-Stelle installations were badly hit, and none of the hangars escaped undamaged. Air operations had to be conducted from Lärz and Roggentin until the work of damage clearance had made reasonable progress some two weeks later. The destruction of workshops, hangars and office buildings made further displacement of individual Referate and Departments to the surroundings necessary.

After that, the sky over the Müritz became peaceful and even reconnaissance sorties subsided, apart from the 13th September and 15th October 1994 when aircraft of the 8th USAAF's 7th Photo Group once more appeared over Rechlin to take damage and activity photographs of the E-Stelle. Here again, they were able to photograph yet another unknown aircraft type which received the designation 'Rechlin 67'. In all probability it portrayed one of the very rare prototypes of the Kalkert Ka 430 transport glider![73]

Apparently unnoticed by the Allies, testing was begun in autumn 1944 in Rechlin of what could be traced back to the desperate thoughts of how to ward off the streams of enemy bombers. The origin of the idea has been claimed by both Hanna Reitsch and Otto Skorzeny, and consisted of a manned Fi 103 flying-bomb (better known under its propaganda name of V-1) whose pilot would dive onto the enemy target but who scarcely had a chance of survival. Since the Fi 103 was now manned, it qualified as an 'aircraft' and hence came within the E-Stelle Rechlin sphere of responsibility; the unmanned Fi 103, as a remotely-guided projectile, having been previously under the aegis of the E-Stelle Peenemünde-West.

The first converted Fi 103 airframes, code-named Reichenberg, stood ready for testing but still without the propulsion unit in late summer 1944 in Lärz.

The flight was to take place following release from an He 111 aircraft which had to carry it to altitude. Initial flights were carried out by Flieger-Haupting. Wilhelm Ziegler of E2, who in a hard landing, suffered spinal injuries and could not partake

Opposite page: The E-Stelle Rechlin during a bombing attack by Boeing B-17s on 25th August 1944 showing massive clouds of smoke from hits already made. Several buildings of the Gruppe Nord, Ost, and West, are already in flames, whilst a further carpet of bombs exploded on the runway. Shortly after this photo was taken, the Gruppe Süd installations at lower right were also struck.

This photograph was taken by the E-Stelle on the day after the first large-scale bombing attack to assess the extent of the damage and to initiate the necessary repairs. A part of the Gruppe Nord hangars and workshops and the seaplane hangars were completely destroyed.

in further flight testing. With his successor, Flieger-Obering. Herbert Pangratz of E2, the cockpit canopy flew off, and in the subsequent landing he too was severely injured.[74] Thereafter – and the first flights confirmable from flight log-book entries – Flieger-Haupting. Heinz Kensche from the RLM, Flugbaumeister Willy Fiedler from the Fieseler firm and Hanna Reitsch, took over further flight trials, including solo flights recorded

by Kensche on the 20th, 23rd, and 29th Sep tember 1944 in what was designated as ε 'V-1 Re 2'.[75] This model consisted of a two seater without propulsion unit. Furthe flights followed with this variant, accompa nied by Augstein, Kachel, Meisner, Pfan nenstein and Schenk in the second seat One test prototype of the Re 3 variant, ε two-seater with propulsion unit was evi dently ready at the beginning of November

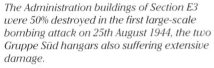

The Administration buildings of Section E3 were 50% destroyed in the first large-scale bombing attack on 25th August 1944, the two Gruppe Süd hangars also suffering extensive damage.

Captured enemy aircraft in Rechlin were not only recognizable by their identification letters but also by the 'Fernruf Mirow 231' inscription on the rudder. Pictured here is the Vickers Wellington Ic 5+4 (ex-LNoF) c/n. T.2501 under camouflage netting at the edge of Rechlin-Roggentin airfield where the majority of the E-Stelle aircraft had to be temporarily parked after the bombing raid.

Kensche being the pilot on an 8-minute flight with it on 4th November 1944. Further flights took place on the following day, but on the second flight after only 56 minutes, a part of the port wing covering parted company due to vibrations caused by the Argus pulsejet and it was only with effort that Kensche was able to make a parachute exit over the Müritz.

On 28th November 1944, Kensche again sat in a two-seater, this time accompanied by Leutnant Walter Starbati, a test pilot seconded from the Luftschiffbau Zeppelin who took over further flight testing of the Reichenberg. Subsequent known flights conducted by Starbati were with the Re 3 (Werk-Nr.10) and the Re 4 V10. He met his fate, however, in an Re 3 on 5th March 1945, the accident report describing in sober words the tragic circumstances:

'The Reichenberg Re 3 aircraft with short-ened wingspan, after a normal start at 1658 hours, was in a climb at around 2,800m (9,200ft) altitude. Speed lay between 400km/h (250mph) and 500km/h (310mph). In a moderate turn to port both wings broke off in succession. With engine still running,

the aircraft went over into an almost vertical dive, without the pilot having been able to leave the aircraft after jettisoning the cockpit canopy ...'

As recalled by one of those who was involved, flight testing resulted in a second victim, an Unteroffizier Schenk, but this cannot be confirmed by documentary evidence. Whatever the case, the previous accidents provided sufficient grounds to discontinue this nonsensical development. In a concise entry of 15th March 1945 in the daily war diary of the Chef TLR Amtsgruppe Flugzeugentwicklung (aircraft develop-ment department unit) is the remark: 'At the suggestion of the Fl-E of KG 200, all further work on the Re-So-Flugzeuge (Reichenberg Special Aircraft) as a result of the last accident, will be relinquished'.

The Year 1945
The war theatres in the East as in the West, were continually drawing closer to Rechlin. The dubious situation, especially after the Soviet Army advances on 12/13th January during the course of a main spearhead drive towards Berlin, caused the Luftwaffe leadership to draw upon the last defensive reserves. Thus, in a conference on 25th Jan-uary 1945 at the office of the KdE Oberst Petersen, it was decided that in the event of a certain situation on the ground, the code word 'Blücher' would be given to signify the 'immediate formation of the KdE flying 'Gefechtsverband' (combat formation).[76] This Verband was to be formed in Rechlin and made up of 'all operationally-ready air-craft consisting of the Me 262, Ar 234, Bf 109, Fw 190, Ta 152, Ju 88, Ju 188 and He 111' and operationally-capable E-Stellen air-crews. The E-Stelle had the task of taking care of the entire technical needs and provisioning of the Verband, at the same time continuing flight test work with crews

that were not fully fit for operational engagement, as stated in the directive. The KdE was envisaged as the 'Verbandsführer' with Combat HQ in Rechlin. Within the Verband there was to have been a 'Recon-naissance and Fast-Bomber Squadron Ar 234' in Lärz, a 'Fighter and Fighter-Bomber Squadron Me 262' as well as other fighter, fighter-bomber and night-fighter squadrons in Lärz and Rechlin-Roggentin. The forma-tion order was actually given as a KR-Telegramme on 1st February 1945 signed by Oberst Petersen. On the same day, Fliegerstabsing. Borsdorff of the E-Stelle Rechlin Department E3 noted in his diary:

'Conference of pilots with the Comman-der. Formation of the Gefechtsverband Rechlin. Reporting for Me 262 (E3+01)'.

Flight testing abated in the days that fol-lowed, the Gefechtsverband remaining in operational readiness. In accordance with the 'Führer-Notprogramm' – the Hitler Emergency Programme instituted in the meantime, flight testing activities resumed on 6th February 1945, the crews who had been deputed to the Gefechtsverband, however, remaining there. On 8th February 1945, the first (documented) actual mis-sions were flown when Fliegerstabsing. Sinram with the Ju 88S-3 (NL+LA) and Fliegerstabsing. Huber with the Ju 88 (BR+BZ) took off from Lärz in 'Operation Oder Bridges'. However, it is reported that on 1st February 1945, an aircraft was said to have been shot down by Soviet flak on a sortie near Küstrin in which Fliegering. Koch of Department E5 and a further crew member was said to have been killed, but the loss is not confirmable from docu-ments.

On 9th February 1945, the Gefechtsver-band consisted of the following aircraft – according to an Allied intercepted and decoded message:[77]

Bf 109 Squadron	9 aircraft
Me 262 Squadron	4 aircraft
Ta 152 HQ Squadron	8 aircraft
Two Fw 190s Ground-attack Squadrons	25 aircraft
Ar 234 Fast-bomber Squadron	9 aircraft
He 111 Night Ground-attack Squadron	10 aircraft
Ju 88/188 Night Ground-attack Squadron	17 aircraft

In the week prior to 17th February 1945, the Ar 234B-1 (Werk-Nr.140102) flew on reconnaissance sorties over the Oder front, whilst the Ar 234Bs that had been earmarked for bombing missions could not be operationally deployed due to bad weather, as noted in the E2 Weekly Report. The dissolution of the Verband has been recorded on 19th February 1945 when Fliegerstabsing. Huber flew the Ju 88 (BR+BZ) over from Lärz to Rechlin and noted in the flight logbook: 'Auflösung Gefechtsverband KdE'.

During the formation of the Gefechtsverband, testing work was completely halted, but in conformity with the 'Führer-Notprogramm' work was now to be resumed and concentrated on a few important aircraft types. Undergoing testing at the time were the Bf 109 and Fw 190, the Ta 152 in various variants, as well as the BV 155 high-altitude fighter which had just made its first flights. In terms of jet aircraft, new variants of the Me 262 kept appearing for testing. He 162 testing ran in parallel with series production and high on the priority list was the four-engined Ar 234C. Flight testing in Rechlin itself became increasingly limited[78] because of deficits in fuel distribution – only 100 tonnes of piston-engine fuel and 600 tonnes of turbojet fuel per month for the entire KdE! The transfer of personnel to frontline units did the rest, as personnel strength at the E-Stelle had now sunk to just over 3,000. Flight testing took place more frequently at the manufacturing firms, which entailed lengthy and dangerous train journeys for the E-Stellen personnel.

Whether this was the underlying reason and the proximity of the Messerschmitt and Dornier firms as also Heinkel in Vienna, or whether the danger of approaching Soviet troops was the reason which led to the decision to relocate jet aircraft flight testing by the Test Detachment Lärz from Rechlin to southern Germany, cannot be determined with certainty. As it happened, preparations were begun in the first half of March 1945 to relocate this activity to Lechfeld, south of Augsburg. Following corresponding preliminary discussions, a forward Detachment started out on 16th March, comprised of Oberleutnant Abels, Fliegerstabsing. Bengsch, Fliegerstabsing. Borsdorff, Oberleutnant Grotewahl and Fliegerstabsing. Spangenberg on their way to Lechfeld.[79] The journey lasted not less than three days before they eventually arrived in the late evening of 19th March.

The days that followed were occupied with meetings as well as arranging accommodation for the individual departments, workshops and storage needs. On 24th March, the first freight train arrived from Rechlin, carrying personnel and materiel followed by a second train a few days later. In all, the transports were made up of 102 wagons with a total of 302 men, to which must be added some truck-convoys. The necessary work on installations began immediately. The conditions under which erection work in Lechfeld took place, can be gleaned from the terse diary entries made by Fliegerstabsing. Heinz Borsdorff.

The twin towers of the Engine Test-Stands lent to the characteristic appearance of the E-Stelle's Gruppe Süd. This view from the roof of the southern hangar looking eastwards after the first large bombing raid, shows only minor building damage in this area

7th April 1945
0530hrs – Arrived in Lechfeld. 1030hrs – departure to Munich, arrival at 1530hrs. 1800hrs – finally at destination (BMW). 2100hrs – departure from Munich, 2330hrs – arrival in Lechfeld. No flight service.

8th April 1945
Unloading freight train with engines from EHAG (Heinkel) Vienna. 0845hrs to 1945hrs – fighter and full alarm alternately. No flight service.

9th April 1945
0900hrs – Conference with Commander re further dispersal. Preparation of lists for men and machines. With Stabsing. Hottinger, Untermeiting – a small village near Lechfeld, transport of parts for the Herbitus (wind-tunnel) installation via airbase trucks, 0800hrs to 2000hrs fighter and full alarm. Air raid on the airfield in 9 waves. Unteroffizier Bischof received shrapnel injuries. No flight service.

10th April 1945
From 0100hrs to 0645hrs – fortification work on the runway. From 1500hrs – workshops. 0700hrs to 2100hrs – fighter alarm. No flight service.

11th April 1945
0800hrs to 0200hrs Spadework on the runway. No flight service.

12th April 1945
Pause until midday. 1400hrs – Meeting with Oberst Petersen. 0915hrs to 1700hrs – fighter alarm. No flying service.

13th April 1945
Loading of 4 Jumo 004s. (He 162A) E2+51 regulation complete. Installation of measuring instruments in E3+51 completed, adjustments begun. No flight service.

14th April 1945
Engine regulator adjustments E3+51 and E3+52. Repair work on 4 engines. No flight service.

15th April 1945
Engine regulator adjustments (Me 262A) E4+E5, (He 162A) E2+53 and E3+52. Modification of test-stand vehicle. 0900hrs – Meeting with Oberst Petersen re testing of Do 335 and He 162. Installation of measuring instruments in E3+52. No flight service.

The Ar 234B (GM+BG, Werk-Nr.140107) with the Rechlin Test ID E2+30 in spring 1945, photographed probably not in Lärz but either in Lechfeld or Kaltenkirchen. Notice that the nosewheel is reversed from its normal position.

The engine of the Me 109G-6 is attached to the static vibration Test Stand to determine the relationship between the rigidity of the engine installation and armament trajectory deviation in turning flight, the test being performed by the Measurement Group of Section E3.

It was only on 16th April 1945 that He 162 flights in the framework of the test programme could begin. First to take off was E3+51 on a Works flight piloted by Stabsing. Borsdorff.

Meanwhile, other aircraft from Rechlin had arrived, among them, those fitted with BMW 003 turbojets such as the Me 262A, Werk-Nr.130164, E3+32 (SQ+WC), in Lechfeld from 14th April; the Me 262 V8, Werk-Nr.130003, VI+AC, in Lechfeld from 17th April; the Ar 234B, Werk-Nr.140111, E4+10 (GM+BK), in Lechfeld from 9th April, and the Ju 88A-5 (GH+FQ) engine test-bed, in Lechfeld from 23rd March 1945.

Test flying with the Ar 234B must have begun earlier, as Fliegerhaupting. Walter Strobel had experienced on 4th April a dangerous encounter with 12 P-47 Thunderbolts of the 316th Fighter Squadron, which he recalled as follows:[80]

'In Lechfeld the flight-support organisations and general peripheral conditions were unfortunately very deficient, so that following the loss of the air raid warning service, whilst on a check-flight at slow speed in a Werknummer where faults had been reported, I was suddenly attacked unawares by 12 American fighters and hit by two firing bursts. Climbing out through

the small exit hatch from the burning aircraft hurtling down in a spiral dive at 4,000m (13,120ft) altitude was extremely difficult and was only managed with the greatest of effort, above all, through my accidental kick on the control lever whereupon, as a result of a rolling movement around the lateral axis, I came free. I opened what was fortunately the latest type of parachute which had an inflation-brake at a still very high speed at around 800m (2,600ft) altitude and landed uninjured in a mountain forest. The wrecked aircraft, which had buried itself deep in the ground, pitted with holes and burning, I was able to make out nearby. After briefly reporting to Oberst Petersen, I travelled on the same day by rail to Alt-Lönnewitz in order to fetch a new Werknummer from there.'

Seen from the American side the incident was unrecorded as follows [the original English text is quoted here.[81]

'Twelve P-47s of 316th Fighter Squadron on fighter sweep mission, up at 0745, down at 1000. At Y-2060 at 0900 hours spotted one Arado 234, flight closed in. Lt Thompson fired a 2 seconds burst, strikes hit in the middle of fuselage, left nacelle started smoking, then exploded – pilot bailed out and e/a crashed at Y-2469. One Arado 234 destroyed.'

A further Ar 234C is reported to have been lost in Lechfeld. On 26th April, dispersal of the E-Stelle remnant to Brunnthal south of Munich, had already been ordered and Fliegerhaupting. Strobl and Oberleutnant Hans-Joachim Abels were assigned the task of ferrying two Ar 234Cs to München-Riem. Whilst Strobl, who was the first to take off on this flight lasting only a few minutes, was able to complete it safely, Abels was killed on take-off, probably through failure of one of the turbojets.

Equally as in Lechfeld in spring 1945, British and American fighter-bombers appeared very frequently in the skies above Rechlin. They were not unaware that the Lärz and Roggentin airfields were now serving as operational and diversionary airfields, used for example by the Me 262s of JG 7. On 22nd February 1945, a low-flying aircraft destroyed an Me 262 whose pilot made a successful parachute jump and damaged another which the pilot Leutnant Fritz G Müller was able to belly-land on the airfield.[82] On 25th March, Leutnant Hans Schätzel of JG 7 became the victim of a US Mustang. 1st Lt Raymond H Littge of the 487th Fighter Squadron caught up near Lärz with the Me 262 which was making a landing approach with his undercarriage

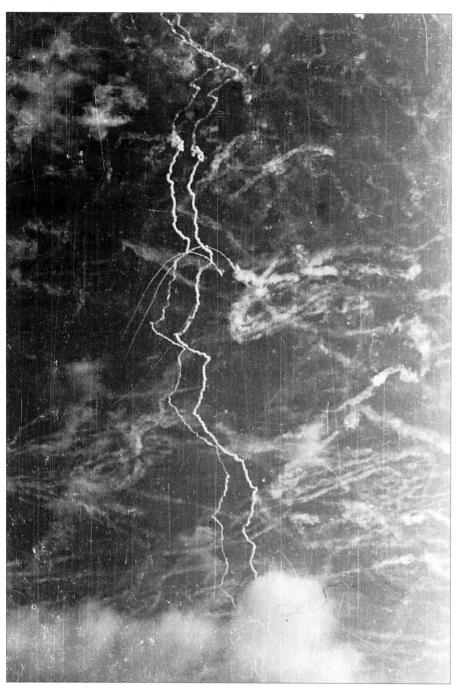

Mischievous omens above Rechlin on 10th April 1945. Whilst the target-markers for American bomber formations already littered the sky, Dipl.-Ing. Georg Hentschel displayed cold-bloodedness on the ground in photographing this spectacle.

extended. Its pilot did not have a chance to get away.[83]

During that same month, there were several schemes earmarked to be put into practice intended to halt the unstoppable advance of Soviet troops, but which in retrospect, could be regarded as of doubtful value and destined to failure from the very beginning. Rechlin was the focal point of this undertaking.

The first of these missions, bearing the code name 'Eisenhammer' (iron hammer), under the leadership of KG 200, was planned as a strike against important energy-producing installations in the Soviet Union. For this purpose, not only had a large

number of Mistel (mistletoe) aircraft combinations been gathered together from the beginning of March in Rechlin and Lärz, but also a large number of the available Ju 290 long-range reconnaissance aircraft of the corresponding FAGr. 5 which operated it.

From flight log-books alone, eleven Ju 290s of this long-range reconnaissance unit have been confirmed as having been dispersed on the Müritz airfields during the period in question. Since the weather conditions necessary for this operation were not met, the plan was cancelled on 30th March 1945. In its place, the Special Operation 'Gertraud' was kept in mind for which the OKL itself had assumed command. Up

to 20th April, using the available Ju 290s equipped with BM 1000 aerial mines slowed by parachute brakes, ten hydro-power stations east of Moscow were to be attacked and destroyed. After more than half of the aircraft had themselves been destroyed in a bombing raid related below, this plan was also abandoned by the OKL.

Rechlin was also to have been the focal point of another operation at the beginning of April 1945 which, in view of the dubious war situation at that time, is difficult to comprehend. The idea was instigated at the OKW of cutting off the rapidly advancing Soviet Armies from their supplies. The targets were specially-selected important bridges behind the frontlines. Following isolated and mostly unsuccessful attacks with conventional bombers as well as with Mistel combinations, a new tactic was considered whereby Do 24 flying-boats, filled with explosives were to land on the Weichsel, float beneath the bridge and exploded there with the aid of a 'Selbstopfer' (suicide) individual.

Flying the heavily-laden aircraft and landing on the Weichsel was to have been undertaken by experienced seaplane crews, who, after landing, were to clamber out and fight their way back to their own lines. How this was supposed to be achieved, was left open.

The starting point for this 'Himmelfahrtskommando' (Heavenly Journey Detachment) under the code name of 'Aktion 24' (Activity 24) was Rechlin airbase, which had a slipway for seaplanes on the bank of the Müritz lake.[84] The first Do 24 arrived in mid March, and on 1st April, several of these aircraft were ferried there. Following removal of all unnecessary equipment, each fuselage was packed full with a large number of crates containing magnesium and dynamite which were connected by a common lead and could be exploded from the pilot's seat. By 4th April, work on the majority of flying-boats had been completed, the aircraft being well camouflaged and anchored in a bay near Röbel on the west bank of the Müritz. On the last of the converted Do 24s, that of Feldwebel Heinz Ottokar Hildenbrandt, still had the 6km (3.7 miles) journey over open water ahead of him, when US fighter-bombers suddenly appeared over Rechlin. This time, it was Mustangs of the 354th Fighter Squadron which attacked the airfield with their weapons and set several parked aircraft on fire. As they flew off westwards, they discovered moving along the water the sole Do 24 of Feldwebel Hildenbrandt, who had no chance of survival. He received fatal injuries whilst his badly-hit aircraft reached the west bank of the Müritz and burned out.

On the same day, a further loss has been documented. The pilot Paul Kahlert of the E-Stelle Rechlin Technical Company was reported as killed. Since in the documents the Müritzsee is given as the place of loss and the term 'low-flying attack' is recorded, it can be assumed that he was in the same Do 24 as Hildenbrandt. The last proof, however, as to why the burial spot of the two crewmen has still not been determined, is still missing to this day.

After these dramatic events, it was only six days before Rechlin became the target of a heavy daylight attack for the second time. At this time, there was almost no flight testing taking place any more. Nevertheless, Lärz was being used more and more as a dispersal and repair centre for the operational Me 262s of JG 7.

For 10th April 1945, the 8th USAAF had planned to deliver a decisive blow against all jet fighter airfields in northern Germany. On that day, bomber formations almost as large as those on 25th August 1944 took off to attack targets in Germany. 170 B-24 Liberators were to attack Rechlin, whilst 105 B-24s, all from the 2nd BD, were to bombard Lärz. Spearheading the formations destined for Rechlin were aircraft of the 466th BG, followed by the 448th BG and the 93rd BG, behind which were the four-engined bombers of the 453rd, 445th and 389th BG.

On their approach to Lärz were bombers of the 467th, 466th and 458th BG. Close support for them was provided by Mustangs of the 4th, 355th and 361st FG, whilst Thunderbolts of 56th BG were given a free hand in the target area. The vast armada took off at 1030 hours, and after a flight of more than five hours, the bombers reached both targets which were attacked almost simultaneously. Prior to that, as on 4th April, Me 262s of JG 7 took off from Lärz to fend off the approaching bombers, but in view of their numerical superiority, the chances of success were extremely low. The airfields themselves were only protected by light flak since the heavier weapons had sometime before been transferred for the defence of large cities or else to the Western or Eastern Front. The Americans were thus able within a quarter of an hour, unhindered, to drop more than 4,200 incendiary, high-explosive, and fragmentation bombs, but without the loss of a single aircraft. Because of cloud cover and co-ordination errors on the approach, three squadrons were not able to drop their bombs on target and had to release their loads on diversionary targets or on open waters.

According to various sources, the raids resulted in 50 deaths, but of these only eleven names are known. After this bombardment, the E-Stelle installations in Lärz were no longer usable, and flight testing came to a complete standstill. After the bombing raid itself, the scores of escort fighters made strafing passes at low level and set a number of the parked aircraft on fire. The camouflaged Do 24 flying-boats, gathered in a bay at Röbel on the Müritz and still awaiting their operational orders to carry-out 'Aktion 24', were discovered by Mustangs of the 61st Fighter Squadron and set on fire. This 'Operation' thus ended before it could even begin and hence avoided the senseless loss of more victims.

The E-Stelle's ability to continue working had been wiped out after these two large air attacks. Nevertheless, low-flying aircraft subsequently appeared quite frequently in the area, and evidently included Soviet aircraft among them. The reason for this was certainly due to increased use of the airfields around Rechlin by fighter, fighter-bomber and transport units which flew out from here in the defence of Berlin. Among others, these included the 'Einsatzkommando (Combat Detachment) Braunegg' from the 'Versuchsverband OKL' trials unit, which in the recollection of the unit's then Intelligence Officer Oberleutnant Wolfgang Mattick, was transferred from Burg to Lärz on 12th April 1945 and from there, undertook reconnaissance missions with the Me 262 over the Eastern Front until 29th April 1945. The remainder of this Detachment thereafter moved to Schleswig, arriving there on 1st May 1945.

Around mid April 1945, a portion of II and III/JG 4 coming from Jüterborg, landed in Rechlin. Its personnel were housed in barracks in Ellerholz Kaserne, the operational headquarters being housed in DF-huts at the conjunction of neighbouring Roggentin. The unit's Fw 190s were stationed on the perimeter of the E-Stelle armaments institute. From here, missions were flown against spearhead routes of the Red Army, against Soviet troops in the suburbs and finally in the government quarter of the Reich capital. On 1st May 1945, the Fw 190s of JG 4 took off on their last operational mission.

The then Unteroffizier Hans Weber of II/JG 4 describes the flight as follows:

'...east of Neustrelitz in a forest clearing we discovered a strung-out Russian supply unit. We each carried an AB 250 besides the aircraft's own guns and a smoke-signal cartridge in the flare pistol. We split up and attacked the column in a cross pattern so that no-one would be able to seek cover. On the first attack, we fired off the smoke cartridges. On the second, we released the AB 250s. On the next approaches, we fired

the aircraft weapons until only 20 rounds/gun remained. On the return flight, we flew over the connecting road between Strelitz and Neustrelitz. Just then, Russian tanks were being rearmed and fuelled there. Acting against orders to conserve the last 20 rounds/gun for our own defence, we attacked the tanks. Shortage of fuel then forced us to continue the flight to Wittstock. (Note: In accordance with the directive, the aircraft were to be transferred there).'

On 20th April 1945, a number of fighters on Rechlin airfield became victims of Tempest fighters from 33 Squadron RAF. After that, the British fighter-bombers discovered, lying some 2km (1.2 miles) north of the airfield, the camp of the RAD, the Reichsarbeitsdienst (Reichs Works Service) erected for the defence of arriving groups of the RAD-Abteilung 6/61 and attacked them in low-level flight. Fortunately, nobody was injured.[85]

A few days later, Lärz became the forward 'jumping-off' airfield for the Fw 190D-9s of the I.&II./JG 26. The IInd Gruppe then flew for the first time on the morning of 23rd April from Uetersen to Lärz, returning the same day in the evening to their home airbase. The action was repeated on the two following days, joined each time by aircraft of the Ist Gruppe from Sülte near Schwerin. From 26th April onwards, the Ist Gruppe remained for three days in Lärz, before they were told to go to their new forward airfield at Klein-Kummersfeld near Neumünster. On 26th April, the Ist/JG 26 from Sülte sent a Technical Detachment on the march to Rechlin and Lärz in order to make the Gruppe's immobile Fw 190D-9s ready for flight. On 27th April, the Detachment reached Rechlin and began with their work. With the last 'Dora 9', the 'brown 11' of the 7th Staffel, Feldwebel Napierski took off at 0635 hours on 30th April from Rechlin for the flight to Klein-Kummersfeld.[86]

In the same period of time, I/JG 11 had received the order to transfer from the threatened Berlin-Gatow airfield to Lärz.[87] The first Fw 190 landed there on 22nd April, followed shortly afterwards by aircraft of the IIIrd Gruppe from Döberitz. Unfortunately, the Staffelkapitän of the 11th/JG 11 Major Schön, was killed when his aircraft overturned during the landing on the severely-bombed airfield in Lärz. Despite this event, JG 11 set out on operational missions the same day. Their operational orders were chiefly to provide cover for ground-attack aircraft flying to Berlin as well as having a free hand as fighters to engage the enemy in the same combat zone.

On 24th April 1945 'Indianer' (Bandits) ie, Allied fighters suddenly appeared in the skies of Rechlin. This time, it comprised Spitfires of 130 Squadron RAF. F/Lts Sibeth and Stowe reported shooting down two

Fw 190s on their landing approach to Rechlin; F/Lt Mertens claimed damaging another.[88] These were apparently the aircraft flown by Feldwebel Paul Berndt who was just able to make an emergency landing in his shot-up Fw 190, whilst Oberleutnant Paul Spangenberg, who had to make a parachute exit, touched down uninjured. Both pilots belonged to I./JG 11. Fighter-bomber activity over Rechlin airfield did not let up on the next day either, when F/Lt Donsford shot-down a Bf 109 and damaged an Fw 190, F/Lt Corbett damaging a Bf 109. On the German side, however, neither the names nor the units to which the shot-down pilots belonged are known.

For the rest of JG 11, the 26th April meant yet another day of special significance, an order to which all machines still available – some 30 Fw 190s – were summoned. The Squadron flew cover for Generaloberst Ritter von Greim, the new Luftwaffe C-in-C, on the flight from Rechlin to Gatow. In the days that followed, further missions in the Berlin area and in Mecklenburg were flown, but on 29th April the move began to airfields further west. On that day, air combat again took place over Lärz, at one time with some 10 Yak-3 fighters and later on with a single Spitfire. One of these aircraft was shot-down by Oberfähnrich Wunderlich, whilst on the German side, Fähnrich Heid was killed. On the next morning, the last aircraft of JG 11 took off from Lärz on missions east of Berlin, landing subsequently in Neustadt-Glewe and Parchim.

Alongside the remaining fighter and fighter-bomber units which flew on defensive missions, there were also transport aircraft which used the airfield during the last days of April. Before this, however, two of the Ju 290s of FAGr. 5 which had survived low-level attacks on 10th April, flew under the leadership of Leutnant Wagner and Hauptmann Eckl on the night of 21st April from Roggentin to Tempelhof to be employed on 'Government Orders' until the end of the war. This meant none other than evacuating hazarded or superfluous individuals from Berlin to southern Germany near to the so-called 'Alpine Fortress'. Another Ju 290 took off on 22nd April 1945 from Rechlin on a flight to southern Germany. On board were at least 15 individuals – members of FAGr. 5, airmen and female intelligence assistants who probably belonged to the Rechlin airbase contingent. At 0320 hours, the aircraft was badly hit by flak northwest of Berlin and caught fire. Only Oberfeldwebel Walter Kroll made a successful parachute exit and was later able to report the incident.[89] Where the aircraft crashed is not known, the remaining crew being regarded as 'missing' to this day. With the ever encroaching advance of the Red Army to Berlin, the airfields there

became endangered. On the morning of 23rd April, Tempelhof and Staaken came under Soviet artillery fire, so that the aircraft of the 'Fliegerstaffel des Führers'[90] received the order to relocate to Rechlin. There, they were to be made available to the OKW which had begun to erect a dispersal centre in a forest camp not far from Rechlin. The first machines of the FdF (the Führer's Air Squadron), an Fh 104 and the Ju 352 (KT+VJ), arrived in Rechlin on the morning of 23rd April. Some of the government aircraft that had remained behind, among them Adolf Hitler's Fw 200 Condor (TK+CV) and a Führer-Escort aircraft, the Fw 200 (CE+IC), also took off and making a detour over Wittstock, arrived in Rechlin-Roggentin on the morning of 25th April. Barely a few hours later, at midday, the ring around the beleaguered capital had closed once and for all.

This circumstance led to the senseless attempt by Wehrmacht leaders to plan an 'air supply' to the besieged city and fly in more troop formations for the 'personal protection of the Führer'. These consisted mostly of badly-trained naval units thrown together from remnants of trained army battalions, and for this purpose, on the night of 26/27th April, the Fw 200 (CE+IC) and the Ju 352 (KT+VJ) among others, flew from Rechlin to Rerik where they took on sailors on board to bring them to Rechlin. The Fw 200, however, was shot down by defensive fire during its approach and crashed south of Potsdam, resulting in the deaths of a portion of the occupants. Only Oberleutnant Schulze in the Ju 352 was able to land in Gatow, where he was able to discharge some 25 sailors and take on board heavily-wounded in exchange. After a dramatic take-off, during which the aircraft came under heavy fire and one engine cut out, Schulze was able to steer the damaged aircraft to Rechlin and land there at 0246 hours. It was possibly the last supply aircraft to be loaded in Gatow, as the airfield was overrun by the Russians that very night. Thereafter, only the provisionally-prepared Charlottenburger Chaussee, the so-called East-West axis on the Tiergarten remained open as a landing-strip.

On the same night, Ju 52s of II/TG 3 had also been given orders to fly from Rechlin on support missions to Berlin. Even these were not accomplished without losses, as the Ju 52/3mg 14e (4V+GR) of Unteroffizier Ernst Martin crashed upon landing after contact with a tree alongside the East-West axis. Already on the outbound flight to Berlin, the Ju 52/3m (4V+AN, Werk-Nr.5111) with Unteroffiziers Wagner, Scharschuch, Villgrattner and Obergefreiter Heuser was lost, the crew posted as 'missing' to this day.

On the following night, only Oberfeldwebel Gerhard Böhm was able to land his

Ju 52/3m on the narrow strip, take off again, and return to Rechlin. Other aircraft of his unit had to leave things unaccomplished and were lucky to come out safely from the inferno. One pilot who wishes to remain anonymous, recalls:

'During the night of 27/28th April 1945 taking-off from Rechlin in the Ju 52/3m (4V+ER), I received the order to land with SS soldiers on the East-West axis. After touching down, there was suddenly a pillar of fire in front of me. I immediately gave full power and in a left turn, with the Victory Monument ahead, got out of there. Renewed attempts were also unsuccessful.'

On the same night, Unteroffizier Geipel of 5./TG 3 in the Ju 52/3m (4V+CN) took off from Rechlin for Berlin. Strong flak fired on the aircraft which received 50 hits on its second sortie, forced the crew each time to turn away prematurely. After that, it was only possible to drop supplies over the Tiergarten before II/TG 3 had to disperse to Güstrow on 30th April, since Rechlin was now immediately threatened by the Red Army.

In the middle of this chaos of material and troop transportation flights to and from Berlin, Rechlin also became the destination or starting-point for a number of special flights. On 23rd April 1945, Reichsminister Speer suddenly appeared in the office of the official on duty, Fliegerstabsing. Hahn, and wanted to be flown to Berlin.[91] After checking with the E-Stelle Commander, a two-seat Fw 190 was made ready, with which Speer was taken to Berlin-Gatow. From there, the journey was continued in a Fieseler Storch to the East-West axis. In the early morning of the 24th April, Speer returned to Rechlin and on 25th April travelled on to Hamburg.

In the same way, the new Luftwaffe C-in-C Generaloberst Ritter von Greim (and successor to the dismissed Reichsmarschall Göring) who had been appointed only two days before to this post, was brought from Rechlin to Berlin on 26th April 1945. The flight took place under dramatic circumstances, for the Fieseler Storch piloted by Flugkapitän Hanna Reitsch, was shot at after take-off in Gatow by Soviet flak; von Greim was wounded and it was only with effort that a successful landing was made close to the Führerbunker.

Hanna Reitsch and von Greim were finally able on 28th April to depart from the capital in an Ar 96 and fly back to Rechlin. From there, the new Luftwaffe C-in-C was flown immediately by Hanna Reitsch to Grossadmiral Karl Dönitz in Plön.

On the morning of 27th April, the Luftwaffe Chief of the General Staff, Generaloberst Karl Koller, coming from Schleissheim, also arrived in Berlin where he became an eyewitness to the precarious

One of the last tasks of Section E3 was the development and testing of a 'combat' Test Stand for the He 162's BMW 003 turbojet.

and mostly unsuccessful attempts to fly in troops to encircled Berlin. His meetings with Generalfeldmarschall Alfred Jodl who was at an OKW dispersal centre in Neuroofen, as well as with Generaloberst Ritter von Greim, did not achieve anything tangible. In view of the military situation, orderly command or any type of countermeasures had long since become useless or impossible, so that Koller flew back on 29th April to Neubiberg near Munich.[92]

The situation on the ground had meanwhile reached a dramatic peak in Mecklenburg. Up until spring 1945, Soviet troops had advanced far into German territory. Along the lower reaches of the Oder river, units of the 2nd White Russian Front had gathered on 20th April 1945 ready to storm the Mecklenburg-Vorpommern region, and following severe fighting, had broken through the thin defensive line of units of the 3rd Panzer Army. On 25th April, the latter were forced to withdraw to the second line of defence – the so-called 'Wotan' position, but were hardly able to remain there for one day. With that, the Red Army was able to make the final breakthrough to Berlin.

In the area south of Prenzlau the Soviet Army made their uninterrupted advance westwards. Neustrelitz, only 45km (28 miles) east of Rechlin, fell on 30th April and on the following day, Weserberg and Mirow were overrun by units of the 191st Rifle Division and the 8th Mechanized Corps. From there, only some 10km (6mls) away from Rechlin, the troops advanced on the next day towards Rechlin.

The approach of the Red Army caused a frenzy of activity. Already some days before, work had begun to pull back the E-Stelle dispersal offices, workshops and laboratories which stretched to Neustrelitz and Weserberg. In the midst of this, on 17th April, the Ju 52/3m (GC+BK) of Department E4 was shot down shortly after take-off, evidently by Soviet fighter-bombers, resulting in at least four fatal casualties whose names are still unknown.[93]

Since Rechlin and its surrounding villages were now directly threatened, the aim was to evacuate remaining personnel, and above all, their families to the west where the Americans had almost advanced as far as Schwerin. The majority of flying and fight-test personnel were, after 10th April 1945 at the latest, called up for non-airborne service in parachute-troop units or in Luftwaffe field divisions to either Travemünde, Schleswig-Holstein or Lechfeld. Flight testing activities in Rechlin had sunk to a minimum from March 1945.

The dangers with which E-Stelle pilots were confronted right up to the final days, is portrayed in the following dramatic description by Flieger-Oberstabsing. Walter Ballerstedt, at that time head of the Department E7 installation group, in his last flight in a Me 262:[94]

'It was Saturday evening before Easter 1945. Somebody had the notion of packing French 2kg (4.4lb) bombs into a 250kg (551lb) container and jettisoning the containers in a dive on enemy bomber formations. A detonator was to open the containers one second after release. On the 'B-Platte', a mock-up of a B-17 had been placed. The container was to have been opened in a diving approach… and then we would see what happens. At an airspeed of 700km/h (435mph) at a height of 70m (230ft) and promptly after one second, hence roughly 5m (16ft) beneath my aircraft the container opened. Hardly had the fuses tasted fresh air when they began to go into action. There was crackling all around me; the elevator became rigid, beneath me there was a hole, and from the port engine a long jet of flame shot out. On the starboard side, everything seemed to be in order. A touch on the trimmer brought the aircraft back to a level flightpath. I closed the port fuel cock; the jet of flame broke away – at least it appeared to do so. But no, the jet stream was now surrounded by a fiery ring, the burning continued and became shorter and shorter. The fiery burden then spread over to the fixed portion of the wing above the engine. I wanted to advise the tracking station, but was unable to make contact. I found myself over the Müritz at about 500km/h (310mph) on a southerly course and wanted to head for

Lärz. With aileron and rudder the 'battering ram' could still be steered to some extent. Now the fire to port had lapped over to the landing flaps. The entire port wing trailing-edge right up to the ailerons was a bright red fiery band which rapidly spread forwards. The properly functioning engine kept pushing the aircraft in a turn to port. I was not able to make the proper approach to the Lärz runway. In front of me lay the large uncultivated field between the Sprottschen Berg, the shooting-ranges, Retzow and Vipperow-Retzow avenue. I wanted to get there before the main spar started to glow. I had no ejection seat, but with a press on the lever, the canopy flew off. I took the Revi gunsight from its mounting and 'ditched it'. I tightened the seat harness as firmly as I could. I then closed the throttle, shut-off the starboard fuel cock and hurtled headlong in a shallow dive towards the ground at about 500km/h (310mph), tensed up to see how it would all end. The aircraft was catapulted upwards and tilted over on its port wing until the lateral axis stood vertical. Now it's all over I thought, and felt how the aircraft tried to do a somersault. But I wasn't able to follow the sequence anymore.'

The aircraft was ripped apart in hundreds of tiny pieces, but Walter Ballerstedt survived the crash despite serious injuries.

In the last few weeks of the war, there were still certain aircraft types, equipment and systems undergoing testing which although technologically highly advanced were still far away in their stage of development from being mature for series production or operational readiness. Pre-eminent among piston-engined aircraft were the Ta152, eg, the Ta152C V8 (GW+QA) as well as the H-0 models (CW+CC, Werk-Nr.150003; CW+CF, Werk-Nr.150006; CW+CI, Werk-Nr.150009, and CW+CJ, Werk-Nr.150010), alongside the Fw 190A-9, D-11 and D-12, as well as the new Ju 88 versions with the Jumo 213 or DB 603 undergoing testing. Gradually, however, the aircraft were handed over to Test Detachments or other units.

Wherever possible, the remainder of the aircraft were to be ferried over to Schleswig-Holstein or to southern Germany. Well-known is the flight by Flieger-Haupting. Hans-Werner Lerche with the Do 335A-02 (VG+PH, Werk-Nr.240102). Taking-off from Rechlin on 20th April 1945, via Prague and Lechfeld, he reached Oberpfaffenhofen on 23rd April 1945. His machine, the sole Do 335 still in existence – and almost certainly the sole survivor of aircraft tested in Rechlin – is at the moment in the Smithsonian Institute in Washington, DC.

Fliegerstabsing. Heinz Fischer was 'lucky in misfortune' when he likewise took off from Rechlin in a Do 335 on 26th April 1945. Due to the failure of the compass, he strayed over French territory and because of lack of fuel, was forced to leave the aircraft over the Vosges. Since neither the explosive tail-surface jettison nor the ejection seat mechanism functioned, he had to leave the aircraft in the normal way using his parachute which he did successfully.[95]

At the turn of 1944/45, helicopter flight testing was also transferred to Rechlin, where the Fa 223 S51 (GW+PA, Werk-Nr.22300051) wound up at the E-Stelle. Sustaining slight damage during the bombing raid on 10th April 1945, after subsequent repairs the machine stood ready to be ferried to Ainring. This flight was to have been undertaken by the 'Musterbegleiter' (Type Supervisor) Dipl.-Ing. Otto Dumke[96] who recalled:

'On 20th April I took off with my mechanic at around 0300 hours on the flight to Ainring near Salzburg. It was difficult since, because of the scarcity of fuel, we had taken aboard a large barrelfull with us and the mechanic had neglected to balance the load with a counterweight. The machine was thus unstable, until I was somehow able to level it. We flew without any illumination since it was known that Russian night-fighters were prying around. Now and again the mechanic lit-up the dashboard with his pocket torch. We flew at a height between 100m (330ft) and 200m (660ft), flew through an air corridor in the neighbourhood of Tegel and landed after a roughly 1.5 hour flight in Finsterwalde.

The landing was spectacular as it was not possible due to its instability to bring the helicopter down in a pancake landing as it always retained some forward speed. Upon contact with the ground, the damaged

nosewheel fork finally gave way. The helicopter's tail end rose high in the air, and the front of the cockpit touched the ground. In the workshops we searched for a welder who had experience of working with metals. To our great surprise, we found such a specialist who welded the nosewheel fork very well, so that we were ready to fly again around noon. After take-off, we flew at the lowest possible altitude in a southerly direction where we landed some time later in Tetschen-Bodenbach. An out-station Detachment of the Siemens firm stationed there brought our engine in order as it was due for a check-up. Two days later, I took-off to continue the journey in the course of which we spotted seven Thunderbolt fighters ahead of us. We quickly turned about face and set the helicopter down in the next forest clearing and ran under cover of the trees. Thank goodness, they had not seen us! Stupidly enough, we had landed in a highland bog, so that the wheels had almost completely sunk in. I had the mechanic climb out so as to reduce the weight. In this way, we were able to lift the helicopter from the swamp; the mechanic climbed aboard again, and we were able to continue the flight. Since the fuel was finally coming to an end, we had to land near a small village and telephone the Transport Squadron in Ainring to request replenishment. After a while, the vehicle arrived and we were able to fill up, so that we were able to fly to Ainring.'

On these ferry-flights, a fatal crash unfortunately occurred when Leutnant Bruno Stellbrink of 6/KG 76 together with Oberfeldwebel Johne were to ferry two Ar 234Cs from Rechlin to Lübeck-Blankensee. Both took off on the afternoon of 28th April 1945 on this flight, but whilst Johne was able to bring his aircraft in safely, Stellbrink was killed in the crash only a few kilometres west of Rechlin following an explosion. This is the last known loss of an E-Stelle Rechlin aircraft.[97]

At this time, the KdE Oberst Petersen together with his staff, as well as the acting E-Stelle Rechlin Commander Major Otto Behrens who held this position since December 1944, had all moved to Lechfeld. From there, they had to relocate again to Brunnthal, south of Munich. On 24th April, the first portion of the E-Stelle remnant started on their journey there, only to find that the location had no decent working and accommodation possibilities. Oberpfaffenhofen was therefore selected as the next destination, where just a few days before the war ended, Oberst Petersen officially declared the dissolution of the E-Stelle Rechlin.[98]

In Rechlin itself there were still members of the Works Department, responsible for electricity and water supply for the airfield

and housing area, as well as a proportion of the Airbase Company responsible for maintaining flying operations of the combat units based on the Rechlin airfields, and last but not least, the wives and children of E-Stelle members who had already been reassigned elsewhere. At the sound of the approaching thunder of guns, a veritable 'escape wave' westwards set in during the last days of April – by car, bicycle or train, even with boats of the ship units or on foot where several deaths occurred as a result of low-flying attacks. Only a few had the good fortune to break out into the unknown with the few flight test aircraft that were still available. One of the last aircraft which took off on such a flight in the early morning of 30th April was the fully-loaded Ju 52/3m (GS+AR) with Fliegerstabsing, Günter Sinram of Department E3 at the controls. At 0517 hours it made a safe landing in Schleswig. On the same afternoon, Oberleutnant Joachim Eisermann of Department E5 took off in the Bü 181 (RE+OS), to make the westward flight in stages, on which he was shot down by American troops two days later and was taken into captivity uninjured.

The last railway cars had already left Rechlin on 29th April, arriving safely in Schwerin. Remaining behind were principally the local employees and workforce as well as many families who had no relatives or who had no jumping-off point in the west, and who were unaware where their husbands were located at the time. They could only hope that they would survive uninjured in the expected Red Army invasion.

Already on 30th April, demolition teams had started work to destroy the buildings and E-Stelle installations which had survived the bombing raids intact. Despite the emergency protective trenches which had been dug out in April, defending the airfield was totally out of the question. Hence the Soviet forward Detachments who had pushed through to Rechlin on 2nd May, met no resistance. It has been reported by many eye-witnesses that the Works Head of the E-Stelle, Obersting. Fischer, together with two other engineers, handed over the installation to the Soviets.

The occupation of Rechlin did not occur without loss of life, injuries, and all the accompanying horrors which had previously been experienced in so many places lying further eastward during the advance of the Red Army. Descriptions about what happened in Rechlin gave no comprehensive picture of events, which is understandable due to the long passage of time. Nevertheless, it seems relatively certain that a young German soldier who was the first to come into contact with the Red Army in Vietzen, was shot by them. In other places in the village, shots were also heard to ring out when several families put an end to their own lives. The incoming troops thereupon began to search all the houses, taking away the occupants' valuables and destroying the furniture and contents. Rapes and shootings followed. As a result of the excesses taking place all around them, up until the evening of that day many of the occupants in Rechlin had chosen to commit suicide. Also, those who had fled to the surrounding farmsteads, forester's houses and villages, were not spared from these happenings. It is thus almost impossible today to determine names and numbers of civilian victims which the occupation of Rechlin had cost. Between 40 and 50 people is the number that can be assumed with relative certainty, to which must be added some 30 servicemen of various German units, of whom a portion fell in combat in the immediate neighbourhood of Rechlin, and a portion who were later taken prisoner by Soviet troops and shot.

Immediately after the occupation, the remaining residents were set to work to fill-in the bomb craters on the Rechlin and Lärz airfields and perform other clearing-up duties, since the locations were occupied by Soviet Air Force units. A large proportion of housing was confiscated by the occupying forces, so that the residents had to seek new accommodation. Nevertheless, with the help of some Works Engineers and handymen who remained behind it soon became possible to provisionally reinstate the energy supplies such that, step by step, life was made more bearable.

The occupiers, however, began simultaneously to dismantle the available or still usable airfield installations right up to the buildings themselves for transport to the Soviet Union. Nothing more should remain in evidence of what had been the Luftwaffe's largest Flight Test Centre.

The Postwar Period

The dismantling work in Rechlin lasted until around 1949 and for many residents, the majority of whom were refugees from Pomerania, Silesia, and East Prussia, who had experienced the end of the war in Mecklenburg, this period was one of the few employment opportunities in the chiefly agriculturally-dominated region. Former E-Stellen installations, nevertheless, were to form the foundation for the establishment in 1947 of the 'Mechanical Workshops, District-owned Plant Rechlin/Vietzen'.[99] Following release of airfield terrain by the Red Army, around 1948 the 'VEB Schiffswerft Rechlin' was established, which soon developed into the largest employer in the region and until 1990 remained an important manufacturer of lifeboats and supplier of equipment for the Baltic Shipbuilding Yards in Rostock, Stralsund, Warnemünde and Wismar.

Beside it, on the grounds of the former Gruppe Nord in 1951, the Water Sports School of the FDJ (Free German Youth) was organised, which from 1952 became the GST (Society for Sport and Technics) Sea Sport School, but was dissolved on 30th March 1956.

Following creation of indigenous armed forces on so-called 'DDR' (German Democratic Republic) territory from 1956 the area became the base of an Intelligence Equipment Depot of the NVA (Peoples National Army) which utilized the surviving buildings of Departments E4 and E5 that had formed a part of the former Gruppe Nord. Today, it houses a Main Equipment Depot of the Bundeswehr (Federal German Army).

Since the end of World War Two, Rechlin airfield itself was non-operational. The hangars had been destroyed by bombing and the remainder dismantled. The aircraft manoeuvring area was used for agricultural purposes. The Ellerholz barracks behind the former Gruppe West remained almost undamaged, and was used as accommodation for units of the Soviet Armed Forces in East Germany. They belonged to Air Force units stationed in Lärz – a fighter-bomber and a combat helicopter regiment. For housing the soldiers' families, the northern portion of the Vietzen settlement had been confiscated and where further tenement blocks were erected. From then on, a concrete wall separated the housing area in the northern Russian Sector from the southern sector for German families. Russian soldiers with their families additionally dwelled in old and newly-erected buildings directly on the grounds of Lärz airfield.

In 1993, the last Russian soldiers left the area. Today, the 'Müritz Airfield Rechlin-Lärz' is used by civilian air transport aircraft and serves as one of the last successors of Rechlin's flying past. Beside it, in the Rechlin surroundings there still remain 'silent witnesses' from the E-Stellen period – dilapidated buildings, blown up observation towers and measurement stations, the foundations of transmission towers and radar emplacements, plus bomb craters and aircraft wreckage. Nature hides these remains with each passing year. In order not to allow the flying period and engineering efforts of Rechlin's historical past to be forgotten, an Aviation Technical Museum Rechlin now stands on the Claas-See directly on the grounds of the former Gruppe Nord which once served as the heart of the Test Centre.

Footnotes

1 Mecklenburg State Archive, Schwerin: War Ministry Nr.2220/11.16.A/L dated 29.11.1916 (Transcript).

2 Mecklenburg State Archives, Schwerin: Letter from Hauptmann Joly to Graf Hahn, aide-de-camp to the Grand Duke of Mecklenburg-Schwerin, of 25.07.1918

3 Georg Wolle: Recollections of Old Rechlin, Rechliner Brief (Letter) Nr.23 (no location) 1987.

4 The existence of the 'Luftfahrtverein Waren' and its ownership re Rechlin airfield are cited in documents (Regional Archive Neustrelitz, usage-acceptance confirmation of 10.04.1928). Other details are only from verbal descriptions.

5 Regional Archive Neustrelitz. Albatros Flugzeugwerke GmbH letter to the Baurat des Landkreises Waren of 23.03.1928, mentioning the 'Rechlin airfield leased by us'. This is the oldest reference to the activities of the Albatros Werke in Rechlin.

6 Letter from Admiral Lahs, President of the RDLI to Generalmajor Ritter von Mittelberger, head of the Inspektion der Waffenschulen In 1 in the Truppenamt, dated 1.10.1929, requesting the In 1 to assume the disguised leadership of the E-Stellen Staaken and Müritz via the RDLI.

7 As portrayed by K H Völker: 'The development of military aviation in Germany 1920-1933', Stuttgart 1962, p247 (Attachment 7) but not confirmed in documents.

8 BA/MA Freiburg, Document RM8v/3604: Library Ref Nr.25/2 25F. Preliminary Draft, Test Programme 1.2.1925 to 30.6.1925 and text of report of Hauptmann Student re Tests in accordance with Test Programme 1.2.1925 to 30.6.1925. Dinos motor = water-cooled 4-cylinder 80hp (59kW) engine of the Dinos company. WGL motor = 30-40hp (22-29kW) engine for light aircraft, developed by Dixi. Grübler motor = No details available. Gast test-firings = Tests with a machine-gun developed by the Gast company. Siemens air-test = No details available. Lübbe = Tests with a machine-gun developed by Heinrich F A Lübbe, who was head of the Fokker Waffenfabrik in Berlin during WW1.

9 BA/MA Freiburg, Doc: RH8v/3604: Ideal (was the camouflage designation). Test Programme 1925/26. Undated, but definitely before 7.4.1925.

10 Walter Hertel: E-Stelle Rechlin within the framework of the 'Technical Air Armament' 1925-33. Rechliner Brief Nr.37 (no location) 1982.

11 Overview of 'Aircraft not included in flying operations in June 1936' with remarks that the He 41a D-IXAZ, Werk-Nr.342 'going to SAM' with handwritten note 'relinquished'.

12 Georg Wolle: 'Rechlin's Early Years', Rechliner Brief Nr.24 (no location) 1978.

13 Ernst Marquard: 'Retrospective glance at the E-Stelle Rechlin', Rechliner Brief Nr.16 Wesselring/Oberbayern, 1976.

14 Walter Hertel: 'E-Stelle Rechlin in the framework of Technical Air Armament 1920-1933', Rechliner Brief Nr.37 (no location), 1982.

15 Volker Koos: 'Aviation between the Baltic and Breitling', Berlin & Allershausen, 1990.

16 From a verbal statement by General der Flieger (retd) Felmy, cited by K H Völker in 'The development of military aviation in Germany

1920-1933', Stuttgart, 1982, p230. No documentary evidence so far discovered.

17 The documentary situation re Lärz and Roggentin is extremely sparse, and recourse can only be made to eyewitness statements which do not always coincide.

18 Karl-Heinz Völker: Documents and documentary photos on the history of the Luftwaffe, Stuttgart, 1968, p420. Report on inspection of the E-Hafen Instruction Course Roggentin on 27th May 1937.

19 BA/MA Freiburg, Document RL 3/206.

20 BA/MA Freiburg, Document RL 3/159: LC Nr.1117/35, II 1, gKdos dated 21st January 1935. R Lucht – Result of discussions … at the E-Stelle Rechlin on 17/18th January 1935.

21 Guido Jungmayr. Report of tests with the Do 17 V2 (D-AHAK, Werk-Nr.257) in Rechlin dated 3rd September 1935.

22 Junkers Motoren (Jumo) document on: Off-field landing of the Ju 86 V1 on 4.6.1935 near Rechlin.

23 Flight log-book Otto Cuno, E3.

24 Deutsches Museum, Munich, Special Collection Document Rech 2: Fw 187 V2 aircraft, type-test and performance, dated 24.6.1938 for PfL Order 152 of 16th August 1937.

25 Details from Dipl.-Ing. Julius Henrici on the DVL out-station and PfL Rechlin office in conversation with the author on 29th May 1997.

26 'Record on the number of take-offs and flying hours for November 1935', also June 1936 as well as the summary of 'Aircraft not flown in 1936' by the E-Stelle Rechlin (no author).

27 BA/MA Freiburg, Document RL 36/29: Department M Monthly Report, April 1936: Continuation of tests with fixed oblique installation in Ar 68 and He 51 by Department M.

28 Flight log-book Kurt Heinrich at Heinkel. Flights with the He 118 V2 (D-UHAH, Werk-Nr.1294) in Rechlin; entries dated 3rd to 6th July. The 3rd July entry presumably refers to the essential technical comparison, whilst the 6th July flight took place in the course of a comprehensive demonstration for the Wehrmacht leaders.

29 National Archives, Washington, Microfilm T 177/9 LC II, 12th May 1934. Results of Meeting between the A-Amt and C-Amt on 11th May 1934 re tactical requirements and priority for aircraft development tests.

30 BA/MA Freiburg, Document RL 3/78: LC II 1 zbV dated 16th Feb 1937, Minutes of Meeting.

31 Karl-Heinz Völker: 'Die Deutsche Luftwaffe 1933-39' Stuttgart 1967, p132. Documentary evidence of a comparative flight not yet discovered.

32 Günter Ott in a letter dated 10th January to the author.

33 Undated Summary 'Personnel Strength' for all E-Stellen, probably compiled in connection with the reorganisation in spring 1938.

34 National Archives, Washington, Microfilm T 177/17: Weekly Report LC II 1 b for the week of 19.2. to 25.2.1938.

35 Karl-Heinz Völker: 'Die Deutsche Luftwaffe 1933-1939', Stuttgart, 1967, p190. Documentary evidence not yet discovered.

36 Fritz Aly: 'The 3rd July 1939', Rechliner Brief Nr.48 (no location) 1984.

37 Kdo.d.E. Nr.15451/42 gKdos (Ia) dated 17th August 1942 '…the first He 177 flew on

20.11.1939…' and Heinkel Flugzeugwerke Announcement Nr.4297 dated 20.11.1939 re 'First flight He 177'. In Flug-Revue 4/1989, Heinz Redemann gives a first flight date of 19.11.1939.

38 BA/MA Freiburg, Document RL 36/75: E-Stelle Rechlin Report of 4.4.1940 re Status of S-tests and Developments/E2 Airframes.

39 BA/MA Freiburg, Document RL 36/75: E-Stelle Rechlin Report of 29.2.1940 re Status of S-tests and Developments/E2 Airframes.

40 BA/MA Freiburg, Document RL 3/124: Luftwaffe equipment and priority steps in Procurement Year 1939/40.

41 Flight log-book Heinrich Beauvais, E2. First entry of Fw 190 V1 (RM+CA) in Rechlin on 28.6.1940.

42 BA/MA Freiburg, Document RL 3/546: Letter GL to PfL dated August 1940 re Certification of Captured Aircraft.

43 Out of the first 19 Partial Reports on Go 244 tests in Rechlin, 15 exist in the Deutsches Museum, Munich, Special Collections.

44 For further details see K von Grasdorff/K Grasmann/H Schubert: 'Flugmotoren und Strahltriebwerke', Bernard & Graefe Verlag, Bonn, 1995.

45 Walter Baist: 'Der Kaltstart', Rechliner Brief Nr.39 (no location) 1982.

46 Walter Baist: 'Rechlin recollections of Dr.-Ing. W Baist' in Der Flieger, 4/1979.

47 Dr.-Ing. Georg Hentschel: 'From the E-Stelle Rechlin to ONERA in Paris', unpublished manuscript (undated), and National Archives, Washington, Microfilm T 321/60 E3L, Weekly Report of 17.7.1943.

48 von Burger/Hottinger: Measurement methods for engine testing. Special printing from Technische Berichte Band 11 (1944), Nr.11.

49 Flight log-books Oskar Huber, E3, and Günter Sinram, E3.

50 Fritz Trenkle: 'Bordfunkgeräte – Vom Funkensender zum Bordradar', Bernard & Graefe Verlag, Koblenz, 1986; also S Ruff/M Ruck/G Sedlmayer: 'Sicherheit und Rettung in der Luftfahrt', Bernard & Graefe Verlag, Koblenz, 1983; and Kurt Kracheel: 'Flugführungssysteme – Blindfluginstrumente, Autopiloten, Flugsteuerungen', Bernard & Graefe Verlag, Bonn, 1993.

51 Hans Westphal/Dr.-Ing. Waldemar-Möller: 'Ein Leben für die Fliegewrei', Rechliner Brief Nr.34 (no location) 1978.

52 E-Stelle Rechlin E4lic, Test Nr.33273, Partial Report 3 ,Düppel mit Würzburg C' dated 13.7.1942.

53 BA/MA Freiburg, Document 3/2570: 'War Diary Chef TLR for the period 16th March to 4th April 1945.

54 Dr. Theodor Benzinger, Medical Department of the Luftwaffe E-Stelle Rechlin, prepared for AAF Aero Medical Center, Heidelberg, 1946.

55 Rudolf Kröber: 'Contribution to the history of Abteilung F', Rechlin Brief, Nr.58 (no location) 1984.

56 Public Record Office, London, Document AIR 34/629: Interpretation Report No C.487 of 29th April 1942 'Dummy Aerodrome near Boek'.

57 F K Utech (former He 177 prototype specialist in Department E2) letter dated 12th June 1982 to Heinrich Beauvais.

58 Walter Hertel: 'E-Stelle Rechlin in the

framework of Technical Air Armament 1925-1933', Rechliner Brief, Nr.37 (no location), 1982.
59 Description of Rechlin, Sheet No 130 of 14.3.1944 with detailed information on existing installations and buildings.
60 Constance Babington-Smith: 'Evidence in Camera – The Story of Photographic Reconnaissance in World War Two', London, 1958.
61 Public Record Office, London, Document AIR 34/272 Interpretation Report No L 40 of 6th June 1942.
62 Public Record Office, London, Doc: AIR 34/273 Interpretation Report No L 77 of 9th July 1943.
63 BA/MA Freiburg, Document RL 36/49: E-Stelle Rechlin 'Nebeleinsatz und Flakschutz Sonderliste' of 7th December 1943.
64 During the so-called 'Big Week' between 20th and 25th February 1944, US bomber formations made concentrated attacks daily on German aircraft and aero-engine factories and caused severe inroads to production.
65 Dipl-Ing. Hans Günter Ploes in letter of 25.11.1996 to the author.
66 Allied Central Interpretation Unit: Interpretation Report S.A.1852 'Attack on Rechlin Airfield' on 24.5.1944 dated 25th May 1944 and Immediate Interpretation Report No K 2261 'Locality: Rechlin/Lärz A/F' of 28th May 1944.
67 Public Record Office, London, Document AIR 34/274.
68 Flight log-books Heinrich Beauvais, Harry Böttcher, Joachim Eisermann: First entries on 14th and 15th June 1944.
69 Flight log-books Heinrich Beauvais, Harry Böttcher: First entries on 15 and 17.8.1944.
70 Oberbayerische Forschungsanstalt Oberammergau, Minutes of Meeting 8/4039/44: Comparison Flights of Me 262 and Ar 234 at the E-Stelle Rechlin, dated 17.6.1944.
71 Weekly Report of Ekdo Lärz and Department E2 from 4.8.1944 to 23.12.1944.
72 Telephonic information from Dipl.-Ing. Hans Günter Ploes to the author on 15.3.1997. In US documents, the loss of only one aircraft is confirmed. German reports of losses (Luftgaukommando XI IcL, Shoot-downs of 25.6.1944) refer to 3 B-17s shot down over Rechlin.
73 Public Record Office, London, Document AIR 34/274: Interpretation Report No L 264 of 31.10.1944 'Unidentified Aircraft at Rechlin/Lärz – Rechlin 67'.
74 Dipl.-Ing. Otto Schneider, E2, in letter of 27.11.1992 to the author. Also Waffen-Revue Nos 92 and 93: The manned German kamikaze projectiles, Parts 6 and 7.
75 Flight log-book Heinz Kensche, GL-C/E2.

76 BA/MA Freiburg, Doc: RL 3/2574: Chef TLR, KR-Telegram to LuFwSt dated 31.1.1945.
77 Public Record Office, London: Ultra-Decoding Report BT 4608, cited in Jet & Prop, 3/1996.
78 BA/MA Freiburg, Document RL 3/2570: War Diary of Chef TLR for the period 5 to 13.5.1945.
79 Diary Hans Borsdorff, E3.
80 Dipl.-Ing. Walter Strobl, E2, in a letter of 6.11.1994 to the author.
81 Hans Grimminger in letter of 23.2.1996 to the author (Transcript of the 324th Fighter Group combat report).
82 Telephonic information from Manfred Boehme on 2.6.1997 to the author.
83 Encounter Report by Lt Raymond H Littge of the 487th Fighter Squadron.
84 Axel Urbanke: 'The history of the Do 24 wreck in the Sinsheim Museum, in Jet & Prop, 2/1994.
85 Diary Maurice Friess, former workman in the RAD Department 6/61 in Rechlin.
86 Axel Urbanke in letter of 24.10.1994 to the author.
87 J Prien/P Rodeike: Jagdgeschwader 1 and 11, Part 3, Eutin, 1995.
88 Dipl.-Ing. Hans Günter Ploes in letter of 25.11.1996 to the author.
89 Undated 'Report based on information by Oberfeldwebel Kroll' re the Ju 290 crash on 22.4.1945.
90 All data re the transport flights to Berlin from G Ott: 'Unternehmen Reichskanzlei', in Jet & Prop, 3/1995 and 4/1995; also G Schlaug: 'The jettisoned articles must arrive at the focal point' in Jet & Prop, 2/1996.
91 Gert Hahn: 'Rechlin's participation in flight regulators and gyro development', Rechliner Brief No 35 (no location), 1978.
92 Karl Koller: 'Der letzte Monat', Esslingen, 1991.
93 Heinz Sommerkorn, E2, in letter of 8.2.1996 to the author.
94 Walter Ballerstedt: 'Murderous tests in and with the Schwalbe (swallow)', Rechliner Brief, No 16, (no location), 1976.
95 Heinz Fischer: 'My Flight to Freedom', Rechliner Brief, No 42, (no location), 1976.
96 Otto Dumke: 'Report of a flight with the Fa 223 from Rechlin to Ainring' in letter of 23.2.1996 to the author.
97 Gerhard Morich (former Hauptmann and Staffelkapitän of 6./KG 76) in letter of 17.9.1945 to Miss Gisela Stellbrink.
98 Diary Heinz Borsdorff, E3, and verbal communication to the author.
99 Various authors: 'Rechlin boatbuilders then and now 1948-1960' Part 1, Rechlin, 1981.

Literature List

Babington-Smith, Constance: Evidence in Camera – The Story of Photographic Intelligence in World War Two, London, 1958.

Boog, Horst: 'Die Deutsche Luftwaffenführung 1935-1945', Stuttgart, 1982.

Hentschel, Dr.-Ing. Georg: 'Von der E-Stelle Rechlin to ONERA Paris', unpublished manuscript, undated.

Koller, Karl: 'Der letzte Monat', Esslingen, 1987.

Koos, Dr. Volker: 'Luftfahrt zwischen Ostsee und Breitling', Berlin, 1990.

Kössler, Karl: 'Transporter – 'Wer kennt sie schon?', Düsseldorf, 1976.

Kössler, Karl & Ott, Günther: 'Die grossen Dessauer- Ju 89, Ju 90, Ju 290, Ju 390', Planegg, 1993.

Krüger, Dieter: 'Militärische Ereignisse zwischen Müritz und Haff 1945', Neubrandenburg, 1991.

Ott, Günther: 'Unternehmen Reichskanzlei' Jet & Prop, 3/1995 and 4/1995, Zweibrücken.

Prien, Dr. Jochen & Rodeike, Peter: 'Jagdgeschwader 1 und 11', Eutin, 1995.

Reitsch, Hanna: 'Fliegen – Mein Leben', Munich, 1974.

Schlaug, Georg: 'Das Abgeworfene muss blitzartig an den Brennpunkte heran', Jet & Prop, 2/1996, Zweibrücken.

Urbanke, Axel: 'Die Geschichte des Do 24-Wracks im Museum Sinsheim', Jet & Prop, 2/1994, Zweibrücken.

Völker, Karl-Heinz: 'Die Entwicklung der militärischen Luftfahrt in Deutschland 1920-1933', Stuttgart, 1962.

Völker, Karl-Heinz: 'Die deutsche Luftwaffe 1933-1939', Stuttgart, 1967.

Völker, Karl-Heinz: 'Dokumente und Dokumentarfotos zur Geschichte der deutschen Luftwaffe', Stuttgart, 1968.

Various authors: 'E-Stelle See', Vols 1 to 3, Steinbach, undated

Various authors: Rechliner Briefe, Vols 1 to 5, Wessling-Fürstenfeldbruck, 1976-1984.

Various authors: 'Rechliner Schiffbauer einst und jetzt 1948-1960', Rechlin, 1981.

Aircraft at the DVL, Abteilung M, Erprobungsabteilung Albatros, E-Stelle RDL Staaken & Rechlin, 1926 to 1934

Registration	Aircraft	Werk-Nr.	Powerplant	Year built	(A) Assigned Unit / (O) Operator	Remarks
D-252	Junkers F 13	572	BMW IIIa		(A) RDL Staaken	In Lipetsk from 01.10.1929
D-586	Albatros L 47b	?	BMW IIIa, later BMW IV	?	(A) DVL	Crashed in Adlershof 19.10.1926
D-677	Heinkel HD 21	7	Mercedes D I later Mercedes D IIa	1925	At Arado from 5.1925 (A) DVL from > 9.1926 (A) Alb. from 4.1928	In 9.1929 to Sweden as SE-ACY
D-713	Junkers A 20	864	BMW IV	1925	(A) DVL from >4.1926 (O) RDL Staaken from 1.1930	(O) DLG from 9.1930
D-720	Junkers A 20	874	BMW IV later BMW Va	1925	(A) DVL from >3.1926 (O) RDL from 3.1930	
D-750	Junkers A 20	878	BMW IV	1925	(O) RDL Staaken	Crashed in Lipetsk 4.8.1931
D-764	Udet U 12	249	Sh 11 later Sh 14	1925	(A) DVL from 7.1928 (O) RDL Staaken (A) RDL Staaken from 12.1932	
D-831	Junkers F 13 Junkers F 13co	781	Junkers L2 later BMW Va	1926	(A) DVL from 9.1926 (O) RDL Staaken from 4.1930 (A) DLG from 5.1932	In Lipetsk 1926/27, later in Rechlin, later D-OBAH
D-868	Junkers A 20be from 3.29 A 35	1052	BMW IV	1926	(A) DVL from 5.1926 (O) RDL Staaken from 2.1930	Broken-up 1.1931.
D-878	Junkers G 24	844	3 x Junkers L2	1925	(A) DVL from 12.1929 (O) RDL Staaken	Tested in Lipetsk
D-970	Dornier B-Bal Merkur	96	BMW VI	1926	(A) DVL from > 5.1927 (O) DLG from 12.1929	In Lipetsk from 1929-1932. Transferred to RDLI, 1932.
D-987	Junkers A 35	1059	BMW IV	1925	(A) DVL from 9.1926 (A) RDL from 7.1930	In Lipetsk 1928, later to Reichsamt für Flugsicherung
D-1001	Junkers F 13de	796	Junkers L5	1926	(A) DVS (O) RDL from 8.1929	
D-1011	Heinkel He 45 A	363	BMW VI 5,5Zu	1930	(A) RDL from >3.1931	Originally HD 41c. To DVS 10.1932, later D-IBEZ
D-1028	Heinkel He 46a	377	Sh Jupiter VIu	1931	(A) RDL from >3.1932	
D-1109	Junkers A 35	1084	BMW IV	1926	(A) DVL from >1.1928 (O) RDL from 2.1930	Later to Reichsamt für Flugsicherung
D-1119	Junkers W 34b W 34 be W 34 b3e	2600	G&R Jupiter VI later SH Jupiter VI later Brist.Jupiter VII	1927	(A) JFA Dessau from 8.1928 (A) RDL from 2.1934	
D-1127	Albatros L 76a	10101	BMW VI		(A) DVL from >1.1928 (O) RDL from >1930	Crashed near Smolensk 11.06.1930 on flight to Lipetsk
D-1128	Albatros L 76a	10104	BMW VI later BMW VI u later BMW VI	1927	(A) DVL from >1.1928 (A) Alb. from 8.1929 (A) RDL from 1.1930	Certification withdrawn 10.1931, later to DVS.
D-1130	Albatros L 76a	10107	BMW VI	1927	(A) DVL from >1.1928 (A) RDL from 12.1929	Certification withdrawn 10.1931, later to DVS.
D-1147	Heinkel HD 22	293	BMW IV		(A) Alb. from > 1.1928	Destroyed in Rechlin 24.7.1928
D-1157	Heinkel HD 20	251	2 x Wright Whirlwind	1926	(A) DVL from >1.1928 (O) Albatros	Damaged on Transport from Warnemünde to Rechlin 21.11.1929.
D-1204	Arado SC I	33	BMW IV	1927	(A) DVL from 1.1929 (O) RDL	Destroyed 5.1932
D-1209	Albatros L 76	10110	BMW VI		(A) DVL from 4.1929 (O) RDL from 12.1929	Broken-up 2.1931
D-1210	Albatros L 76	10111	BMW VI		(A) DVL from 12.1928	Crashed in Rechlin 13.6.1929
D-1232	Dornier B-Bal Merkur	166	BMW VI, later BMW VI u	1927	Assigned to RDL 1931	
D-1283	Albatros L 76	10113	BMW VI	1927	(A) DVL from 7.1928 (O) RDL from 1.1930	Crashed in Rechlin 5.12.1933
D-1306	Heinkel HD 22	294	BMW IV	1927	(A) Alb. from > 1.1928	Destroyed 2.1932
D-1311	Arado SC I	37	BMW IV	1927	(A) Alb. from 2.1928	Destroyed 4.1928

D-1345	Focke-Wulf A 17 later A 17a	38	G&R Jupiter 9Ab later Sh Jupiter VI u	1927	(A) DVL from 3.1928 (A) Alb. from 9.1929	Flown in Rechlin, later to DVS
D-1423	Junkers W 33b later W 33c	2519	Junkers L5		(A) DVL from 10.1929 (O) Luftdienst (O) RDL Travemünde from 4.1930	Flown in Rechlin, 1930/31 for a while, military tests in Sweden as SE-ACH
D-1524	Albatros L 78u	10121	BMW VI u	1928	(A) DVL from 7.1930 (O) RDL	
D-1546	Albatros L 77v	10136	BMW VI	1928	(A) Alb. from 1.1929 (A) RDL from 12.1929	Certification withdrawn 10.1931, later to DVS
D-1547	Albatros L 77v	10137	BMW VI	1928	(A) Alb. from 1.1929	Crashed near Rechlin 6.3.1929
D-1548	Albatros L 77v	10138	BMW VI	1928	(A) Alb. from 1.1929 (A) RDL from 12.1929	Certification withdrawn 10.1931, later to DVS
D-1549	Albatros L 77v	10139	BMW VI	1928	(A) Alb. from 1.1929 (A) RDL from 12.1929	Certification withdrawn 10.1931, later to DVS
D-1569	Klemm L 251	113	Salmson 9 Ad	1928	(A) Alb. from 4.1929 (O) DLG from 4.1930	Crashed in Staaken 31.5.1932
D-1573	Albatros L 77v	303	BMW VI	1928	(A) Alb. from 3.1929 (A) RDL from 12.1929	Certification withdrawn 10.1931
D-1574	Albatros L 77v	304	BMW VI	1928	(A) Alb. from 3.1929 (A) RDL from 12.1929	Certification withdrawn 10.1931, later to DVS
D-1592	Dornier Do 10	226	HS 12 Ybre, later BMW VI	1930/31	Assigned to RDL 1931	
D-1624	Heinkel HD 22	306	BMW IV	1928	(A) Alb. from 5.1929	Certification withdrawn 3.1934
D-1652	Heinkel HD 22c	307	BMW Va	1928	(A) Alb. from 6.1929	Crashed in Staaken 4.5.1931
D-1694	Heinkel HD 41a	321	BMW VI 7,3Zu	1929	(A) Alb. from 7.1929	From 1934, D-IDYM
D-1698	Junkers W 33d	2547	Junkers L5		(A) DVL from 7.1929 (O) RDL from 1.1930	Later D-ONIR
D-1702	Heinkel He 46b	376	Sh Jupiter VI		Assigned to RDL 1931	
D-1705	Albatros L 82c	10161	Sh 14		(A) RDL from 3.1930	Crashed in Staaken 9.4.1933
D-1708	Focke-Wulf Fw 39	98	Sh Jupiter VI u	1931	Assigned to RDL 1931	Registered for Focke-Wulf 4.1932
D-1791	Albatros L 78	10157	BMW VI		(A) RDL from 2.1930	
D-1795	Heinkel HD 41b	342	Sh Jupiter later Sh 20	1930	(A) RDL from 3.1930	Later D-IXAZ. Confirmed in Rechlin as He 41a up to 25.5.1936, then transferred to SAM
D-1840	Raka Kl Ic	93	Sh 12	1930	(A) RDL from 5.1930	Later to DVL Berlin
D-1844	Junkers W 34f Junkers W 34fao	2589	G&R Jup.9AF later Sh 20	1930	(A) RDL from 5.1930	For a time in Russia
D-1845	Junkers W 34fi	2590	P&W Hornet	1930	(A) RDL from 5.1930	For a time in Russia, later D-ONYS
D-1871	Albatros L 79	10165	Sh 12	1930	(A) RDL from 6.1930	Later D-ETIZ, flown in Rechlin 11.1935
D-1887	BFW M 23c	522	As 8	1930	(A) RDL from 3.1931	Certification not renewed 12.1936
D-1888	BFW M 23c	523	As 8	1930	(A) RDL from 3.1931	Later to Akaflieg, Aachen, D-EKER
D-1898	Dornier Do 10	227	Hs 12 Ybre, later BMW Viu	1930/31	Assigned to RDL 1931	
D-1899	Albatros L 84	10187	BMW VI u		Assigned to RDL 1931	Later D-IBIM, flown in Rechlin 1935
D-1908	Focke-Wulf A 40	99	Sh Jupiter	1931	Assigned to RDL 1931	Later to Reichsamt für Flugsicherung, D-IJEF. Registered for Focke-Wulf 2.1933
D-1973	Arado SD III	54	Sh Jupiter	1932	(A) RDL	Flown in Rechlin. Registered for Arado 10.1932
D-1982	Dornier Do P-Sil	180	4x Sh Jupiter	1930	(A) RDL from 8.1931	Previously registered as CH 302
D-1984	Arado SC II	62	BMW V a	1931	(A) DVL from 1.1931 (O) RDL	Later to DLG
D-1994	Albatros L 75 D	10181	BMW V a	1931	(A) DVL from 2.1931 (O) RDL	
D-1998	Albatros L 75 D	10182	BMW V a	1931	(A) DVL from 2.1931 (O) RDL	Later D-INAV
D-2041	Klemm L 26 Va	265	As 8	1931	RDL from 2.1934	
D-2063	Junkers F 13ko	2062	BMW V a	1931	(A) DVL from 6.1931 (O) RDL	Later D-OHUV, in Rechlin 1936

D-2064	Heinkel HD 45a	364	BMW VI u	1931	(A) DVL from 5.1931 (O) RDL	Later to DVS
D-2075	Arado Ar 64 D	70	Sh Jupiter VI u		Assigned to RDL 1931	Later to DVS
D-2086	Albatros L 84	10190	BMW VI u		(A) RDL from >3.1932	Crashed near Melverode 21.9.1932, Crew saved by parachutes.
D-2131	Albatros L 78	10188	BMW VI		Assigned to RDL 1931	Later to DVS
D-2132	Albatros L 78	10189	BMW VI		Assigned to RDL 1931	Later to DVS
D-2198	Albatros L 81	10164	BMW Va		(A) DVL from 1.1932	Later D-IDUK, flown in Rechlin 11.1935
D-2218	Arado Ar 65	71?	BMW VI		Assigned to RDL 1931	Flown in Rechlin 11.1932
D-2238	Heinkel He 45b	391	BMW VI Zu		Assigned to RDL 1931	Registered later for EHF Warnemünde
D-2251	Heinkel He 45b	394	BMW VI Zu		Assigned to RDL 1932	
D-2262	Heinkel He 45b	400	BMW VI u		Assigned to RDL 1932	Later as D-IQAZ
D-2270	Dornier Do 11a	230	2xSh Jupiter VI u	1931/32	Assigned to RDL 1932	Flown in Rechlin
D-2277	Arado Ar 64 D	68	Sh Jupiter U		Assigned to RDL 1931	Later registered for DVS
D-2278	Arado Ar 64 D	69	Sh Jupiter U		Assigned to RDL 1931	Later registered for DVS
D-2279	Arado Ar 64 E	72	Sh Jupiter U		Assigned to RDL 1931	Later registered for DVS
D2280	Arado Ar 64 E	73	Sh Jupiter U		Assigned to RDL 1931	Later registered for DVS, D-IPEF
D-2281	Arado Ar 64 E	75	Sh Jupiter U		Assigned to RDL 1931	Later registered for DVS
D-2282	Arado Ar 64 E	76	Sh Jupiter U		Assigned to RDL 1931	Later registered for DVS
D-2286	Heinkel He 45 B	392	BMW VI u		Assigned to RDL 1931	Later registered for EHF
D-2287	Heinkel He 45 B	405	BMW VI u		Assigned to RDL 1932	Later registered for EHF
D-2303	Heinkel He 64 C	423	As 8R	1932	Assigned to RDL 1932	
D-2316	Junkers F 13ko	2079	BMW V a	1932	Assigned to RDL 1932	Later registered for DLG
D-2329	Heinkel He 63 A	407	As 10	1932	(A) RDL from 8.1932	Flown in Rechlin 8.1934
D-2335	Arado Ar 66	78	As 10 R	1932	(A) RDL from 9.1932	Later D-IHAV, in Rechlin 11.1935
D-2356	Junkers Ju 52cai	4005	BMW IXu	1933	(A) RDL from 2.1933	Emergency landing near Zechliner Hütte 27.5.1933
D-2368	Heinkel He 45 B	398	BMW VI u		Assigned to RDL 1932	Later D-IPIM
D-2369	Heinkel He 45 B	399	BMW VI u		Assigned to RDL 1932	
D-2406	Heinkel He 45 B	395	BMW VI u		Assigned to RDL 1932	Registered later for DVS
D-2407	Heinkel He 45 B	397	BMW VI u		Assigned to RDL 1932	Registered later for DVS
D-2465	Focke-Wulf Fw 44 a	155	Sh 14a		RDL evtl. only user?	Crashed near Rechlin 5.9.1933
D-2470	Arado Ar 64 D	65	Sh Jupiter U		Assigned to RDL 1931	Later registered for DVS
D-2557	Arado Ar 66b	99?	As 10 c		(E?) RDL	
D-2663	Klemm L 25dVII	543	HM60	1933	(A) RDL from 12.1933	Later D-ELUT
D-2766	Arado Ar 64 C	86?	Sh 22			In Rechlin 3 x 100 hours Sh 22
D-2767	Arado Ar 64 C	87?	Sh 22			In Rechlin 3 x 100 hours Sh 22
D-2768	Arado Ar 64 C	88?	Sh 22			In Rechlin 3 x 100 hours Sh 22
D-2821	Arado Ar 69 A	?	As 8B			In Rechlin
D-2860	Junkers F 13ke	2078	Ju L5	1933	(A) RDL from 12.1933	Later D-OPIT
D-2919	Fieseler F 5R	219	HM 60 R	1933	(A) RDL from 12.1933	
D-3047	Junkers W 34d2i	2574	P&W Hornet	1934	(A) RDL from 3.1934	Later D-OBAK, in Rechlin 11.1935
D-3347	Waco U Ic	3818	Continental R-670		(A) RDL Berlin from 3.1934	
none	Arado SD I	31	Brist.Jupiter IV	1927		Crashed in Rechlin 11.10.1927
?	Arado Ar 64 E	74			Assigned to RDL 1931	Later D-IGOR, in Rechlin 11.1935
?	Arado Ar 65 B	77			Assigned to RDL 1931	Later D-IGIL, in Rechlin 11.1935

Abbreviations

>	from at least (date)	DVL	Deutsche Versuchsanstalt für Luftfahrt	JFA	Junkers Flugzeugwerke, Dessau
Alb.	Albatros-Flugzeugwerke GmbH	DVS	Deutsche Verkehrsflieger-Schule GmbH	RDL	Reichsverband der Deutschen Luftfahrtindustrie, E-Stelle Staaken
DLG	Deutsche Luftfahrt GmbH	EHF	Ernst Heinkel Flugzeugwerke GmbH	SAM	Siemens Apparate & Maschinen GmbH

Aircraft with Rechlin Identification Codes

Aircraft	Call-Sign	Werk-Nr.	Departed	Remarks
Ar 66	GJ+AA		03.1940	Ferried to Schwerin 15.03.1940
Ar 79	GJ+AG		05.1941	Used for Communications
Ar 79	GJ+AH		06.1943	Used for Communications
Ar 79	GJ+AI		12.1940	Used for Communications
Ar 79	GJ+AJ		08.1940	Used for Communications
Ar 96 V6	GJ+AL	2069	09.1940	
Ar 96A-0	GJ+AM	2880 (?)	12.1939	Crashed at Fighter Training School 07.10.1941
Ar 96	GJ+AO		05.1944	
Bf 108	GJ+AP		07.1940	At E3 for Tests, otherwise Communications
Bf 108	GJ+AQ		06.1940	Used for Communications
Bf 108	GJ+AR		05.1942	Used for Communications
Bf 108	GJ+AS		06.1941	Used for Communications
Bf 108	GJ+AT		05.1940	Used for Communications
Bf 108	GJ+AU		(?)	Confirmed in Tarnewitz for Communications
Bf 108	GJ+AV		06.1942	Used for Tests at E3 (Propellers)
Bf 108	GJ+AW		03.1940	Used for Communications
Bf 108B-1	GJ+AX	1993 (?)	05.1942	10% damaged in Bombing Raid on 30.05.1944 at EKdo 16
Bf 108	GJ+AY	1995	06.1944	Used for Tests at E3 (Propellers)
Bf 108	GF+AZ		12.1941	Used for Tests at E2 and E3
Bf 109	GK+AB		06.1941	Used for Tests at E2
Bf 109	GK+AC		08.1941	Used for Tests at E2
Bf 109E	GK+AD		04.1942	Used for Tests at E3
Bf 109E	GK+AE	719	07.1941	ex-D-IIGR, from 07.1944 at DFS Ainring (Mistel-Tests)
Bf 109E	GK+AF	1254	09.1940	Used for Tests at E3
Bf 109E	GK+AG	1256	08.1940	Used for Tests at E3 (Engine Cooler Tests)
Bf 109E	GK+AK		11.1939	
Bf 109E	GK+AL	1788	06.1940	Damaged 26.06.1940, later JG 103, 80% damaged there 03.1944
Bf 109	GK+AM			Accident Report 01.1941, location unknown
Bf 110	GK+AO		10.1941	
Bf 110B	GK+AP		06.1940	Used for Tests at E3
Bf 110	GK+AS		07.1940	
Bf 110B	GK+AT	919		Confirmed in Neubiberg 04.1941
Bf 110	GK+AW	940	11.1940	Crashed at Zerstörer Schule 1, 11.1940
Bf 110	GK+AX		08.1942	Confirmed later in Fassberg
Bf 110	GK+AY		06.1940	Used for Tests at E3
Bf 110C	GK+AZ	3302 (?)	08.1941	To Schönefeld 08.1941, later at Argus for Argus-Rohr Tests
Bü 181	GL+AF		04.1943	Used for Tests at E3 (HM 500)
BV 141	GL+AG		12.1940	Confirmed last in Tarnewitz (also entered as Do 17)
BV 141	GL+AH		05.1941	Used for Tests at E2 ('Ente')
Do 17	GL+AI		07.1940	
Do 17 V6	GL+AJ	656	03.1941	ex-D-AKUZ, confirmed at LG 1 04.1943
Do 17	GL+AK		12.1939	
Do 17M V1	GL+AL	691		ex-D-AELE, at DLH Staaken for course-control installation, later as D-AELE at DFS Ainring
Do 17	GL+AN		03.1942	Confirmed last at FF-Schule
Do 17	GL+AO		10.1941	Used for Tests at E3 (BMW 132 N)
Do 17P	GL+AP		09.1941	Used for Tests at E3
Do 17M	GL+AR	2164	07.1941	80% damaged at Perleberg (Training unit) 08.1941
Do 17M	GL+AT	2159	11.1940	Crashed in Bomb Tests 21.11.1940
Do 17Z V2	GL+AU		10.1941	ex-D-APRT, at E7 for Bomb Tests, crashed 10.1942, location unknown
Do 17Z	GL+AV		10.1944	Used for Tests at E5
Do 17Z	GL+AW		06.1942	ex-D-ABWA, at E7 for Bomb Tests
Do 17	GL+AX		06.1940	
Do 17Z	GL+AY	2517	05.1944	ex-D-APFF; for Tests at E3, crashed 21.05.1944
Do 17Z	GL+AZ		11.1944	ex-D-ATDE (?); for Tests at E3, E4, E5 and E7
Do 17Z	GM+AA		05.1942	ex-D-ACJJ; for Tests at E3 and E7 (Parachutes & Bombs)
Do 17Z	GM+AB		04.1941	Used for Bomb Tests at E7
Do 17Z	GM+AC		(?)	In Logbook Gleuwitz, 01.1942 confirmed at Fieseler
Do 17Z	GM+AD		12.1943	Used for Tests at E4 (Navigation instruments)
Do 17	GM+AE		10.1942	ex-D-APDC, at E7 for Bomb Tests
Do 217 V5	GM+AF	2703	05.1940	Used for Tests at E3, 95% damaged near Lübben, 02.1941
Fh 104	GM+AG		08.1940	
Fi 156 V3	GM+AI	603	11.1942	ex-D-IGQE, used for Communications by Dept. F
Fi 156	GM+AJ		01.1940	
Fi 156	GM+AK		10.1940	
Fi 156 (?)	GM+AL			
Fw 44	GM+AM		10.1941	Used as Communications and tow-craft for gliders
Fw 44	GM+AN			Confirmed until 07.1941, location unknown
Fw 44	GM+AO		08.1941	Used as Training aircraft
Fw 44	GM+AP		05.1941	Used as Training aircraft
Fw 56	GM+AQ		05.1941	ex-D-INIO, used for Communications
(?)	GM+AR		10.1940	
Fw 58	GM+AT			At Erg. Aufkl. Gr. Ob.d.L., 04.1941
Fw 58	GM+AU		07.1941	Used at Dept. F as Communications and Transport aircraft
Fw 58	GM+AV		03.1944	Used for Tests at E3 and E5 (course-control)
Fw 58	GM+AW		12.1940	
Fw 58	GM+AX		04.1940	
Fw 58	GM+AY		09.1940	
Fw 58C-1	GM+AZ	2099	08.1940	Used for Instrument Tests at E5, crashed 28.08.1940
Fw 58	GN+AA		05.1941	Used for Tests at E3 (HM 508)
Fw 58	GN+AE		05.1942	Used as Training- and Communications aircraft
Fw 189	GN+AI		02.1940	
Go 145	GN+AJ		09.1941	
Go 145	GN+AK		12.1939	
Go 145	GN+AL		04.1941	
He 46D	GN+AS			Photographed at a Field airbase in the East (?)
He 50	GN+AT			At an A/B School Neukuhren, 04.1942
He 70	GN+AW		05.1941	Used as Communications aircraft, confirmed in Dresden 10.1941
He 70	GN+AX		06.1940	ex-D-UHIH (?), used for Communications
He 70	GN+AY			
He 70	GP+AA			
He 72d	GP+AD		04.1942	Used for Tests at E2 (wheels) and as tow-craft
He 72	GP+AE			Collision with GP+AF, 07.1942
He 72d	GP+AF		04.1941	Used as tow-craft, collision with GP+AE, 07.1942
He 100	GP+AG	3005 (?)	06.1940	Used for Tests at E3
He 100	GP+AI		06.1940	Used for Tests at E3
He 111	GP+AJ			Confirmed in Finsterwalde 11.1941
He 111	GP+AK			Confirmed in Neubrandenburg 08.1940
He 111	GP+AM		06.1940	
He 111	GP+AN			in Logbook Wallischek, Firma Fieseler 08.1941
He 111	GP+AO		12.1939	Used for Tests at E3
He 111	GP+AP		05.1941	Used for Tests at E7
He 111B	GP+AR			
He 111P	GP+AU		06.1942	Used for Tests at E3 (DB 601E)
He 111P	GP+AV	2428	10.1940	Used for Tests at E3
He 111P	GP+AX	2470	07.1940	Used for Tests at E3 (Cooler, heating), at Erg. KGr.2, 10.1940
He 111	GP+AY		10.1942	ex-D-AEAB, used for Tests at E7 (Bombs and target instruments)
He 111P-2	GQ+AA			Confirmed at LN-Reg. Köthen, 12.1941
He 111P	GQ+AB	2755	11.1941	ex-D-ASVS, used for Tests at E4, (Radio instruments)

Type	Code	W.Nr.	Date	Notes
He 111H-1	GQ+AC		06.1940	Crashed during gyro-test on 04.06.1940
He 111H	GQ+AD	5115	09.1940	Ultra-short wave measurement flights for Dept.F, at EHF Marienehe 07.1941
He 111H	GQ+AE			Confirmed in Krakow, 08.1940
He 111H-1	GQ+AF	5251	07.1943	ex-D-APFK, used for Bomb Tests at E7
He 111	GQ+AG		01.1941	
He 111H-3	GQ+AH		05.1943	Used for Tests at E3 and E4
He 118 V4	GQ+AJ	1963	09.1940	ex-D-OQYF, used for Tests at E3
He 172	GQ+AM		02.1941	Used for Tests at E2, also as tow-craft and Communications
Hs 126	GQ+AR		01.1942	
Hs 126	GQ+AT		01.1942	
Hs 126	GQ+AV		06.1941	
Ju W 34 hi	GS+AA		10.1941	Used as Training aircraft
Ju W 34	GS+AB		05.1944	Used as Training aircraft
Ju W 33	GS+AC			Confirmed in Gatow, no date
Ju W 34	GS+AD		08.1940	Used as Training aircraft, ferried to Thorn 08.1940
Ju W 34	GS+AE			Confirmed in Braunschweig-Völkenrode, 07.1941
Ju W 34	GS+AF			Photographed on a West-German Airfield at war's end, Blind-flying school
Ju W 34	GS+AG		06.1940	Used as Training aircraft
Ju W 34	GS+AH		06.1942	Used as Training and Transport aircraft
Ju 52/3m	GS+AI		05.1944	
Ju 52/3m	GS+AJ	1347 (?)		At KGr z.b.V. 900, 1942
Ju 52/3m	GS+AK		09.1940	Used as Training and Communications aircraft
Ju 52/3m	GS+AL		02.1942	
Ju 52/3m	GS+AM		05.1940	
Ju 52/3m	GS+AN		02.1942	ex-D-ADEH, Ultra-short wave measurement flights by Dept. F
Ju 52/3m	GS+AO	4027 (?)	10.1941	ex-D-AZEV
Ju 52/3m	GS+AP		06.1942	Used for Tests at E3 (Jumo 208)
Ju 52/3m	GS+AQ	5035	08.1944	Used for Tests at E3 (DB 603D, E and G)
Ju 52/3m	GS+AR		05.1945	Used for Tests at E3 (DB 601, DB 605)
Ju 52/3m	GS+AS		07.1941	
Ju 52/3m	GS+AT			Confirmed in Gatow, no date.
Ju 52/3m	GS+AU	5353	10.1943	ex-D-AHUX, used for Tests at E3 (Jumo 213)
Ju 52/3m	GS+AV		03.1941	
Ju 52/3m	GS+AW			Confirmed at Blind-flying school Belgrade-Semlin, 02.1942
Ju 52/3m	GS+AX	5848	12.1941	ex-D-AIMA, Communications and Training aircraft, at TG1 05.1943
Ju 52/3m	GS+AY	5885	02.1942	Used as Training and Transport aircraft, later 1Z+LW
Ju 52/3m	GS+AZ	5929		Crashed near FFS B 19, 01.1944
Ju 52/3m	GT+AA	5930 (?)	03.1942	ex-D-ABWR (?), Tests of landing brake-chutes, crashed 05.07.1942
Ju 52/3m	GT+AB	6020	02.1942	Training and Communications aircraft, later 4V+JU at KGr. zbV 4.
Ju 52/3m	GT+AC		12.1941	Used at Dept. F for Radio tests.
Ju 52/3m	GT+AD	6038	03.1941	ex-D-ADBP, used for Tests at E4, at TG 1 as 1Z+EQ, 04.1943
Ju 52/3m	GT+AE		02.1942	Used at Dept. F for Radio tests, transferred ca. 04.1942 to LLG 1
Ju 52/3m	GT+AF		08.1944	ex-D-AXLA, used for Tests by E4 and E5
Ju 86	GT+AG	0018 (?)	01.1942	ex-D-AXEQ, used for Tests by E3
Ju 86	GT+AH			Confirmed in Laibach (Zagreb), 03.1941
Ju 86	GT+AJ	0066	09.1942	Used for Tests at E3, modified at JFM, 04.1942
Ju 86	GT+AK		05.1941	
Ju 87	GT+AN			Confirmed at Pilot instructor school Brandenburg-Briest, 11.1940
Ju 87A	GT+AO	0004 (?)	12.1939	Confirmed at Stuka Vorschule 1, 03.1943
Ju 87A-1	GT+AQ	0028 (?)		Confirmed in Bad Aibling, 11.1942
Ju 87B-2	GT+AR		06.1941	Used for Tests at E3
Ju 87B	GT+AS		04.1944	Used for Tests at E2 and E5 (Snow-skis)
Ju 87B-1	GT+AT	0230	11.1940	Crashed during Bomb Test on 28.11.1940
Ju 87	GT+AU		12.1939	
Ju 87B	GT+AV		11.1939	Used for Tests at E2
Ju 87	GT+AW		12.1939	
Ju 87	GT+AX	0279	11.1940	Ferried to Tarnewitz on 23.11.1940
Ju 87B	GT+AY	0307		At III/StG 1, 01.1942, shot down by Flak
Ju 87B	GT+AZ		06.1940	Used for Tests at E3
Ju 87B-1	GU+AA	0361	10.1942	Used for Tests at E5
Ju 87	GU+AB	0459	07.1942	Used for Tests at E2, confirmed at I./SG 103, 04.1944
Ju 87B	GU+AC		04.1940	Used for Tests at E3
Ju 88 V7	GU+AE		12.1939	ex-D-ARNC
Ju 88 V11	GU+AF	0003	11.1939	
Ju 88 V12	GU+AG	0004	11.1940	Confirmed at Bordfunkerschule 6, 06.1943
Ju 88	GU+AH		02.1941	
Ju 88	GU+AJ		01.1940	Entered as Ju 87
Kl 32	GU+AL		05.1940	
Kl 35	GU+AM		08.1940	Crashed 10.08.1940
Kl 35	GU+AO		08.1942	
Kl 35	GU+AQ		10.1940	
Kl 36	GU+AR		05.1941	

Captured Aircraft with Rechlin Identification Codes

Manufacturer	Aircraft	Code	From	Until	Remarks
Fokker	G Ia	0+9	06.1940	07.1940	Captured in Waalhaven 05.1940
Handley-Page	Hampden	1+1	07.1940		
Curtiss	H 75 A	1+2	06.1940	07.1940	Crashed Rechlin 08.07.1940
Hawker	Hurricane Mk.1	1+4	06.1940	07.1940	
Curtiss	H 75 A	1+5	06.1940		
Curtiss	H 75 A	1+6	06.1940		
Curtiss	H 75 A	1+8	07.1940		
Curtiss	H 75 A	1+9	06.1940		Confirmed in Tarnewitz from 07.1940, crashed there 26.09.1940
Supermarine	Spitfire	2+1	06.1940	03.1941	Used in film sequences
Ilyushin	Il-2	2+2	(?)		Confirmed only from photo without location and date
Curtiss	H 75	3+2	07.1940		
(?)	(?)	3+4	08.1940		
Arsenal	VG 33	3+5	(?)		Confirmed only from photo without location and date
Caudron	Goéland	4+1	03.1941		At Messerschmitt Augsburg as Communications aircraft from 07.1941
Morane-Saulnier	MS-230	4+2	05.1941	06.1941	
Handley-Page	Hampden	4+4	04.1941	05.1941	
Supermarine	Spitfire I	4+5	10.1940		At Messerschmitt 11.1940, crashed 07.1941, location not known
(?)	(?)	4+6	10.1940		
Vickers	Wellington	5+1	11.1940		Possibly Wellington Ia, ex-KXoE, c/n L7788, made emergency landing in Holland, transferred to Rechlin 10.1940
Supermarine	Spitfire Mk.1a	5+2	12.1941	09.1942	
Hawker	Hurricane	5+3	06.1941		
Vickers	Wellington	5+4			Possibly Wellington Ic, ex-LNoF, c/n T2501, made emergency landing in France, transferred to Rechlin 02.1941
Bristol	Blenheim Mk.4	5+5	05.1941	09.1941	Possibly ex-TIoD, probably destroyed in Rechlin in target practice
Ilyushin	DB 3	5+8	06.1941		
Mikoyan-Gurevich	MiG-3	6+1	08.1941		Confirmed only from photo without location and date
Lockheed	Ventura	6+?	(?)		Confirmed only from photo without location and date
Caproni	Ca 313	6+4	03.1942	05.1942	
Lockheed	Hudson	6+6	02.1942	04.1942	Made emergency landing near Carpriquet 01.1942, transferred to Rechlin 08.-11.02.1942
Short	Stirling	6+8			Captured in Holland 09.1942, destroyed in Rechlin in target practice
Caproni	Ca 111	7+0	03.1943		
Savoia-Marchetti	SM 82	7+6	10.1943		
Boeing	B-17F-100-B0	7+8	10.1943	06.1944	Made emergency landing in Denmark 10.1943, s/n 42-30336
Republic	P-47 Thunderbolt	7+9	11.1943	12.1943	s/n 42-68274
Caproni	Ca 314	8+0	03.1944		
Fiat	G 55	8+4	02.1944		
S.A.I.M.A.N.	202	8+5	02.1944	03.1944	
Republic	P-47 Thunderbolt	8+6	06.1944		
North American	P-51 Mustang	8+7	06.1944		Made emergency landing near Cambrai 06.1944

Jet Aircraft with Rechlin Test Identification Codes

Aircraft	Test Code	Parent Code	Werk-Nr.	From	Until	Remarks
Ar 234 B	E2+10	GM+BI	140109	8.44	2.45	Tests with FuG 203 for Hs 293 pole-tow at DFS Ainring. At KG 76 in Kaltenkirchen 04.1945
Ar 234 B	E2+20	GM+BJ	140110	8.44	2.45	Tests with high-speed brake-chute, ETC 2000, Hs 293
Ar 234 B	E2+30	GM+BG	140107	8.44	3.45	Flight testing in dives, performance measurements, undercarriage tests
Ar 234 B	E2+40	GM+BQ	140117	9.44	07.12.44	Crashed in Lärz, Arado pilot Jakob Kunz killed (in Hirschberg's logbook an E2+40 again mentioned in Jan. 1945, but is probably a writing error)
Ar 234 B	E3+10	GM+BE	140105	7.44	3.45	Engine tests, fuel consumption measurements
Ar 234 B	E4+10	GM+BK	140111	8.44	4.45	W/T tests (FuG 217, FuG 136, FuG 102). Ferried to Lechfeld 09.04.1945
Ar 234 B	E5+10	GM+BF	140106	7.44	3.45	PDS (three-axis course-control) tests, simplified statoscope switching. Initially coded E7+15 then E5+10 from 08.1944
Ar 234 B	E5+20	GM+BM	140113	8.44	12.44	Undercarriage and brake-chute tests
Ar 234 B	E7+10	GM+BB	140102	8.44	2.45	Tests with course-control and Lotfe periscope. In ops with Gefechtsverband KdE 02.1945, thereafter used in de-icing tests
Ar 234 B	E7+20	GM+BH	140108	8.44	3.45	Measurements of flight characteristics, u/c endurance tests, BZA tests. At DFS, 03.1945
Ar 234 B	E7+30	SM+FJ	140150	10.44	3.45	Tests with TSA 2D
He 162 A	E2+51	?	?		4.45	Confirmed in Lechfeld
He 162 A	E2+52	?	?		4.45	Confirmed in Lechfeld
He 162 A	E2+53 (?)	?	?		4.45	Confirmed in Lechfeld (probably E3+52)
He 162 A	E3+51	?	?		4.45	Confirmed in Lechfeld
He 162 A	E3+52	?	?		4.45	Confirmed in Lechfeld
Me 262 A	E2+01	SQ+WB	130163	8.44	1.45	Undercarriage tests, transferred to 11./JG7
Me 262 A	E2+02	SQ+WI	130170	7.44	12.44	Performance measurements as A-1 and A-2 versions, re-engined with BMW 003A, thereafter E3+36
Me 262 A	E3+01	VI+AR	130018	6.44	3.45	Used for Jumo 004 tests
Me 262 A	E3+02	SQ+WG	130168	8.44	3.45	Used for Jumo 004 tests with hollow blades
Me 262 A	E3+03	KI+IR	170038	8.44	05.09.44	Crashed in Lärz, Fliegerstabsing. Johann Ruther of E3a5 killed
Me 262 A	E3+04	SQ+WO	130176	11.44	12.44	Two-seater used for training flights and turbojet tests
Me 262 A	E3+31	SQ+XA (ex-E7+01)	130188	7.44	02.02.45	ex-E7+01. Crashed in Lärz on conversion training, Hauptmann Hans Furchner killed
Me 262 A	E3+32	SQ+WC (ex-WA+TA)	130164	1.45	4.45	ex-WA+TA. Re-engined with BMW 003A. Ferried to Lechfeld 14.04.1945
Me 262 A	E3+33	?	?		1.45	Used for BMW 003A tests
Me 262 A	E3+34	?	?	1.45	2.45	Used for BMW 003A tests
Me 262 A	E3+35	SQ+WM (ex-EK+L2)	130174	7.44	2.45	Ferried to Burg 17.02.1945
Me 262 A	E3+36	? (ex-E2+02)	?	2.45	3.45	ex-E2+02. Ferried to Burg 07.03.1945
Me 262 A	E4+E5	SQ+WD	130165	8.44	4.45	Last confirmed in Lechfeld
Me 262 A	E7+01	SQ+XA	130188	6.44	02.02.45	Damaged on landing in Ballerstedt. Re-engined with BMW 003A as E3+31
Me 262 A	E7+02	KL+WX	170070	8.44	3.45	With I./JG7 as 'white 12', 04.1945
Me 262 A	EK+L1	SQ+WK	130172	6.44	9.44	Suffered engine failure on take-off end of 09.1944, aircraft destroyed by fire
Me 262 A	EK+L2	SQ+WM	130174	7.44	11.44	Re-engined with BMW 003A, thereafter E3+35, transferred to BMW Flight Test Department
Me 262 A	EK+L3	KI+IS	170039	7.44	3.45	
Me 262 A	EK+L4	SQ+XC	130190		25.08.44	Severely damaged in air raid on Rechlin, not repaired

In addition to the above, there were at least 15 other Me 262s and 14 other Ar 234s undergoing testing at the E-Stelle Rechlin and the Erprobungskommando Lärz.

Losses of the E-Stelle Rechlin and its Predecessors 1926 to 1945

The following abbreviations are used in this table

Column 2 - Aircraft Firms

Alb	Albatros Flugzeugwerke GmbH	He	Ernst Heinkel Flugzeugwerke GmbH
Ar	Arado Flugzeugwerke GmbH	Hs	Henschel Flugzeugwerke AG
Bf	Bayerische Flugzeugwerke AG	Ju	Junkers Flugzeug- & Motorenwerke AG
Do	Dornier-Werke GmbH	Kl	Hans Klemm Flugzeugbau GmbH
Fw	Focke-Wulf Flugzeugbau AG	Me	Messerschmitt Flugzeugwerke AG
Go	Gothaer Waggonfabrik,	Pe	Petlyakov (Russia)
	Abt. Flugzeugbau	Re	Reichenberg (piloted V-1)
HD	Heinkel-Doppeldecker (biplane)	Si	Siebel Flugzeugwerke Halle KG

Column 5 - Crew

inj	injured	pd	parachute descent
He	Heinkel	Me	Messerschmitt

Column 6 - Personal Grade

A (Diploma)

Ing.	Ingenieur	*Engineer*
DI	Diplom-Ingenieur	*Graduate Engineer*
DPh	Diplom-Physiker	*Graduate Physicist*
DOpt	Dipolom-Optiker	*Graduate Optician*

B (Specialist)

		Approximate equivalent
FBM	Flugbaumeister	*Master of Aircraft Engineering*
FI	Flieger-Ingenieur	*Engineer-Pilot (EP)*
FHI	Flieger-Hauptingenieur	*Chief EP*
FOI	Flieger-Oberingenieur	*Senior EP*
FOSI	Flieger-Oberstabsingenieur	*Senior (HQ) Staff EP*
FSI	Fliegerstabs-Ingenieur	*(HQ) Staff EP*
Flkpt	Flugkapitän	*Flight-Commander*
Mech	Mechaniker	*Mechanic*
Mstr	Meister	*Head Foreman/Master*
O-Ing	Oberst-Ingenieur	*Engineer-Colonel*
O-Mstr	Obermeister	*Senior Head Foreman*
Prüfer	Prüfer	*Evaluator/Examiner*
T.Ang.	Technischer Angestellter	*Technical Employee*
T.Ass.	Technischer Assistent	*Technical Assistant*

C (Military)

		WW2 Royal Air Force equivalent
Flg	Flieger	*Aircraftman 2nd Class*
Gef	Gefreiter	*Aircraftman 1st Class*
Obergef	Obergefreiter	*Leading Aircraftman*
Uffz	Unteroffizier	*Corporal*
Ufw	Unterfeldwebel	*[Senior Corporal]*
Fw	Feldwebel	*Sergeant*
Ofw	Oberfeldwebel	*Flight Sergeant*
Stfw	Stabsfeldwebel	*Warrant Officer*

Lt	Leutnant	*Pilot Officer*
Oblt	Oberleutnant	*Flying Officer*
Hfw	Hauptfeldwebel	*[NCO Admin Head]*
Hptm	Hauptmann	*Flight Lieutenant*
Maj	Major	*Squadron Leader*
Kptn	Kapitän	*Commander*
Oberst	Oberst	*Group Captain*

D (Civilian)

Arb	Arbeiter	*Workman/Labourer*
Gast	Gast	*Invited Guest*
	Maurer	*Mason/Bricklayer*
Oberfwk	Oberfeuerwerker	*Senior Firefighter*

Column 7 - Aircrew Function

BF	Bordfunker	*W/T Operator*
BM	Bordmechaniker	*Flight Mechanic*
BO	(Mess)-Beobachter	*(Measurement) Observer*
BS	Bordschütze	*Air Gunner*
FF	Flugzeugführer	*Chief Pilot*
2.FF	2. Flugzeugführer	*Co-Pilot*

Column 8 - Organisation

Abt.F	Abteilung F	*Department F*
B-(Platz)	B-Nord/Mitte/Süd	Rechlin Location North/Centre/South
DVL/M	DVL Abteilung M	*DVL Department M*
EKL	Erprobungskommando Lärz	*Test Detachment Lärz*
E-leiter	Erprobungsleiter	*Head of Testing*
E1 to E9	E-Stelle Rechlin	Specialist Departments
Fl. Ltg.	Flugleitung	*Air Traffic Control*
GL/C-E	Abteilung in RLM	German Air Ministry Specialist Dept
LC4, LC7	Abteilung in RLM	German Air Ministry Specialist Dept
HWA	Heereswaffenamt	*Army Ordnance Office*
OKL	Oberkommando der Luftwaffe	*Air Force Supreme Commander*
Prüfst.	Prüfstelle	*Evaluation Centre*
VKP	Versuchskommando für	*Test Detachment for*
	Panzerbekämpfung	*Anti-Tank Warfare*
Est 177	Erprobungsstaffel He 177	Test Squadron He 177
Est 210	Erprobungsstaffel Me 210	Test Squadron Me 210
FlH.Kdtr.	Fliegerhorstkommandantur	*Air Base Command*
FlH.Kp.	Fliegerhorstkompanie	Air Base Company
Kdo. Re	Kommando Reichenberg	Test Detachment Reichenberg (piloted V-1)
T.Kp.	Technische Kompanie	E-Stelle Technical Company
KG	Kampfgeschwader	*Bomber Wing*

Date	Aircraft	Code	Werk-Nr.	Crew	Mil. Grade	Function	Department	Location	Remarks
19.10.26	Alb L 47b	D-586	?	Seefeld, Max	DI	FF	DVL/M	Adlershof	Crashed in spin after stall
22.07.27	Alb L 76a	RR 32	10106	Mühlhan, Fritz		FF		Berlin-Rudow	Crashed in spin
				Wedekind, Erich			Telefunken		
11.10.27	Ar SD1		31	Bienen, Theodor	DI	FF	DVL/M	Rechlin	Crashed
06.03.29	Alb L 77v	D-1547	10137	Arens, Hans	Oblt	FF		near Kotzow	Crashed due to material failure
				Düring		BO			
13.06.29	Alb L 76	D-1210	10111	Dr. Jeschonnek, Paul	Hptm	FF	HWA	North of Kotzow	Crashed due to inverted spin
11.06.30	Alb L 76a	D-1127	10101	Künne		BM	HWA	East of Smolensk	Crashed on take-off from emergency
				Thuy, Emil		FF	HWA		landing field
14.10.30	Bf M22		444	Mohnicke, Eberhard		FF		Augsburg	Crashed on test flight at Messerschmitt
04.05.31	HD 22c	D-1652	307	v. Kamecke, Peter	Ing			Staaken	Crashed on take-off
				Waschinski, Gottfried	Ing				

Date	Aircraft	Reg.	W.Nr.	Crew	Rank	Role	Unit	Location	Remarks
27.05.33	Ju 52cai	D-2356	4005	Isert, Max	Mech			nr Zechliner Hütte	Emergency landing after engine fire
				Bauer, Otto (inj)					
				v. Bornstedt, Horst (inj)					
				Heller, Paul (inj)					
05.09.33	Fw 44a	D-2465	155	v. Rochow, Paul		FF	Flugleitung	near Rechlin	Crashed in spin in characteristics test
05.12.33	Alb L 76	D-1283	10113	Kneeser, Walter		FF		Rechlin	Crashed in jettison of dummy in parachute-test
				Haubold, Karl	Ing	BO			
19.07.35	Kl 35 V1	D-EHXE	959	König, Helmuth		FF		near Vietzen	Crashed after wing failure
				Lipke, Alfred	Gefr	BM	T.Kp		
17.01.36	Kl 35	D-EBRA	1009	Jordan	Mech	FF		near Waren	Crashed after sideslip in low curve
14.05.36	Ju 86 V8	D-AVEE	6004	Heisig, Helmut	Uffz		T.Kp	near Meseritz (Warthegau)	Crashed during endurance test
				Paul, Erich	Fw		T.Kp		
07.07.36	Ju W 34hi	D-ONAN	508	Andersen, Harald		FF		near Kempten	Crashed in bad weather
				Pfeiffer, Alfred	DI	BO	E3		
				Winkler, Kurt	Ing	BO	E3		
				Schüler, Erich	Gefr	BM			
24.03.37	He 111B-1	D-ARAU	1449	Voelskow		FF	E1	Triebsee/Pommern	Wing failure after unintentional dive due to pilot high-altitude sickness
				Wolf					
				Höfle		BM	Heinkel		
				Sievers	Ufw	BF	T-Kp		
				Kalbitzer, Edmund	Ing	BO	E1		
01.04.37	Hs 123			Wulf, Heinz		FF	Fieseler	Rechlin	Crashed
27.04.37	Do 23G	D-ABOP	352	Illgen, Werner	Mech	BM	E5	Leppinsee	Drowned after fighter attack following bomb explosion in aircraft
				Bienek, Erich (inj)	Ing	FF	E5		
				Zincke, Werner (inj)	Gefr	BM	T.Kp		
05.06.37	Ju 86D-1	D-AOXE	860184	Nagel, Adolf	Uffz	BS	II./KG 245	B-Platz Mitte	Crashed during bomb testing following bomb explosion in aircraft
				Paeper, Lothar	Uffz	BS	II./KG 245		
				Steinbrecher, Paul	Ufw	FF	II./KG 245		
				Tarruhn, Adolf	Ogefr	BM	II./KG 245		
				Wolff, Kurt	Lt	BO	II./KG 245		
17.07.37	Bf 109B-0	2	1014	Dr. Jodlbauer, Kurt	DI	FF	E1	Müritzsee	Crashed during diving-flight test
13.08.37	Boeing 247	D-AKIN	1944	Behn, Robert	DI	BO	E3	Hannover-Vahrenwald	Crashed on take-off for course-control test flight
				Chun, Hans	DI	FF	E1		
				Knaak, Walter	Ogefr	BF	T.Kp		
				König, Gustav	Mstr	BO	E3		
				Nowak, Johann		BM			
				Schalla, Rudolf	Mech	BO			
				Weyland, Ernst	Mech	BO	E3		
				Schütze, (inj)	Ing	BO	E3		
23.11.37	Ju 52/3mge	D-AFYV	5352	Kötke, Henry	Uffz	BM	T.Kp	Roggentin	Ground contact in blind-landing attempt in fog
				Kurth, Friedrich	Kptn	BO	E3		
				v.Medem, Otto		FF	E3		
				Merten, Walter	Kptn	BO	E3		
				Schröder	FBF	2.FF			
				Bülte, Friedrich (inj)	Ing /FBF	BO			
				Rackow (inj)		BO	Lorenz		
18.07.38	?			Holtermann, Ernst		FF	E1	Roggentin	Crashed due to collision during filming
				Selter, Horst	Uffz	FF	T.Kp		
11.10.38	Do 217 V1		687	Köppe, Rolf	DI	FF	E1	near Tettnang/Bodensee	Crashed in single-engine flight test
				Bausenhart, Egon		BM	Dornier		
15.11.38	Bf 110 V7	D-AEDO	912	Nietruch, Friedrich-Karl		FF	Abn. Kdo/LC4	nr.Schwastorf	Air collision with Ju W34
26.11.38	Ju 90 V2	D-AIVI	4914	Schwendler, Heinz	FSI		E9	Bathurst/Africa	Crashed due to engine failure on take-off
				Sutter, Walter	Kptn		E9		
				(+10 men)					
31.03.39	Ju 88 V9	D-ADCN	1	v. Moreau, Rudolf	Hptm	FF	E7	B-Platz West	Crashed in bomb-test flight in a dive
				Schräwer (pd)		BO	E7		
				Beck, Bernhard (pd)		BM	Junkers		
24.06.39	Do 17M	D-AAQU		Lange, Willi	Prüfer	BO		Fleesensee nr. Göhren	Crashed upon contact with water-surface in low-level flight
				Sydow, Herbert	Uffz	BM	T.Kp		
				Visintini, Herbert		FF			
23.11.39	?			Blattmann, Theodor	DI		E5	unknown	Missing in combat with 2./(F) 122
				(+3 men)			2./(F) 122		

Date	Type	Code	No.	Name				Location	Remarks
22.02.40	Ju 88			Gluud, Hans-Ferdinand	DI	FF	E2	near Rambow	Crashed during diving-flight training
13.03.40	Ju 88A-1	TP+AS		Beck, Bernhard		BM	Junkers	near Rechlin	Crashed during tests of a Zeiss-Ikon dive bomb-sight
				Denecke, Herbert		FF			
				Dr. Müller, Wolfgang	FSI	BO	LC 7		
24.04.40	He 177 V3	D-AGIG	3	Riekert, Hans-Friedrich (+2 men from He)	FBM	FF	E2	Gehlsdorf	Crashed probably through tailplane failure
04.05.40	He 111H-4	TM+AS	6986	Drössler, Adolf		BM		Lärz	Wing failure in diving flight during parachute test
				Tengler, Willi		BO	E5		
				Vogel, Erich	T.Ang	BO	E7		
				Weisser, Hans		FF	E7		
10.05.40	?			Issel, Emil		BO	E7	near Reims	Unsuccessful pd in combat flight in France
04.06.40	He 111H-1	GQ+AC		Böttger, Rudolf	FBM	BO	E5	near Prenzlau	Crashed after engine fire in gyro test flight
				Dr. Hierholzer, Wilhelm	DPh	BO	E5		
				Peters	FBF	FF	E5		
				Reitis	FSI	BO	E5		
				Wilke, Rudolf	FSI	BO	E5		
				Leitreitner (pd)		BM	T.Kp		
				Wüst, Helmut (pd)	FSI	BO	E5		
27.06.40	He 177 V2	CB+RQ	2	Ursinus, Fritjof (+3 men from He)	FBM	FF	E2	Müritz-Graal	Crashed in test of minimum flying speed
09.07.40	H 75A6	1+2		Arlt, Werner	FSI	FF	E3	Rechlin	Crashed on t.o. 08.07., died in hospital 09.07.40
10.08.40	Kl 35	GU+AM		Böhm, Georg	Ing	FF	E7	Rechlin	Crashed, died in hospital on 14.08.40
				Michael, Fritz	Flg	BM	T.Kp		
28.08.40	Fw 58C-1	GM+AZ	2099	Duhnkrack, Heinz	Ing	BO	E2	Schneeberg/ Erzgebirge	Unintentional ground contact in bad weather
				Meyer-Probst, Robert	Ing	FF	E5		
				Winkel, Johann	Ing	BO	E2		
21.11.40	Do 17M	GL+AT	2159	Gembus, Erich		BM	T.Kp	Rechlin	Crashed after take-off for flare-bomb test flight Winzer died in hospital 23.11.40
				Winzer, Wolf-Eberhard	Ing	FF	E7		
28.11.40	Ju 87B-1	GT+AT	230	Grundmann, Alfred	DOpt	BO	E7	Schillersdorf	Unintentional ground contact during pull-out
				Maurer, Helmut	FHI	FF	E7		
16.12.40	Do 17R	CT+NA	2194	Hangleiter, Otto	FBM	FF	E3	Rechlin	Crash-landing after measurement flight
				Bermann, Max (inj)	DI	BO	E3		
				Kocimski, Paul (inj)		BM			
16.12.40	Hs 129			Balke, Hermann	Ing	FF	E2	Braunschweig	Crashed during service instruction
20.12.40	Ju 87R-1	PC+XV	5554	Othmer, Erich		FF	E7	Schwarzenmoor	Crashed from inverted flight condition
14.03.41	Ju 88A-1	JB+RI	65	three-man crew				Waltersdorf	Unsuccessful take-off
18.03.41	Go 242			Thomas		BM	GWF	Lärz	Crashed through airframe rupture in speed-test
				Harmens, Hugo (pd)		FF	GWF		
26.04.41	Go 242			Kirschke, Helmut	Ing	FF	E2	near Bremen	Crashed on overland tow-flight
				Quitter, Rolf	Ing	2.FF	E2		
10.05.41	He 111H-6		3780	Schadl		BM		Neustrelitz	Crashed
				Waibel		BO	E3		
				Wittmann, Heinrich	Ing	FF	E3		
28.05.41	Me 321		452	Flinsch, Bernhard (+4 men from Mtt.)	Fw	FF	E2	Obertraubling	Crashed due to tailplane failure
04.07.41	Do 217C	D-ADBD	2710	Lapp, Anton	Ogefr	BF		near Gladau	Crashed for unknown reason
				Ostermaier, Adolf	FBM	FF	E7		
				Renz, Eduard	Uffz	BM			
02.08.41	Ju 88A-4		1019	v. Mallinckrodt, Friedrich	Hptm	FF	Prüfstelle	near Krienke	Emergency landing due to engine fire
				Haus (pd)	Gefr	BM			
				Chemnitz (pd)	Ofw	BF			
31.08.41	He 111H-5	PH+EK	3921	Freyer, Fritz	Flg	BM		Mittelmeer	Missing on flight from Derna to Athens
				Fritsche, Kurt	FOSI	BO	E-Leiter		
				Lück, Rolf	Fw	FF	Fl.ltg.		
				Müller, Kurt	Fw	BF			
				Schütz	Oberst	Guest			
03.09.41	Pe-2			Förschler, Friedrich	DI	FF	E2	Müritz	Crashed due to engine problem after take-off
23.09.41	Me 210A-1	SJ+GG?	117	Forgatsch, Heinz	Oblt	FF	E-Stf 210	Gut Ankershagen	Crashed due to engine problem
				Hoffmann, Kurt	Fw	BF	E-Stf 210		

Date	Type	Code	W.Nr	Name	Rank	Function	Unit	Location	Remarks
22.10.41	Do 217E-2	RB+YB	1180	Becker, Otto	Prüfer	BO		Rechlin	Crashed on take-off, probably due to trimming problem
				Hasenclever, Ludwig	DI	FF	E2		
				Heidbrecker, Paul		BM			
07.11.41	Ju 87D-1	BK+ES	2019	Parr, Josef	Uffz	BF		near Neustrelitz	Somersaulted on field-landing following engine problem
				Bewerbung, Heinrich (inj)	Fw	FF			
06.01.42	Hs 129		17	Bewermeyer, Konrad	Fw	FF	E7	Rechlin	Crashed due to technical defect
20.01.42	Fw 190		12	Steffen, Alfred	FHI	FF	E5	Müritz	Crashed possibly due to being sun-blinded
30.01.42	Fw 189			Jabzinski, Albert	Uffz			near Gnesen	Crashed
08.02.42	He 111H-6	GA+SP	4206	Berz, Karl		BF		Müritz	Unintentional ground contact
				Hannebohn, Werner	FSI	FF	E3		
				Kaubisch, Egon (inj)	Ogefr	BM			
18.02.42	He 177 A-011	GA+QT	26	Wiegand, Heinrich	FHI	FF	E7	Müritz	Crashed after engine fire
				Borocuth, Horst (pd)	Ogefr	BS			
				Nelke, Otto (pd)	Ofw	BM	T.Kp		
				Riebold, Rudolf (pd)	FHI	BO	E7		
				Schräwer, Karl (pd)	FHI	BO	E7		
26.02.42	He 111H-4	DC+BN	3239	Wiebe, Hans-Joachim	Uffz	FF	FIH.Kdtr.	Burg nr Magdeburg	Crashed due to engine fire
07.03.42	none			Hansen, Karl	Ofw	BF	T.Kp	Pleskau	Succumbed in hospital to injuries of 25.02.42
15.04.42	none			Kottwitz, Günter	Uffz		E3	Rechlin	Hit by propeller
28.04.42	Bf 110F-2	BD+WT	2658	Vogler, Werner	Gefr	BM		near Zielow	Crashed due to engine problem
				Zeh, Albin	Gefr	FF	E2		
01.06.42	Si 204 V3		3	Demel, Gerhard	Uffz	BM		near Buchholz	Crashed following tailplane failure
				Trudrung, Max	FOI	FF	E2		
11.06.42	He 177			Fischer, Otto	Ofw	BF	E-Stf 177	near Franzburg	Parachute jump from spinning He 177. Parachute ripped due to too high a speed.
				Scherleitner, Johann	Ofw	BM	E-Stf 177		
				Seitz, Emil	Stfw	BO	E-Stf 177		
23.06.42	Go 242			unknown airman		BM	T.Kp	Lärz	Crash landing upon brake-chute test
16.07.42	He 177 A-013	GA+QV	28	Gerds, Heinrich	Ofw	BM	E-Stf 177	Stuer, Kreis Malchow	Crashed due to wing failure during dive
				Schiering, Otto (inj)	Fw	FF	E7		
19.07.42	Fw 190A-3	DF+GM	0514?	Elble, Franz	FSI	FF	E3	Castel Benito	Crashed on test flight
16.08.42	Do 217E-2	SK+WZ	1270	Gebauer, Alfred	Ofw	2.FF	EKL	Roggentin	Crashed on landing due to engine problem
				Knauss, Karl	Uffz	FF	T.Kp		
				Kamp, Hans (inj)	Uffz	BM	EKL		
20.08.42	Ju 87 V22	SF+TY	540	Rudhart, Hans	FBM	FF	E2	Rechlin	Crashed as a result of CO-poisoning
22.08.42	Bf 109G-1		14019	Leschhorn, Hans	Uffz	FF		Leussow	Crashed
05.09.42	He 177A-1	VE+UN	5214	Baier, Gerhard	Ofw	BM	KG 40	Müritz	Crashed due to side-slip after steep curve
				Kocks, Hermann	Uffz	BS	KG 40		
				Köppel, Richard	Ofw	FF	KG 40		
				Scholz, Oskar	Ofw	BF	KG 40		
17.09.43	Ju 88A-4	BD+SF	1016	Brose, Otto	Fw	FF	EKL	Wuticke near Wittstock	Crashed
				Evers, Karl	Gefr	BF	EKL		
				Reitberger, Hermann	Uffz	BM			
				Weisse, Helmut	Uffz	BM			
01.10.42	He 111H-6	CC+SE	4838	Brinkhoff, Egon	Uffz	BO	T.Kp	Berg Veroli/Italy	Unintentional ground contact on flight to Foggia
				Garczyk, Johannes	Gefr		EKL		
				Sieber, Martin			E7		
				Weichert, Erich	FI	BO	E7		
				Weist, Helmut	Uffz	FF	EKL		
11.10.42	Do 217N-1	GG+YA	1401	Ritter, Günther	Fw	FF	EKL	Müritz	Crashed
				Weißmann, Wolfgang	Gefr	BM	EKL		
30.10.42	Bf 109G-2	CC+PF	14235	Kaufmann, Egon	DI	FF	E2	near Demmin	Crashed probably due to altitude sickness
03.11.42	Si 204A-0	DI+IM	107144	Ernsting, Arnold	FSI	FF	GL/C-E2	Bonn Airfield	Crashed due to technical defects
				Sott, Hermann	Uffz	BM	T.Kp		
06.11.42	He 111	3E+PZ		Dr. Becker, Heinrich	FHI	BO	Abtl. F	near Brünn	Crashed on cross-country flight in bad weather
25.11.42	Ju 88			Kalenski, Georg	Gefr	BO		nr Latronico/Italy	Crashed on ferry flight
				Ringe, Wilhelm	Uffz	BM	T.Kp		
				Willer, Herbert	Fw	FF			

Date	Type	Code	W.Nr.	Name	Rank	Function	Unit	Location	Remarks
02.12.42	Ju 52/3m g8e	DG+KO	7565	Schröder, Heinz	Lt	FF		Mittelmeer	Missing on transport flight Tripolis to Trapani
				Volz, Konrad (+2 men)	Uffz	BM	T.Kp		
04.12.42	Ju 88A-4		140420	Bender, Wilhelm	Oblt	FF		near Fahrenkrug	Crashed on ferry flight
				Schreiber, Johann	Uffz	BM			
08.12.42	Ju 87D-1	BK+EP	2016	Vogel, Alfred	Uffz	BO		Woterfitzsee	Crashed during bomb-test flight
				Winkler, Fritz-Albrecht	Lt	FF	E7		
08.12.42	Do 217E-5		119	Jähnichen, Walter (+4 men)	T.Ass.			Taille-Fontaine	Shot down in enemy low-level attack
16.12.42	Ju 88C-4		375	Koch, Claus	Uffz	BS		near Rechlin	Crashed upon landing
				Möws, Günther	Fw	FF			
				Steuerwald, Horst	Uffz	BF	T.Kp		
28.12.42	Do 217		5141	Schober, Franz	Uffz	BM		Rechlin	Belly landing due to operating error
				Brandt, Rudolf (inj)	Fw	FF	T.Kp		
				Weber, Hans (inj)	Fw	BF			
26.01.43	Do 217E-2	RH+EN	140	Walch, Manfred	Fw	FF	EKL	Mittelmeer	Missed on transport flight Iraklion to Naples
				Stanies, Günter	Uffz	BM	T.Kp		
				Opitz, Ernst	Uffz	BF	EKL		
				Donner, Heinz	Uffz	BF	EKL		
28.01.43	He 177A-3	ND+SK	35016	Blume, Eduard	Ogefr	BS		near Lärz	Crashed after take-off
				Joos, Eugen	Oblt	FF	E-Stf 177		
				Joos, Otto	Uffz	BO	E-Stf 177		
				Nagel, Herbert	Fw	BM	E-Stf 177		
				Wunderlich, Johannes	Fw	Bf	E-Stf 177		
05.02.43	Bf 109G-2	BJ+WL	13515	Willinger, Franz	Oblt	FF	EKL	Mirow	Crashed due to engine problem
06.02.43	Ar 232A-01	VD+YA	3	Fieg, Paul	Uffz	FF	EKL	nr Crossen/Oder	Crashed due to engine problem
				Gruphofer, Fritz (inj)	Ogefr	BF	EKL		
				Verhöven, Heinrich (inj)					
				Warm, Heinz (inj)					
12.02.43	Ju 88D-1	BL+EU	1351	Fischer, Helmut	Fw	FF	EKL	near Rechlin	Crashed in bad weather emergency landing
				Klein, Kurt	Ogefr	BM	T.Kp		
				Trojer, Anton	Uffz	BF	EKL		
				Voelcker, Kurt	O-Ing	BO	GL/C-E7		
13.04.43				Boschow, Heinz	Uffz	BF	VKP	Rechlin	Fell out of the aircraft
18.04.43	Ju 52/3m	IZ+MZ	5527	Lustig, Gerhard +3 men	Flg	BM	E3	S/WCape Bon Tunis	Shot down on transport mission
27.04.43	Bf 110G-4	G9+DX	5361	Möller-Holtkamp, Albert	Oblt	FF	Fl.ltg.	near Rottumeroog	Crashed during training flight
14.05.43	Do 215B-5	NO+TP	66	Krutzke, Franz	Uffz	BM	EKL	near Kotzow	In-flight collision in parachute-test flight
				Pahlen, Engelbert	Uffz	BF	EKL		
				Weihard, Johann	Uffz	FF	EKL		
				Werner, Helmut	Uffz	BO	E5		
14.05.43	Do 217M-03	BD+KQ	1243	Matheis, Willi	Flg	BM	T.Kp	near Kotzow	Mid-air collision during take-off on measurement flight
				Sprung, Heinz	Lt	FF			
26.05.43	Bf 109G-6		15436	Knöfel, Horst	Oblt	FF	E3	Rechlin	Rammed into Ju 87 on take-off
02.06.43	He 177 A-3	ND+SE	35010	Reck, Willi	Fw	BM	E-Stf 177	near Buchholz	Crashed due to technical problems during bomb-target training
				Schwarz, Roland	Oblt	FF	E-Stf 177		
				Tarrach, Herbert	Fw	BO	E-Stf 177		
				Wagner, Josef	Fw	BF	E-Stf 177		
				Koch, Hermann (inj)	Fw	BS			
10.08.43	He 111H-6	CC+SZ	4859	Elsner, Günter	Uffz	BF	T.Kp	near Cleve	Crashed during test flight
				Konschak, Wilhelm	Ofw	BM	T.Kp		
				Noetzel, Alfred	Ofw	FF	T.Kp		
				Dr. Herzog (inj)		BO	Abtl. F		
				Dr. Netzer (inj)		BO	Abtl. F		
16.08.43	Bf 109E-7	CP+MY	3298	Manthey, Alwin	Ofw	FF	T.Kp	Cazaux	Crashed due to wing failure in BZA-testing
19.08.43	Ju 88D-1	NF+KV	1587	Pötzelberger, Josef	Fw	FF	EKL	near Retzow	Emergency landing due to engine problem
				Tappenbeck, Werner (inj)	Uffz	BF	EKL		
				Weisbrodt, Gustav (inj)	Uffz	BF			
07.09.43	Bf 110F-2 trop	CE+UI	4536	Hesse, Werner	Lt	FF	E3	Müritz	Crashed during test flight
				Scheffler, Gerhard	Fw	BO			
10.09.43	Fw 190A-3		130270	Schmid, Lorenz	FSI	FF	E2	near Neu-Gaarz	Somersaulted on landing following engine problem

Date	Type	Code	W.Nr.	Name	Rank	Duty	Unit	Location	Remarks
15.09.43	He 177A-3	GJ+RH	535446	Brommundt, Heinz	Uffz	BM	6./KG 40	near Rechlin	Crashed due to technical deficiencies
				Görlitz, Friedrich	Ogfr	BS	6./KG 40		
				Greibich, Josef	Ofw	FF	6./KG 40		
				Junge, Helmut	Ogefr	BO	6./KG 40		
				Moews, Harry	Uffz	BF	6./KG 40		
				Lensch, Hans (inj)	Gefr	BS	6./KG 40		
01.10.43	none			Kaule, Paul	FHI		E7	Feldkirch/Vorarlbg	Killed in hospital through bomb emergency jettison
16.10.43	Bf 109G	KL+ZV	27180	Heinig, Gottfried	Gefr	FF	EKL	near Wittstock	Crashed
04.11.43	Go 244	VC+WC	884	Knaebe, Heinz	Gefr	FF	EKL	near Gotha	Crashed
				Schröder, Fritz	Uffz	BM	EKL		
10.11.43	He 111		70	Gerlach, Helmut	Uff	BM	T.Kp	Albi, near Toulouse	Crashed on test flight
				Hartung, Walter	Oberfwk		T.Kp		
29.12.43	He 111H-11	GL+EJ	110060	Güttler, Gerhard	Uffz	BF	EKL	Müritz	Contact with water surface on beacon approach
				Gruchmann, Konrad	Fw	BM	T.Kp		
				Wanninger, Hans	Uffz	FF	E7		
24.02.44	Bf 109G-6	SU+XS	15435	Pohl, Rudolf	Lt	FF	EKL	Plauer See	Shot down on approach to enemy
26.02.44	Bf 110G-4		4860	Kucera, Walter	FHI		E5	near Neustrelitz	Crashed due to engine problem
				Nöding, Rudolf	FHN		E4		
				Paveljak, Wilhelm	T.Ang.		E5		
01.03.44	Ju 87D-3	NJ+VZ	1260	Stößel, Walter	FSI	BO	E5	near Hamburg	Emergency landing following engine fire
03.03.44	none			Nagel, Kurt	Gefr		T.Kp	Rechlin	Killed in test-shooting due to tube-burst
06.03.44	Bf 110G-2	PG+XJ	210010	Wächter, Ernst	Uffz	FF	EKL	near Perleberg	Shot down on approach to enemy
				Lindenbaum (inj)	Uffz	BF			
13.03.44	Bf 109G-6	BL+ZB	19210	Fischer, Herbert	Ofw	FF	EKL	Schwinkendorf	Shot down on approach to enemy
28.03.44	He 219 V13		190052	Jurk, Otto	Lt			near Treptow	Crashed
15.04.44	Do 335 V2	CP+UB	230002	Altrogge, Werner	FHI	FF	E2	near Memmingen	Crashed due to engine fire
23.04.44	Ju 88		39550	Eiermann, August	Gefr	FF	T.Kp		Crashed during test flight
09.05.44	Do 17M	RG+NW	2153	Bloch, Karl	FHj.Fw	FF	T.Kp	Lärz	Crashed due to being blinded by searchlight
				Dührkop, Karl	FOI	BO	E5		
				Knack, Gerhard	Uffz	BM	T.Kp		
				Miltenberger, Kurt	Ofw	BF	T.Kp		
21.05.44	He 111H-6	KI+XA	4093	Autheried, Ladislaus	Oblt			Teutoburger Wald	Ground contact in bad weather
				Beck, Georg	FOI	BO	E4		
				Heimann, Josef	Uffz	FF	T.Kp		
				Indisteln, Gerhard	Uffz	BF	T.Kp		
				Wiehle, Herbert	Ofw	BS	T.Kp		
21.05.44	Do 17Z	GL+AY	2517	v.Clanner, Bertram	Uffz	BF		near Minden	Crashed in bad weather
				Mann, Eberhard	FSI	FF	E3		
				Wegerle, Wilhelm	Uffz	BM	T.Kp		
14.06.44	Ar 232 B-010	QD+XP	110032	Goedicke, Theo (+6 men from Arado)	DI	FF	E2	Lärz	Crashed due to technical deficiencies
16.06.44	He 219 A-011	RL+AA	190061	Friedmann, Helmut	T.Ass.	BO	E5	near Mirow	Crashed due to tailplane failure during course-control test
				Huß, Karl-Heinz	FSI	FF	E5		
22.06.44	Bf 109G-4	TQ+LW	730023	Behrmann, Günter	FI	BO	E2	near München	Crashed during de-icing test
				Pernthaler	DI		Junkers		
				Barczykowski, Paul (inj)	Oblt	FF			
24.06.44	Ju 87D-5	BG+LW	130523	Geiger, Gerhard	Uffz	BM	T.Kp	Kemijärvi/Finland	Crashed due to operating error
				Hildenbrand, Fritz	FHI	FF	E2		
25.07.44	Ar 234B-2	GM+BA	140101	Lissau, Herbert	Lt	FF		Lärz	Somersaulted on take-off due to engine problem
12.08.44	none			Spengemann, Herbert	FHI		E4	near Coulommiers	Low-level attack on railway train
25.08.44	none			Andreoli, Emilio	Maurer			Rechlin	Killed in enemy air raid
				Becker, Hermann	Ogefr		T.Kp		
				Behrendt, Betty	Stabsh				
				Bohlig, Rudi	Ogefr		T.Kp		
				Frank, Gottlieb	Gefr		T.Kp		
				Godglück, Alfred	Mstr				
				Hartlef, Johannes	Ogefr		FlH.Kp		
				Hoof, Wilhelm	Ogefr		FlH.Kp		

				Keil, Philipp	Ogefr		FlH.Kp		
				Kipping, Hubertine	Stabsh				
				Könncke, Wilhelm	Mech				
				Matthes, Günther	Gefr		T.Kp		
				Pikoleit, Herbert	Gefr		T.Kp		
				Ranft, Karl	R.Ang.				
				Roloff, Karl	Ogefr		FlH.Kp		
				Schmidt, Hans	Ogefr		T.Kp		
				Schwarz, Josef	Ogefr		T.Kp		
				Steinfeldt, Gertrud	R.Ang.				
				Uhlrich, Hans-Joachim	Ogefr		T.Kp		
05.09.44	Me 262A-1	E3+03	170038	Ruther, Johann	FSI	FF	E3	Lärz	Crashed for unknown reason
17.09.44	Ju 188E-1		260308	Dietz, Friedrich	Uffz	FF	T.Kp	nr Schillersdorfer Teerofen	Crashed due to operating error
				Ecker, Richard	Uffz	BF	T.Kp		
				Günther, Kurt	Uffz	BM	T.Kp		
25.09.44	Fw 190D-9	TR+SD	210004	Thoenes, Alexander	FOSI	FF	E2	Roggentin	Contact with obstacle on landing
30.09.44	Me 323F V16	DU+QZ	160001	Popin, Herbert	Fl	BO	E5	Heuberg/ Württemberg	Crashed during load-parachute test
12.10.44	Ar 234B	GM+BP	140116	Arndt, Hans-Egon	Lt	FF	KG 76	Lärz	Contact with obstacle on take-off, died in hospital
16.10.44	none			Bellingrath, Ewald	Obermstr		B-Nord	Rechlin	Deceased
27.11.44	Fw 190? Bf 109?			Neidhart, Karl-Gustav	FSI	FF	E2	Roggentin	Crashed, probably due to CO-poisoning
07.12.44	Ar 234B-2	GM+BQ	140117	Kunz, Jakob		FF	Arado	Lärz	Crashed for unknown reason
01.02.45?	?			Koch, August	Ing	FF	E5	near Küstrin	Shot down on approach to enemy
				?		BO			
02.02.45	Me 262A-1	E3+31	130188	Furchner, Hans	Hptm	FF	OKL	Lärz	Crashed due to engine cut-out (ex-SQ+XA)
05.03.45	Re 3			Starbati, Walter	Lt	FF	Kdo.Reichenberg	near Buchholz	Crashed due to wing-panelling breaking off
04.04.45	Do 24?			Hildenbrand, Fritz		FF		Müritz	Low-level enemy attack
				Kahlert, Paul	Flg		T.Kp		
ca.04.45	Ju 52/3m	PB+UA		Hausmann, Walter and Crew	Flg	BM	E3	between Rechlin and Travemünde	Shot down by fighter-bombers on evacuation flight
10.04.45	none			Delz, Hans	FHI		E2	Rechlin	Killed in enemy air raid
				Heinemann, Wilhelm	T.Ang.		E7		
				Hintze, Fritz	Uffz		E3		
				Kendelbacher, Leo	Ofw		B-Süd		
				Marten, Arthur	Mech		E3		
				Nisch, Heinz	FHI				
				Pape, Heinz	Arb				
				Radtke, Franz	Flg				
				Räder, Max			T.Kp		
				Rehner, Rudolf	Mech				
				Schiering, Otto	Flkpt		E7		
17.04.45	Ju 52/3m	GC+BK		Piatschek, Joachim (+3 unknown persons)	FHI		E4	Neu-Wustrow	Shot down by fighter-bombers
26.04.45	Ar 234C			Abels, Hans-Joachim	Oblt	FF	E2	Lechfeld	Crashed following engine failure at take-off
27.04.45	Me 262			Gebel, Kurt	Uffz	FF	EKL	Oberpfaffenhofen	Landing accident on ferry flight
28.04.45	Ar 234C			Stellbrink, Bruno	Lt	FF	KG 76	near Rechlin	Exploded in the air
02.05.45	none			Schneider, Adolf	Hfw		Fl.ltg	Eastern Front	Died during ground warfare
04.05.45	none			Voigt, Hans	FSI		E2	Westermarkelsdorf	Low-level enemy attack
13.06.45	none			Gladebeck	Obermstr		B-Nord	Neubrandenburg	Died from injuries in hospital, incurred 10.04.45

Organisation of the E-Stelle Rechlin 1928 to 1945

During the years of its existence, the organisational structure of the E-Stelle Rechlin and its predecessors underwent various transformations, partly covered in the Chapter dealing with the organisation of development and testing activities. A chronological listing of the detailed structure and leadership of its various Referate (Advisory Boards) and Gruppen (Sections or Groups) are provided below, wherever these are supported by documentary evidence.

Based on personnel lists dated 25th October 1928 for the Gruppe Wa.Prw.6F (headed by Hauptmann Student), the following sub-divisions can be discerned:

The Referate I to V consisted of Entwicklungs- (Development) or else Verwaltungs- (Administration) Referate, located in Berlin. The Erprobungsreferate (Test Advisory Boards) designated as Aussenstellen (Out-Stations) were probably located in Staaken or Rechlin.

Outstations

Advisory Board	Activity		Activity Head
Referat VI	Erprobungsgruppe 1	*Test Group 1*	Currently unoccupied
Referat VIa	Flugzeuge	*Aircraft*	Dipl.-Ing. von Massenbach
Referat VIb	Bordgerät	*Aircraft Equipment*	Dr. Karl Genthe
Referat VIb-N	Nachtflug	*Night Flying*	Dipl.-Ing. Gillert
Referat VIb-F	Fallschirm	*Parachutes*	Rittmeister a.D. Kempte
Referat VIc	Motoren	*Powerplants*	Ing. Sachse
Referat VId	Betrieb	*Works/Operations*	Ing. Hans Leutert
Referat VIe	Bildgeräte	*Photography*	Rittmeister a.D. Poetsch
Referat VIf	F.T. Gerät	*W/T Equipment*	Dr. von Seelen
Referat VII	Erprobungsgruppe 2	*Test Group 2*	Oblt. a.D. Mohnicke
	Taktische Aufträge	*Tactical Tasks*	
	Training	*Training*	

The amalgamation of Gruppe Wa.Prw.6F and Gruppe Wa.B.6. into the Wa.L. shortly after, resulted in the creation of a new Gruppe Wa.L.Prw. headed by Hauptmann Dr. Paul Jeschonnek.

Within the sphere of responsibility for testing and evaluation, the Gruppe III structure was as follows:

Advisory Board	Activity		Activity Head
–	Leiter Erprobung	*Head of Testing*	Dipl.-Ing. von Massenbach
–	Leiter Betrieb	*Head of Works*	Dipl.-Ing. von Gerlach
(Deputy)			
Referat IIIa	Flugzeuge	*Aircraft*	Chief Pilot Hoppe
Referat IIIb	Ausrüstung	*Equipment*	Dr. Karl Genthe
Referat IIIc	Kraftanlagen	*Power Installations*	Ing. Sachse
Referat IIId	F.T.	*W/T Equipment*	Dr. von Seelen
Referat IIIe	Bild	*Photography*	Rittmeister a.D. Poetsch
Referat IIIf	Waffen	*Armament*	–
Fl. Staffel Berlin			Ing. Hans Leutert
Fl. Staffel Rechlin			Oblt. a.D. Mohnicke
Verwaltung		*Administration*	Hauptmann a.D. Brandt

There was thus no significant re-organisation, and since the responsible Referat Heads remained unchanged, only the designation became altered. Equally unchanged was the Erprobungsgruppe in the subsequent re-organisations in 1929, becoming subsequently known as Wa.L III and a short while later, as Wa.Prw.8, Gruppe III – the E-Stelle of the RDL Staaken-Rechlin, Geschäftsführer (Business Manager) continued to be Dipl.-Ing. Freiherr von Massenbach, who evidently led the Erprobungsgruppe in a unified position. Under him were:

a) Verwaltungsreferat	(Admin. Advisory Board)	Hauptmann a.D. Brandt
b) Erprobungsgruppe	(Test Section)	Dipl.-Ing. von Massenbach
Referat Flugzeuge	(Adv. Board Aircraft)	Chief Pilot Hoppe
Referat Motoren	(Adv. Board Powerplants)	Currently unoccupied
Referat Ausrüstung	(Adv. Board Equipment)	Dipl.-Ing. Schwencke
Referat F.T.	(Adv. Board W/T Equipmt)	Dr. von Seelen
Referat L.B.	(Adv. Board Photography)	Rittmeister a.D. Poetsch
c) Betriebsgruppe	(Operating Group)	Dipl.-Ing. von Gerlach
Betrieb Rechlin	E-Stelle Rechlin	Dipl.-Ing. K Bader
Betrieb Staaken	E-Stelle Staaken	Ing. Karl Leutert

Following the establishment of the RLM, the first known composition of the E-Stelle (most probably dating from 1934) was as follows:

Commander of the Flight Test Centres and Rechlin Airbase Kommandant			Flieger-Kommodore Stahr
Head of the E-Stelle Rechlin			Dipl.-Ing. von Massenbach
Head of T (Technik)			Dipl.-Ing. Reidenbach

Gruppe T1   Flugwerk   *Airframes*   Dipl.-Ing. K Bader
(Encompassing: combat, reconnaissance, fighter, sports and special aircraft, aerodynamics, propellers, statics, materials and prototype testing).

Gruppe T2   Triebwerke   *Powerplants*   Dipl.-Ing. W Eisenlohr
(Encompassing: engines, accessories, installation, test-stands, airfield equipment, materials, oils and lubricants).

Gruppe T3   Ausrüstung   *Equipment*   Dipl.-Ing. Schwencke
(Encompassing: mechanical, W/T, photographic and navigational equipment).

Gruppe T5   Bewaffnung   *Armament*   Dipl.-Ing. Koch (?)
(Encompassing: bombs, chemicals and protectives).

Gruppe B   Betrieb   *Works/Operations*   Dipl.-Ing. von Massenbach (?)

Abteilung M   Militärische Erprobung   *(Military Testing)*   Fl.Kptn. Baier

From mid 1938, activities were further sub-divided into specialist test groups and new designations were introduced. As related elsewhere, it eventually led to separation of leadership of the E-Stellen and Test Departments.

E-Stelle and Airbase Kommandant was Major (E) Haagen, and Head of Testing Dipl.-Ing. K Fritsche. The sub-divisions are set out in the first table on the following two pages.

Organisational changes in the RLM in spring 1939 led to the almost definitive final internal structure of the E-Stelle Rechlin, as outlined in the second table on the two pages which follow. From this time on, no further evidence has been uncovered for the existence of a separate, Abteilung M', whereas no changes occurred affecting the existence and functions of the Airbase Command, whose Airbase Commander was Major Haagen, and Dipl.-Ing. Fritsche, its Chief of Testing and Head of the E-Stelle.

At the turn of 1944/45, the applicable E-Stelle divisions set out in the third of the tables on pages 128-129 – subject to revision – can only be determined on hand from partially-surviving German documents as well as from an Allied document based on captured records, and from statements made by former participants. The E-Stelle Rechlin Kommandeur was Major Behrens.

Organisation of the E-Stelle Rechlin from mid 1938

Dept	Activity	(Translation)	Activity Head
E7	**Flugzeuge**	*Aircraft*	Dipl.-Ing. Francke
E7a	Serienflugzeuge (?)	*Series Aircraft*	
E7b	Kampfflugzeuge	*Bombers*	
E7c	Jagdflugzeuge & Zerstörer	*Fighters/Heavy Fighters*	
E7d	Enteisung	*De-icing*	
E7s	Flugzeugschutz	*Aircraft Protection*	
E8	**Triebwerke**	*Powerplants*	Dipl.-Ing. Cuno
E8a	Motoren	*Engines*	
E8b	Triebwerke & Einbau	*Engines & Installation*	
E8c	Kraft- & Schmierstoffe	*Fuels & Lubricants*	
E8d	Prüfstände	*Test Stands*	
(?)*	Luftschrauben	*Propellers (*It is not certain whether Propellers had at this time been assigned to the Powerplant Department)*	
E9	**Nachrichten & Navigation**	*Comm & Navigation*	Dipl.-Ing. v. Hauteville
E9b	Navigation	*Navigation*	
E9c	Funkgeräte, Funknavigation	*W/T Equipment & Navigation*	
E10	Ausrüstung	*Equipment*	Dr. Wendroth
E10a	Bord- u. Kreiselgeräte	*Aircraft & Gyro Instruments*	
E10d	Bildgeräte	*Photographic Equipment*	
E10e	Bordelektrik	*Aircraft Electricals*	
E10h	Rettungs- u.Sicherheitsgerät	*Rescue & Safety Devices*	
E10med	Luftfahrtmed. Erprobungen	*Aero-medical Testing*	
E11	**Schusswaffen**	*Rifle-barrelled Weapons*	Dipl.-Ing. Koch
E11 IIA	Starre u. bewegl. Schusswaffen	*Fixed & movable Weapons*	
E11 IID	Lafetten	*Gun turrets*	
E11 IIE	Ballistik	*Ballistics*	
E11 IIF	Zieleinrichtungen (?)	*Target-aiming Installations (?)*	
E11 IIIA	Bordmunition	*Aircraft Ammunition*	
E11 IIIB	Rauch- u. Signalmunition	*Smoke & Signal Cartridges*	
E 11 IIIC	Behälterschutz	*Container Protection*	
E12	**Abwurfwaffen**	*Air-drop Weapons*	Dipl.-Ing. Koch
E12 IVA	?		
E12 IVB	?		
E12 IVC	?		
E12 Eb	Einbauten	*Installations*	
E13	**Bodengeräte**	*Ground Equipment*	Dr. Göttmann (?)
E13 I	?		
E 13 II	?		
E 13 III	?		
E 13 IV	Licht- u. Elektrotechnik	*Optical & Electrical Engineering*	
F	**Leitstrahlverfahren,**	*Guide-beam Systems*	Dr. Plendl
	Ionosphärenforschung	*Ionospheric Research*	
M	**Militärische Prüfung**	*Military Evaluation*	Hauptm. Restemeyer
	Jäger, Bomber, Erkunder	*Fighters, Bombers, Scouts*	
B	**Betrieb**	*Operations*	Dipl.-Ing. Fischer

Organisational changes in the RLM Spring 1939

Dept	Activity	(Translation)	Activity Head
E2	**Flugzeuge u. Einbau**	*Aircraft & Installations*	Dipl.-Ing. Francke
E2a	Serienflugzeuge	*Series Aircraft (until end 1941)*	
E2b	Kampfflugzeuge	*Bomber Aircraft*	
E2c	Jagdflugzeuge u. Zerstörer	*Fighters & Heavy Fighters*	
E2d	Enteisung	*De-icing (until end 1940, then E2g)*	
E2f	Fahrwerke	*Undercarriages*	
E2g	Enteisung	*De-icing*	
E2s	Flugzeugschutz, Panzerung	*Aircraft Protection, Armour Plating*	
E3	**Triebwerke**	*Powerplants*	Dipl.-Ing. Cuno
E3a	Motoren	*Engines*	
E3b	Triebwerke u. Einbau	*Engines & Installations*	
E3c	Kraft- u. Schmierstoffe	*Fuels & Lubricants (in summer 1943, E10)*	
E3d	Prüfstände	*Test-Stands*	
E3e	Messwesen für Triebwerke	*Engine Measurement Systems*	
E3f	Luftschrauben	*Propellers*	
E4	**Nachrichten u. Navigation**	*Comm & Navigation*	Dipl.-Ing. v. Hauteville
E4a	(bisher nicht nachgewiesen)	*(not confirmed in documents)*	
E4b	Navigation	*Navigation*	
E4c	Funkgeräte, Funknavigation	*W/T & Navigation Devices*	
E5	**Ausrüstung**	*Equipment*	Dr. Wendroth
E5a	Bordgeräte	*Aircraft Instruments*	
E5d	Bildgeräte	*Photographic Equipment*	
E5e	Elektr. Energieversorgung	*Electrical Energy Supply*	
E5g	Kreiselgeräte (?)	*Gyro Equipment (?)*	
E5h	Rettungs- u. Sicherheitsgeräte	*Rescue & Safety Devices*	
E5med	Luftfahrtmedizinische Erprobungen	*Aeromedical Testing*	

E6	**Bordmunition**	*Aircraft Ammunition*	**Dr. Burgsmüller**
E6 IIIA	Zünder	*Igniters/Fuses*	
E6 IIIB	Leucht- u. Signalmittel, Sonder-Kampfmittel	*Visibility & Signal Flares, Special Combat Devices*	
E6 IIIC	Wirkung im Ziel, Aussenballistik	*Target Effectiveness, External Ballistics*	

E7	**Abwurfwaffen**	*Air-drop Weapons*	**Dipl.-Ing. Koch**
E7 I	? (in Udetfeld)		
E7 IIA	Zünder	*Igniters/Fuses*	
E7 IIB	Abwurfbehälter	*Jettison Containers*	
E7 IIC	Sprengbomben	*Demolition Bombs*	
E7 IID/E	Leucht-, Brand- u. Markierungsbomben	*Flares, Incendiary & Marker Bombs*	
E7 IILab	Sonderzünder	*Special Fuses*	
E7AG	Aufhängungen	*Suspension Gear*	
E7Eb	Einbauten	*Installations*	
E7RS	Rauchspurmunition (= Raketenbomben)	*Rocket -propelled Bombs*	

E8	**Bodengeräte**	*Ground-based Equipment*	**Dipl.-Ing. Schnittke**
E8a	Flugbetriebsanlagen u. Geräte	*Flight Operations Installations & Equipment*	
E8b	Fahrzeuge	*Vehicles*	
E8c	Wärmeversorgung, Feuerlöschwesen	*Heating Supply & Fire Extinguishers (only until 1940)*	
E8d	Starkstromtechnik, Bodenbefeuerung u. Lichttechnik	*Strong-Power Supply, Ground Flare & Lighting Equipment*	

F	**Leitstrahlverfahren**	*Guide-Beam Systems*	**Dr. Plendl**
	Funkberatung	*Wireless Systems Advice*	
	Ionosphärenforschung	*Ionosphere Research (removed from the E-Stelle 1943 and assigned to Research Institutes)*	

E-Stelle Rechlin Divisions at the turn of 1944/45

E2	**Flugzeuge**	*Aircraft*	**Fl. Oberstabsing. Böttcher**
E2b	Bomber	*Bombers*	
E2c	Jäger	*Fighters*	
E2d?	Schul- u. Sonderflugzeuge	*Training & Special Aircraft*	
E2e	Flugleistungen	*Flight Performance*	
E2f	Fahrwerke	*Undercarriages*	
E2g	Flugzeug-u. Behälterschutz, Panzerung	*Aircraft & Container Protection, Armour-plating*	
E2w	Wartung, Fertigung, Reparaturfragen	*Maintenance, Assembly & Repair Matters (initially from Summer 1943)*	

E3	**Triebwerke**	*Powerplants*	**Fl. Oberstabsing. Cuno**
E3a	Motoren	*Engines*	
E3b	Triebwerksanlagen, Einbau	*Engine Systems & Installations*	
E3d	Prüfstände	*Test-Stands*	
E3e	Messwesen	*Measurement Techniques*	
E3f	Luftschrauben	*Propellers*	

E4	**Funk- u. Nachrichtentechnik**	W/T & Communications	**Fl. Oberstabsing. von Hauteville**
E4 I	Navigationsgeräte	*Navigation Equipment (Assigned to E5 at the end of 1944/45 as E5/I)*	
E4 IIa	FT-Nachrichtentechnik	*W/T Techniques*	
E4 IIb	Peil- u. Adcockanlagen	*Homing & Direction-finding Installations*	
E4 IIc	Funknavigationstechnik	*Radio Navigation Technology*	
E4 IId	Drahtnachrichtentechnik u. Elektrotechnik	*Cable-type Communications & Electrical Technology*	
E4 IIe	Bordfunkanlagen	*Airborne Wireless Installations*	
E4 IIf	Sonderaufgaben	*Special Tasks*	

E5	**Ausrüstung**	*Equipment*	**Fl. Oberstabsing. Roloff**
E5/I	Navigation*	*Navigation*	
E5/II	Bordgeräte	*Aircraft Equipment*	
E5/III	Bildgruppe	*Photography Group*	
E5/IV	Rettungs- und Sicherheitsgeräte	*Rescue & Safety Equipment*	
E5/V	Elektrische Energieversorgung	*Electrical Energy Supply*	
E5/VI	Steuerungen u. Kreiselgeräte	*Control & Gyro Equipment*	
E5/VII	Pneumat.u. Hydraul. Energieversorg	*Pneumatic & Hydraulic Energy Supply*	

E6	**Bordmunition**	*Aircraft Ammunition*	**Fl. Oberstabsing. Dr. Burgsmüller**
E6 IIIA	Zünder	*Fuses*	
E6 IIIB	Leucht- u. Signalmittel, Sonderkampfmittel	*Flares & Signals, Special Weapons*	
E6 IIIC	Außenballistik, Wirkung im Ziel,	*External Ballistics, Effectiveness at target,*	
	Ausländische Munition	*Foreign Ammunition*	
E6 IIID	Hochgeschwindigkeitsmunition	*High-speed Ammunition (begun in 1941)*	

E7	**Abwurfwaffen**	*Air-dropped Weapons*	**Fl. Oberstabsing. Schürfeld**
E7a	Zünder	*Fuses*	
E7b	Bomben	*Bombs*	
E7c	Aufhängungen, Lanciergeräte	*Suspensions, Launchers*	
E7d	Zielgeräte und Ballistik	*Target Devices & Ballistics*	
E7e	Einbau	*Installation*	

E8	**Bodengeräte**	*Ground Equipment*	**Fl. Oberstabsing. Lauschke**
E8a	Flugbetriebsanlagen- u. geräte	*Flying Operations Installations & Equipment*	
E8b	Fahrzeuge, Feuerlöschwesen	*Vehicles, Fire Extinguishing Equipment*	
E8c	Tankanlagen u. Geräte für Kraft- und Schmierstoff	*Storage Installations for Fuels and Lubricants*	
E8d	Bodenelektronik, Bodenbefeuerung u. Lichttechnik	*Ground Electronics, Ground Igniting & Lighting Equipment*	

E10	**Kunststoffe, Kraft- u. Schmierstoffe**	*Synthetics, Fuel & Lubricants*	**Fl. Oberstabsing. Dr. Giessmann**
E10 I	Kunststoffe?	*Synthetics?*	
E10 II	Chemie	*Chemicals*	
E10 III	Kraftstoffe	*Fuels*	
E10 IV	Schmierstoffe	*Lubricants*	
E10 V	Motorische Prüfung	*Engine Testing*	

Chapter Six
by Karl Kössler

The E-Stelle (See) Travemünde

The Seaplane Test Centre Travemünde is traceable back to the intention of the Reichswehr Navy Command, similar to that which existed during World War One, to establish a naval air arm that would come directly under their jurisdiction. The leading personnel of the establishment consisted exclusively of former Navy aviators who brought the benefit of their experience with them. Disguised at first as a normal enterprise, a suitable team provided with the necessary equipment was built up within a few years from 1928. Whilst the concept of independent navy flyers had to be finally given up in 1933, the E-Stelle, which had also been in the service of the Luftwaffe, continued its functions although the seaplane was reduced in significance to the role of supporting land-based aircraft engaged in naval operations.

Quick-Reference Abbreviations

DLH   Deutsche Lufthansa AG
       German Airlines

DVL   Deutsche Versuchsanstalt für Luftfahrt
       German Experimental Institute for Aviation

DVS   Deutsche Verkehrsflieger-Schule GmbH
       German Civilian Pilots School

HWA   Heereswaffenamt
       Army Ordnance Office

MLD   MarineLuchtvaartdienst
       Navy Aviation Service (Holland)

RDL   Reichsverband der Deutschen Luftfahrtindustrie
       Reich Union of German Aircraft Industry

RKL   Reichskommissar für Luftfahrt (later RLM)
       Reich Commissioner for Aviation

RLM   Reichsluftfahrtministerium
       German Air Ministry

RVM   Reichsverkehrsministerium
       Reich Ministry of Transport

RWM   Reichswehrministerium
       Imperial Army and Navy Ministry

SES   Seeflugzeug-Erprobungsstelle (des RDL)
       Seaplane Test Centre (of the RDL)

TVA   Torpedo-Versuchsanstalt
       Torpedo Test Institute

It is difficult to determine exactly when seaplane testing under commission of the Navy Command commenced in strict secrecy at the Priwall near Travemünde. It can only be confirmed that this indeed took place and that the Caspar-Werke GmbH owned and established by Dr. jur. Karl Caspar and operating there since 1918, was

The Priwall and the town of Travemünde in 1928, photographed from 4000m (13,120ft).

The former Caspar-Werke AG installations, which became the home of the RDL E-Stelle Travemünde in 1928/29.

The Caspar-Werke AG Administration building on the Priwall, and from 1928, home of the newly-created RDL E-Stelle.

best suited to support this disguise. The firm, which had designed and manufactured aircraft up until the beginning of 1928, possessed all the prerequisites required for testing seaplanes which had also stemmed from elsewhere. From this time on, the path led directly to the RDL 'Seeflugzeug-Erprobungsstelle', referred to by the abbreviation SES. The extent of the installations at that time can be seen in the map on page 156.

The Reichsmarine and Versailles

As already mentioned in Chapter 4 dealing with Lipetsk, because of the harsh conditions of the Treaty of Versailles imposed upon the nation by the Victorious Powers, the Navy Command under Admiral Hans Zenker as early as February 1920 had formed a disguised Aeronautical Advisory Group known as Referat A II 1, led by Kapitänleutnant Walther Faber, a renowned World War One navy aviator who was succeeded by Kapitänleutnant Hans Ritter on 23rd March 1923. During his period of office, an important decision was taken. Since close co-operation already existed with

Sweden, the Navy Command saw no necessity to participate in the Soviet Red Army proposal to establish a combined German Army and Navy land- and seaplane testing centre in Odessa, the Army Command under Generaloberst Hans von Seeckt therefore opting for Lipetsk.

On 1st June 1925, Kapitän zur See Rudolf Lahs was appointed as successor to Hans Ritter. Contemporaneously, the Referat was expanded into a larger body comprising five Referate (Advisory Groups) under the designation BSx. As an organisation, it

belonged initially to the 'BS' or sea-transport division under Kapitän zur See Walter Lohmann from the Navy General Office (B), but became independent later on.

The Caspar-Werke GmbH (Co Ltd), had meanwhile been transformed into an AG (Share Company), and it was none other than Captain Lohmann who was appointed to its Board of Directors on 8th April 1927. For some time, the firm's own activities had not been going at all well, and published literature often refers to the 'Caspar-Werke purchase' by Walter Lohmann in 1926. It is more than probable, however, that he merely purchased a portion of the share capital as a camouflage figure for the Navy Command. Otherwise, how else could it have been possible that at the decision of the firm's General Meeting on 10th May 1930, the entire assets of the company passed into the hands of the Reich, as announced by the Berlin-Mitte County Court on 1st July 1930?

As it happened, prior to being relieved of this position in September 1927, Lohmann had already purchased property which lay not on the Priwall but on the other side of the strait on Mecklenburg territory and upon which the Luftzeugamt was later erected. It soon became recognizable in which direction the enterprise was heading. On 31st October 1927, Kapitänleutnant and retired navy pilot Hermann Moll, who since April 1925 had been the Commercial Director on the GmbH Board, was now appointed the sole Chairman of the AG Board. At this time, the enterprise had already received an increasing number of contracts which apparently came from the RDL but which in fact concerned seaplane testing within the framework of the so-called first 'armament period' and intended to form the initial equipment of the planned naval air arm despite the restrictions of the Treaty of Versailles.

An impetus for development for such aircraft was accorded when the Navy Command earlier in the year had issued requirements for the 'German Seaplane Contest' which took place in Warnemünde from the 11th to 31st July 1926. Of a total of 18 aircraft tested, 14 participated in the contest. The event was made possible since only two months previously the 'Paris Agreement' came into effect where, in an exchange of diplomatic Notes between the victorious powers Permanent Legation Conference and the German ambassador in Paris, the very restrictive 'Begriffsbestimmungen' (Definitions of Understanding)

concerning aircraft construction in Germany which had been in force up until then, where largely lifted.

For its intended purpose, the contest was deemed highly successful, in which among others, the Junkers W 33 and W 34 appeared for the first time. The Caspar C 29 reconnaissance aircraft, disguised as a 'mail-carrying aircraft' was also to have taken part but was destroyed by fire during a test flight a few days earlier. One of the two winning Heinkel aircraft, the HD 24 biplane trainer incidentally, was flown by Dipl.-Ing. Rudolf Spies who at that time belonged to the RWM Department T2V (L) and shortly afterwards was appointed as Specialist Advisor on Airframes in the Gruppe BSx.

The Priwall is Expanded

Towards the end of 1926, work had begun to enlarge the Priwall into a land- and seaplane base as a 'northern focal point'. According to facility planning by the Lübeck Board of Constructions Chief Fritz Neufeldt, the Priwall area was to be considerably expanded, and included the erection of a large seaplane hangar of surface area 60 x 60m (197 x 197ft) with a 12m (39½ft) high doors. When one considers that at around this time when the Dornier-Metallbauten GmbH was undertaking design work on the Do X flying-boat under contract to the Navy Command, that the new hangar in Travemünde was 'coincidentally' dimensionally capable of housing exactly this flying-boat, one can clearly see the effects of the many connections which existed at that time. Just as 'coincidental' also, was the Travemünde seaplane floating dock built by the Flender-Werft (dockyard) in Lübeck, dimensioned to fit the Do X flying-boat.

This assumption is further strengthened by the fact that the Hanseatische-Flughafen-Gesellschaft (airfield company) of Lübeck-Travemünde had only been established on 2nd November 1927 as the

enterprise responsible for expansion of the airfield, whereas the large hangar was already completed and fully in use a mere two weeks later. The Navy General Office of the Naval Command had almost certainly played a definite role in all of these plans.

Director of this industrial company and one who energetically pursued the establishment of this new Lübeck-Travemünde land- and seaport was Kapitänleutnant (retd) Hermann Mans colloquially referred to as 'Mans – der kann's' (Mans – the man who can).

On 26th May 1927, the RWM issued the directive to carry-out measures for the so-called 'Air Armament Period' 1927 to 1930, which included expansion of the naval air arm and improving its equipment. It also raised the possibility of having an independent E-Stelle especially tailored to meet its needs, just as the Army already had available in Lipetsk, and which was in the process of adding to it Staaken and Müritz (the later Rechlin).

The RDL E-Stelle Appears

At the beginning of 1928, the SES (Seaplane E-Stelle) of the RDL as a title appeared for the very first time, headed by none other than the former Caspar-Werke director Hermann Moll. His deputy, first 'Chefpilot' and head of the 'Fluggruppe' established shortly afterwards on 1st April 1928 was Ernst-August Roth, who had been discharged as Kapitänleutnant from Navy service the previous day. They were joined by another pilot, Walter Hagen, who had previously been with the SEVERA or See-Versuchsabteilung (Navy Test Department). A team was gathered around them, built up partially from well-trained Caspar employees and partially from capable engineers and technicians from elsewhere. A few months later, they were already capable of carrying out the seaborne-suitability trials of the trimotor Rohrbach Roland (Werk Nr.29) flying-boat which, intended for DLH admirably acquitted. It had only been four weeks before, on the night of 16/17th November 1928, when the aircraft had survived an extremely heavy storm in the Pötenitzer Wiek (bay or cove) without suffering any damage, although it had been blown landwards complete with the base of its mooring-buoy and had to withstand the breakers for two whole days. The Con

The Heinkel HD 24 (Werk-Nr.249), with which Dipl.-Ing. Rudolf Spies of the RWM secured third place in the 1926 German Seaplane Contest. Shortly afterwards, he became the Referent (Expert Advisor) on airframes in the Navy Gruppe BSx and in 1934, was appointed Technical Head of the E-Stelle.

The land-and seaport Travemünde during its expansion in 1928. In the hangar is a Rohrbach Roland with another outside it together with a Rohrbach Rocco. To the right is a Dornier Superwal.

Members of Gruppe F pictured in front of the Administration building in 1929. Starting second from left are Arthur Rengies, Werner Damasko, Ernst-August Roth, Rudmai and Paul Schenck. Identity of the others is not known.

The appearance of the larger Rohrbach Romar (Werk-Nr.29) attracted much attention in Travemünde. At this time, the flying boat, without markings, still had a small fin and rudder and mid-positioned tailplane susceptible to water spray.

cluding Report E1/29 of the incident was compiled by Roth on 3rd January 1929.

The first aircraft received by the SES for experimental and test purposes was the four-engined Dornier Superwal (Do R Nas, D-1337, Werk-Nr.143) which Roth, after demonstrating it on the Wannsee in Berlin on 27th April 1928, flew over to Travemünde together with the Dornier flight mechanic Josef Hörhager who joined the SES staff. The second aircraft to follow, on 7th June 1928 was the Heinkel HE 1 float-plane (D-938, Werk-Nr.205). None of the aircraft tested by the SES at that time had been reassigned to them as 'own' property. The records mostly mention the SEVERA or the DVL as owners, and for a time a SEVERA-used a non-existent camouflage organisation called the 'Abteilung Küsten-flug der DLH' (DLH Coastal Flight Depart-ment). As a result of DLH objections, it became renamed the 'Luftdienst GmbH' (Air Service Co Ltd).

The SES received its first Head of Works, Dipl.-Ing. Kurt Fritsche, on 1st January 1929, simultaneously changing its title to the 'RDL, Gruppe Flugzeugbau, Travemünder Erprobungsstelle' (RDL Aircraft Construc-tion Section, E-Stelle Travemünde). A superb engineer, Fritsche soon made a name for himself as the creator of the res-cue vessel 'Phönix' and its particular instal-lations, and for his foresighted planning and expansion of Travemünde itself, to which was later added the completely new E-Stelle Tarnewitz in 1934.

Despite its clearly military significance, Travemünde had to maintain the appear-ance of a purely civilian installation. For this reason, it had only civilian employees who wore civilian clothes, the only sign of their attachment to the centre being the letters RDL on the patent-leather peaks of their dark blue caps. After 1933, It was changed to 'EST' – for E-Stelle – and still later, Luftwaffe uniforms became more frequently seen.

On 25th June 1929, the free and Hanses-tadt Lübeck received a communication signed by Hermann Moll of the RDL that:

The Rohrbach Romar (Werk-Nr.29) admirably proved its seaworthiness and high-seas capabilities in tests conducted in December 1928.

A Dornier Do R Nas (possibly Werk-Nr.143), piloted by Egon Fath on a test flight on Lake Constance, still without markings.

The RDL nose emblem and the name 'Pottwal' on the fuselage identifies this flying boat as the Do R Nas (D-1337, Werk-Nr.143), the first aircraft used by the E-Stelle. Standing ahead of the engine is the flight mechanic Josef Hörhager who came with the aircraft.

'From 1st January 1929, the previous sea-plane testing work undertaken by the Caspar-Werke AG at RDL request has been carried-out by the latter, whereby the entire Caspar personnel has been taken over.' With this, the E-Stelle Travemünde thus officially came into being. The dissolution of the Caspar-Werke which subsequently took place and the transfer of its entire assets to the Reich has already been mentioned. The E-Stelle was now able to be expanded in line with Dipl.-Ing. Fritsche's plans. In addition to the three hangars and the administration building taken over from Caspar, it also had half of the large airport hangar available for housing aircraft, the other half being used by DLH whose flying operations to and from Travemünde continually increased.

Among the most noteworthy events with which the E-Stelle was involved in 1929 was the departure of Rudolf Lahs from naval service, being promoted to Konteradmiral (Rear Admiral) and becoming President of the RDL, remaining as such until the end of World War Two. The maiden flight of the DoX took place on 12th July in Altenrhein, the Gruppe BSx, taken over by Kapitän zur See Konrad Zander on 24th September being simultaneously renamed the Luftschutzgruppe (Air Defence Group) or LS, and the drawing-up of specifications for aircraft developments during the second so-called Armament Period 1930-1933. An endeavour was thereby made, through mutual agreements between the up until then independently-operating Army centres (the Waffenamt Wa.L) and the Navy (BSx, now LS) to avoid duplication in aircraft development.[1]

There were also changes in E-Stelle personnel. A number of new pilots were added, among them Karl Wiborg (who met with a fatal accident in 1931), Gerhard Hubrich, Hugo Dobberthien, and Erich Gundermann. How the E-Stelle was organised, is unfortunately not traceable from existing documents. It seems, however, that for fulfilling its tasks, an organisational form was chosen which was continuously further developed but in its basic form was retained until the very end. The rapidly increasing number of aircraft naturally brought about a growth in personnel in individual Referate and Gruppen.

Under the date of 16th June 1930 for the purpose of advising all responsible centres and for the first and only time, an aircraft type-list complete with drawings, diagrams and performance charts was compiled of all seaplanes tested between 1928 and 1930. Responsible for its contents was Wilhelm Huth, head of the Flugerprobung (Flight Testing) Gruppe F. The listing included the Heinkel HD30 first prototype which had arrived at the E-Stelle shortly before, and

Admiral Erich Raeder, Chief of the Naval Command, upon his first visit to Travemünde, in conversation with Gruppe F head Walter Hagen. Wearing a cap is the E-Stelle director Hermann Moll and in the centre is Kapitän zur See Konrad Zander, head of the Navy Command Gruppe BSx. All are dressed unobtrusively in civilian clothing.

The Heinkel HD30a (D-1463, Werk-Nr.288) on approach to the Pötenitzer Wiek (bay).

rather prematurely, was intended to serve as the first series production observation and training aircraft for the Navy, but which did not advance beyond the two prototypes built.

Travemünde Flying Meeting
During this period, Travemünde was often the showplace of large air sporting events, one of which took place in July 1930 when E-Stelle aircraft and crews participated. Among the guests of honour was Günther Plüschow, the famous 'Aviator of Tsingtau' who subsequently achieved world renown for his pioneering research flights undertaken in the southernmost regions of South America. Travemünde also became the venue for large national as well as international air contests.

Several documents from the years 1931 to 1933 relate how the E-Stelle received its complement of aircraft.[2, 3, 4] The RVM purchased the aircraft, their engines and necessary substitute parts from the 'domestic promotion of the German aircraft industry' or from the 'aviation vehicle development' funds and transferred them without reim-

bursement 'as material assistance' to the centres involved in aeronautical activities. These included the RDL or its E-Stelle, the DVL, the DVS, the Luftdienst GmbH, and the University Flying Academies. The previous practice of mostly registering aircraft intended for Travemünde under the names of other centres was terminated. The RDL E-Stelle Travemünde now appeared directly in the assignments of aircraft to be tested, starting with the two ArLIIa, (D-1875 and D-1876), and the HE9d (D-1947).

On 16th December 1931 – and not on the 6th as often related – the E-Stelle suffered its first tragic loss when Karl Wiborg crashed whilst demonstrating the second prototype HD60a (D-2176) when parts of the aircraft disintegrated in a dive through overstressing. The HE60, together with the He59 and DoJII Bis Wal actually formed the initial types of naval seaplanes.

Initial Decision for Series Production Aircraft – The He59 and He60
Stemming from Heinkel aircraft designer Reinhold Mewes and originally known as the HD59 (later He59), the first proto-

type (D-2214) of this large multi-purpose biplane was test flown in seaplane form in Travemünde. The second He 59 prototype (D-2215), fitted with a fixed trousered mainwheel undercarriage, was transferred to Lipetsk for flight trials (from 6th July to September 1932) as this would not have been possible at Travemünde or elsewhere on German soil. The Navy Command's section LS welcomed usage of the Lipetsk facilities. Its crew, consisting of Heinz Simon who had joined Travemünde on 1st March 1932, and German Cornelius as head of testing, were both provided by the E-Stelle.[5] The He 59 and He 60 were thus the first floatplanes tested by the E-Stelle which then went into large-scale series production and which absolved themselves well in subsequent operational trials.

The E-Stelle was also visited twice that year by the Do X, initially on 22nd July and again on 27th August 1932. On the occasion of its second visit, the dimensionally-large Flender dry dock was used for maintenance and repair work on it. The seaplane hangar which had been originally designed large enough to accommodate the flying-boat, however, was never used. Both visits of this large flying-boat understandably drew a considerable amount of public attention and interest.

Towards the end of the year, far-reaching changes took place in the hierarchy of the Army and Navy flying organisations. On 30th September 1932, Kapitän zur See Konrad Zander, head of the Navy's section LS, was replaced by Fregatten-Kapitän Rudolf Wenninger. Despite the already-mentioned

The 'real' Heinkel HD 24W (D-1313, Werk-Nr.271) christened 'Tsingtau', which became world-famous through exploration flights over the Andes and southermost Argentinean island groups by its pilot Günther Plüschow. The photograph was taken on the aircraft's acceptance flight, on which he was accompanied by Ing. Ernst Dreblow of Askania, lent for the occasion as a flight mechanic.

The 'fake' Tsingtau – the same Heinkel HD 30a (D-1463, Werk-Nr.288) pictured above, which had been so presented for the 'Flying Day' held on 6th July 1930 in Travemünde. Günther Plüschow was also present as Guest of Honour, and not much more than 6 months later, both he and Dreblow were killed in a fatal accident in Argentina. In 1934, a flight safety ship bore his name.

The He 60a (D-2176, Werk-Nr.381) crashed directly in front of the Air Traffic Control Building. It was piloted by Karl Wiborg, who was the first E-Stelle fatality.

The funeral ceremony for Karl Wiborg.

*Nearest the camera is the Heinkel HD 59b
(D-2215, Werk-Nr.379) seaplane, specially
fitted with a fixed undercarriage for armament
testing prior to its flight to Lipetsk.*

*On 27th August 1932, the Do X (D-1929),
alighted for the second time in Travemünde
for maintenance purposes in the floating dock
that had been erected for this aircraft.*

agreements between the largely independently-functioning Army and Navy flying units, it was not considered permanently tangible by the Reichswehr leadership. Hence, in a directive issued by the Chef des Truppenamtes (Armed Forces Office) on 8th November 1932,[6] an investigation was to be made to determine whether or not it would be practical to combine all Army and Navy flying activities, including that of the RVM, into a single new Office which would be known as the Luftschutzamt (Air Raid Precautions Office) reporting directly to the RWM.

In comparative flight trials that were taking place at that time from 7th to 22nd November 1932 in Rechlin to decide upon a fighter for the planned fighter squadrons, Heinz Simon from the E-Stelle Travemünde also took part.[5]

The RLM Takes Up the Reins

The take over of power by the Nazi Party on 30th January 1933 resulted in the creation on 2nd February of the Office of Reichskommissar für Luftfahrt (Reich Commis-

sioner for Aviation) headed by Hermann Göring. With this measure, all flying activities whose pursuit had only been previously possible with difficulty, was now given strong support. The Luftschutzamt previously suggested, and including the Navy Gruppe LS, became a reality effective 1st April 1933.[7] The aim of establishing an independent Navy Air Force was finally obliterated when the Navy LS Department, in the decree signed by the Reichswehrminister Generaloberst Werner von Blomberg on 10th May 1933, was incorporated in the newly-established Reichsluftfahrtministerium (German Air Ministry).[8]

Expansion of the available facilities, including those of the E-Stelle Travemünde planned by Dipl.-Ing. Kurt Fritsche, could now be energetically pursued under the aegis of the RLM. The first aircraft rescue vessel, the 'Phönix', entered service at this time. Outwardly, nothing had changed, the RDL still managed the E-Stelle with Hermann Moll as its director.

According to records in the Bundesarchiv Kornelimünster, the first changes

took place later in the year, when Hermann Moll was promoted to Fregatten-Kapitän in September 1933, this service grade being redesignated Oberstleutnant (E) only one month later. This, however, is not apparent in a document dated 30th November 1933 containing a list of all organisations and staffing which existed at that date. Even the SES designation had not yet been altered, as visible in the illustration on page 157. Newly created was the position of an SES Commander, not held by Moll, however, but by Kapitänleutnant Eugen Bischoff.[6] At this time, the E-Stelle comprised the following:

Gruppe A   Navigation, wireless/telegraphy, naval personnel equipment and special installations (military).

Gruppe B   Operation of aircraft, ships, docks, catapults, vehicles and ground-based services.

Gruppe E   Air services, pilot readiness.

Gruppe F   Aircraft flight testing, preparation, carrying-out measuraments and evaluations, reports and judgements.

Gruppe G   Testing of airborne equipment, flight measurement instruments, laboratory, precision-mechanics workshops, photographic service and multi-copy printing.

Gruppe M   Motors, propellers, apparata, workshops and test-stands

Gruppe K   Administration of personnel, material, buildings and installations.

Top: *The E-Stelle Administration building, like most of the other buildings, was of brick construction.*

Below: *The aircraft rescue/recovery ship 'Phoenix' designed by Dipl.-Ing. Kurt Fritsche and put into service in 1933, is pictured here with the He 59c (D-ARAN, Werk-Nr.529).*

Expansion of the E-Stelle and its range of tasks not only resulted in the engagement of new specialists but also to changes in positions of leadership. In the Gruppe A for example, the Referat Funkwesen (W/T Advisory Group) was led by Dr. Gerhard Gresky who came from Jena University, whilst the Gruppe itself, headed by Kapitänleutnant Fritz Schily, was taken over by Hans Ulrich Klintzsch on 1st April 1934, joined also by Dr.-Ing. Josef Dantscher.

On 14th July 1934, the entire civilian air traffic to and from Travemünde was terminated. The Priwall now belonged solely to the E-Stelle which, based on Kurt Fritsche's plans, was able to be expanded to allow completion of installations to fulfil its tasks.

An informal group of Section Leaders. Pictured from left to right are Dobberthien und Schily (Gruppe A), Dr. Weidinger (M), Wollé (G) and Hagen (E), probably in autumn 1933.

Grouped in front of the He 60b (D-2325) and the He 59b (D-2215) are the most important men of the Naval Flying Unit of the time. Pictured from left to right are Manche Haagen, Heinz Simon, Hugo Dobberthien, Walter Hagen, Walter Schmidt-Coste, Hans Siburg, Wilhelm Huth, Alfred Ritscher, Konrad Zander, Hermann Mans, Hermann Moll, Kurt Fritsche, Hanns Weidinger, Wilhelm Bock, Fritz Schily, Erich Schumacher and Heinrich Wollé.

The large hangar was the only building retained by DLH for overhaul purposes until the end of World War Two.

Only seven months later, military conscription limitations were eliminated with the Führer Decree of 26th February 1935. The E-Stellen now abandoned their previous painstakingly-upheld guise as 'civil' installations, and showed themselves to be – as they had been for some time – military establishments directly subordinate to the RLM (LC) from whom they received their instructions. Several of the most important E-Stelle members who remained until the end of World War Two, began their service there at about his time, when planned increases in personnel were raised considerably, continuing further in 1936. Flugkapitän Carl Hense, who assumed the position of Flugleiter (Air Traffic Controller) remained as such until 1945. It has also been established that to bolster its own personnel expansion, the RLM increasingly spirited away leading specialists from the E-Stellen to its Berlin offices.

A good deal of the flight testing operations in Travemünde were no longer confined to water-based aircraft. The Report dated 20th February 1935 listing a total of 44 aircraft on hand, included only 17 seaplanes, mostly He 59s and He 60s, the remaining 27 being landplanes.[9] A report of this aircraft strength and the multifarious tasks of the E-Stelle was demonstrated and explained on the occasion of a visit on 10th and 11th April 1935 to the Air Zone (Luftkreis VI(See)) former Rear Admiral and now Supreme Commander Generalmajor der Luftwaffe Konrad Zander, his staff, and to representatives of the RLM, including especially those from the Technisches Amt (LC).[10]

These range of tasks included their involvement with the dive-bombing concept, the methods relating to it, and the development of suitable bombsights, testing of which had already been undertaken in Lipetsk. The aircraft mostly used in flight trials for this purpose was the He 50, which had been increased in number in Travemünde from two in February to six in November 1935. At exactly this date, however, the entire field of endeavour was whisked away and handed over to the E-Stelle Rechlin.[11]

The Heinkel HD 38a (D-1609, Werk-Nr.320) in its landplane form.

The same HD 38a, this time on floats. The aircraft was destroyed in November 1936.

Almost unknown is the fact that as early as 1935, direct-injection fuel tests had been carried-out in Travemünde. The system, developed by the Bosch firm, was tested in the Albatros L84 (D-INYK, Werk-Nr.278) whose BMW VI U motor was accordingly equipped. Initial difficulties which almost led to the idea being abandoned, were soon overcome through the efforts of Dr. Heinrich, head of the Bosch Development Department and thus paved the way for the subsequent widespread use of this system. Flight testing at Bosch was chiefly conducted by Siegfried Holzbauer who at Junkers, later played a prominent role in development of the Ju 88.

Weapons Testing Moves to Tarnewitz

Weapons testing, better described as Special Equipment testing, in the camouflage term of that time, led to an increasing work-load for the E-Stelle Travemünde following the closure of Lipetsk. Since the much-used neighbouring coastal region made this rather unsuitable, Dipl.-Ing. Fritsche drew up plans for a new E-Stelle specially suited for such a purpose. The location selected was a spit of land near the village of Tarnewitz, whose site erection was approved by the RLM on 2nd September 1935 and described in Chapter 7.

Fighter Decision –
Heinkel or Messerschmitt?

Surprisingly enough, passing judgement on the new types of fighter aircraft designs was one of Travemünde's tasks at that time. This sphere of activity for which Rechlin was really responsible, was closely connected with Dipl.-Ing. Carl Francke who presumably from the beginning of 1935, had taken-over as head of the Flugzeug-

gruppe (now designated T1) from his predecessor Dipl.-Ing. Werner Damasko who had been summoned to work at the RLM. Carl Francke had already made a name for himself as the author of the so-called Trave-münde Ringbuch, a standard manual for flight testing. In November 1933 a newly-created course of training as a Flug-baumeister (Master of Aircraft Engineering) had been established, and out of its first term, there emerged Dipl.-Ing. Gerhard Geike, Dr.-Ing. Kurt Jodlbauer and Dr.-Ing. Hermann Wurster who joined Carl Francke's team on 8th July 1935. Whereas only Geike remained in Travemünde, both Jodlbauer and Wurster went to Messer-schmitt in Augsburg on 1st January 1936.

Out of the four new fighter aircraft designs – the Ar 80, Fw 159, He 112 and Bf 109, as a result of earlier comparative flight testing which had apparently not taken place in Travemünde, only the latter two remained in the running. Starting on 8th February 1936 at the Priwall, trials began with the He 112 V1 (D-IADO) and a few days later, with the Bf 109 V1 (D-IABI). The Bf 109 V2 (D-IILU) followed on 21st February 1936, brought over by Dr.-Ing. Wurster to Travemünde, where he flew it on the 26th and 27th February and on 2nd March at its foremost and rearmost cg positions in dives from 7,000m (23,000ft) pulling out just above the ground as well as performing left and right stall turns.[12] The competing He 112 V2 (D-IHGE) on the other hand, was first brought over to Travemünde by Heinkel Chief Test Pilot Gerhard Nitschke on 15th April. During his demonstration flight, he was not able to recover from a spin and had to bail out.[13] The Bf 109 V2 had previously been lost on 1st April when the forward, fixed portion of the cockpit canopy flew away on take-off for a duration test flight and the pilot Trillhaase, sitting directly in the slipstream was forced to land practically without vision, where-upon the aircraft overturned.

Of the two unsuccessful designs, only the Fw 159 V2 (D-INGA) remained in Trave-münde from 13th August to 9th September 1936, the Ar 80 not being listed in any of the available flight log-books.

In the comparative flights which continued into October 1936 with the above contenders, but also in simulated dogfights against their He 51 and Ar 68 precursors, it appears that both Ernst Udet, now a Luft-waffe Oberst and 'Inspekteur der Jagd- und

Sturzkampfflieger' (Inspector of Fighters and Dive-bombing Aircraft) and the preceding holder of the title, Robert Ritter von Greim, had taken part in the tests or at least, been keen observers. Besides Carl Francke, the E-Stelle had also supplied Leo Conrad and Helmut Schuster as pilots.[14] The final decision in favour of the Bf 109 as against the He 112 was taken sometime later in Rechlin, although further evaluation and endurance trials of both aircraft continued in Travemünde. The record of aircraft on hand as of 30th September 1936 lists no less than four prototypes of the He 112 – the V1, V3, V5 and V6, but only two of the Bf 109 – the V3 and V4. The last two aircraft, piloted by Geike and Jodlbauer and led by a third piloted by Francke, flew in a close three-aircraft formation on the 3rd October 1936 Harvest Thanksgiving Feast over the spectators at Bückeberg, showing off the new fighters in public for the very first time.

Changes – Not Only in the Technical Office
After Ernst Udet had taken over the RLM Technisches Amt on 9th July 1936, reorganisations followed not only there but in the E-Stellen as well. The former spheres of activity carrying designations beginning with T – certainly for 'Technik', were now designated with the letter E for 'Erprobung' (test), although the activities themselves remained almost the same. A new addition was in the area of 'Sichtschutz' (vision protection) which was transferred from Rechlin to Travemünde effective 15th June 1936. Almost simultaneously, the E-Stelle was in receipt of a whole series of new planning positions, turning the Priwall into a seaplane airbase in order to make clear, its subordination to Luftkreiskommando VI (Air Zone Detachment VI).[15]

In terms of personnel, there were several changes. The first director and subsequent long-serving head, Oberstleutnant Moll, left the E-Stelle on 30th June 1936 to take over the newly-established Luftzeugamt (Air Ordnance Office) located on the other side of the Pötenitzer Wiek. Its commander at this time was Oberstleutnant (E) Walter Friedensburg, succeeded on 1st October 1936 by Hauptmann Martin Mettig. The E-Stellen and airbase headquarters were simultaneously amalgamated so that both functions had only one superior. In the Waffengruppe E5, Fliegerstabsing. Willy Emonds, an old seaplane pilot from World War One, on 1st July took-over the leadership from Heinz Simon who took-up a post at the Mauser company. Out of this section, a new special unit known as the 'Sondergruppe T' was formed to take over the running of the meanwhile almost-completed E-Stelle Tarnewitz, headed by Fliegerstabsing. German Cornelius who was able to relocate there in February 1937. The

In the early 1930s, almost all E-Stelle aircraft bore names, such as this He 59 C (D-AKYH, Werk-Nr.530) 'Lachmöve'. Above the name appeared the emblem, an anchor with wings at whose centre were the letters EST.

Shown during their naval training in Neustadt/ Holstein to become Flugbaumeister were from left to right Dipl.-Ing. Gerhard Geike, Dr.-Ing. Kurt Jodlbauer and Dr.-Ing. Hermann Wurster.

Shown here is the Bf 109 V2 (D-IILU, Werk-Nr.759) which crashed on 1st April 1936 during flight testing in Travemünde. The pilot Trillhaase escaped only slightly injured.

Waffengruppe remaining in Travemünde was thus noticeably reduced in size.

In addition to the fighter trials, the most extensive work of the year 1936 included:
- Type-testing and evaluation of the Do 18 – the V3 serving as the Do 18E civil variant for DLH, as well as the V2 and V4 prototypes of the military Do 18C for the 'See' long-range reconnaissance squadrons.
- Trials of the special equipment set 'Sonderausrüstung 2' or So 2 for aircraft movable defensive armament, as also the So 3 'Abwurfwaffen' (air-drop weapons) consisting of 50kg (110lb) bombs, their suspension gear and target-sighting devices.

Alongside this, type-testing was in progress with the He 51D floatplane fighter variant as well as trials with several USA-purchased Vought V-85-G biplanes that could be either fitted with a central float or wheeled undercarriage. In order to operate these aircraft and the series-built He 60 from ships, the catapult built by the Deutsche Werke Kiel at the side of the previously- mentioned Flender dry dock was used for the tests. Problems occurring in connection with the subsequent modification of new and older large naval fighting ships to take shipboard vessels were also expected to be solved.

Trials also began at the end of 1936 which extended over a number of years of aircraft and their accompanying take-off and landing aids that were expected to be based on board the planned 'Graf Zeppelin' aircraft carrier.

Carl Francke, who had meanwhile been transferred back to Rechlin, as a result of his experiences at Travemünde, once more drew attention with his compilation entitled 'Guidelines and Proposals for Seaplane Development'.

Travemünde Tests Not Only Aircraft
Even when the testing of both land- and water-based aircraft naturally plays a prominent part in the activities at Travemünde, the effects of the excellent rearguard work in other spheres at the E-Stelle must not be forgotten. Deserving of special mention (from around the beginning of 1937) is the equipment of Gruppe E3 under the leadership of Dipl.-Ing. Kurt Rehder with its Referate for Surveillance and Aerial Photography (Dipl.-Ing. Roling); Navigation and Rescue Equipment (Fliegerhaupting. Hugo Dobberthien); W/T Development and Testing (Dr. Gerhard Gresky); and Electrical Equipment and Ground Installations for Sea Operations (Dipl.-Ing. Pannier). The Gruppe E4 Airfield Equipment (Dipl.-Ing. Kurt Eich) also contributed valuable experience, which all assisted the goal of 'safer flying operations'. A series of Test Reports summarized the activities of all these spheres covering the period 10th October 1934 to 15th July 1936.[16] To attempt to go into all of the highly interesting details,

however, would far exceed the scope of this narrative.

The year 1937 brought a flood of testing demands for the E-Stelle. The German aviation industry, firmly centrally controlled by the RLM Technisches Amt (LC), precipitated several new developments resulting each time in two or three proposals submitted by various firms to fulfil the same purpose. These were now to be compared and evaluated by the E-Stelle. The results had to be accompanied by a recommendation for the decision-making bodies ie, for the Technisches Amt and for the Luftwaffe Air Staff who thereupon decided upon procurement and introduction to service use.

As indicated in available Reports, type-testing was continued with the Do 18 V4 and the He 51 V5, the latter powered by a Jumo 210 motor not fitted to series-produced aircraft already in service. The first comparison mentioned above concerned the Ar 95 and He 114 shipboard reconnaissance aircraft. The large Arado biplane, capable of being fitted with floats as well as a wheeled undercarriage was soon judged to be less suited for the task and was freed for export. A few examples were purchased by Chile. The He 114, whose first prototype was powered by a Jumo 210 but later replaced with a BMW 132K, was somewhat better, but was not rated very highly.[17] Most of the He 114A- and 0-series aircraft produced, nevertheless, went to Spain. The

The Heinkel HE 5e (D-1511, Werk-Nr.302) on take-off. It was mainly used for equipment testing.

This Dornier Wal (D-AHUU, Werk-Nr.640) built in 1934, bears the E-Stelle emblem on the nose. It was principally used by Gruppe M. All three armament stations are equipped with the British Scarff rotatable turret mounts.

This view shows the So 1 (MG 17) installation in the He 114, which bears the E-Stelle emblem above the Heinkel name.

Photograph on the opposite page:

The Waffengruppe E5 pictured in front of the He 59 (D-AQEV, Werk-Nr.1513) prior to their transfer to Tarnewitz. Fifth from left is Evers, then Pätz, Denzinger, Frost, Gessner, Simon, Loose, Blecher and Semrau.

Top: *On its ferry flight from Friedrichshafen to Travemünde in July 1937, this Do 18D made an emergency landing but was not seriously damaged.*

Centre: *The Ha 140 V1 (D-AUTO, Werk-Nr.281) on take-off in choppy conditions.*

Bottom: *An He 115B-1 taking off in similar conditions in Lübeck Bay in June 1939.*

Above: *Visiting Travemünde is the Navy C-in-C Generaladmiral Erich Raeder together with Generaloberst Milch (right). Announcing him is the Base Commander Major Minner.*

end result of this comparison was that the requirements were altered and led to the Ar 196. Alongside further involvement with the Do 18F for DLH and the Do 18D-1 to D-3 versions entering series production, next to follow as a possible successor to the aged He 59 were the Ha 140 and He 115 multi-purpose competitors. The decision in this case was no doubt influenced by the accident which occurred to the Ha 140 during seafaring trials when the starboard engine dislodged from its mountings on landing, the propeller tearing open the upper decking of the float causing its forward section to bend upwards. The Concluding Reports recommended introduction of the He 115, which in fact happened.[18]

At the beginning of 1937, the RLM LC had ordered that the entire development structure be reorganised,[19] which placed the E-Stellen Commanders directly under their LC Chief, Ernst Udet. The E-Stelle Rechlin Commander thus became only a military superior whose principal task was to maintain an appropriate balance of personnel and material between the E-Stellen.

On 31st March 1937, Fliegerstabsing. Rudolf Spies left the E-Stelle to return to the RLM LC II from where he had come in 1934. His place as Technical Head was assumed by Dipl.-Ing. Kurt Fritsche whose previous position as head of the Gruppe B Betrieb (Operations) was now filled by Fliegerstabsing. Paul Bätzner. The position of

Werftleiter, held by Ing. Bernd Langhoff who transferred to industry, was taken by Fliegerstabsing. Horst Hädrich, formerly 'Ing. z.b.V.' (engineer for special assignments) in Gruppe E1. Dipl.-Ing. Fritsche was only able to exercise the functions of his new position for just eight months, as he became transferred with the same functions to Rechlin on 15th November 1937. His successor was Fliegerstabsing. Paul Schenck who had since 1928 been with Caspar and hence with the E-Stelle.

The E-Stelle Commander also changed, Major Heinrich Minner taking over the office on 1st October 1937 from Major Martin Mettig.

First of the A-0 series flying boats, the BV 138A-01 (Werk-Nr.148, D-ADJE, later TW+BC) during trials in Travemünde from April 1939 onwards.

One of the Do 24 K-1 flying boats (probably Werk-Nr.764) destined for Holland. Together with D-AYWI, a total of 25 aircraft were delivered.

The rescue/recovery ship 'Greif' (Griffin) with retracted crane, had taken aboard the He 60D (D-IBER, Werk-Nr.495).

The New Seaplane Reconnaissance Aircraft – The Do 24 or Ha 138?

The next large task of comparison to be fulfilled came in mid 1937. As intended successor to the stop-gap Do 18 there appeared the Ha 138 and the Do 24, both patrol and reconnaissance aircraft. Use of the Jumo 205 Diesel engine with its very favourable fuel consumption was required of both manufacturers. The Ha 138, which initially had severe teething troubles was ready for trials after several important design changes had been made, but not so with the Do 24. For political reasons, the German government had agreed to give priority to a version fitted with US engines for the Netherlands – the Do 24 V3, the E-Stelle, however, being involved in its trials. In conducting the seafaring trials,[20] the E-Stelle gained knowledge which could be applied to the V1 and V2 prototypes intended for application in Germany. Comparison between the available Blohm & Voss aircraft and the not yet available Dornier aircraft had to be partially made from data gained from the Dutch variant. Despite all its known shortcomings, it was decided in favour of the Ha 138, later designated BV 138 to the detriment of the Dornier aircraft[21] from the Bodensee (Lake Constance). Used in another role a few years later, the Do 24 was indeed built in large numbers for the Luftwaffe and proved itself an excellent aircraft, but that is another story. Several years after the end of World War Two at a gathering of former Travemünde personnel, one of those who had played an important part in the evaluation of both types and the subsequently recommended BV 138 remarked 'I believe we had indeed chosen the wrong aircraft!'

Blohm & Voss nevertheless received a large production order for the BV 138, whilst it took Dornier more than one year to be able to deliver the Jumo 205-powered Do 24 V1 to the E-Stelle, the Do 24 V2 following as late as April 1940. Even so, the firm built a total of 29 aircraft as the Do 24 K-1 and one K-2 for use in the Dutch East Indies, until the Dutch firm of Aviolanda took over licence production of the Do 24 for the MLD, the Dutch Naval Air Arm.

Landing Aboard Ships

To ascertain the possibility of operating land-based aircraft on board shipping vessels, an auxiliary forward-facing short landing deck some 25m (82ft) in length was built at the stern of the aircraft recovery ship 'Greif' (Griffon) which had entered active service only a few months previously. The only suitable aircraft happened to be the Fieseler Storch, two examples of which were available in Travemünde. Following preliminary trials on land with the Fi 156A-0 (D-IJSN, Werk-Nr.608), two landings were

attempted on 1st November 1937, the first, with Leo Conrad proving successful, whilst at the second, with Albert Wahl, the aircraft went overboard and sank but the pilot was able to be rescued. It is presumed that previously unsuspected strong turbulence behind the ship's platform had led to the uncontrollable roll movement which prevented the aircraft making a deck landing. After appropriate corrective measures had been effected, the trials were resumed in August of the following year when 13 successful landings and subsequent take-offs were made from the Greif's rear deck.[14] Conrad was again the pilot, but no practical use was made of the scheme.

In the course of 1937, the aircraft listed below appeared for trials at the E-Stelle, the date column recording the earliest known that is traceable from available flight logbooks.

Date	Aircraft	Regn	Werk-Nr.	Pilot
22.02.37	Ar 95 V1 S	D-OHEO	946	Conrad
25.02.37	He 114 V2	D-UGAT	1971	Conrad
26.02.37	Do 18 V4	D-AHOM	662	Conrad
12.03.37	Ha 139 V1	D-AMIE	181	Conrad
01.04.37	Ha 138 V1	D-ARAK	114	Conrad
23.04.37	Ha 137A-0	D-IFBA	187	Mlodoch
14.05.37	Fw 56A	D-IPOP	2008	Mlodoch
24.05.37	Hs 123A-0	D-IKHA	788	Mlodoch
26.06.37	He 114 V3	D-IDEG	1972	Geike
09.07.37	Do 18D-0	D-AMIU	665	Conrad
20.07.37	Fi 156A-0	D-IJSN	608	Schuster
11.08.37	He 114 V4	D-IOGD	2255	Schuster
02.09.37	Fi 156A-0	D-IGSF	609	Geike
08.09.37	Do 17E-1	D-AMOO	833	Conrad
10.09.37	Ar 196 V1	D-IEHK	2589	Schuster
10.11.37	He 115 V1	D-AEHF	1553	Geike
11.11.37	Kl 35A W	LN-EAV	1142	Schuster
13.11.37	Ha 138 V2	D-AMOR	113	Conrad
01.12.37	Ar 196 V3	D-ILRE	2591	Conrad
08.12.37	Ha 140 V1	D-AUTO	281	Geike

Helmut Schuster flight tested the Kl 35A W fitted with floats and destined for Norway, not in Travemünde but in Konstanz for its type certification.

1938 – Organisational Changes Yet Again

In yet another RLM reorganisation on 9th May 1938, E-Stellen changes took place. Instead of the military Commanders who previously reigned supreme, the office of an 'Erprobungsleiter' (Chief of Testing) was now introduced, the position in Travemünde occupied by Fliegerstabsing. Paul Schenck.[22] Major Minner now designated as Kommandant was henceforth only responsible for military testing and operations undertaken by the Airbase and its Technical Company. Since the E-Stellen Erprobungsgruppen had now been made directly subordinate to each of the corresponding specialist branches in the RLM, they were also redesignated accordingly. E1 (Aircraft) thus became E7 (Aircraft and Installations), and E3 (Engines) now

E8, disappeared completely since Rechlin was to be solely responsible. E9 was now the Surveillance and Navigation Section, E10 the Equipment Section, with E12 handling 'Abwurfwaffen (See)' naval air-dropped weapons and E13 in charge of 'Bodengeräte' or surface-based equipment. Section E11 for 'Schusswaffen' or Rifle-barrelled armament existed but only in Rechlin and Tarnewitz, where it was further sub-divided into four subordinate sections.

In mid 1938, the E-Stelle had a personnel strength of 1,339, of whom 17 were Officers and 316 NCOs and airmen working together with 47 officials, 289 office employees and 670 manual workers.[23]

The larger proportion of testing activities involved continuation of comparative trials between the He 115 V1 (D-AEHF) and the meanwhile repaired Ha 140 V1 (D-AUTO), to which was added the Ha 140 V2 (D-ATEK) on 11th June 1938. The former type was supplemented on 1st February by the He 115 V2 (D-APDS) and on 14th August 1938 by the He 115 V3 (D-ABZV). Various forms of nose and cockpit sections for this aircraft had also been tested by Fliegerstabsing. Gerhard Geike and his crew in the He 59D (D-AXAL) in Travemünde between April and August 1937.[24]

Part of the type-testing work was conducted with the Ha 138 V2, including a long-distance evaluation flight. Between 24th and 28th July 1938, the flying-boat was flown from Travemünde, at first to Thorshavn in the Faroes (6 hours 20 mins away), accompanied by the 'Greif' vessel which provided sleeping accommodation for the pilots Conrad/Schuster, navigator Kapitän Ewald Andrae and W/T operator Hans Schröder. On the second stretch of the flight heading for and some 60 sea miles before Iceland, a landing had to be made on the open sea in order to examine the central motor's engine cowlings. The flight was able to continue 15 minutes later back to Thorshavn and on 28th July, after a flying time of 6 hours 54 mins, the aircraft landed again in Travemünde.

The Ar 196 Appears

To the requirement for a 'small, cata-pultable shipboard reconnaissance aircraft' and based on the Vought V 85 G, two contenders were to be compared. One was the already-mentioned Ar 196 and the other, the Fw 62, a conventional biplane that could be fitted with either one central float or two separate floats. A new feature was the springing in the float support intended to dampen the effects of hard landings on water. Although the aircraft fulfilled all demands, it lost out in favour of the more modern Ar 196 of simpler construction. Despite repeated references in pub-

Two experimental nose armament stations intended for the He 115, mounted for test purposes in the He 59D (D-AXAL). These were installed in this form on the He 115 V1 and V2 prototypes, but following machines had the later Ikaria cupola-type nose gun mount.

On the Ar 196 V4 (D-OVMB) fitted with a central float, the engine broke away upon landing and set the aircraft on fire.

The Fi 167 V2 (Werk-Nr.2502, TA+AA – originally D-OFWP) seen in a brake-landing test where the hook has engaged the cable and is holding the fuselage horizontal.

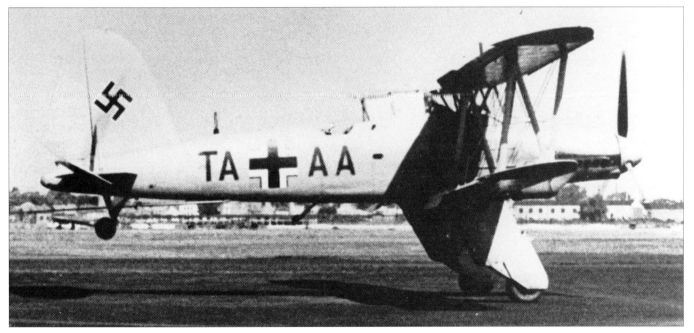

lished literature to only two Fw 62 examples built, there were in fact four, of which the first two, the Fw 62 V1 (D-OFWF) and V2 (D-OKDU) each had twin-floats, whilst the Fw 62 V3 (D-OHGF) and V4 (D-OMCR, later D-IMGD) each had one central float. The V1 prototype was evidently transferred subsequently out of category B2 to B1, since from March 1939 it was no longer coded D-OFWF but D-ICDS as recorded in a flight log-book. Two of the four prototypes, the V1 and V4, were lost during trials.

In seaworthiness trials with the Ar 196 V4 (D-OVMB) fitted with a central float, the single fuselage nose-mounted engine broke away on landing with Helmut Schuster at the controls on 8th December 1938, setting

the aircraft on fire. As he recorded in his flight log, Schuster thereupon had to 'go for a dip' and let himself be 'fished out' later. The fate of the not particularly well regarded single-float Ar 196 variant was thus sealed.

From 21st September onwards the Fw 167 V2 (D-OFWP) became available for trials, intended to operate as a multi-purpose aircraft aboard the aircraft carrier 'Graf Zeppelin' scheduled for launching on 8th December 1938. At around the same time, the E-Stelle pilots Conrad and Schuster were also involved in type-testing the Do 26 V1 flying-boat destined for DLH, particularly with regard to its high-seas behaviour and flying characteristics.

The E-Stelle organisation underwent a change on 1st November 1938, when Fliegerstabsing. Schenck, carrying out duties commensurate with that of a Head of Testing up until then, was appointed Head of the E-Stelle. Thus, for the first time, an engineer and not a ranking officer held the foremost position.

Ernst Udet's nomination as Generalluftzeugmeister (Chief of Procurement and Supply) on 1st February 1939 resulted in the RLM Technisches Amt, still continuing under his leadership, being redesignated from LC to GL/C, the organisational structure remaining as before.

In the months leading up to the outbreak of World War Two, there were no signifi-

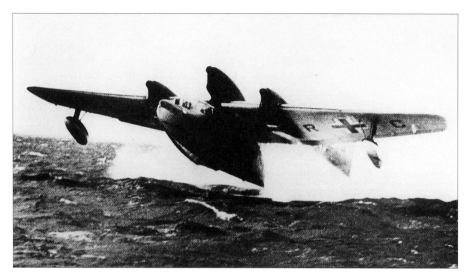

The BV 138 A-1 (NG+RC, Werk-Nr.367) in a turbulent sea test, was the first of 25 examples of the A-1 series built.

Seen here during testing is the Do 24 V1, perhaps unjustly regarded as inferior to the BV 138. With this prototype, Adolf Mlodoch, together with the Do 26 of 9./KGr.z.b.V. 108, was able to fly twice to Narvik during a critical period, the second time using the Do 24 V2.

other aircraft such as the Avia B 534, Bf 109T, Ju 87C and the Ar 196, the latter conceived as a training aircraft for this new technique. Thanks to its high-lift aids, only the Fi 167 was able to leave the deck without any take-off assistance. These flight trials were mainly conducted by Rudolf Hertle, Karl-Friedrich Königs, Adolf Mlodoch, Rauchenberger and Fritz Reccius, but others also participated.

From July 1939 onwards, trials began with the new Ar 199 V2 (D-ISBC) seaplane trainer intended to replace the aged He 42, being joined by the Ar 199 V3 (D-ITLF) in September and the Ar 199 V4 (BH+AN) in November 1939.

Especially equipped for seaborne rescue missions was the He 59N (D-AROO), which following modifications by the Bachmann firm in Ribnitz, was tested in Travemünde between April and August 1939. A BV 138N variant had also been planned, for which the corresponding requirements had been issued by the Technisches Amt on 21st June 1939.[25] It appears that the Do 24 was not considered for such a purpose.

Introduction of 'Stammkennzeichen'

Shortly before the beginning of World War Two, the Luftwaffe Generalstab introduced a new aircraft identification or call-sign system. According to the accompanying definitions, all aircraft operated by E-Stellen regardless of function, were classified as military machines and had to display the new military identifiers. Previous civilian markings which began with the letter D- or since spring 1939 with the letters WL- had to be replaced with those newly defined. These consisted of four alphabet letters two of which had to appear before the Luftwaffe 'Balkenkreuz' (cross emblem) and two behind it on the fuselage sides whilst one each of the same letters appeared on either side of the portside underwing 'Balkenkreuz', the remaining two separated by the underwing 'Balkenkreuz' on the starboard side. Like the other E-Stellen, flying schools, etc a specific group of letters which had to be applied to all its aircraft on hand was assigned to Travemünde from the responsible office of issue – the GL Prüfstelle für Luftfahrzeuge in Berlin-Adlershof (Aircraft

cantly new trials undertaken at Travemünde. The Ar 196 and BV 138 still had to contend further with enormous difficulties, whilst 0-series pre-production models of the Fi 167 and He 115 appeared, which had to be flight tested and verified to be in agreement with the corresponding prototypes. The Do 24 V1 (D-AIBE) made its debut in March 1939 and underwent trials, if only half-heartedly. Following the previously made decision in favour of the BV 138, comparative trials of this aircraft with the Do 24 only now becoming available, was rendered superfluous. For this reason the Do 24 V2 was not brought over to Travemünde but remained with its manufacturer at Manzell on Lake Constance.

Under construction and completely new was the twin-float He 119 V3 (D-ADPQ) whose fuselage-mounted DB 606 engine consisted of two DB 601s mounted side-by-side. Power was transmitted via a collector assembly gearbox and an extension shaft to large four-bladed propellers in the fuselage nose. It was flown by Schuster several times between March and June, and on one occasion in November 1939.[14] The design, however, was still too futuristic for its day and had to contend with various technical difficulties, so that it was not pursued further. Its flight characteristics also appeared to have been critical.

Aircraft for the Aircraft Carrier

The He 50 and both the Fi 167 V2 and V3 flown from January until June 1939 had absolved a comprehensive programme of trials involving installations for arrested landings on the decks of aircraft carriers. One such deck surface, appropriately sized, had been built for this purpose on the Priwall, the braking mechanism stemming from the Atlas-Werke in Bremen. The catapult take-off system for land-based aircraft had also to be tested. This initially took place with the Ar 197, continuing later with

Certification Centre). The system comprised a total of 104 'Kennzeichen' (aircraft identification markings) which, with the exception of a few, had to be applied to the aircraft stationed there. At that time, the E-Stelle had around 95 aircraft.

The Stammkennzeichen (parent markings) assigned all had two fixed letters out of the four, the first being a T and the third an H. In the second position, the letters H, I, J, and K could be used whilst in the fourth and last position, all 26 alphabet letters could be used. Under this system for example:

An E-Stelle Ju 52 (Werk-Nr.4033, formerly D-AHIP) on floats, showing its new call-sign TK+HB.

The He 115 V3 during winter trials in 1939/40.

- He 59D formerly D-ADYU, became TH+HM.
- Ju W 34hi formerly D-OGFT, became TI+HM.
- Do 17M formerly D-AQJO, became TJ+HM.
- Bf 109B-1 formerly D-IKAC, became TK+HM.

Clearly recognizable is the exactitude exercised by the compilers in the Flugleitung (Air Traffic Control), at least at the very beginning, to ensure that the markings were correctly recorded in flight records. All aircraft which subsequently arrived featured their own individual markings which had been assigned to the manufacturer from the same Prüfstelle.

Floatplanes Land on Ice

The severe winter of 1939/40 made the problem of floatplanes landing on ice one requiring urgent attention. Almost one year before, from 7th to 20th March 1939, with

Schuster at the controls, the He 115 V2 had made a whole series of landings on ice in the presence of high Swedish military officials at Östersund in central Sweden.[14] Trials were now successfully continued in January and February 1940 in and ahead of Travemünde with the He 115 V2 and CA+BP, and the Ar 199 V1 and V3 piloted by Ing. Hans Schippers, where the floats had been specially fitted with ice-skids.

It was also a time of changes in the personnel sphere. In February 1940, Dipl.-Ing. Horst Hädrich as head of the Betriebsabteilung (Operations Department) replaced the former holder Fliegerstabsing. Paul Bätzner who had been transferred to Rechlin. Replacing Hädrich as Werftleiter on 1st March was Flugbaumeister Dipl.-Ing. Fritz Reccius. Likewise in February, the E-Stelle was assigned a new task area, now

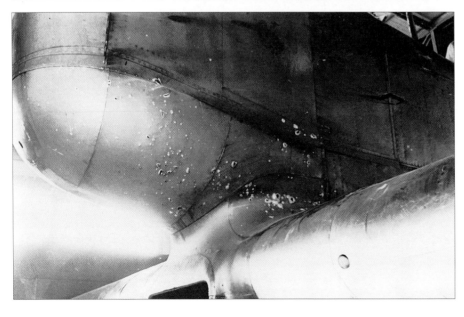

made responsible for evaluating the usefulness of Polish and Czech aircraft for the Luftwaffe. In the period which followed, entries have been found in Travemünde flight log-books of a number of Czech aircraft, whereas no entry of a single Polish aircraft has been found. Of Czech origin, besides an Avia 122 (SE+BZ), at least 5 Avia B 534s (D-IPLD, IUIG, IWNF and IQSV, later TK+HU and SE+DZ) and a Praga E 114 Baby (SD+TB). The last named, a two-seater shoulder-wing sports aircraft with side-by-side seating, was very much liked and used as a communications aircraft. A twin-engined Aero A 304 (VB+HT) was later added. A Letov S.328 (SG+SV) was also test flown by Schippers in Olmütz.

E-Stelle Components on Wartime Missions

The preparations for Operation 'Weserübung' – the occupation of Norway, affected the E-Stelle in particular. All available transport aircraft, above all water-based aircraft, were requisitioned. It made no difference that some, like the BV 138 and Do 24, were still undergoing flight testing. The crews that flew them, almost all civilians, were hastily clad in uniform and made members of the Luftwaffe. They were subjected to a rapid course of shooting practice after which their transformation into military crews was complete. Together with the Do 26 and Ha 139 belonging to the 'Sonderstaffel Transozean' (Transocean Special Squadron), the former DLH Atlantic aircraft, they formed the 9./KGr.z.b.V.108 special purpose combat unit.

On 12th April 1940, one day before the last combat operations of ten German destroyers in Narvik against a far inferior enemy, three BV 138s, each piloted by Conrad, Dobberthien and Schuster as well as the Do 24 V1 flown by Mlodoch, were to bring in supplies to Narvik. Only the Do 24 was able to take off on 12th April, the 3 BV 138s following the next day. The Do 24 was the only one to reach its destination the other three flying-boats having to abor the mission due to fog and return to Sta

The BV 138 A-03 (BH+AT, Werk-Nr.150), shot at 'successfully' by German defensive A/A fire, prevented by its pilot Dobberthien from sinking upon landing by beaching the aircraft. During the recovery operation, the aircraft suffered further damage.

The effects of a 20mm A/A projectile. Seen here is the entry hole on the BV 138A-03 central engine nacelle.

The other side of the engine nacelle showing the projectile exit hole. Several more hits were registered.

The Flettner Fl265 helicopter was demonstrated in summer 1940 to Generalluftzeugmeister, Generaloberst Ernst Udet at Leuchtenfelde near Travemünde.

vanger. Upon their arrival there, German flak positions opened fire on the unfamiliar machines and rather severely damaged the BV 138A-03 piloted by Dobberthien. It was only the nearness of the life-saving embankment that prevented the aircraft from sinking after landing. It had to be subsequently retrieved by the Greif rescue vessel and returned to Blohm & Voss for repairs. The other two flying-boats, after discharging their loads, flew back to Travemünde on the same day. Adolf Mlodoch with his crew, flight mechanic Hans Demuth and W/T operator Steiner as well as two armament operators, flew twice more with the Do 24V1 and lastly one final mission with the Do 24V2 (DP+BH) to Narvik.[26] One other BV 138A-1 (NG+UC, Werk-Nr.369) met an early end on 16th May 1940 in Finneidfjord. It was hit by ground fire and sank immediately after landing. Of the crew, flight mechanic Bruno Dreyer was killed, whilst the pilot, now promoted to NCO Schuster and two crew members were taken into captivity in Norway, his period of captivity ending in Canada.[27] When the Norwegian campaign was over, the Do 24V2 was returned to Dornier in Friedrichshafen.

E-Stelle activity had meanwhile continued unaffected. Since the November/December 1939 period, three Ar 197A-0 aircraft as well as the three Ar 199s were available for testing, joined in January 1940 by the V1 (NH+AM).

Testing Demands Sacrifices
The E-Stelle suffered a heavy loss on 23rd April 1940 when the He 115C (DC+GG, Werk-Nr.2756) crashed, killing Flugbaumeister Hans Petersen and his two crew members.

When Generaloberst Ernst Udet visited the E-Stelle on 27th August 1940, he was given an extensive appraisal of the ongoing work. Special emphasis was laid upon the demonstration of carrier-based aircraft, the Fi 167, Ar 197, Ju 87C and Bf 109T which made arrested landings.[28]

A short while later, on 11th September 1940, the E-Stelle bemoaned another heavy loss when the BV 142 V3 (PC+BD, Werk-Nr.437) piloted by Wilhelm Schwarzlose crashed near Rettin, taking the lives of all on board.[29]

Soon after the beginning of the following year, on 21st February 1941, the flags again flew at half-mast after the Do 24N-1 (KD+GF, Werk-Nr.006) crashed on a test flight at the Aviolanda firm in Dordrecht,

Holland. W/T operator Hans Schröder was the sole survivor.

Fate again intervened on 9th June 1941, when the Werftleiter, Fliegerstabsing. and Flugbaumeister Fritz Reccius, on a works flight with the BV 138B-1 (Werk-Nr.2013) crashed with fatal results on the Mecklenburg coast. Several highly experienced installation colleagues perished with him. On 1st July 1941, his position was filled by Fliegerstabsing. Herbert Kabisch who came from Rechlin and was able to exercise its duties until February 1945.

In June 1941 a series of unusual trials took place with the Ju 52 (TK+HB, Werk-Nr.4033) flown by Uwe Petersen. The goal was to test newly designed floats from the Heinkel Werke fitted to the Ju 52, which similar to those on the He 115, would enable landings to be made on snow or ice. In an attempt to find suitable conditions, the aircraft was taken to the extreme north

of Norway, but even there the snow and ice were insufficient to permit extensive tests to be carried out.[30]

Not quite in keeping with the period were the trials undertaken between May and December 1941 with the Wn 11 sports amphibian of which only one prototype was built by the Wiener-Neustädter Flugzeugbau.

The Do 24 Appears Again –
As a Sea Rescue Aircraft
In that same year, trials with the BV 138 continued to increase. The C-version had now entered the picture, its performance raised with the Jumo 205D. Only the planned N-version intended for sea rescue duties was rejected outright due to its unsuitability for this role. A marvellous opportunity for this duty, however, was presented in the shape of the Do 24. When Holland was overrun, the Aviolanda firm in Papendrecht was discovered complete with all its installations

Operational trials of the Ar 196 (BB+YF) in Kiel in August 1941, with catapult take-offs from the cruiser 'Leipzig' at the hands of pilot Hans Schippers.

The Do 24 (CM+IA, Werk-Nr.0035), one of the initial batch of the T-2 variant on a practice gunnery flight with a Hispano-Suiza 20mm MK 404 in the dorsal fuselage B-Stand. Practically all Do 24T-2s were equipped with this weapon.

as well as a number of flying-boats in various stages of construction. What could be more welcome than to commence manufacture of the rejected Do 24 and operate it as a sea rescue aircraft? Already at the end of 1940 the first Do 24N-1 (Werk-Nr.001, initially D-AEAV and later KD+GA), still with its US Wright engines, came to the E-Stelle and was followed by others. When the supply of American engines ran out, the German Bramo 323R-2 radials were installed. The Do 24 (KD+GJ, Werk-Nr.003) served as the

prototype for the T-1 variant, followed later by the T-2 and T-3, and created for the E-Stelle a new, rich field of activity led by Fliegerstabsing. and Flugbaumeister Gerhard Geike.

Sighting Aids for Nightfighting

The growing significance of nightfighting brought the desire for aids to vision in conditions of darkness. This task was assigned to Travemünde where the Gruppe E4/5, in close co-operation with the AEG and

Siemens firms and the Reichspost developed and tested night-vision aids. They worked at that time with invisible ultra-red light which was beamed from a searchlight in the fuselage nose either directly forwards or upwards. Reflected back by the target, they were made visible by a converter. Under the code-names 'Spanner I to III', various devices were tested, mostly in the Do 17. With the appearance of the Telefunken-developed FuG 202 'Lichtenstein' radar, however, they lost much of their significance. Despite this, following transfer of the testing Gruppe at first to Werneuchen and finally to Stade, work was still continued on it until the end of the war.

At the turn of the year 1941/42, one of the most experienced of the E-Stelle pilots, Leo Conrad, left the station to enter combat service. Shortly before, as type specialist, he had completed and handed over the final report on frontline testing of the BV 138B and C-versions. On 17th January 1942, the BV 138B-1 (NA+LW, Werk-Nr.2001) somersaulted on take-off in adverse conditions. Fortunately, the crew and its pilot Rosarius survived suffering only shock, but the flight mechanic Hans Beitel unfortunately lost one of his hands.

A New Testing Task – The Autogyro
In the middle of the year, the E-Stelle was confronted with a new technology with which they had already had contact in the early 1930s. At that time, it was a Juan de la Cierva helicopter built under license as the Focke-Wulf Fw C 30, and in the shape of the small motorless Focke-Achgelis Fa 330 Bachstelze autogyro, was destined for operation from submarines. Both Flugbaumeister Fischer and Geike as well as Otto Dumke were able to gather initial experience in tethered flights with it in the large Chalais-Meudon wind-tunnel near Paris. Trials were later continued aboard ships and finally, on submarines for which the seemingly fragile craft was intended. The Bachstelze (water-wagtail) was followed a few months later by two powered

General Hermann Moll conversing with Focke-Achgelis Chief Test Pilot Carl Bode during the Fa 330 gyrocopter's visit aboard a submarine, the U-boot's Commander, Kapitänleutnant Linke, listening attentively.

Deck landing trial on the 'Greif' in September and October 1943. Dipl.-Ing. Carl Bode is seated in the Fl 282 V12 (CJ+SF) helicopter.

The Fl 282 V17 (CJ+SK) helicopter after a crash landing on 13th April 1944.

helicopters, the small Flettner Fl 282 and the large Fa 223 on which the above-mentioned pilots as well as Flugbaumeister Helmut Lechner of the DVL received instruction from the Flettner works pilots Hans Fuisting and Ludwig Hofmann, and the Focke-Achgelis works pilot Dipl.-Ing. Carl Bode.

The E-Stelle position of Commander, previously dissolved by Ernst Udet, was reinstated on 1st October 1942. Major Richard Linke now took charge of the E-Stelle as well as the Airbase. The former head, Paul Schenck, was transferred to the HQ staff of Luftflottenkommando 4 (Air Fleet Detachment 4).

The BV 222 – The Last Flying-Boat
The last new aircraft to arrive at the E-Stelle was the BV 222 flying-boat. Initial acquaintance with it had been made in December 1941 by Fliegerstabsing. Geike, when he flew in it as an active observer and second pilot in a flight with the BV 222 V2 to Athens and back. This aircraft now came to Travemünde where henceforth Flugbaumeister Ewald Kursch and the pilots Mlodoch and Wismar were principally occupied with it. In particular, it was the BV 222 V7 prototype, the first to be fitted with Jumo 207C diesel engines that was extensively tested, and with interruptions, remained in Travemünde until the end of the war.

At the beginning of March 1943 the Fl 282 V12 (CJ+SF) was the first to be taken over by the E-Stelle and to undergo flight testing. Since the Kriegsmarine (Navy) showed a special interest in the helicopter for shipboard use, deck-landing trials became a focal point of the trials. In a landing attempt on a raised platform on the afterdeck of the 'Greif' vessel on 13th April 1944, however,

the Fl 282 V17 (CJ+SK) was badly damaged. Three months later, in June 1943, Travemünde received its first Fa 223.

Returning to the subject of flying-boats, on the Etang de Berre near Marseilles, lay a number of various large French flying-boats, some of them six-engined, whose take over was planned by the Luftwaffe. Groups of E-Stelle staff, mostly headed by Fliegeroberstabsing. Eduard Elbelt, paid a number of visits there for this purpose. Part of the task was undertaking test flights with the aircraft, performed mainly by Flugbaumeister Gerhard Full of the DVL, and Paul Niessen.

Operational Flights Once More
At the same time as the above events, the E-Stelle once more received an operational order. This time, they were to use the Do 26 V6. It was to make an initial supply flight to a Navy weather service stationed in Greenland, and in a second flight ten days later, return with all its personnel. Both missions were successfully accomplished under difficult conditions by Hauptmann Walter Blume (who had joined the E-Stelle) and his crew. In November 1943 it was the turn of the BV 222C-09 (TB+QN) to accomplish a similar mission to provide supplies to another weather station also located in Greenland. Because of prevailing adverse weather conditions, however, the station could not be found and having arrived at its destination, the crew had to return without accomplishing its mission.

On 1st December 1943, Fliegeroberstabsing. Elbelt was assigned the technical leadership of the entire E-Stelle testing activities. In 1944, its activities suffered under the growing pressure of reduced supplies of fuel. Even though flying contin-

ued with the Ar 196, BV 138 and Do 24, and series production BV 222s were being prepared for operational use, more and more landplanes, mostly Do 217s as also the Ju 88, were being tested for night-fighting duties.

Parallel to an Ar 232 which had been fitted at Arado's with a 'cold' Walter boundary-layer suction system in the wings, a Do 24 was also planned to have an identical system. Dornier reported the flying-boat as being flight-ready in Friedrichshafen at the end of July 1944, but only one day later received the order to cease all such development with this aircraft. Three months later, all testing work on seaplanes was declared terminated and the corresponding Gruppe E2/3 was dissolved. Simultaneously, autogyro testing was transferred to Rechlin. The flight log-book of Fliegerstabsing. Geike shows the 25th October 1944 as his last helicopter flight at the Priwall. It is regrettable that from around November 1944 almost no entries were made in flight log-books anymore, so that concerning the few later flights, almost nothing is available for comment.

One of the praiseworthy exceptions is that of W/T operator Hans Schröder who kept records in his log-book[31] until the very end, on 25th April 1945. From this it can be noted that besides the installation of the FuG 200 in a few Do 18s for submarine detection in the Baltic, testing work was still continued up to the very end with the FuG 241 and FuG 243 'Biene' (Bee) radars in the BV 138C-1 (Werk-Nr.055). Participating in these trials were the pilots Georg Leschke, Heinrich Petry and Henry Wismar. In addition, Ing. Königs[32] flew almost to the very end in trials on development of the 'Kurt' spherical rolling-bomb, flying the Fw 190 (BQ+QV) as bomb-carrier.

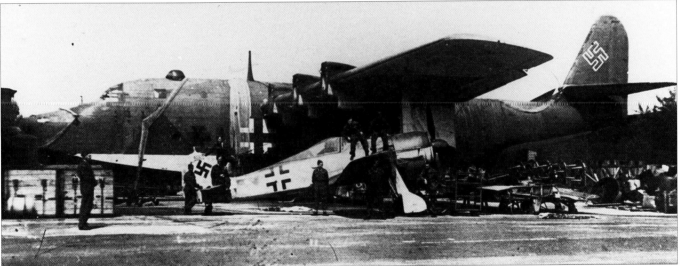

Top: *Damage during the last days of the war was only slight, presenting an otherwise deserted appearance. The Allies were mostly disappointed that almost no documents could be found.*

Above: *The picture of the E-Stelle as seen by the British – almost forlorn and with only a few aircraft rendered unusable, such as this engineless BV 222C-09, some parked or still afloat. Some new Fw 190 aircraft assembled there completed the picture.*

Opposite: *One of the last E-Stelle activities was to equip the Do 18G – long since relegated to training schools – with an FuG 200 in the search for Russian submarines in the Baltic. These aircraft were again put into operational use since no more fuel was available for the Do 24 which it replaced, whereas Diesel fuel supplies were.*

The End Draws Near

Despite the reduced amount of E-Stelle activity taking place, its Commander was once more changed on 1st December 1944, when Obersleutnant Richard Linke was succeeded by Oberstleutnant Wolfgang Lenschow. A proportion of the engineers were transferred to the E-Stelle Tarnewitz, others to the TVA (Torpedo Test Institute) Eckernförde, whilst the majority of those remaining were summoned for active duty with the Wehrmacht.

The 'Greif' vessel, under the command of the Navy sea transport chief for the Baltic eastern region, right up to the last days of the war, served for the rescue of thousands of refugees from the Kurland and East Prussia. After the end of World War Two, the ship, well over 30 years later, was still in the service of the French Navy as 'Marcel di Bihan'.

On 5th May 1945, the last Commander handed over the practically undamaged E-Stelle to the British, after the aircraft on hand had been rendered unusable with the exception of the Fl 282B V20 (CJ+SN) helicopter, certainly of interest to its captors. Documents which had not previously been moved to Eckernförde or elsewhere had been destroyed. The E-Stelle now became a central prison camp for some 3,700 servicemen as well as about 1,000 refugees. Wolfgang Lenschow himself was retained by the British as Commander to organise the care and control of all those at the Priwall. After 17 years of tradition and successful activity, the E-Stelle Travemünde had now ceased to exist.

Today, only a few remnants of buildings and a monument in front of the former sentry post serve as remainders of its former glory. An ever-decreasing number of former E-Stelle members gather there annually, to pay tribute to their injured, fallen and deceased colleagues.

Footnotes

1 Conference Minutes of 27.1.1930 In 1 No 19/30 III gKdos.

2 Letter Reichsminister of Transport to Reichsminister of Finance, Document L.7. 6979/31 of 20.8.1931.

3 Letter Reichsminister of Transport to Reichsminister of Finance, Document L.7. 6362/32 of 6.7.1932.

4 Letter Reichsminister of Aviation to Reichsminister of Finance, Document 10998/33 of 6.10.1933.

5 Flight log-book Heinz Simon.

6 K H Völker: Die deutsche Luftwaffe 1933-1939, p233 and Dokumente und Dokumentarfotos zur Geschichte der deutschen Luftwaffe (Documents and documentary photos on the history of the German Air Force), DVA, p115.

7 Reichswehrminister decree of 21.3.1933, Document 401/33 gKdos. In 1 (L)V, in K H Völker, p118.

8 Reichsminister of Defence decree of 10.5.1933, Document LA 617/33 gKdos. L 1(H)IIA, in K H Völker, p131.

9 E-Stelle Travemünde: Record of the number of take-offs and flying hours from 21.1. to 20.2.1935.

10 Letter RLM LC II to Luftkreis VI of 5.4.1935,

LC 6084/35 gKdos, and Minutes of discussions on the occasion of the visit of 16.4.1935 gKdos.

11 E-Stelle Rechlin File Remark of 23.10.1935

12 Flight log-book Dr. Hermann Wurster.

13 Report by Gerhard Nitschke of 20.4.1936.

14 Flight log-books of Just Schuster and Flugkapitän Leo Conrad.

15 Letter RdL and ObdL to Luftkreis VI of 22.6.1935, LA 2350/36 gKdos. LA II 2B.

16 Index of Reports of the E-Stelle Travemünde of 28.8.1936, LC II 1214/36 gKdos.

17 Bundesarchiv Freiburg, File RLM 1325.

18 Bundesarchiv Freiburg, File RLM 1322.

19 New organisation in the sphere of Development, LC/LA 4140/36 of 21.12.1936,

20 E-Stelle Travemünde File Remark of 15.10.1937, Library Ref 18876 E 1.

21 Report on BV 138 V1 high-seas trials of 23.7.1937, Library Ref 12947.

22 New Structure of the Technisches Amt of 28.5.1938, LCAdj. 2250/38 geh.

23 Luftwaffe E-Stellen organisational disposition of 31.8.1938, RLM Chef des Stabes (Adj. 2), 3333/38 geh.

24 Flight log-book Flugbaumeister Gerhard Geike.

25 Sea-rescue aircraft BV 138N, Technische Richtlinien (Technical Guidelines), Bundesarchiv Freiburg, File RLM 1325/11.

26 Report and flight log-books Flugkapitän Adolf Mlodoch.

27 Report of Losses dated 16.5.1940.

28 Internal Programme for the Demonstration to the GL Generaloberst Ernst Udet, dated 23.8.1940.

29 Accident Report, General Flight Safety, of 12.9.1940.

30 Bundesarchiv Freiburg, File RLM 1325/8.

31 Flight log-book, W/T op Hans Schröder.

32 Flight log-books Karl-Friedrich Königs.

Note: Flight log-books of several other E-Stelle Travemünde pilots were also made available.

Literature List

Wollé, Heinrich/Caspari, Dr. H A/Passoth, Oskar: Die E-Stellen Travemünde und Tarnewitz – Die Geschichte der Seeflugzeugerprobungsstelle Travemünde und der daraus hervorgegangen E-Stelle für Flugzeugbewaffnung in Tarnewitz (History of the Seaplane test centre Travemünde and the resulting E-Stelle for aircraft armament in Tarnewitz), 3 Volumes, Luftfahrtverlag Axel Zuerl, Steinbach am Wörthsee.

Flugzeug (Bi-monthly periodical), Flugzeug Publikations GmbH, Illertissen (up to Issue No 3/1990).

E-Stelle Travemünde Site Plan, 8th March 1929

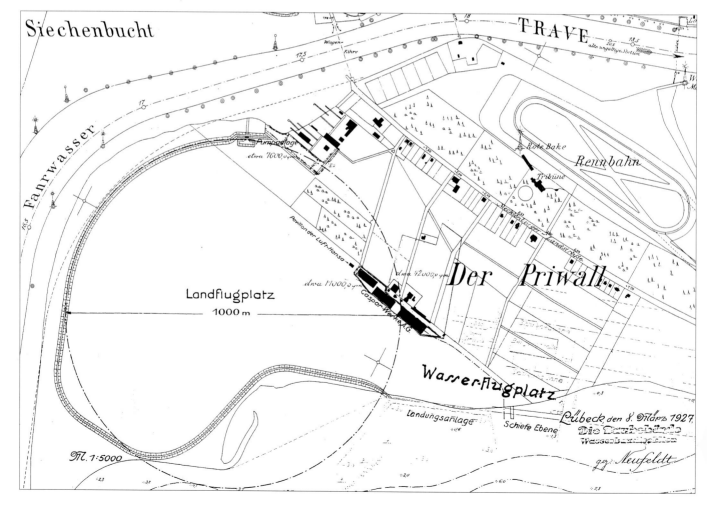

RDL E-Stelle Travemünde Personnel List, 30th November 1933

Betr. Verteilung und Unterzeichnung der Post.

Ab 1. Dezember tritt nachfolgende Änderung bezüglich der Verteilung der Post und Unterzeichnung der Post in Kraft:

a) Posteingang:

Es gehen nachfolgende Schreiben direkt von Ds an K, der das Weitere entsprechend Postverteilungsvorschrift veranlasst:

1.) Rechnungen unter RM. 250.--
2.) Normale Auftragsbestätigungen.
3.) Zahlungsbestätigungen unter RM. 250.-- .
4.) Empfangsbestätigungen.
5.) Versandanzeigen mit Ausnahme von "Bau".
6.) Bewerbungen von Lohnempfängern.

b) Postausgang:

Es gehen nachfolgende Schreiben direkt von K mit Unterschrift i.A. (im Auftrage) zum

Postausgang:

1.) Rechnungen unter RM. 150.--.
2.) Bestellungen unter ca. RM. 150.-- .
3.) Lieferscheine.
4.) Überweisungsmitteilungen.

Sind bei den unter a) und b) aufgeführten Schreiben besondere Punkte zu beachten oder zu klären, so hat K rechtzeitig D zu informieren, gegebenenfalls dessen Entscheidung einzuholen.

Im Posteingangs- und Postausgangsbericht sind wie bisher sämtliche Schreiben aufzunehmen.

Reichsverband
der Deutschen Luftfahrt-Industrie
Gruppe Flugzeugbau
Travemünder Erprobungsstelle

30.11.33.

Umlaufschreiben Nr.61.

Zur Kenntnis bei :

Chiffre	Name
D =	Herr Direktor Moll
Ds =	Frl. Brüggen
A =	Herr Schily
A1 =	" Kaerger
A2 =	" Bock
A3 =	" Schumacher II
A4 =	" Dobberthien
A5 =	" Hoyer
A6 =	" Geßner
B =	" Fritsche
B1 =	" Hartmann
B2 =	" Hein
B3 =	" Krüger II
B4 =	" Langhoff
B5 =	" Kröger
Bau =	" Schneidt
Bau1 =	" Fechter
Bau2 =	" Tinneberg
Bau3 =	" Zülehner
Bau4 =	" Wundenberg
Bau5 =	Frl. Geißelbrecht
E =	Herr Hagen
E1 =	" Simon
E2 =	" Schmidt-Coste...
F =	" Huth
F1 =	" Damasko
F2 =	" Schenck
F3 =	" Hermann
F4 =	" Fischer
F5 =	" Emonds
Fr. =	" Bischoff
Fr1 =	" Hefele
Fr1 =	" Wollé
G =	" Passoth
G1 =	" Bresler
G2 =	" Rengies
G3 =	" Mettel

Zur Kenntnis bei:

Chiffre	Name
G5 =	Herr Pannier
K =	" Schumacher
K1 =	" Krüger I
K2 =	" Burmeister
K3 =	" Grabe
Kr =	Frl. Vollert
Kr1 =	" Bock
Kr2 =	Frau Hinrichsen
Kl =	Herr Schmlt
M =	" Dr.Weidinger
M1 =	" Dr. Auer
M2 =	" Stahl
M3 =	" Pauls
TR =	" Paeprer

Personnel at E-Stelle Travemünde

Last Name	First Name	Title	Military Grade	Last Name	First Name	Title	Military Grade
Andrae	Ewald	Kapitän		Leschke	Georg	Flugzeugführer	
Auer	Ludwig	Dr.-Ing., Triebwerksgruppe		Linke	Richard	Kommandeur	Major
Bätzner	Paul	Dipl.-Ing., Gruppenleiter B	Flieger-Stabsingenieur	Lohmann	Walter	Leiter Seetransportabt. BS	Kapitän zur See
Beitel	Hans	Flugmaschinist (BM)		Mans	Hermann	Flughafendirektor	Kapitänleutnant a.D.
Bischoff	Eugen	Kommandeur SES	Kapitänleutnant	Mettig	Martin	Kommandeur	Hauptmann, Major
		Travemünde 1933		Mewes	Reinhold	Ing., Konstrukteur b. Heinkel	
Blomberg, von	Werner	Reichswehrminister	Generaloberst	Minner	Heinrich	Kommandeur	Major
Blume	Walter	Flugzeugführer	Hauptmann	Mlodoch	Adolf	Flugkapitän	
Bode	Carl	Dipl.-Ing., Flugzeugführer		Moll	Hermann	Direktor, Kommandeur	Kapitänleutnant,
Caspar	Karl	Dr. jur.					Oberstleutnant (E)
Conrad	Leo	Flugzeugführer		Neufeldt	Fritz	Oberbaurat	
Cornelius	German	Dipl.-Ing.,		Niessen	Paul	Dipl.-Ing., Flugzeugführer	
Damasko	Werner	Dipl.-Ing., Gruppenleiter		Nitschke	Gerhard	Flugzeugführer (Heinkel)	
Dantscher	Josef	Dr.-Ing., Ref. Funkwesen		Pannier		Dipl.-Ing., Referent in E3	
Demuth	Hans	Flugmaschinist (BM)		Petersen	Hans	Dipl.-Ing., Flugbaumeister	
Dobberthien	Hugo	Flugzeugführer, Kapitän		Petersen	Jens-Uwe	Flugzeugführer	
Dreblow	Ernst	Ingenieur bei Askania		Petry	Heinrich	Flugzeugführer	
Dreyer	Bruno	Flugmaschinist (BM)		Plüschow	Gunther	Pilot und Forscher	Kapitänleutnant a.D.
Dumke	Otto	Dipl.-Ing., Flugbaumeister	Flieger-Stabsingenieur	Raeder	Erich	Chef der Marineleitung	Admiral, Generaladmiral
Eich	Kurt	Dipl.-Ing., Gruppenleiter E4		Rauchenberger		Flugzeugführer	
Elbelt	Eduard	Dipl.-Ing., Techn.Leiter	Flieger-Oberstabsingenieur	Reccius	Fritz	Dipl.-Ing., Flugbaumeister	
Emonds	Willy	Gruppenleiter E5	Flieger-Stabsingenieur	Rehder	Kurt	Dipl.-Ing., Gruppenleiter E3	
Faber	Walther	Referatsleiter A II 1	Kapitänleutnant	Rengies	Arthur	Versuchsingenieur	
Fath	Egon	Chefpilot Dornier		Ritscher	Alfred	E-Stelle	
Fischer	Hans	Dipl.-Ing., Flugbaumeister		Ritter	Hans	Referatsleiter A II 1	Kapitänleutnant
Francke	Carl	Dipl.-Ing., Gruppenleiter		Ritter von Greim	Robert	Inspekteur Flugsicherheit	Oberstleutnant
Friedensburg	Walter	Kommandeur	Oberstleutnant (E)	Roling		Dipl.-Ing., Referent in E3	
Fritsche	Kurt	Dipl.-Ing.,Techn.Leiter		Rosarius	Josef	Flugzeugführer	
Fuisting	Hans	Flugzeugführer Fa.Flettner		Roth	Ernst-August	Leiter der Fluggruppe	Kapitänleutnant
Full	Gerhard	Dipl.-Ing., Flugbaumeister		Rudmai		Ingenieur bei Caspar,	
Geike	Gerhard	Dipl.-Ing., Flugbaumeister	Flieger-Stabsingenieur			dann E-Stelle	
Göring	Hermann	Reichskommissar,	Gen, Gen feldmarschall,	Schenck	Paul	Dipl.-Ing., Techn.Leiter	Flieger-Stabsingenieur
		Reichsminister d.L.	Reichsmarschall	Schily	Fritz	Leiter Gruppe A (Navigation)	Kapitänleutnant
Gresky	Gerhard	Dr.rer.nat., Ref. Funkwesen		Schippers	Hans	Ing., Flugzeugführer	
Gundermann	Erich	Flugzeugführer		Schmidt-Coste	Walter	Flugzeugführer	
Haagen	'Mannche'	Flugzeugführer		Schröder	Hans	Bordfunker (BF)	
Hädrich	Horst	Dipl.-Ing., Werftleiter		Schumacher	Erich	Flugzeugführer	
Hagen	Walter	Flugzeugführer		Schuster	Helmut	Flugzeugführer	
Heinrich		Dr.-Ing., Fa. Bosch		Schwarzlose	Wilhelm	Ing., Flugzeugführer	
Hense	Carl	Flugkapitän, Flugleiter		Seeckt, von	Hans	Chef der Heeresleitung	Generaloberst
Hertle	Rudolf	Dipl.-Ing., Flugzeugführer	Flieger-Stabsingenieur	Siburg	Hans	Referatsleiter Technik	Fregattenkapitän
Hofmann	Ludwig	Flugzeugführer Fa. Flettner				in Gruppe LS	
Holzbaur	Siegfried	Flugzeugführer		Simon	Heinz	Flugzeugführer, Leiter T5	
Hörhager	Josef	Flugmaschinist (BM)		Spies	Rudolf	Dipl.-Ing., Referent in BSx	
Hubrich	Gerhard	Flugzeugführer		Steiner		Bordfunker (BF)	
Huth	Wilhelm	Ing., Leiter Flugerprobung		Trillhaase		Flugzeugführer	
Jodlbauer	Kurt	Dr.-Ing., Flugbaumeister		Udet	Ernst	Inspekteur Jagd- u. Stukaflieger	Oberst
Kabisch	Herbert	Werftleiter	Flieger-Stabsingenieur	Wahl	Albert	Dipl.-Ing., Flugbaumeister	Flieger-Stabsingenieur
Klintzsch	Hans Ulrich	Leiter Gruppe A (Navigation)		Weidinger	Dr.Hanns	Leiter Triebwerksgruppe	
Königs	Karl-Friedrich	Ing., Flugzeugführer		Wenninger	Rudolf	Leiter Gruppe LS	Fregattenkapitän
Kursch	Ewald	Dipl.-Ing., Flugbaumeister		Wiborg	Karl	Flugzeugführer	
Lahs	Rudolf	Referatsleiter A II 1	Kapitän zur See,	Wismar	Henry	Flugzeugführer	
			Konteradmiral	Wollé	Heinrich	Leiter Gruppe G	
Langhoff	Bernd	Ing. Flugzeugführer		Wurster	Hermann	Dr.-Ing., Flugbaumeister	
Lechner	Helmut	Dipl.-Ing., Flugbaumeister		Zander	Konrad	Leiter Gruppe BSx, dann LS	Kapitän zur See
Lenschow	Wolfgang	Kommandeur	Oberstleutnant	Zenker	Hans	Chef der Marineleitung	Admiral

Note: The above-mentioned titles and grades refer to the time when the Names appear in the text. Possible subsequent changes have in general not been taken into account.

Names given to Aircraft at E-stelle Travemünde from 1930 to c1936

Aircraft	Werk-Nr.	Powerplant	Code No	Registration	Name
Do R Nas	143	Napier V u	1337		Pottwal
HD 38 b	63	BMW VI	2077		Meise
HD 49 a	371	Ju L 5	2363	IREH	Falke
He 59 a	378	BMW VI u	2214	ARAR	Silbermöwe
He 59 b	379	BMW VI u	2215	ABIF	Raubmöwe
He 59 B	442	BMW VI u	2622	AKIV	Seemöwe
He 59 C	529	BMW VI u		ARAN	Sturmmöwe
He 59 C	530	BMW VI u		AKYH	Lachmöwe
HD 60	380	BMW Vi	2157		Seeadler
He 60 C	431	BMW VI u	2486		Seeschwalbe
He 60 D	485	BMW VI u	3124	IGOQ	Condor
He 60 D	486	BMW VI u	3128	IGEH	Pelikan
He 60 D	494	BMW VI u	3162	IRIT	Cormoran
He 72 A	482	As 8 R	2574	EZOQ	Amsel
He 72 D	831	Sh 14 A		EZYS	Sperling
Do J II d Bis	218	BMW VI	2474	ABER	Pottwal
Do J II d Bis	247	BMW VI	3018	ABEF	Narwal
Do J II d Bis	296	BMW VI	3024	ADOR	Blauwal
Do J II d Bis	547	BMW VI		AHYS	Finwal
BFW M 35	630	Sh 14 A		EGYT	Hummel
Kl 32	406	Sh 14 A		EKIQ	Spatz
Kl 32	898	Sh 14 A		EJOZ	Fink
Vought V-85-G	1069	BMW 132 A		IBAX	Pinguin

Use of Stammkennzeichen (ST.Kz.) at E-Stelle Travemünde from October 1939

E-Stelle Code	Previous	Aircraft	Werk-Nr.	Powerplant	Assigned to	E-Stelle Code	Previous	Aircraft	Werk-Nr.	Powerplant	Assigned to
TH+HA	?	Ju 52	?	BMW 132 A		TI+HY	OBDB	Ar 195 V-1	2439	BMW 132 M	E2
TH+HB	?	Ju 52	?	BMW 132 A		TI+HZ	OCLN	Ar 195 V-2	2440	BMW 132 M	E2
TH+HC	?	?	?								
TH+HD	?	Ju 87	?			TJ+HA	ODSG	Ar 195 V-3	2441	BMW 132 M	E2
TH+HE	?	?	?			TJ+HB	ISFD	Ar 196 A-01	2522	BMW 132 K	E2
TH+HF	UFOH	Ju 160 B-0	4239	BMW 132		TJ+HC	ISLD	Ar 196 A	12	BMW 132 K	E2
TH+HG	?	Fi 156	?	As 10 C		TJ+HD	?	?			
TH+HH	?	?	?			TJ+He	?	?			
TH+HI	IRKI	He 42 E	1403	L 5 c	?	TJ+HF	ILRE	Ar 196 V-3	2591	BMW 132 K	E2
TH+HJ	ISIH	He 50 E	406	SAM 322	E2/8	TJ+HG	IEMX	Ar 197 A-02	3666	BMW 132 K	E2
TH+HK	ITNY	He 50 V-18	2/967	SAM 322 H1	E2/8	TJ+HH	IPCA	Ar 197 A-01	3665	BMW 132 K	E2/3
TH+HL	IJDA	He 50 G	765	SAM 322	E2/8	TJ+HI	IRHG	Ar 197 A-03	3667	BMW 132 K	E2/3
TH+HM	ADYU	He 59 D	1831	BMW VI	E2/7	TJ+HJ	IVLE	Ar 197 V-3	2073	BMW 132 K	E2/8
TH+HN	AZUK	He 59 D	1524	BMW VI	E6/7	TJ+HK	?	?	?		
TH+HO	AZOX	He 59 D	1516	BMW VI	E4	TJ+HL	ITLF	Ar 199 V-3	3673	As 410 A	E2/5
TH+HP	IEQU	He 60 D	301	BMW VI	E4/3	TJ+HM	AQJO	Do 17 M	2190	Bramo 323	E5
TH+HQ	IPZI	He 60 E/V-8	1573	DB 600	F	TJ+HN	AJII	Do 18 D-0	664	Jumo 205 C	
TH+HR	EVIH	He 72 D	342	Sh 14 a	F	TJ+HO	AGRT	Do 18 D-3	V802	Jumo 205 C	E4/5
TH+HS	ETUK	He 72 D	344	Sh 14 a	F/E2/3/5	TJ+HP	ADBA	Do 18 G	V 841	Jumo 205 C	E2/5
TH+HT	AREP	He 111 B-1	1011	DB 600	E2/3	TJ+HQ	ADFG	Do 18 H	V 901	Jumo 205 C	E2/3
TH+HU	ADBS	He 111	2762	DB 601	E4/5	TJ+HR	AIBE	Do 24 V-1	760	Jumo 205 C	E2/F/6/7/4
TH+HV	AERJ	He 111 P-2	2598	DB 601 A	E6/7/4/5	TJ+HS	ARZT	BV 138 A-02	149	Jumo 205 C	E2/4/5/6/7
TH+HW	IADO	He 112 V-1	1290	RR Kestrel	E/2	TJ+HT	AVEK	Ha 140 V-2	282	BMW 132 K	E6/7
TH+HX	?	?	?			TJ+HU	?	?	?		
TH+HY	?	?	?			TJ+HV	AETR	Ju 52/3m S	6005	BMW 132 A	E7
TH+HZ	IPEW	He 114 B-1	2546	BMW 132	E/2	TJ+HW	AKCD	Ju 52/3m g3e	5970	BMW 132 A	E7
						TJ+HX	AMOS	Ju 52/3m	5575	BMW 132 A	B/E2
TI+HA	APDS	He 115 V-2	1554	BMW 132 K	E4/5/2/3	TJ+HY	ACBQ	Ju 52/3m	5965	BMW 132 A	E7
TI+HB	ABZV	He 115 V-3	1555	BMW 132 K	E6/7	TJ+HZ	AZAF	Ju 52/3m	5372	BMW 132 A	E4/2
TI+HC	AHME	He 115 V-4	1977	BMW 132 K	E2						
TI+HD	ABBI	He 115 V-5	1862	BMW 132 K	E6/7/2/4	TK+HA	ADUE	Ju 52/3m	1368	BMW 132 A	E5/4
TI+HE	ASLD	He 115 A-02	1852	BMW 132 K	E4/5	TK+HB	AHIP	Ju 52/3m S	4033	BMW 132 A	E4/5
TI+HF	AKPS	He 115 A-06	1856	BMW 132 K	E2/5	TK+HC	IEXC	Ju 87 A-1	870013	Jumo 210	E7/2/3
TI+HG	ADJL	He 115 A-05	1855	BMW 132 K	E2	TK+HD	IHJH	Ju 87 V-10	4928	Jumo 211 A	E2/4/5/8
TI+HH	ADBT	He 115 B	1873	BMW 132 K	E6/7/2	TK+HE	IAGR	Ju 87 A-1	5000	Jumo 210	E2
TI+HI	IISI	Hs 122	645	SAM 322	E5	TK+HF	?	Ju 160	?		
TI+HJ	EJOZ	Kl 32	898	Sh 14 a	B	TK+HG	IBVF	Bf 108 B-1	1082	As 10 C-3	E
TI+HK	EPDF	Kl 35	1138	HM 504	F	TK+HH	IHCR	Bf 108 B-1	2015	As 10 C-3	B
TI+HL	OYAG	W 34 hi	1024	BMW 132 A	B/F	TK+HI	IACU	Bf 108 B-1	1639	As 10 C-3	MP
TI+HM	OGFT	W 34 hi	1025	BMW 132 A	F	TK+HJ	INHR	Bf 108 B-1	1617	As 10 C-3	E
TI+HN	OZDS	W 34 hi	1026	BMW 132 A	F	TK+HK	IYMS	Bf 109 C-1	1776	Jumo 210 G	E2
TI+HO	OLOA	W 34 hi	2884	BMW 132 A	E4/2	TK+HL	IECY	Bf 109 E	1781	DB 600	E2
TI+HP	OSIF	W 34 hi	1558	BMW 132 A	F	TK+HM	IKAC	Bf 109 B-1	301	Jumo 210 D	E2
TI+HQ		W 34				TK+HN	EAEP	Fw 44 J	948	Sh 14 a	F
TI+HR	IGSF	Fi 156 A-0	609	As 10 C	E2	TK+HO	EMRI	Fw 44 J	596	Sh 14 a	F
TI+HS	INBC	Fi 156 C-1	629	As 10 C		TK+HP	IPOP	Fw 56 A	2008	As 10 C	F/E2
TI+HT	OCML	Fi 167 V-1	2501	DB 601	E2	TK+HQ	OLCH	Fw 58 C-2	G200	As 10 C	F/E2/3
TI+HU	IIAO	Go 145	1464	As 10 C	F	TK+HR	IBAX	V-85-G	1069	BMW 132	B
TI+HV	IMEH	Go 145	210	As 10 C	F7E2	TK+HS	ITIX	V-85-G	1074	BMW 132	E2
TI+HW	?	?	?			TK+HT	IRIN	V-85-G	1071	BMW 132	B
TI+HX	IRAS	Ar 76	364	As 10 C	B	TK+HU	IQSV	Avia B 534	440	HS 12 Y	E6/7

Note: Entries denote no documentary evidence discovered

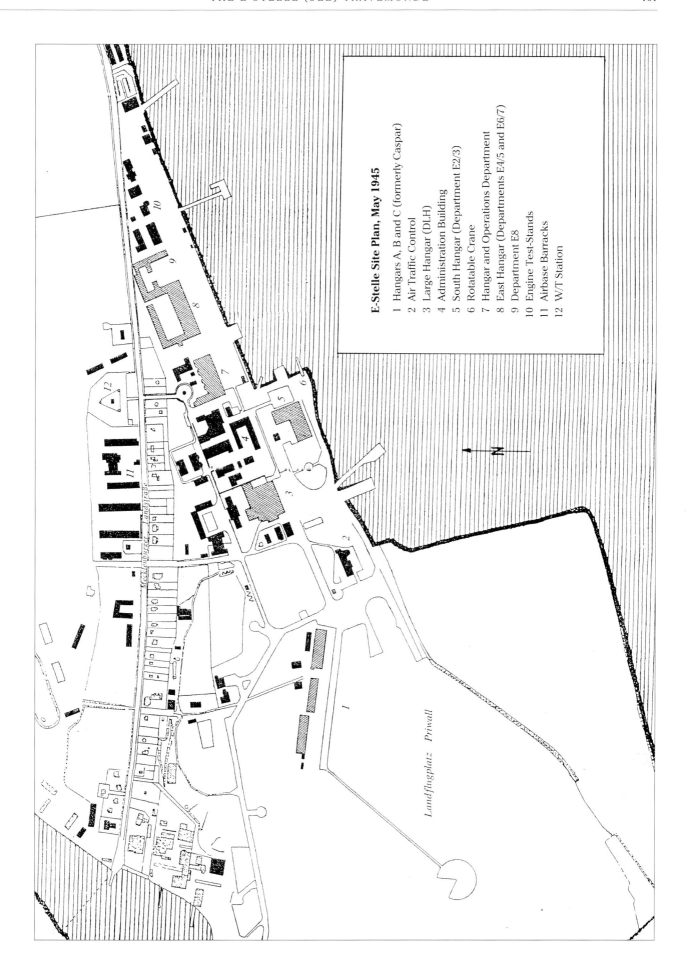

E-Stelle Site Plan, May 1945

1 Hangars A, B and C (formerly Caspar)
2 Air Traffic Control
3 Large Hangar (DLH)
4 Administration Building
5 South Hangar (Department E2/3)
6 Rotatable Crane
7 Hangar and Operations Department
8 East Hangar (Departments E4/5 and E6/7)
9 Department E8
10 Engine Test-Stands
11 Airbase Barracks
12 W/T Station

Landflugplatz   Priwall

Chapter Seven
by Mathias-Jens

The E-Stelle Tarnewitz

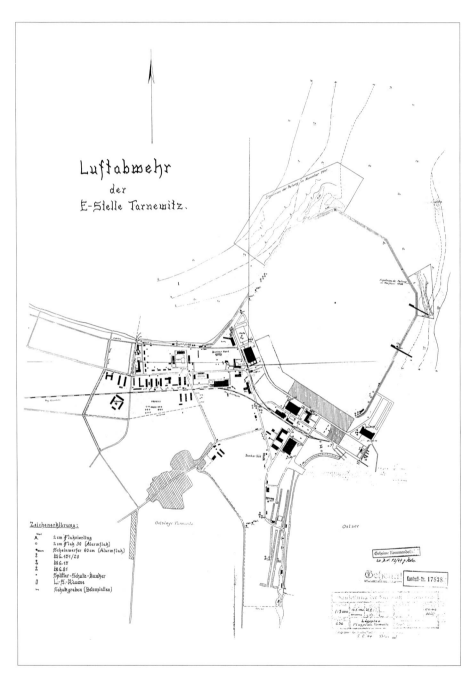

The E-Stelle Tarnewitz in 1944. On this 'Anti-Aircraft Emplacements Plan', the most important structures and buildings are shown, as well as projects such as the proposed railway connection which was not realized.

The growth of Luftwaffe testing activity after 1933 soon revealed the need for a new organisation to conduct these tests undertaken in the existing locations. The Luftwaffe leadership's demands for increasingly stronger aircraft armament resulted in an immense increase in weapons testing. However, neither Rechlin nor Travemünde had the capacity or potential available for devotion to this task. It was predictable that with the advent of new weapons, existing shooting-ranges would no longer be adequate since the weapons and their operational usefulness had to be evaluated and tested and theoretical knowledge accumulated for further development.

These were the underlying reasons which from 1934 led to plans for a new, independent E-Stelle which would be primarily concerned with the testing and development of aircraft armament. The E-Stelle Travemünde was accordingly commissioned to take care of its needs since a weapons testing section had already existed there prior to 1933. Construction planning was placed largely in the hands of Dipl.-Ing. Kurt Fritsche, the Travemünde Head of Works who had previously been responsible for expanding the E-Stelle's facilities there.

At the new location, a number of prerequisites had to be met. A coastal environment was deemed necessary for the erection of new, widespread firing-ranges which would offer safety and security during the course of trials. It also had to possess good transportation connections in order to facilitate co-operation with other existing E-Stellen. In addition, it was expected that the construction project should sacrifice the least amount of arable land and so save on costs.

The Station Site
For the new E-Stelle, an area on the eastern Baltic coast was found, halfway between Lübeck and Wismar. A site near to the Untiefe Lieps (coastal shallows) near the village of Tarnewitz, just a little east of the seaside hamlet of Boltenhagen, was selected. This extremely shallow coastal stretch at the Tarnewitzer Huk (hook) between the Boltenhagener Bucht (bay)

and the Wohlenberger Wiek (creek or cove) as the remnant of a sunken spit of land, would prove ideal in several respects to construct an airfield.

The site fulfilled all the location requirements. Shooting-ranges extending far out to sea were possible here as well as its proximity to other E-Stellen, even though the infrastructure in this weak northernmost Mecklenburg district was rather poor. Construction of the largely artificial airfield whose manoeuvring area would extend to the Untiefe Lieps, moreover, occupied very little of the cultural hinterland.

Following RLM approval on 2nd September 1935, work began on the site, where 80% of the surface area was to project beyond the existing coastline, only 20% occupying terrain inland. Due to the shape of the shoals, the manoeuvring area took the shape of an irregular quadrangle which enclosed an area of 1,000m² (10,760ft²). Dependent upon the need to build up the artificial land surface, it was proposed to level it with some 5.5 million m² (194.2 million ft²) of Baltic sea sand-sediment using dredging and irrigation machines. This surface was separated from the sea by a bulkhead or sheet-piling wall and heaps of stone, the new manoeuvring area being made firm by an artificial embankment 3m (9¾ft) high. After the sand-pourings had settled, the whole area was sealed with a layer of bitumen. Employing a vast amount of manpower and materials enabled this work to be completed as early as autumn 1936, a trial landing testifying to its operational readiness. The 1937 winter caused severe damage to the dyke, for which reason improvements to protect the manoeuvring area were underway well into 1938.[1]

Since almost the entire quantity of construction material, particularly the rinsing-sand, had to be transported there by barges and ships, a harbour at the site had also to be built. At the south-eastern end of the site, a breakwater and a jetty were therefore erected and continually in use until the end of 1938. In view of the meagre travel network on the landward side, sea travel appeared to be more advantageous. The presence of ice on the Baltic, however, was a hindrance to shipping in the winter months.

Parallel to construction work on the manoeuvring area, the first airfield buildings appeared, built exclusively on existing firm ground and grouped around the south and west perimeters of the airfield. The first and centrally-located Hangar I, like all subsequent hangars in Tarnewitz, had extensive annexes primarily intended to house the initial staffing complement. The first set of rooms became available for use at the beginning of 1937, the hangar itself being completed at the end of the year.

An overall perspective of the E-Stelle Tarnewitz from the air, seen from the south. At right is the artificial peninsula; at centre, Tarnewitz village and at far left, the first house of Boltenhagen bathing resort.

The E-Stelle pictured during construction work around 1939, from an east-west perspective.

At the southern end, directly overlooking the airfield, erection work was begun on Hangar VII – the shooting hall. Firing trials were to take place from here directly out into the Baltic, tangential to the airfield. Separated by distances of 500m (1,640ft) and 800m (2,625ft) north-eastward and firing directly out to sea were two target

bridges, later fitted with target discs which were fired at from the hangars.

A further hangar was built at the south-western end of the site, consisting of Hangar II, whose construction was completed around the end of 1937. Behind this hangar to the west, erection of an extensive complex of various workshop buildings was begun in early 1938. To the east appeared a seaplane harbour and landing ramp. The installations, together with the E-Stelle's built-up harbour, was able to be put into operation from autumn 1938.

The northwest firing-range represented another constructional focal point. Begun in 1937, this complex with its shooting stands, shooting tower and armament workshops, comprised the most important

*The landing approach from a southerly
direction shows clearly how the aircraft flew
over Tarnewitz village on their approach path
to the runway.*

E-Stelle test installations. Firing trials out to
sea, westwards from the manoeuvring
area, took place from here.

To expand the southern portion of the
E-Stelle, considerable earthwork was necessary on the steep coast heading towards
Wohlenberg. In the second quarter of 1938,
a laboratory together with an accompanying test-stand, was readied for trials with
rockets.

Work on the most important buildings
and installations was completed during the
course of 1938. As in every military airbase
environment, barrack blocks, a command
centre and works buildings without which
air traffic could not operate, were also built
in 1938. Following the completion of
Hangar V on the western perimeter and
storage depots at the entrance, the E-Stelle
was virtually complete by the end of 1939.

Up to 1945, Tarnewitz was constantly
enlarged and expanded. The appearance
of new aircraft necessitated lengthening
the runways between the hangars towards
the south and southwest. A new shooting-
tower at the northern tip of the tarmac
runway relieved the overstressed shooting-
ranges situated at the eastern and western
peripheries. A railway terminus, planned
from the very beginning of construction
work, was not realized.[2] This proved to be a
great disadvantage for the E-Stelle, as the
transport of all materials had to be handled
at the nearest Klütz railway station 10km
(6.2 miles) away. The 1937/38 Annual
Report of the new E-Stelle contains the following assessment:

'From the flying aspect, the airfield location is ideal. It is a great comfort to the pilots
involved in frequent shooting-practice
flights over water with land-based aircraft,

to have an airfield in the immediate neighbourhood of the firing-ranges. There are no
hindrances in the surroundings which
could in any way influence take-offs and
landings. The extent of the airfield is such
that even landing approaches over the
hangars present no danger, once the pilot
becomes familiar with the relative size of
the location. Since there is no background
on each of three sides and thus no land-
marks as a guide, estimating distances is
rendered difficult so that to pilots new to
the station, it appears much smaller than it
really is. Night landings with landing-lights
requires a certain amount of practice for
the pilots since, because of the colour and
evenness of the airfield the light becomes
absorbed, which makes an estimation of
his exact height difficult …The bituminized
surface of the tarmac has proved itself to be
generally good. In winter as well as in summer, it remained constantly firm but nevertheless 'springy'. Following long periods of
rainfall, large pools of water form, so that in
landings with fast aircraft, the spray thrown
up causes damage to the landing flaps.
After a few hours, however, the airfield has
dried out so much that flying operations
can recommence without danger…'

Its Personnel
Especially in the early years following its
erection, the E-Stelle was faced with the
significant problem of obtaining qualified
personnel. Although individual test groups
had been transferred from Travemünde
and Rechlin to Tarnewitz and thus occupied a certain amount of the planned positions, these experts did not suffice by far to
allow work to commence in its planned
sphere of activities. Despite generous job

descriptions, the attractions for the sought-
after specialists to go to Tarnewitz were not
very high. Tarnewitz possessed neither
favourable travel connections nor ample
accommodation and in the beginning, the
salaries paid also left much to be desired.

A big problem was the need to provide
accommodation. As early as 1936, housing
construction had been commissioned by
the E-Stelle Travemünde, but there were
sheer insurmountable obstacles of a
bureaucratic nature and of ownership
rights which continually delayed the commencement of construction. Some of its
personnel at first even had to seek quarters
in guest-houses and private homes in the
surroundings. The first apartments finally
became ready for occupation at the beginning of 1938 and in accordance with project
plans, others appeared at the entrance to
the E-Stelle, in Tarnewitz village, as well as
in large measure in Boltenhagen.

In principle, the organisation plan for
Tarnewitz followed that of the E-Stellen
Rechlin and Travemünde. The E-Stelle itself
was a Luftwaffe seaplane airbase with all
the installations that were necessary for the
accomplishment of military flying activities.
The Airbase Commander's office was
responsible for all the station installations. It
also handled security matters as well as the
supervision of property. The E-Stelle
Tarnewitz proper was actually located on
the grounds of the airbase which in principle resembled a civilian research institute.

The E-Stelle and Airbase Commander
fulfilled the duties corresponding to a military service rank. Explicitly for the E-Stelle
there was an Erprobungsleiter (Head of
Testing) who, contrary to the Commander
reported to the RLM Technisches Amt (LC).
Fundamentally, the E-Stelle was sub-
divided into a number of Test Sections
whose specialist task areas considerably
simplified accomplishment of work of a
complex nature. In their designations, the
sections corresponded to the Technische
Amt Development Advisory Boards, where
changes in the latter had direct effects at
the E-Stelle.

To avoid any hindrances to co-operation
with the armaments industry, from the very
beginning there were two independent
specialist groups from the Rheinmetall-Borsig
and Mauser firms in Tarnewitz. Having
their own personnel and equipment, these
groups were able to execute tests themselves, without having to rely upon outside
assistance.

The E-Stelle leadership ensured support for the testing groups by providing them with subordinate Works groups, without whose efforts their work would not have been possible. These groups maintained and checked the aircraft for the E-Stelle and got them ready for the scheduled tests. They ensured readiness of the test-bed aircraft, vehicles, and shipping, so as to guarantee a problem-free facility. All subordinate units of the Works groups were tailored to match the test environment in Tarnewitz. The 'experimental workshops' took care of modifications and additional installations in aircraft scheduled to conduct the tests, and developed and manufactured the constantly-required experimental devices for the E-Stelle. A further subordinate group for 'ships and boats' was of particular significance. Registering impacts on sea targets and ensuring the safety and security of seaborne shooting-ranges could only be conducted over water, for which purpose the E-Stelle had a large number of various vessels.

The precise organisation of all daily tasks discharged in Tarnewitz had to be thoroughly prepared with a watchful eye. The combination of flying and shooting practice with only a minute slip in planning, could cause fatal results. The head of flight testing had the duty, in co-operation with the heads of planning and air traffic control, to ensure that such mistakes did not occur, and by taking responsible action, to maintain irreproachable safety.

E-Stelle personnel recruitment consisted mainly of civilian workers drawn from the most varied professions who were listed as office employees. Even those obliged to perform military service during the war years also held the status of civilians in instances where they were not part of the airbase Technische Kompanie.

On 1st October 1936 the special 'Sondergruppe Tarnewitz' was formed in Travemünde whose task was the planning and execution of all work necessary for the new

Three high-ranking personalities at the service of the E-Stelle visitors on 'open day' to answer questions. Pictured at left is Obersting. Niedlich, head of the works section, Dipl.-Ing. Puls and the pilot von Guenther.

The Tarnewitz Mess shows the typical building style adopted in and around the vicinity. The beach pine trees, remnants of former coastal woodland, were retained to preserve camouflage.

To preserve a record during testing, members of the photography service were continually at the scene and are seen here filming the take-off of an He 111 on the snow-covered manoeuvring area.

E-Stelle. Headed by German Cornelius, this group moved to Tarnewitz on 1st February 1937 and formed the core of the E-Stelle there. In the following month, Major Umlauff took up his post as the first Commander, Cornelius becoming the Chief of Testing. Since 1st January 1936, Dipl.-Ing. Kurt Fritsche had already been the Technical Chief. His office was dissolved when testing operations, in accordance with an order, commenced on 1st April 1937.

Personnel changes in authoritative positions took place in 1939, when Obersting. Maximilian Bohlar took over as the E-Stelle Chief of Testing. During the course of World War Two, he also became the Commander, so that the organisationally separate positions were united in one person. In August 1939, the Flight Test Chief Helmut Rolf Zeising was tragically killed, his place being taken by Ekkehard von Guenther who served in this function until the end of the war.

The Pre-war Years 1937 to 1939

The task of the E-Stelle Tarnewitz consisted in general of testing aircraft armament corresponding to its intended operational use right up to combat maturity. The stimulation and demand for new or improved armament came from the RLM, the Services, or the E-Stelle itself and were turned into projects by the industrial firms. These then arrived in Tarnewitz where the trials, expressed very simply, were undertaken in two phases. The first was a purely stationary functional test of the new weapon in which, among other things, its characteristics in climatic tests, duration firings and projectile flightpath measurements were established. Necessary improvements followed in co-operation with the manufacturing firms. If the weapon fulfilled the requirements demanded of it, it then entered the second phase. After detailed preliminary examination, weapon installation was then checked out, its centring aids,

and the corresponding gunsight installation in the test-bed aircraft. The entire weapons system was thereafter tested statically and in the air under conditions which would most closely approximate to those met in combat operations.

The most modern instruments and equipment were used in Tarnewitz to enable the trials to be conducted with the highest degree of quality. For the measurement and evaluation of projectile trajectories, two cinetheodolite tracking stations of different sizes were available. With the aid of a low-temperature chamber, it was possible to test the behaviour of weapons and ammunition at temperatures down to –60°C, so that flights at correspondingly high altitudes could often be eliminated. The superbly-equipped Photographic Centre in Tarnewitz produced documentation and evaluation of all tests conducted. The Optical Laboratory was the starting point for the development and testing of all

A glance into the optical laboratory with its wall-mounted check-panel. Directly in front of it are two Zeiss optical benches and at far left above the wooden trestle is an aircraft periscope.

During the early formative years, simple aids were often resorted to for capturing the results of required tests. The first head of the photographic service, Hans Schibbach, is seen here with an aviator hand-camera in the rear fuselage position of a Ju 52 (ND+AN).

An everyday scene in Tarnewitz. Two weapon mechanics are centring the 4 MG 17 fuselage nose guns of a Bf 110.

An everyday scene in Tarnewitz. Two weapon mechanics are centring the 4 MG 17 fuselage nose guns of a Bf 110.

The Ju 52/3m (ND+AN) belonging to the E-Stelle Tarnewitz was experimentally fitted with a rotatable HD 151 machine-gun in a dorsal turret. Flying ahead of it is the Tarnewitz Fieseler Storch equipped with inflatable auxiliary floats on its main undercarriage for emergency landings on water.

new aircraft target-search and gunsighting mechanisms.

The entire work of the E-Stelle Tarnewitz exemplified how the status of German weapons development had altered between 1937 and 1945, and how futuristic some weapons tested actually proved to be. On the other hand, the tests also showed how development capacity was spread over such a wide range of diverse projects whose simultaneous realization was just not possible.

An effective flight and testing operation parallel to ongoing construction work was first noticeable in Tarnewitz in the second half of 1937. The following numerical example epitomizes the train of events on the airfield:

In the period from the beginning of August to the end of December 1937, there were 862 take-offs in Tarnewitz. Of these, 330 were carried out by E-Stelle aircraft and 532 by aircraft from elsewhere. Out of a total of 129 test flights and airborne firing trials in the same space of time, only 27 originated from the E-Stelle.

During the preliminary stage of its existence, Tarnewitz was not in a position to itself conduct an extensive amount of work. The E-Stelle suffered under the dearth of personnel. The incomplete state of installations under construction also hindered all its activities. They were lacking in workshops, W/T installations and shooting-targets on obsolete barriers and at the airfield periphery. The lack of boats meant that defining the boundaries and ensuring safety and security of an area for shooting trials was not possible. Despite this, a series of tests did take place. For several firms as well as other E-Stellen, the testing possibilities offered here were obtainable nowhere else.

In August 1937, the first air-launch of a model glider aircraft from an He 111 took place via the E-Stelle Rechlin. For this purpose, the entire Tarnewitz airfield had to be cordoned off, but because of the meagre testing activity at that time, caused little disruption. From October 1937 onwards, the armament manufacturer Rheinmetall-Borsig had a standing presence there two or

three aircraft. They began with trials of the new 13mm MG 131. Work commenced thereafter in a continuous field of endeavour – gunsighting and firing tests from aircraft; initial velocity and gas-pressure measurement, as well as projectile and detonator testing. At first, there was little experience to draw upon, but with each new test, the expertise and knowledge of all the participants grew. Headaches were caused for example, by the demand to conduct lateral (sideways) weapons-firing tests from aircraft, as it was expected to be established in what measure the projectile trajectories altered and how the aircraft gunners were expected to react accordingly. At the beginning, these tasks could only be carried out at night since the optical trace from the projectile could only be ideally tracked in darkness. In order to take measurements, high flying speeds and low

flying heights over the tracking station were necessary. In darkness, however, this increased the danger of accidents. Trials were repeatedly unsuccessful because of technical failures.

Even at the beginning of 1938 the situation in Tarnewitz had changed little. Tests that had been planned could only be undertaken under great difficulty. The necessary installations had meanwhile progressed in construction to the stage where extensive operations could take place, but there was still the lack of suitable personnel and test aircraft as the E-Stelle had to continually relinquish aircraft. Neither the towing of target discs nor the lateral shooting trials could be commenced because no suitable test aircraft were available.[3]

In March 1938, despite intensive negotiations, the establishment of a permanent area for shooting trials on the Baltic sea

The E-Stelle was opened to visitors for the very first time in 1940. Aircraft exhibited outside Hangar 1 from left to right are a Bf 110, He 72, Fw 44 and two Bf 109s.

A weapons-firing demonstration in Tarnewitz was not always a pleasant experience for the ears of the visitors.

The firing-range in front of Tarnewitz in the Bay of Wismar extended more than 7.4km (4.6 miles) northward and 4.3km (2.67 miles) eastward into the Baltic and was continually in use from 1939.

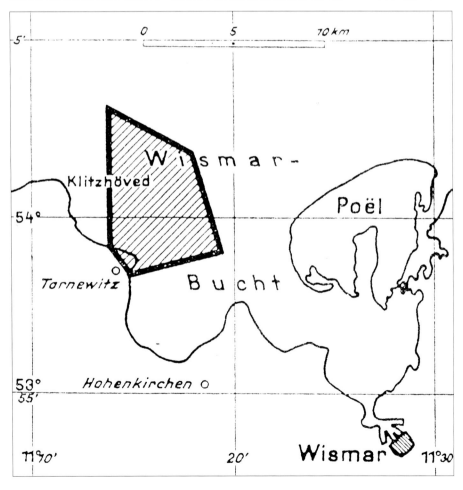

ahead of Tarnewitz was still questionable. The boat group urgently needed vessels in order to be able to set up even a provisional prohibited area. It often happened that fishing boats lingered in the E-Stelle shooting-range and scheduled tests had to be cancelled due to the lack of their own water craft.

As had happened the previous year, a strong separation between E-Stellen and 'outside' tests was established for the year 1938. As far as the means allowed, the E-Stelle continued the sideways-directed airborne firing trials. A new system of measurement developed by Tarnewitz engineers made test evaluations easier. Two MG 131s were tested under their own direction, a movable installation being the focal point of the tests.

Trials also began with the MG 151. This development by the Mauser firm resulted from a Luftwaffe requirement for ammunition of greater calibre. The MG 151 could be used to fire either 15mm or 20mm ammunition and was intended for both fixed and movable installations. Because of its weight, it could not be hand-operated in an open airstream, for which reason aiming aids such as the Hydraulische Drehring (hydraulic rotation ring) HD 151 was tested.

Endurance trials largely occupied the work in Tarnewitz. Besides the above new weapons, the 7.9mm MG 17 and the 20mm MG FF also took their turn at the shooting-stands. The transfer of ammunition development to Rechlin was regarded as an annoyance by the teams, and often led to delays in the development of weapons systems.

Of 'outside' testing conducted at Tarnewitz, the majority came from the E-Stellen Travemünde, Rechlin, and Peenemünde. Airborne and static firing-tests as well as those of long duration using various types of aircraft, formed the customary usage of its installations. Rechlin carried out a further test-drop of a glider and a glider model, whilst Peenemünde undertook measurements of special ammunition and high-speed bombs. Rheinmetall-Borsig in particular, had conducted numerous armament tests. To the trials which had begun in 1937 in Tarnewitz with the MG 131, were added the 30mm MK 101 in December 1938. At first, theoretical questions were dealt with, since hardly any experience was available with such heavy-calibre weapons. The MK 101 was expected to be able to destroy the enemy in air combat with only a single hit from a great distance, initial firing-trials indicating positive results.

In 1938, high-ranking visitors were often seen at the Test Centre, a noteworthy occasion having been on 23rd March 1938. Among the visitors were Generalinspekteur Erhard Milch, the RLM LC Chef Ernst Udet, General der Flieger Hermann Göring and Generalstab representatives who came to the new E-Stelle Tarnewitz. In-flight weapons-firing was conducted by seven aircraft, and all of the shooting-ranges which had been completed up until then put on a demonstration.

After the harsh winter of 1938/39, there was a noticeable increase in testing activity in Tarnewitz during the course of the new year. All planned installations had now been completed, the personnel situation allowing a wider range of work to be taken up and the establishment of a permanent 'prohibited area' considerably added to operating safety and security. Lateral-firing trials were continued, raising new problems which could often not be answered with existing knowledge. Tests with the MG 131 and MG 151 continued in close co-operation with the manufacturers. New gun-mountings and methods of installation were designed and built, endurance trials revealing previously unsuspected weapon deficiencies. Another weapon which appeared on the test-stands was the Mauser-developed 7.9mm MG 81 in which

the Luftwaffe became very interested as it offered more advantages in a movable turret than the customary MG 15 of the same calibre. The ammunition belt-feed in particular, was impressive. Tarnewitz also played a decisive role in the development of single and twin gun-mounts. As a traversable aircraft weapon, the MG 15 was soon displaced.

Tests by Rheinmetall-Borsig's own crews with the MK 101 were successfully accomplished. In comparative firing trials against tank targets, the superiority of the 30mm weapon as opposed to the 20mm MG 151/20 was to be determined.[4] It was hoped to obtain an answer to the question as to whether a fixed or semi-fixed installation in an aircraft would achieve better impact results. In corresponding trials at the Letzlinger Heide (heath) on 3rd August 1939, the E-Stelle's MG 151/20-equipped Bf 110 crashed due to contact with the ground, resulting in the deaths of its crew, Helmut R Zeising and Paul Berners, for whom an hour of mourning was held in Tarnewitz.

The outbreak of World War Two in September 1939 had few noticeable effects on Tarnewitz,[5] and did not alter until the end of the year since German aircraft armament appeared to have been vindicated.

Special Trials
Besides relating the chronological sequence of events in Tarnewitz, it is deemed necessary at this juncture to describe in detail some of the testing work seldom connected with the E-Stelle although it embodied a significant proportion of its activities, covering three aspects in particular.

Aircraft Rocket Armament
From the very beginning, trials with aircraft rocket-powered weapons had been conducted. It had been shown that to achieve a greater effectiveness at the target, weapons of larger calibre were necessary in order to strike the enemy with a larger quantity of explosive, or alternatively, attain a higher impact velocity. It was recognized that this could not be achieved with traditional machine-gun types of armament. Recoil forces exerted on turrets, weapons and ammunition, made the installation of large-calibre weapons difficult. Rocket projectiles were the alternative.

Under the strictest of secrecy, initial trials with rocket-driven projectiles began in Tarnewitz as early as 1937 with the Rheinmetall-Borsig spin-stabilised 'Rauchzylinder' (smoke cylinder) RZ 65 of 65mm calibre, but initial results were unsatisfactory. Its dispersal at the target was too great and it could therefore not be precisely aimed, the cause being due to the immature state of its propulsion. Further tests with the new weapon were nevertheless enthusiastically pursued following an improvement in the number of target impacts achieved, leading to its installation in specially-equipped test-bed aircraft. Progress, however, was negligible, with no discernible improvements achieved until the end of 1940. The usefulness of rocket armament for fighters was nonetheless recognized, the RZ 65 being fitted to the Bf 109 and Fw 190 at the beginning of 1943. For the Bf 110, projectiles of larger calibre were intended. At the end of 1943, trials were conducted with an RZ 65-equipped Ju 88 to

The He 111 (ND+AR) approaching the E-Stelle from a south-easterly direction, flying over the Bay of Wismar south of Poel Island. It was one of the establishment's complement, and served as a touring and communications aircraft.

Left: *Making a film sequence on RZ rockets in the E-Stelle film studio. To the left of the platform is an RZ 100; in the foreground are several RZ 15/8 propulsion sets.*

Below left: *This Ha 137 was used in Tarnewitz for firing trials with RZ rockets.*

Below: *For aircraft fitted with rocket armament, extensive preliminary tests were particularly necessary. This firing platform for RZ 100 rockets was intended to show the effects of gas impact on the Me 210 fuselage nose. Behind it is Hangar VII with its seaward-facing control tower.*

investigate its suitability for attacks on railway targets. In combat trials, however, the projectile did not prove successful.[6]

Parallel tests had meanwhile been in progress for some time with further developments of spin-stabilised rocket weapons. Alterations were made in terms of dimensions and calibres, trials being conducted with the larger-calibre 73mm RZ 73, the 150mm RZ 15/8, and the 420mm RZ 100. As in the case of machine-guns, the larger the calibre, the more difficult was its installation in aircraft. In the end, the entire RZ development was forbidden by the RLM GL/C Technisches Amt in April 1944 and work on the subject in Tarnewitz was ter-

minated. Apparently, interest in spin-stabilised rocket projectiles had ceased, whilst at the same time, tests with other types of rocket weapons had already begun.

In 1943, trials had commenced in Tarnewitz with the 21mm calibre Wgr 21 'Werfergranate' (mortar grenade), derived from the 'Nebelwerfer' (smoke thrower) mortar used by the Army. In operations by the Luftwaffe, its enormous destructive effectiveness against ground targets and against bomber formations was envisaged. At the forefront of trials in Tarnewitz were examinations of its trajectory and development of suitable launching apparatus for

its use on a large variety of aircraft. Besides its relatively simple suspension in firing-tubes beneath the wings of fighters and twin-engined interceptors, a six-tube arrangement was tested in an Me 410. In co-operation with the Erprobungskommando (Test Detachment) EK 25, vertical installation and firing-tests with several Wgr 21s were executed from the He 177 and Ju 88. Further development of this rocket projectile as well as comprehensive ballistic trials continued into 1945.

From November 1944, tests began in Tarnewitz with the 'Panzerblitz' (Tank lightning) and 'Panzerschreck' (Tank terror) anti-tank weapons, consisting of 88mm and 130mm calibre fin-stabilized rocket projectiles, mounted in bundles beneath the wings of Fw 190 ground-attack aircraft and intended to be introduced as an immediate means of combatting tank targets. Firing-trials to determine trajectories and impacts were undertaken in Tarnewitz and an important feature was the development of related installation accessories. A priority task at the end of 1944 was equipping the Fw 190 with the 'Panzerblitz' since an effective weapon was needed quickly.

Besides these rockets, the 55mm calibre R4M missile arrived in Tarnewitz at about the same time. It was very successfully employed at the end of the war in combat against bomber formations and was one of the most advanced developments in the sphere of rocket technology. It was installed in the Bf 110, Fw 190, Me 262 and Ba 349, but testing was hindered by its lack of availability in the quantities needed.

Following the termination of RZ trials, rocket testing in Tarnewitz was almost exclusively concerned with tests of launching apparatus, development of the rockets themselves having taken place elsewhere.

Target Simulation
For the trials conducted in Tarnewitz, it was very important that the theoretical knowledge gained be evaluated and turned to practical use. Shooting-trials at target-markers served an extremely important function. These recordings, providing particularly valuable information on weapon performance, were generally obtained by shooting at a target disc. Intensive development of such target markers was conducted at Tarnewitz in order to obtain a sufficiently high evaluation of the various impacts.

For firing-practice in air-to-ground and ground-to-ground trials, practice target discs of various sizes were located at specific target spots in the Baltic and on floating pontoons. These target markers were either positioned vertically or inclined at particular angles. Additionally, 'real' targets were used to determine the effectivity of the various weapons, where practice firings were directed against discarded aircraft or parts thereof, or against submarines and tanks.[7]

For the unavoidable employment of aerial targets for testing aircraft armament, markers were especially developed for this purpose. Since they were not capable of becoming airborne themselves, aircraft suitable as target-towers had to be used. The Gruppe E5z had already been formed in Travemünde specifically for the development of towed targets, and on 1st September 1938, moved over to Tarnewitz. Responsibility for the entire field of towed-target testing and development was passed to this E-Stelle where at first, corresponding trials were the concern of Gruppe W4, and later, Gruppe IId.

From then on, various aircraft types were modified for the target-towing role,[8] the aim being to make the aircraft as safe as possible. Reeling-out the target for aerial practice and jettisoning it for exposure to allow impacts to be achieved, however, was not without its dangers.

Just as exacting and not less painstaking, was the testing of suitable towed targets, as these had to possess sufficiently stable flying characteristics. At first, the targets resembled large square kites, but were soon replaced by more complicated constructions, especially when the multi-part 'Sternscheiben' (star-shaped discs) were eventually used.

Gunsight Development
The wide spectrum of involvement at the E-Stelle included not only the development of aircraft armament and their accessories, but corresponding gunsights as well. Ludwig Röhm, the head of Gruppe IIe in charge of gunsight development, in his 1942 LGL Report 153 entitled 'Experimental Results with Gunsights and Firing Systems' stated:

'On the subject of sighting devices for aircraft armament, it can be said on the whole today, that it is apparently much more important to raise the combat effectiveness of the aircraft by improving the impact accuracy by means of target-finding and centring instruments as well as the training of gun-aimers, than by increasing the amount of gun-barrels, ammunition, armour-protection and men involved. The latter path necessitates a much greater expenditure in man-hours, weight, and

The Fw 190 appeared to be pre-destined for almost all kinds of weapons trials, and is seen here with three WGr.21 firing tubes. The rockets were fired rearwards opposite to the direction of flight.

In order to prepare servicing instructions, the view from a rear-facing remote camera is being photographed. The Zeiss periscope formed part of the gunsight installation for the fixed rearward-firing armament that was fitted to some Bf 110s.

space. In other words, [aim for] more hits [and] not just more ammunition'.

For each new weapon, aircraft, and weapons bay, it became necessary to install a sighting mechanism which because of ever-changing requirements, meant that new gunsights had to be developed. In the course of time and in co-operation with the manufacturing firms, a whole series of new optical instruments appeared.

Up to the beginning of World War Two, the Luftwaffe used two types of gunsights. The inherent velocity-controlled VE sight,

based on the 'ring and bead' open-sight principle, was primarily used for traversable defensive armament. A considerable increase in target accuracy with fixed and movable weapons was afforded by introduction of the 'Revi' reflex sight in which the open-sight was replaced by an optical indicator.

When trials of rearward-firing armament began in 1940, sighting mechanisms in the shape of rear-view periscopes became developed. The incorporation of special 'Waffenstände' (weapons positions) in combat aircraft made development of corresponding electrically-operated VSE sighting stands necessary. Due to the separate location of the gun-aimer from the weapons, these sighting systems required special attention. Up to the end of the war, therefore, tests with PVE periscopic sights were conducted which gave good results

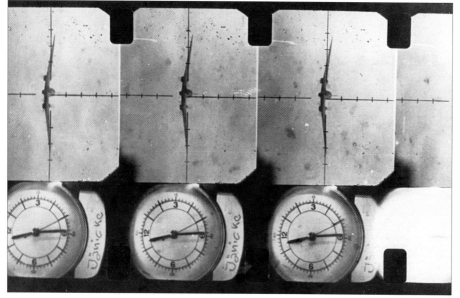

with remote-controlled armament. Large-calibre aircraft armament from 30mm upwards, partially required well-developed sights. The ZFR target telescopes allowed heavy weapons to be centred, but considerably limited the gunner's field of vision because of the degree of magnification.

Despite the advances made in gunsight development, one factor nevertheless still played a decisive role in air combat – namely, the ability of the user in being able to successfully engage the opposing target. Distance from the target, or alternatively, the lead-angle correction necessary, could not always be measured precisely. A revolutionary improvement was the gyro-controlled reflex sight with which the gunner could fire the weapons without having to take into account his own speed and direc-

tion as well as that of the target. From the data supplied, the sight itself calculated the required lead-angle correction. Instruments of this type were tested from 1942 onwards, and development had made such advances that by 1945, the first combat tests had been successfully accomplished. The Askania EZ 42 'Adler' (Eagle) gyroscopic gunsight was intended at the end of 1944 to be installed in almost all of the latest aircraft developed until the collapse,[9] but the majority of such projects did not pass the experimental stage.

The War Years 1940 to 1945

Technical testing of the MG 131 was concluded in 1940 and the weapon, declared ready for procurement purposes, was successfully employed as aircraft armament,

Tarnewitz continually serving as the starting point for new installation variations. With or without centring aids, remote-controlled or hand-operated, the 'Abwehrstände' (defensive positions) of almost all German combat aircraft were laid out to take the MG 131. As an example, the commencement of testing of the FDL rotating ring-mounted B-131/2 with remote centring-drive for the B-Stand in the He 177 may be cited.

When weaknesses in German day fighter and bomber aircraft armament were revealed at the beginning of the Battle of Britain, the E-Stelle was instructed to provide rapid assistance. The first task was to increase the defensive armament of bombers and 'Zerstörers' (heavy fighters) so that these would still remain usable for operations against England. The simple installation of rearward-firing weapons promised good chances of success. Already at the beginning of 1940, trials were conducted with 'Störkörpern' (nuisance bodies) which, fired opposite to the direction of flight, were expected to hinder the enemy in air combat.

In 1941, development and testing work on fixed rearward-firing armament for combat aircraft was completed. Various types of installations and firing methods, together with corresponding rear-view sighting periscopes, had been evaluated and the efficiency and effectiveness of these new weapons determined. Further development of defensive armament for combat aircraft was expected to progress towards remote-controlled defensive positions, the fixed rearward-firing armament being regarded as only an interim solution. Towards the end of the year, defensive positions with the MG 131 – the FDL-C 131/2 – were tested, intended for newer aircraft such as the Ju 288.

With the expansion of the war, especially after the invasion of the Soviet Union, the Luftwaffe demanded means for combatting large-area targets. Tarnewitz thereupon began trials with 'Waffenbehälter' (weapons containers) containing a combination of three MG 81Zs (the WB 81A and B), or two MG 151/20s (the WB 151), each in bomb-shaped ventral containers, expected to be highly effective against ground targets.

Development and testing of the MK 101, successfully carried out in 1939, reached its zenith with its installation in a number of Bf 110 heavy fighters and Hs 129 ground-attack aircraft. At an early date, however, this weapon's disadvantages were also revealed. It was too heavy, and performance was still too weak to be able to become really effective. At that time, however, there were no 30mm calibre weapons available. Although newer designs for weapons in this category did exist, there were many differing viewpoints in internal Luftwaffe circles regarding their necessity. As a result, development at first stagnated.

In 1942, importance focused in Tarnewitz on development of an effective defensive armament for the Luftwaffe's new combat aircraft. Predominantly, it concerned MG 131 defensive positions: the nose Stand for the He 177 and Ju 288 (the FDL 131Z), the eye-ball turret for the Ju 188 and the tail tur-

ret (FHL 131Z) for the Ju 388 and Ju 287 with which new remote directional-steering was tested for the first time. A particular achievement was development of the defensive remote-controlled twin lateral-fuselage FDSL-B 131 turrets for the Me 210 and Me 410 which made almost optimum use of available space.

Testing work on suitable gunsights became a special task to be fulfilled, which presented greater difficulties than weapons-testing itself. As soon as prototypes of any new aircraft became available, one of them was sent to Tarnewitz to undergo armament trials. When the armament installation Gruppe Ellf was switched from Rechlin to Tarnewitz, the proportion of test aircraft at the airfield steadily increased. Whilst this simplified trials with new armament

directly, it placed more responsibility on all groups at the E-Stelle. Accidents happened more often, aside from difficulties with the new technology.

Trials with the MG 151/20 advanced towards new gun-mounts, the focus lying on a wing-mounted armament gondola for the Bf 109.

The wartime events of summer 1942 involved the E-Stelle's manpower once more. Up until then, the large-calibre weapons of Luftwaffe aircraft had proved adequate for combatting tanks on the Eastern Front. The introduction of new models of tanks, however, dramatically reduced the superiority of German aircraft. A 50mm cannon which would become available in the near future was demanded. In Tarnewitz, an interim solution suggested by

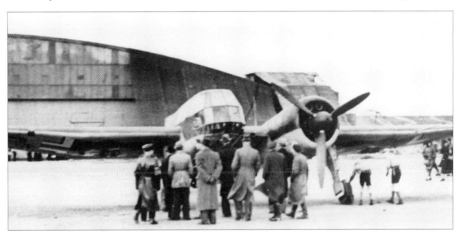

Tarnewitz 1940. On 'open day' the BV 141 (BL+AA) displayed aroused considerable interest among the visitors. In the background is Hangar V, already partly camouflaged at this time.

Hangar VII offered the opportunity of conducting armament firing tests with aircraft in flying attitude and with engines running, at two target discs. The He 177 (GI+BL) seen here was fitted with a ventral nose-mounted MK 101 cannon.

Landing accidents such as this Ju 88PV-1 with its BK 7.5cm cannon were not an infrequent occurrence on the airfield. The cause could often be attributed to technical immaturity or to pilots' errors of judgement of prevailing airfield conditions.

Mock-ups formed a significant part of the testing process. Depicted here is the experimental installation from front to rear, of two MK 108s, two MK 103s and two MG 151/20s in the nose of an Me 262.

Oberst Hans-Ulrich Rudel was turned into reality, involving fitting a Ju 87 with a 37mm cannon beneath each wing. This weapon was derived from the old Rheinmetall-Borsig Flak 18 gun and was relatively simple to install beneath the Ju 87 wings. The test-bed aircraft was correspondingly modified in Tarnewitz and successfully tested under operational conditions. The weapon showed such good results that it led to the first Bf 110 equipped with a single 37mm cannon being made ready in autumn 1942 and it was reckoned that this large-calibre weapon could also be employed against enemy bomber formations. At the turn of 1942/43, this weapon, known as the BK 3.7 (cm) cannon, was installed in Hs 129 aircraft.

At about the same time, the MK 101 once more came into use as aircraft armament, finding a slot in the ventral nose turret of the He 177, the last installation variant of this weapon.

After the long-enduring resistance exercised in influential places had slackened off, the MK 108 made its appearance in 1943 as a new weapon to be tested. This Rheinmetall-Borsig development from the year 1941 had long been blocked because of its unconventional design, and now, it was to be tested under the highest priority. The MK 108 consisted of a 30mm calibre weapon specially developed for combat against bombers. Because of its small dimensions when installed, it was also termed a 'short device' and represented the most advanced and mature weapons system. This electric-pneumatic recoil loader soon became the standard armament for all German fighters. Prior to that, however, the obligatory preliminary testing work was conducted in Tarnewitz. Installation arrangements were tested in the Fw 190; as a central motor-cannon in the Bf 109; as nose armament in the Bf 110, and also for the Me 262. Upon the recommendation of night-fighter leaders, it was also tested in an oblique-firing arrangement known as the 'Schräge Musik' (Jazz music) in the Bf 110 and Ju 88. Since it represented a new, very promising armament variation, the oblique-firing arrangement was also tested with the MG 151/20. Work in this respect initially met with rejection by higher authority,

for which reason further trials were carried out in Tarnewitz on their own initiative.

The Rheinmetall-Borsig firm had meanwhile brought another MK 101 development to a state of maturity. This, the MK 103, turned out to be smaller, lighter and faster than its predecessor. Together with the MK 108, there were two weapons of equal calibre available. It was a matter of free production capacity as to which would become the standard weapon adopted by the Luftwaffe. To enable a decision to be made, both weapons were tested in parallel.

Further weapons tested were the hand-operated as well as remote-controlled defensive positions with the MG 131, where tail twin and quadruple gun-mounts – the HL 131Z and HL 131V, were intensively investigated. For remote-controlled single gun positions, the remotely-driven FA 15 was envisaged.

A focal point at the E-Stelle in 1943 concerned super-heavy armament. The point of view prevailed that increasing the calibre was the decisive factor in raising the fighting power of airborne cannon. Every target, whether bomber or tank, was to be destroyed with a single hit. On the Eastern Front, where such weapons were urgently needed to combat tanks, correspondingly good results had been achieved in surface combat with the 75mm PaK 40L cannon. This artillery weapon was modified and latterly tested for use as airborne armament. In the summer of 1942, a Ju 88A-4 had been fitted with the PaK 40 derivative now known as the BK 7.5 (cm) cannon. The heavy armament of what was now designated as the Ju 88PV-1 machine caused enormous problems for the test engineers. In firing trials, difficulties were experienced with exhaust gases from the cannon which caused partial damage to both the propellers and the airframe.

Alongside it, work was continued on the BK 3.7. The weapon itself as well as its installation in the Bf 110 and Me 210 in 1943, and finally as a twin mount in the Ju 88, certainly fulfilled all the requirements, but was nevertheless soon rejected for frontline use as it was too weak and had insufficient rounds of ammunition. The tank combat crews still demanded a 50mm cannon which ought to be ready for use by the end of 1943. Rheinmetall-Borsig thereupon redesigned the KWK 39 without significant changes into the BK 5 (cm) cannon which, other than for use against tanks, was also envisaged for use against bombers. A trial installation was effected in an Me 210 in August 1943, followed shortly afterwards in a few Me 410s for testing purposes in Tarnewitz. Only a little later, a Ju 88 was also fitted with this 50mm weapon.

Some of the numerous series-configured equipment packs should likewise be mentioned which were to involve Tarnewitz from 1943. The MG 17 in the Fw 190 and Me 410 were replaced by the MG 131, the Ju 88 in its heavy-fighter variant receiving a six-barrel MG 151/20 as nose armament. At the end of 1943, testing of the Me 323WT (weapons-carrier) was carried out. This aircraft was conceived as a 'Flakkreutzer' (flak cruiser) which, fitted with heavy armament, was to accompany formations of the large Me 323 transports, but the idea was not adopted.

Work in Tarnewitz had reached its peak in 1944. It involved such a large assembly of weapons and aircraft as had not been seen in any of the preceding years. Tests which had started in previous years continued on insofar as they had not already been concluded, with new ones being added to them. Noticeable was the drift away from the primary testing of defensive combat aircraft armament due to the 'Jäger-Notprogramm' (Fighter Emergency Programme). Testing now suffered partly from the lack of fuel as well as from spare parts, which of course, among other things, led to delays in being able to fulfil various testing tasks.

With regard to tail turrets, the HL 131Z equipped with two MG 131s were undergoing testing at this time specially for the Ju 388, whilst the HL 131V was projected for

the Ju 290. For planning reasons, a comparison was made between the HL 131V (4 x MG 131)) and the HL 151Z (2 x MG 151/20) tail barbettes which revealed that the larger-calibre twin mount would in the long run be superior to the quadruple mounting.

Meanwhile, the MG 151 was subjected to further testing, principally as oblique-firing and fixed fighter armament. The MK 103 and MK 108 also underwent further testing for this purpose, for use in wing-mounted or central motor arrangements as well as oblique-firing 'Schräge Musik'. Newer aircraft types such as the Do 335 and Me 262 in particular, were equipped and tested with them, revealing time and again the superi-

ority of the MK 108. Due to its dimensions and difficult mounting, the MK 103 proved unsuitable as wing armament, as well as being less suitable as nose armament in the Me 262. An armament comparison in the Me 262 with 4 x MK 108s or 2 x MK 103s and 2 x MG 151/20s showed the clear superiority of the MK 108 cannon.

Although a number of Hs 129s were converted and equipped with the BK 7.5, testing work was not concluded when the anti-tank aircraft had to be sent to the Eastern Front in summer 1944. This resulted in a continuation of flight testing, most of which took place whilst in use with combat units.

The manned tail-gunner's HL 131V cupola with its 4 MG 131 machine-guns was one of several He 177 armament variations. The weapons were electro hydraulically adjusted.

Tarnewitz, 1st May 1943. Up to the end of World War Two it had its own gliding unit, whose leader Heinz Schaefer is seen here in the Grünau Baby IIb (3-1212) cockpit. The Russian tank parked behind it served as a target for projectile firing tests.

Target No.   Illustration No.
3/AIR/125   3/AIR/125/1

AIRFIELD and   —   TARNEWITZ near WISMAR
SEAPLANE STATION   (GERMANY)

Photographed 8 October 1943   (1 : 12,000) approx   Issued March 1944

Illustration
3/AIR/125

As the war progressed, it became more and more evident that the aircraft machine-guns and cannon so far developed, despite their advanced technology, would not bring about an end to the war. A search was made for new, unconventional yet practicable designs which would bring a last-minute 'turn of the tide'. The 'Schräge Musik' development of 1943 had laid the cornerstone for new projects that now appeared in Tarnewitz. Based on the idea of firing vertically upwards, the 'Sonder-gerät' (special weapon) SG 116 'Zellen-düsche' (cellular shower) was proposed, consisting mostly of a trio of 30mm MK 103s installed at an almost vertical angle in the fuselage aft of the Fw 190 cockpit. Upon flying beneath a bomber, the shells in the recoil-free gun barrels would be fired, activated by photocell sensors in the wings. To test this weapon, voluminous time-consuming preparatory work was necessary at the E-Stelle, since the field of automatic target-guided projectile release was something completely new and presented the engineers with a host of new problems. How should a vertically-installed weapon be centred, and what angle of inclination was the most suitable? Solutions were eventually found and a few Fw 190s were fitted with this weapon. A test-firing in near-operational conditions with an He 177 showed that the SG 116 was undoubtedly usable.[10]

Parallel to the SG 116, there were other projects based on the same principle, the majority of which arrived for trials in Tarnewitz towards the end of 1944. Comparative tests revealed the merits of each design in terms of characteristics, performance and combat suitability, and showed that the SG 117 'Rohrblock' (barrel block) and SG 500 'Jägerfaust' (fighter fist) held the greatest prospects of success. The SG 117 consisted of a group of seven MK 108 barrels where, by ejecting a counterweight each time a shot was fired, was thus recoilless. The SG 500, intended for vertical installation, consisted of single projectiles of 50mm calibre and was also made recoilless. By combining several of these, an effectiveness similar to the SG 116 was produced.

Photograph on the opposite page:

The Reconnaissance Report accompanying this Allied photograph of 8th October 1943 shows clearly how precisely they were informed of the activities in Tarnewitz, and is all the more puzzling why no air raid subsequently took place.

Since the problem of engaging tanks was still one of considerable importance, the vertical-firing idea was also applied for this type of target. Upon flying over, the projectile would be triggered in reaction to the tank's magnetic field, penetrating its lightly-armoured upper surface. Preliminary tests were conducted from December 1944 with the single-barrel 75mm calibre recoilless SG 113 'Förstersonde' (forester's probe) in Tarnewitz. Equipping the Fw 190 with two barrels under each wing was envisaged for this project.

In connection with the development of newer armament and gunsights, new firing systems were also tried out in Tarnewitz. The designations 'März' (March) and 'Natter' (Viper) symbolized trials of the ram-attack method of air combat, whose realization was faced with enormous difficulties.

Until the activities of the E-Stelle were brought to a total standstill in 1945, a vast spectrum of tasks had been worked upon. All testing became severely limited due to weather conditions, test-bed aircraft unfit for flying, and the lack of fuel and ammunition.

The SG 113-equipped Fw 190s, completed in the meantime, appeared several times in Tarnewitz for weapons testing.[11] Problems with the projectile and its electronic triggering caused some delays so that tests ultimately came to a standstill with the end of the war.

At the end of January 1945, besides the 'Sondergeräte' SG 113, SG 117 and SG 500, there were a number of various rocket-propelled projectiles undergoing testing. The 'Panzerblitz' Pb 1 and Pb 2, the 'Werfergranate' Wgr 42 and R4M, were only a few of the innumerable projects which had not been brought to completion, in addition to the Revi 40 and EZ 42 gunsights which had formed the focal point of testing.

The last aircraft armament to arrive in Tarnewitz was the MG 213C, working on the revolver system and laid out for both 20mm and 30mm calibre rounds. The project resulted from an RLM requirement for a rate of fire of 1000 rds/min and an initial velocity of 1000m/sec (3,280ft/sec). At the end of the war, two prototypes were at the E-Stelle.

The End of the War
Tarnewitz did not suffer the fate of the majority of German airfields during World War Two. It was spared from bombing attacks and enabled the E-Stelle to continue its work almost unhindered into the year 1945.

Although the Allied Air Forces were aware of the location and its importance, the feared bombing attacks did not materialize. The first low-level attack by American

fighters took place on 13th May 1944, when several aircraft on the airfield were damaged. Towards the end of the war, Tarnewitz was more frequently attacked by marauding fighters, but suffered only limited damage.[12]

Detailed emergency plans had been made in the event that the E-Stelle Tarnewitz would be occupied by Allied troops. Its capture by the Red Army would have resulted in destruction of the entire facility. When it became apparent that the Western Allies would be the first to reach and occupy Tarnewitz, E-Stelle dispersal to Gettorf near Eckernförde was organised. The facility itself was to remain intact. Important equipment and documents were prepared for transfer elsewhere by ship, the most secret items being sunk in the sea. The most important test aircraft were flown to Schleswig in the course of which an Me 262 met with disaster. The pilot, Eugen Speier, was killed when he stalled the aircraft on take-off and it crashed into a storage depot. The E-Stelle's uniformed Engineer Corps, the employees and their families, had the choice of making their way over water to Eckernförde or remaining where they were. Everyone had to decide by 2nd May 1945. Just a few days after a freighter had reached Eckernförde unscathed, American soldiers appeared in Tarnewitz, the remaining employees giving themselves up without any resistance. All uniformed individuals were taken to a provisional prisoner-of-war camp north of Grevesmühlen. E-Stelle installations still intact were searched and materials confiscated.

In June 1945, the British moved into Tarnewitz. Everywhere in the former Reich they assembled and evaluated technical new developments, the E-Stelle proving to be of great interest. The Ju 388 V6 for example, which was still in Tarnewitz, was ferried to Lübeck.[13] Portions of ammunition stock that were in over-abundance were sunk in the harbour.

In July 1945, the E-Stelle region passed into the territorial zone of the Red Army, which began to systematically dismantle the installations and when this had been completed, began to blow-up or make unusable the approach roads, buildings, and parts of the runway manoeuvring area. With the exception of the employee housing settlement and living quarters in Boltenhagen, the location soon became one big expanse of debris.

After the Red Army withdrew in 1946 and the local population had scattered the last remnants of the former E-Stelle in all directions, the Tarnewitz peninsula remained behind as a monotonous wilderness. It was only in the 1950s that the grounds were again used as a military base.

Tarnewitz, 25th February 1945. Apparently, peace reigns at the E-Stelle. Parked in front of Hangar V are the E-Stelle's own gliders – a Schempp Hirth Gö 4 (XI-22) and a single-seat Grünau Baby IIb (LJ+GP). Behind them in the uncamouflaged hangar is an He 177.

E-Stelle Tarnewitz Organisation

Commensurate with the official order, testing activities commenced in Tarnewitz on 1st April 1937, the Truppenamt (TA) Test Departments and their Chiefs being initially as follows:

Commander (Abteilung LC6 in the TA)			Umlauff
Head of Testing			German Cornelius
W1	Ballistik u. Vermessung	*Ballistics & Measurements*	Ludwig Röhm
W2	Ziel- u. Richtmittel	*Targeting & Navigation Systems*	Rudolf Pätz
W3	Gewehre u. Laffetten	*Weapons & Turrets*	Walter Denzinger
W4	Munition u. Zieldarstellung	*Ammunition & Target Representation*	Walter Segitz
Head of Flight Testing			Helmut R Zeising

In mid November 1938 the specialist groups were re-arranged since restructuring took place in the TA (Abt. LC11/II/E11).

E11 / IIA	MG und Munition	*Machine Guns & Ammo*	Walter Segitz
E11 / IID	Lafetten und Luftscheiben	*Turrets & Target Discs*	Rudolf Pätz
E11 / IIE	Ballistik und Visiere	*Ballistics & Gunsights*	Ludwig Röhm

In May 1942 the structure of the Test Sections was again altered, so that the picture at the end of the war was as follows:

Commander & Head of Testing			Maximilian Bohlan
Head of Test-Flights			Ekkehard von Guenther
E 6	Versuchkoordinierung mit TA	*Test coordination with TA*	Walter Segitz
E 6 / IIA	Schusswaffen, Bordraketen, Waffenelektrik	*Firearms, Airborne Rockets, Weapons Electricals*	Walter Denzinger
E 6 / IID	Lafetten, Antriebe, Fernsteuerungen, Hydraulik	*Turrets, Drives, Remote-Steering, Hydraulics*	Rudolf Pätz
E 6 / IIE	Ballistik, Messwesen, Zielgeräte, Optik	*Ballistics, Measurement Systems, Targeting Devices, Optics*	Ludwig Röhm
E 6 / IIF	Waffen – Einbau	*Weapons – Installation*	Ernst Pfister

Footnotes

1 For the circumstances existing at that time, the work in Tarnewitz was really superlative. Not only was the filling-up of a 2.5m (8ft) high layer of sand spectacular, but also sealing it with a continuous layer of bitumen. In one single day, some $37,500m^2$ ($1,174,252ft^2$) of Baltic sediment was dredged and poured out.

2 A pre-requisite for a rail connection to the E-Stelle was an extension of the railway line from Klütz to Boltenhagen. This had been planned since 1938, but was not realized on cost grounds. The Reichsbahn at that time wanted the necessary properties to be handed over without reimbursement.

3 In 1938, a number of test aircraft had to be handed over for a so-called 'Mobilization Exercise' in connection with the occupation of Czechoslovakia.

4 On 3rd July 1939, Hitler and Göring visited the E-Stelle Rechlin. The demonstration of the Bf 110 fitted with Rheinmetall-Borsig MK 101 armament and which was ferried over from Tarnewitz, made an imposing impression.

5 Camouflage schemes adopted on all buildings, however, were visible everywhere in the locality.

6 The tests referred to were carried out in co-operation with the EK 25 Test Detachment.

7 The submarine supplied by the Navy served principally to test the MK 101 ammunition. The armour-piercing rounds were specially intended to be directed against the pressure tanks of surfaced U-boats.

8 Modifications of the following aircraft types have been verified from documents: the Do 17, Ju W 34, Ju 52, He 60 and Avia B.71.

9 In November 1944, installation examinations were being undertaken with the EZ 42 in the Ar 234C, BV 155, Do 335, Fw 190, Go 229 He 162, Me 109, Me 262 and Ta 152.

10 Automatic projectile release of the vertically-firing armament was tested at the end of 1944 from an Fw 190. The blind projectile hit the target He 177 precisely. A further live test-firing directed at a remote-controlled He 177 was unsuccessful due to failure of the SG 116 fuze.
11 A Russian tank, which travelled under its own power from Klütz railway station to Tarnewitz was used for target representation. The few tests carried out proved very positive.
12 On 8th May 1944, the following communication was sent to the Kommando der E-Stellen (here an extract): '…Active flak troops have not been previously engaged at the E-Stelle Tarnewitz, so that the entire flak protection has been carried out by our own personnel … As long as active flak personnel are not available, all weapons stations will only be manned after a preliminary alarm is sounded, which means that if a low-level surprise attack occurs … there will be no reaction from the ground defences.'
13 For the Ju 388 transfer flight, the pilot Hermann Gatzemeier was brought back from internment near Grevesmühlen to Tarnewitz. He and his flight mechanic were not allowed to wear parachutes and were not to exceed certain speeds and altitudes. The aircraft, which carried RAF insignia, flew under the protection of Spitfire fighters.

Documentary Sources

Abbreviations

DRG   Deutsche Reichsbahn Gesellschaft
      German State Railway Company
EST   E-Stelle Tarnewitz
      Test Centre Tarnewitz
LGL   Lilienthal Gesellschaft für Luftfahrt
      Lilienthal Society for Aviation
NfL   Nachrichten für Luftfahrer
      Information for Air Travellers
RLM   Reichluftfahrtministerium
      German Air Ministry
OKL   Oberkommando der Luftwaffe
      Supreme Command of the Air Force
USAAF United States Army Air Force
USSBS United States Strategic Bombing Survey

DRG Berlin: Communications re rail connection Boltenhagen, August/September 1934.

EST Documents:

Flight log-books Gatzemeier and Kowalewski.

Annual Reports 1937/38 and 1938.

Quarterly Reports II/38, III/38 of 30.9.1938 and IV/38 of 15.12.1938.

Document Remark 'Status of RZ 65 Tests', 6.9.1939.

Communication re Ve-bombsights, 1.5.1940.

Proposals for a new type of Armament and Combat Procedure, 28.10.1940.

Letter re 'Warning device for Fighters', 31.10.1941.

Contribution to Annual Report 1940, Section D II, 18.3.1941.

Report: Tests of VSE-B 288/1 device, 20.1.1942.

Document Remark: Status of work on aircraft for the VfB, 28.4.1943.

Activity Test reports Nos 9, 16, 18, 26/1943.

Report: Installation and Functional Checks of the MK 108 in … the Bf 109, 21.7.1943.

Chart of Sailplane slope Klütz-Höved, 9.12.1943.

Report: MK 108 Testing, 8.3.1944.

Letter to Kdo.d.E. re 'Order for E-Stelle Safety/Security', 18.4.1944.

Building works, Anti-aircraft and Site-plan, last entry 5.5.1944.

Letter to Kdo.d.E. re 'Anti-aircraft Defences', 8.5.1944.

Report: Armament comparisons of the tail-positioned four-barrel MG 131 and the two-barrel MG 151/20 gun-mounts, 22.5.1944.

Extract from the Commander Order No 18/44, 9.6.1944.

Document Remark re SG 116, 29.11.1944.

Activity Test Reports Nos 30-37/1944, 39-41 and 43-51/1944.

Summary re Equipment Dispersal, etc, 1944.

Report: Armament Proposal 8-262 with 4 x MK 108 or 2 x MK 103 and 2 x MG 151/15s, 30.1.1945.

Activity Test Reports 1, 7 and 9/1945.

E-Stelle Travemünde: Catalogue of E-Stelle Travemünde Reports, 10.10.1934.

E-Stelle Rechlin, Report: Airscrew Stress measurements … with the Ju 88P1…, 9.7.1943.

Gemeinde [Community] Boltenhagen, Tarnewitz Boundary Map, circa 1935.

Gendarmeriekreis [Police District] Schönberg: Accident Notice, 6.12.1941.

Gendarmeriekreis Schönberg: re Report on Air Raids, 18.7.1944.

Gerhard Fieseler Werke GmbH, Kassel: Status of Development, 31.3.1939.
LGL Report 153, 1942.

Luftgaukommando XI, IcL: Aircraft shot down from 24 to 25.3.1944.

Mecklenburg State Ministry, Department of the Interior: Exchange of correspondence – Gemeinde Boltenhagen, Gemeinde Tarnewitz, Kommandantur E-Stelle Tarnewitz, 1940-1944.

Messerschmitt AG: Minutes 'Bf 110 with MK 108', 13.7.1943.

Messerschmitt AG: Minutes 'Me 262 with 4 x MK 108', 6.4.1944.

Messerschmitt AG: Minutes '8-262, Various Matters re Armament', 15.12.1944.

NfL: Supplement to Announcement in NfL 1939/1933, New Permanent Danger Area (Tarnewitz Shooting-range), 27.12.1939.

OKL: Primary Task – Shooting Trials of Panzerblitz Projectiles in 8-190, 7.1.21944.

OKL: Letter to E-Stelle Tarnewitz re Wgr 42 and R 100BS, 2.1.1945.

RLM Technisches Amt GL/C-E: Transfer of development tasks: Bombsights, 23.5.1944.

RLM Technisches Amt GL/C-E: Transfer of development tasks: Ju 290 etc, 31.5.1944.

RLM Technisches Amt GL/C-E: Record of meetings 14.6. to 26.6.1944.

USAAF Air Photo E-Stelle Tarnewitz of 8.10.1943 and 22.2.1944.

USAAF Report No 512/1943, Tarnewitz1943.

USAAF Record Group 243 (USSBS), Reconnaissance Report Tarnewitz, 3.5.1944.

Literature List

Bukowski, Helmut/Griehl, Manfred: 'Junkers Flugzeuge 1933-1945 – Bewaffnung, Erprobung, Prototypen' (Junkers Aircraft 1939-1945 – Armament, Testing, Prototypes), Podzun-Pallas –Verlag, Friedberg, 1991.

Galland, Adolf: 'Die Ersten und die Letzten – Die Jagdflieger im Zweiten Weltkrieg' (The First and the Last – Fighter Pilots in the Second World War), Franz Schneekluth Verlag, Munich, 1953.

Held, Werner: 'Die deutsche Tagjagd – Bildchronik der deutschen Tagjäger bis 1945' (German Day Combat Operations – Chronicle of German Day Fighters until 1945), Motorbuch Verlag, Stuttgart, 1982.

Held, Werner: 'Reichsverteidigung – Die deutsche Tagjagd 1943-1945' (Defence of the Reich – German Day Combat Operations 1943-1945), Podzun-Pallas-Verlag, Friedberg, 1988.

Meyer-Scharfenberg, Fritz: 'Wismar, die Insel Poel und der Klützer Winkel', VEB Hinstorff Verlag, Rostock, 1984.

Mittler, E S (Publisher): 'Luftfahrt – Bilder, Texte, Documente' (Aviation – Photographs, Texts, Documents), Vols 1, 7 and 9, Herford, 1978.

Ries, Karl/Dierich, Wolfgang: 'Fliegerhorste und Einsatzhäfen der Luftwaffe – Planskizzen 1935-1945' (Luftwaffe Airbases and Operational Airfields – Overhead Views 1935-45), Motorbuch Verlag, Stuttgart, 1993.

Schliephake, Hanfried: 'Flugzeugbewaffnung – Die Bordwaffen der Luftwaffe von den Anfängen bis zur Gegenwart' (Aircraft Armament – Airborne Weapons of the Luftwaffe from the Beginnings to the Present), Motorbuch Verlag, Stuttgart, 1977.

Sefzig, Udo: '40 Jahre deutsche Flugerprobung –2. Teil' (Forty Years of German Flight tests – Part 2, Tarnewitz), Jahrbuch der Wehrtechnik, Part 6, Darmstadt, 1971.

Magazines:
Jet & Prop (bi-monthly), Verlag Heinz Nickel, Zweibrücken.

Jet & Prop Foto-Archiv, Vols 1 to 6, Verlag Heinz Nickel, Zweibrücken Waffenrevue (quarterly), Karl. W Pawlas, Nürnberg.

Chapter Eight
by Max Mayer

Luftwaffe Test and Experimental Establishment Peenemünde-West/Usedom

Peenemünde is in essence a minute location in Germany, but as the 'Birthplace of Space Travel' is known worldwide. The date of 3rd October 1942 marks the successful commencement of space travel for it was on this day for the first time that a ballistic, liquid-fuelled A4 rocket was despatched above the stratosphere to an altitude of approximately 90km (56 miles) over a distance of 192km (119 miles).

This rocket was a successful achievement of the Heeresversuchsanstalt (Army Experimental Establishment) Peenemünde-East. Even when the A4 was developed with the means of the then HWA (Army Ordnance Office) Berlin, and latterly as a weapon became known under the propaganda designation V-2, there can surely

be no doubt today – even worldwide – that it comprised a superb technical achievement. It served as the basis and precursor for later comparable developments in other countries.

In relation to the A4/V-2 and its origin, a considerable amount of literature is available both at home and abroad. On the other hand, little has become known concerning the activities of the Luftwaffe Test- and Experimental Establishment at Peenemünde-West. The following narrative is devoted primarily to this Versuchsstelle (Experimental Station), its sphere of tasks, organisation, working methods, and results. All important aspects are covered hereunder without, however, according too much emphasis to technical detail.

Preliminary Remarks
This report consists of my recollections as an eye-witness, supported by notebook jottings and flight logbook entries, expanded and enlarged using information from former colleagues and assisted by critical knowledge of recent literature. Such a retrospective portrayal cannot take place without taking into account the ambivalent circumstances at that time. The recollections, nevertheless, do not lack a certain

Flight navigation chart of the Pomeranian Baltic coastline showing the location of air-launch and easterly flight-path of missiles from the Versuchsstelle Peenemünde.

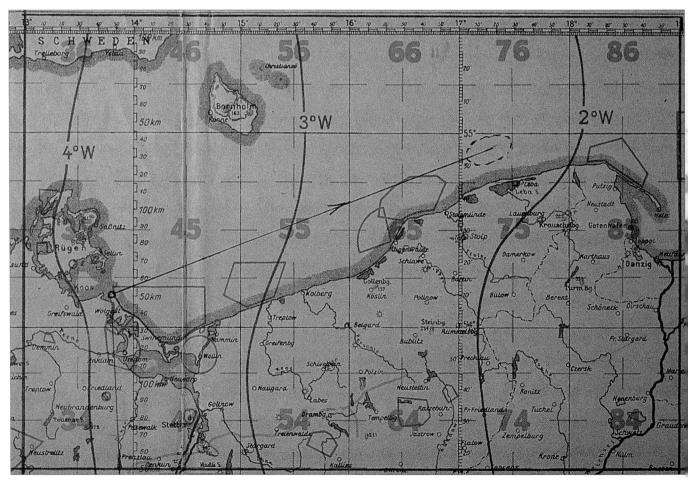

Right: *Peenemünde and its surroundings.*

Bottom: *Dr. Wernher von Braun (left) and Dr.-Ing. Walter Dornberger (right).*

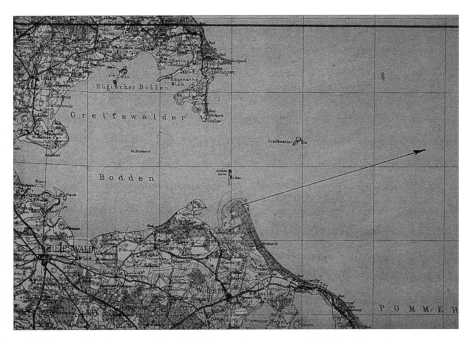

personal touch. This Versuchsstelle was, like all other comparable or similar establishments, a product of this period which determined the path to be followed.

Departure to Peenemünde
Following an RLM initiative, I undertook a three-year course of study to qualify as a 'Flugbaumeister' which was linked upon conclusion to a university Dipl.-Ing. examination. When I commenced my service at the DVL in Berlin-Adlershof in 1936, nobody among my circle of friends and relations entertained the least suspicion of an approaching military conflict. Rather, the viewpoint prevailed that the build-up of an indigenous German Luftwaffe then in train, was intended to bring about parity with those of neighbouring European countries.

The second half of the year 1938 was earmarked for the continuation of my flying training to qualify as an engineer-pilot in the Flight Department of the DVL in Brunswick-Volkenrode. Surprisingly, on 31st August 1938, this Flight Department was temporarily closed. As it turned out, the reason for this was the so-called 'Sudeten-crisis' which had cast its shadow and resulted in the addition of the Sudetenland to the German Reich in accordance with the Munich Agreement of 29th September 1938. On 1st October 1938, German troops marched into the territory.

During September, I was detailed to report to the RLM (German Air Ministry) in Berlin. On 15th September 1938, I met there Dipl.-Ing. Werner Hartz, who suggested I should visit the then strictly secret Luftwaffe Experimental Establishment Peenemünde-West on the island of Usedom, which careerwise, could be extraordinarily interesting for me. It should also be possible there for me to prepare for my second state examination as a 'Flugbaumeister'. Upon my visit there, I found a whole group of very competent, mainly young, specialists, and extraordinarily favourable assumptions with regard to future working conditions. They attracted me equally as well as the geography of the location – a former nature reservation at the northern tip of the island, surrounded by the Stettiner Haff (lagoon), the Peene estuary, the Greifswalder Bodden and the Baltic sea, together with excellent recreational opportunities.

I commenced my service in Peenemünde on 11th December 1938 and already on the first evening, I came to know the currently active Flugbaumeister Gerd Reins

and Johannes Fischer, as well as Dr. Wernher von Braun, head of development of the HVA Peenemünde-West. Thus began some of the most interesting years of my career.

Spheres of Activity in Peenemünde
The development and experimental tasks in Peenemünde were oriented into two basically different spheres of activity:
a) Devices which primarily followed a ballistic trajectory, eg, projectiles.
b) Devices which primarily flew like an aircraft.

a) Preliminary Experimental Station Kummersdorf-West
The development of devices which followed a ballistic trajectory were primarily the prerogative of the HWA (Army Ordnance Office). It was there, at the beginning of the 1930s that Captain Dipl.-Ing. Walter Dornberger had already in 1932 taken pains to bring about some kind of order to the multifarious activities of the so-called rocket pioneers and enthusiasts. He wanted exact measurements to be carried out on an engineering basis so that the capabilities of a rocket propulsion unit could be consistently examined and tested. His eventual aim was the development of a new weapon which – unlike artillery – would not fall under the range limitation imposed by the Treaty of Versailles at the end of World War One.

The tests promoted by the HWA initially took place on the Army-owned proving grounds in Kummersdorf-West, south of Berlin. Among the several individuals of the team engaged there were Walter Thiel, Rudolf Nebel, Prof. Hermann Oberth, and Wernher von Braun. Soon, however, a new location was sought from where it would

become possible to achieve longer ranges.

In his book 'V2 – The Shot Into Space' published in 1952, Walter Dornberger has described this in detail, hence, the preliminary tests and further stages of development which finally led to the A 4 rocket, will not be elaborated here.

b) Preliminary Experimental Station Neuhardenberg
The work of the HWA in Kummersdorf-West was followed with increasing interest by the RLM where for some time rocket propulsion problems were also tackled, but for quite different purposes than was the case in Kummersdorf – namely as an aircraft propulsion unit. With the aid of rocket-assistance [RATO units], it would facilitate or even make possible heavily-laden aircraft to take-off from the then customary grass airstrips. For this purpose, the firm of Hellmuth Walter KG, Kiel (HWK), had submitted proposals and developed the corresponding devices.

Left: *Observing the fourth test flight at Neuhardenberg of an He 112 equipped with a von Braun (HWA) rocket motor and piloted by Erich Warsitz.*

Bottom left:
Test Pilot Erich Warsitz.

Bottom right:
On 18th June 1940, Flugbaumeister Dipl.-Ing. Gerd Reins met with a fatal accident in the He 112R.

The first flight tests took place from mid 1937 onwards from a small field airstrip near Neuhardenberg, some 60km (37 miles) east of Berlin. Test pilot was Erich Warsitz who had come from the German Commercial Pilots School in Stettin to the Luftwaffe E-Stelle Rechlin and had volunteered his services to the RLM as a pilot for new types of flight tests.

Warsitz was at first familiarised in Kummersdorf with the trials undertaken on liquid-propellant rocket motors, as conducted by the HWA under the leadership of von Braun.

The principle involved the use of liquid oxygen and ethyl alcohol. Combustion took place at very high temperatures of around 2200°C, which the materials of the combustion chamber initially did not always withstand. Von Braun had proposed to the RLM Technisches Amt (Technical Office), responsible for development tasks, that the rocket motor under development in Kummersdorf be also employed as a propulsion unit for aircraft or as a RATO unit. To enable preparation for flight testing, Prof. Ernst Heinkel had placed the fuselage of an He 112 single-seat fighter at their disposal. As a result of several mishaps experienced during static ground tests, Heinkel's gen-

erosity had to be called upon several times. Warsitz, who had good connections with Heinkel, commenced his activity at the beginning of 1936 at Kummersdorf, but no flights were able to take place from here. In the spring of 1937, therefore, the von Braun group, together with the Heinkel technicians concerned with the use of the rocket motor for aircraft, relocated to Neuhardenberg where the necessary preparatory work for flight testing had meanwhile been completed.

In the meantime, in mid 1936, Dipl.-Ing Uvo Pauls from the E-Stelle 'See' in Travemünde, was transferred to take over the 'Referat für Raketentriebwerke' (Expert Advisory Group for Rocket Propulsion Units) incorporated in the RLM where he would be responsible for erection of the Neuhardenberg airfield. A visit to Kummersdorf made him familiar with the results of development that had been achieved thus far.

In Neuhardenberg, the static tests that had begun in Kummersdorf with the von Braun rocket motor on an He 112, were continued. Prior to the first flight, when a final static test of rocket motor ignition was conducted by Warsitz himself from the cockpit, the aircraft exploded. Heinkel again donated a flyable He 112 for further tests.

Finally, at the end of May 1937, the first flight with rocket power took place. It ended, however, with the rocket motor on fire and a belly landing, but Warsitz himself remained uninjured.

The von Braun rocket motor for aircraft was continually developed further until successful flights could be carried out, but it nevertheless remained a risky undertaking. When testing was resumed – despite serious doubts – from 1938 onwards in Peenemünde-West, Flugbaumeister Gerd Reins suffered a fatal accident on 18th June 1940. On his test flight, the rocket combustion chamber burned through; a hot gas stream emanating sideways melted the He 112 elevator control rods whereupon the aircraft crashed out of control.

Further development of a rocket motor based on the Army-employed liquid oxygen and alcohol combination was rejected by the Luftwaffe as it appeared to be too dangerous for use in aircraft.

The propulsion system developed by Hellmuth Walter, Kiel, proved itself to be surprisingly reliable. It was based on the use of highly concentrated 80% hydrogen peroxide as oxygen supplier, which was decomposed in a combustion chamber with a catalyst, calcium permanganate. A decomposition temperature of a little over 500°C was attained, which became known as the 'Kaltes Verfahren' (cold system) and which could easily be withstood by the combustion chamber materials.

Hellmuth Walter proposed this system to the RLM for use as a rocket drive for aircraft or as a RATO unit. Initial flights with an He 72, an Fw 56 and an He 112 were so successful that the HWK was commissioned to develop the 109-500 assisted take-off unit. It was tested from 1937 onwards in Neuhardenberg on an He 111. Again, Warsitz was the test pilot. The jettisonable RATO units were mounted beneath the wings on both outer sides of the He 111 undercarriage wheels; they each delivered an auxiliary thrust of 500kg (1102lb) for a duration of 30 seconds. At burnout, the RATO units were jettisoned mechanically by the pilot, descended to earth by parachute, were refilled, and re-used on the next operation. The fact that these RATO units could be used on up to 60 consecutive occasions without any problems encountered, testified to the safety of the Walter system and robust design of the devices.

In Neuhardenberg, more than 100 test flights were carried out with the He 111E, partly at high overload without noticeable problems. Towards the end of 1937, a status of maturity had been attained in the development of these RATO units, so that the tents in Neuhardenberg could be dismantled. Further development and testing was then continued in Peenemünde-West.

Review of the Site Erection and End in Peenemünde

As in Kummersdorf-West, the limited possibilities available in Neuhardenberg were not commensurate with the expected tasks of development and experimentation.

Already in late autumn 1935, the area at the northern tip of the island of Usedom near the Peenemünder Haken (Hook) was proposed to fulfil these tasks – a lonely, largely undisturbed nature preservation area in the neighbourhood of the small fishing village of Peenemünde. The Peenemünde area was undoubtedly excellently suited for its intended purposes and could be well guarded. Here, the possibility existed, despite difficult subsoil, to erect extensive installations which – at least initially – could remain largely undetected.

In a Chefbesprechung (conference of leading figures) on 2nd April 1936 between the RLM and the HWA, it was jointly agreed by dividing the expenses, to erect a Luftwaffe and Army experimental establishment. On that same day the estate, owned by the Wolgast community, was purchased for RM 750,000 and thus enabled the erection of both experimental centres to commence.

Laboratories, test installations, as well as generous housing quarters, were erected in rapid succession in accordance with typical Luftwaffe guidelines. Already in early summer 1937, the first buildings of the Army Experimental Establishment and the first housing units intended for use by personnel of both experimental establishments could be occupied. For the large Prüfstände (Test Stands) and test installations, the concept took into account future needs such as had been realised nowhere else up until then and which were completed in a surprisingly short space of time. Out of Peenemünde was created a precedent for the erection of large installations that followed very much later abroad, eg, in Cape Canaveral in the USA.

It was only after the completion of a connecting road built over metres-deep swampland that construction of important installations could be started at Peenemünde-West at the end of July 1937. By the end of the year, a considerable amount of work had been completed. For that portion of the area reserved for the airfield, which lay only a little above sea-level, a considerable amount of earth had to be moved by dredging from the Peene estuary. Peenemünde-West commenced operations on 1st April 1938 only two years after the agreement of 2nd April 1936. At this juncture, Peenemünde-East had already been in operation for some months. Even when further expansion of both experimental establishments required more time for completion, it nevertheless displayed an excellent performance on the part of the construction groups and leadership, and set an example of how efficiently and swiftly decisions could be realized when largely unbureaucratic methods could be adopted.

One has to view these and the later development of Peenemünde in the light of the dynamics of that time. Following the Machtergreifung (Assumption of Power) by the NSDAP (National Socialist German Workers Party) in 1933, rapid steps were taken to further the military preparedness of the nation. The armament limitations imposed by the Treaty of Versailles were eliminated. In 1935, conscription was introduced. In 1936, the Rheinland was re-occupied and in Berlin, the world-famous Olympic Games were held. One has to understand that these years especially, constituted a time of national revival and engendered a high level of enthusiasm.

The circumstance that the experimental establishments in Peenemünde stood under the utmost secrecy, was in several respects of considerable value: on the one hand even high-ranking visitors – with exceptions – could be prevented from visiting the location, and on the other hand – at least during the early years – unwelcome and disruptive external influences, particularly from Party circles, could be kept well away from the experimental establishments.

It was a particular characteristic of the Peenemünde experimental establishments that a circle of mostly young, knowledgeable, and enthusiastic individuals could work on programmes which evidently lay on the border of the then known technical and scientific possibilities, and in all probability, promised to open the door to an interesting future. Only a few felt the presentiment of an approaching war.

Whatever could in any way promote the work of test and development, was approved without extensive formality. It was thus possible to bring a considerable number of projects to functional efficiency

An Fw 56 'Stösser' is being prepared (1937) for the installation of a Walter (HWK) rocket motor at Neuhardenberg.

RATO trials were conducted with an He 111 at maximum load. Test pilot Erich Warsitz is at the extreme right of the group, not all of whom flew in the aircraft.

Entry portal to the Peenemünde Siedlung (housing area).

The Peenemünde housing area with its street leading to the shore.

Entrance point to the Luftwaffe Versuchsstelle Peenemünde-West showing the central office building.

Workshops and hangars in Peenemünde-West.

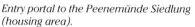

and partly even to operational readiness despite the lack of precedent and experience in an astonishingly short space of time.

Whilst Peenemünde-East took care of development, manufacture, experimentation and testing largely on its own grounds, Peenemünde-West worked, like other Luftwaffe E-Stellen, on the 'contract-out' principle. Following determination of the aim of development by the responsible departments of the RLM Technisches Amt (Technical Office), industrial firms, often in competition, were commissioned to carry out development and provide proof of the functional efficiency of their development. The task of the test and experimental establishments thereafter was to check out the functional capabilities and establish the principal suitability for the eventual user, or alternatively, to put forward suggestions for alteration and further development. This regularly led to close contact with industry and hence to an accelerated realisation or else to conclusion of a development task.

The immediate neighbourhood of Peenemünde-East and Peenemünde-West under a joint local administration was characterised by an extensive close co-operation which was promoted by reason of related tasks of a scientific and technical nature. Over the years, however, there were occasions of petty jealousy. Such was the case for example, concerning the differing judgements regarding the method of operation and cost analyses of the later V-1 versus V-2. In general, however, it turned out to be a thoroughly peaceful and successful 'co-existence' and symbiosis.

During the period of the most intensive activity – 1942/1943 – there were more than 12,000 people employed in Peenemünde, of whom around 1,000 belonged to Peenemünde-West. Numerous test and experimental groups from industry and the services temporarily enlarged these numbers. The deficit in specialists, increasing noticeably during the erection and later, expansion stages, were partly compensated with the support of the Armed Forces personnel offices through recall from the frontline of technically qualified soldiers, who were housed in command quarters. The call-up of team members during the

A part of the Army Heeresversuchsstelle Peenemünde-East after the large Royal Air Force bombing raid on 17th/18th August 1943.

war years on the other hand, again caused gaps which could only partly be provisionally filled.

As a result of the well-prepared and widespread British air raid on Peenemünde-East with 596 bombers during the full-moon night of 17/18th August 1943, activities were appreciably disturbed but not interrupted. 40 aircraft failed to return. [1,2]

The housing area and foreign workers' barracks were almost completely destroyed in this night attack in which 735 people lost their lives.

Daylight raids aimed primarily at Peenemünde-West by large American bomber formations followed on 18th July, 2nd August and 25th August 1944, but despite more extensive damage, did not substantially hinder the continuation of activities. Peenemünde-East, however, relocated a large part of its activities, especially manufacture of the large A4 rocket, to central Germany.

Finally, in April 1945, Peenemünde-West relocated almost completely to the Wesermünde-Weddewarden air base near Bremerhaven, where the end of hostilities was awaited. Only a few members of the experimental establishment personnel, together with their families, remained behind in neighbouring villages. Laboratory, test and

experimental installations, were destroyed prior to the arrival of Soviet forces. Buildings suitable for living accommodation, including the administration building were, however, left largely undamaged.

Following this survey of the 'Birth and Evolution' of the Luftwaffe experimental establishment Peenemünde-West, the organisation, tasks, and projects of the E-Stelle will now be considered.

Organisation and Working Methods of the Luftwaffe Versuchsstelle Peenemünde-West

The Luftwaffe Versuchsstelle Peenemünde-West, later renamed the Luftwaffe E-Stelle (Experimental Establishment) Peenemünde-West, and finally 'E-Stelle Karlshagen' was just seven months in being when I commenced my period of service there. Head of the Versuchsstelle was Uvo Pauls, who had previously been the Referent für Raketentriebwerke (Specialist for rocket propulsion units) in the RLM Technisches Amt (Technical Office).

At my introductory visit, he informed me about the two most important tasks on which practically all the experimental groups and related areas on which the Versuchsstelle were more or less involved, namely:

The entrance portal to the Peenemünde housing area after the RAF bombing raid of 17/18th August 1943.

- All problem areas connected with rocket propulsion units for aircraft.
- All problem areas connected with the development and testing of unmanned, self-guided or remote-controlled missiles with or without reaction propulsion.

These two main task areas were technically related to several individual tasks, whose examination were each critical towards development and testing of devices themselves, as for example the chemistry of fuels used, remote- and guidance-control installations, ground equipment and so forth. The Versuchsstelle was thus correspondingly so divided. The separation into various development and specialist groups followed basically the way that other, already existing Luftwaffe E-Stellen were organised, such as Rechlin or Travemünde, with which Peenemünde-West occasionally closely co-operated.

The Chief Office was that of the GL or Generalluftzeugmeister (Chief of Procurement and Supply) under which came the RLM Technical Office (GL/C), together with its Development Departments (C-E). Generalluftzeugmeister and Chef des Technischen Amtes (Head of the Technical Office) until his suicide on 17th November 1941 was Generaloberst Ernst Udet. Thereafter, these offices were assumed by the Staatssekretär der Luftfahrt im RLM (RLM State Secretary for Aviation) Generalfeldmarschall Erhard Milch (see RLM organisations chart on page 220).

Uvo Pauls, the first head of Peenemünde-West, had already gathered experience at the E-Stelle 'See' in Travemünde. He succeeded in establishing a model of planning in co-operation with the Luftwaffe leaders responsible for construction, which henceforth fulfilled all required expectations. He also succeeded in winning individuals of proven ability who had been deputed from other E-Stellen to carry out the duties of a high-performance air base. The engineers

Albert Plath as Head of Works and Hans Waas as Head of Repairs were his reliable supports, as also Inspector Lange for general administration.

Daily tasks were co-ordinated in the morning Group Leader conferences held under the chairmanship of the Head of the Versuchsstelle. Above the Head of the Versuchsstelle, insofar as no particular expert matters were involved, was obtaining the agreement of the Army Versuchsstelle in Peenemünde-East in relation to general station/location matters and the Army authorities established for this purpose, such as for example, matters concerning the Works railways and electrical power.

In 1941 the office of a 'Kommando der E-Stellen' (Test Establishment Detachment) was established, initially subordinate to the RLM GL/C Technisches Amt. (Technical Office). Oberst Edgar Petersen was charged with the leadership of this Detachment. From this time on, Peenemünde-West was subject to this Kdo.d.E. on matters of discipline, whereas the technical co-operation with the GL/C Development Departments continued as before.

The disciplinary subordination of Peenemünde-West under a Kdo.d.E. did not, however, remain without consequences for the civilian leadership of the Versuchsstelle, which had held office up to 1942:

Following a test flight on 1st September 1942, I was engaged in recording the flight duration in the Flight Operations Office of the Versuchsstelle, when a Bf 108 Taifun (Typhoon) landed, a Ritterkreuz-decorated and heavily war-disabled Major (Otto Stams) climbed out and shortly thereafter introduced himself at the Operations Office with the words 'Heil Hitler, I am the new Commander'. The civilian head who held this office up until that moment and who had meanwhile been promoted to Flieger-Oberstabsingenieur, Uvo Pauls, had not been informed of this change at all.

Despite an evident lack of technical knowledge, Otto Stams undoubtedly took pains to understand and consider the peculiarities of a technically-oriented E-Stelle. Because of his human characteristics, co-operation ran in the main without problems. Additionally, the Commander of the E-Stelle, Oberst Edgar Petersen, took pains to come to terms with his new position.

The hoped-for tightening and accelerating the winding-up of experimental tasks by the Oberkommando der Luftwaffe (Luftwaffe Supreme Command) under military leadership largely did not materialise. There surfaced instead numerous leadership problems, competence arguments and expertise discord, because the time and means for the technical solution of new types of problems which were connected with the risk that mishaps occurred without visibly traceable causes, could not be 'commanded'.

Over the years, and especially as a result of the war, considerable changes took place in the organisation and subordination of various offices and functions, but will not be mentioned here in detail.

Otto Stams, promoted in the meantime to Oberstleutnant, remained as Commander and Head of the E-Stelle until the end of 1944. He was succeeded by Major Karl Henkelmann who headed Peenemünde-West until the end of the war, including the period of its relocation to Wesermünde-Weddewarden.

For the maintenance of contact with the RLM GL/C and its C-E Development Departments, working meetings took place each Monday morning in Berlin at which, under the chairmanship of the Generalluftzeugmeister, the heads of Development Departments of the various E-Stellen were in attendance. Following establishment of the Kdo.d.E., these Monday conferences concentrated on matters agreed between the GL/C-E and the Kdo.d.E.

Peenemünde-West was largely involved with project conception of the Development Departments, and by reason of preparation of test installations, was involved at an early date on developments involving industry participation.

The Versuchsstelle had therefore, besides technical equipment testing, yet another important general task:

The concepts and equipment developed by industrial firms could only be tested by them in a limited capacity. The firms mostly did not possess their own airfields and

Buildings and Installations in Peenemünde-West

1 W 25 Accommodation for engineers, officers and visitors.
2 Police Precinct.
3 Sentry-post.
4 West station with waiting room.
5 W 21 Administration building.
6 W 22 Vehicle department.
7 W 26 Acceptance and Despatch centre.
8 Barracks.
9 T-L1 Fuel storage for special fuels.
10 Barracks.
11 T-L2 Fuel storage for special fuels.
12 W 7 Engine Test-bed: Prüfstand 1
13 W 15 Engine Test-bed: Prüfstand 2
14 W 20 Junkers hangars with fixed aircraft fuel depot
(Total area 1,400m² = 15,069ft²)
15 Three barrack buildings for laboratories and offices.
16 W 3 Large hangar of total area ca. 5,000m² (53,818ft²).
17 W 23a Air-conditioning installation, Vibration Table,
Weapons and Tools distribution centre.
18 W 23 Air Traffic Control, Fire Brigade, Laboratories
and Workshops.
19 W 4 Heating station.
20 W 5 Locksmiths, Blacksmiths, Tailors and
Examination Group.
21 W 2 Hangars.
22 Wooden hangar for Me 163 test aircraft.

23 W 1 The Reins-Hangar.
24 The Schneise Measurement building.
25 Large assembly hangar for the Fi 103 test vehicles.
26 Barracks for Training and Lectures.
27 Facility Barracks
28 Storage Barracks
29 W 19 Canteen 'Dörres' with cinema.
30 Air raid bunker

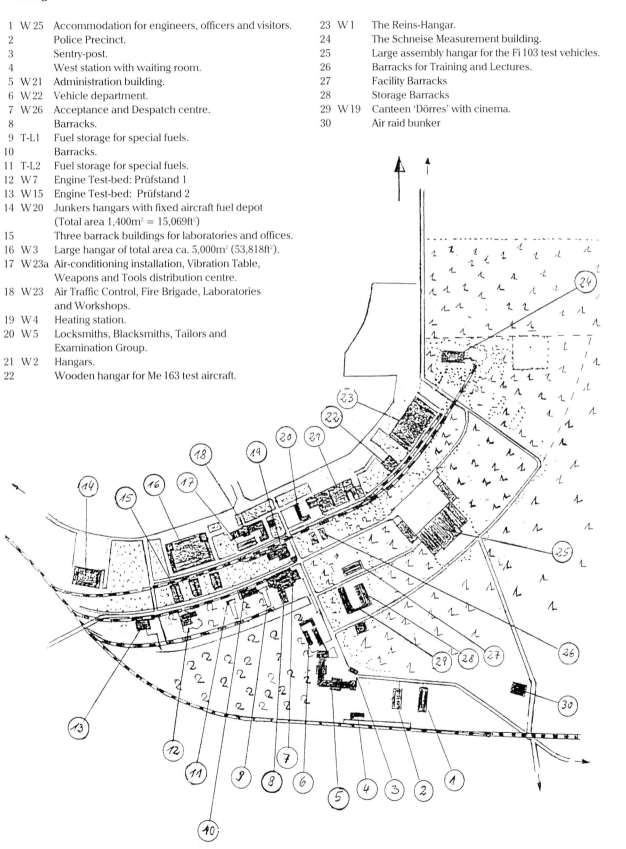

flightpath/trajectory measuring equipment, and for example, had no suitable grounds for air-launched tests. Furthermore, the troops were dependent from a military point of view upon the development results and upon competent support. Additionally, the Versuchsstelle required on their part, for the testing of industry-manufactured equipment, the participation of industry and co-operation with the military departments in order to take into account their possibilities and proposals. Out of this, there developed an extraordinarily close, and for all sides involved, fruitful co-operation of the participating groups.

The Versuchsstelle thus played, by reason of its acknowledged possibilities, a stimulating, co-ordinating and system-integrating function, such as no other group could exercise in a comparable manner.

Organisation of the Versuchsstelle and Delegation of Task Areas
A central point available for all experimental groups was the Flugleitung (Air Traffic Control) responsible for operation of the aircraft parks of the Versuchsstelle. Up to the end of 1941, Erich Warsitz was Head of the Flugleitung. He was succeeded by Gerhard Rackenius, who headed the Flugleitung until the end of the war. The individual test groups largely determined the test flights which took place, in agreement with the Flugleitung. The weather station, reporting to the Flugleitung in connection with current atmospheric conditions, was of special importance during test flying. It exceeded the standards of a normal weather station, since the atmospheric conditions mostly played a part in the evaluation results of flight tests and measurement criteria.

In keeping with the expected tasks, the Versuchsstelle was divided into the following experimental groups:
E2 Aircraft and missile systems with rocket propulsion.
E3 Powerplants and fuels.
E4 Radio and remotely-guided installations.
E5 Equipment: Energy supply, control installations, photographic section, measurement systems.
E7 Jettison installations, target and target-practice equipment.
E8 Ground installations.

Test Section E2
Following my arrival in Peenemünde-West, I was deputed to the E2 Test Section and as a specialist, took over the 'missile' task area. Head of the Test Section was Dipl.-Ing. Werner Hartz, who came from the DFS Darmstadt, and following a period of activity in the RLM, came to the Versuchsstelle in July 1938. In March 1940, he transferred to the Messerschmitt AG in Augsburg in

order to work on tasks related to the development of rocket-powered tailless aircraft. In his place came the engineer and pilot Hermann Kröger from the E-Stelle Rechlin, until I myself in 1944 assumed the position of Head of this Test Section until the end of the war.

The extent of the tasks encompassed the following:
- Continuation of flight testing of high-thrust RATO units.
- Development and test of load-carrying parachutes.
- Testing and accompanying development of the DFS 194 and Me 163 rocket-powered tailless aircraft.
- Progressive development whilst testing of self-guided and remote-controlled missiles.
- Flight testing of carrier aircraft following their conversion for operations with missiles.
- Supervision of the conversions by the industrial firms.

Furthermore, it was the task to carry out test and experimental flights in which special technical problems came to the fore. The E2's extent of tasks included taking care of the military troop Test Detachments which, with successfully-running technical tasks, had to take over preparations for field operations. These detachments were partly attached to E2 up to the point where they moved to their intended operational airfields.

The ever-increasing workload over the years led in 1943 to separation of the Hs 117 anti-aircraft rocket and the Fi 103 projects. For the former, an additional Experimental Group was established, which Hermann Kröger took over, and for the latter, the 'Experimental Group Temme' was established in May 1943, responsible for all matters dealing with testing and progression to operational readiness, as far as it was possible to carry out in Peenemünde.

Test Section E3
Head of the Section was initially Fliegerstabsing. Hillermann, who was succeeded at the beginning of 1940 by Fliegerstabsing. Heinrich Weigand. The latter came from the E-Stelle Rechlin and led the section until the end of the war.

The task area encompassed all questions which dealt with propulsion, in particular the rocket units for aircraft and missiles. To it belonged also continuation of technical testing of RATO units, the erection and management of the necessary Test Stands for such powerplants, and examination and association with rocket fuels, right up to the testing of solid fuels such as those used in RATO units for the Hs 117 Schmetterling (Butterfly) or Enzian (Gentian) anti-aircraft missiles. In this area there was particularly close co-operation with the representatives

seconded by the industrial firms for the purpose of providing support for the tests, above all, those of the Hellmuth Walter Werke and the Schmidding firm.

Test Section E4
The task area of this Section encompassed almost the whole range of radio communication. It was responsible for the parallel-running development of remote-control systems, radio communication of all types and including television as a basis of implementing commands for the remote steering of the missile under test. In the last years of the war, testing of automatic fuses was also undertaken, which as proximity fuses for remotely-guided rocket-missiles carried by fighters, promised to be of high significance. Head of Section E4 from the beginning of its activities until the end of the war was Fliegerstabsing. Dr. Josef Dantscher who was transferred from the E-Stelle 'See' in Travemünde to Peenemünde, and had at his disposal a staff of highly-qualified colleagues. Principal partners from industry were: Telefunken, the Stassfurter Rundfunk Gesellschaft (Broadcasting Company), the Reichspost Forschungsanstalt (Research Institute), the Fernseh GmbH (Television Co Ltd) the Siemens & Halske AG, and the Donauländische Apparatebaugesellschaft (Danubian Apparatus Manufacturing Company) in Vienna.

Test Section E5
The most important components of missiles and aircraft are the power supply and control systems, which can be electrically, hydraulically, or pneumatically driven. Even when basic principles are known, the necessary devices have to be configured to fit the limited space available and be developed anew. Dr. Arthur Späth, in co-operation with industry, carried out this task with considerable success. His chief partners were the Luftfahrtgerätewerk (Aviation Instrument Works) in Hakenfelde, the Anschütz company in Kiel, and the Askania-Werke AG in Berlin.

Head of the Test Section from 1st April 1938 was at first Fliegerstabsing. Dr.-Ing. Gerhard Hengst who came from the Measurement Section at the E-Stelle 'See' in Travemünde, being succeeded from 15th September 1944 until the end of the war by Fliegerstabsing. Alfred Fritz.

This Section was also responsible for measurements conducted by cinetheodolites, which with eight stations spread over a 24km (15 miles) length of coastline played an important role in flight test evaluation, since unmanned automatically guided or remote-controlled missiles did not often fly without mishap during the development and testing phase. They crashed and disappeared in each case into

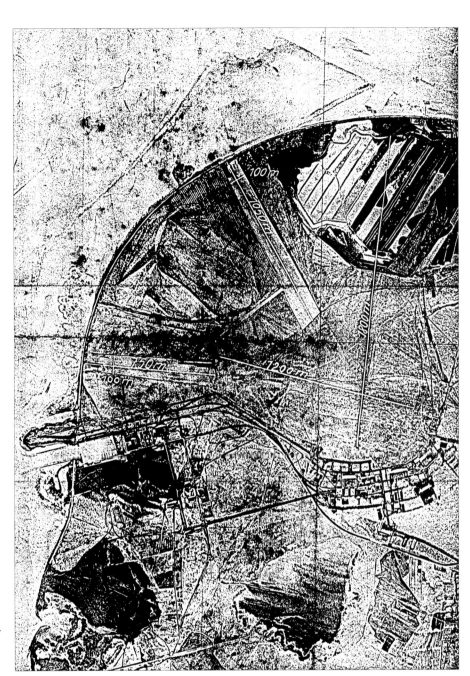

The Versuchsstelle-West seen from the air by the British on 19th August 1943, the day after the large-scale RAF bombing raid.

the Baltic, so that the causes of the crash or failures could not be established from examination of the equipment itself. It was only from the in-flight behaviour that certain functional failures could be determined. Each missile release from a carrier aircraft was therefore not only filmed and observed from an accompanying aircraft, but was also tracked from the measurement station mostly until the end of the flight.

Measurement results were recorded cartographically such that at each point of time the location, altitude, direction of flight and speed, were thus known. This system of measurement was also partly used for the A4 trials carried out from Peenemünde-East, for which Fliegerstabsing. Dr. Reissig and Dr. Francke were responsible, as also for the evaluation results.

Finally, there was the subordinate Photographic and Film Section, of considerable importance since it was responsible for the documentation and creation of training films for the instruction of servicemen in the field, who had to be made aware of significant procedures in operations with missiles.

Test Section E7

Whilst Test Section E2 was responsible for co-ordinating the testing of all 'flying' missiles, Section E7 was responsible for the 'free-falling' but nevertheless guidable bombs such as the SD 1400X, which will be described later. This guided bomb was conceived by Dr. Max Kramer of the DVL and manufactured by the firm of Rheinmetall-Borsig. In order to simulate the release and guidance phase, he had developed an ingenious target-training device which was not only used within the framework of trials carried out at Peenemünde, but was later used in military service for training the bomb-aimers. Head of Section E7 until war's end was Dr. Hans Bender whose responsibility included bombsights such as the Lotfe 7 installed in the carrier aircraft, and the ignition systems and installations in both aircraft and missiles. The welfare of personnel who were trained as firemen was also one of its functions. From 1944 onwards, Dr. Bender was also made familiar with the X4 'Jägerrakete' rocket missile carried by fighters, and the X7 anti-tank 'Rotkäppchen' (Little Red Riding Hood) missile. The latter, however, did not reach the testing stage in Peenemünde.

Test Section E8

The use of aircraft requires the availability of ground installations such as fuelling, engine starter equipment and loading apparatus for bombs or missiles. For missiles, special ground installations are necessary, especially when they are surface-launched as is the case with anti-aircraft missiles or the longer-range Fi 103 flying-bomb. Supervising the development of such ground installations produced by industry and their testing in Peenemünde in connection with missile trials right up to their use by service troops was the responsibility of Section E8. Head of this Section initially was Dipl-Ing. Gümbel, who was succeeded after 1942 by Fliegerstabsing. Dr. Erich Wondratschek.

Experimental and Testing Functions

The activities of the Luftwaffe Versuchsstelle are now described by way of examples, without entering into specific details of the aircraft, missiles, or other items that are mentioned.

RATO Units

From the very beginning of work carried out in Peenemünde, activities were concentrated at first on continuing work that had started at the predecessor experimental station in Neuhardenberg, ie, the testing and further development of RATO units for aircraft as well as aircraft rocket motors as installed in the He 112.

The 109-500 assisted take-off unit had already proved itself to be extremely reli-

Above: *The HWK 'hot' RATO unit equipped with a parachute pack to avoid damage to the unit upon landing following fuel burnout.*

Top left: *An He 111 on take-off, equipped with two HWK 'hot' RATO units, one under each wing.*

Left: *High-ranking visit to Peenemünde. From left to right – Uvo Pauls, head of the Versuchsstelle Peenemünde-West, Generalbauinspektor Albert Speer and Oberst Walter Dornberger of the HWA.*

Centre: *Unsuccessful take-off of the He 116 on its long-distance record flight attempt of 27th July 1939 when an underwing RATO unit became unexpectedly dislodged.*

Bottom: *Heinkel Works pilot Rolf Jöster after landing in Peenemünde-West on 1st August 1939 at the conclusion of his World Record 10,000km (6,210 miles) duration flight in the He 116.*

able, so that preparations for service use could be considered. Series production maturity was attained in 1939 and almost all the aircraft earmarked to use RATO units such as the He 111, Ju 88, Do 18 and others up to the Ar 234, were equipped with the necessary auxiliary installations. A suspension mechanism for the RATO unit which was jettisoned after fuel burnout, a rocket ignition system with automatic cut-off switch and an emergency jettison capability, were all envisaged. Especial credit was earned by Ing. Wilhelm Dettmerling from Test Section E3 for his supervision of trials and troop familiarisation. Several thousand take-offs with these RATO units were carried out during active service with frontline units of the Luftwaffe in all theatres of occupied Europe without experiencing any serious problems which could be attributed to these RATO units. It is interesting to note that later on, the Gigant (Giant) transport glider developed by the Messerschmitt AG and equipped with 8 RATO units, was used with success on the Eastern Front.

Heinkel for instance, had intended to use the He 116, developed as a mail-carrying aircraft, to set up a world long-distance record. Due to its high flying weight as a result of the auxiliary fuel tanks installed, the aircraft was to take off from Peenemünde-West with the aid of HWK RATO units. The first take-off attempt took place on 27th July 1939 with the He 116 'Rostock' (D-ARFD), but after rocket ignition, one of the units suspended beneath the port wing broke loose from its mounting, which caused the main undercarriage and inner motor propeller to suffer damage. Following a further take-off attempt on 29th July with a replacement He 116 aircraft when one engine failed, another take-off attempt finally followed with the He 116 'Rostock' at 0605hrs on 30th July with all four RATO units functioning successfully. Pilot was the Heinkel Werkspilot Rolf Jöster. After a duration of more than 49 hours covering a flying distance of around 10,500km (6,525 miles), the attempt had to be broken off at 0709hrs on 1st August due to a fuel-feed problem. The aircraft landed once more at Peenemünde and with the remaining fuel on board, could have flown a total distance of some 14,400km ((8,950 miles). A short time later, this record was surpassed by Japan.

It had already been established in 1938 that the previously-used 'cold' RATO units of 500kg (1,102 lb) thrust would not in the long run be adequate. The HWK therefore developed a more powerful RATO unit – the 109-501, which likewise had 80% hydrogen peroxide decomposed by a liquid catalyst, but to which petroleum was added. As a result, decomposition not only took place in the rocket combustion chamber, but resulted in combustion at a much higher temperature of 2,200°C and higher thrust. This 'hot' RATO unit, depending on combustion chamber layout, delivered a thrust of 1,000kg (2,205 lb) for a duration of 43 seconds, or alternatively, 1,500kg (3,307 lb) thrust for 30 seconds. These newer RATO units were also tested on the Prüfstände (static Test Stands) of Section E3, followed by a series of take-off tests with aircraft. I can still recall very well these RATO take-off tests with various types of aircraft which were not without mishap. On one take-off with 'hot' rocket units mounted beneath an He 111 on 28th November 1939, the star-

board RATO unit exploded just at the moment when I was beginning to climb after lift-off from the runway. I was, however, able to land the aircraft safely again, but the fuselage, the wing undersides, and landing flaps were so badly damaged that the aircraft was out of service for a while. Thanks to the safety switch that had been introduced, the port RATO unit was able to be switched off immediately.

Testing a rocket motor on an aircraft was in any case much more dangerous than on a static test stand situated behind thick concrete walls. Hence, with the majority of tests conducted, the question of safety became paramount. Even so, in many instances there was still a high risk involved.

Noteworthy is the fact that the more powerful RATO units gave the pilots at the start of rocket power operation, a 'lifting' acceleration which became more pronounced as a result of the climbing attitude. Very often, an altitude of 800 to 900m (2,625 to 2,950ft) was attained at the end of the runway. It was, however, necessary to go over into horizontal flight prior to RATO unit burnout.

Heinkel He 176 Rocket Aircraft

Ernst Heinkel's receptiveness to new technical innovations and for fast aircraft in particular, led in the mid 1930s to contact with engineers working on rocket propulsion development. He commissioned his well-known aircraft designers, the brothers Walter and Siegfried Günter, to design a small high-speed aircraft to be powered by a 'cold' Walter rocket motor. Initial trials with this type of powerplant mounted inside an aircraft fuselage had already taken place in Neuhardenberg parallel to the already-mentioned tests with the He 112. This then led to the concept of the He 176 high-speed research aircraft in close co-operation with

its eventual test pilot Erich Warsitz, the Heinkel team led by Walter Künzel, and Asmund Barthelsen of the HWK.

The aircraft was conceived to accommodate the stature of Erich Warsitz who had to be positioned semi-reclining, like stepping into a shoe, inside the clear-vision cockpit capsule. For pilot safety reasons, the whole capsule was made jettisonable whereby, following its release and retardation with the aid of a capsule parachute, the pilot was to climb out and descend to earth with his own parachute.

The first roll tests with the aircraft, carried out in autumn 1938 in Peenemünde-West, soon showed the necessity for a regulable rocket motor. This unit, which bore the designation HWK RI-203, delivered a thrust of 500 to 600kg (1,102 to 1,323 lb). Numerous rocket motor static tests and aircraft roll tests were necessary before the first straight-line 'hops' with functioning rocket motor took place. Since construction of a hard runway had only just begun, initial ground rolls in spring 1939 had to be undertaken on the normal airfield grass surfaces. Due to the unusually small dimensions of the He 176 with its main undercarriage track of only 70cm (27½in), this often led to deviations from the straight-line roll direction, and even to a complete 'carousel' or circular wheelspin. The aircraft could only be held straight by alternate application of the wheelbrakes, especially because the normal vertical rudder on the aircraft first became effective upon full rudder deflection

On 25th May 1939, a large group of leading RLM personalities inspected the He 176 in Peenemünde-West. In the presence of Heinkel, Warsitz conducted a straight-line 'hop'. In his capacity as State Secretary for Aviation in the RLM, Milch used the opportunity presented and spontaneously

A model of the high-speed variant of the He 176 rocket-powered experimental aircraft, based on early post-war information supplied by several former Heinkel design staff. The wingspan was a mere 5.00m (16½ft) and all-up weight 1,600kg (3,530 lb). The actual prototype, of which a single photograph surfaced many years later, shows that the aircraft in fact had a fixed tricycle nosewheel undercarriage, different fuselage nose and canopy, high-positioned mid-wings with fixed underwing outrigger skids and horizontal tailplane mounted on the fin and rudder.

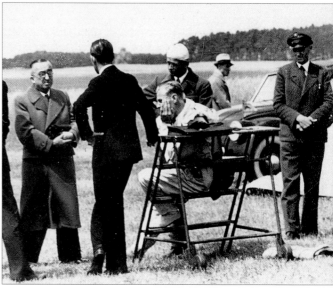

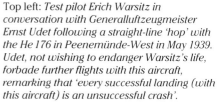

Top left: *Test pilot Erich Warsitz in conversation with Generalluftzeugmeister Ernst Udet following a straight-line 'hop' with the He 176 in Peenemünde-West in May 1939. Udet, not wishing to endanger Warsitz's life, forbade further flights with this aircraft, remarking that 'every successful landing (with this aircraft) is an unsuccessful crash'.*

Top right: *The meeting in May 1939. What happens now with the He 176 following Udet's flying ban? Pictured from left to right are Ernst Heinkel (with overcoat), Uvo Pauls, Erich Warsitz (seated) and behind him, Josef Wrede.*

Above left: *Erich Warsitz in conversation with Staatssekretär Erhard Milch after demonstrating a straight-line 'hop' with the He 176 in Peenemünde-West on 25th May 1939. On the right of Erich Warsitz in the white protective clothing is Erhard Milch, behind whom is Ernst Heinkel. The author, with hat, is on the left.*

Bottom left: *In commemoration of the first successful airfield circuit-flight of the He 176, artist Hans Liska sketched an animated picture of an extremely pleased Erich Warsitz at the centre of a group of well-wishers and photographers. At the end of World War Two, this illustration fell into the hands of the British in Berlin, and on the occasion of a 'round-decade' birthday of Erich Warsitz in the 1960s or 1970s, was given to him as a birthday present by the British – a noble gesture. The text at lower left reads 'On 20th June 1939, Flugkapitän Erich Warsitz was the first man to successfully accomplish the first flight in the world with a rocket-powered aircraft – the Heinkel 176'. This drawing of the forward cockpit and low-positioned wing-root leading-edge it seems, formed the basis for 3-view drawings of the 'high-speed' He 176 variant that was never built and flown in that form.*

Hermann Göring and Adolf Hitler (second and third from left), Ernst Udet (fifth from left) and Ernst Heinkel (extreme right), watch the He 176 demonstration by Erich Warsitz in Rechlin on 3rd July 1939.

Erich Warsitz (in white coat) being greeted after his demonstration flight upon his return to Rechlin by (from left to right) Stabsing. Hillermann, Dr. Gerhard Hengst, Uvo Pauls, Josef Wrede, Dr. Hans Bender, Albert Plath, Frau Warsitz and Hans Scholz.

awarded Warsitz the title of Flugkapitän. Udet on the other hand, remarked: 'Every fortunate landing with this aircraft is an unsuccessful crash', and forbade Warsitz to carry out further flight tests with the He 176. Because of the good relations which Warsitz had with Udet, however, the ban was soon lifted.

The exact date of the first extremely short airfield circuit flight under rocket power is controversial in published literature. Even Warsitz in an interview on 24th October 1952 could not remember exactly. According to my notes, the first brief circuit flight occurred on 15th June 1938 which, at Warsitz's wish, was not previously advised to Heinkel or to others, especially the RLM. This airfield circuit flight with this completely novel aircraft was in fact a master piece of flying by the pilot, since the rocket fuel tank capacity allowed a combustion duration of only 50 seconds, whereby the aircraft quickly accelerated to a speed of 600 to 700km/h (373 to 435mph) and guiding it to the correct approach path for a landing presented a serious problem. This first airfield circuit of a high-speed rocket-powered aircraft represented a milestone in the history of aviation.

A further 'sharp' take-off and airfield circuit took place in Peenemünde-West on 20th June 1939 in the presence of Heinkel and RLM officials. Milch and Udet were again present. Following a final 'sharp' airfield circuit flight made from Rechlin-Roggenthin on 3rd July 1939 in the presence of Hitler, Göring, Keitel, Milch, Udet, and others, further development and testing was terminated by the outbreak of war. The He 176 was dismantled and via the Ernst Heinkel works in Rostock-Marienehe, was transferred to the Aviation Museum in Berlin, where it is said to have been burned in a 1944 bombing raid.

Heinkel He 178 Turbojet Aircraft

In the course of a discussion on the He 176 on 31st May 1939, I inspected together with Erich Warsitz the world's first turbojet-powered aircraft – the He 178, at Rostock-Marienehe, and at 1000hrs on 23rd June 1939 witnessed the first ground roll tests of this aircraft at the E-Stelle Rechlin airfield.

First flight of the He 178 took place on 27th August 1939 at the Heinkel works in Rostock-Marienehe.

DFS 194 Rocket Aircraft

At the time when a development order from the RLM for the DFS 194 and its successor was being debated, the HWK RI-203 rocket motor used in the He 176 had reached a stage of high performance and reliability in 1939. In the course of his activity at the RRG, Dr. Alexander Lippisch had already commenced design work on tailless aircraft. In 1933, the RRG was transformed into the DFS. Although flights with existing tailless aircraft at that time had already resulted in several deaths, among them Günther Groenhoff, with the support of Dr. Adolf Baeumker, head of the RLM Research Department, Lippisch in 1937 began development of a new tailless aircraft design – the later DFS 194, whose manufacture was undertaken by the Messerschmitt AG in Augsburg. On 2nd January 1939, Dr. Lippisch and his team moved to the Messerschmitt AG, where he established Department L (for Lippisch).

Whereas the RLM exercised little influence during development of the He 176, in the case of the DFS 194, especially in view of later developments, the RLM exercised its influence continuously. RLM Flugbaumeister Dipl.-Ing. Hans Antz became the Referent responsible.

The aircraft initially underwent intensive trials in towed flights, landing as a glider on its central skid. Heini Dittmar piloted these flights and thus became one of the most experienced pilots on this type of aircraft. After several towed flights in Augsburg, the DFS 194 was transferred at the end of 1939 to Peenemünde-West and modified for installation of its 'cold' unit under the auspices of the Versuchsstelle Sections E2 and E3. Following a further series of towed flights culminating in landings after gliding flight, Heini Dittmar undertook the first flight of the DFS 194 under rocket power in the summer of 1940. In the period thereafter, some 45 flights were successfully accomplished. Contrary to the He 176, the DFS was not conceived as a high-speed aircraft. It attained about 550km/h (342mph) at 3,000m (9,840ft) altitude, and according to Heini Dittmar's testimony, displayed surprisingly good flying characteristics.

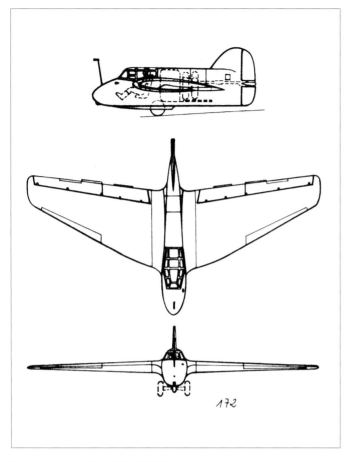

Three-view drawing of the DFS 194.

*The experimental DFS 194 rocket-powered aircraft,
the forerunner of the Me 163.*

Peace Comes to an End

A retrospective look at general development at the Peenemünde Versuchs-stellen
allows one to picture the initial exhilaration
and the changes in tasks and circumstances which took place. For both Peenemünde-West and East, the year 1939
appeared to develop extremely positively.
Several new tasks were taken up; recipro-
cal assistance was provided in a spirit of
co-operation wherever it was possible and
needed. Co-operation between the two
Versuchsstellen tended towards being pro-
fessionally-oriented, on a friendly basis,
and even to follow common paths. Peenemünde-West made its aircraft available for
tests conducted by Peenemünde-East, and
the Army invited the 'Men of the West' to
witness their latest rocket motor and
launching trials. Even recreational activities did not suffer, although it was necessary on occasions to work until late hours
at night during preparations for tests. Mutu-
ally-organised entertainment events were
often a contributory factor.

All this, however, changed suddenly
from one day to the next. A few days after
the previously-mentioned landing of the
He 116 after its world duration flight record,
we were summoned on 2nd August 1939 to
attend a 'roll-call' in one of our large aircraft
hangars. Uvo Pauls, head of the Versuchsstelle Peenemünde-West, explained
that war would most probably break out
and that the workplace as well as the
remaining population must now be prepared to face restrictions. The opening of
hostilities on 1st September 1939 with
Poland, and the declaration of war by
Great Britain and France on 3rd September
1939, determined events from now on.

The basic thoughts behind our work thus
began to take another course. Where formerly it had primarily been technical problems which interested us, the foremost
question which now arose was how soon
would the new devices under test become
fit for military use. This, however, was a
gradual process, as the initially successful
course of the war from the Wehrmacht
(Armed Forces) point of view, permitted
the Versuchs-stelle to pursue an essentially
undisturbed set of activities in the years
1939/1940.

On 23rd February 1940, the current Section Head of E2, Werner Hartz, handed
over the files to the new Section Head Hermann Kröger, whom I had brought over
from the E-Stelle Rechlin on 31st January
1940.

During the course of progressive developments at the Front, secrecy was continually intensified under the motto 'Beware –
the enemy is listening too', so that only a
few were made aware of the whole picture. Measures taken included a dramatic
increase in barricades and personal identification controls which extended considerably beyond and around the Versuchsstelle
facilities. Many things happened of which
the workforce were told nothing.

Der Führer und Oberste Befehlshaber
der Wehrmacht   Berlin, den 11.1.1940.

Grundfäßlicher Befehl.

1. Niemand: Keine Dienststelle, kein Offizier dürfen von einer
geheimzuhaltenden Sache erfahren, wenn sie nicht aus dienst-
lichen Gründen unbedingt davon Kenntnis erhalten müssen.

2. Keine Dienststelle und kein Offizier dürfen von einer geheimzuhaltenden Sache mehr erfahren, als für die Durchführung
ihrer Aufgabe unbedingt erforderlich ist.

3. Keine Dienststelle und kein Offizier dürfen von einer geheimzuhaltenden Sache bzw. dem für sie notwendigen Teil früher
erfahren, als dies für die Durchführung ihrer Aufgabe unbedingt
erforderlich ist.

4. Das gedankenlose Weitergeben von Befehlen, deren Geheim-
haltung von entscheidender Bedeutung ist, laut irgendwelcher
allgemeiner Verteilerschlüssel ist verboten.

Adolf Hitler.

**The Führer and Supreme Commander of
the Armed Forces – Berlin, 11.1.1940**

Basic Directive

1. Nobody – no duty station, no officer, may be
advised of any secret order, when it is not necessary to have such knowledge in the course of
his duty.

2. No duty station and officer may be advised of
any secret matter, more than is absolutely necessary in the performance of his duties.

3. No duty station and no officer may be advised
of any secret matter, or of that portion which is
essential to know, earlier than is required in the
performance of his duty.

4. The thoughtless passing-on to others – in
compliance of a generally-established distribution list – of orders whose secrecy is of decisive
importance to be maintained, is forbidden.

Adolf Hitler.

New Tests and Experimental Tasks

Me 163 Rocket Fighter

After he joined the Messerschmitt AG in
Augsburg, Prof. Alexander Lippisch initiated a further development of the DFS 194,
intended to lead to an operational rocket-
propelled fighter. Flight testing of the
Me 163A prototype was likewise carried out
initially under air-tow, landing after free
flight as a glider. The first prototype, the
Me 163 V4, was transferred to Peenemünde-West, where installation of the
HWK RI-203 rocket motor, more powerful
than that in the DFS 194, with a thrust regulable up to 750kg (1,653lb), was undertaken.

The first 'sharp' take-off with the Me 163A
took place on 10th August 1941. Heini
Dittmar enthusiastically remarked: 'This is
the start of a new type of flying!'. On 2nd
October 1941, after being towed to an altitude of 4,000m (13,120ft), under the full
power of the rocket motor Dittmar attained
a speed measured by cinetheodolite of just
over 1,000km/h (621mph). A second pilot
trained to fly the Me 163A was Rudolf Opitz,
who had landed in a DFS 230 transport
glider on the roof of Fort Eben Emael in Belgium at the beginning of the French campaign.

During the testing phase of the Me 163A,
development of the Me 163B rocket fighter
intended for operational use, began with
the strengthened support of Ernst Udet
in autumn 1941. The planned installation

of the Walter HWK 109-509 'hot' rocket
motor of 1,500kg (3,307 lb) thrust, with an
increased fuel capacity, plus the numerous
alterations that were shown to be necessary as a result of tests carried out with the
Me 163A in addition to fitting the aircraft
with military equipment, resulted in an
almost twofold increase in take-off weight,
and led basically to an extensive redesign
of the aircraft.

The first V-models were still manufactured in Augsburg, whereas production of
the initial series of 70 airframes took place
at the Messerschmitt works in Regensburg.
Following preliminary tests in towed flight
from Lechfeld airfield begun in June 1942,
the first 'sharp' flights with the Me 163B
began in Peenemünde-West in summer
1943.

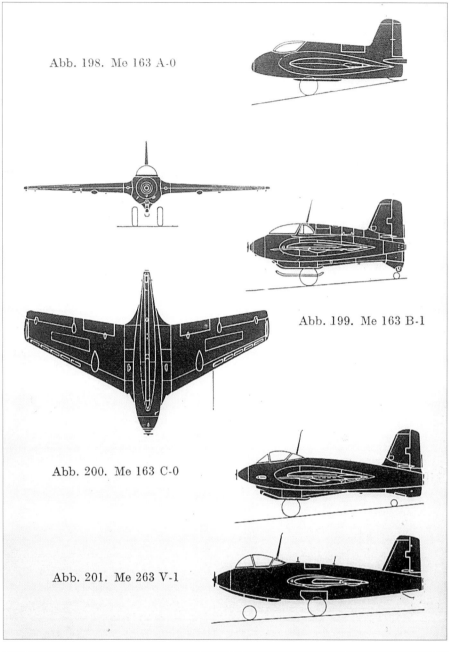

Abb. 198. Me 163 A-0

Abb. 199. Me 163 B-1

Abb. 200. Me 163 C-0

Abb. 201. Me 263 V-1

The Me 163 development series.

After the Me 163A with HWK rocket motor had been demonstrated by Heini Dittmar in summer 1941. From left to right Reichsminister Fritz Todt, Staatssekretär Erhard Milch, Heini Dittmar, Hellmuth Walter (partly hidden with hat) and Hermann Kröger.

Meanwhile, at the wish of the Versuchsstelle, Flugkapitän Dipl.-Ing. Hans Boje from Test Section E3 and the pilot Ing. Bernhard Hohmann from Test Section E2, were trained to fly the Me 163A. Hans Boje, involved with supervising the functional safety of the rocket motor, as a result of an engine failure in January 1943, had to make an emergency landing 6km (3.6 miles) away from shore on the waters of the Baltic and in so doing, sustained such a severe eye injury upon impact, that his flying career was brought to an end. Bernhard Hohmann, who took care of the entire systems, had better luck during flight testing, and after the war worked in the USA on the Gemini project.

In the meantime, in April 1942, through the auspices of General der Jagdflieger Generalmajor Adolf Galland, the 'Erprobungskommando 16' (Experimental Detachment 16) was ordered to be set up under the leadership of Hauptmann Wolfgang Späte. This unit was to accompany development and testing of the Me 163B from the military perspective, train Luftwaffe personnel on the aircraft, and prepare the way for operational use of this rocket fighter which, because of its rotund shape, was accorded the nickname 'Kraftei' (Power-Egg).

It was only on 24th June 1943 that the first 'sharp' start with the Me 163B V21 took place in Peenemünde-West, with Rudolf Opitz as the pilot. After several initial teething troubles, the HWK 109-509 'hot' rocket motor of 1,700kg (3,747 lb) thrust now functioned without problems. Despite a dangerous situation caused by surface unevenness, Opitz was able to effect take off and carry out a completely successful test flight.

Despite considerable efforts by industry series manufacture of the Me 163B was considerably delayed due to several necessary alterations and new demands as well as dispersal of the manufacturing centres caused by the war situation. Following the bombing raid on Peenemünde on 17/18th August 1943, with the support of the E-Stelle technical personnel, Ekdo 16 moved from Peenemünde via Anklam to Bad Zwischenahn, and at the latter airbase, began in earnest with training of pilots and ground crew as well as preparations for operational use.

The Peenemünde-West Section E2 specialist, Dipl.-Ing. Carl Ruthammer, responsible for the Me 163, listed on his Test Report dated 6th June 1943 critical remarks on the aircraft's deficiencies, which were also confirmed by Ekdo 16. In order to support industrial efforts to eliminate the deficiencies, relevant personnel from the Versuchsstelle formed a Detachment known as 'Kommando Hummel', initially based in Lechfeld but later also providing assistance to Bad Zwischenahn.

The enormous limitations which soon manifested themselves with regard to operations with a rocket fighter, above all, because of its short duration under rocket power and the unavoidable landing in gliding flight thereafter, led to several successive variants of the Me 163B. These, however, were limited to factory tests and V-models, and did not make their appearance in Peenemünde-West.

Concerning combat operations with the Me 163, also known as the 'Power Egg' and Komet, the reader is referred to published literature.[3,4,5,6,7] In all, 364 examples are reported to have been delivered.

Unmanned Missiles

The years 1938 and 1939 were still largely devoted to the erection and expansion of the Versuchsstelle. This involved the airfield in particular and the widely-spaced measurement stations. Even so, a start was made at the beginning of 1939 with the test and development of unmanned missiles – an advance into technically new territory. The problem lay in the high speed of the aircraft intended to launch the missiles in flight. The earliest missiles tested proposed by the DVL and the DFS, were based on the premise that with a highly-streamlined aerodynamic configuration and exceedingly precise manufacture, even without automatic course control, it should be possible to produce a directionally-stable straight-line flight. But this proved to be a false assumption. The glide-bomb missile bodies 'GV', conceived by Dr. Oskar Tietjens of the DVL and the 'GS' by Horst Muttray of the DFS, could be looked upon by reason of painstaking manufacture as excellently-conceived missiles, were not able to achieve the required in-flight behaviour. Initial air-launchings of the DVL GV-1 model took place in April 1939 at the E-Stelle Rechlin, and from 5th May 1939 at Peenemünde-West. The slight manufacturing errors led at high speeds to both models

entering a curved flight path which ended with such regularity in a spiral dive and ensuing crash, that it was no longer possible for observers in the accompanying aircraft to follow the missile up to the moment of impact. The consequences resulting from a series of flight tests was that it was only possible to obtain straight flight by installing a course-control system.

The extraordinarily elaborate precision manufacture of the DVL and DFS missiles led to the consideration whether it would not be more favourable to change to much simpler manufacturing methods and with the use of an appropriate course control, attain the required results.

With the help of a simple-to-make apparatus, a normal Luftwaffe SC 250 bomb body was equipped with flat, dihedral steel-sheet wings having arrow-shaped and slightly depressed leading edges. The usual cruciform tail surfaces of the bomb were replaced by a long pointed cone at the rear, which carried the horizontal and vertical flying surfaces and allowed space for the insertion of course-control equipment. A simple model known as the GB 200, con-

ceived by this author and whose introduction appeared to have chances, was completed in the Versuchsstelle workshops on 26th May 1939, tested in the DVL wind-tunnel on 21st/22nd July 1939, and demonstrated on 30th August 1939 to the Rheinmetall-Borsig firm for manufacturing purposes.

Course-control systems for the missiles were developed by the firms Askania-Werke in Berlin, Anschütz in Kiel, Kreiselgeräte GmbH in Berlin, Patin, and the Siemens-Luftfahrtgerätewerk in Berlin. Equipped with such – as air-launch tests had shown from spring 1940 onwards – perfectly straight flights could be achieved, except that functional reliability did not occur in all cases.

It is appropriate to mention at this point that missiles of the type described were unsuitable for use against 'point' targets. Further development was thus later terminated, since attacks against so-called 'area' targets was not included in the OKL operational doctrine. It had to be 'point' targets, and ships were ideally suitable for this purpose.

The Me 163B V6 prior to take-off.

The DFS RSA-160 glide-bomb with Askania course-control (1941).

The Fi 156 Storch broke its undercarriage landing on the ice-covered Baltic sea in the attempt to recover an unpowered glide-bomb missile on 5th February 1940. Both missile and aircraft were recovered a few days later.

Carrying out and tracking the release of such missiles was not without problems. The severe winter of 1939/40 had iced-up the Baltic sea, so that a continuous sheet of ice right up to Sweden was only interrupted by a navigable lane between Swinemünde, Sassnitz, and Kattegat. In conditions of bright sunshine in February 1940, several test-drops were made from an He 111 of the GV, GS, and GB 200 missiles. On 5th February 1940, I accompanied the pilot in a Bf 110 to film the behaviour of the missiles upon separation from the carrier aircraft and track them until impact. Surprisingly, one of the missiles made a flat belly-landing on the frozen surface of the Baltic sea. It lay there in its aerodynamic beauty on the snow-covered ice layer as a secret 'something' which obviously had to be retrieved. We noted the landing spot in our charts and started out again in an Fi 156 Storch, taking along tools to dismantle the missile. A landing area which appeared to be completely even was soon found nearby, but turned out to be deceptive. Shortly before coming to a halt, the undercarriage sank through the flat layer of snow and remained suspended on an icefloe beneath, whereupon with creaking and cracking noises, it collapsed. Both missile and aircraft now lay on the ice in the glistening sun, and we had to make our way back to shore on foot, clambering up over very high ice drifts at the edge of the shore. However, with the help of vehicles, both aircraft and missile were retrieved in the next few days.

Automatically-Controlled Missiles

Blohm & Voss BV 143

One of the first promising proposals for a glide-bomb featuring both internal automatic control an external remote guidance for course corrections was the BV 143, developed by the Blohm & Voss Flugzeugbau in Hamburg-Finkenwerder.[8,9] The concept was by no means new, as this had already been tried out with the so-called Lufttorpedo (air-launched torpedo). In order to make an effective strike at the target, however, the unavoidably short distance from its point of release made it necessary for the controlling aircraft to be positioned within the range of the ship's anti-aircraft defences.

Blohm & Voss, familiar with both ships and aircraft, tackled the problem under the leadership of Dr. Richard Vogt, Chief of Aircraft Development, in spring 1939. Within the scope of a missile team led by Dr. Zeyns and Flugbauführer Jürgen Cropp, the rocket-powered BV 143 glide-bomb was created, capable of flying long distances. Designed from the outset to be suitable for operational use, it had a flying weight of about 1,000kg (2,205 lb) and was to be jettisoned from an aircraft at some distance – more than 10km (6.2km) away from the target. The HWK 109-501/2 rocket motor having a cruising chamber, was to accelerate it to around 450km/h (280mph), whereupon it would in diving flight descend toward the sea surface but without submersing. By means of a mechanical, optical or electrical precision altimeter, it would level out and fly at a very low height above the water. For the terminal phase of the flight, a remote

course guidance, and finally even an automatic target-seeking device was planned.

Flight testing took place mainly in Peenemünde-West. I saw the first completed BV 143 in Hamburg-Finkenwerder on 16th July 1940. The first air-launch took place over the Baltic on 5th September 1940 from an He 111 from Peenemünde. In-flight behaviour of the glide-bomb equipped with a three-axis control – at first from Anschütz and later from Askania, but not yet fitted with a propulsion unit, was fully satisfactory until impact with the sea.

On 17th October 1940, the BV 143V3 prototype was prepared for air-launching, namely, rocket motor ignition beneath the He 111. I observed the procedure from the accompanying Bf 109 but had to abort the drop as the rocket motor did not function. Air-launch of the BV 143 subsequently took place on 24th October 1940. I again flew as an observer in a Bf 109 and much to our disappointment, had to witness that the BV 143V3 flew faultlessly at first, but then went over into a roll and crashed. There thus began a whole series of continual mishaps with the BV 143, many of whose causes despite numerous air-launch tests, could not be satisfactorily determined. Since all releases had to take place over the sea, the missiles could not be recovered. Even the installation of measuring instruments inside a floatable capsule which was ejected in the event of a fault arising, and descending with the aid of a parachute to enable recovery, proved mostly of little help. A particular problem encountered was that the powered missile, after an initial period of faultless flight and upon reaching a certain flying speed, without any visible reason suddenly entered a steep climb, stalled, and crashed out of control. The cause was suspected to lie in local sonic-speed influences on the elevators which could not be overcome by the automatic-control system.

Some BV 143s were latterly released over land on a troop training ground near Radom in Poland, in order to safely retrieve the measuring-instrument capsule. But despite all efforts by Blohm & Voss and the relevant E-Stellen participants from Peenemünde West, not all of the many and diverse causes of mishaps were established, let alone eliminated.

One unsolved problem, among others, was the automatic 'pull-out' mechanism whose function was to change the flight path from a descent into horizontal flight at a low height above the water. The mechanical feeler originally intended by Blohm & Voss, which upon contact with the water surface was to activate suitable flap and elevator movements, was quickly discarded due to its unreliability. But even optical or electrical fine-precision altimeters, regarded as promising and even used in trials, did not bring the desired results. I myself conducted several flight tests with these devices, flying in an He 111 and Do 217 over the Peene estuary right up to treetop height – in other words, up to about 5m (16ft) proximity to the sea surface. These trials, however, still provided no conclusive evidence regarding the indispensable reliability of the BV 143's automatic 'pull-out' mechanism.

Although during the course of test and development of the BV 143, several alterations and subsequent improvements were introduced, this missile, which could also have been employed on ship-to-ship and shore-to-ship launchings, never reached operational maturity. Further development was therefore stopped in autumn 1943.

Blohm & Voss BV 246

Another development by this firm from 1943 onwards was an 'ideal' unpowered long-range glide-bomb – the BV 246 Hagelkorn (Hailstone), completed in various versions to fulfil a variety of tasks. A speciality of this missile, which carried a 500kg (1,102 lb) bomb, was its externally suberbly fine aerodynamic form. The wing, with a span of 6.5m (21ft 4in), had an extremely narrow mean chord of some 24cm (9¼in), which corresponds to a wing aspect ratio of 28, with which the BV 246 could attain a gliding angle of 1:25 to 1:28. This means that when released from an altitude of 7,500m (24,600ft), it had a gliding range of 200km (124 miles).

This missile, initially equipped with an automatic course control, could likewise only be used against area targets. It was therefore a clear rival to the Fi 103 described later, and this intention was clearly mentioned by the firm's Chief Designer Dr.-Ing. Richard Vogt to Hitler and Speer in summer 1943. He related this to me personally on the occasion of his visit to Peenemünde.

It was only in December 1943 that the BV 246 also found favour with the RLM elite. Numerous BV 246s from the summer of 1943 onwards were air-launched over the Baltic from Peenemünde to test in-flight behaviour and in various configurations. Aircraft employed in air launchings were the He 111 and Fw 190. In the majority of cases the release tests produced positive results, even when take-offs and landings with the ventrally-suspended Hagelkorn on

the Fw 190, in my view, were not without problems. Further development and testing of this long-range glide-bomb was stopped in July 1944 in favour of a variant capable of serving as a high-speed target for the anti-aircraft rockets that were undergoing testing and development at that time. For this purpose the missile, now known as the BV 246E, was equipped with a curved-flight control system which imitated the course corrections made by bomber formations. Tests were so far advanced up until April 1945, that faultless automatically-con-

trolled curved flight according to programme could be carried out. The entire BV 246 programme suffered under frequently changing and partly contradictory requirements, approvals, and restrictions – occurrences which, as in other instances, hindered consistent testing and development.

The Report dated 15th August 1944 entitled 'Status of Tests of the BV 246 Glide-bomb', prepared by the project specialist Werner Hermann at the E-Stelle Karlshagen, provides particulars on the subject.[10]

The BV 143 rocket-powered automatically-controlled anti-ship missile.

The 'Hamburg' infra-red target-seeking device developed by Elektro-Akustik of Kiel for the terminal phase of the BV 143.

The BV 143 missile under rocket power.

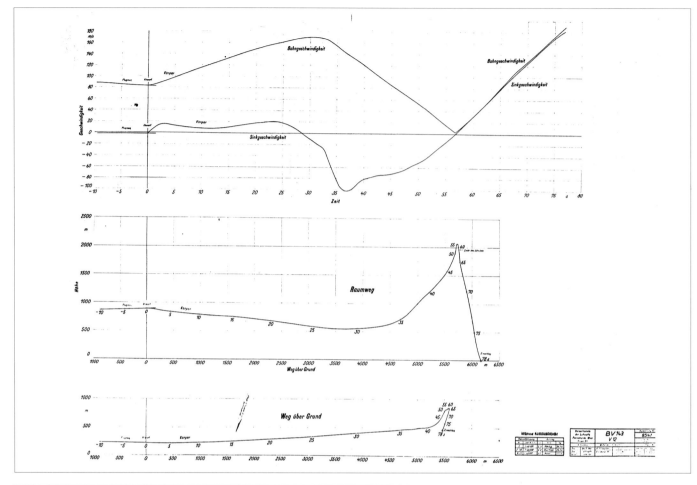

Tracking-station measurements of the BV 143 V12 flightpath on 24th March 1941.

The author at the controls of an He 111 on a 5th June 1941 test flight. At left is the flight mechanic Medzlewski, killed on a test flight on 18th June 1941, and in the middle, Dipl.-Ing. Thiele of E5.

Guided Missiles

Following the outbreak of war, contracts issued by the RLM Development Departments for missile development concentrated on guided bombs having as their main purpose, attacks on point targets.

Statistical evaluation of target strikes of normal bombs dropped from aircraft flying at high altitude had for some time displayed a very low impact quota against point targets. Even the use of the Ju 87 and Ju 88 dive-bombing aircraft initially favoured, brought only marginal improvements. For particular operational tasks, especially attacks against naval targets where the ships represented movable point targets, remote guidance of the bomb following release was selected.[11]

As early as the First World War attempts had been made – even though futile – to improve the results of bomb hits by means of remotely influencing the free-fall trajectory. Since then, attempts had been made by both industrial and private individuals to advance from remote-controlled boats to remote-controlled missiles, occasionally even successfully. From the equipment point of view the results, however, were not suitable for the intended missile objective, even when the basic principles were not altogether new.

The BV 246 long-range glider bomb.

An Fw 190G with a BV 246 beneath the fuselage. The flexible long-span narrow-chord wings were held firm by auxiliary struts to prevent damage prior to missile release.

A group of observers during the 'Siemens-gespann' demonstration in Peenemünde-West on 17th May 1940. From left to right Hans Hillermann, Uvo Pauls, Albert Plath, Dr. Fritz Gosslau of Argus and Generaling. Roluf Lucht of the RLM.

'Siemens-Gespann'

A demonstration of remote control and remote guidance.

In mid April 1940, two Ju 52s appeared in Peenemünde-West, with Flugbaumeister Armand Protzen on board. They came from the Siemens Luftfahrtgerätewerk in Berlin-Hakenfelde and rather furtively at the end of the airfield runway, became very occupied near to a newly-arrived instrument truck. On 30th April 1940 the two aircraft, known as the 'Siemens-Gespann' (a cattle yoke or team), flew a circuit of the Peenemünde-West airfield, whereby one of the aircraft was remotely controlled and guided from on board the other. For safety reasons both aircraft were manned.

'Remote control' is referred to when, for example, from another location such as from the 'Geräte-LKW' instrument truck, aircraft engines are started, run up to full speed and switched off, whereas 'remote guidance' refers to the aircraft roll or flight direction being influenced from another location, hence remotely guided.

On 15th May 1940 I received the unexpected order to fly in a Bf 109 fighter to Garz airfield on Usedom, in order to conduct shooting trials with live ammunition. For a civilian pilot, this was an exciting opportunity. The reason for this measure was the 'Siemens-Gespann' demonstration on 17th May 1940 in front of the GL/C head, Generaling. Lucht and a number of high-ranking RLM representatives. On this occasion, however, one of the Ju 52s was flown completely without a crew aboard, and therefore functioned partly as a both automatic and remote-controlled, remotely guided 'missile'.

The Ju 52 was at first parked on the edge of the airfield. By means of radio commands, the engines were started, the brakes released, and the flaps extended to the take-off setting. The aircraft then taxied under remote guidance to the take-off point and began its run. It then flew a large circuit of the airfield with changes in height and performed turns, returning finally to the airfield with throttled engines during the descent, thereafter landing without any

problem and rolling to its parking spot. The engines were then shut down by radio command – a flawless and impressive demonstration.

But how easily something could have gone wrong: the radio transmissions and with it the remote guidance could have been distorted or even failed so that the Ju 52, flying in an undesired direction, could have got out of control. That would have been the reason to have to shoot it down. For this purpose, I circled in the armed Bf 109 within sight of the unmanned Ju 52, ready to intercept in the event that this was signalled by the ground command post or else the other Ju 52.

The demonstration proved the availability of equipment with whose assistance even large and modern aircraft could be remotely controlled and guided, but whose dimensions and weight were still a long way from being suitable for installation in missiles then under development. It would therefore become necessary to develop items possessing much smaller dimensions.

Remote-controlled Missiles

I had participated in several discussions with the RLM GL/C-E2 in late autumn 1939 and at the end of February 1940, concerned with the aim of developing remote-controlled missiles. Taking part in these discussions were Dr.-Ing. Max Kramer from the DVL, Prof. Dr. Herbert Wagner of Henschel, the RLM Referat heads Rudolf Bree and Dr. Theodor Benecke as well as colleagues from Peenemünde-West. The development of remote-controlled missiles was now to be taken up in earnest.

SD 1400X (FX)

Dr. Max Kramer had already tackled the problem as early as 1937. On an experimental basis, he had adapted a normal SC 250 free-falling bomb equipped with a radio-command receiver unit and control devices and tested it at the E-Stelle Rechlin, with which the DVL had a good relationship. The RLM was interested in this concept, but preferred the use of a heavy, armour-piercing SD 1400 bomb dropped from high altitudes. The project was supervised by the RLM GL/C-E7 department head Generaling. Marquard together with his Referent Dr. Theodor Benecke and involved Peenemünde-West, where already in autumn 1939, Test Section E7 supervised the testing in co-operation with E2, E4 and E5.

The first air-launch of a remote-controlled SD 1400X, also known as the 'Fritz X' or simply 'FX', took place on 21st June 1940, dropped from a height of 4,000m (13,120ft). On 23rd November 1940, the first air-launch from 7,000m (23,000ft) followed. Both release tests were extremely promising, but only a limited number of releases were possible in Peenemünde, and until the end of December 1941, only nine FX bombs were dropped in the course of remote-controlled trials. This was in part due to the weather, but mainly because of the time-consuming and widespread testing involving trials of the missile parts and individual components.

Since the missiles were remotely guided using the optical 'Zieldeckungsverfahren' (target-covering method), the controlling operator in the aircraft had to be able to follow the path of the bomb up to impact in order to obtain a direct hit. A minimum altitude of around 4,000m (13,120ft) and a cloudless sky were prerequisites for a successful remote-controlled drop test which could be confirmed by measuring instruments. Bad weather conditions thus considerably delayed the continuation of tests. This was unfortunately the case in the Baltic, above all, in the semi-annual winter months. Test Section E7 therefore transferred air-launch tests to the sunny south to Foggia on the southernmost Adriatic coast of Italy.

Branch Station 'Süd'

Following the erection of a Measurement Unit consisting of 3 cinetheodolite stations in the region surrounding the Italian Air Force bombing range near Manfredonia, the project was relocated there in December 1941 under the leadership of the E7 Gruppenleiter Dr. Hans Bender. Comprehensive check- and measuring instruments of Test Section E4 and E7 had previously been transported to the newly-erected housing quarters of this Peenemünde-West out-station.

From the beginning of March until mid May 1942, some 20 remote-controlled FX bombs were dropped from altitudes between 6,000m (19,700ft) and 8,000m (26,250ft) and guided to the target 'cross' with increasing measures of success. With this achievement, the E-Stelle 'Süd' (South) testing programme was wound up and the Peenemünde personnel withdrew.

Up to the end of June 1942, another 10 air-launches from 6,000m (19,700ft) altitude took place in Peenemünde-West aimed at a target cross marked on the neighbouring peninsula named 'Struck'. Nine of these tests were a complete success. Impact results showed that 50% of the impacts lay within a circle of radius 7m (23ft), and all 100% lay within a circle of radius 14.4m (47ft) from the centre of the target cross. The functional capability of the remote-guidance method and that of the SD 1400X and aircraft remote-control systems were thus proven.[12]

FX Target-Training Device

A particularly important part of the system was the 'target-training device'. The missile controller, who had to guide the FX from the aircraft release point to the target, needed thorough training before he was able to carry out his first successful air-launching. For this purpose, Dr. Max Kramer had developed an excellently-contrived – even if somewhat complicated but nevertheless very efficient training device which functioned as follows:

From a raised platform and looking through a Lotfe target telescope, with the aid of a command joystick the movement of a small white disc over a surface representing a bombing 'carpet' as seen beneath the aircraft according to the flying speed could be controlled (forward/back or left/right). On this bombing 'carpet' was marked the outline of a ship, onto which the disc had to be brought, ie, using the previously-mentioned 'target-covering method'.

The SD 1400X, alias 'Fritz X' or 'FX' armour-piercing remote-controlled free-falling anti-shipping glide-bomb.

A photo sequence showing the two 'Fritz X' impacts on the Italian battleship 'Roma' on 9th September 1943 which, despite evasive manoeuvring, was hit and sunk.

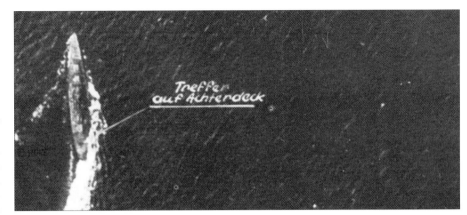

The command implement did not control the speed but instead, the acceleration of the disc, which moved in the commanded direction with either increasing or decreasing speed over the bombing 'carpet'. Stopping the speed, as for example, on approaching the desired target cover, was equivalent to applying the brakes in an automobile that had to be brought to a halt on a roadway white line.

After a short period of practice, individuals who were sensitive to accelerations, were reliably able to measure and hold the disc over the target and upon any deviation from it, could correspondingly react and return the disc over the target. All of the operators intended to serve on actual operations – as a general rule they accompanied the aircraft crew as observers – had to undergo this training. Their suitability for this task was rather diverse. Like other members of the Versuchsstelle, I was able to convince myself of the suitability of the target-training device.

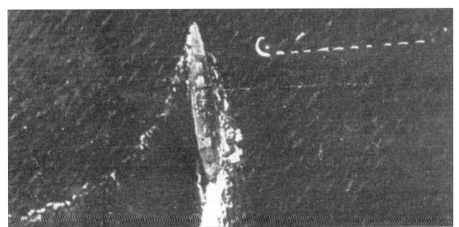

Lehr- und Erprobungskommando 21 (FX)
Instructional & Test Detachment 21 (FX)
Already during the course of ongoing technical development and testing of the FX, EK 21 was established in order to quickly familiarise military personnel. The war events of 1941/42 hardly allowed another choice. EK 21 had the task of preparing the military prerequisites for operational use of the FX and undertaking crew training. Despite efficient collaboration between the Versuchsstelle, industry, and EK 21, everything did not always go smoothly.

Led by Major Hetzel, EK 21 was initially stationed in Schwäbisch Hall/Hessenthal. It commenced its activities at the end of 1941 and from the end of 1942, transferred the trained crews to III/KG 100 which later used the FX operationally. Since series manufacture of the FX by Rheinmetall-Borsig in Berlin-Marienfelde suffered delays from several causes, and the conversion of aircraft and missiles took longer than planned, active use of the FX only began from July 1943 onwards. In mid July 1943, III/KG 100 moved to Istres in southern France, where a missile depot was established. Other missile depots were in Banak and Trondheim in Norway; Istres, Toulouse and Cognac in France, and Kalamaki in Greece. Operations were partly very successful. On 9th September 1943 for example, the Italian battleship 'Roma' was sunk by two SD 1400X direct hits whilst on its way from

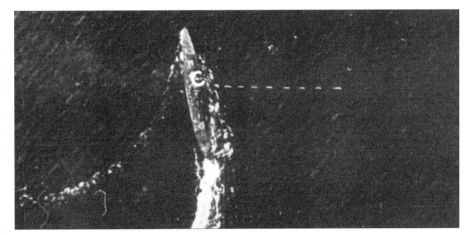

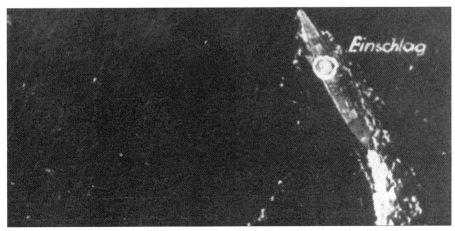

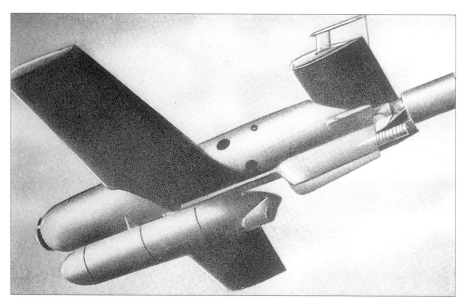

Hs293 component parts. Clockwise from top. Command elevator, suspension lug, electrical fuse, warm-air heating connection, transformer, receiver, aileron, elevator, tracing light,flare, pitot head, elevator servo, rocket motor, aileron steering, explosive, and trimming weight.

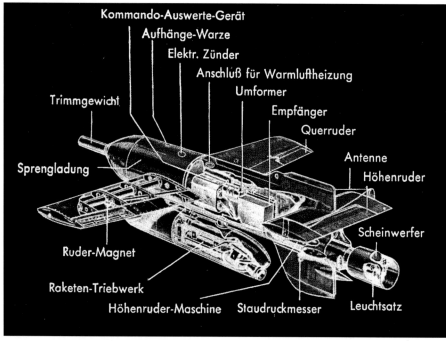

Kommando-Auswerte-Gerät
Aufhänge-Warze
Elektr. Zünder
Anschlúß für Warmluftheizung
Umformer
Empfänger
Querruder
Trimmgewicht
Antenne
Höhenruder
Sprengladung
Scheinwerfer
Ruder-Magnet
Raketen-Triebwerk
Höhenruder-Maschine   Staudruckmesser   Leuchtsatz

down to impact. With well-trained controllers, impact accuracy, as with the SD 1400X, lay within a 5 x 5m (16 x 16ft) box. With this missile it was possible, depending on visibility and the tactical opportunities offered in the target area, to operate it in a very wide range: from a minimum altitude of around 400m (1,300ft) and from 3.5 to 5km(2.2 to 3.1 miles) distance, right up to over 10,000m (32,800ft) altitude and up to 18km (11.2 miles) distance from the target.

Under the leadership of the very energetic, imaginative and resolute Prof. Herbert Wagner, who had with him a very capable team of co-workers at the Henschel Flugzeugbau (Aircraft Company) in Berlin-Schönefeld, the project made rapid progress. Whilst Telefunken undertook development of the 'Kehl' remote-control transmitter-receiver equipment (FuG 203a for the SD 1400X and FuG 203b for the Hs 293), the Stassfurter Rundfunk GmbH developed the 'Strassburg' guidance receiver equipment (FuG 230a for the SD 1400X and the FuG 230b for the Hs 293). It was soon recognised that the operating range of the Hs 293 and above all in cloud conditions, without an additional means of acceleration following air-launch, was insufficient. After evaluating several types of auxiliary propulsion units, among which the Schmidding firm had developed a liquid-propellant rocket motor and Rheinmetall-Borsig a solid-propellant rocket motor, the decision fell in favour of using the already-tested Walter system. For this particular purpose, HWK had developed the short-duration auxiliary 109-507 'cold' rocket unit which was suspended beneath the Hs 293 fuselage and automatically ignited upon missile release.

Prior to essential jettison trials, the Test Sections E3, E4 and E5 in numerous other tests had to establish the checklists and instruments needed for the propulsion and remote-control transmission and receiving installations. This task was basically concluded in autumn 1940, but during the entire phase of testing, had to be continued into the year 1943.

On 3rd September 1940 an Hs 293, as yet without rocket motor, was dropped from Henschel's own He 111 (KC+NW) over the Greifswalder Bodden in order to test the

Toulon to Malta. As a result of the very considerable enemy air superiority, operations often resulted in severe losses and were stopped following the invasion of France by enemy forces in June 1944.

Henschel Hs 293

Following studies involving various other possibilities, Prof. Herbert Wagner was commissioned by the RLM in the winter of 1939 to develop a remotely-guided glide-bomb. On the occasion of a meeting in the RLM at which Dipl.-Ing. Josef Dantscher, Section Head of E4 and myself attended, the involvement of Peenemünde-West was discussed and agreed upon.

The Hs 293, similar in form to an aircraft and weighing 800kg (1,763 lb), had ailerons of a special type for longitudinal control and

for lateral axis steering, had an elevator operated by a crankless motor. Both types of movable surfaces could be operated through radio commands with which the missile could be remotely controlled.

Technical details of the Hs 293, its components and how they functioned, as well as the configuration and effectiveness of the remote-control devices, are all detailed later.

The warhead portion of the missile was filled with Trialen, and having the effectiveness of an SC 250 bomb, enabled effective operations to be carried out against merchant vessels, light cruisers and destroyers. For night operations, a tracer flare or alternatively a searchlight with colour filter housed in the rear fuselage extremity, enabled the missile to be followed right

in-flight behaviour of the missile and the problem-free release from the carrier aircraft. On 18th December 1940, only six months after the commencement of development, Prof. Herbert Wagner himself steered the Hs 293, still without rocket motor, for the first time successfully from a distance of 3.5km (2.2 miles) from the target – a haystack on the 'Struck' peninsula on the Peene estuary, and scored a direct hit. This gave rise to an evening of celebration among the participants whom I joined just in time, having just returned from a BV 143 conference at Blohm & Voss in Hamburg-Wenzendorf.

It required, however, more than two years until all important teething-troubles with both missile and aircraft installations were overcome and a sufficient number of series-produced glide-bombs and transmission equipment were all available, as well as training of the operators.

Trials of the various auxiliary rocket motors on static test stands and air-launch tests in Peenemünde-West unfortunately did not proceed without incidents. In one of the numerous air-launch trials, shortly after commencement of the steering phase towards the target ship, the Hs 293's remote-control failed and under its own stability the missile could no longer be influenced in its flight over the neighbouring HVA Peenemünde-East, where it crash-landed between the platforms of the 'Siedlung' (Community) railway station and the Werksbahn (Works railway). Fortunately, no one was waiting there at the time and damage was marginal.

On 18th June 1941 one of our air-launch test aircraft, the He 111 (DC+CD), crashed together with its suspended FX missile shortly after take-off; pilot Bärsch and mechanic Medzlewski lost their lives, whilst the other crew members mostly sustained heavy injuries. Up until the accident, I myself had flown on several test flights with Medzlewski, who had shown himself to be a skilful, cautious, and reliable aircraft mechanic.

On 13th January 1944 one of the rocket motors exploded on the test stand as the result of an ignition fault, resulting in one death and several seriously injured.

Hs 293 Target Training Device

In a similar manner to that developed by Dr. Max Kramer for the SD 1400X, Prof. Herbert Wagner likewise developed a target-training device for the Hs 293. Whereas the SD 1400X was steered by cartesian co-ordinates, ie, left/right or forward/back for longitudinal axis stabilisation, the Hs 293 was steered by polar co-ordinates. With this system the missile 'attitude' along its longitudinal axis was remotely steered via ailerons, and aerodynamic lift varied via the elevator. The resulting flight path was equivalent to flight in a curve performed by a normal aircraft without the need to employ a normal vertical rudder.

The target-training device developed by Wagner stood out because of its simplicity in superb simulation exercises using the 'target-covering method'. It consisted of a flat plate nicknamed the 'Wackeltisch' (rocking-table) which, with the aid of a 'Knüppel' (joystick) for giving command signals, could be inclined from the horizontal. A ball on top of the plate simulated the missile and moved according to the inclination, accelerating under the influence of gravity in the direction of inclination, and through an opposing tilt, could be arrested and brought to a standstill or else made to move by tilting the plate in any desired direction. This target-training device proved very successful for the training and gaining of practical experience by service operators.

Lehr- and Erprobungskommando EK 15 (Hs 293)

The EK 15 was formed in winter 1941/42 under the leadership of Hauptmann Franz Hollweck stationed in Garz air base near Swinemünde. In comparison to the then attained but by far still incomplete state of testing and development of the Hs 293, its establishment – due to wartime events – took place very early. The enforced result was advantageous in that it led to a very close collaboration between EK 15 and the various experimental teams from Peenemünde-West. EK 15's tasks were identical to those of EK 21. In the course of the training of EK 15 officers and crews, I flew several training flights in approach and jettison procedures and carried out an asymmetric-load and take-offs and landings where the Hs 293 was suspended on only one side of the aircraft. Later on, during the period 7th May 1943 until 10th August 1943, I often visited the operational air bases of II/KG 100 under Kommandeur Hollweck in Istres and Cognac in southern France, in order to determine the causes of failures encountered or to introduce measures to eliminate them. Military operations with the Hs 293 begun in mid 1943 on the Atlantic coast and in the Mediterranean were notably successful, but suffered increasingly from the air superiority of the opposing forces.

A sortie with a Do 217 in the Aegean, reported to us at that time (summer 1943), serves to indicate the efficacy of the Hs 293 attack: the aircraft, which started out from northern Greece, carried two Hs 293s, one under each wing. Only one approach and air-launch for each missile was said to have been necessary to sink two destroyers 'in passing flight'.[13]

Remote-guidance operator in an He 111H-12 holding the command joystick for the Hs 293 missile.

The wreck of a beached merchant ship served as the target for trials with remotely-guided missiles.

A Do 217E-5 of II./KG100 on an airfield in the south of France in August 1943. Beneath the port wing is a 900 litre auxiliary jettisonable fuel tank, and beneath the starboard wing, an Hs 293 missile.

An Fw 200 Condor with two Hs 293 missiles beneath the outboard engines.

it was also one of the aircraft in which I had already carried out several test flights. One can therefore understand in retrospect, the annoyance I felt when the following incident is related:

At the end of June 1943, I was returning from a test flight and was on the point of landing on the airfield at Peenemünde-West when I saw a large A 4 rocket which had just risen from Prüfstand VII in the Army Versuchsstelle Peenemünde-East. After a few seconds the rocket turned sideways and flew horizontally, heading directly towards Peenemünde-West airfield, exactly in the direction of my landing approach. Making a sharp turn to the left, I broke off the planned landing and after flying a circuit of the airfield, I noted that the rocket had impacted and exploded beside the runway directly beside the parked He 111 (PH+EI). The aircraft was thus totally unusable, with the result that test work was considerably delayed.

Despite all exertions from July 1943 onwards, whereby some 70 to 80 Hs 293D examples were air-launched in trials, operational status was not achieved. Development of this highly interesting and very promising weapon was terminated in autumn 1944.

Hs 294

Another very promising Hs 293 variant intended for use against ships was the Hs 294. In its basic concept, it had a similar overall form to the Hs 293 and was to be remote-controlled in a similar manner. Instead of the bomb body of the Hs 293, however, it was fitted with a WLK or 'Unterwasserlaufkörper' – a streamlined fuselage shape suitable for travelling submerged, having a nose profile similar to the upper part of a bowling-alley skittle or ninepin. An annular 'Stolperkante' or drag surface just behind the tip of the rounded nose produced the desired boundary-layer turbulence surrounding the WLK such that, in conjunction with a marked conically-shaped extension at the rear extremity of the WLK, a straight-line underwater path was attainable without the need for additional steering equipment. The Hs 294 was to be remotely guided up to a point where it would submerge about 30m (98ft) away from the target ship. At this instant the

Hs 293 Variants and 'One-Offs'

As with all other development projects, the first missile project realised by the Henschel Flugzeugbau was the Hs 293, the starting point for a whole series of developments.[14] It epitomised the imagination and wealth of ideas of Prof. Herbert Wagner and his colleagues. In the following narrative, only a few of the projects will be discussed which during trials in Peenemünde-West acquired a notable significance.

Hs 293D

Missiles of the Hs 293D-series were equipped with a complete television camera in the fuselage nose as well as picture transmission and remote guidance equipment, the television receiving and remote guidance transmission equipment being housed in the carrier aircraft. This variant had been proposed by Prof. Wagner to enable the aircraft launching the Hs 293D, following missile release, to be protected by cloud cover or else immediately turn away from its approach course to the target.

In co-operation with the Reichspost-Forschungsanstalt, the Fernseh GmbH, Telefunken and Loewe companies, appropriate trials were undertaken at an early stage. Initial discussions took place in early summer 1940 between Peenemünde-West, the RLM and Henschel. Preliminary

trials conducted by the Fernseh GmbH (Television Co Ltd) in Peenemünde-West rapidly followed, in the course of which night flights took place on 18th July 1940. Despite considerable efforts by the industrial firms, the research institutes and above all, the Versuchsstelle Section E4, initial experimental flights and release trials were first carried out from mid 1943 onwards. Continual problems were encountered with remote guidance connected with the transmitted television picture which appeared on a monitor screen in the aircraft. As a consequence of the rapidly-changing size of the target image on the small TV screen during the missile's final approach to the target, it proved difficult for the missile controller to give the correct commands needed. Prof. Wagner and myself as well as other controllers had also established this fact during air-launched tests. Nevertheless, direct hits were secured on a building simulating the target and on a fixed merchant vessel wreck placed near the Peene estuary.

The expenditure necessary for development of recording and test instrumentation was considerable. Two carrier aircraft from Section E4 were modified for the TV-guided Hs 293D trials. One of these was the He 111 (PH+EI), whose special equipment was not only comprehensive and expensive but also unique up until that time. Additionally,

entire wing and tail surfaces, including steering installations would be blown off, leaving the streamlined WLK, driven solely under its own kinetic energy, to proceed a certain distance under water. A distance-counter was to effect detonation of the explosive-filled WLK beneath the vulnerable ship's hull. For impacts against the side of the ship, a percussion fuse was provided. To provide initial acceleration after release of this 2000kg (4,409 lb) weight missile, two underslung HWK 109-507 rocket motors mounted side by side were to be used.

Numerous air-launched trials with the WLK were carried out during 1942 and 1943. From an Me 110 at the torpedo Versuchsstelle Hexengrund/Gotenhafen, I repeatedly jettisoned the WLK in diving flight near to the water surface whose boundaries were indicated by buoys. Attached to these buoys, positioned at short intervals, were deep underwater nets which the WLK was to penetrate, the resulting perforations indicating the underwater path the WLK had followed. The trials were later continued in Peenemünde-West where, during 1943 and 1944, numerous air-launches of the Hs 294 complete with remote guidance via radio or wire carried out, and these were partly successful. During this period, the tactical and material superiority of the enemy air forces had become exceedingly great.

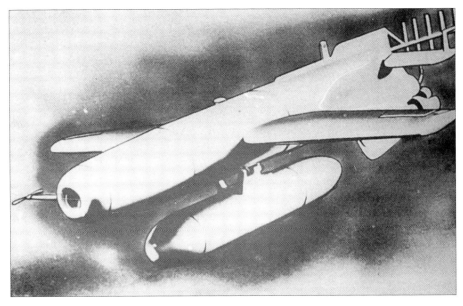

Above: The Hs 293D variant with nose-mounted television equipment and tail Yagi antenna.

Below left: The Fernseh GmbH 'Tonne' TV camera developed and installed in the Hs 293D.

Below right: The Seedorf TV receiver was installed in the controlling aircraft above the joystick command console, visible in the He 111H-12 photo on p205.

Out-Station Jesau

From the beginning of the war, Peenemünde had often been overflown by the British Mosquito high-altitude reconnaissance aircraft. It was apparent that sooner or later Peenemünde would also become of interest to bomber formations, so the possibilities offered by an out-station were sought. In autumn 1943, Jesau was selected for this purpose, an isolated air base some 25km (15 miles) south of Königsberg.

On 10th August 1943 I flew to Jesau in order to inspect and discuss with Fliegerstabsing. Albert Plath, head of our preliminary Versuchsstelle contingent, the possibilities presented for carrying out air-launchings there. Following the already-mentioned devastating air raid on Peenemünde-East on 17/18th August 1943, a partial relocation to Jesau took place at the beginning of September 1943 in order to continue tests there with the SD 1400X, Hs 293 and Hs 293D missiles in parallel with Peenemünde. In the second half of September, discussions took place concerning air base expansion, erection of a measure-

ment station on the Kurischer Nehrung and the usefulness of continuation of trials in view of the situation developing on the Eastern Front.

On the 29th and 30th October 1943 I was again in Jesau to fly across the measurement station that had meanwhile been erected immediately next to an anti-aircraft prohibited area, to determine the approach flight paths for air-launch trials. Jesau showed itself, at least for a number of months, to be useful and usable. As a result of the war situation on the Eastern Front, this out-station had to be abandoned in early summer 1944. Complete dismantling of the installations and their return transportation to Peenemünde-West was completed in mid July 1944.

Carrier Aircraft for Missiles

To establish the suitability of various types of aircraft as missile launchers, thorough examination and testing were undertaken. This was valid for both the SD 1400X and Hs 293 as well as other missiles to be mentioned later on. The trials concerned the

An Army A4 rocket shortly after lift-off from Prüfstand VII at the Heeresversuchsstelle Peenemünde-East.

The rocket-powered Hs 294 remotely-guided anti-shipping missile. Not seen in this view are the twin underslung rocket motor nacelles.

Opposite page: *The spooling arrangement for the 0.2mm-diameter wire on the carrier aircraft and on the missile for the wire-guided remote-control system.*

possibility of missile suspension beneath the aircraft, examination and test of the remote guidance installations on aircraft and missile relating to function and reliability, determination of in-flight performance of the aircraft with attached missiles, testing of the industry-manufactured components and equipment parts and especially their functional ability under various environmental conditions such as temperature, moisture and air pressure both on the ground and at extreme altitudes, coupled with the danger of extreme icing and extremely low temperatures. Time and again the mechanical or electrical connections between aircraft and missile were disrupted, or else failures occurred in the special installations on the aircraft to provide missile heating. Additionally, the development and test of measuring and test instruments necessary for safety and functional testing of missile and aircraft systems under operational conditions, formed part of the most important and work-intensive tasks of the various experimental detachments. From 1943 onwards, all bomber aircraft under construction were equipped with the necessary installations for missile operation, and in selected cases, for use of either the SD 1400X or Hs 293.

With the war continuing, there was an urgency to accomplished the numerous conversion discussions and inspections and the transfer and test flights with the Do 217E, K and M, the He 177, Fw 190, Fw 200, Ju 88, Ju 188 and Ju 290 right up to the Ar 234. It was astonishing that despite the continual and increasing pressure of the Allied air forces flying to various parts of continental Europe right across Reich territory, these flights – only occasionally interrupted by warnings of enemy aircraft – were conducted mostly without any problems.

Remote-Control Evasion Solutions

It became clear from the very outset that remote-control via radio was susceptible to interference. All the more so since the transmission frequencies used, reserved especially for remote-control purposes, were in accordance with those agreed at the previously-held 'Wavelength Distribution Conference' held in Cairo in 1936.

The outbreak of war on 1st September 1939 had a shock effect upon us. It had only been a few years – or so it seemed to us – that we had experienced a stimulating period of reconstruction. Should all this be now set at risk in a war which definitely had to be won against allied forces which, since the end of World War One had been able to build up their strength continuously and undisturbed? The lightning successes of the Wehrmacht in Poland, Belgium, Holland and France, threw a euphoric veil over these increasing apprehensions which could not without personal danger be openly elucidated or discussed, especially since widespread slogans put out by Reichspropaganda such as 'endemic excitement', 'defeatism' and 'undermining military potential', could very quickly result in strong countermeasures against the individual concerned. Anonymous denunciation was always a fear, hence in such conversations, the greatest care had to be exercised.

The dramatically increased losses suffered in the autumn of 1940 in the 'Battle of Britain' by Luftwaffe aircraft and crews to whom we in Peenemünde–West felt affiliated, intensified our fears. On the night of 21st/22nd June 1941, when the opening of hostilities against the USSR was announced, we discussed the prospective results of 'Operation Barbarossa'. In view of the vast expanse of territory to be occupied by our troops and the human reserves and industrial potential of the USSR, we regarded the whole undertaking as an arrogant Napoleonic overconfidence whose aspired success would in the end result in total failure. Even the early successes of German troops in the central sector of the Eastern Front and the purposeful optimism expressed in radio broadcasts and Wehrmacht reports, could not deceive us about the actual developments. The Far-Eastern manpower reserves brought in by the USSR as well as the war materials delivered under Lend-Lease by the USA, had to eventually exhaust the energy of the Wehrmacht.

On 11th December 1941, when the Axis Powers Germany and Italy both declared war on the United States, it became clear to us that with the far superior Allied production capacity, the war could no longer be won. Even Wernher von Braun and his deputy Dipl.-Ing. Eberhard Rees from Peenemünde-East, who occasionally took part in such discussions, agreed with our opinions. Comments expressed from time to time, that everything would possibly and hopefully not turn out to be as bad as they might seem, were just not convincing anymore.

One of the 'Ausweichlösungen' (evasion solutions) tested was the use of several close-lying frequency bands, which could be rapidly altered by means of an exchangeable quartz inserted in the transmission and receiver equipment. In this way it was possible to conduct the remote guidance of up to 18 missiles simultaneously without enemy interference.

Another evasion solution regarded as exceptionally interference-free was wire-guided remote control. It was developed to a high state of reliability and used in trials in several releases of both SD 1400X and Hs 293 missiles dropped from high altitudes and release distances. Two wire spools or bobbins were installed on both aircraft and missile. The aircraft-mounted spools each contained insulated steel wire up to 12km (7.5 miles) in length, and on the missile side, up to 20km (12.4 miles) of the 0.2mm (0.008in) diameter wire. At the moment of release, reeling-out of the spools could take place simultaneously, so that the wire connection between aircraft and missile appeared to remain stationary during the further flight of both vehicles. Modified transmitter and receiver equipment allowed, in case of need, to switch quickly from radio to wire guidance. Development and testing had advanced to operational maturity, but it did not prove necessary to employ wire guidance.

Scepticism Increases

As had already happened with previous occurrences, the war situation and its foreseeable outcome had been discussed and doubts were expressed in close circles among friends and colleagues regarding the usefulness of certain development projects being tackled. In retrospect, it must be said that the alarming fears expressed at that time as a result of passing events were confirmed.

In order to 'turn over a new leaf' – in the event that this was still possible – what ought we, and what could we in the Versuchsstellen in Peenemünde do?. We all more or less found ourselves in an apparent dilemma. We were torn on the one hand between the necessity and the obvious aim to bring test and experimental work on new technical devices to a speedy success, whilst on the other hand the sheer number of projects worked upon may well have had military usefulness but were nevertheless of doubtful value, requiring a considerable amount of material, personnel, and expenditure of work which could be better utilised for needs elsewhere.

The oft-exercised changes in organisation and command structure as well as frequent reversal of orders from 'above', only added more 'fuel to the fire' of these deliberations. The increasingly difficult situation at the Front served to raise the motivation of the workforce (despite doubts and despite repeated bombing raids) to continue our work with determination and with increasing imperativeness. The constantly-necessary discussions and review of the multifarious programmes and projects with official departments and industrial firms, the ongoing flight testing of various types of aircraft converted by industry as missile carriers which over the years were faced with increasing difficulties on their journeys all over Europe – often traversing destroyed or burning cities, provided an impetus for the increasing haste to solve existing tasks. Examination of the physical possibilities and what was technically feasible to produce, however, retained its fascination.

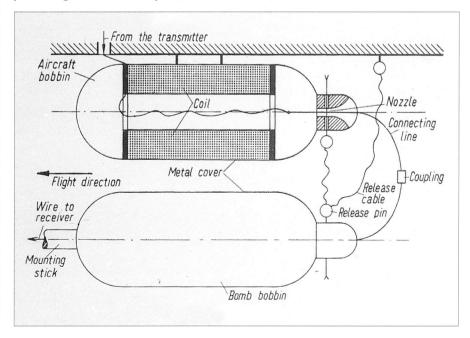

War-Stipulated Programmes

Combating Long-range Targets

Attacking widely-spaced land targets using unmanned missiles was already a subject of military consideration in World War One. The French marine Chief Engineer Camille Rougeron had given extensive consideration to this means in his book 'Bombing Aviation', where unguided rocket-powered glide-bombs formed the basis of his proposals. New types of propulsion units, based partly on older patents, gave rise to new ideas. Paul Schmidt for example, devoted himself to development of a pulsating jet engine also known as a pulsejet which was fully functional, but due to insufficient financial support, only made slow progress. In a largely independent effort led by Dr.-Ing. Fritz Gosslau, the Argus Motoren GmbH in Berlin, commissioned by the RLM, developed a similar propulsion

unit which soon entered the flight test stage. In order to give recognition to Paul Schmidt's pioneering work on pulsejets, the resulting unit was designated the 'Argus-Schmidt' duct.

At the beginning of the war, Dr. Gosslau had submitted proposals for several unmanned, automatically-controlled long-range flying-bombs. The suggestion was initially rejected by the OKL as well as by the RLM Technisches Amt since it did not cater for attacking point targets, and attacks against large area targets was not part of an OKL strategic concept at that time. It was only from autumn 1941 onwards that the increasingly noticeable lack of combat aircraft and crews caused technical circles responsible for Luftwaffe development to undergo a radical reversal of normal methods employed for bombing. An additional factor was the area bombing raids conducted on German cities.

Fieseler Fi 103 (V-l) Flying-Bomb

At the end of April 1942, the Work-study Group of companies consisting of Argus (propulsion unit), Askania/Siemens (remote control), and the Fieseler-Werke GmbH of Kassel (missiles), submitted a new proposal to the RLM for an unmanned, medium-range flying-bomb which already embodied all the important characteristics of what was later to become the Fi 103 or

An Fi 103 after leaving the launching ramp. The HWK accelerator piston is seen falling away.

The pulsejet-powered pre-set automatically-guided long-range Fi 103 flying bomb, also known under various designations such as 'Flakzielgerät 76', Kirschkern (cherry stone), 'Richard' and latterly as the 'V-1'.

The Walter (HWK) catapult ramp launcher for the Fi 103 flying bomb.

'V-1' flying-bomb.[15,16] Generalfeldmarschall Erhard Milch approved the project on 19th June 1942, the Fieseler firm being assigned the task of heading development under the highest priority.

A project was thus set in motion which was pursued with such exemplary energy by all those involved that, after the war, even commanded the respect of the former enemy with the remark: '(the) Fi 103 – this never-to-be-forgotten ground-to-ground medium-range flying-bomb'.[17]

After just four months, in mid October 1942, two acceleration ramps were erected for trials of the initial variant of the Fi 103 on the north shore of Peenemünde-West. Rheinmetall-Borsig had proposed the use of a solid-propellant rocket unit with a short combustion time which, with a deafening noise at burnout, would accelerate a ballast-weight body representing the as yet unavailable Fi 103 to a speed of around 400km/h (250mph) into the nearby Baltic sea. Unfortunately, it caused the temporary wooden building that provided weather protection for the crew working at the ramp, to be blown away. Tests and discussions on the ramp topic led to the decision in summer 1943 to utilise the HWK WR.2 catapult, ie, a Walter Rohrschleuder (cylinder accelerator) for the missile weighing 2.3 tonnes (5,070 lb) and functioned as follows:

In a 48m (157½ft) long hollow cylinder or tube having a dorsal opening slit along its length, a cylindrical piston fitted with a hook would engage the missile placed above the aperture. As a result of the expanding gases generated through the spontaneous decomposition of hydrogen peroxide and potassium permanganate, the piston would be accelerated at around 18g through the catapult tube, simultaneously closing the aperture behind the engaging hook by means of a metal band running the length of the tube. At the upper end of the ramp the Fi 103 was disengaged from the piston and continued its flight at a speed of some 350km/h (220mph).

On 23rd October 1942, Flugbaumeister Willy Fiedler, responsible at Fieseler for the Fi 103 project, appeared with an Fw 200 Condor equipped with an underslung Fi 103 – but without propulsion unit – for the first air-launch test at Peenemünde-West. In the days that followed, I trained on the Fw 200 and a few days later, took over the Fi 103 air-launch tests to establish its suitability for flight under various conditions. From the very first test, the flying characteristics proved to be very good. In preparation

for forthcoming flight tests, an additional measurement station to those already existing was built on the island of Bornholm in order to gather measurement data on the longer-ranging Fi 103 test flights.

Although until then not a single Fi 103 had undergone a catapult launch, I had already received at the beginning of November 1942 together with Fiedler, the order to search in the St Omer/Lille area along the Channel coast, for sites suitable for later Fi 103 operations and advise the Luftwaffe construction departments accordingly. We carried out this task during very bad weather conditions from 12th to 20th November, passing on the results to Fieseler Director Dr. Lusser on the occasion of a visit to the Fi 103 manufacturing centres in Kassel, and finally to the RLM.

I was unfortunately not able to witness the first catapult launch of the Fi 103 which now carried the camouflage designation Kirschkern (Cherry stone), and later, FZG 76. The launch took place on 24th December 1942 using the Borsig accelerator (ramp). At that time – from the end of November 1942 until 7th January 1943 – I was at the Blind-flying School in Radom for instrument-flight training. The blind-flying Certificate II for which I qualified there, allowed me to fly all types of civilian and military land-based aircraft on instrument-only flights.

Upon my return from Radom, testing of the entire missile systems which had begun in parallel, continued apace. For the Fi 103, the simultaneous testing and development of each new airframe and engine configuration, automatic remote-control, catapult and individual components, resulted in enormous problems. Even more astonishing was the progress made in rapid succes-

sion. Characteristic of this were the following incidents:

The pulsating combustion of the Argus-Schmidt 109-014 pulsejet with its frequency of about 48 cycles/sec, as a result of sound pressure generated upon duct ignition, caused certain individuals among test crews at the static test-beds and catapults to suffer such damage to internal body organs whose natural frequency were set in resonance, that they had to receive attention in Greifswald Hospital, and were out of action for several weeks.

These low-frequency sound pressure waves were particularly felt in the immediate neighbourhood of the duct exhaust orifice. With an Argus-Schmidt pulsejet to one side beneath an He 111 fuselage, I carried out for our Section E3 several test flights up to altitudes of 3,000m (9,850ft) to test the ignition and combustion behaviour at various heights and speeds and to define the setting of the fuel-injection regulator. Located in the ventral gondola, members of the aircraft crew who had to critically follow and form an opinion of the pulsejet ignition and flame behaviour, were so shattered by the combustion process and the noise that, following the landing, they were hardly able to report anything worth knowing.

On one of these flights in 1943 I had gained the impression that the aircraft's control behaviour had become somewhat 'milder'. Upon conducting checks after landing to determine the possible cause, I noticed that in the region of the Argus-Schmidt pulsejet exhaust nozzle, as a result of the pulsating sound pressures, the fuselage skin rivetting had partially worked loose, so that the aircraft had to undergo a long period of repairs. For the substitute

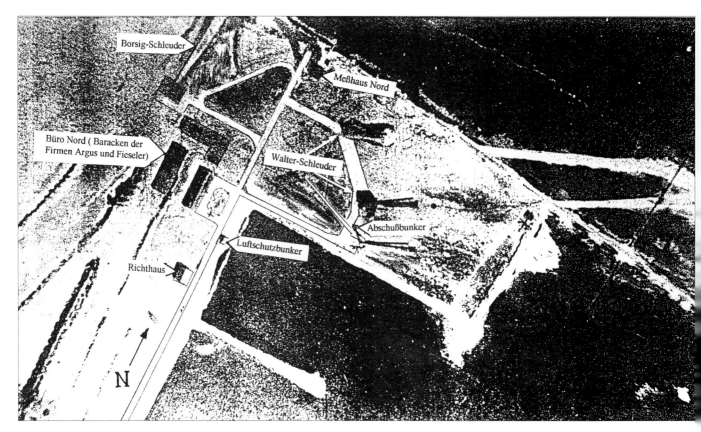

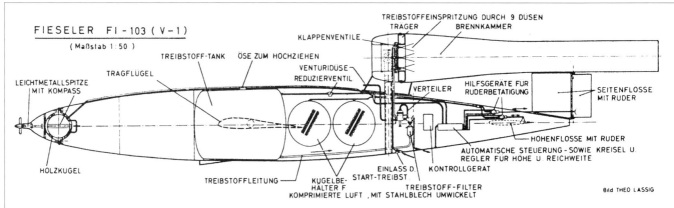

aircraft, special sound pressure protector shields were installed.

In the course of 1943/44, numerous Fi 103 air-launches were carried out from various aircraft where the pulsejet was ignited each time just before release. The Fi 103 automatic control device developed and minutely tested in the meantime by Askania/Siemens had made such progress that automatically-steered flight following both air-launch and catapult take-offs functioned perfectly up to the maximum range of 230km (143 miles). Not all such flights, however, were without problems. On one occasion, instead of the intended straight-line flight, it flew in a circle; the workforce of both Versuchsstellen held their breath for the whole time that the Fi 103 with droning engine flew some 500m (1,640ft) high,

for 20 minutes, in circles over the northern tip of Usedom island. Because it was not always possible to satisfactorily determine the cause of a mishap since the missile as a rule ended with an impact or crashed into the sea, lack of time placed pressure on the testing. Finally, in May 1943, crews involved in testing were strengthened, and a special Gruppe 'ET' under the leadership of Dr.-Ing. Heinrich Temme of the DFS, was created solely for the Fi 103.

Under the overall supervision of Sections E5 and E7, testing of various types of ignition fuses for the Fi 103 warhead took place. Because of the unsuitability of the terrain foreseen for this purpose in the surroundings of Peenemünde, fuse testing was then transferred to the E-Stelle Udetfeld in southern Poland. Long-distance flights of the

A British aerial view of the Fi 103 installations on the northeastern shore of Peenemünde-West.

Principal internal components of the Fi 103 flying bomb.

Fi 103 were also carried out from this location to ascertain the probable circle of impact. For surveillance of the actual flight path and survey of the point of impact, Section E4 in co-operation with individual firms developed and tested various 'Funkmess Peilverfahren' (radar tracking methods) which were later used operationally and proved trustworthy.

Parallel to ongoing trials but without the direct participation of Peenemünde-West all preparations for the commencement of series manufacture had been instituted, in which, however, constant alterations resulting from test results established, had to be incorporated.

Introduced at a likewise comparably early date was the training and field testing by service troops to prepare for operational use of the Fi 103. On 1st July 1943, 'Erprobungskommando Wachtel' with headquarters in Zempin, not far from the Versuchsstelle, was set up. It later formed the Flakregiment 155(W) under the leadership of Oberst Max Wachtel, charged with conducting operations with the Fi 103. As a consequence of reorganisation in the higher leadership structure, series manufacture from the end of 1943 became more and more subject to influences exercised by Party offices which strove to become involved not only in development, test and manufacture, but also in operational use of the so-called V-weapons. In the end, control of the programme was assumed by Waffen-SS Generalleutnant Dr.Ing. Hans Kammler, who since the beginning of 1944 had already been a member of the 'Jägerstab' (Fighter Committee) and its successor, the 'Rüstungsstab' (Armaments Committee), as the individual responsible for the 'Sonderbauaufträge' (Special Construction Orders).

As an alternative solution to the catapult start, Fi 103 operations carried out from aircraft were also tested. For this purpose, 'Erprobungskommando Banneick' was established at the end of 1943, stationed in Peenemünde-West. Led by Leutnant Graudenz who worked most closely with the E-Stelle, Fi 103 operations from aircraft by service personnel were prepared and executed and the crews duly trained. Within this framework, I carried out numerous test, demonstration and training flights with the He 111, He 177, Do 217 and Ju 188 with asymetrically-slung Fi 103s, and even demonstrated landings with an underslung Fi 103. Because of the very limited ground clearance of just 15cm (6in), this was associated with a degree of risk, but which could nevertheless be accomplished.

A manned version of the Fi 103 with 'joystick steering' known as the Fi 103R (Project Reichenberg) was tested in flight. Since the E-Stelle Rechlin provided the pilots, some of whom suffered severe injuries upon landing the aircraft, testing took place in Rechlin. Peenemünde-West made the He 111 carrier aircraft available with which the manned Fi 103 was carried aloft and released to fly as a glider and then land. The project was terminated at the end of 1944.

Soon after the beginning of Fi 103 test and development, improvements – especially for raising the flying speed, flight duration and target impact accuracy, were examined and tested out in Peenemünde-West and were partially introduced.[18]

Not quite two years after receipt of the development order of 19th June 1942, the first planned Fi 103 operations against England (with a reserve of 5,000 missiles) were carried out in the early morning hours of 13th June 1944 – seven days after the Invasion by Allied Forces on the Channel coast. From then on, the Fi 103 was publicized as the V-1 or Vergeltungswaffe (Vengeance Weapon) Number One. Shortly afterwards, on 7th July 1944 – but according to author Botho Stüwe, initially on 16th September 1944 – V-1 operations commenced from aircraft of III/KG 3, followed later by KG 53 which carried out these sorties with He 111H-22s over the North Sea towards England, but which suffered heavy losses. According to one British source, V-1 operations using aircraft ended after some 1,200 air-launches on 14th January 1945. The last V-1 was reported to have fallen on London

On the occasion of an Fi 103 test-launch at the EdL Peenemünde-West on 16th April 1943, members of the test team together with the E-Stelle head, Major Otto Stams, were greeted by Generalluftzeugmeister Erhard Milch. From right to left Dr.-Ing. Fritz Gosslau (Argus), Dr.-Ing. Robert Lusser (Fieseler), Hermann Kröger (E2) shaking hands, and Arthur Schäfer (E3).

An Fi 103 test prototype prior to release from the He 111 carrier craft.

The air-to-air rocket-powered wire-guided X4 missile.

A perspective view of the X4 missile.

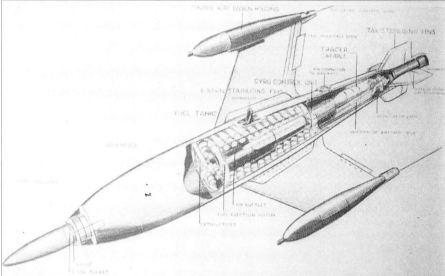

'If the Germans had been able to complete and bring these weapons into operation six months earlier, that would have made our invasion of Europe extremely difficult, perhaps even impossible. Operation Overlord (the code name for the Allied invasion on the Channel coast in June 1944) might possibly have had to be written off'.[20]

In my opinion, the run of events would have been delayed, but certainly not prevented. The remarks clearly indicate that on the part of the British and the Americans, tribute was paid to German developments in the field of unmanned missiles and rockets.[21,22,23]

At the invitation of the British Royal Aeronautical Society (RAeS), I gave a lecture on 25th January 1962 on the development of German guided missiles in Bristol. At RAeS request, the lecture was repeated one year later in various other locations in England.

Combating Airborne Targets

'Air-to-Air' Missiles
The increasing operational use from 1941 onwards of large, closely-knit bomber formations against the civilian population, and above all, the cover provided to the bombers by long-range fighters, led to the search for means which would enable the home-based fighters to remain outside the range of the bombers' anti-aircraft defences and yet safely achieve their destruction successfully.

X4 Guided Fighter Rocket
Modelled on his development of the SD 1400X, Dr.-Ing. Max Kramer conceived for this purpose the X4 missile which was developed by the Ruhrstahl AG in Brackwede. Like the SD 1400X, it had cruciform wings and cruciform tail surfaces mounted at 45° to the wings. As a result of a pre-set adjustment, the wings rotated the missile along its longitudinal axis. The tail surfaces were equipped with protruding spoilers or drag-producing vanes which were magnetically operated. To provide 'high-low' or 'left-right' commands, the magnets received remote-control signals via wire connections in the aircraft. The incoming remote-control commands were distributed in the missile by means of a gyro known as the 'command distribution gyro via the spoiler magnets, such that despite missile rotation, it could be remote-controlled by cartesian co-ordinates.

on 29th March 1945. Of the more than 32,000 Fi 103s manufactured, more than 21,000 were actually launched, and according to British data some 4,900 impacts were achieved. Other sources[19] speak of more than 13,000 impacts in the target area. Around 27% of the V-1s launched fell victim to massive countermeasures – anti-aircraft artillery, barrage balloons and fighter aircraft – concentrated in a narrow corridor. The biggest failure was attributed to 2,500 V-1s immediately after leaving the catapult launching ramps.

If one considers the elapsed time from the commencement of V-1 development, test and manufacture, right from the date of its commencement up to its operational use in 1944 as a coherent whole, one cannot help but come to the conclusion that the realisation of this project under the circumstances existing at that time, was a masterpiece of technical and organisational talent. This performance cannot be judged merely with an all-to-simple and one-sidedly coloured evaluation, since it consisted ultimately of a deadly weapons system. Rather, this performance must be considered among all prevailing efforts conducted by all the leading belligerents whose aim was to provide their own armed forces with the most effective weapons systems.

As an unmanned medium-range flying-bomb, the Fi 103 became the precursor for several comparable weapons systems known as 'cruise missiles' in both East and West, and found its place in the history of technology.

In his memoirs relating the knowledge of British military intelligence concerning the so-called German secret weapons, Winston Churchill quoted the American General Eisenhower as follows:

The rocket-powered remote-controlled Hs 298 air-to-air missile.

During the air-launch of the Hs 298 V2 proto-type on 7th January 1945, the missile motor exploded just after launching. A large piece of debris snagged in the port Ju 88G propeller which slammed it into the top of the cockpit canopy and severely injured the author.

The X 4 was accelerated in flight by the 109-548, a storable liquid-propellant rocket motor developed under the leadership of Dr.-Ing. Helmut Zborowski of BMW. Following release from the aircraft it attained some 250m/sec (559mph) and a horizontal range of 3,000 to 5,000m (1.86 to 3.1 miles) within which distance the missile could be guided. The X 4 was to be equipped with an acoustic proximity fuse which responded to propeller noise upon meeting or overtaking the target aircraft, whereupon the 20kg (44 lb) warhead would detonate.[25]

Numerous RLM planning conferences with Dr.-Ing. Max Kramer or with the Ruhrstahl AG led to the decision from early summer 1944 to commence flight trials in Peenemünde-West with the X 4 which, because of its wire-guidance method, was not without risk. Carrier aircraft employed were the Ju 88 and Fw 190. Tests were partially successful, but time was insufficient to enable a status of reliable operational readiness to be achieved. Despite ongoing series production, development had to be stopped in spring 1945 when the BMW works in Stargard was destroyed.

Hs 298 Guided Fighter Rocket

Prof. Herbert Wagner's proposed Hs 298, developed out of the remote-controlled Hs 293 glide-bomb, suffered a similar fate. Like the X 4, it was expected to be a very promising remote-controlled missile carried by fighter aircraft, especially as guid-ance and control components within the missile had been meanwhile successfully tested within the framework of Hs 293 trials.

In contrast to the Hs 293, the Hs 298 had a two-stage Schmidding 109-543 rocket motor, furnished with a WASAG solid-propellant. The motor developed for five seconds an initial thrust of 150kg (331 lb) – raised later to 250kg (551 lb), continuing finally with a thrust of 50kg (110 lb) for 20 seconds. After release from a guide rail beneath the wing of a Ju 88, Ju 188 or Fw 190, the Hs 298 was thus accelerated to a speed of 100m/sec (224mph) higher than that at launch, and with a cruising speed of around 700 to 800km/h (435 to 500mph), dependent upon the rocket motor variant used, would achieve a range of some 5km (3.1 miles).

Flight testing began in Peenemünde-West in early summer 1944. For initial trials, the He 111 and Do 217 were used; Prof. Wagner himself acted as the guidance con-troller on several flights. Whilst guidance and flying behaviour of the Hs 298 was mostly satisfactory, serious problems were encountered with the solid-propellant rocket motor; it revealed that in moulding the solid fuel, cavities and cracks appeared in the propellant cylinders, which upon ignition, could lead to an explosion. Thrust was initially shown to be too weak, and the unit insufficiently resistant to low ambient temperatures.

Several working meetings on the X 4 and Hs 298 were held at the RLM and with industrial firms regarding aircraft conversion for missile operation. These took place in parallel with missile tests. It was also necessary to carry out numerous overflights to check out the acoustic or electromagnetic proximity fuses then under development and test for both missiles, the fuses being installed in a laboratory environment atop a wooden tower and serviced by Section E4 engineers.[26] The wooden tower had to be

flown over at the lowest possible height by the He 111 and Do 217, which often caused the tower crew to duck their heads.

On 27th December 1944, I took off on yet another test flight with a Ju 88 carrying two Hs 298s in cold weather. The first missile launched flew perfectly and responded to remote guidance without any problems. Upon release of the second missile, however, at a certain distance ahead of the aircraft, the rocket motor exploded.

On 7th January 1945, I took off once more with the Ju 88G, this time to test the Hs 298V2, now equipped with a higher-thrust rocket motor, over the iced-up Baltic sea within sight of our measurement station. Air-launched at 2,000m (6,560ft) altitude, the Hs 298 cleared the guide rail beneath the aircraft's port wing but the rocket motor unfortunately again exploded, this time only slightly ahead of the aircraft. A massive piece of missile debris became snagged in the Ju 88's port engine propeller and was slammed into the cockpit, causing me severe head injuries. I regained consciousness after what must have been several seconds later, the accompanying test engineer and my radio operator preparing to bale out. I managed to talk them out of it just in time, switched off the port engine and except for the blood streaming down my face, landed without further problems at our airfield where the ambulance, already forewarned by radio, was waiting. Up to the end of January 1945, I carried out a further number of Hs 298 test flights, but further test and development ceased shortly thereafter since no further prospect for operational use existed.

'Surface-to-Air' Missiles
The almost nightly bombardment of German cities had already led in the early 1940s to consider enhancing conventional Flak (anti-aircraft) artillery with remotely guided surface-to-air missiles with which a higher number of target strikes could be expected. Although target-seeking systems had meanwhile undergone research and development, none were so far advanced as to be capable of use in surface-to-air missiles. As a result, overall concentration was confined to the already proven radio-command remote guidance employing the 'target-covering method', whether by radar or optical means. Various enterprises endeavoured to fund a solution.[27, 28]

The Army Versuchsstelle Peenemünde-East, renamed in the interim HAP 11 or Heimatartilleriepark (Homeland Artillery Park), had undertaken development of an anti-aircraft surface-to-air missile derived from the large liquid-propellant A 4 rocket. Known as the Wasserfall (Waterfall), it underwent trials near the newly-erected Luftwaffe Flak-Versuchsstelle Karlshagen.

The Rheinmetall-Borsig firm had initiated development of a Flak rocket using solid propellants as fuel. Known as the Rheintochter (Rhine Daughter), its trials were carried out on the Leba firing-range in East Prussia.

Using the basic design of the Me 163 rocket fighter, the Messerschmitt AG also sought to develop a Flak rocket of which several variants were proposed. Known as the Enzian (Gentian), some 60 examples of these variants were built and a portion were tested from May 1944 at the edge of Peenemünde-West under the surveillance of the Flak-Versuchsstelle. The trials, carried out with minimal participation of Peenemünde-West, were not successful. The project was certainly so diverse in its planned and tested variants that it was not possible in the circumstances of 1944 to carry out a consistent test programme.

Hs 117 'Schmetterling (Butterfly)
Particularly promising was the Henschel Hs 117 remote-controlled anti-aircraft rocket ultimately developed under the leadership of Prof. Herbert Wagner. Success with the Hs 293 glide-bomb had spurred him to propose development of a surface-to-air Flak rocket to the RLM, from whom a positive response was not at first forthcoming. It was only later, under the advent of increasing area bombardment of German cities that the project was again taken up in 1943 and its realisation accelerated. Peenemünde-West was tasked to take care of accompanying development and testing, and for this purpose established a special 'EF' Test Section headed by Hermann Kröger.

The Hs 117, 4.3m (14ft) long and weighing 460kg (1,014lb) loaded, was launched with the aid of two Schmidding 109-533 solid-propellant RATO units from a rotatable launching platform which could be adjusted in inclination and direction. After about four seconds, the RATO units were jettisoned by means of explosive bolts, whereupon the missile's own cruising rocket motor, in its final version capable of being regulated to provide variable thrust, took over. Power supply in flight was provided via a small windmill propeller which drove a dynamo that had previously been brought to its planned rpm by an external power source. Altitudes of something over 10,000m (32,800ft) could be attained.

Flight testing commenced in early summer 1944, following comprehensive and thorough testing of all component parts, in particular the rocket motor and remote control systems. According to my notes, the first Hs 117 air-launch took place on 24th May 1944 from an He 111 to determine its in-flight behaviour. Evaluation of the missile, filmed from an accompanying aircraft,

showed a flawless flight. An Hs 117 model built to test the ground-zero launch from an improvised starting ramp, was fired for the first time one day later. Successive ground-launch tests took place from 26th July 1944 onwards – only a few days after the large air raid of 18th July 1944 carried out by successive waves of American bombers. To these must be added the previously-mentioned further development of the long-range BV 246 glide-bomb into a high-flying programme-controlled target for Flak-rocket tests.

From autumn 1944, the Luftwaffe Versuchsstelle Karlshagen took over further testing and the co-ordinated supervision of all surface-to-air Flak missiles with specialist and laboratorial support provided by the Army and Luftwaffe E-Stellen in Peenemünde.

Up to the end of December 1944, a total of some 70 Hs 117s were utilised in trials. Further testing and continuation of Hs 117 series production which had started in December 1944, were stopped together with the Wasserfall on 6th February 1945.

Bachem Ba 349 Natter (Viper)
The group of anti-aircraft rocket-powered missiles in the summer/autumn 1944 period was associated with the project for a manned, vertical-take-off rocket-powered aircraft, initially automatically, but in the course of its flight, steered by the pilot. It was to have been extremely simple to manufacture, but for the operational usage intended, incorporated a combination of complex assemblies. Known as the Ba 349 Natter and conceived by the Erich Bachem-Werke in Bad Waldsee, situated half-way between Ulm and Friedrichshafen, it was to take off with the aid of four Schmidding 109-533 solid-propellant RATO units burning for ten seconds, whereafter the main suitably-adapted HWK 109-509A-2 variable-thrust rocket motor would provide power during the climb. The pilot was to engage a bomber formation, fire a salvo of rockets, and descend separately from the aircraft using his parachute.

On 24th October 1944 I received the order to evaluate the project from the aspect of an experienced Peenemünde test and experimental engineer. Following a preliminary meeting with the RLM-TLR concerning the project and a visit to the Messerschmitt AG in Oberammergau regarding 'Further development of the Me 163 rocket fighter', I inspected the Natter on 30th October 1944 in the course of an extensive presentation by Erich Bachem and his colleagues in the Waldsee-Aulendorf factory. The project was again discussed on 3rd November 1944 at the RLM, and on the 11th with the commander of the E-Stelle in Rechlin.

On 11th December 1944 – there being no aviation fuel available at this time even in the E-Stellen for cross-country flights – I travelled by rail via Dessau-Raguhn to the Junkers firm for the purpose of discussing the Ju 248 project as an eventual successor to the Me 163, and then on to Bad Waldsee-Aulendorf where we discussed the Natter proposal in detail, on 18th and 19th December 1944.

Although the in-flight behaviour of the Natter in towed flight behind an He 111 was regarded as good, my judgement turned out to be negative for the following reasons:

The hardly-manageable vertical take-off and approach to a high-flying target by young, inexperienced pilots in a new and untested manned aircraft; the combination of several new or altered components and assemblies that had not yet been tested, coupled with the pressure of time under which development was faced, despite all the optimism displayed by the manufacturer, would not in my view urgently lead to the expected success of the Natter project.

From 22nd December 1944 onwards, scarcely a dozen unmanned vertical launches from a ramp with the aid of RATO units – but without the main rocket motor, took place. On 1st March 1945, the pilot Lothar Siebert on his first Natter flight, ascended vertically using the RATO units and with the main rocket motor switched on. He had reached a height of roughly 150m (500ft) whereupon an external part of the aircraft failed, the flight ending in the pilot's death. To my knowledge, no further manned take-offs with the Natter were made, although limited production was already being undertaken.

Frustrations

From the summer of 1944, working conditions at Peenemünde-West became noticeably more difficult, the prospects of success ever diminishing. Problems with the remote-control missile systems from the point of view of technical progress proved to be of a multifarious nature, so that testing became very time-consuming. In the monthly RLM working meetings on the 'air-to-air' and 'surface-to-air' subjects, attempts were made to master the situation, co-ordinate the activities of industrial firms, official Departments, experimental

Detachments as well as the E-Stellen and effect measures against the withdrawal of personnel from important spheres of activity. The increasing intervention and influence exercised by military and party-political circles did little to help the situation, neither did fundamental changes to spheres of responsibility. These more often led to confusion rather than clarifying competency, as the following demonstrates:

On 1st March 1944, the 'Jägerstab' (Fighter Committee) was established, headed by Reichsminister Albert Speer and Generalfeldmarschall Erhard Milch.

On 26th May 1944, the RLM C-Amt (Office) was dissolved.

At the end of July 1944, the Luftwaffe C-in-C Hermann Göring in agreement with the OKL – certainly as a pre-emptive countermeasure to Speer's planned 'Rüstungsstab' (Armaments Committee) – proclaimed the establishment of an Office entitled 'Chef der Technischen Luftrüstung' (Chief of Technical Air Armament) or Chef TLR, at the same time disbanding the areas of responsibility of the former Generalluftzeugmeister (Milch) with effect from 1st August 1944.

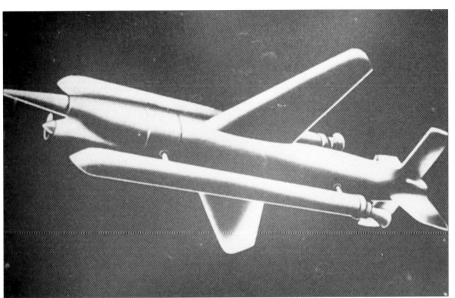

The rocket-powered remote-controlled ground-to-air Hs 117 Schmetterling (Butterfly) missile.

The Hs 117 shortly after leaving its inclined take-off launcher.

The duties and responsibilities of the Chef TLR on 27th July 1944 made it clear that he was to be responsible for (among other articles):

- 2a) Research, development, testing and control of all Air Force equipment including fuels – for control purposes only, insofar as these are not managed by the Army and Navy.
- The Chef TLR represents the OKL opposite the 'Reichsminister für Rüstung und Kriegsproduktion (RM for Armament and War Production) in all matters concerning air Armament.
- Subordinate to the Chef TLR re (a) Operations are E-Stellen Detachments and all Luftwaffe E-Stellen.

On 1st August 1944 Speer, at the same time dissolving the 'Jägerstab' established shortly before, signed the decree establishing the 'Rüstungsstab' whose leadership he personally assumed at the elimination of Milch. The 'Rüstungsstab' was to have the task 'without bureaucratic restraints by means of immediate orders, to carry out the following programmes with all due

The Ba 349 M17 prototype just after leaving its near-vertical launcher on the power of its four solid-fuel booster rockets on 29th December 1944.

The rocket-powered manned Ba 349 Natter (Viper) point-defence interceptor. The plastic nosecap illustrated was not used on test prototypes.

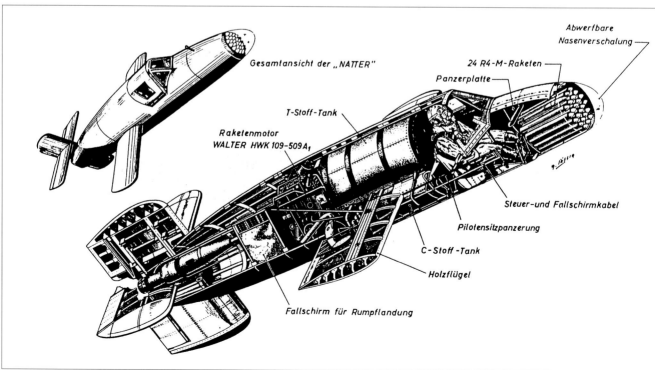

vigour: '(a) the Luftwaffe Programme, (b) the Flak Programme, (c) the V-Weapons Programme …'

It was obvious that by the definition of each of the centres of activity that some duties cut across each other, which led to cases of obscurity in the establishment of responsibility. These changes in structure also had turbulent effects in Peenemünde-West, and led among other things, to the workforce being uniformly channelled, as also changes being postulated and practised in leadership positions.[29,30,31]

The Finale

Despite all difficulties and growing stresses in autumn and winter 1944/45, the work in Peenemünde-West ran according to the aims set. It was not the foreseeable uselessness of the efforts exacted, but rather, solution of the continually occurring technical problems which determined the daily events of test and experimental work.

At the end of January 1945, Commander Otto Stams, who up until then still held this position, was replaced by Major Karl Henkelmann. Programme and project work were either run down or stopped. The sinking by torpedoes of the overloaded 'Wilhelm Gustloff' passenger liner carrying thousands of refugees from East Prussia close to the nearby Swine estuary hit us like a bombshell on our own doorstep.

As already mentioned, between the end of March and in April 1945, Peenemünde-West was relocated to the Wedderwarden air base north of Bremerhaven. We flew back and forth several times with our test aircraft in order to retrieve important instruments, documents, colleagues, and military stores. The majority of the workforce, at times under fire from enemy aircraft, were brought westwards by rail, road, or ship. A few small experimental units conducting special tasks were allocated to other locations.

On 25th April 1945, I wanted to ferry over to Wedderwarden the last of our test aircraft, the jet-propelled Ar 234B (GM+BI). Shortly before reaching Wedderwarden the port Jumo 004 turbojet cut out as a result of turbine blade failure, so that a landing there was not possible. I therefore flew on the remaining engine to Nordholz north of Cuxhaven, where I landed. Following installation of a new engine, I flew this aircraft on 30th April 1945 to Lübeck-Blankensee, from where it was to have been flown by a Luftwaffe pilot to drop a supply container onto the Charlottenburger Chaussee highway in Berlin. After a concluding meeting with Oberst Siegfried Knemeyer, the RLM Chef-TLR and Oberst Werner Baumbach, Kommodore of KG 200, in the Luftwaffe E-Stelle 'See' in Travemünde on the Priwall, I flew before sunrise on 1st May 1945 in an Si 204 at treetop height back to Wedderwarden, taking with me eight co-workers who had experienced a ventureful tramp on foot from Peenemünde to Travemünde.

Following the unconditional Wehrmacht (Armed Forces) surrender on 7th May 1945, the air base was occupied in a fair and problem-free manner by a Scottish contingent clad in kilts. With this action, the former Luftwaffe Versuchsstelle Peenemünde-West, subsequently designated EdL Karlshagen/Wedderwarden, ceased to exist.

If one reviews the events in Peenemünde-West without bias and prejudice, it will be realised that the industrial development conducted there, the tests carried out, the changes, improvements or new developments instigated there, lay mostly on the border of the then known state of technology, edging almost always into technically new ground and serving worldwide as a starting point for new or further improved but in principle equivalent devices or systems which came into use. All the basic functions of modern missile systems at that time brought to operational maturity, were in part solved at the very outset or tested with promising results. Much more ought to have been accomplished through consistent leadership on the part of responsible authorities. But despite deficiencies in leadership and organisation, much was realised astonishingly quickly. We became convinced that the automatically-controlled, remotely-guided or target-seeking missile would just as much revolutionise the air warfare of tomorrow as the aircraft in the past had done.

Footnotes

1   RAF 'Target Information Sheet' of July 1943 (p222 of this book).

2   M Neufeld: 'Die Rakete und das Reich' Brandenburgisches Verlagshaus, 1997, pp238-40.

3   R Kosin: 'Die Entwicklung der deutschen Jagdflugzeuge' Bernard & Graefe Verlag, 1983, Vol 4, p198-201.

4   O Pabst: 'Kurzstarter und Senkrechtstarter' Bernard & Graefe Verlag, 1984, Vol 6, 124-129.

5   W Wagner: 'Die ersten Strahlflugzeuge', Bernard & Graefe Verlag, 1989, Vol 14, pp162-173.

6   H J Ebert/J Kaiser/K Peters: 'Willy Messerschmitt – Pioneer der Luftfahrt und des Leichtbaues' Bernard & Graefe Verlag, 1992, Vol 17, pp255-269.

7   W Späte: 'Der Streng Geheime Vogel', Verlag für Wehrwissenschaften, 1983.

8   Th. Benecke/K H Hedwig/J Hermann: 'Flugkörper und Lenkraketen' Bernard & Graefe Verlag, 1987, Vol 10, p115 ff.

9   B Stüwe: 'Peenemünde-West', Bechtle Verlag, 1995, p270 ff.

10   Karlshagen Partial Report 2412/44 gKdos E2a of 15.8.1944, p1-2 (p223 of this book).

11   M Mayer: 'Selbstgesteuerte und ferngelenkte Flugkörper', Nautilus Jahrbuch, 1953, Verlag Mittler & Sohn, p153.

12   Peenemünde-West Report 1887/42 gKdos of 30.6.1942 'Fritz X Impact Circle from körper und Lenkraketen', Bernard & Graefe Verlag, 1987, Vol 10, p122 ff.

13   B Stüwe: 'Peenemünde-West', Bechtle Verlag, 1995, p473 ff.

14   Th. Benecke/K H Hedwig/J Hermann: 'Flugkörper und Lenkraketen', Bernard & Graefe Verlag, 1987, Vol 10, p122 ff.

15   B Stüwe: 'Peenemünde-West', Bechtle Verlag, 1995, p473 ff.

16   J R Smith/A Kay: 'German Aircraft of the Second World War', Putnam & Co Ltd, 1972, p666.

17   Th. Benecke/K H Hedwig/J Hermann: 'Flugkörper und Lenkraketen', Bernard & Graefe Verlag, Vol 10, p95.

18   Th. Benecke/K H Hedwig/J Hermann: 'Flugkörper und Lenkraketen', Bernard & Graefe Verlag, Vol 10, p94/95.

19   W Churchill: 'The Second World War' (Cassell & Co, 1950), Vol V, Chapter XIII, p208.

20   H Hibbard: 'Unbemannte Flugkörper', Luftfahrttechnik, April 1958, p98.

21   F Ross: 'Guided Missiles', Lothrop, Lee & Shephard, 1951, p99 ff.

22   R A Young: 'The Flying Bomb', Ian Allan Ltd, 1978, pp152-154.

23   Th. Benecke/K H Hedwig/J Hermann: 'Flugkörper und Lenkraketen ' Bernard & Graefe Verlag, 1987, Vol 10, p170.

24   Th. Benecke/K H Hedwig/J Hermann: 'Flugkörper und Lenkraketen', Bernard & Graefe Verlag, Vol 10, 1987, p173 ff.

25   B Stüwe: 'Peenemünde-West', Bechtle Verlag, 1995, p761 ff.

26   Th. Benecke/K H Hedwig/J Hermann: 'Flugkörper und Lenkraketen', Bernard & Graefe Verlag, Vol 10, 1987, p129 ff.

27   B Stüwe: 'Peenemünde-West', Bechtle Verlag, 1995, p713 ff.

28   Reichsminister für Rüstung und Kriegsproduktion: 'Anordnung über die Errichtung des Jägerstabes' (Directive re the Establishment of a Fighter Committee) of 1.3.1944 (p224 of this book).

29   Oberkommando der Luftwaffe, Generalquartiermeister re 'AufstellungChef TLR und Auflösung GL (Establishment of Chef TLR and Dissolution of GL) per 1.8.1944 (p225 of this book).

30   Reichsminister für Rüstung und Kriegsproduktion: 'Erlass über die Bildung eines Rüstungsstabes' (Decree on the Formation of an Armaments Committee), p1-2 (p226 of this book).

31   H D Kohler: 'Ernst Heinkel – Pionier der Schnellflugzeuge', Bernard & Graefe Verlag, 1983, Vol 5, p170 ff.

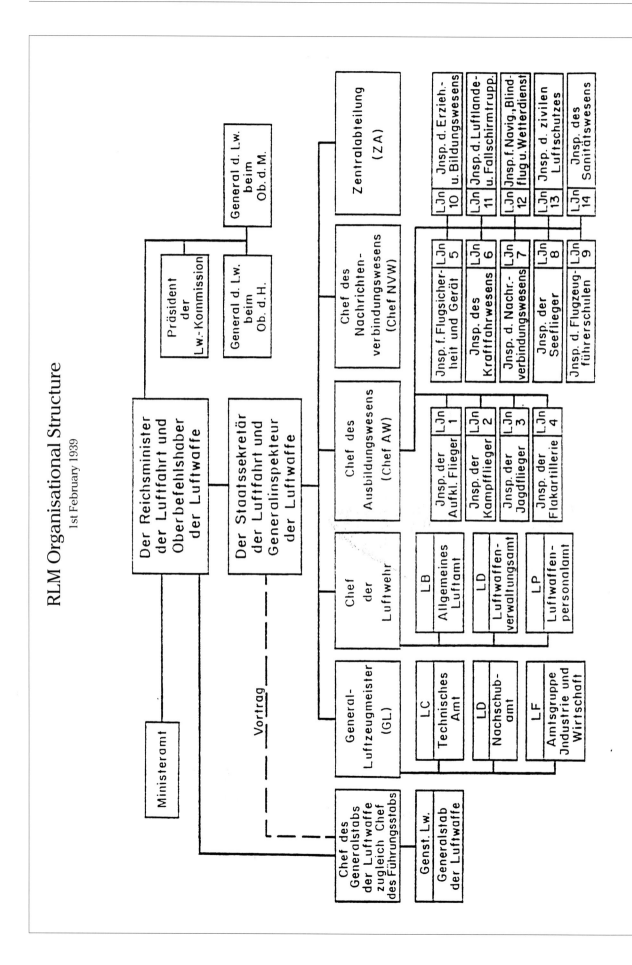

RLM Organisational Structure
1st February 1939

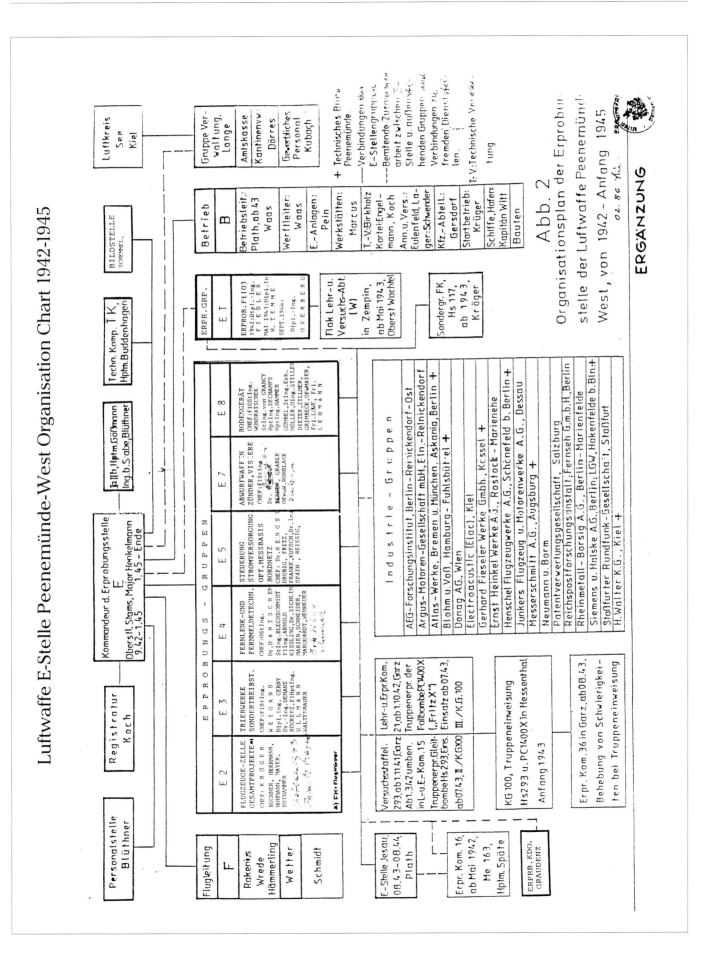

Luftwaffe E-Stelle Peenemünde-West Organisation Chart 1942-1945

Royal Air Force Target Information Sheet

July 1943 – Pages 1 & 2

DRAFT TARGET INFORMATION SHEET.

NOT TO BE TAKEN INTO THE AIR.

GERMANY

INFORMATION SHEET dated July 1943

OP.NO. _____

PLACE: PEENEMUNDE

Lat: 54° 09' N.

A.M.NO. _____

CATEGORY: _____

Long: 13° 48' E.

DISTRICT TARGET
MAP NO. _____

SUB-CATEGORY: _____

Altitude: 10 feet

ALL PREVIOUS INFORMATION SHEETS AND AMENDMENTS THERETO ARE CANCELLED

TARGET MAP: Draft map dated: 4th July 1943.

DESCRIPTION: The target is the EXPERIMENTAL ROCKET PROJECTILE ESTABLISHMENT at PEENEMUNDE situated on a tongue of land on the Baltic Coast about 60 miles N.W. of STETTIN.

The whole complex, which covers an area of some 8,000 x 2,000 yards, includes experimental station, assembly plant, living quarters etc, as follows:—

A.   Experimental Station at the north end of the site, and comprising 4 main component parts as follows, the annotations being shown on the plan attached:

     (W)   A tall building believed to be for the erection and possible loading of the rocket apparatus.

     (X)   An isolated installation near the coast

     (Y)   A further isolated installation between (W) and (X).

     (Z)   A crane like structure and associated installations at the north-west end of an oval earthwork.

B.   Two large factory workshops situated side by side in a wood between the general factory area (E) and the living quarters (F). It is believed that these buildings are intended for the manufacture and assembly of the rocket or firing apparatus.

C.   Power plant situated to the west of the complex.

D.   Apparatus within circular emplacements to the S.W. of the site believed to be possible firing points for the rocket apparatus.

E.   Old established technical and manufacturing establishments probably now largely concerned with experiments and production of the rocket apparatus. One building within this area (T) is believed to be the administrative offices and mess or canteen for specialist and high level workers.

F.   Sleeping and living quarters for personnel employed in the various parts of the works.

G.   Experimental airfield for use in testing rocket projected aircraft etc.

VULNERABLE POINTS: It appears that the greatest damage can be effected to the productive capacity of this plant by making attacks on the following sections of the plant:—

(1)   The experimental establishment (E), destruction of which would interfere with research work and the development of the rocket apparatus.

(11)   The two large factory workshops (B) where it is believed the rockets and/or projecting apparatus are being finally assembled.

(111)   The living and sleeping quarters (F) with the object of killing or incapacitating as many of the scientific and technical personnel as possible.

DECOYS: Particulars of decoys can be obtained from Bomber Command "Gazetteer of Decoys" and subsequent amendments.

CAMOUFLAGE:

FURTHER INFORMATION:

ILLUSTRATIONS:

   /1   -   Vertical aerial photograph of complete site.

   /2   -   Vertical aerial photograph of the experimental portion of the plant (Section A of the target)

   /3   -   Vertical aerial photograph of the two large factory workshops (Section B of the target)

   /4   -   Vertical aerial photograph of the manufacturing establishment (Section E of the target)

   /5   -   Annotated plan of the complete site.

A.I.3c(1).

Luftwaffe E-Stelle Karlshagen 'Status of BV 246'

15th August 1944 – Pages 1 & 2

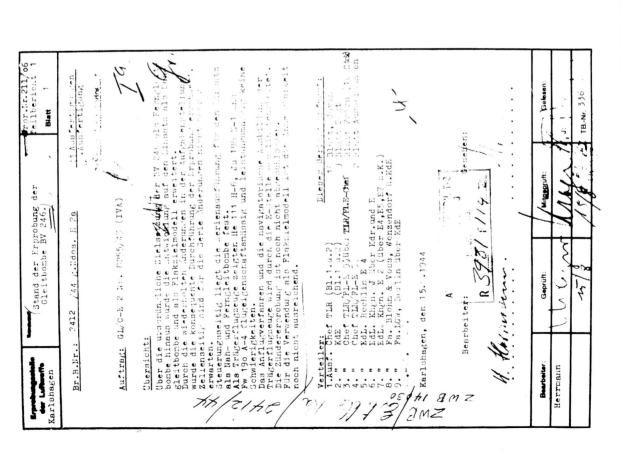

Establishment of the 'Jägerstab' by Albert Speer

1st March 1944 – Pages 1 & 2

Der Reichsminister für
Rüstung und Kriegsproduktion
320 - 922/44 g

Berlin, den 1.März 1944

2. Fassung

A n o r d n u n g

Über die Errichtung der "Jägerstabes"

1) Zur Sicherstellung des Jägerprogramms wird beim Reichsminister für Rüstung und Kriegsproduktion mit sofortiger Wirkung der "Jägerstab" vorläufig auf die Dauer von 6 Monaten
gebildet. Er hat die Aufgabe, ohne bürokratische Hemmungen
durch unmittelbare Befehlsgebung ~~~~ beschädigter Werke oder deren
Verlegung durchzuführen.

Diese Aufgabe steht - insbesondere soweit es sich um die
baulichen Arbeiten handelt - vor allen anderen in letzter
Zeit als besonders wichtig erkannten Aufgaben. Die Beseiti-
gung der durch Fliegerangriffe hervorgerufenen Schaden in
den Städten ist ebenso wie die Luftschutzmaßnahmen und alle
Rüstungsbauten daher hinter diese Aufgabe zu setzen. Ausge-
nommen hiervon sind lediglich die Kugellagerproduktion, die
Betonstartbahnen für Tag- und Nachtjagd, die Versorgungsbe-
triebe (Gas, Wasser, Strom) sowie die Verkehrseinrichtungen
der bombengeschädigten Städte.

Zur Durchführung der Baumaßnahmen ist es notwendig, auf die
in Deutschland befindlichen Bauarbeitskräfte ohne Rücksicht
auf etwaige Einbrüche zurückzugreifen.

2) Der Jägerstab setzt sich wie folgt zusammen:

L e i t u n g :

Reichsminister Speer

Gemeinsamer Stellvertreter und Chef des Stabes
Generalfeldmarschall Milch
Hauptdienstleiter Dipl.Ing. Saur.

M i t g l i e d e r :

verantwortlich für
Bauangelegenheiten   Dipl.Ing. Schlempp

verantwortlich für
Sonderbauaufträge   SS Gruppenführer
Dr. Ing. Kammler

verantwortlich für
Fertigungsplanung   Dr. Ing. Wegener

vegantwortlich für
Zulieferung   Dir. Schaf

verantwortlich für Arbeitseinsatz   Dr. Schmelter

verantwortlich für
die Beschlagnahme von
Verlegungsobjekten   Min. Rat Speh

verantwortlich für
Transportangelegenheiten   NSKK-Gruppenführer Nagel

verantwortlich für
Energieversorgung   Generaldirektor
Dr.Ing. Fischer

verantwortlich für
Programm 262   Hauptmann Dr. Krome

verantwortlich für
alle Maschinenfragen   Ing. Otto Lange

verantwortlich für zu-
sätzliche Sozialbetreuung   Ing. Oberregierungsrat
Dr. Birkenholz.

verantwortlich für
Angelegenheiten der
Reichsbahn

verantwortlich für
Angelegenheiten der
Reichspost.

Entscheidungen des Jägerstabes gelten als Weisungen des
Reichsministers für Rüstung und Kriegsproduktion sowie des
Reichsministers der Luftfahrt und Oberbefehlshabers der
Luftwaffe (Generalluftzeugmeister). Die sachliche Bearbei-
tung erfolgt durch die einzelnen Mitglieder des Jägerstabes,
die unter Verwendung ihres bisherigen Briefkopfes mit dem
Zusatz "Jägerstab" zeichnen.

Soweit bei Fertigung, Zulieferung, Verlagerung und Arbeitseinsatz in Kapazitäten des Heeres und der Kriegsmarine eingegriffen werden soll, ist von den entsprechenden Mitgliedern des Jägerstabes die Zustimmung der beteiligten Amtschefs des Reichsministers für Rüstung und Kriegsproduktion
einzuholen, die erforderlichenfalls meine Entscheidung herbeiführen.

3) Der Jägerstab errichtet bei den in Frage kommenden Produktionsstätten Außenstellen. Der Chef des Stabes bestimmt die
verantwortlichen Leiter der Außenstellen, die nicht Mitglieder des Jägerstabes sind.

Die Außenstellen haben bei der Erfassung und Behebung der
Schäden den Vorsitzer der zuständigen Rüstungskommission zu
beteiligen, um die Auswirkung des Schadens, Verlagerungsmög-
lichkeiten und Wiederaufbaumaßnahmen im einzelnen festzustel-
len. Kommen die Leiter der Außenstellen und Vorsitzer der
Rüstungskommissionen dabei zu keiner Einigung, so entscheidet
der Chef des Stabes im Benehmen mit dem Chef des Rüstungsam-
tes des Reichsministers für Rüstung u. Kriegsproduktion innerhalb 48 Stunden.

4) Die Obersten Reichsbehörden bitte ich, dem Jägerstab jede Unterstützung zu gewähren und ihre beteiligten Dienststellen
anzuweisen, Ersuchen des Jägerstabes weitestgehend zu entsprechen.

P.d.R. gez.Vizepräsident Dr.
Frank. Verteiler A 1,C 1 und 2

gez. S p e e r

Establishment of the Chef TLR by the OKL
27th July 1944

Oberkommando der Luftwaffe   H.Qu., den   Juli 1944
Generalquartiermeister
/44 geheim (2.Abtlg. (I)

Bezug 1) Der Reichsmarschall des großdeutschen Reiches und
    Oberbefehlshaber der Luftwaffe (Generalquartiermei-
    ster 2.Abt. (I)Nr. /44 geheim von .Juli 44.
    2) Oberkommando der Luftwaffe Generalquartiermeister
    (2.Abt.(I)) geheim Nur. /44 geheim v. .Juli 1944.

Betr.Aufstellung Chef der Technischen Luftrüstung und auflösung Generalluftzeugmeister.

In Durchführung zu o.a.Bezug 1) und 2) wird verfügt:
    I.

1) Mit Wirkung vom 1.8.1944 wird die Dienststelle
    Chef der Technischen Luftrüstung (Chef TLR)
    aufgestellt.
2) Durchführung durch Chef der Technischen Luftrüstung.
3) Vorläufige Gliederung gemäß Anlage 1.
4) Aufgaben gemäß Entwurf der vorläufigen Dienstanweisung.
    (Anlage 2)
5) Vorschlag für endgültige Gliederung, Dienstanweisung so-
    wie Dienst- und Stellenplan ist dem Generalquartiermeister
    Durch Chef der Technischen Luftrüstung nach Vorliegen von
    Erfahrungen in der Bewährung der Neuorganisation einzurei-
    chen.
6) Unterstellung: Der Chef der Technischen Luftrüstung un-
    tersteht dem Chef des Generalstabes unmittelbar.
7) Durchführung der Aufstellung ist durch Chef der Technischen
    Luftrüstung bis zum 1.9.44 den Genralquartiermeister zu
    melden.
    II....
    III....
    IV....
    V.

Dem Chef der Techn. Luftrüstung werden unterstellt:
a) einsatzmäßig:
    das Kommando der Erprobungsstellen mit den Erprobungsstel-
    len der Luftwaffe
b) zur Durchführung von Versuchen:
    Die Techn. Akademie der Luftwaffe
c) in jeder Beziehung:
    Die Forschungsführung der Luftwaffe mit ihren Forschungs-
    stellen.

Chef TLR Duties and Responsibilities
27th July 1944

Anlage 2 zu OKL Gen.Qu.Nur19327/44 geh.
(2.Abt.(I))vom 27. Juli 1944

Vorläufige Dienstanweisung für den
Chef der Technischen Luftrüstung. (TLR)

1) Der Chef der Techn. Luftrüstung (TLR) ist dem Chef des Gene-
    ralstabes unmittelbar unters ellt.
    Er hat die Dienststellung eines Kommandierenden General
    d.Lw. und die Disziplinarbefugnisse eines Höheren Befehlshab
    bers gemäß L.Dv. 3/9.
2) Der Chef der Techn. Luftrüstung ist verantwortlich für:
a) die Forschung, Entwicklung, Erprobung und Übernahme des
    gesamten Luftwaffengerätes einschl. der Betriebsstoffe,
    (für Übernahme nur soweit diese nicht durch Heer oder Ma-
    rine erfolgt)
b) Bearbeitung und Auswertung der Entwicklungs- und Rüstungs-
    forderungen, die von Führungsstab, den Waffengeneralen usw.
    über Gen.Qu.6.Abt. gestellt werden.
c) Bearbeitung der durch Gen.Qu.6.Abt.und dem Chef des Nach-
    schubwesens gestellten Gesamtforderungen auf Rüstungsgegen-
    stände nach Menge, Art und Güte und Vertretung dieser Ge-
    samtforderungen gegenüber dem Reichsminister für Rüstung
    und Kriegsproduktion.
d) Einführungsreifserklärungen für das zu beschaff. Gerät.
e) Anregungen für vorausschauende Maßnahmen bei Einführung neu-
    artiger Geräte in Verbindung mit dem Führungsstab,Gen.Qu,
    Gen.d.Fliegerausbildung und den Waffengeneralen.
f) die Bereitstellung der Techn. Vorschriften, Bedienungsan-
    weisungen, Ersatzteillisten und Lehrmittel für das von ihm
    zu erstellende Gerät.
g) Sammlung und Auswertung der Beanstandungen für die Truppen-
    einweisung am techn. Gerät und die techn. Beratung der Trup-
    pe.
h) die Herausgabe techn. Anweisungen und Mitteilungen an die
    Truppe.
3) Der Chef TLR überwacht alle für die Luftwaffe im Verantwor-
    tungsbereich des Heeres und der Marine bzgl. Forschung, Ent-
    wicklung und Erprobung technischen Geräts lfd. Aufgaben.
4) Der Chef TLR wirkt vertritt ien OKL gegen-
    über dem Reichsminister für Rüstung und Kriegsproduktion in al-
    len Fragen der Luftwaffenrüstung.
5) Der Chef TLR wirkt mit bie Aufstellung von Stärke- und Aus-
    rüstungs-Nachweisungen, bei Neueinführung von Gerät.
6) Der Chef TLR ist bei der Ausfuhr von Luftwaffengerät in techn.
    Hinsicht zu beteiligen.
7) Der Chef TLR it in allen, sein Arbeitsgebiet betreffenden Fra-
    gen an enaste Zusammenarbeit mit den übrigen zuständigen
    Dienststellen des OKW u.RLM,insbesondere mit den Waffengene-
    ralen angewiesen.
8) Dem Chef TLR sind unterstellt:
a) Einsatzmäßig
    das Kommando der Erprobungsstelle n mit sämtl. Erprobungs-
    stellen der Lw.:
b) bezügl. Durchführung von Versuchen:
    die Techn. Akademie der Lw.:
c) in jeder Beziehung:
    die Forschungsführung d.Lw. mit ihren Forschungsstellen.
9)Anordnungen, Weisungen und Verfügungen, die vom Chef TLR
    herausgegeben werden, tragen den Briefkopf
    "Oberkommando der Luftwaffe
    Chef der Technischen Luftrüstung"
    und sind "I.A." zu unterzeichnen.

Establishment of the 'Rüstungsstab' by Albert Speer

1st August 1944 – Pages 1 & 2

ABSCHRIFT!

Der Reichsminister für Rüstung
und Kriegsproduktion.

Berlin W.8, den 1.8.1944
Pariserplatz 3.

G e h e i m !

Erlass über die
Bildung des Rüstungsstabes.

1) Um weiteren Schwerpunktprogrammen die Möglichkeit zu geben, aus der bewährten Arbeitsweise und Organisationsform des Jägerstabes den unbedingt erforderlichen Nutzen zu ziehen, ordne ich die Bildung eines
R ü s t u n g s s t a b e s
an. Er hat die Aufgabe, ohne bürokratische Hemmungen durch unmittelbare Befehlsgebung die nachstehenden Programme mit allem Nachdruck durchzuziehen:
Das Luftwaffenprogramm einschl.
das Marineprogramm
das Infanterieprogramm einschl.
des Kraftfahrzeug- und Sturmgeschützprogramms
das Panzerprogramm
das Lokomotivprogramm
das Flakprogramm
das Artillerieprogramm
das V-Programm und
die Reparaturprogramme.

Der Umfang dieser Programme wird jeweils auf Vorschlag meines Vertreters von mir festgelegt. Sie haben sowohl fertigungsmäßig als auch baulich den Vorrang vor allen übrigen Rüstungsendfertigungen.

2) Der Rüstungsstab setzt sich wie folgt zusammen:
Leiter: .... Reichsminister S p e e r
Stellvertreter und
Chef des Stabes .. Hauptdienstleiter Dipl.Ing. S a u r

Persönliche Mitglieder: verantwortlich für:

Generalstabsing. Lucht	Sofortmaßnahmen
Obering. Lange	Flugzeugprogramm
Ing. Desch	Marineprogramm
Ing. Krömer	Panzerprogramm
Direktor Purucker	Waffenprogramm
Dipl.Ing. Groth	Munitionsprogramm
Dipl.Ing. Nobel	Kraftfahrzeugprogramm
Direktor Kunze	Lokomotiv- u. V-Programm
Ing. Oestreich	Reparaturprogramme
Dipl.Ing. Knipping	Bauangelegenheiten
SS-Gruf. Dr.Ing. Kammler	Sonderbauaufträge
Direktor Schaaf	Zulieferungen
Direktor Dr. Heyne	Ausrüstung der Programme

Dr. Stoffregen	Rohstoff-Fragen, Kontingente.
Dr. Wegener	Fertigungsplanung
Dr. Werner	Fertigungsmittelplanung
Dr. Schnelter	Arbeitseinsatz
Min.Rat. Dr. Birkenholz	zusätzl. Sozialbetreuung
Min.Rat Speh	Beschlagnahme von Verlagerungsobjekten.
Grufu Nagel	Transportangelegenheiten
Obering. Pauly	Energieversorgung
Präsident Puckel	Reichsbahnangelegenheiten
Min. Rat Zerbel	Reichspostangelegenheiten
Oberreg. Rat. Dr. Schnauder	Werkluftschutz
Oberberghauptmann Gabel	angelegenheiten der Berverwaltung

Das OKW und die Wehrmachtteile stellen Verbindungsleute.

3) Entscheidungen des Rüstungsstabes gelten als Weisungen des Reichsministers für Rüstung und Kriegsproduktion.

Um auch in Zukunft zu vermeiden, dass sich der Rüstungsstab mit der Zeit zu einer umfangreichen Dienststelle entwickelt, bleibt die Regelung der reinen persönlichen Mitgliedschaft- wie es beim Jägerstab der Fall war - bestehen.
Die sachliche Arbeit erfolgt daher in den intern bzw. Dienststellen, zu denen die persönlichen Mitglieder gehören unter Verantwortung des zuständigen Amtschefs bzw. Dienststellenleiters.

Soweit bei Fertigung, Zulieferung, Verlagerung und Arbeitseinsatz in Kapazitäten anderer Fertigungen eingegriffen werden soll, ist von den entsprechenden Mitgliedern des Rüstungsstabes die Zustimmung der beteiligten Amtschefs des Reichsministers für Rüstung und Kriegsproduktion einzuholen, die erforderlichenfalls meine Entscheidung herbeiführen.

Der Rüstungsstab kann bei den infrage kommenden Produktionsstätten Werksbeauftragte einsetzen, die von meinem Vertreter ernannt werden. Sie sind nicht Mitglieder des Rüstungsstabes. Die Werksbeauftragten, die dem Rüstungsstab unmittelbar unterstehen, haben bei der Durchführung ihrer Aufgabe den Vorsitzer der zuständigen Rüstungskommissionen zu beteiligen. Kommen diese bei ihren Entschließungen zu keiner Einigung, so entscheidet mein Vertreter innerhalb 24 Stunden.

4) Die obersten Reichsbehörden, die Reichsverteidigungskommissare und Gauleiter und die sonstigen Dienststellen bitte ich, dem Rüstungsstab jede Unterstützung zu gewähren und ihre nachgeordneten Dienststellen anzuweisen, Ersuchen des Rüstungsstabes weitestgehend zu entsprechen.

6) Die Verfügung vom 1.März 1944 - 320-922/44 g - betreffend Anordnung über die Errichtung des Jägerstabes wird aufgehoben.

gez. S p e e r

Verteiler wie SB
An.

Luftwaffe E-Stelle Peenemünde-West Report
Fritz X Impact Results 30th June 1942

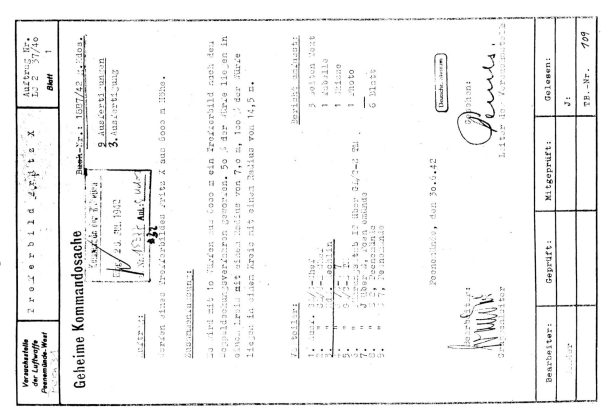

Chapter Nine
by Christoph Regel

Other Test Centres

In view of the ever-increasing number of special requirements for aircraft and equipment, the necessity grew to establish suitable testing installations. These were partly in the form of temporary out-stations, and partly in the form of new E-Stellen which were progressively put into operation. The most important of these centres are described below.

E-Stelle Udetfeld
As a result of increases in flying speeds and altitudes of newer aircraft, the bomb-release ranges east of Berlin had already reached the limits of their usability even before the beginning of World War Two. Added to this, the geological conditions did not allow a proper evaluation of certain types of bombs, so that the establishment of out-stations suitable for these special needs came into consideration.

Bomb release tests undertaken in Mandal, Norway, selected for its granite subsoil, can be initially traced back to August 1941.[1] Test flights started out from Kristiansand, where individual crews with their aircraft and specialists from Section E7 were stationed for the duration of the tests. Drop-tests were carried out in Mandal far into 1944, but without any permanent out-station personnel having been assigned there.

Around 1940 on the other hand, a permanent installation for bomb-testing was established north-east of Beuthen in Upper Silesia. It was initially known as the 'E-Stelle Oberschlesien',[2] but later, probably after the death of Ernst Udet, became the 'E-Stelle Udetfeld'. Its first Commander was Major Werner Zober who came from the E-Stelle Rechlin, being succeeded by Oberstleutnant von Riesen. Fliegerstabsing. Rudolf Noch from Section E7, performed the duties of head of testing. In Udetfeld, tests were mainly carried out with small explosive and incendiary bombs housed in canisters and containers, as well as tests with special detonators and acceptance detonator tests for all types of bombs. A considerable number of tests likewise took place in Udetfeld with parachute bombs, parachutes, and ejection seats. Following progressive expansion, the E-Stelle was equipped with measurement stations, several drop zones, and a photographic section.

Having served for many years as the Reich 'air-raid shelter' and therefore suffering no air attacks whatsoever, Udetfeld suddenly became endangered at the beginning of 1945 due to the advance of Soviet troops. Whilst the location was still being used by units of SG 2, SG 4 and SG 177 as a base of operations, the last tests and evaluations took place on 16th January 1945 before the onset of events occurred in rapid succession. On 17th January 1945, the evacuation of personnel consisting of 350 soldiers, engineers, officials and civilian employees began. The very next day, a train loaded with materiel rolled westwards and crews from the E-Stelle Rechlin flew out the test aircraft which remained. On 20th January 1945, all the field installations and aircraft incapable of being transported were blown up, the location falling into Soviet hands a few days later.

Technical personnel were largely redeployed in their former Rechlin 'home' Detachments as were a portion of the Technical Company soldiers. The majority, however, were summoned for frontline service. The dissolution order for the E-Stelle Udetfeld on 15th February 1945, was a purely administrative act which sealed its end in writing.

E-Stelle Tropen (Tropics)
In the Mediterranean area, the Luftwaffe was confronted with particular climatic conditions. From 1941 onwards, single- and twin-engined fighter units were stationed in North Africa in support of the German Army – later termed the 'Afrikakorps', under Generaloberst Erwin Rommel to assist the cornered Italian Army. It soon became clear, however, that in many respects the aircraft and equipment were unsuitable for this theatre of war. At the behest of the GL/C-E, the E-Stelle Rechlin had already in autumn 1940 involved specialists in all departments, headed by Fliegerstabsing. Fitjer of E2, with tropical matters. Problems soon arose dealing with undercarriages, cockpit canopies, surface covering materials and protection, and wooden structural parts which were affected by high day and night temperature differences and the effects of sand and dust as well as soil structure in the North African coastal regions.

In order to gather experience with functional and operational conditions in Africa, the E-Stelle at first sent individual specialists directly to the units stationed there. On one such visit, Fliegerstabsing. Walter Baist from Section E3 travelled at the beginning of June 1941 for 10 days to Tripoli, Benghazi and Derna, and assembled his findings thereafter in a report entitled 'General Requirements for Tropical Operations of Aircraft Engines'. Since this form of 'testing' did not by far keep abreast with the needs of the troops for operationally-capable flying equipment, the E-Stelle Tropen (Tropics) was established in the summer of 1941, initially having several aircraft of it own – one example of each of the Ju 52, Ju 87R, Ju 88A, Bf 109E, Hs 126B and Fi 156C, and which directly accompanied the various German-Italian units. One supporting base remained at Castel Benito airfield near Tripoli. Appointed as head of the E-Stelle was Fliegerstabsing. Schürfeld, formerly Gruppenleiter E7Eb in Rechlin. Equipping the E-Stelle with personnel, it appears, took place only sporadically, for even in November 1941, individual specialists came with the order to 'collect, evaluate and pass on the experiences and problems encountered'.[4] It was thus still a far cry from planned testing!

In the meantime the Afrikakorps was again on the advance, which led to the E-Stelle being transferred to Derna. This transfer and base supply followed progressively using the Ju 52 (GG+BR) and He 11? (GD+FH) which flew back and forth between Castel Benito and Derna, but had to continually fetch materials from Catania or even Foggia. At the beginning of December 1941, when personnel in Derna were finally at full strength, a British counter offensive forced Rommel to retreat and the base had to be abandoned. Because of shortage of aviation fuel, a part of the equipment had to be returned by road, under constant attack from British low-flying aircraft. In mid December 1941, E-Stelle personnel were reunited at their regular base at Castel Benito. After the British advance had been stopped and equipment and supplies had been flown out in numerous flights from Italy, the activities of the E-Stelle could again commence at the beginning of 1942 in a somewhat regular form. During the first half of the year, Fliegerstabsing. Erich Fleischhauer became the new head of the E-Stelle Tropen. Besides general trials conducted on all aircraft types in operation, interest centred chiefly on the Bf 109 and Fw 190 fighters, since air superiority in the Mediterranean area was almost exclusively in the hands of the Allies. The need for functionally-operational fighters for defence against the ever-increasing bomber formations or the ever-present fighters, received the highest priority. Testing was largely concluded in October 1942. At this point, unfortunately, an accident happened, for on 19th July 1942, Fliegerstabsing. Franz Elble from Section E3, flying the Fw 190A-3 (DF+GM, Werk-Nr.514), crashed in Castel Benito with fatal injuries.

The next machine whose special Africa trials were scheduled was the Hs 129 ground-attack aircraft. At least three examples of the Hs 129B-2 variant, equipped with tropical filters and altered engine cowlings since cooling proved insufficient in the series-built version, were provided for this purpose. Testing, however, suffered delays due to the increasingly unfavourable war situation for the Axis partners and was finally overdue when units of the Afrikakorps and the Army in Tunis had to lay down

Testing snow-skis were not without problems at the Dorpat out-station. Insufficient rigidity led to twisting in flight and damage on landing which were not always so negligible as happened here with the Fw 198A (KD+RO) of the E-Stelle Rechlin.

their arms in May 1943 before the overwhelming British-American forces. E-Stelle Tropen personnel were able to be completely returned to Germany, but Hs 129B-2 (ZN+DQ, Werk-Nr.277), remained behind and was captured by the Allies in La Depienne, Tunisia. Its tailplane still visibly bore the E-Stelle Rechlin telephone number 'Murow 231'.

E-Stelle Süd (South)

A further location for testing air-drop weapons was in Foggia, situated on the heel of the southern Italian peninsula, where during the second half of 1944, the E-Stelle Süd (South) commenced its activities. Decisive factors for the selection of this location were first the limestone strata, and second, its proximity to the bay of Manfredonia where testing of air-launched torpedoes and underwater weapons (air mines) could be conducted. The bay, however, proved to be unsuitable for the latter task, so that trials were soon moved Grosseto on the Italian west coast in the region of the Isle of Elba. It was simultaneously established that Foggia had unsuitable conditions for conducting tests. The location was constantly occupied by other flying units; the harbour was not allowed to be used by the E-Stelle; living quarters, furniture and technical equipment were not available, and the allotted aircraft hangar proved to be unusable. In addition, there was the long supply route over the Brenner Pass – up to four weeks! – and for that time, the still-dangerous ferrying of test aircraft over the Alps and Appenines. These anxieties were not unfounded, as on 1st October 1942, He 111C-6 (CC+SE, Werk-Nr.4838), was lost en route to Foggia when it crashed on Mount Veroli with the loss of all five crew members belonging to Section E7,

the Technical Company Rechlin, and the E-Stelle Lärz.

It was therefore only logical that the E-Stellen Commander, Major Petersen, following an inspection in Foggia on the 21st and 22nd February 1942, agreed with the proposal of the E-Stelle head Fliegerstabsing. Fleischhauer, to relocate the E-Stelle.[3] An eminently suitable location was found in the former French experimental airfield in Cazaux, southwest of Bordeaux. This sparsely-inhabited airfield had been expanded in peacetime, sported over 15 hangars as well as a dockyard, and offered comparably favourable weather conditions as in Foggia. A very large bombing range with measurement station was available nearby, as also the Biscarosse naval air base which was suitable for the experimental tasks of the E-Stelle Travemünde. The KdE proposal met with a positive response, so that from July 1942 onwards, work at Cazaux could begin. Up to its dissolution, the new E-Stelle Süd Commander was Hauptmann Henno Schlockermann, whose deputy was Hauptmann Schwering. Most flights served to make ballistic measurements of various types of bombs or jettisonable containers, eg, the BZA 1, BZA 20, Lotfe 7, TSA and Stuvi. (level- and dive-bombing sights), in-flight release of rocket-bombs, as well as 'normal' drops in the target area known as 'Steingarten' (stone-garden) and 'Storchennest' (stork's nest) used for low- and high drops. The test contingent, consisting of members of Rechlin Section E7 in Cazaux, were temporarily strengthened by test personnel from the Rheinmetall-Borsig and Zeiss firms and with the DVL's own test aircraft. As recollected with satisfaction by the then Commander, a total of some 1,800 flights were carried out at the E-Stelle Süd with only one

The trousered spring coverings and snow-skis have an unusual plump appearance on this Fw 190A (RI+KW) seen here in front of a hangar in Dorpat. In addition to the principal ski trials, a whole series of tests were necessary to determine the best form and treatment of the wooden trellis surfaces to prevent the skis from being firmly frozen when resting on them for a long period.

fatality, involving Oberfeldwebel Alwin Manthey on 16th August 1943 during the testing of a reflex sight as a bomb-aiming device (BZA), when the wings of his Bf 109E-7 (CP+MY, Werk-Nr.3298), disintegrated during the dive and the aircraft crashed and exploded on the airfield at Cazaux.

When the Allies began to make their Invasion preparations by the systematic bombardment of all French airfields located in rear areas, it became only a matter of time before Cazaux would be targeted in the cross-wires of American bombsights. On 27th March 1944, the E-Stelle was the target of a daylight raid in which installations were badly hit and a large number of test aircraft, among them two Ju 88s, two He 111s, two Fw 190s, an Fi 156 and the Do 217P V2 used for high-altitude bomb releases, were destroyed or badly damaged. As a result, testing had to be severely reduced and the first batch of E-Stellen personnel returned to Rechlin or Udetfeld. But it was only after the unstoppable advances made by Allied troops who had landed in Normandy and the low-level attack on 1st September 1944 in which several more test aircraft were destroyed, that the E-Stelle Süd in Cazaux as well as the Technical Company contingent was disbanded by official order on 1st October 1944.

Winter Tests – Out-Station Dorpat

With the increasing escalation of the war in northern and eastern Europe, the Luftwaffe and other branches of the armed forces were confronted more and more with the problems of snow and severe long-duration cold-weather conditions, posing extremely bad maintenance and housing possibilities.

One of the main problems encountered here was the start-up of aero-engines in polar climatic conditions that had already been investigated by the E-Stelle Rechlin since the mid 1930s, and which led to development of the Rechlin 'cold-start' procedure.[5]

In the meantime, further testing tasks were added, eg, the increasing use of hydraulically-operated aircraft systems; the attainment of ever-higher flying altitudes and the necessity to install crew heating; requirements for airframe and canopy de-icing, as well as accelerating operational readiness under extreme winter conditions such as by the use of snow skids. Operational readiness of the necessary ground-support equipment had also to be taken into account, ranging from tarpaulin protective coverings up to complete fuel tankers. Related tests had already been started even before the war at air bases in southern Germany and were continued in Rechlin in the winter of 1939/40. This work, however, suffered under the disadvantage that the attainable temperatures and snow conditions were neither extreme nor held up for long periods. Thus, in the winter of 1940/41, an additional series of tests were conducted in Gardermoen, Norway, where snow skids were evidently the focal point of trials. This resulted at the end of January 1941 in the loss of a Bf 109E-1 where the port skid whilst in flight, had skewed outwards and downwards so that a landing approach appeared to be too risky, causing the pilot to eject using his parachute.[6] This incident highlighted one of the main problems with the use of snow skids, namely, its anchoring in the horizontal position in flight. A solution for this was still not found when the next series of tests began in

autumn 1941, so that a number of fortunate single-engined landings also occurred at this time. The location chosen for these tests was Dorpat in Estonia, as it offered ideal winter test conditions. It became possible there to test the majority of standard Luftwaffe operational aircraft with skids as also engines and equipment. Engine manufacturers such as BMW also used this location for their investigations. Tests were provisionally terminated at the end of April 1942 and the personnel, which had been under the leadership of Fliegerhaupting. Kloppe from Referat E2f (Undercarriage Test), were transferred back to Rechlin.

In September of that year Oberfeldwebel Friedrich Böhle from the Technical Battalion Rechlin was ordered to establish an advance Kommando which was to make preparations for the installations at Dorpat to be occupied by an out-station Detachment. This time, the testing contingent with some 100 men, was more than twice as strong as in the previous winter. Fliegerstabsing. Helmut Roloff from Rechlin Section E5 was appointed as its head. The range of tasks remained the same, the items to be tested corresponding to the newer aircraft and engine models coming into service in the meantime, and is reported to have included a BMW 003 turbojet.[7] With the onset of the thaw, winter testing was no longer possible from April 1943 onwards; the out-station was finally dissolved and personnel returned to Rechlin.

E-Stelle Werneuchen

Note: This contribution concerning the E-Stelle Werneuchen, published by Helmut Bukowski in 'Jägerblatt' 6/1996, is based upon the recollections of Klaus Müller, the then adjutant to the E-Stellen Commander and who is thanked especially for making additional documents available.

In April 1942 at Werneuchen air base 24km (15 miles) northeast of Berlin, a special E-Stelle placed directly under the charge of the RLM Technical Office Department GL/C-E4, was established for the testing of radio and radar equipment. Working together with the FFO or Flugfunkforschungsanstalt (Aerial Radio Research Institute) at Oberpfaffenhofen the following basic tasks were to be investigated:

- Comprehensive naval air reconnaissance and methods of combatting targets from the air.
- Swift determination and perception of the aerial situation.
- Operational response for day and night air defence and providing fighter direction for destroying targets from the air.
- Combatting enemy air forces' jamming and deceptive tactics.
- Testing new techniques and methods of electronic warfare.

Out-stations for testing ground radar installations were located at Weesow, 3km (1.8 miles) northwest of Werneuchen and at Tremmin, 10km (6.2 miles) southwest of Nauen. The proximity of Berlin with its industrial and research facilities, the RLM, and the Chief of the Communications Services (NVW), General Wolfgang Martini, enabled problems which surfaced to be easily and directly solved.

Construction of the E-Stelle Werneuchen was directed by Major I G August Hentz, who required for Werneuchen, hand-picked personnel from Rechlin and from Lufthansa's Funkversuchsstelle (Radio Research Centre) in Berlin-Tempelhof. From 1st April 1942, for exactly two years, Hentz was Commander of the E-Stelle Werneuchen before taking over the post of Section Head for Radar Equipment, reporting to the Chef NVW/ObdL until the end of the war. His successor in Werneuchen was Major i.G Cerener.

Flight testing of newly-developed devices was carried out initially by the Erprobungsstaffel (Test Squadron) of the E-Stelle TVK or Technisches Versuchskommando (Technical Test Detachment) prior to April 1944, when Nachtjagdgruppe NJG 10, and especially its Versuchsstaffel 3 under Hauptmann Gustav Tham, set up for this purpose, took over. A Training Company led by Oberleutnant Hans Malchow, for airborne radar, trained Luftwaffe flight crews on the new devices.

In 1942, the E-Stelle Werneuchen tested a blind-nightfighting system with the 'Lichtenstein U' radar apparatus. The downward-directed ventral antenna-array (here beneath an He 111) was expected to enable the pilot to detect enemy aircraft flying beneath and attack them with downward-firing ammunition having delayed fuses, such that the aircraft itself would not come within range of the enemy's defensive weapons. Nothing is known concerning combat experience with this system.

Stabsing. Poppendieck of the E-Stelle Werneuchen with the 'Spanner II' infra-red target-sighting periscope.

Despite considerable ignorance by the Luftwaffe leadership for this new technology, the E-Stelle Werneuchen tested a large number of radar types and was able to hand over a portion to service units. In the first half of 1942, tests were undertaken in Werneuchen with the AEG-developed 'Spanner III' (Trigger), an infra-red target-seeking device aimed at combatting enemy jamming of indigenous airborne radar. A proposal made in the summer by Fliegerstabsing. Poppendieck to equip nightfighters with a vertically-upward-directed infra-red beam for target-capture for aircraft equipped with the FuG 'Lichtenstein' and Schrägebewaffnung (oblique-firing armament) did not see operational use. In 1942, tests were conducted at Werneuchen with the nightfighter radars FuG 202 'Lichtenstein B/C' and 'Lichtenstein U', the latter intended for operations against low-flying

targets. Testing of the FuG 212 'Lichtenstein C1' lasted until May 1943. Other tasks for the E-Stelle Werneuchen during its first year of existence, were testing of the ship target-seeking FuG 200 'Hohentwiel' device installed from September in an He 111H-18 and testing series-produced models of the FuMG 65 'Würzburg-Riese' and 'Freya' ground-based radar, intended for anti-aircraft and fighter direction.

In 1943 it became necessary to develop at short notice, means to counter radar jamming by the British. The very first use of the so-called Düppelstreifen (chaff strips) during the large-scale raid on Hamburg, had paralysed the German nightfighters and required immediate countermeasures. Indeed, the method whereby the release of tinfoil strips having half the wavelength of the enemy radar, causing the monitor screens to become blanked-out by the

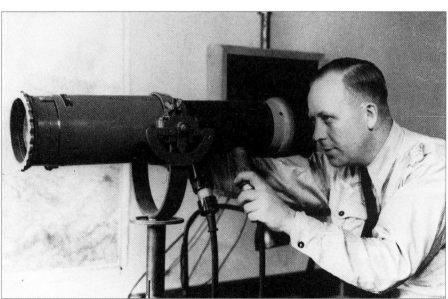

reflexion disturbances, had already been tested the previous May by the E-Stelle Rechlin above the Müritz.[8] Operational use of it had been postponed by the Luftwaffe in order not to betray this simple and effective expedient to the enemy. In Werneuchen, methods had been developed which, by making use of the Doppler effect, bombers could be distinguished from fake targets. On the viewing screen, a so-called 'Laus' (louse) crawled away over the disruptive jamming, and was given code-names such as 'Fack-Laus' or 'Würzlaus' after its inventor Dr. Fack, or else named after the FuMG 'Würzburg' radar. The devices were immediately put into production and introduced into service by conversion and training units. Also developed in 1943 was the 'Freya-Halbe' flight target receiver which reacted passively to the disturbances of the ground-support Freya stations. In spring 1943, the E-Stelle tested the rearward-directed FuG 216 'Neptun R' and FuG 'Lichtenstein BC/R' warning devices, which homed onto the radar signals of British long-range nightfighters which lay in wait to catch the German fighters on take-off.

Other developments comprised the FuG 220 'Lichtenstein SN-2' wide-angle search device derived by Telefunken from a shipboard search device; the Lorenz FuG 200 'Hohentwiel' which was the competitor to the FuG 213 of Telefunken; the rearward-warning device FuG 217 'Neptun J' nightfighter device derived from the FuG 216 rearward-warning device, and the passive target-approach devices FuG 227 'Flensburg-Halbe' and the FuG 350Z 'Naxos Z' which reacted to the impulses of British rearward-facing warning apparatus. The first two ground-supported all-round search devices were erected in Tremmin – the FuG 403 'Panorama', and in Weesow – the FuG 404 'Jagdschloss'. Tests on a third device, the FuMG 41 'Wassermann L' had to be terminated in February 1944.

The end of 1943 witnessed the equipping of He 111H-20 training aircraft in Werneuchen with the 'Lichtenstein SN-2' airborne radar and the testing of the first Ta 154 aircraft with this apparatus. The Lufthansa Werft housed in Hangar 1 and Hangar 2 also assisted with the conversions in Werneuchen, from where the auxiliary Fw 189 and Fw 58 nightfighters, equipped with the FuG 212 'Lichtenstein C-1' originated, and which actually saw operational service with NJG 100 on the Eastern Front.

Testing began in 1944 with 'Identification Friend-Foe' devices such as the FuG 25a 'Erstling' (First-born), the FuG 226 'Neuling' (Novice), and the FuG 225 'Biene W' (Bee W). Based on the British 'Rotterdam' device, the E-Stelle working group 'Berlin', led by Fliegerstabsing. Arved von Schubert, in co-operation with Telefunken, developed the centimetre wavelength 'Berlin nightfighter radar, used for the first time in the Ju 88G-7c. In Werneuchen, nightfighting equipment was also installed and tested in the Ar 234 and Me 262. First to be modified in the Lufthansa Werft in Werneuchen was the Ar 234B-2/N (Werk Nr.140145), and in January 1945, three further machines were in process of modification. Ground-supported long-distance and all-round search devices were tested in 1944 in Göhren on the island of Rügen – the 'Würzmann', and in Weesow near Werneuchen, the Propeller. The equally successful mobile all-round search device 'Jagdwagen' was also tested in Werneuchen. Due to the approach of the Front in February 1945, the E-Stelle had to be moved to Stade, where the entire materiel fell into British hands at the end of the war.

In January 1944, the E-Stelle Werneuchen prepared a Testing Report on the 'Lichtenstein SN-2' radar. Despite its low close-resolution and susceptibility to disturbances from radio waves and other 'Lichtenstein' radars, the SN-2 was declared to be the 'currently most effective nightfighter search device'. It is seen here installed in a Ju 88 at the E-Stelle.

Photographs on the opposite page:

The Do 17Z 'Kauz' aircraft experimentally fitted with an infra-red target searchlight and the 'Spanner' search apparatus in the nose.

Out of the Do 217E-2 variant equipped with the FuG 202, the Do 217J-2 radar-equipped nightfighter was developed.

E-Stelle Munster-Nord

The E-Stelle Munster-North, located near Munster in the Lüneburger Heide (Luneburg Heath), existed since spring 1938 at the latest. Its task was testing poison-gas bombs for high-altitude attacks and poison-gas spray containers for low-altitude attack, in co-operation with the HWA (Army Ordnance Office). Hardly any documents are available concerning the activities of this E-Stelle. All that is on record is that this E-Stelle conducted a presentation in the presence of Staatssekretär Milch on 9th April 1943 and further, that the Do 217E-3 (KH+CR, Werk-Nr.5068), crashed on 8th September 1944 near Munsterlager with its crew consisting of Oberfeldwebel Brandt, Unteroffizier Dubberke and an industrial employee Obering. Bauer, the crash apparently being in connection with a presentation.

Footnotes

1 Pilot's Logbook Hans Schwenk, E7.
2 BA/MA Freiburg File RL 3/2091 Letter LC 7 Ref: 66p16 (IAI) to LD 12 dated 12.2.1941 re 'Bauvorhaben Dringlichkeitsstufe 0' (Construction Proposal Priority Rating 0).
3 E-Stelle Tropen (Tropics), Service Commission for Fliegerstabsing. A. Kr. A Kuhn of 3.11.1941.
4 National Archives, Washington, Microfilm T 321/59 Kommando der E-Stellen Nr.15108/42 gKdos 'Bericht über Besichtigung der E-Stelle Foggia durch KdE am 21 und 22.2.1942' (Report on Inspection of the E-Stelle Foggia by Commander on 21 & 22.2.1942.
5 K Gersdorff/K Grasmann/H Schubert: 'Flugmotoren und Strahltriebwerke' Bernard & Graefe Verlag, Vol 2, 1995.
6 Deutsches Museum, Munich, File Rech 31: Rechlin E2f, Test Nr.1767, Partial Report 4 'Bf 109 Snow-ski testing' of 14.2.1941.
7 Letter dated 30.11.1994 from Friedrich Bohle to author.
8 See footnote 52 in Chapter 5 – 'E-Stelle Rechlin'.

Chapter Ten
by Christoph Regel

Test Squadrons and Test Detachments

Following the technical type-testing and suitability for series manufacture conducted by the manufacturers or by the Luftwaffe E-Stellen from around 1939, very often for single-engined aircraft or types of equipment, the Erprobungskommandos (Test Detachments) or Erprobungsstaffeln (Test Squadrons) were established for the following duties:
- Testing under operational conditions the item intended for introduction into service use.
- Development of tactical procedures.
- Providing support for service introduction.
- Testing of technical and tactical proposals for the services.

The following portrays the known tasks of the various E-Staffeln and E-Kommandos:

Erprobungskommando 4
Its formation order, approved on 1st December 1944, was carried out through Luftflotte (Air Fleet) 10 in agreement with the Kdo.d.E. and the General der Jagdflieger. It was intended to have a personnel strength of 16 men in addition to the 1st FK-BK or Flugkörper-Betriebskompanie (Missile Operating Company). The exchange of trained personnel for the X4 missile from the 5th FK-BK with personnel from the 1st FK-BK was arranged by KG 200 in close agreement with the Kdo.d.E.

Task of the Detachment was service-testing the X4 guided rocket, testing operational methods and flight testing its operational possibilities. The Detachment had nine aircraft available for this purpose, consisting of Bf 109s and Fw 190s.

Erprobungskommando 15
This Detachment was formed out of the Versuchsstaffel (Test Squadron) Hs 293 and had the task of carrying out service testing the Hs 293 glide-bomb. Further details are related in Chapter 8 – The E-Stelle Peenemünde-West.

Erprobungskommando 16
The formation of this E-Kdo took place via the Detachment route around April 1942 in Peenemünde-West. The Detachment was budgeted for on 1st September 1943 and transferred to Bad Zwischenahn. Its task

was the testing and service preparation of the Me 163 tailless fighter, and for this purpose it was assigned various Me 163As for training and Me 163Bs for trials, alongside several gliders, towing and touring aircraft. In October 1944, the unit moved to Waldpolenz near Brandis, but on 14th February 1945, E-Kdo 16 received the order for immediate disbandment. The tasks still open were to be undertaken by JG 400 which took over the operationally-usable aircraft. Personnel thus freed reverted to various service units or were transferred to operational flying units.

Erprobungskommando 17
This Detachment was originally formed out of the 2nd Staffel of KG 100 which in November 1941 relocated for freshening-up to Hannover-Langenhagen. It latterly moved to Chartres in France, where in January 1942, it was renamed Erprobungskommando XY. From there, a number of operational flights were made against England with noticeable losses. Since the designation of the Detachment gave an all too apparent clue to its activities, ie, the further development of the X- and Y-Verfahren – the target-alignment beams, it was renamed E-Kdo 100 from March to May 1942 and was finally budgeted as the E-Kdo 17, under which designation further flights were made. As early as September 1942, the Detachment was renamed 15/KG 6, serving as the cornerstone for the newly-intended I/KG 66 Pfadfinderverband (Pathfinder Formation).

Erprobungs- und Lehrkommando 18
This Test- and Instruction Detachment was formed on 1st August 1942 in Pillau, being placed simultaneously under the command of the General der Luftwaffe in the Ob.d.M. (Supreme Command of the Navy). Its task consisted of testing the aircraft intended for use aboard the aircraft carrier 'Graf Zeppelin' including the necessary equipment as well as providing familiarisation and training for the flight and shipboard crews. Exactly when the detachment was dissolved is not known, but presumably occurred at the time when construction work on the sole German aircraft carrier

was definitely terminated in January 1943.

Erprobungskommando 19
This Detachment was formed on 1st July 1942 at Castel Benito airfield near Tripoli for the temporary duration of two months. Its task was to test the Bf 109G and Fw 190 for their tropical suitability as fighter and ground-attack aircraft. The Detachment was assigned two fighter instructors and six fighter trainees who came from the Ergänzungsgruppen (Replacement Training Squadrons) of JG 27 and JG 53.

Erprobungs- und Lehrkommando 20
This Test- and Instruction Detachment was established on 1st October 1942, initially in Trave-münde and later in Kamp. It was to carry out all testing needs in connection with ship-based special aircraft as well as the familiarisation and training of air and ground crews for such aircraft. How long this unit existed is not known.

Erprobungs- und Lehrkommando 21
This Detachment was established on 1st August 1942 in Garz on Usedom, its personnel and equipment coming largely from the disbanded II/KSG 3. Its task involved service testing of the PC 1400X guided bomb. Further details are related in Chapter 8.

Erprobungs- und Lehrkommando 22
Established in autumn 1942 in Lärz, the Detachment had the task of testing the Fw 190 fighter-bomber with increased range, known as the 'Jaborei'. Its personnel came from KG 40, JG 2 and JG 26, as well as from a twin-engined Zerstörerschule (heavy-fighter school). In spring 1943, the Detachment was transferred to St André in France, and in December 1942 it merged with the established I/SKG 10.

Erprobungs- und Lehrkommando 24
This Detachment was established on 1st March 1943 in Mark Zwuschen for the purpose of testing all aircraft types intended for the reconnaissance role but excluding high-altitude aircraft. It is known that trials were carried out on automatic flight control and navigation devices in the Bf 109, Bf 110 and Fw 190 reconnaissance versions as

well as with target-approach flights with these aircraft. On 14th October 1944, the Detachment received the order to disband, and its personnel were transferred to the Versuchsverband OKL (OKL Test Flight) or to other units, the former then assuming the tasks of the Detachment from that date.

Erprobungskommando 25

The order for its establishment was announced on 17th April 1943, and in a further order of 22nd January 1944, its range of tasks were expanded. It had additionally to conduct testing under frontline conditions of all aircraft required for day-fighter use, airborne radar equipment, weapons, and combat methods as well as operations within the framework of Reichsverteidigung (National Defence). Testing included defensive tactics by bomber formations against horizontal and vertical attack by use of the WGr 21 or the SG 116 'Zellendusche' installed in an Fw 190F-8. Out of this Detachment, Jagdgruppe 10 was later established, performing the same range of tasks.

Erprobungskommando 26

Upon an order dated 29th December 1943, this Detachment was set up through the redesignation of the former 11th(Pz)/SG 9, and was stationed at the E-Stelle Udetfeld. It had at its disposal 4 Ju 87s, 4 Fw 190s and 4 Hs 129s, as well as 4 nightfighters, one touring and 1 transport aircraft. The Detachment existed until 14th February 1945, whereupon its personnel were seconded to the General der Schlachtflieger. Tasks still not carried out were to have been undertaken by the Ergänzungsstaffel of SG 151.

Erprobungskommando 36

This Detachment was formed in Garz on 10th August 1943 through the renaming of 13/KG 100 (ex-4th/EK 21), and was to test the service suitability of successive Hs 293 variants which either already existed as prototypes or were under development. In addition, He 177 Operators were to be familiarised with the FuG 203 'Kehl', but training on the latter was, however, broken off. In the first half of 1944 alone, the Detachment lost 5 aircraft during trials.

By an order of 12th July 1944, the Detachment was immediately disbanded. Personnel thus freed were mostly transferred to E-Kdo 25 for the purpose of continuing trials with missile-equipped fighters, the remainder being placed at the disposal of the General der Jagdflieger and the General der Kampfflieger.

Transportstaffel 40

Although not designated as an Erprobungskommando, this unit, by reason of its duties, ought to be mentioned here. Transport Squadron 40 was officially established on 14th February 1945 in Muhldorf/Inn, and was subordinate to the 'Operational Testing of Helicopter Aircraft'. On paper, the Squadron was to receive 12 examples of the Fa 223, but this was never attained since a large number of these helicopters were destroyed in bombing raids on the manufacturing centres. Only two Fa 223s actually reached the Squadron in April 1945, but could by no means undergo operational testing at that time. At the end of the war, the unit was in the Austrian mountains and the two Fa 223s were captured by the Americans.

Erprobungskommando 40

This Detachment came into being on 1st January 1944 through the renaming of the former 'Flieger-Forstschutzverband' (Aerial Forest Protection Unit) which, since its inception, was responsible for combatting forest termites and in this function since 1939, had sprayed around 61,000 Hectares or 610km² (235.4mls²) of forest in some 3,500 flights. The aircraft park consisted mainly of Fw 58s but also had old Do 23s. The Detachment, which until then had been stationed in Göttingen, was dissolved by order on 3rd September 1944. Remaining aircraft were transferred to the E-Stelle Munster-Nord and Werneuchen or to other air bases, the Do 23s being scrapped. The E-Stelle Rechlin took over the majority of its materials, whereas its personnel were sent to pilot assembly centres to await operational orders.

A Detachment remainder stayed on in Göttingen and moved in November 1944 to Coburg where prior to this, parts of the Detachment had already been stationed. The rest then served as the core for E-Kdo 41.

Erprobungskommando 41

Formed on 22nd January 1945, this Detachment and its tasks were apparently the same as that of E-Kdo 40. Nothing, however, is known of its activities.

Erprobungsstaffel Ju 88

A unit bearing this designation is known solely through mention in post-war literature, but documentary evidence has up to now not been seen by this author. The Squadron is reported to have been formed in Rechlin in summer 1939, and from it the later I/KG 30 (previously designated I/KG 25) is said to have been formed.

It is possible that in this instance, the 1st/ Lehrgruppe 88 is meant, which with effect from 21st September 1939, was formed in Greifswald. The unit, which had the strength of a Squadron at the beginning, and in gradual stages expanded to Gruppen strength, had the task of training air and ground crews for the Ju 88. The frontline flying units scheduled to be equipped with this aircraft were looked after by this Lehrgruppe right up to their operational readiness stage.

In the last half of 1940 the Gruppe was renamed the Ergänzungskampfgruppe 4 (Replacement Combat Training Group 4).

Erprobungskommando 100

For details see Erprobungskommando 17.

Erprobungsstaffel Bf 109G

This Squadron reported its arrival in Rechlin on 15th March 1942. It is known that in July 1942, it had eleven Bf 109G-1s and seven pilots, but no further details of its activities or inventory are available.

Erprobungskommando Ta 152

This unit, established in Rechlin on 2nd November 1944, had the task of testing the Ta 152 up to operational readiness. With effect from 9th January 1945, its existence was extended until 1st April 1945 and at the same time, the Detachment was expanded and restructured. Thereafter, it was to consist of a Gruppenstab (Group HQ) with a Stabskompanie (HQ Company) and five Staffeln, of which four were to be assigned on operations and one for technical test work. This directive, however, was promptly altered on 15th January 1945, whereby the four combat squadrons were discarded since operational trials were to be undertaken by III/JG 301. Twelve Ta 152s were to remain under the auspices of the KdE, and formed the Stabsstaffel (HQ Squadron) of JG 301. The remaining aircraft were to be transferred to II/JG 301.

The Detachment was disbanded with effect from 23rd January 1945. As related elsewhere in this book, the KdE Gefechtsverband (Combat Unit) reported on 9th February 1945 an inventory of eight Ta 152s in a Stabsstaffel. In all probability, it can be assumed that this referred to the E-Kdo Ta 152 renamed as the Stabsstaffel of JG 301.

Erprobungskommando Ta 154

This Detachment was established at Hannover-Langenhagen air base with effect from 9th December 1943 with the Ta 154, in order to determine its suitability for operational use. In July 1944, it had only one airworthy machine available. The disbandment order for the unit was dated 1st August 1944, following cancellation of the Ta 154 from the aircraft programme. A heavy air attack on Langenhagen on 5th August 1944 resulted in the destruction of all hangars and available test aircraft save one. At the suggestion of the KdE, personnel of the disbanded unit were to be transferred to the Erprobungskommando Me 262 since the Ta 154s still available were intended to be used there for conversion training on twin-engined aircraft.

Erprobungskommando He 162

A Detachment bearing the above designation did not exist, even though the establishment order was given on 9th January 1945, when it was intended to form a Detachment having Gruppen strength in Lärz. A change had already been requested on 21st January 1945, whereby a Gruppe and a Stabsstaffel of a new JG 200 were to undertake these duties. A few days later, I/JG 80 with a Stabsstaffel was formed, and again a week following, it was now I/JG 1 which was equipped with the He 162 and simultaneously took over operational testing, this status finally remaining as such. Equipped in Leck with the new aircraft, I/JG 1 thereafter flew isolated sorties with it in April 1945.

Erprobungsstaffel He 177

This Squadron was set up in Lärz on 1st February 1942. The Allocation of test aircraft was, however, sporadic, so that up until August 1942 only 372 flying hours on a total of eight aircraft had been accomplished. Restricted as a result of enormous difficulties encountered with the development and testing of this aircraft, the Squadron remained active for a relatively long period until its dissolution order on 20th September 1943. Its personnel were transferred to I/FKG 50 as also to KG 40 where it formed the II Gruppe equipped with the He 177.

Erprobungsstaffel Ju 188

Of this Squadron it is known only that it was established on 1st March 1943 and that in June and July 1943 was stationed in Rechlin before it relocated at the end of that month to Chièvres near Brussels. In December 1944, the Squadron was merged into 4/KG 66.

Erprobungsstaffel Me 210

This Squadron was apparently established in Lechfeld in late spring 1942, its personnel coming from the Zerstörer schools and Ergänzungsgruppen. A few of its members had previously been ordered to Rechlin to take part in type-testing. In July 1942, the unit transferred for operational trials to Evreux in France, but suffered heavy casualties including their Staffelkapitän. Following several redesignations – for a while as 16/KG 6 and then 11/ZG 1 – the unit finally became Erprobungsstaffel 410 (qv).

Erprobungskommando Ar 234

This Detachment commenced its activities in Lärz in July 1944, where operational use of the Ar 234 was to be as a bomber. Pilots came exclusively from KG 76, the aircraft comprising the initial series-built Ar 234B version. During trials, several deficiencies surfaced, particularly involving engine, undercarriage, automatic guidance and bomb-aiming, but which were able to be progressively eradicated. After a relatively short period, the pilots returned to KG 76 where they undertook familiarisation training so that the unit, itself later equipped with the Ar 234, was able to conduct operations with the type.

Erprobungskommando Me 262

Established on 9th December 1943, the Detachment was intended to accelerate Me 262 testing at Lechfeld air base. Due to the general programme delays experienced, only a few prototypes were available which were required exclusively for the manufacturer's own test purposes. In April 1944 the unit finally received its 'own' aircraft – the Me 262 V8, series-produced machines following in May 1944. It was only after this date that the Detachment's personnel could be brought to full strength from parts of III/ZG 26. At the beginning of June the unit had about 8 aircraft, but most had to remain grounded pending the elimination of various deficiencies. From August onwards, the first Einsatzkommandos (Combat Detachments) such as in Lärz were formed, made up of the Test Detachment's own pilots. At the end of September 1944, 'Kommando Nowotny' was formed, consisting of contingents from the E-Kdo, III/ZG 26 and the Einsatzkommando. The official dissolution of E-Kdo 262 took place on 2nd November 1944.

Erprobungskommando Do 335

The establishment order on 4th December 1944 envisaged an initial duration of six months, and was to have been accompanied by the Kdo.d.E. The entire III/KG 2 was ordered to report to the Dornier firm in Friedrichshafen, where the contingent was disbursed to the various sections dealing with production, maintenance and test flying, the Detachment being tasked with carrying out service testing in the roles of Mosquito nightfighter, fighter, reconnaissance, and bomber. Upon an order from the KdE, the Detachment was transferred to Rechlin on 20th November 1944 where it became involved with maintenance of the test aircraft stationed there and was able to conduct a few test flights. The many technical difficulties experienced with the Do 335 permitted only a slow advance to be made in test work. Added to this, it no longer offered any advantage performance-wise over the Allied aircraft which in the meantime were being engaged operationally. Following cancellation of the type from the aircraft programme on 14th February 1945, official dissolution of the Detachment followed as an orderly consequence. This was, however, rescinded shortly afterwards, since the aircraft was again included in the 'Führer-Notprogram' (Emergency Programme).

Erprobungskommando Ju 388

Its official establishment was on 15th July 1944, and the task of the Detachment was service-testing the Ju 388 up to operational readiness. The task programme, however, was again revised at the beginning of October 1944, so that only type-testing as a night-fighter was to be pursued.

At the end of July 1944, an advance Detachment arrived in Rechlin. At this time, there were already eight Ju 388s there, of which three examples were reserved for the Detachment. An air raid on the E-Stelle resulted in the loss of two aircraft which were 100% destroyed and a further example 70% damaged. Even so, the Detachment had over seven aircraft available in September 1944. Due to adverse weather conditions and the poor quality of series-aircraft manufacture, testing was constantly delayed. Not only that, performance established did not meet the prescribed requirements so that this aircraft displayed no significant improvement in performance. The Detachment was thus disbanded by official order on 14th February 1945 and its personnel transferred to KG 76, to Erprobungskommando Do 335, or to various other units.

Erprobungsstaffel 410

This unit was derived from the former, often-renamed Erprobungsstaffel 210 (qv), evidently with the task of conducting service tests with the Me 410 successor. In keeping with a redisposition order of 11th May 1943, the unit was incorporated as the 9th Staffel of KG 101 and was to function there as an Erprobungsstaffel für Schnellkampf (Rapid-Combat Test Squadron). Here also, several redesignations took place. It became 12/KG 2 in October 1943, then 13/KG 51 in April 1944, before finally being terminated a few days later from the unit lists.

Erprobungskommando 600

The directive which established this Detachment was dated 1st April 1945. Its task was to bring development and testing of the manned, rocket-powered Ba 349 Natter target-defence interceptor-missile to operational readiness. It could not be established up to the present, whether this directive was actualised or whether testing of this aircraft in its previous form was still continued by the DFS and the E-Stelle Rechlin in co-operation with the Bachem firm until further work on it was terminated.

Erprobungskommando 'Kolb'
A Test Detachment 'Kolb' is reported to have been established on 20th November 1944 evidently in Fürstenfeldbruck or in its vicinity. Although its task is not mentioned in the directive, its Detachment strength with only six men was exceedingly small. No other details are known.

Erprobungskommando 'Nebel'
In a directive of 26th July 1944, this Detachment in Offingen near Günzberg, established for the purpose of 'Testing and Manufacture of Me 264 Aircraft', discovered in December 1944 that their tasks had undergone an important extension. There-

after, long-range aircraft 'based on up-to-date aerodynamic and flight-technical standpoints' were to be developed in support of the newly-produced U-boat weapons. This Sonderkommando (Special Detachment) was to be responsible for projection, design and prototype manufacture, right up to maturity of introduction, and thereby count upon the support of civilian industrial capacity. In view of the overall war situation and experience with the Me 264, these intentions were utopian, and even with the Detachment's budgeting which followed in February 1945, could no longer exert any influence. It is not known if and in what form the Detachment became active.

Further Erprobungskommandos
Besides those mentioned above, still other Test Detachments are reported to have existed, such as an Erprobungskommando 9 as also an Erprobungsstaffel 190 and an Erprobungsstaffel 167. Concerning their activities, however, no documentary proof has as yet been found.

The documentation situation re the Erprobungskommandos is on the whole, very insufficient, so that for any additional information, the authors would be very thankful.

Index to Aircraft and Missiles

Index to Personalities

Four of the few known colour photographs of the E-Stelle Rechlin, showing the experimental building camouflage schemes after the commencement of World War Two.

Top: An overall view of the Gruppe Nord complex.

Left: A close-up of the Hangar A workshops.

Above: The Halle Ost (east hangar) seen from the north.

Left: The Halle Ost (east hangar) office wing.

Top: *This view to the northwest shows, behind Halle Ost, the firing range for collimating aircraft-mounted weapons, with the C-Platz in the background. At the left corner of the picture the Gruppe Nord compass-base can be made out.*

Above: *On the grounds of the former Gruppe Süd, completely overgrown by bushes and trees, can still be seen the concrete foundation remains for the compressor motor of Powerplant Measurement Stand I.*

Left: *In May 1938, a tandem-wheel main under-carriage was tested on an Fi 156 Storch in Rechlin. The aircraft is seen here during the war on active service as an airborne ambulance in a Sanitätsstaffel.*

Above: *Even after 50 years, the foundation of the former rectangular Halle Westhangar and the barrack blocks built to the front of it can still be recognized in this aerial view (centre of picture), whilst to the west of it, the still-existing buildings of the Ellerholz-Kaserne are almost completely hidden by trees.*

Below: *The former Gruppe Nord E4 building, following thorough renovation and now in superb condition, serves as a central equipment depot for the Bundeswehr.*

Above: *A view to the southeast of the Rechlin shipyard hangars and central equipment depot of the Bundeswehr leaves only a few buildings recognizable from the former E-Stelle. In the centre of the picture is the former manoeuvring area, whilst in the background, trees thickly cover the area where the Gruppe Süd installations formerly existed.*

Bottom left: *The Bundeswehr central equipment depot in its coat-of-arms, combines the emblem of the E-Stelle Rechlin with that of the Rechlin community.*

Left: *Two of the authors – Heinrich Beauvais and Christoph Regel, seen standing in front of the former E4 building on the occasion of their visit to Rechlin in 1992.*

Below: *Enclosed rescue boats with high-seas capability count among the successful products of the Schiffswerft Rechlin since the foundation of this enterprise. The tower building in the background was formerly an office wing of the seaplane hangars in the E-Stelle Rechlin.*

Above: *The Priwall today looking northwards. Nothing can still be recognized to indicate that this was once a heavily-frequented airfield, the 'Air-hub of the North'.*

Top left: *The DLH catapult-ship 'Friesenland' lay at anchor in Travemünde from the end of 1939 until summer 1940 and is seen here with the Do 26 V5 on deck, belonging to the Sonderstaffel Transozean (Trans-Ocean Special Squadron).*

Top right: *At the beginning of World War Two, all E-Stellen received their own strong flak protection, mostly with the tower-mounted four-barrel 20mm gun emplacements as seen here in Travemünde.*

Left: *Only the harbour installations and the preserved runway strip serve as a reminder in this aerial view that this used to be an airfield. The peninsula that had once been transformed by human endeavour has now been recaptured by nature.*

Top: *The territory of the former E-Stelle Tarnewitz has since developed into a solitary nature reserve. The entire flying area is overgrown and the huge bituminous surfaces have almost completely disappeared.*

Above left: *To determine the causes of failure, the BV 143 missile was released over land. It was a trying task to salvage the data recorder.*

Above right: *Retrieving the data recorder from the wreck of the air-launched BV 143 was no easy matter on 27th August 1941.*

Left: *Loading the BV 143 remains for transport and examination.*

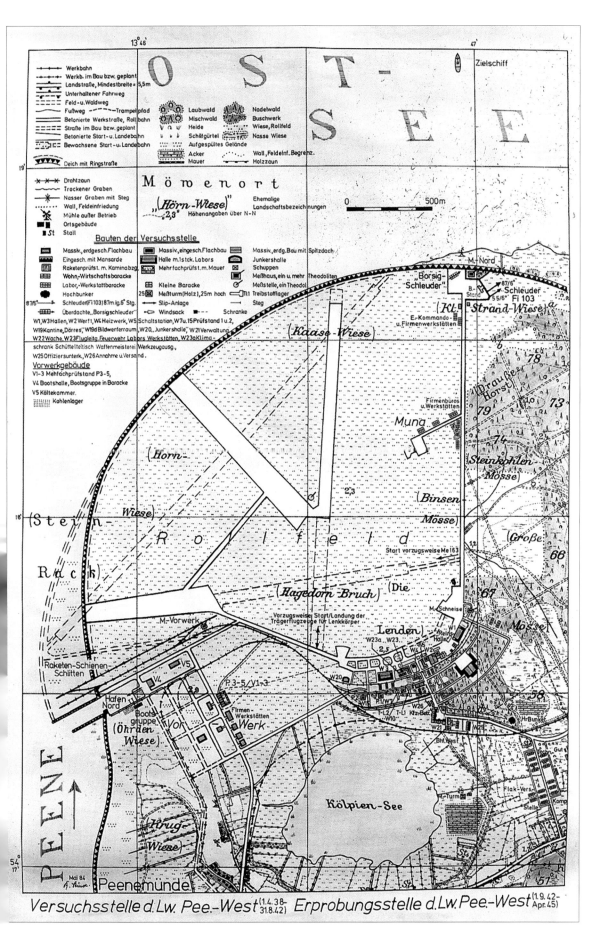

An annotated overhead map of the Peenemünde-West Versuchsstelle (1.4.1938 to 31.8.1942) at left and the Luftwaffe Erprobungsstelle (1.9.1942 to April 1945) at right.

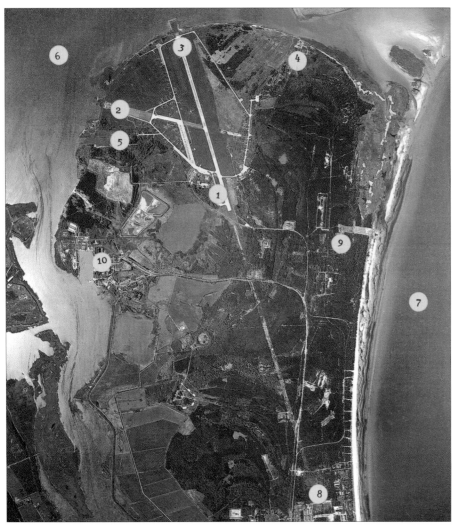

The Peenemünde Peninsula.

1. *The former Luftwaffe Versuchsstelle Peenemünde-West.*
2. *The first runway.*
3. *The second runway, extended after 1945.*
4. *The Fi 103 launching ramps.*
5. *The Versuchsstelle North Harbour.*
6. *The Peene estuary outlet into the Greifswalder Bodden.*
7. *The Baltic sea coastal region.*
8. *The Peenemünde/Karlshagen housing area.*
9. *The Army Heeresversuchsstelle Peenemünde-East.*
10. *The almost preserved but inoperative power station*

Still-recognizable remains of the Fi 103 launching installations.

We hope you have enjoyed this book...

Midland Publishing book titles are carefully edited and designed by an experienced and enthusiastic team of specialists. A catalogue detailing our aviation publishing programme is available upon request from the address on page two.

Our associate company, Midland Counties Publications, offers an exceptionally wide range of aviation, railway, spaceflight, naval, military, astronomy and transport books and videos, for purchase by mail-order and delivery around the world.

To order further copies of this book, or to request a copy of the appropriate mail-order catalogue, either write, telephone, fax, e-mail or order online from:

Midland Counties Publications
4 Watling, Hinckley, Leics, LE10 3EY
Tel: 01455 254 450   Fax: 01455 233 737

E-mail: midlandbooks@compuserve.com
www.midlandcountiessuperstore.com